TRAIL ATLAS OF
MICHIGAN

Nature • Mountain Biking • Hiking
Cross Country Skiing

Dennis R. Hansen

Hansen Publishing Company — Okemos, Michigan

First Printing — October 1994
Second Printing— February 1995
Third Printing — April 1995
Fourth Printing — August 1995
Fifth Printing — March 1996
Sixth Printing — September 1996

TRAIL ATLAS OF MICHIGAN — Nature, Mountain Biking, Hiking, Cross Country Skiing is published by
Hansen Publishing Company, 1801 Birchwood Drive, Okemos, MI, 48864.

Printed in the United States of America.

Library of Congress Catalog Card Number: 94-76438
ISBN: 0-930098-05-6

With All My Love,
      to my wife Barbara
      and daughters Stephanie and Lisa,

without who's continued understanding and
support for the last seventeen years, this book
would not have been possible.

CONTENTS

INTRODUCTION

The *Trail Atlas of Michigan* is a greatly expanded version of a series of publications that began in 1977 with the 134 page *Michigan Cross Country Skiing Atlas*. You will find that this new book is the most comprehensive non-motorized trail publication available, with more than 520 trails presented.

Two major changes have taken place for non-motorized trail users since my last publication, the *Michigan Trail Atlas*. Most notable is the increase in development of rail trails throughout the state. They can be found from the southern part of the lower peninsula to the Keweenaw Peninsula in the UP. Therefore, I have included all rail-trails that are completed, under construction or purchased.

The second major change is the dramatically increased use of trails by mountain bikers. This new user group has demonstrated their willingness to maintain existing trails and, where possible, develop new trails to accommodate increased demand. This increase has also been reflected in the number of existing trails that permit mountain bikes, including rail trail conversions and ski trails in both the public and private sectors. By allowing mountain biking and mountain bike racing, the financial position of private cross country ski trail providers has improved with this new source of off season income. Michigan mountain bikers are fortunate to have an active and responsible mountain bike user group, the Michigan Mountain Biking Association (MMBA). This association has demonstrated its willingness to put in the volunteer time to maintain existing trail systems, develop strategies to resolve conflict with other user groups, and develop new trail systems where appropriate.

The *Trail Atlas of Michigan* also has more nature trails. Previously, only nature centers that allowed cross country skiing were listed. Realizing that interpretive trails and nature sanctuaries have much to offer, I have included as many as possible.

In addition to interpretive trails, I have included separate indexes for hiking, cross country skiing, mountain biking and paved trails (for in-line skaters, road cyclists and handicapper trail users).

Similar to my previous Atlas, there is no detailed description of each trail. For those who desire more information, I have included a bibliography of additional publications for further reading.

To aid you in your trip planning, a comprehensive listing of travel and tourist organizations is found in the index. I encourage you to contact these organizations, many of which have toll free numbers.

I have provided the most current information available. Unfortunately, with the dramatic increase in trail development in recent years, along with many changes and improvements made to existing trails, this information may become quickly outdated. For this reason I have included addresses and phone numbers with each trail listing. I encourage you to contact the trail manager/owner should you need to confirm critical information.

I welcome and encourage your comments. Please send your suggestions, corrections and additions to me at the address found on the copyright page.

Sincerely,
Dennis Hansen
Okemos
September 1994

HOW TO USE THIS ATLAS

LOCATING A TRAIL

The *Trail Atlas of Michigan* has adopted, with permission, the *Michigan Atlas and Gazetteer* grid system by DeLorme Mapping of Freeport, Maine. This location system will easily locate and identify the large number of trails that are in this trail atlas.

Although you do not need the *Michigan Atlas and Gazetteer* to find the trail of your choice, having a copy will make the task considerably easier. However, the *Trail Atlas of Michigan* will function very adequately if you have one of several Michigan map books organized by county rather than this grid system. Each entry also lists the county(ies) where the trail is located. Regardless of the type of map book you use, you should easily find any trail you desire.

By trail name...

For purposes of simplicity, trails are listed in alphabetical order in the Master Index. For trails that go by several names, the master index also lists multiple entries to aid in locating the specific trail of interest.

By grid or map location...

To find a specific trail or several trails in a specific area of the state, the *Trail Atlas of Michigan* is organized by uniform size geographic areas called grids. These grids are designated by consecutive numbers from 18 through 119 beginning in the southwest corner of the lower peninsula and ending in the north end of the Keweenaw Peninsula in the upper peninsula. The grid number is also the page number in the *Michigan Atlas and Gazetteer*. In the *Trail Atlas of Michigan*, the grid number is found in the top right corner of each trail data page.

For trails that cover more than one grid, the lowest grid number is used to identify the location of the trail information. There is a separate listing in the index for all trails that extend beyond a single grid. When locating all the trails in a specific geographic area, this listing should be reviewed to insure that trails in the geographic area that are located elsewhere in the Atlas are included in your review.

By trail type or special characteristic...

To easily identify trails with specific characteristics, several specialty lists have been provided. They include the following headings:

Cross County Ski Trails
Hiking Trails
Interpretive Trails
Mountain Bike Trails
Paved Trails
Handicapper Accessible Trails
Multiple Grid Trails

ABOUT THE TRAIL INFORMATION

Trail Location

The *Michigan Atlas and Gazetteer* location is a series of numbers and letters that designates the exact location(s) where the trail can be found in the *Michigan Atlas and Gazetteer* map book. For trails that span more than a single page (grid), the additional page entries are separated by a comma. Each entry begins with a page number. The page number is followed by letter(s) which are the horizontal axis locators found on the right or left edge of the page. The letter(s) are then followed by numerals which are the vertical axis locators found only on the top of each page.

For example: a typical entry could read "56A6." This entry means that the trail is found on page 56. On page 56, the trail is located within the "A" horizontal axis and "6" on the vertical axis. Multiple axis references such as "ABC," "234" or "2-7" indicates the trail extends over a greater length.

Trail Type

Trail type is represented in both text form and as an icon at the top of each entry.

The purpose of an **interpretive** trail is to allow the user to experience the natural environment of the surrounding landscape. In some cases, trail side information may not be provided. Information when provided may be about the flora, fauna, or history of the area. Often no distinction is made because many interpretive trails mix historical and natural information. In addition, the historical content could be either natural and/or human. Overall, the information provided may vary greatly in quality, content and quantity.

A **walking/hiking** trail may be used separately or in combination with other designations. Walking is included since the shorter trails might not be considered a "hike" by some individuals.

A **mountain biking** trail refers to the specific type of trail most commonly associated with the activity, namely loose surfaced trails, single track, 2 track, or gravel roads. Paved trails will not list mountain biking as a trail type if only a paved trail exists. Only trail systems that have at least an additional natural surface trail such as Maybury State Park will list mountain biking. For those who desire to use their mountain bike on a paved trail, a separate Paved Trail index is provided. Since mountain biking is

a very rapidly evolving recreation, each entry should be confirmed by the managing organization to verify that the specific trail is of sufficient length and that mountain biking is currently permitted.

A **cross country skiing** trail includes both groomed and ungroomed trails. Many manmade and weather factors contribute to the current condition of the trail. Therefore, the author suggests that a call ahead may be appropriate to reduce disappointment.

Handicapper Accessibility

The handicapper symbol is added near the top right corner of the page to easily identify trails that offer some type of accommodation for handicappers. The type and amount of accommodation is not listed, but usually consists of at least one paved trail segment. Often more facilities are provided. If handicapper accommodation is important to you, the author suggests you contact the trail manager/owner for current information.

Terminology

To save space, frequently used terms or names are abbreviated as follows:

DNR — Michigan Department of Natural Resources
HNF — Hiawatha National Forest
HMNF — Huron Manistee National Forest
ONF — Ottawa National Forest
SFCG — state forest campground
NFCG — national forest campground
FH — forest highway — usually paved and a major road in a
      national forest (national forest designation)
NCT or NCNST — North Country National Scenic Trail
NCTA — North Country Trail Association

Legend

The following is a legend of some of the typical graphic symbols that are found on the maps or in the text. Even though the maps do not all have identical symbols, the symbols used are easily identified, and should be easily understood.

 cross country skiing trail

 walking/hiking trail

 mountain bike trail

 interpretive trail

 trail with some type of accommodation for handicappers

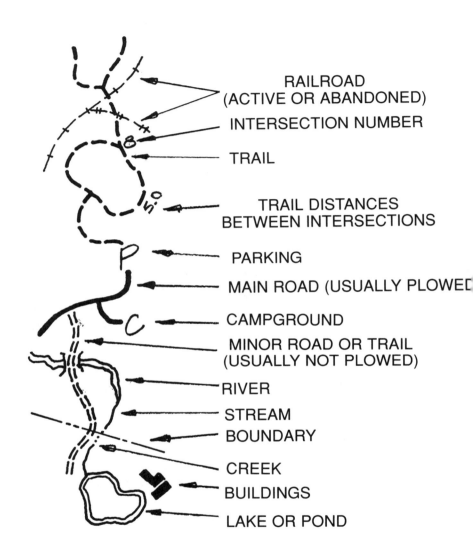

RAILROAD
(ACTIVE OR ABANDONED)

INTERSECTION NUMBER

TRAIL

TRAIL DISTANCES
BETWEEN INTERSECTIONS

PARKING

MAIN ROAD (USUALLY PLOWED

CAMPGROUND

MINOR ROAD OR TRAIL
(USUALLY NOT PLOWED)

RIVER

STREAM

BOUNDARY

CREEK

BUILDINGS

LAKE OR POND

Michigan Atlas & Gazetteer Index Map

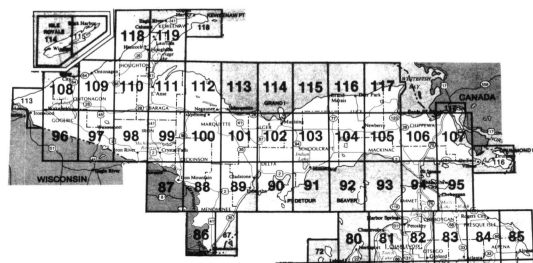

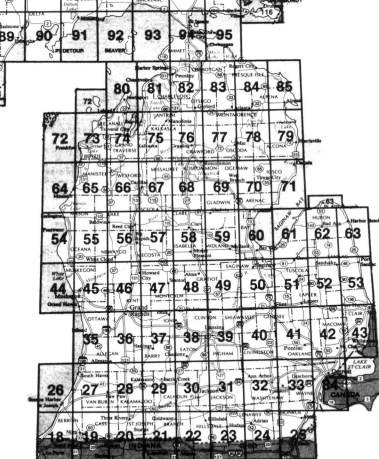

Use this map to identify trails in any specific location in the state, by following these simple instructions:

First, locate the portion of the state where the trail(s) you desire to investigate

Second, identify the grid number(s) that covers that part of the state

Third, turn to the portion of the Atlas where the trail information is presented

Fourth, turn to the specific pages where the grid number(s) is/are found in the top right corner of each page that corresponds to the grid number(s) on the map.

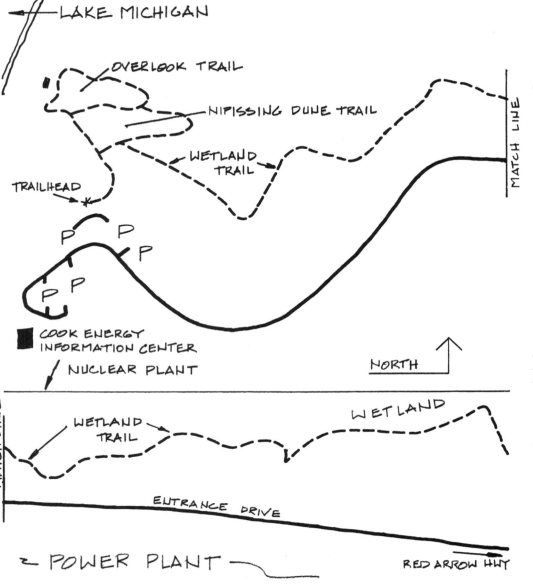

LAKE MICHIGAN

OVERLOOK TRAIL

NIPISSING DUNE TRAIL

WETLAND TRAIL

TRAILHEAD

P P P P P P

COOK ENERGY INFORMATION CENTER

NUCLEAR PLANT

NORTH

MATCH LINE

WETLAND TRAIL

WETLAND

MATCH LINE

ENTRANCE DRIVE

POWER PLANT

RED ARROW HWY

Cook Energy Information Center
PO Box 115
Bridgeman, MI 49106

800-548-2555

Michigan Atlas & Gazetteer Location: 18A2

County Location: Berrien

Directions To Trailhead:
Off I-94 at exit 16, just south of Bridgeman. Then 3.5 miles north on Red Arrow Highway.

Trail Type: Hiking/Walking, Interpretive
Trail Distance: 2.5 mi   Loops: 3   Shortest: .5 mi   Longest: 1 mi
Trail Surface: Natural
Trail Use Fee: None
Method Of Ski Trail Grooming: NA
Skiing Ability Suggested: NA
Hiking Trail Difficulty: Easy to moderate
Mountain Biking Ability Suggested: NA
Terrain: Steep 20%, Hilly 20%, Moderate 20%, Flat 40%
Camping: Public and private campgrounds nearby

Owned by Indiana - Michigan Power.
Site of a nuclear power plant.
Two existing nature trails that were recently constructed make up the trail system. They are the Nipissing Dune Trail and the Overlook Trail. The Overlook trail covers the Lake Michigan shoreline and the primary dune area. The Nipissing Dune Trail covers the secondary dune area. A third trail called the Wetland Trail is presently under construction.

NIPISSING DUNE TRAILS

Tabor Hill Vineyard
185 Mt Tabor Rd.
Buchanan, MI 49107

616-422-2787
800-283-3363

Michigan Atlas & Gazetteer Location: 18A3

County Location: Berrien

Directions To Trailhead:
7 miles east of Bridgeman and 6 miles west of Berrien Springs, just south of Snow Rd on Mt Tabor Rd.
Take exit 16 from I-94, then Lake St. east and follow signs.

Trail Type: Cross Country Skiing
Trail Distance: 11mi   Loops: MAny   Shortest: Longest:
Trail Surface: Natural
Trail Use Fee: None
Method Of Ski Trail Grooming: None
Skiing Ability Suggested: Novice to intermediate
Hiking Trail Difficulty: NA
Mountain Biking Ability Suggested: NA
Terrain: Steep 5%, Hilly 45%, Moderate 25%, Flat 25%
Camping: None

Privately operated vineyard with trails.
Warming shelter, wine tasting and tours and snack bar.
Panoramic views of Lake Michigan dunes

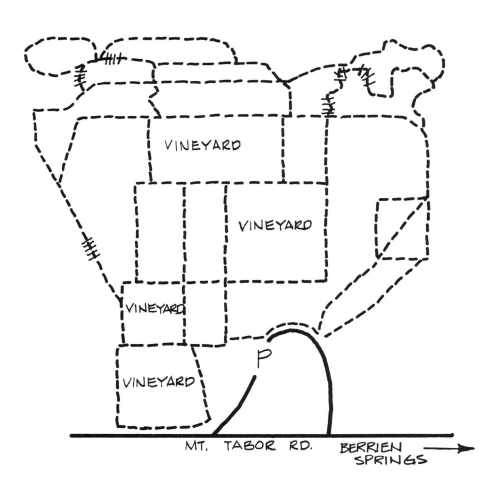

VINEYARD

VINEYARD

VINEYARD

VINEYARD

P

MT. TABOR RD.   BERRIEN SPRINGS →

NO SCALE ↑

TABOR HILL VINEYARD

Warren Dunes State Park
Red Arrow Hwy
Sawyer, MI 49125

616-426-4013

DNR Parks and Recreation Divison

517-373-1270

Michigan Atlas & Gazetteer Location: 18A2

County Location: Berrien

Directions To Trailhead:
On Lake Michigan about 16 miles south of Benton Harbor at exit 16

Trail Type: Hiking/Walking, Cross Country Skiing, Interpretive
Trail Distance: 6.75 mi   Loops: Several   Shortest: Longest:
Trail Surface: Natural
Trail Use Fee: None, but vehicle permit is required
Method Of Ski Trail Grooming: None
Skiing Ability Suggested: Novice to intermediate
Hiking Trail Difficulty: Easy to Moderate
Mountain Biking Ability Suggested: NA
Terrain: Steep 0%, Hilly 0%, Moderate 20%, Flat 80%
Camping: Available on site

Maintained by the DNR Parks and Recreaton Division
Terrain above is for trails, except where noted below.
Trail length listed above to total length for all trails.
Ski trail - 2.75 miles
Hiking trail -3 miles Terrain: Steep 15%, Hilly 15%, Moderate 45%, Flat 25%
Nature trail is 1 mile long. Trailhead is at parking lot located between the
campground and the main entrance.

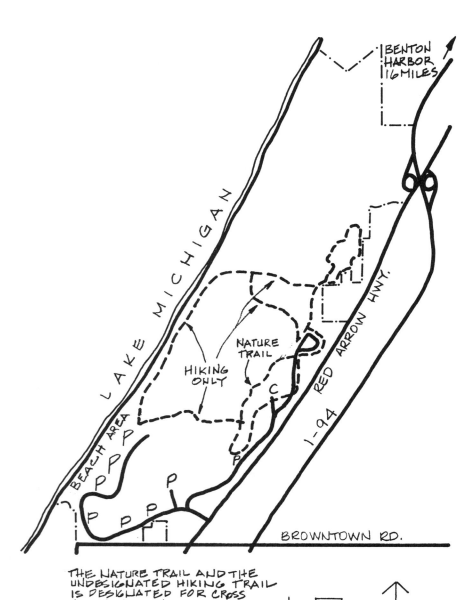

THE NATURE TRAIL AND THE
UNDESIGNATED HIKING TRAIL
IS DESIGNATED FOR CROSS
COUNTRY SKIING.
ALL TRAILS AVAILABLE FOR HIKING

3200 FT.

WARREN DUNES STATE PARK

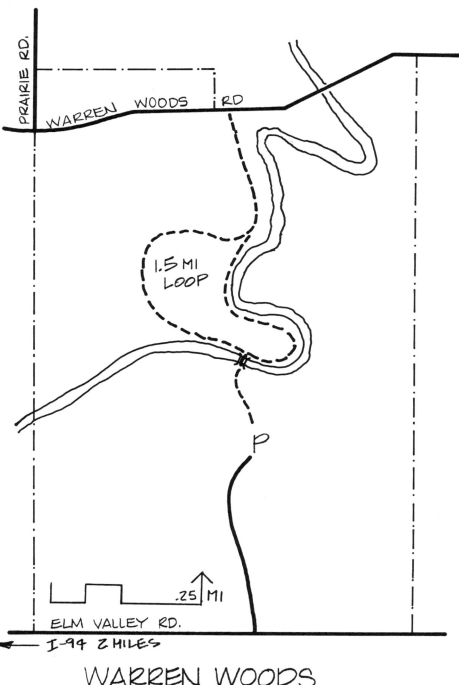

PRAIRIE RD.

WARREN WOODS RD

1.5 MI LOOP

P

.25 MI

ELM VALLEY RD.

← I-94 2 MILES

WARREN WOODS
NATURAL AREA

Warren Dunes State Park
Red Arrow Hwy
Sawyer, MI 49125

616-426-4013

DNR Parks and Recreation Division

517-373-1270

Michigan Atlas & Gazetteer Location: 18B2

County Location: Berrien

Directions To Trailhead:
3 miles from Lake Michigan and 5 miles from Indiana state line Exit I94 at Union Pier Rd., then west 2.5 miles on Elm Valley Rd. to the park, which is on the north side of the road.
Warren Woods State Park is about 7 miles north of Warren Dunes State Park

Trail Type: Hiking/Walking, Cross Country Skiing, Interpretive
Trail Distance: 1.5 mi   Loops: 1   Shortest: Longest:
Trail Surface:
Trail Use Fee: None, but vehicle permit required
Method Of Ski Trail Grooming: None
Skiing Ability Suggested: Novice
Hiking Trail Difficulty: Easy
Mountain Biking Ability Suggested: NA
Terrain: Steep 10%, Hilly 20%, Moderate 10%, Flat 60%
Camping: Camping at Warren Dunes State Park to the north

Maintained by the DNR Parks and Recreation Division
Mostly undeveloped park except for the trails and picnic area.
A primeval forest 200 acre preserve of virgin hardwoods.

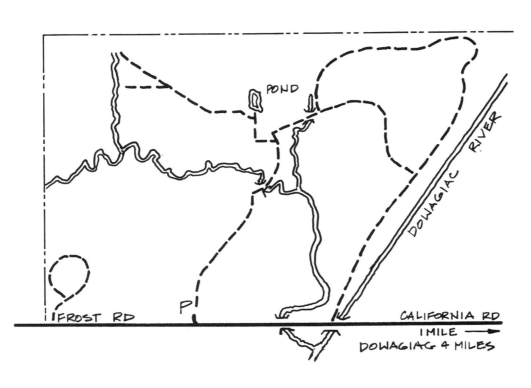

POND

DOWAGIAC RIVER

P

FROST RD
CALIFORNIA RD
1 MILE ⟶
DOWAGIAC 4 MILES

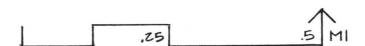

.25
.5 MI

DOWAGIAC WOODS
NATURE SANCTUARY

Michigan Nature Association
7981 Beard Rd, Box 102
Avoca, MI 48006

810-324-2626

Michigan Atlas & Gazetteer Location: 19A5

County Location: Cass

Directions To Trailhead:
Take M62 west of Dowagiac about 2 miles to California Rd, then south on
California Rd for 1 mile to Frost Rd.. Then west on Frost Rd for 1 mile to
sanctuary entrance.

Trail Type: Hiking/Walking, Interpretive
Trail Distance: 2.5 mi   Loops: 3   Shortest: .25 mi Longest: 2 mi
Trail Surface: Natural
Trail Use Fee: None
Method Of Ski Trail Grooming: NA
Skiing Ability Suggested: NA
Hiking Trail Difficulty: Easy to moderate
Mountain Biking Ability Suggested: NA
Terrain: Steep 0%, Hilly 0%, Moderate 20%, Flat 80%
Camping: None

Owned by the Michigan Nature Association.
A truely unique property.
Considered the largest moist virgin soil woodland in Michigan. Other than
occasional lumber harvesting, this property has never been tilled.
In the spring, this sanctuary is filled with an abundance of wildflowers.
The most outstanding is the Blue -eyed Mary flower.
Almost 400 plants have been catalogued.
An area not to be missed for those interested in Michigan"s flora.

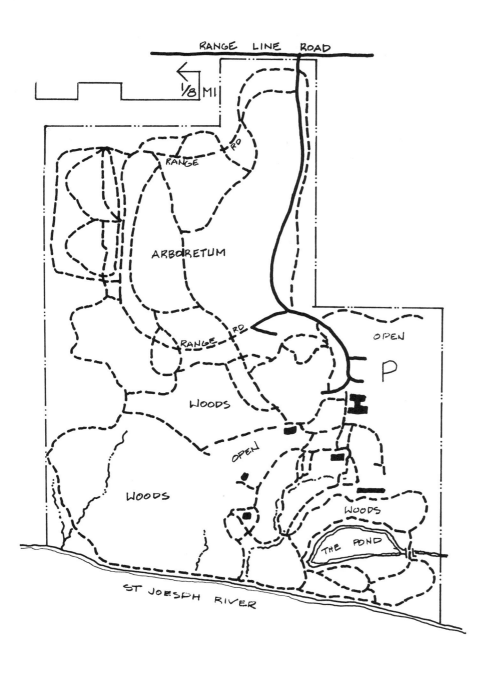

Fernwood Botanic Garden
13988 Range Line Rd
Niles, MI 49120

616-695-6491

Michigan Atlas & Gazetteer Location: 19B4

County Location: Berrien

Directions To Trailhead:
From M12, take US31 north to Walton Rd, then southwest to Range Line Rd, then north to entrance

Trail Type: Hiking/Walking, Interpretive
Trail Distance: 4 mi   Loops: Many   Shortest: .5 mi   Longest: 1 mi
Trail Surface: Paved, gravel and natural
Trail Use Fee: Yes, memberships available
Method Of Ski Trail Grooming: NA
Skiing Ability Suggested: NA
Hiking Trail Difficulty: Easy
Mountain Biking Ability Suggested: NA
Terrain: Steep 15%, Hilly 25%, Moderate 20%, Flat 40%
Camping: None

A non-profit Botanic Garden.
Visitor Center, Fern House, Nature Center Building, Art Studio, Boydston Winter House, Summer House, Pottery Studio, Gazebo, Herb Garden Terrace Garden, Tea Room and many gardens and collections.
100 acres and over 125' of elevation change along the bank of the St. Joseph River.
Many facilities and programs are available.
Extensive and varied collections.
Call or write for their brochure.

FERNWOOD

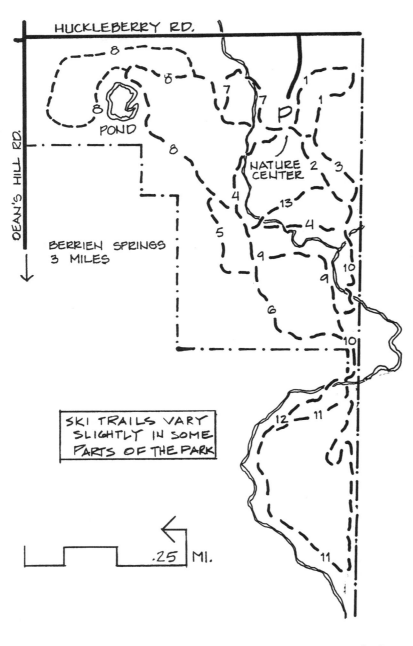

HUCKLEBERRY RD.

8
8
7 7
1
1
8
POND
8
P
NATURE CENTER
2 3
4
13
4
5
4
DEAN'S HILL RD.
9
10
9
6
10
BERRIEN SPRINGS 3 MILES
12 11
SKI TRAILS VARY SLIGHTLY IN SOME PARTS OF THE PARK
11
.25 MI.

LOVE CREEK COUNTY PARK & NATURE CENTER

Love Creek Nature Center
9228 Huckleberry Rd.
Berrien Springs, MI 49102

616-471-2617

Berrien County Parks and Recreation Department
Berrien County Courthouse
St Joesph, MI 49085

616-983-7111
ext 435

Michigan Atlas & Gazetteer Location: 19A4

County Location: Berrien

Directions To Trailhead:
From Berrien Springs, take US31 south about .75 mile to Deans Hill Rd., then turn left, then turn immediately right on Pokagon Rd. for 2 miles to Huckleberry Rd., then north 1 mile to the park entrance.

Trail Type: Hiking/Walking, Cross Country Skiing, Interpretive
Trail Distance: 6 mi   Loops: Many   Shortest: Longest:
Trail Surface: Natural
Trail Use Fee: Yes for skiing
Method Of Ski Trail Grooming: Track set
Skiing Ability Suggested: Intermediate to advanced
Hiking Trail Difficulty: Easy to moderate
Mountain Biking Ability Suggested: NA
Terrain: Steep 5%, Hilly 25%, Moderate 70%, Flat 0%
Camping: None

Operated by the Berrien County Parks and Recreation Department.
Separate classic cross country ski and skating trails.
Rentals and ski instruction available.
Lake effect snow provides excellent conditions throughout season.
Addition trails available for hiking during the rest of the year.
Separate winter hiking and snowshoeing trails are provided.
Some trails are different for summer hiking.
Spectacular spring woodland wildflower show in late April & early May.
Call or write for their brochure.

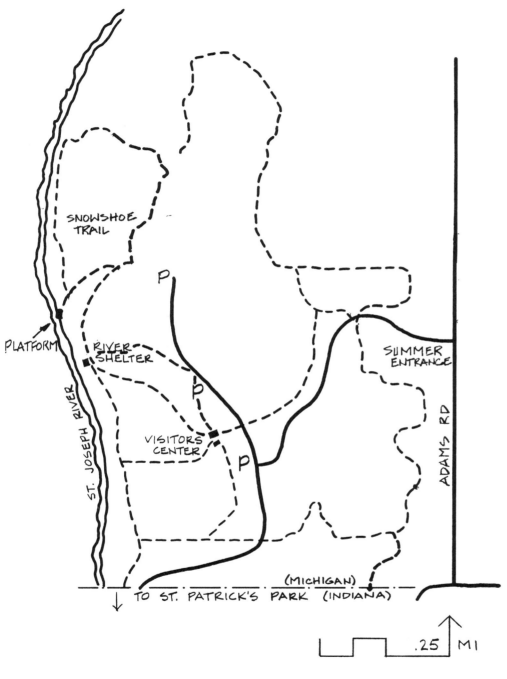

PLATFORM

SNOWSHOE TRAIL

ST. JOSEPH RIVER

RIVER SHELTER

VISITORS CENTER

P

P

P

SUMMER ENTRANCE

ADAMS RD

(MICHIGAN)
↓ TO ST. PATRICK'S PARK (INDIANA)

.25 MI

MADELINE BERTRAND PARK

Madeline Bertrand County Park
3038 Adams Rd.   616-683-8280
Niles, MI 49120

Berrien County Parks and Recreation Department
Berrien County Courthouse   616-983-7111
St. Joseph, MI 49085   ext. 435

Michigan Atlas & Gazetteer Location: 19BC45

County Location: Berrien

Directions To Trailhead:
4 miles south of Niles on the St. Joseph River at the Michigan/Indiana state line
Take US31 south from Niles to Stateline Rd., then west to Adams Rd., then
north to the park entrance

Trail Type: Hiking/Walking, Cross Country Skiing, Interpretive
Trail Distance: 3.5 mi   Loops: 2   Shortest: .2 mi   Longest: 1 mi
Trail Surface: Natural
Trail Use Fee: Yes, vehicle and trail fee on weekends
Method Of Ski Trail Grooming: Track set
Skiing Ability Suggested: Novice
Hiking Trail Difficulty: Easy
Mountain Biking Ability Suggested: NA
Terrain: Steep 0%, Hilly 0%, Moderate 2%, Flat 98%
Camping: None

Maintained by the Berrien County Parks and Recreation Department
Park closed Monday and Tuesday. Hours W-F 12 noon to sunset, weekends
10am to sunset. Park is adjoining the St. Patrick's County Park in Indiana, with
connecting trails for added skiing and hiking trail distance. Heated visitor center.
Picnicing/resting area in Bertrand Lodge. The lodge is dominated by a large
stone fireplace. Trails wind through a stately evergreen forest. Torch-lighted
skiing is available on most weekends. Snowshoe rental available. Ski rentals are
available at adjoining St. Patrick's Park. Separate snowshoe trails provided.
Scheduled naturalist activities throughout the year. Facilities available for rent
and/or private torch-light skiing.

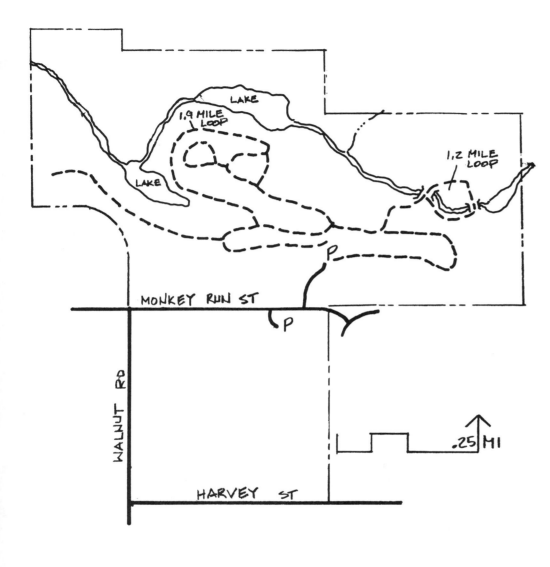

Cass County Parks Department
340 N. O'Keefe St.   616-445-8611
Cassopolis, MI 49031

Dr T.K. Lawless Park
15122 Monkey Run St.   616-476-2730
Vandalia, MI 49095

Michigan Atlas & Gazetteer Location: 20A1

County Location: Cass

Directions To Trailhead:
Between Cassopolis and Three Rivers off of M60. 12 miles east of Cassopolis
and about 3 miles southeast of Vandalia. Take Lewis Lake St. south off of M60
about 1 mile, then east on Monkey Run Street to the park entrance .

Trail Type: Hiking/Walking, Cross Country Skiing, Interpretive
Trail Distance: 5+ mi   Loops: 7   Shortest: .3 mi   Longest: 1.2 mi
Trail Surface: Natural
Trail Use Fee: None, but vehicle entry fee required
Method Of Ski Trail Grooming: Track set
Skiing Ability Suggested: Novice to advanced
Hiking Trail Difficulty: Easy to difficult
Mountain Biking Ability Suggested: NA
Terrain: Steep 25%, Hilly 25%, Moderate 25%, Flat 25%
Camping: Group camping only.

Operated by the Cass County Parks Department.
Tubing hill, warming shelter with fireplace, ice fishing and picnic area with grills
and restrooms.

DR T.K. LAWLESS PARK

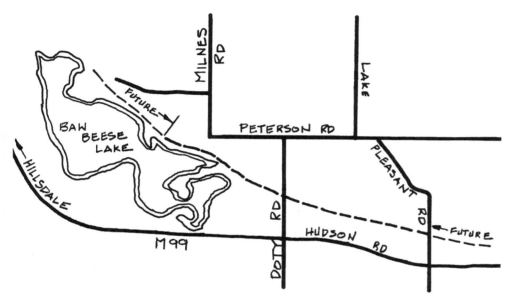

Baw Beese Trail

Hillsdale Parks and Recreation Department
43 McCollum St
Hillsdale, MI 49242

518-437-3579

Michigan Atlas & Gazetteer Location: 22A34

County Location: HIllsdale

Directions To Trailhead:
Trail begins on the northeast side of Baw Beese Lake and ends at Lake Pleasant Rd. just north of Hudson Rd (M99) southeast of Hillsdale. Trail crosses Doty Rd about .3 mile north of M99. East trailhead - Follow Water Works Ave on the north side of Baw Beese Lake past several parks to Sandy Beach park. The trailhead is .3 mile east at bollards in corridor.

Trail Type: Hiking/Walking, Cross Country Skiing,
Trail Distance: 2 mi   Loops: NA   Shortest: NA   Longest: NA
Trail Surface: Paved
Trail Use Fee: None
Method Of Ski Trail Grooming: NA
Skiing Ability Suggested: Novice
Hiking Trail Difficulty: Easy
Mountain Biking Ability Suggested: NA
Terrain: Steep 0%, Hilly 0%, Moderate 0%, Flat 100%
Camping: None

Owned by City of Hillsdale.
When completed the trail will be 6 miles long. Extensions will be in both directions into Hillsdale and eastward.
Part of the North Country Trail.

BAW BEESE TRAIL

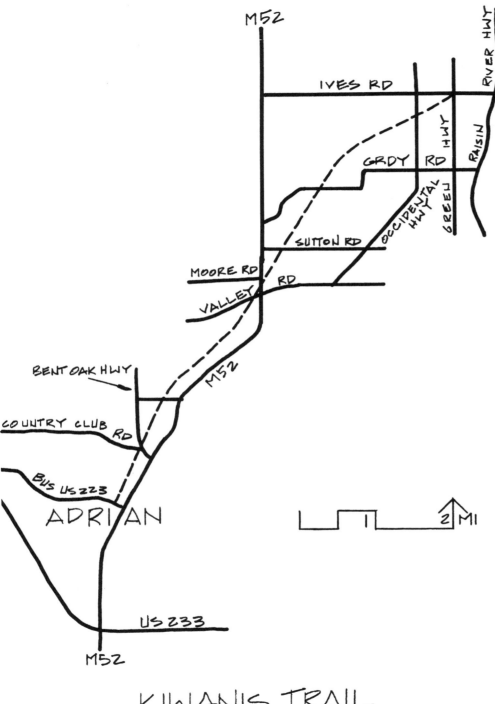

M52

IVES RD

RIVER HWY

GRDY RD

RAISIN

GREEN HWY

OCCIDENTAL HWY

SUTTON RD

MOORE RD

VALLEY RD

BENT OAK HWY

M52

COUNTRY CLUB RD

BUS US 223

ADRIAN

US 233

M52

KIWANIS TRAIL

Kiwanis Trail

♿

Director of Community Service, City of Adrian
100 E. Church
Adrian, MI 49221

517-263-2161

Michigan Atlas & Gazetteer Location: 24A1

County Location: Lenawee

Directions To Trailhead:
South trailhead - Parking lot for the Country Market/Arbor Drugs off Maumee Rd west of downtown
No parking at north trailhead.

Trail Type: Hiking/Walking, Cross Country Skiing
Trail Distance: 7 mi   Loops: NA   Shortest: NA   Longest: NA
Trail Surface: Paved
Trail Use Fee: None
Method Of Ski Trail Grooming: ?
Skiing Ability Suggested: Novice
Hiking Trail Difficulty: Easy
Mountain Biking Ability Suggested: Novice
Terrain: 100% Flat
Camping: None

Owned by the City of Adrian
According to the Roger Storm, Director, Michigan Chapter of the Rails-to-Trails Conservancy "Trestle Park puts this trail in a league all its own. Of all the facilities developed thus far along a rail-trail, this could well be the finest. The City of Adrian truly did themselves proud. Trying to describe Trestle Park is almost a disservice. You have to see it to really get a feel for what has been created here....Oh yes, the trail is nice too."
Plans call for the trail to extend to Tecumseh in the future.

LAKE
ERIE

The Nature Conservancy, Michigan Chapter
2840 East Grand River, Suite 5   517-332-1741
East Lansing, MI 48823

SWAMP

POND

Michigan Atlas & Gazetteer Location: 25B6

County Location: Monroe

Directions To Trailhead:
Take I-75 south to exit 2. Exit on Summit Rd and pass over I-75 to Brewer's Boat Livery(at the intersection with Sterns Rd). Make a U-turn at Sterns Rd and head north .2 mile to Bay Creek Rd, which is the first road to the right. Follow Bay Creek Rd .8 mile north to Dean Rd. Turn right onto Dean Rd and travel 1 mile to the Erie Shooting Club cottages. Park here. Follow the dikes that traverse the preserve .

I-75

BAY CREEK RD

DEAN RD

P

POND

POND

POND

Trail Type: Interpretive
Trail Distance: 5+ mi   Loops: Shortest: Longest:
Trail Surface: Gravel and natural
Trail Use Fee: None
Method Of Ski Trail Grooming: NA
Skiing Ability Suggested: NA
Hiking Trail Difficulty: Easy
Mountain Biking Ability Suggested: NA
Terrain: Steep 0%, Hilly 0%, Moderate 0%, Flat 100%
Camping: None

MAUMEE BAY

I-75

SUMMIT ST

.5   1 MI

Owned by the Nature Conservancy
Follow dikes. No marked trails.
Closed in October and November.
Don't block roads or private property at trailhead

OHIO
1 MILE

ERIE MARSH PRESERVE

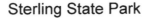

MONROE
3 MILES
I-75
1 MILE

DIXIE HWY.

SANDY CREEK RD.

C

P

2.6 MILE
LOOP

MARSH

LAGOON

LAGOON

P

P

P

P

P

P

BEACH

LAKE ERIE

NO SCALE

STERLING STATE PARK

Sterling State Park

25

Sterling State Park
2800 State Park Rd., Rte 5
Monroe, MI 48161

313-289-2715

DNR Parks and Recreation Division

517-373-1270

Michigan Atlas & Gazetteer Location: 25A6

County Location: Monroe

Directions To Trailhead:
East of Monroe on Lake Erie Take Dixie Hwy east from the I75 exit about 1 mile to park entrance

Trail Type: Hiking/Walking
Trail Distance: 2.6 mi   Loops: 1   Shortest: Longest: 2.6 mi
Trail Surface: Natural
Trail Use Fee: None, but vehicle permit required
Method Of Ski Trail Grooming: NA
Skiing Ability Suggested: NA
Hiking Trail Difficulty: Easy
Mountain Biking Ability Suggested: NA
Terrain: Flat
Camping: Campgound in park

Maintained by the DNR Parks and Recreation Division
Trail along backwater marsh of Lake Erie, and includes a small open air shelter and several displays with an observation tower to overlook the marsh area. Swimming available at beach area.

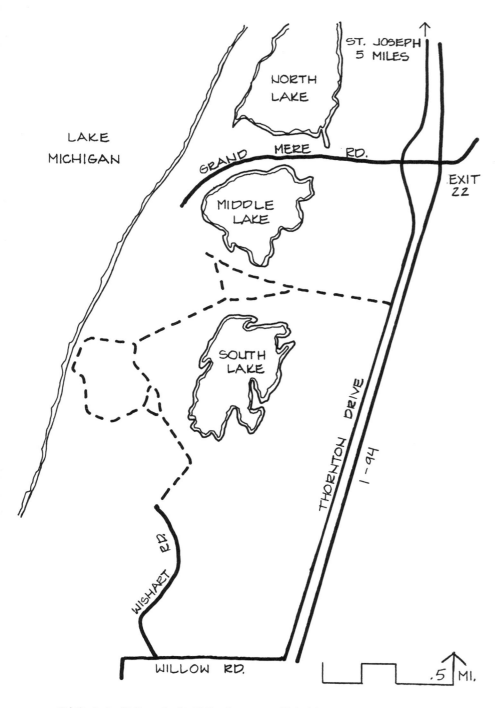

LAKE MICHIGAN

ST. JOSEPH 5 MILES

NORTH LAKE

GRAND MERE RD.

EXIT 22

MIDDLE LAKE

SOUTH LAKE

THORNTON DRIVE

I-94

WISHART RD.

WILLOW RD.

.5 MI.

GRAND MERE STATE PARK

Warren Dunes State Park
12032 Red Arrow Highway
Sawyer, MI 49125

616-426-4013

DNR Parks and Recreation Division

517-373-1270

Michigan Atlas & Gazetteer Location: 26D2

County Location: Berrien

Directions To Trailhead:
5 miles south of St Joesph on I94 at exit 22, then west to the park

Trail Type: Hiking/Walking, Cross Country Skiing, Interpretive
Trail Distance: 3.5 mi   Loops: Several   Shortest: Longest:
Trail Surface: Paved and natural
Trail Use Fee: None, but vehicle entry permit required
Method Of Ski Trail Grooming: None
Skiing Ability Suggested: None
Hiking Trail Difficulty: Easy to moderate
Mountain Biking Ability Suggested: NA
Terrain: Rolling to hilly
Camping: Campgound available at Warren Dunes SP, 10 miles south of this park

Maintained by the DNR Parks and Recreation Division
Trails in Lake Michigan dune area. Some wooded trails. Great for bird watching.
The park has a 1/2 mile paved nature trail.

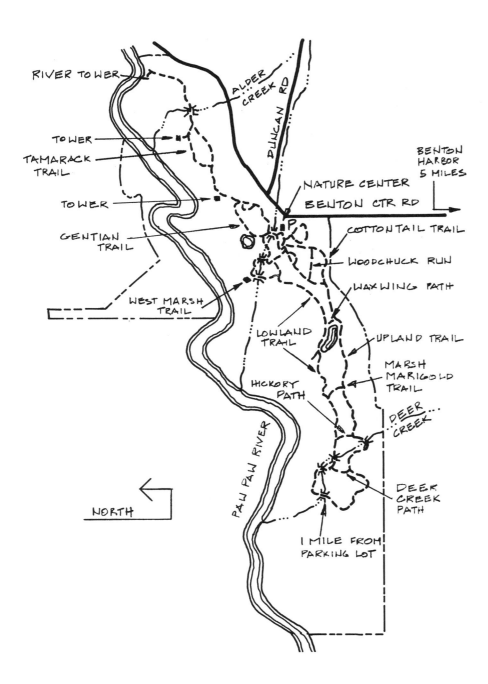

Sarett Nature Center
2300 Benton Center Rd
Benton Harbor, MI 49022

616-972-4832

Michigan Atlas & Gazetteer Location: 26C34

County Location: Berrien

Directions To Trailhead:
From I-94, take esit 35, then exit 1(Red Arrow Hwy), then left onto Red Arrow.
Drive .12 , turn right(north) onto Benton Center Rd. for .75 mile to the center

Trail Type: Hiking/Walking, Cross Country Skiing, Interpretive
Trail Distance: 5+ mi   Loops: 3   Shortest: .25 mi Longest: 3 mi
Trail Surface: Natural
Trail Use Fee: No, but donations accepted
Method Of Ski Trail Grooming: None
Skiing Ability Suggested: Novice
Hiking Trail Difficulty: Easy
Mountain Biking Ability Suggested: NA
Terrain: Steep 0%, Hilly 0%, Moderate 20%, Flat 80%
Camping: None

Owned by the Michigan Audubon Society
Trails have boardwalks, towers, elevated platforms and benches throughout the
350 acre preserve.
A trail guide is available.

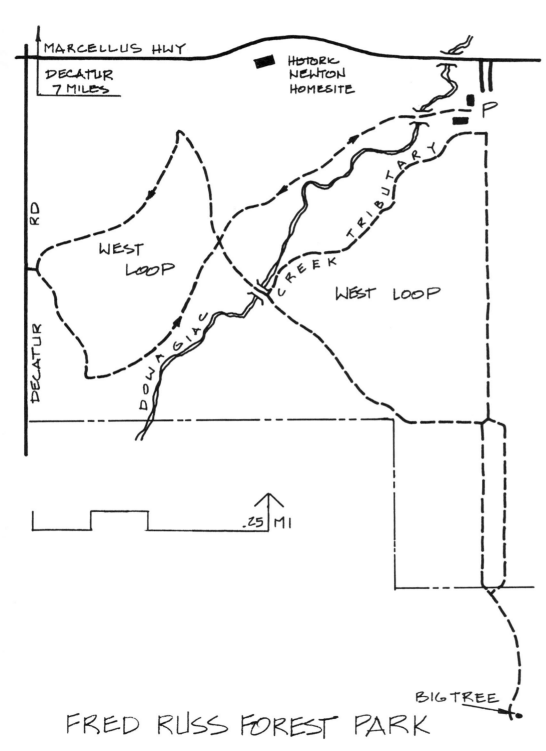

MARCELLUS HWY

DECATUR
7 MILES

HISTORIC
NEWTON
HOMESITE

P

WEST
LOOP

WEST LOOP

CREEK TRIBUTARY

DOWAGIAC

RD

DECATUR

.25 MI

FRED RUSS FOREST PARK

BIG TREE

Cass County Parks Department
340 N. Okeefe St
Cassopolis, MI 49031

616-445-8611

Michigan Atlas & Gazetteer Location: 27D7

County Location: Cass

Directions To Trailhead:
.5 mile east of the intersection of Marcellus Hwy and Decatur Rd

Trail Type: Hiking/Walking, Cross Country Skiing, Interpretive
Trail Distance: 2 mi   Loops: 2   Shortest: 1 mi   Longest: 1.5 mi
Trail Surface: Natural
Trail Use Fee: None
Method Of Ski Trail Grooming: Not known
Skiing Ability Suggested: Novice to intermediate
Hiking Trail Difficulty: Easy
Mountain Biking Ability Suggested: NA
Terrain: Steep 0%, Hilly 0%, Moderate 10%, Flat 90%
Camping: None

Managed by the Cass County Parks Department
Part of the 640 acre MSU research station

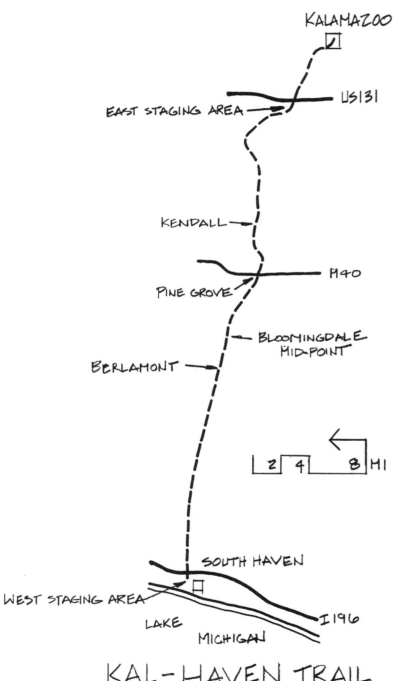

KALAMAZOO

US131

EAST STAGING AREA

KENDALL

M40

PINE GROVE

BLOOMINGDALE MIDPOINT

BERLAMONT

| 2 | 4 | 8 | MI |

SOUTH HAVEN

WEST STAGING AREA

LAKE MICHIGAN

I196

KAL-HAVEN TRAIL SESQUICENTENNIAL STATE PARK

Van Buren State Park
23960 Ruggles Rd., PO Box 122-B
South Haven, MI 49090

616-637-2788

DNR Parks Division and Recreation

517-373-1270

Michigan Atlas & Gazetteer Location: 27A567,28B123

County Location: VanBuren & Kalamazoo

Directions To Trailhead:
Between Kalamazoo and South Haven "Station Sites" are located at Berlamont, Bloomingdale, Pine Grove and Kendall. East staging area-Just west of US131 on 10th St between G & H Avenues West staging area-West of I196 on the Blue Star Hwy, north of South Haven

Trail Type: Hiking/Walking, Cross Country Skiing, Mountain Biking
Trail Distance: 34 mi   Loops: NA   Shortest: NA   Longest: NA
Trail Surface: Crushed limestone
Trail Use Fee: Yes, daily, family and annual passes are available
Method Of Ski Trail Grooming: None
Skiing Ability Suggested: Novice
Hiking Trail Difficulty: Easy
Mountain Biking Ability Suggested: Novice
Terrain: Steep 0%, Hilly 0%, Moderate 5%, Flat 95%
Camping: Some campgrounds along or near the trail

Maintained by the DNR Parks and Recreation Division and the Friends of the Kal-Haven Trail, a nonprofit organization.
Very popular rail trail.
The trail passes through farm land, wooded areas and over rivers.
Equestrian use is limited to a parallel and separate trail from 68th St to 51st St.
Write or call for more information.

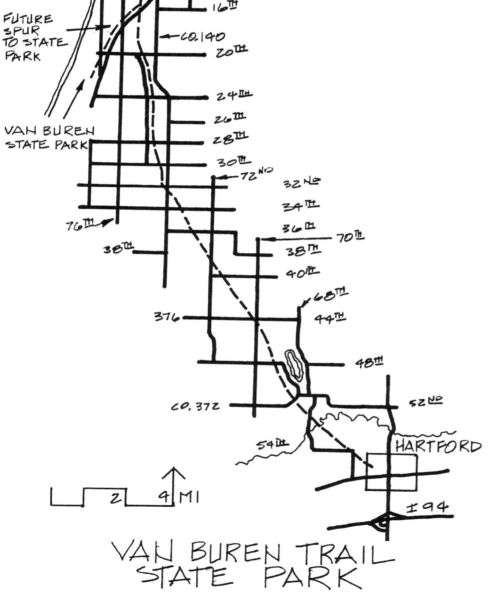

SOUTH HAVEN

LAKE MICHIGAN

8TH
LOVEJOY
12TH
14TH — 73RD
16TH

FUTURE SPUR TO STATE PARK

CO.140
20TH

VAN BUREN STATE PARK

24TH
26TH
28TH
30TH — 72ND
32ND
34TH
36TH — 70TH
38TH
40TH

76TH

38TH

376
68TH
44TH

48TH

CO.372
52ND

54TH
HARTFORD

2 4 MI

I 94

VAN BUREN TRAIL
STATE PARK

Van Buren State Park
23960 Ruggles Rd, Box 122B
South Haven, MI 49090

616-637-2788

DNR Parks and Recreation Division

517-322-1300
517-373-1270

Michigan Atlas & Gazetteer Location: 27AB45

County Location: Van Buren

Directions To Trailhead:
North trailhead - Lovejoy Rd, .5 mile west of Bus I-196, just south of South Haven
South trailhead - Hartford, northwest corner of town

Trail Type: Hiking/Walking, Cross Country Skiing, Mountain Biking
Trail Distance: 14.3 mi   Loops: NA   Shortest: NA   Longest: NA
Trail Surface: Ballast and natural
Trail Use Fee:
Method Of Ski Trail Grooming:
Skiing Ability Suggested:
Hiking Trail Difficulty:
Mountain Biking Ability Suggested:
Terrain: 100% Flat
Camping: Van Buren State Park

Managed by the DNR Parks and Recreation Division
Acquired in late 1994. Development in next 2 years.
Contact DNR for current status.
Spur trail proposed to contect main trail with Van Buren State Park

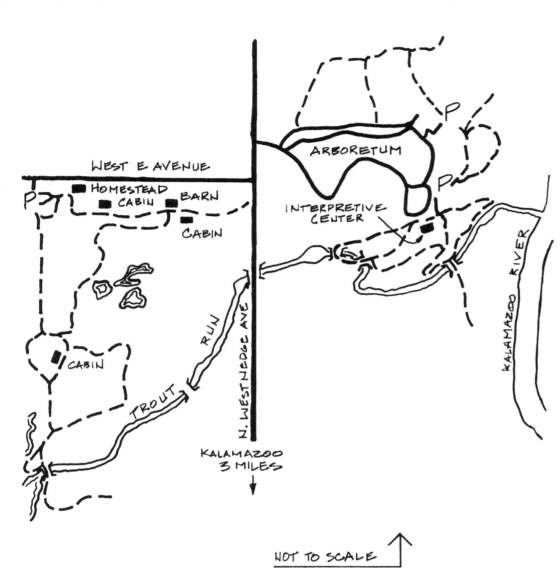

Kalamazoo Nature Center
7000 N. Westnedge Ave
Kalamazoo, MI 49004

616-381-1574

Michigan Atlas & Gazetteer Location: 28B3

County Location: Kalamazoo

Directions To Trailhead:
At US131 and D Ave. go east on D Ave about 3 miles to Westnedge Ave., then south on Westnedge Ave one mile. Entrance is on the left.

Trail Type: Hiking/Walking, Cross Country Skiing, Interpretive
Trail Distance: 10 mi   Loops: Many   Shortest: Longest:
Trail Surface: Natural
Trail Use Fee: No, but addmission fee is requried.
Method Of Ski Trail Grooming: None
Skiing Ability Suggested: Novice
Hiking Trail Difficulty: Easy
Mountain Biking Ability Suggested: NA
Terrain: Steep 0%, Hilly 10%, Moderate 80%, Flat 10%
Camping: None

Maintained by The Nature Center,a non-profit, scientific, environmental education and land-conservancy institution originally founded to save the property from development.
Cooper's Glen, site of the Nature Center, was named for James Fenimore Cooper, a frequent visitor to this area in the 1840's.
Trails, interpretive center, barnyard, farm, arboretum, botanic garden, DeZLano Homestead and a gift shop are part of the nature center.
Call or write for their brochure.

KALAMAZOO NATURE CENTER

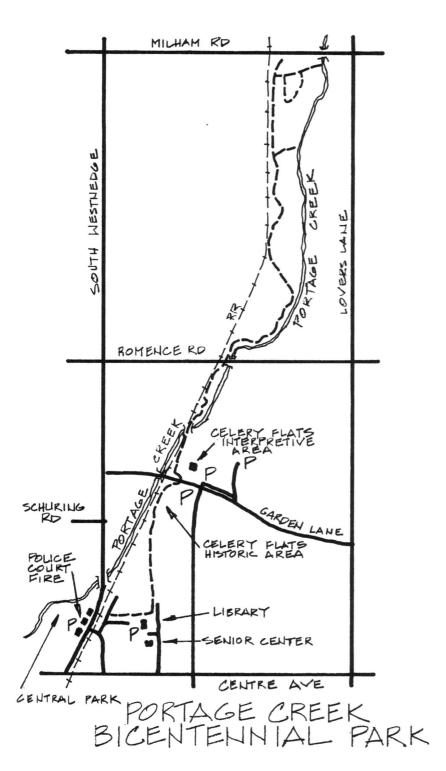

MILHAM RD

SOUTH WESTNEDGE

PORTAGE CREEK

LOVERS LANE

RR

ROMENCE RD

CELERY FLATS INTERPRETIVE AREA

PORTAGE CREEK

P

P

SCHURING RD

GARDEN LANE

CELERY FLATS HISTORIC AREA

POLICE COURT FIRE

LIBRARY

P

P

SENIOR CENTER

CENTRE AVE

CENTRAL PARK

PORTAGE CREEK
BICENTENNIAL PARK

City of Portage, Parks and Recreation Department
7900 S. Westnedge   616-329-4522
Portage, MI 49002

Michigan Atlas & Gazetteer Location: 28C3

County Location: Kalamazoo

Directions To Trailhead:
I-94 to exit 76A(S. Westnedge), then take Westnedge about .5 mile to Milham Rd., then left for about .5 mile to the park entrance.

Trail Type: Hiking/Walking, Cross Country Skiing, Interpretive
Trail Distance: 2.25 mi   Loops: NA   Shortest: NA   Longest: NA
Trail Surface: Paved
Trail Use Fee: None
Method Of Ski Trail Grooming: None
Skiing Ability Suggested: Novice
Hiking Trail Difficulty: Easy
Mountain Biking Ability Suggested: NA
Terrain: Steep 0%, Hilly 0%, Moderate 20%, Flat 80%
Camping: None

Maintained by the City of Portage, Parks and Recreation Department
100 acre linear park.
The Celery Flats Interpretive and Historical Area is along this trail.
Call or write for the brochure.

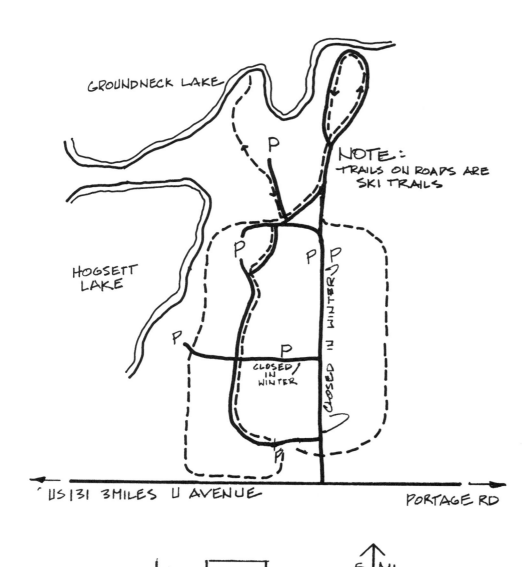

GROUNDNECK LAKE

P

NOTE: TRAILS ON ROADS ARE SKI TRAILS

HOGSETT LAKE

P

P

P

P

CLOSED IN WINTER

CLOSED IN WINTER

P

P

US131 3 MILES   U AVENUE

PORTAGE RD

.5 MI

PRAIRIE VIEW PARK

Kalamazoo County Parks and Recreation Department
2900 Lake St.
Kalamazoo, MI 49001

616-383-8778

Michigan Atlas & Gazetteer Location: 28C3

County Location: Kalamazoo

Directions To Trailhead:
South of Kalamazoo about 9 miles on US131, then east on U Ave 3 miles to the park entrance

Trail Type: Hiking/Walking, Cross Country Skiing
Trail Distance: 5 km   Loops: Several   Shortest: Longest:
Trail Surface: Natural
Trail Use Fee: None, but vehicle entry fee required
Method Of Ski Trail Grooming: Track set
Skiing Ability Suggested: Novice
Hiking Trail Difficulty: Easy
Mountain Biking Ability Suggested: NA
Terrain: Steep 0%, Hilly 0%, Moderate 5%, Flat 95%
Camping: None

Operated by the Kalamazoo County Parks Department
Ski trails use some vehicle roads that are closed during the winter.
Sledding hill, warming shelter, beach, concessions, picnic shelters and play fields.
Park is about 210 acres

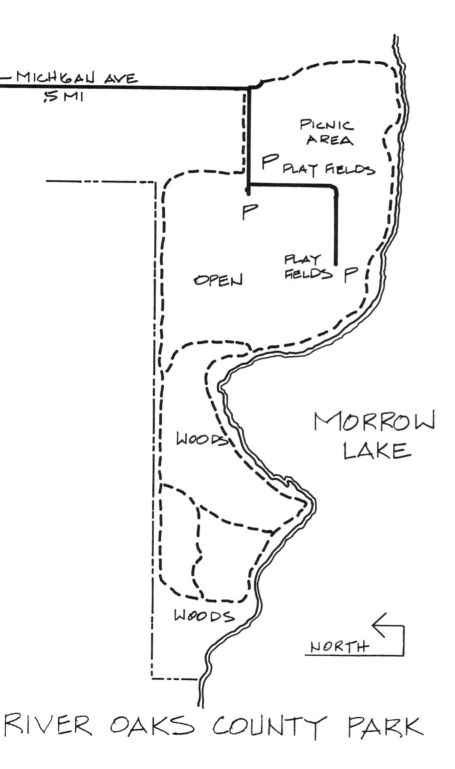

Kalamazoo County Parks and Recreation Department.
2900 Lake St
Kalamazoo, MI 49001

616-383-8778

Michigan Atlas & Gazetteer Location: 28B34

County Location: Kalamazoo

Directions To Trailhead:
North on 35th St from I-94 to M96, then west .75 mile to park

Trail Type: Hiking/Walking, Cross Country Skiing
Trail Distance: 2 mi   Loops: Several   Shortest: Longest:
Trail Surface: Natural
Trail Use Fee: None, but entry fee required
Method Of Ski Trail Grooming: None
Skiing Ability Suggested: Novice
Hiking Trail Difficulty: Easy
Mountain Biking Ability Suggested: NA
Terrain: 100%Flat
Camping: None

Maintained by the Kalamazoo County Parks and Recreation Department
Park is along the north shore of Morrow Lake.

RIVER OAKS COUNTY PARK

City of Portage, Parks and Recreation Department
7900 S. Westnedge
Portage, MI 49002

616-329-4522

Michigan Atlas & Gazetteer Location: 28C3

County Location: Kalamazoo

Directions To Trailhead:
I-94 to exit 76A(S. Westnedge), then south on Westnedge about 5 miles to
Osterhout Rd., then right about 3/4 mile to Schrier Park

Trail Type: Hiking/Walking, Cross Country Skiing, Interpretive
Trail Distance: 1.5 mi   Loops: 3   Shortest: .25 mi Longest: .75 mi
Trail Surface: Natural and paved
Trail Use Fee: None
Method Of Ski Trail Grooming: None
Skiing Ability Suggested: Novice
Hiking Trail Difficulty: Easy
Mountain Biking Ability Suggested: NA
Terrain: Steep 0%, Hilly 0%, Moderate 30%, Flat 70%
Camping: None

Maintained by the City of Portage, Parks and Recreation Department
Park with playground, pavilion and picnic area
50 acre park.
Handicapper facilities include restrooms, .25 mile paved trail, paviliion and
playground

MARSH TRAIL

INTERPRETIVE
TRAIL

ORCHARD
TRAIL

P

NORTH

S. WESTNEDGE
3/4 MILE

OSTERHOUT RD

SCHRIER PARK

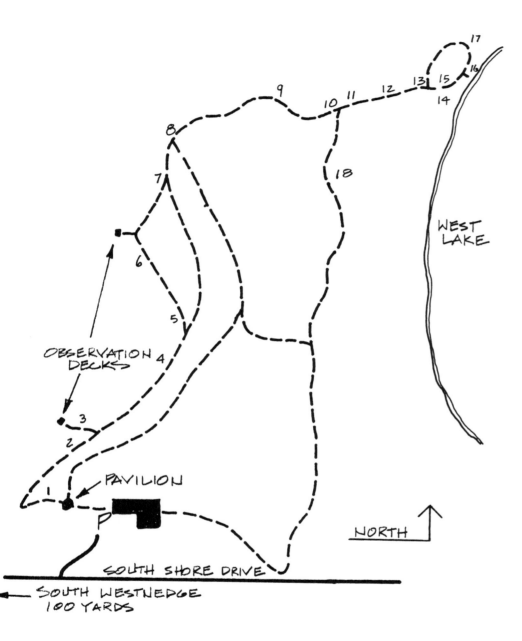

City of Portage, Parks and Recreation Department
7900 S. Westnedge
Portage, MI 49002

616-329-4522

Michigan Atlas & Gazetteer Location: 28C3

County Location: Kalamazoo

Directions To Trailhead:
I-94 to exit 76-A(S. Westnedge), then south on Westnedge about 4 miles to South Shore Drive, then left about 100 yards to the park entrance.

Trail Type: Hiking/Walking, Cross Country Skiing, Interpretive
Trail Distance: 1.5 mi   Loops: 2   Shortest: .25 mi Longest: 1 mi
Trail Surface: Bark, natural, boardwalk and paved
Trail Use Fee: None
Method Of Ski Trail Grooming: None
Skiing Ability Suggested: Novice
Hiking Trail Difficulty: Easy
Mountain Biking Ability Suggested: NA
Terrain: Steep 0%, Hilly 0%, Moderate 20%, Flat 80%
Camping: None

Maintained by the City of Portage, Parks and Recreation Department
Three interpretive trails available.
80 acres preserve with extensive wetland area and observation decks
Handicapper faclities include a .25 mile handicapper trail with overlook, restrooms, shelter and playground.

WEST LAKE NATURE PRESERVE

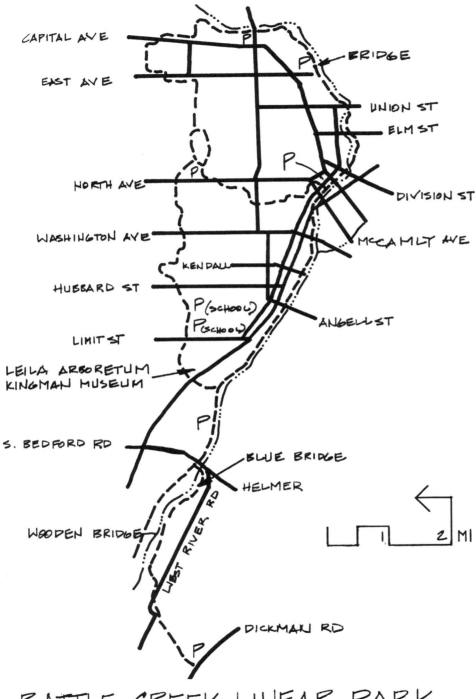

City of Battle Creek, Parks and Recreation Department
124 E. Michigan Ave
Battle Creek, Mi 49017

616-966-3431

Michigan Atlas & Gazetteer Location: 29B56

County Location: Calhoun

Directions To Trailhead:
In downtown Battle Creek and west to Dickman Rd

Trail Type: Hiking/Walking, Cross Country Skiing, Interpretive
Trail Distance: 17 mi   Loops: 3   Shortest: 2 mi   Longest: 8 mi
Trail Surface: Paved
Trail Use Fee: None
Method Of Ski Trail Grooming: None
Skiing Ability Suggested: Novice
Hiking Trail Difficulty: Easy
Mountain Biking Ability Suggested: NA
Terrain: Steep 5%, Hilly 5%, Moderate 40%, Flat 50%
Camping: None

Owned by Battle Creek
Excellent looped city trail system.
Restaurants and shops along the trail.
During the winter holiday season, a light show is presented along the trail.
Great trail for roller blading and other hard surfaced trail activities.

BATTLE CREEK LINEAR PARK

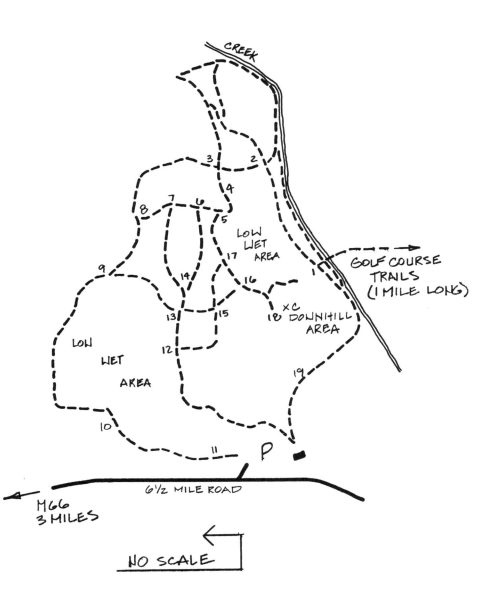

Binder Park Inc.
123 E. Michigan Ave.
Battle Creek, MI 49017

616-966-3431

Michigan Atlas & Gazetteer Location: 29C6

County Location: Calhoun

Directions To Trailhead:
South of I94 on M66, then east on B Drive South. about 1.75 miles to intersection. Enter to the left.

Trail Type: Hiking/Walking, Cross Country Skiing
Trail Distance: 7 mi   Loops: 6   Shortest: .25 mi Longest: 3 mi
Trail Surface: Natural
Trail Use Fee: Yes
Method Of Ski Trail Grooming: Packed with snowmobile
Skiing Ability Suggested: Novice to advanced
Hiking Trail Difficulty: Easy to moderate
Mountain Biking Ability Suggested: NA
Terrain: Steep 10%, Hilly 40%, Moderate 25%, Flat 25%
Camping: None

Operated by Binder Park Inc., a non-profit corporation.
Rentals, snack bar, instruction and sledding area is available.
Additional 1 mile long cross country skiing loop is on adjacent golf course accessable from Binder Park.
Picnic area and playground available in the summer.

BINDER PARK

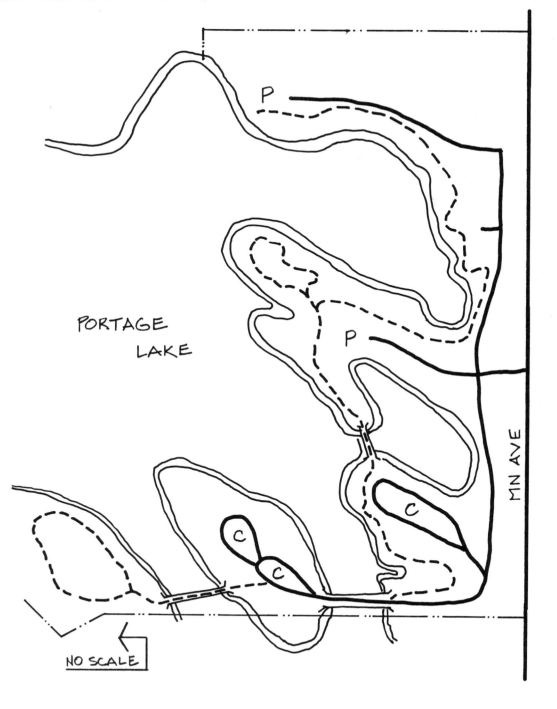

PORTAGE

LAKE

NO SCALE

COLDBROOK COUNTY PARK

Coldbrook County Park

Kalamazoo County Parks and Recreation Department
2900 Lake St.   616-383-8778
Kalamazoo, MI 49001

Michigan Atlas & Gazetteer Location: 29B5

County Location: Kalamazoo

Directions To Trailhead:
Between Battle Creek and Kalamazoo, just south of I64. Exit I64 at 35th Street
for about 1.5 miles to MN Ave. Then turn left (east) to the park entrance which
will be on the left about 4 miles, just past 42nd Street..

Trail Type: Hiking/Walking, Cross Country Skiing
Trail Distance: 4.5 mi   Loops: 2   Shortest: Longest:
Trail Surface: Natural
Trail Use Fee: None but vehicle entry fee required
Method Of Ski Trail Grooming: None
Skiing Ability Suggested: Novice
Hiking Trail Difficulty: Easy
Mountain Biking Ability Suggested: NA
Terrain: Flat to slightly rolling
Camping: Summer camping with both rustic and improved sites available

Maintained by the Kalamazoo County Parks and Recreation Department.
This is complete recreation area with swimming, boat rentals, camping picnic
grounds with shelters, ice fishing, ice skating, boat ramp and access to three
lakes. The park contains about 275 acres.

Fort Custer Recreation Area
5163 W. Fort Custer Drive
Augusta, MI 49012

616-731-4200

DNR Parks and Recreation Division

517-373-1270
517-322-1300

Michigan Atlas & Gazetteer Location: 29B5

County Location: Kalamazoo

Directions To Trailhead:
5 miles west of Battle Creek and .25 mile east of Augusta on M96 (Dickman Rd.)
Trailhead - At Whitford and Lawler Lakes picnic area
Trailhead - Trailhead parking lot just east of the campground parking lot

Trail Type: Hiking/Walking, Cross Country Skiing, Mountain Biking, Interpretive
Trail Distance: 13+ mi   Loops: Many   Shortest: .75 mi Longest: 5+ mi
Trail Surface: Paved(some rough), gravel and natural
Trail Use Fee: None, but vehicle entry fee required
Method Of Ski Trail Grooming: None
Skiing Ability Suggested: Novice
Hiking Trail Difficulty: Easy
Mountain Biking Ability Suggested: Novice to intermediate
Terrain: Steep 0%, Hilly 10%, Moderate 35%, Flat 55%
Camping: Campground available in the recreation area

Maintained by the DNR Parks and Recreation Division
Many old military reservation road, old trails, new trails and DNR trails available for use.
Horse back riding is permitted in the area but little used in recent years.
Recently the members of the Michigan Mountain Biking Association have been expanding the trail system with additional excellent technical single track trails.
All trails are open to mountain biking. Reviewed in the 1994 Summer issue of the Michigan Cyclist Magazine
Campground located along the lake.
Cabin rentals available.
Group camping area available.

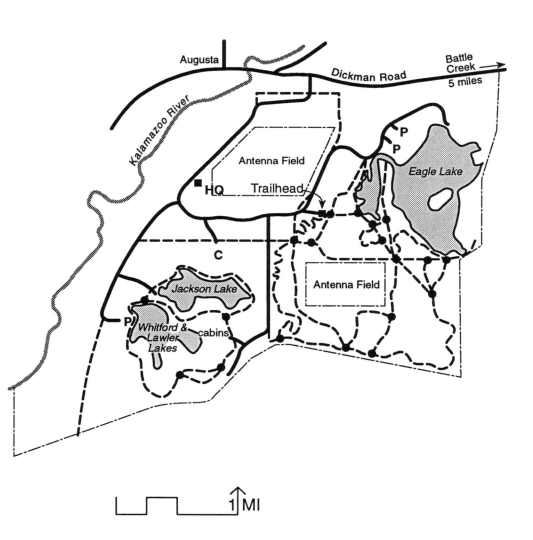

Fort Custer Recreation Area

Eaton County Parks and Recreation Area
3808 Grand Ledge Hwy
Grand Ledge , MI 48837

517-627-7351

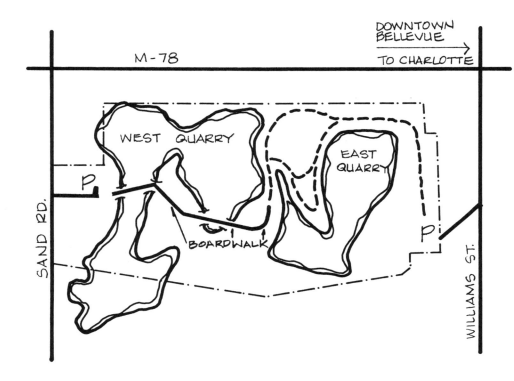

Michigan Atlas & Gazetteer Location: 29A7

County Location: Eaton

Directions To Trailhead:
I-96 to exit 98A (27/I69 south) towards Charlotte. Travel 23 miles to exit 48(Bellevue exit M78 west). Turn right on west M78 to park

Trail Type: Hiking/Walking, Cross Country Skiing, Interpretive
Trail Distance: 1.5 mi   Loops: 2   Shortest: .3 mi   Longest: .5 mi
Trail Surface: Natural
Trail Use Fee: None
Method Of Ski Trail Grooming: Track set
Skiing Ability Suggested: Novice
Hiking Trail Difficulty: Easy
Mountain Biking Ability Suggested: NA
Terrain: Steep 0%, Hilly 0%, Moderate 2%, Flat 98%
Camping: Campground available in Olivet

Operated by the Eaton County Parks and Recreation Department
Picnic area availible.
Naturalist programs available with reservations.
Fishing and ice skating available.

KEEHNE ENVIRONMENTAL AREA

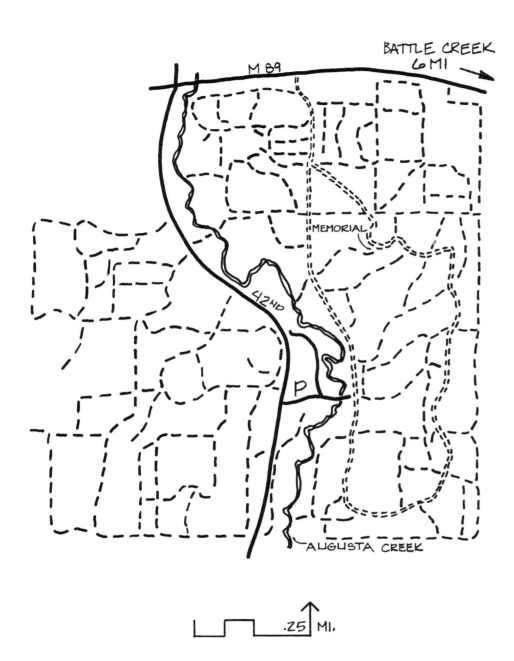

Kellogg Forest
42nd Street
Augusta , MI 49012

616-731-4597

Michigan Atlas & Gazetteer Location: 29B5

County Location: Kalamazoo

Directions To Trailhead:
9 miles west of Battle Creek on M89 at 42nd St.
Parking lot on 42nd St. about .5 mile south of M89.

Trail Type: Hiking/Walking, Interpretive
Trail Distance: 40 mi   Loops: Many   Shortest: Longest: 2.25 mi
Trail Surface: Gravel and natural
Trail Use Fee: None
Method Of Ski Trail Grooming: None
Skiing Ability Suggested: Novice to intermediate
Hiking Trail Difficulty: Easy
Mountain Biking Ability Suggested: NA
Terrain: Steep 0%, Hilly 15%, Moderate 60%, Flat 25%
Camping: None

Operated by Michigan State University as a forestry research station
Trails used for skiing and hiking are lanes developed for research purposes.
Off trail skiing is not permitted.
Some snowmobiles in the general area but they usually do not use the lanes
that are used for hiking and skiing
Open 8am to 5pm everyday except holidays

KELLOGG FOREST

Scotts Mill Park
8507 S. 35th St   616-626-9738
Scotts, MI 49088

Kalamazoo County Parks an Recreation Department
2900 Lake St   616-383-8778
Kalamazoo, MI 49001

Michigan Atlas & Gazetteer Location: 29C4

County Location: Kalamazoo

Directions To Trailhead:
I-94 to exit 85, south on 35th St to MN Ave, then west on MN Ave to 34th St.,
then south on 34th St. to Q Ave, then east on Q Ave to 35th St, then south on
35th St to the park.

NO MAP

Trail Type: Interpretive
Trail Distance: 1 mi   Loops: 1   Shortest: NA   Longest: 1 mi
Trail Surface: Natural
Trail Use Fee: Yes, varies
Method Of Ski Trail Grooming: NA
Skiing Ability Suggested: NA
Hiking Trail Difficulty: NA
Mountain Biking Ability Suggested: NA
Terrain: 100%Flat
Camping: None

Maintained by the Kalamazoo County Parks and Recreation Department
1870 working Grist Mill powered water wheel
Fishing docks pedal and row boats and picnic area, ball field, play equipment

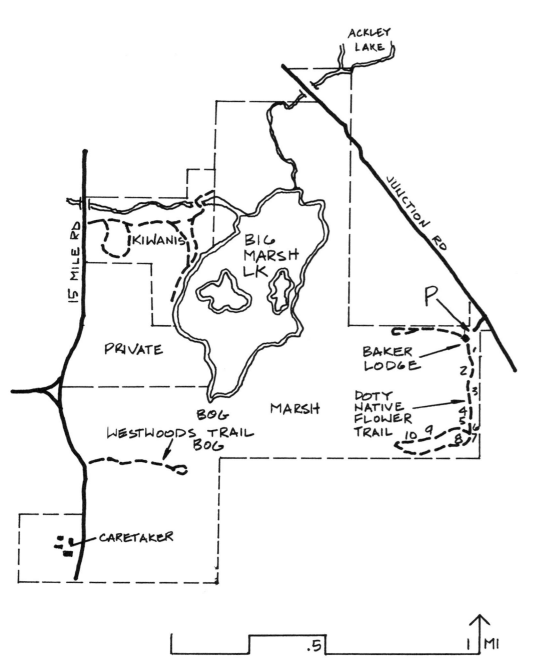

Michigan Audubon Society
21145 15 Mile Rd
Bellevue, MI 49021

616-763-3090

Michigan Atlas & Gazetteer Location: 30A1

County Location: Calhoun

Directions To Trailhead:
North on I-69 from I-94 to the first exit(N Drive North), then west to first road north(16 Mile Rd), then take 16 Mile Rd to first fork to left(Junction Rd), then take left fork about 1/3 mile to the sanctuary.

Trail Type: Hiking/Walking, Interpretive
Trail Distance: 1.25 mi   Loops: 2   Shortest: .25 mi Longest: 1 mi
Trail Surface: Paved and natural
Trail Use Fee: None
Method Of Ski Trail Grooming: NA
Skiing Ability Suggested: NA
Hiking Trail Difficulty: Easy
Mountain Biking Ability Suggested: NA
Terrain: Steep 0%, Hilly 0%, Moderate 50%, Flat 50%
Camping: None

Owned by the Michigan Audubon Society.
The main trail in the sanctuary is the Doty Native Flower Trail. This is a 10 station interpretive trail.
Lodge on site is available for rent.
Resident manager is present.
Call or write for brochures on the sanctuary and the trail.

BAKER SANCTUARY

City of Albion
112 W. Cass St   517-629-5535
Albion, MI 49224

NO MAP

Michigan Atlas & Gazetteer Location: 30BC23

County Location: Calhoun

Directions To Trailhead:
Exit I-94 at exit 121, then south on Eaton St. to first light, then turn right onto
Austin Ave to the first light, then left onto Albion St to Brownswwod Rd. and to
the Park

Trail Type: Hiking/Walking, Cross Country Skiing, Mountain Biking

Trail Surface: Wood chips
Trail Use Fee: None
Method Of Ski Trail Grooming: None
Skiing Ability Suggested: Novice
Hiking Trail Difficulty: Easy
Mountain Biking Ability Suggested: Novice
Terrain: 100% Flat
Camping: None

Owned by the City of Albion
Underdevelopment at this time (1994)

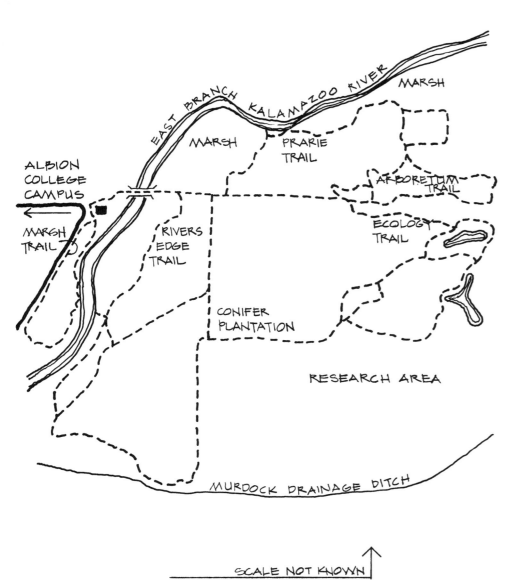

EAST BRANCH KALAMAZOO RIVER

MARSH

ALBION COLLEGE CAMPUS

MARSH

PRARIE TRAIL

ARBORETUM TRAIL

MARSH TRAIL

RIVERS EDGE TRAIL

ECOLOGY TRAIL

CONIFER PLANTATION

RESEARCH AREA

MURDOCK DRAINAGE DITCH

SCALE NOT KNOWN

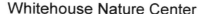

Whitehouse Nature Center
Albion College
Albion, MI 49224

517-629-2030

Michigan Atlas & Gazetteer Location: 30C3

County Location: Calhoun

Directions To Trailhead:
Located 1/4 mile southeast of Albion College main campus, on the east branch of the Kalamazoo River at the end of the athletic field.

Trail Type: Hiking/Walking, Interpretive
Trail Distance: 5 mi   Loops: 5   Shortest: Longest:
Trail Surface: Natural
Trail Use Fee: None
Method Of Ski Trail Grooming: NA
Skiing Ability Suggested: NA
Hiking Trail Difficulty: Easy
Mountain Biking Ability Suggested: NA
Terrain:
Camping: None

Owned and maintained by Albion College
Established in 1972
Six self guiding nature/hiking trails are provided:
　　　Rivers Edge Trail - 1.3 miles
　　　Prairie Trail - 1.1 miles
　　　Ecology Trail - 2.4 miles (1.5 miles short loop)
　　　Marsh Trail - .5 mile
　　　Ewell A. Stowelll Arboretum Trail - 1 mile
　　　History Trail -
Brochure available

Dahlem Environmental Education Center
7117 S. Jackson Rd
Jackson, Mi 49201

517-782-3453

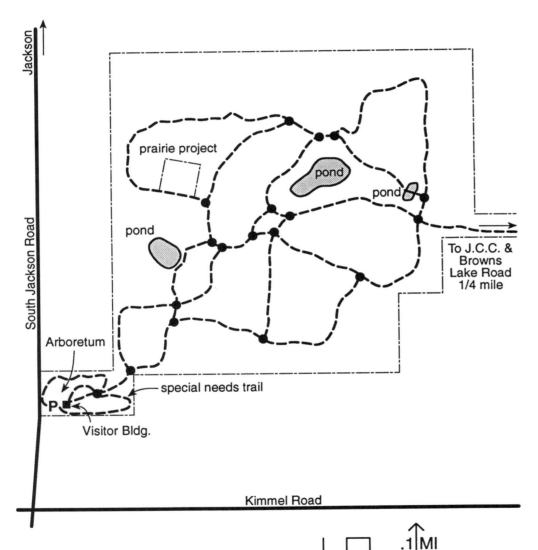

Michigan Atlas & Gazetteer Location: 31C5

County Location: Jackson

Directions To Trailhead:
I-94 to exit 142, then south on M127 to Monroe exit, then left on McDevitt to the 1st traffic light, then left(south) and follow signs to the Dahlem Center. Center is located just west of Jackson Community College on west side of Browns Lake Rd.

Trail Type: Hiking/Walking, Cross Country Skiing, Interpretive
Trail Distance: 5 mi   Loops: 8   Shortest: .4 mi   Longest: 2 mi
Trail Surface: Paved and natural
Trail Use Fee: Skiing for members only, otherwise free
Method Of Ski Trail Grooming: None
Skiing Ability Suggested: Novice and intermediate
Hiking Trail Difficulty: Easy
Mountain Biking Ability Suggested: NA
Terrain: Steep 0%, Hilly 0%, Moderate 75%, Flat 25%
Camping: None

Public non-profit environmental education center
Visitor Center building houses exhibits, offices and gift shop.
Many activities for the family.
Many special programs held seasonally.
Cross country skiing is limited to members and guests only.
Contact the center to become a member.

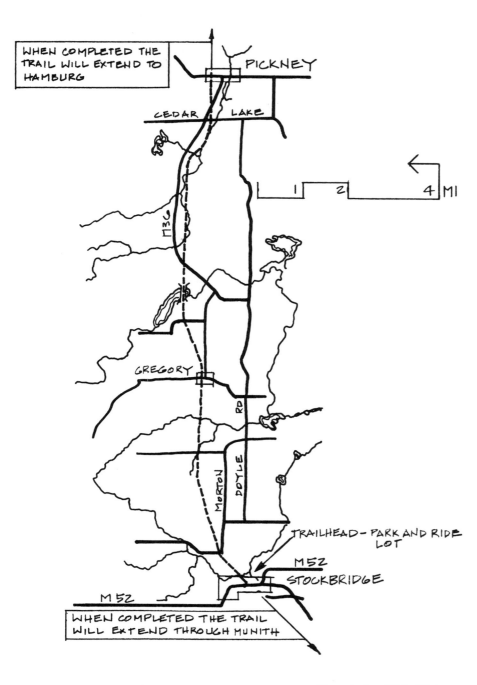

WHEN COMPLETED THE TRAIL WILL EXTEND TO HAMBURG

PICKNEY

CEDAR LAKE

M36

1 2 4 MI

GREGORY

RD

DOYLE

MORTON

TRAILHEAD - PARK AND RIDE LOT

M52

STOCKBRIDGE

M52

WHEN COMPLETED THE TRAIL WILL EXTEND THROUGH MUNITH

LAKELANDS TRAIL STATE PARK

Lakelands Trail State Park

Pinckney Recreation Area
8555 Silver Lake Rd
Pinckney, MI 48169

313-426-4913
fax 426-1916

DNR Parks and Recreation Division

517-322-1300
517-373-1270

Michigan Atlas & Gazetteer Location: 31A7,32A12

County Location: Livingston, Ingham

Directions To Trailhead:
Temporary east trailhead - Pinckney, north side of the village at the old railroad station
Temporary west trailhead - M52 in southside of Stockbridge
Future east trailhead - Hamburg (1995)

Trail Type: Hiking/Walking, Cross Country Skiing, Mountain Biking
Trail Distance: 12 mi   Loops: NA   Shortest: NA   Longest: NA
Trail Surface: Crushed stone
Trail Use Fee: None, but subject to change
Method Of Ski Trail Grooming: None
Skiing Ability Suggested: Novice
Hiking Trail Difficulty: Easy
Mountain Biking Ability Suggested: Novice
Terrain: 100% Flat
Camping: None along trail but nearby at adjacent recreation areas

Managed by the DNR Parks and Recreation Division
New rail trail opened in 1994.
Future expansion will extend trail eastward to Hamburg (in 1995) adding 7.5 miles and westward to Munith area in Jackson Co. with total of 36 miles.
Many nearby trails in Waterloo, Brighton, Pinckney Recreation Areas; Huron Meadows Metropark, Independence Lake County Park and more.

Waterloo Recreation Area
16345 McClure Rd, Rte 1
Chelsea, MI 48118

313-475-8307

DNR Parks and Recreation Division

517-373-1270

Michigan Atlas & Gazetteer Location: 31AB67,32AB1

County Location: Jackson & Washtenaw

Directions To Trailhead:
Adjacent to and NW of I94 and M52 and the city of Chelsea. Winter trailhead-From Chelsea east on Cavanaugh Lake Rd. to Pierce Rd., then north .5 mile to the Cedar Lake Outdoor Center. Summer trailhead-Mill Lake Outdoor Center or Eddy Geology Interpretive Center

Trail Type: Hiking/Walking, Cross Country Skiing, Interpretive
Trail Distance: 41 mi   Loops: Many   Shortest: .13 mi Longest: 23 mi
Trail Surface: Natural
Trail Use Fee: None, but vehicle entry fee required
Method Of Ski Trail Grooming: None
Skiing Ability Suggested: Novice to advanced
Hiking Trail Difficulty: Easy to difficult
Mountain Biking Ability Suggested: NA
Terrain: Steep 15%, Hilly 40%, Moderate 25%, Flat 20%
Camping: Two modern and two rustic campgrounds available

Maintained by the DNR Parks and Recreation Division.
Eddy Geology Center features many exhibits and a staff naturalist.
Eddy Geology Center is the trailhead for the trails listed on the map.
Warming shelter & snack bar open winter weekends at Cedar Lake Lodge.

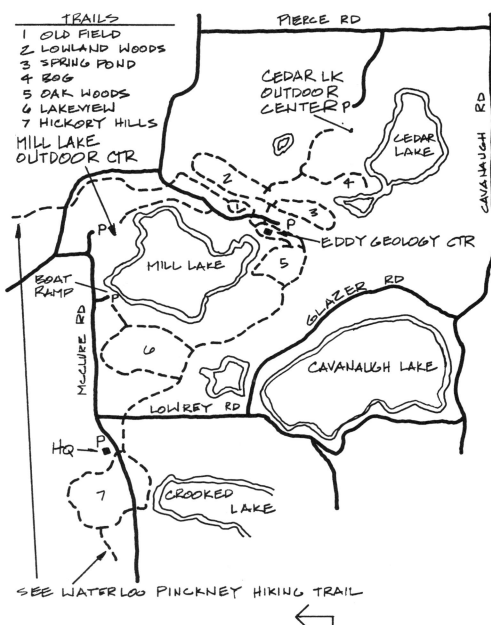

TRAILS
1 OLD FIELD
2 LOWLAND WOODS
3 SPRING POND
4 BOG
5 OAK WOODS
6 LAKEVIEW
7 HICKORY HILLS

MILL LAKE OUTDOOR CTR

PIERCE RD

CEDAR LK OUTDOOR CENTER P

CEDAR LAKE

CAVANAUGH RD

EDDY GEOLOGY CTR

MILL LAKE

BOAT RAMP

McCLURE RD

GLAZER RD

CAVANAUGH LAKE

LOWREY RD

HQ

CROOKED LAKE

SEE WATERLOO PINCKNEY HIKING TRAIL

.5   1 MI

EDDY GEOLOGY CENTER HIKING TRAILS
WATERLOO RECREATION AREA

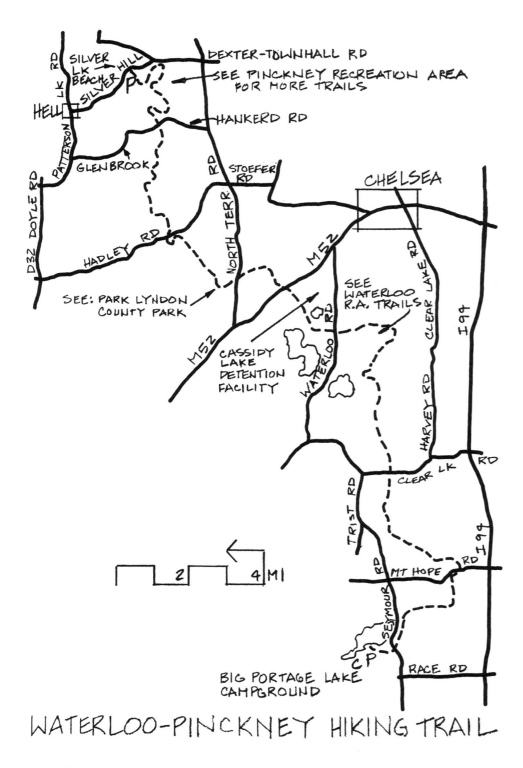

Waterloo Recreation Area
16345 McClure Rd, Rte 1   313-475-8307
Chelsea, MI 48118

Pinckney Recreation Area
8555 Silver Hill Rd., Rte 1   313-426-4913
Pinckney, MI 48169

Michigan Atlas & Gazetteer Location: 31B7,32AB12

County Location: Jackson, Washtenaw & Livingston

Directions To Trailhead:
Between Waterloo and Pinckney Recreation Areas, NW of Ann Arbor
East trailhead-Silver Lake Beach in Pinckney Recreation Area
West trailhead-Big Portage Lake Picnic Area in Waterloo Recreation Area
Other trailhead - Waterloo Recreation Area Headquarters

Trail Type: Hiking/Walking, Cross Country Skiing
Trail Distance: 25 mi   Loops: NA   Shortest: NA   Longest: NA
Trail Surface: Natural
Trail Use Fee: None, but vehicle entry fee required
Method Of Ski Trail Grooming: None
Skiing Ability Suggested: Advanced
Hiking Trail Difficulty: Moderate
Mountain Biking Ability Suggested: NA
Terrain: Steep 2%, Hilly 20%, Moderate 60%, Flat 18%
Camping: Campgrounds available at both recreation areas

Maintained by the DNR Parksand Recreation Division
This trail was not designed for skiing, but portions can be skied. Trail is connected to the Waterloo Recreation Area ski trail at the Cedar Lake Outdoor Center on Pierce Rd and the Potawatomi Trail system in the Pinckney Recreation Area and Big Portage Lake Campground. Trail marking may not be complete is some sections. Be prepared by taking   a compass along with you. Call to confirm adequacy of trail markings. The trail section between McClure Rd west of the Hq's and Katz Rd is used by horseback riders. The Pond Lily Lookout has a spectacular view. Many side trails are not shown. See also Waterloo Recreation Area and Pinckney Recreation Area for more trails.

WATERLOO-PINCKNEY HIKING TRAIL

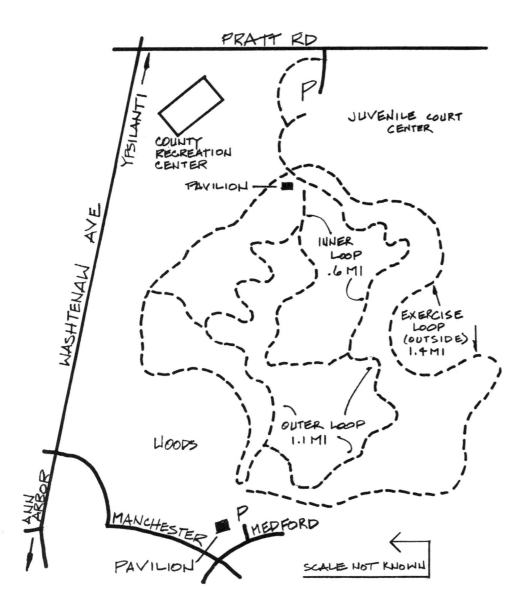

Washtenaw County Parks & Recreation Commission
PO Box 8645
Ann Arbor, MI 48107

313-971-6337

Michigan Atlas & Gazetteer Location: 32B4

County Location: Washtenaw

Directions To Trailhead:
Between Ann Arbor and Ypsilanti on Washtenaw Ave, just east of the Washtenaw and East Stadium Blvd intersection. West trailhead-Take Pratt Rd. south from Washtenaw Ave to parking lot. East trailhead-Take Manchester south from Washenaw Ave past a water tower to the first intersection, then east(left) on Medford to parking lot.

Trail Type: Hiking/Walking, Cross Country Skiing, Interpretive
Trail Distance: 3.5 mi   Loops: 4   Shortest: .5 mi   Longest: 1.4 mi
Trail Surface: Natural
Trail Use Fee: None
Method Of Ski Trail Grooming: None
Skiing Ability Suggested: Novice to intermediate
Hiking Trail Difficulty: Easy to moderate
Mountain Biking Ability Suggested: NA
Terrain: Steep 15%, Hilly 25%, Moderate 50%, Flat 10%
Camping: None

Maintained by the Washtenaw County Parks and Recreation Commission
Open and wooded landscape in the heart of the Ann Arbor metro area.
Shelter with restrooms, Par course along one trail.
The 18 acre Britton Woods Nature Area is located in the northwest corner of the park. .
The Parcour exercise trail is 1.4 miles long.

COUNTY FARM PARK

Furstenberg Park

32

City of Ann Arbor, Department of Parks and Recreation
PO Box 8647
Ann Arbor, MI 48107

313-994-2780

Michigan Atlas & Gazetteer Location: 32B4

County Location: Washtenaw

Directions To Trailhead:
From US23, take Geddes Rd exit westbound. At Huron Parkway, intersection go straight (Geddes Rd turns into Fuller Rd). Park is located on the south side of the road.

Trail Type: Hiking/Walking, Cross Country Skiing, Interpretive
Trail Distance: .75 mi   Loops: 2   Shortest: .25 mi Longest: .5 mi
Trail Surface: Paved
Trail Use Fee: None
Method Of Ski Trail Grooming: None
Skiing Ability Suggested: Novice
Hiking Trail Difficulty: Easy
Mountain Biking Ability Suggested: NA
Terrain: 100%Flat
Camping: None

Maintained by the CIty of Ann Arbor Department of Parks and Recreation
Additional trails are planned for construction in 1994 and 1995 to double existing trail distances.
Adjacent to Gallup Park. Proposed bridge to link the two parks in the future.

HURON HIGH SCHOOL

FULLER RD

CP

FUTURE

HURON RIVER

GALLUP PARK TRAIL

TRAILS

SEE GALLUP PARK

BRIDGE

NORTH

FURSTENBERG PARK

45

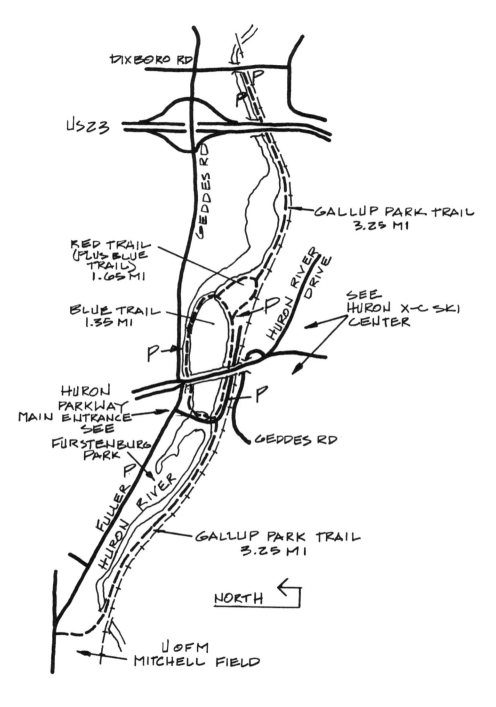

GALLUP PARK

City of Ann Arbor, Department of Parks and Recreation
PO Box 8647
Ann Arbor, MI 48107

313-994-2780

Michigan Atlas & Gazetteer Location: 32B4

County Location: Washtenaw

Directions To Trailhead:
From US 23 take Geddes Rd exit westbound, then at Huron PArkway intersection go straight (Geddes Rd becomes Fuller Rd) take first left hand turn into park.

Trail Type: Hiking/Walking, Cross Country Skiing, Interpretive
Trail Distance: 5.28 mi   Loops: 2   Shortest: 1.35 mi Longest: 1.65 mi
Trail Surface: Paved and wood chips
Trail Use Fee: None
Method Of Ski Trail Grooming: None
Skiing Ability Suggested: Novice
Hiking Trail Difficulty: Easy
Mountain Biking Ability Suggested: NA
Terrain: 100% Flat
Camping: None

Maintained by the City of Ann Arbor, Parks and Recreation Department
In addition to the two loop trails mentioned above there are additional point to point trails. They are the Dixboro Mile - 1.0 mi; Arboretum Mile - 1.0 mi and the Mitchell Filed Link - .28 mi. In addition the Gallup Park Trail (which include the above three) is designated a National Recreation Trail that is 3.25 miles long. The park facilities include a bike, paddleboat and canoe rentals, picnic shelters, fishing pond for youth, ball fields, meeting bldg, boat launch, play grounds, and and interpretifve display.
Site of frequent competitive events held annually.
See Furstenburg and Huron Golf Course and Cross Country Ski center trails which adjoin this park.
In addition to other city parks listed in this Atlas, Ann Arbor has many other city parks.

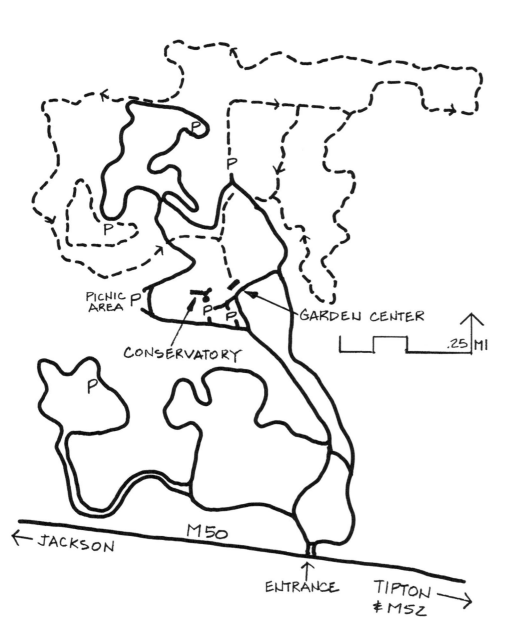

Director
Hidden Lake Gardens   517-431-2060
Tipton, MI 49287

Division Of Campus Park & Planning
412 Olds Hall, Michigan State University   517-355-9582
East Lansing, MI 48824

Michigan Atlas & Gazetteer Location: 32D1

County Location: Lenawee

Directions To Trailhead:
SE of Jackson on M50 west of Tipton

Trail Type: Hiking/Walking, Interpretive
Trail Distance: 5 mi   Loops: 4   Shortest: .2 mi   Longest: 3 mi
Trail Surface: Paved and natural
Trail Use Fee: None, but entry fee required
Method Of Ski Trail Grooming: NA
Skiing Ability Suggested: NA
Hiking Trail Difficulty: Easy to moderate
Mountain Biking Ability Suggested: NA
Terrain: Steep 0%, Hilly 80%, Moderate 10%, Flat 10%
Camping: None

Maintained by Michigan State University and administered by the Division of
Campus Park & Planning.
This facility is a landscape arboretum. The gardens include 670 acres on which
is a Plant Conservatory that contains a tropical dome, arid dome and
greenhouse; a Visitor Center with informative exhibits, auditorium, meeting
rooms, library and gift shop; a picnic area; and over 6 miles of one way roads.
The Gardens are set in the scenic Irish Hills which provides many scenic vistas
along the many trails .
Open 365 days from 8AM to dusk during April through October and 8AM to 4PM
weekdays and 9AM to 4:30 weekends and holidays during November to March.

HIDDEN LAKE GARDENS

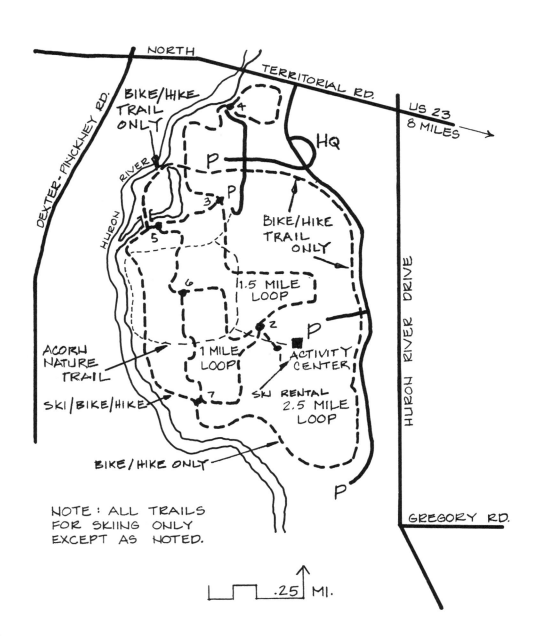

HUDSON MILLS
METROPARK

Hudson-Mills Metropark
880 N. Territorial Rd.
Dexter, MI 48130

313-426-8211
800-47-PARKS

Huron-Clinton Metropolitan Authority
13000 High Ridge Drive, PO Box 2001
Brighton, MI 48116-8001

810-227-2757

Michigan Atlas & Gazetteer Location: 32B2

County Location: Washtenaw

Directions To Trailhead:
NW of Ann Arbor on the Huron River. On North Territorial Rd just west of Huron River Drive, 8 miles west of US23

Trail Type: Hiking/Walking, Cross Country Skiing, Interpretive
Trail Distance: 7.5 mi   Loops: Several   Shortest: .5 mi   Longest: 2.5 mi
Trail Surface: Paved and natural
Trail Use Fee: None, but vehicle entry fee required
Method Of Ski Trail Grooming: Track set
Skiing Ability Suggested: Novice to intermediate
Hiking Trail Difficulty: Easy
Mountain Biking Ability Suggested: NA
Terrain: Steep 0%, Hilly 0%, Moderate 30%, Flat 70%
Camping: Group campground only, reservations required

Operated by the Huron-Clinton Metropolitan Authority.
Ski rentals, snack bar, picnic grounds and bike rentals.
Separate skiing, bike/hike and nature trails.
Ski trail loops are 1, 1.5, 2.5 and 2.5 miles.
The bike/hike trail is paved.
Ice skating when weather permits.
Typical summer recreation facilities are available.
Call or write for their Metropark Guide, published each year.

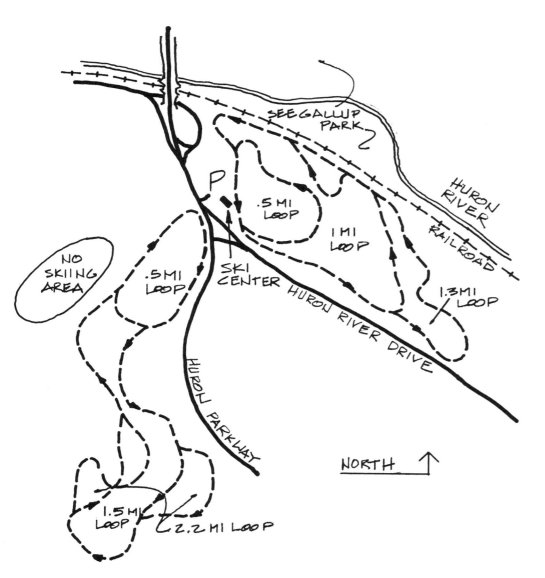

City of Ann Arbor, Parks and Recreation Department
PO Box 8647   313-994-2780
Ann Arbor, MI 48107   313-971-6840

Michigan Atlas & Gazetteer Location: 32B4

County Location: Washtenaw

Directions To Trailhead:
Take US23 to Washtenaw Ave exit west, then right onto Huron Parkway, then right onto Huron Drive, parking on left with overflow on right

Trail Type: Cross Country Skiing
Trail Distance: 2.2 mi   Loops: 6   Shortest: .5 mi   Longest: 2.2 mi
Trail Surface: Natural
Trail Use Fee: Yes, daily fee varies with day of the week
Method Of Ski Trail Grooming: Track set
Skiing Ability Suggested: Novice to intermediate
Hiking Trail Difficulty: NA
Mountain Biking Ability Suggested: NA
Terrain: Steep 1%, Hilly 10%, Moderate 19%, Flat 70%
Camping: None

Maintained by the City of Ann Arbor Parks and Recreation Department
135 acre golf course used for cross country skiing.
Trailhead and Ski Center at golf course club house.
Ski rental available at the Ski Center.

HURON HILLS GOLF COURSE
CROSS COUNTRY SKI CENTER

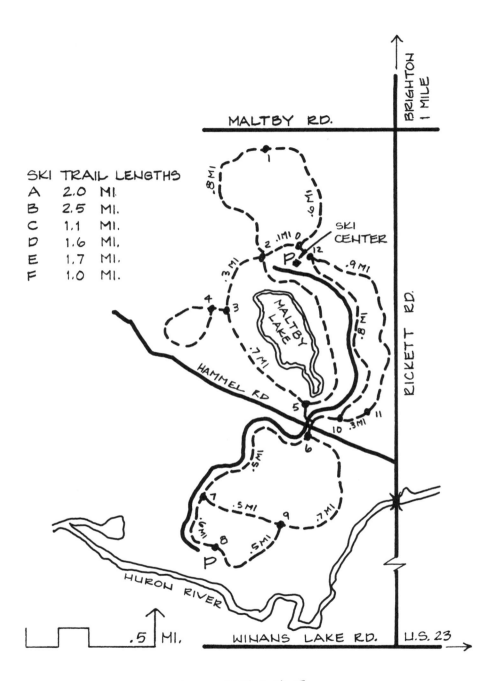

SKI TRAIL LENGTHS
A   2.0 MI.
B   2.5 MI.
C   1.1 MI.
D   1.6 MI.
E   1.7 MI.
F   1.0 MI.

SKI TRAILS
HURON MEADOWS METROPARK

Huron Meadows Metropark
8765 Hammel Rd.   810-227-2757
Brighton, MI 48130   800-47-PARKS

Huron-Clinton Metropolitan Authority
13000 High Ridge Drive   810-227-2757
Brighton, MI 48116-8001

Michigan Atlas & Gazetteer Location: 32A3

County Location: Livingston

Directions To Trailhead:
South of Brighton on US23, exit Silver Lake Rd. west, then south on Whitmore Lake Rd. 500 ft to Winans Lake Rd., then west .5 mile to Rickett Rd., then north on Rickett Rd. 1 mile to Hammel Rd., then west to park entrance

Trail Type: Cross Country Skiing
Trail Distance: 9 mi   Loops: 4   Shortest: 1.5 mi Longest: 6.1
Trail Surface: Natural
Trail Use Fee: None, but vehicle entry fee required
Method Of Ski Trail Grooming: Track set
Skiing Ability Suggested: Novice to intermediate
Hiking Trail Difficulty: NA
Mountain Biking Ability Suggested: NA
Terrain: Steep 5%, Hilly 20%, Moderate 50%, Flat 25%
Camping: None

Operated by the Huron-Clinton Metropolitan Authority.
Warming area, ski rentals and snack bar available.
Just east of the Brighton Recreation Area.
Some trails on the golf course.
Summer recreation includes golf course and picnic grounds.
Call or write for their Metropark Guide, published each year.

Independence Lake Park
3200 Jennings Rd.
Whitmore Lake, MI 48189

313-449-4437

Washtenaw County Parks and Recreation Commission
PO Box 8645
Ann Arbor, MI 48107

313-971-6337

Michigan Atlas & Gazetteer Location: 32A3

County Location: Washtenaw

Directions To Trailhead:
NW of Ann Arbor 2 miles west of US23 off Jennings Rd., 3 miles SW of Whitmore Lake

Trail Type: Hiking/Walking, Cross Country Skiing, Interpretive
Trail Distance: 1.3 mi   Loops: 1   Shortest: Longest: 1.3 mi
Trail Surface: Natural
Trail Use Fee: None, but an entrance fee is required
Method Of Ski Trail Grooming: None
Skiing Ability Suggested: Novice
Hiking Trail Difficulty: Easy
Mountain Biking Ability Suggested: NA
Terrain: Flat to rolling
Camping: None

Maintained by the Washtenaw County Parks and Recreation Commission
Restrooms available.
A nature area open only in the spring through fall seasons.
Pavilions available for rent.
Call ahead for park hours.

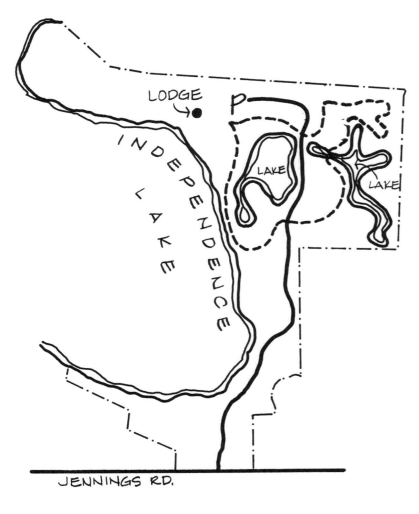

INDEPENDENCE LAKE COUNTY PARK

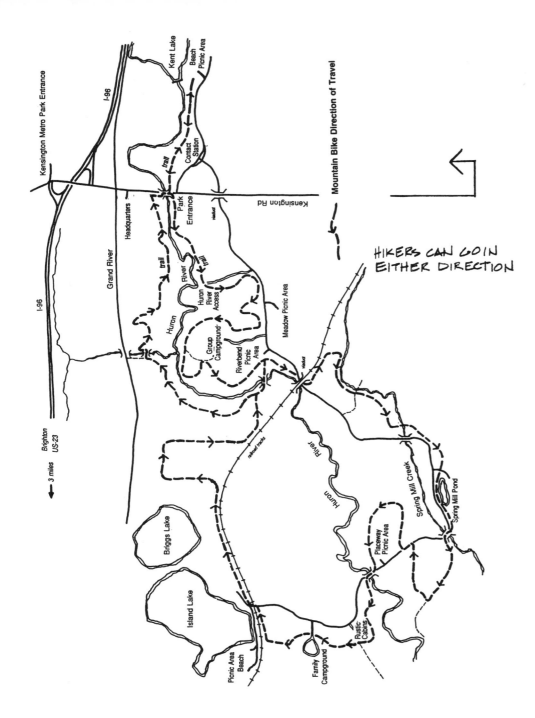

HIKERS CAN GO IN
EITHER DIRECTION

Island Lake Recreation Area
12950 East Grand River
Brighton , MI 48116

313-229-7067

DNR Parks and Recreation Division

517-373-1270

Michigan Atlas & Gazetteer Location: 32A4,40D4

County Location: Livingston

Directions To Trailhead:
West of Brighton on Grand River Ave to Kensington Rd., then south to the park entrance; or I-96 exit 151at Kensington Rd., then south to park entrance.
Trailhead at Riverbend Picnic Area and others throughout the park.

Trail Type: Hiking/Walking, Cross Country Skiing, Mountain Biking
Trail Distance: 14 mi   Loops: 2   Shortest: 6 mi   Longest: 8 mi
Trail Surface: Natural
Trail Use Fee: None, but vehicle entry fee required
Method Of Ski Trail Grooming: None
Skiing Ability Suggested: Novice to intermediate
Hiking Trail Difficulty: Easy
Mountain Biking Ability Suggested: Novice to intermediate
Terrain: Steep 1%, Hilly 20%, Moderate 60%, Flat 19%
Camping: Rustic, semi modern and organized campgrounds avaiable

Maintained by the DNR Parks and Recreation Division
Trails have recently been improved by park staff and members of the Michigan Mountain Biking Association. Trails are clearly marked. A large trail map is posted at the Riverbend Picnic Area. The 7 miles of the Huron River within the park boundary is designated as "country scenic", under the Natural Rivers Act. Adjacent to Kensington Metropark on the north. Swimming areas are available at two locations in the park. Other typical state park facilities are available including canoe rental by a private concession.
Some snowmobile conflict on summer non-motorized trails. Open to hunting - wear hunter orange during hunting season.

ISLAND LAKE RECREATION AREA

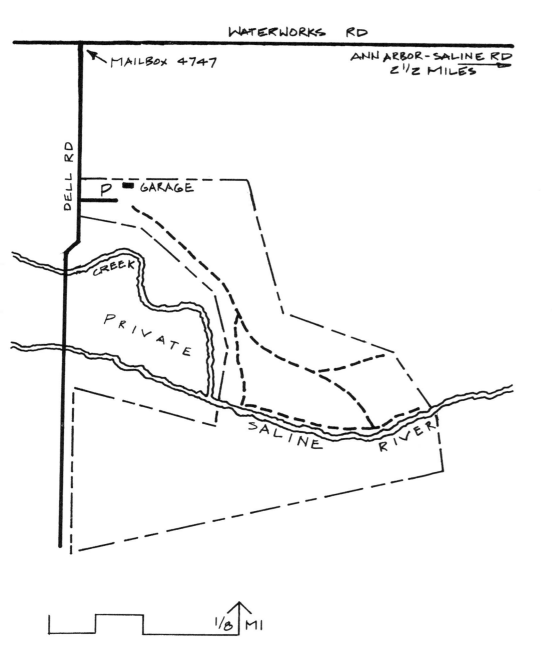

Michigan Nature Associaton
PO Box 102
Avoca, MI 48006

810-324-2626

Michigan Atlas & Gazetteer Location: 32C3

County Location: Washtenaw

Directions To Trailhead:
From Saline, take Ann Arbor -Saline Rd to the edge of town, then left (west) on Saline Waterworks Rd. Go about 2 miles and turn left(south) on a long straight drive marked with a mailbox 4747. Go about 500' south and take the fork to the left. Park by the MNA storage building (garage).

Trail Type: Interpretive
Trail Distance: .5 mi   Loops: 1   Shortest: NA   Longest: .5 mi
Trail Surface: Natural
Trail Use Fee: None
Method Of Ski Trail Grooming: NA
Skiing Ability Suggested: NA
Hiking Trail Difficulty: Easy
Mountain Biking Ability Suggested: NA
Terrain: Steep 0%, Hilly 0%, Moderate 20%, Flat 80%
Camping: None

Maintained by the Michigan Nature Association
Mostly floodplain area of the Saline River for 750' on both sides of the river.

RODMAN MEMORIAL PLANT PRESERVE

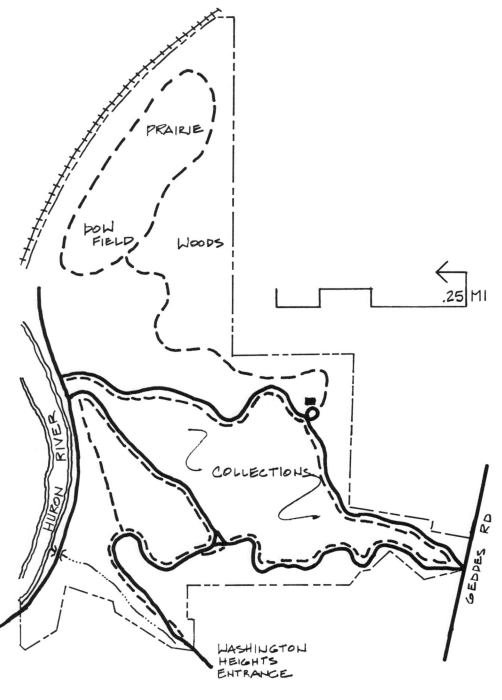

NICHOLS ARBORETUM

PRAIRIE

DOW FIELD

WOODS

HURON RIVER

COLLECTIONS

GEDDES RD

WASHINGTON HEIGHTS ENTRANCE

.25 MI

Nichols Arboretum

Nichols Arboretum
3012 D Dana, UM
Ann Arbor, MI 48109-1115

313-763-5823

Michigan Atlas & Gazetteer Location: 32B4

County Location: Washtenaw

Directions To Trailhead:
From I-94, take US23 north, then take Washtenaw Ave west , then right onto Observatory St., then right onto East Medical Campus Drive to Hosipital lot M29.

Trail Type: Hiking/Walking, Cross Country Skiing, Interpretive
Trail Distance: 3.5 mi   Loops: 4   Shortest: .25 mi Longest: 2.5 mi
Trail Surface: Natural and gravel
Trail Use Fee: None
Method Of Ski Trail Grooming: None
Skiing Ability Suggested: Novice
Hiking Trail Difficulty: Easy to moderate
Mountain Biking Ability Suggested: NA
Terrain: Steep 20%, Hilly 25%, Moderate 30%, Flat 23%
Camping: None

Owned by the University of Michigan.
124 acres, 1/2 mile of the Huron River shoreline
Write for their brochure.

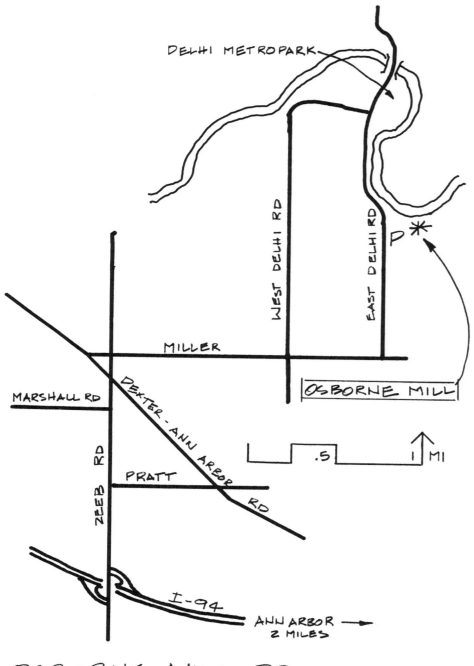

Washtenaw County Parks and Recreation Commission
PO Box 8645
Ann Arbor, MI 48107

313-971-6337

Michigan Atlas & Gazetteer Location: 32B3

County Location: Washtenaw

Directions To Trailhead:
I-94 to Zeeb Rd, then north to Miller Rd, east on Miller to E. Delhi, then left on E. Delhi to trailhead on right side of the road.

Trail Type: Hiking/Walking, Interpretive
Trail Distance: .25 mi   Loops: 1   Shortest: Longest:
Trail Surface: Natural
Trail Use Fee: None
Method Of Ski Trail Grooming: NA
Skiing Ability Suggested: NA
Hiking Trail Difficulty: Easy
Mountain Biking Ability Suggested: NA
Terrain: Steep 0%, Hilly 25%, Moderate 0%, Flat 75%
Camping: None

Maintained by Washtenaw County Parks and Recreation Commission

OSBORNE MILL PRESERVE NATURE TRAIL

Map

SEE WATERLOO PINCKNEY TRAIL

LADYSLIPPER CREEK

EMBURY WOODS

ESKER

OAK ISLAND

OAK ISLAND BOG

YELLOW LOOP

SHELTER

P

N. TERRITORIAL ROAD

M-52 1 MILE

P

SHELTER

ANN ARBOR

P

GREEN LOOP

BLUE LOOP

LAKE GENEVIEVE

SEE WATERLOO PINCKNEY TRAIL

.25 MI

Park Lyndon

Washtenaw County Parks and Recreation Commission
PO Box 8645
Ann Arbor, MI 48107

313-971-6337

Michigan Atlas & Gazetteer Location: 32A1

County Location: Washtenaw

Directions To Trailhead:
5 miles north of Chelsea and northwest of Ann Arbor 1 mile east of M52 on North Territorial Rd.

Trail Type: Hiking/Walking, Interpretive
Trail Distance: 2.75 mi   Loops: 3   Shortest: .75 mi Longest: 1.3 mi
Trail Surface: Natural
Trail Use Fee: None
Method Of Ski Trail Grooming: None
Skiing Ability Suggested: Intermediate to advanced
Hiking Trail Difficulty: Easy to moderate
Mountain Biking Ability Suggested: NA
Terrain: Steep 30%, Hilly 30%, Moderate 30%, Flat 10%
Camping: None

Maintained by the Washtenaw County Parks and Recreation Commission.
Restrooms, picnic grounds, restrooms, shelter and water available.
The 47 mile Waterloo-Pinckney Trail passes through this park.
Park Lyndon South contains the Embury Swamp Natural Area Preserve.
Naturalist available to lead walks for groups of 15 or more if advance arrangements are made.

PARK LYNDON

TRAIL NOTES

Pinckney Recreation Area
8555 Silver Hill Rd., Rte 1
Pinckney, MI 48169

313-426-4913

DNR Parks and Recreation Division

517-373-1270

Michigan Atlas & Gazetteer Location: 32A12

County Location: Livingston & Washtenaw

Directions To Trailhead:
15 miles NW of Ann Arbor at the Washtenaw County line. Trail head - From US23 west on N. Territorial Rd. about 10 miles to Dexter-Townhall Rd., turn north for 1.2 miles to Silver Hill Rd., bear left to parking lot at Silver Lake Beach.

SEE MAP ON NEXT PAGE

Trail Type: Hiking/Walking, Cross Country Skiing, Mountain Biking, Interpretive
Trail Distance: 26 mi   Loops: 3   Shortest: 1.9 mi Longest: 17.5 mi
Trail Surface: Natural and geoweb
Trail Use Fee: None, but vehicle entry fee required
Method Of Ski Trail Grooming: None
Skiing Ability Suggested: Intermediate
Hiking Trail Difficulty: Easy to moderate
Mountain Biking Ability Suggested: Intermediate to advanced
Terrain: Steep 5%, Hilly 15%, Moderate 65%, Flat 15%
Camping: Campgrounds available in the recreation area

Maintained by the DNR Parks and Recreation Division
Complete 10,000 acre recreation area with camping, beaches, picnic areas and trails.
Mountain biking and hiking permitted on the trail system. Mountain biking restricted to one-way travel as shown on the trail map. Trail maintenance by the Michigan Mountain Biking Association. Two 2 rustic campgrounds open in the snowless months. The Bruin Lake Campground is open all year. This system is the east end of the Pinckney-Waterloo Hiking Trail(46 mi). Mountain biking is not permitted on the Pinckney-Waterloo Hiking Trail beyond the Potawatomi Trail. Because of the heavy use of this trail for mountain biking, consider other trails in the area such as the Island Lake, Pontiac Lake, Holly, Bald Mountain and Brighton Recreation Areas and Maybury State Park.

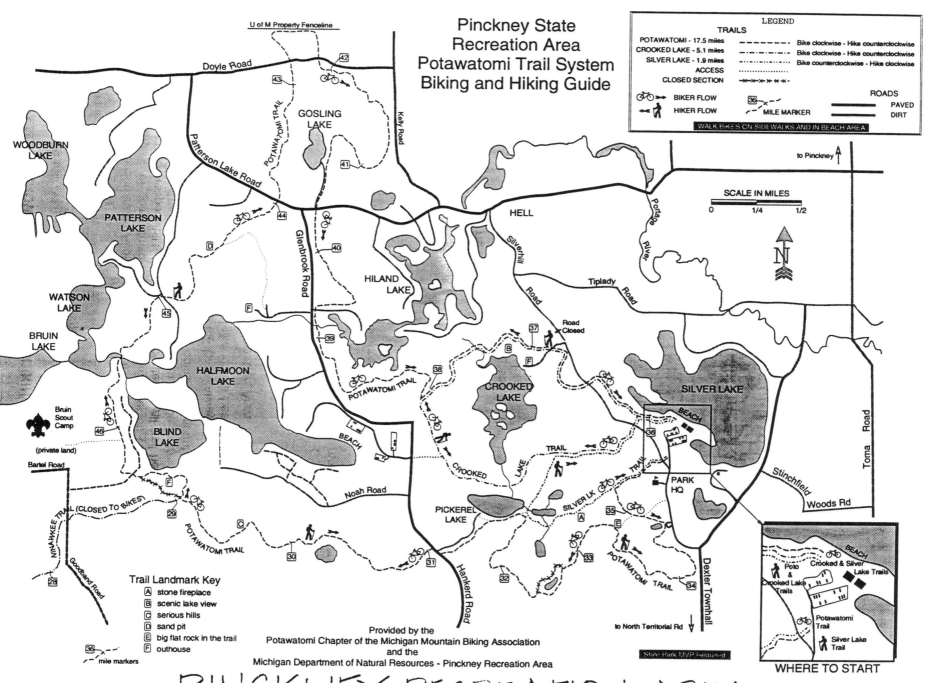

Pinckney State Recreation Area Potawatomi Trail System Biking and Hiking Guide

LEGEND

TRAILS
POTAWATOMI - 17.5 miles — Bike clockwise - Hike counterclockwise
CROOKED LAKE - 5.1 miles — Bike clockwise - Hike counterclockwise
SILVER LAKE - 1.9 miles — Bike counterclockwise - Hike clockwise
ACCESS
CLOSED SECTION

🚲 BIKER FLOW
🚶 HIKER FLOW
36 MILE MARKER

ROADS
PAVED
DIRT

WALK BIKES ON SIDEWALKS AND IN BEACH AREA

SCALE IN MILES
0   1/4   1/2

to Pinckney

N

U of M Property Fenceline

Doyle Road

WOODBURN LAKE

GOSLING LAKE

Patterson Lake Road

Kelly Road

PATTERSON LAKE

HELL

Portage River

Silverhill Road

Tiplady Road

WATSON LAKE

Glenbrook Road

HILAND LAKE

Road Closed

BRUIN LAKE

HALFMOON LAKE

CROOKED LAKE

SILVER LAKE

BEACH

Bruin Scout Camp

(private land)

BLIND LAKE

BEACH

PARK HQ

Stinchfield Woods Rd

Toma Road

Bartel Road

POTAWATOMI TRAIL

CROOKED LAKE TRAIL

SILVER LK TRAIL

Noah Road

PICKEREL LAKE

NINAWKEE TRAIL (CLOSED TO BIKES)

POTAWATOMI TRAIL

Goodband Road

POTAWATOMI TRAIL

Hankerd Road

Dexter Townhall

to North Territorial Rd

State Park MVP Required

Trail Landmark Key
Ⓐ stone fireplace
Ⓑ scenic lake view
Ⓒ serious hills
Ⓓ sand pit
Ⓔ big flat rock in the trail
Ⓕ outhouse

36 mile markers

Provided by the
Potawatomi Chapter of the Michigan Mountain Biking Association
and the
Michigan Department of Natural Resources - Pinckney Recreation Area

WHERE TO START
BEACH
Polo & Crooked Lake Trails
Crooked & Silver Lake Trails
Potawatomi Trail
Silver Lake Trail

PINCKNEY RECREATION AREA

FARMINGTON RD

ENTRANCE

WINDBREAK

P VISITOR CENTER

■

P

ORCHARD

P

ESTATE

RIVER

VALLEY

RIVER

WINDBREAK

BOG

MEADOW

BOG

ROUGE RIVER

1 MILE LOOP

RIVER

SCALE NOT KNOWN

City of Farmington Hills
31555 11 Mile Rd.
Farmington Hills, MI 48018

810-473-9570

Michigan Atlas & Gazetteer Location: 33A6

County Location: Oakland

Directions To Trailhead:
Located on Farmington Rd between 10 and 11 Mile Rds in Farmington Hills

Trail Type: Hiking/Walking, Cross Country Skiing, Interpretive
Trail Distance: 3 mi   Loops: Many   Shortest: .5 mi   Longest: 1.5 mi
Trail Surface: Paved and natural
Trail Use Fee: None
Method Of Ski Trail Grooming: Track set
Skiing Ability Suggested: Novice to intermediate
Hiking Trail Difficulty: Easy
Mountain Biking Ability Suggested: NA
Terrain: Steep 0%, Hilly 0%, Moderate 50%, Flat 50%
Camping: None

Maintained by the City of Farmington Hills.
Year around 211 acre park with some paved trails.
Ski rental, warming area, sledding hill, hockey rink, and ice skating available.
Along the banks of the Rouge River.

HERITAGE PARK

Wayne County Divsion of Parks
33175 Ann Arbor Trail
Westland, MI 48170

313-261-1990

Michigan Atlas & Gazetteer Location: 33B6

County Location: Wayne

Directions To Trailhead:
Farmington Rd south of I96 at Hines Drive.

Trail Type: Hiking/Walking, Interpretive
Trail Distance: 12 mi   Loops: 6   Shortest: .5 mi   Longest: 12 mi
Trail Surface: Natural
Trail Use Fee: None
Method Of Ski Trail Grooming: NA
Skiing Ability Suggested: NA
Hiking Trail Difficulty: Easy
Mountain Biking Ability Suggested: NA
Terrain: Steep 0%, Hilly 40%, Moderate 10%, Flat 50%
Camping: None

Managed by the Wayne County, Division of Parks
Preserve includes the Nankin Mills Nature Center and 500 acres along the
Tonquish Creek.
The Middle Rouge Parkway Trail (see other listing) passes through the area.
Trails open during daylight hours.
Call for hours of the nature center.

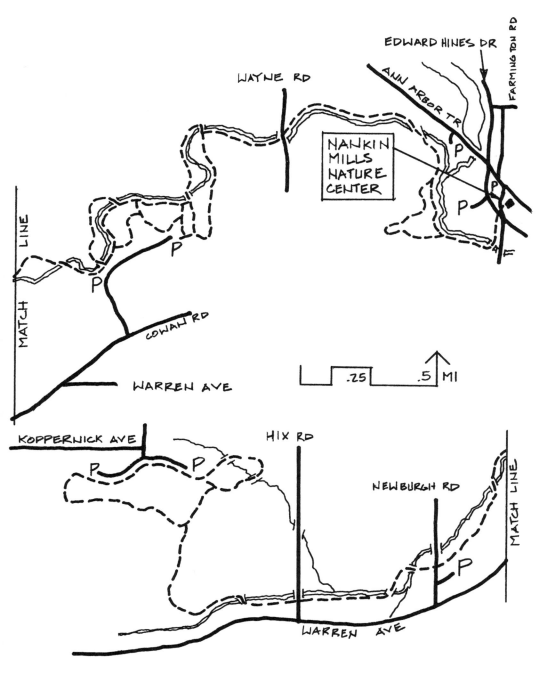

HOLLIDAY NATURE PRESERVE

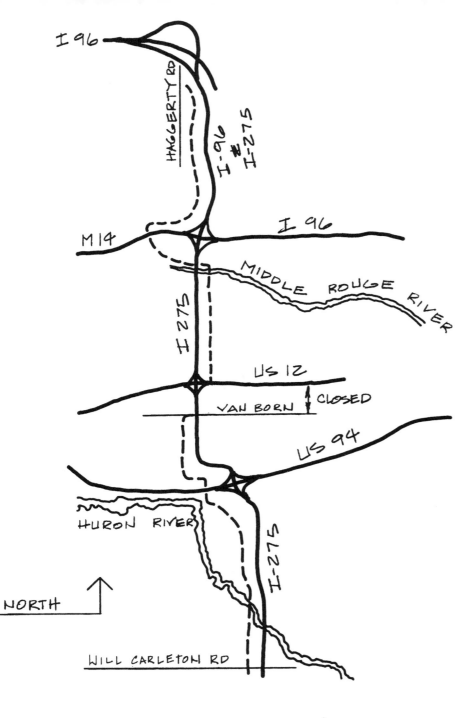

I96

HAGGERTY RD

I-96 & I-275

I96

M14

MIDDLE ROUGE RIVER

I 275

US 12

VAN BORN   CLOSED

US 94

HURON RIVER

I-275

NORTH

WILL CARLETON RD

I-275 BIKE PATH

Michigan Department of Transportation
425 West Ottawa St., PO Box 30050
Lansing, MI 48909

517-373-9049

Michigan Atlas & Gazetteer Location: 33A-D6

County Location: Oakland, Wayne

Directions To Trailhead:
Along the I-275 Interstate from Haggerty Rd to Will Carleton Rd with one exclusion from US12 to Van Born.

Trail Type: Hiking/Walking
Trail Distance: 33.5 mi   Loops: NA   Shortest: NA   Longest: NA
Trail Surface: Paved
Trail Use Fee: None
Method Of Ski Trail Grooming: NA
Skiing Ability Suggested: NA
Hiking Trail Difficulty: Easy
Mountain Biking Ability Suggested: NA
Terrain: Steep 0%, Hilly 0%, Moderate 10%, Flat 80%
Camping: None

Maintained by the Department of Transportation
Some trail sections accessible for handicappers.

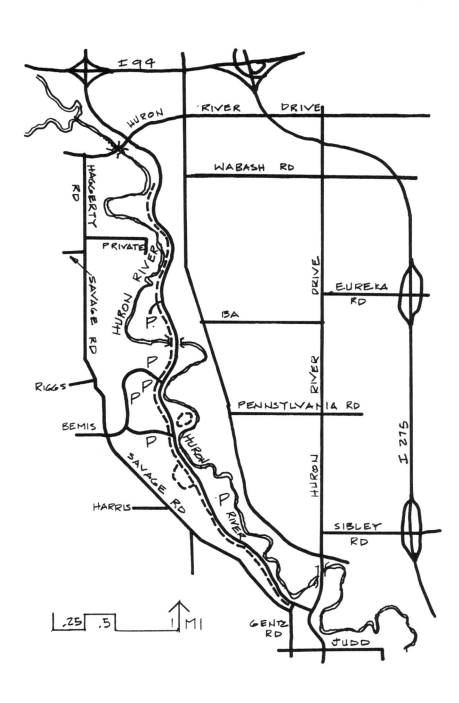

LOWER HURON METROPARK

Huron Clinton Metropolitan Authority
13000 High Ridge Drive, PO Box 2001
Brighton, MI 48116

810-227-2757
800-47-PARKS

Michigan Atlas & Gazetteer Location: 33C6

County Location: Wayne

Directions To Trailhead:
Exit I-94 at Haggerty Rd exit south .5 mile to park entrance

Trail Type: Hiking/Walking, Cross Country Skiing, Interpretive
Trail Distance: 2 mi   Loops: 2   Shortest: .75 mi Longest: 1.25 mi
Trail Surface: Paved and natural
Trail Use Fee: None, but vehicle entry fee required
Method Of Ski Trail Grooming: None
Skiing Ability Suggested: Novice
Hiking Trail Difficulty: Easy
Mountain Biking Ability Suggested: NA
Terrain: Steep 0%, Hilly 0%, Moderate 40%, Flat 60%
Camping: None

Operated by the Huron Clinton Metropolitan Authority
Pool, Par 3 golf, picnic areas and ball fields are available in this park.
Two nature trails are connected by a paved "bike-hike" trail along the main park road.
Call or write for their Metropark Guide, published each year.

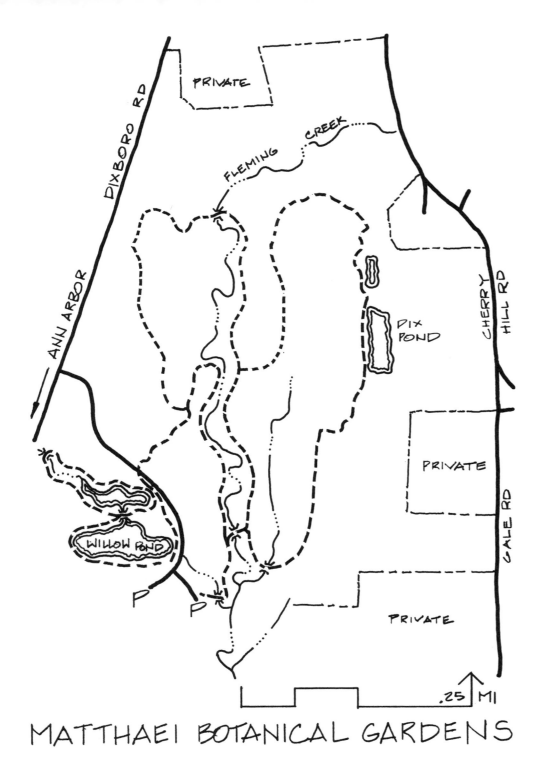

Matthaei Botanical Gardens
1800 N. Dixboro Rd
Ann Arbor, MI 48105

313-998-7061

Michigan Atlas & Gazetteer Location: 33B4

County Location: Washtenaw

Directions To Trailhead:
Exit US23 at the Plymounth Rd exit, then 1 mile east to Dixboro Rd, then south on Dixboro. Garden is .5 mile down
Dixboro/Plymouth Rd.

Trail Type: Hiking/Walking, Interpretive
Trail Distance: 3.6 mi   Loops: Several   Shortest: .6 mi   Longest: 1.8 mi
Trail Surface:
Trail Use Fee: None
Method Of Ski Trail Grooming: NA
Skiing Ability Suggested: NA
Hiking Trail Difficulty: Easy
Mountain Biking Ability Suggested: NA
Terrain: Steep 0%, Hilly 0%, Moderate 10%, Flat 90%
Camping: None

Owned by the University of Michigan
Including the trails, there is a conservatory , display gardens, shade garden, wildflower display and praire plantings
The four main trails are:
Parker Brook Trail - .6 mile
Musclewood Trail - .6 mile
Fleming Creek Trail - 1.2 miles
Dix Pond Trail - 1.8 miles

MATTHAEI BOTANICAL GARDENS

MAYBURY STATE PARK

Horseman's & Riding Stable Entrance **Beck Rd**

I-275
5 MI

M14
3 MILES →

Eight Mile Rd

Riding Stable Toilets

Private

Main Entrance

Private

Seven Mile Rd

Sports Fields

Living Farm

Ski and Bike Rental Concession

Toilets

Rain Shelter

Private

Private

Rain Shelter

Rain Shelter

Toilets

Loop Trail

Bike Mountain Trail

Rain Shelter

MB — — — Mountain Bike Trail
PT — · — Paved (hiking, walking, biking) Trail
H — — Hiking Trail
· · · · · Horse Trail
P Parking

Napier Rd

Maybury State Park

33

Maybury State Park
20145 Beck Rd.
Northville, MI 48167

810-349-8390
810-348-1190

DNR Parks and Recreation Regional Office

517-322-1300

Michigan Atlas & Gazetteer Location: 33A5

County Location: Wayne

Directions To Trailhead:
The exact NW corner of Wayne County
5 miles west of I-275 on 8 Mile Rd., between Napier and Beck Rds
Or take Beck Rd north from M-14 about 3.2 miles to the park's Horseman's and Riding Stable Entrance, or farther to 8 Mile Rd, the west (left) on 8 Mile Rd to the main park entrance. The mountain biking trailhead is easily reached from the Horseman's and Riding Stable parking lot.

Trail Type: Hiking/Walking, Cross Country Skiing, Mountain Biking, Interpretive
Trail Distance: 19 mi   Loops: Many   Shortest: 1 mi   Longest: 8 mi
Trail Surface: Paved and natural
Trail Use Fee: None, but vehicle entry fee required
Method Of Ski Trail Grooming: Track set
Skiing Ability Suggested: Novice to intermediate
Hiking Trail Difficulty: Easy
Mountain Biking Ability Suggested: Intermediate
Terrain: All types depending on trail
Camping: None

Maintained by the DNR Parks and Recreation Division.
This is a multi use park with trails for most everyone. Trails overlap seasonally.
The "Living Farm" is open daily.
Warming area, rentals(bike and ski), snack bar, lighted ski trail on some weekends and picnic grounds.
The asphalt paved hike/bike trail appears to have been a vehicle road in the past.
A 5 mile long single track mountain bike trail designed and built under the direction of the Michigan Mountain Biking Association was added to the trail system in 1994. The best trailhead for the bike trail is located at the Horseman's and Riding Stable parking lot off Beck Rd. The mountain bike trailhead is accessed from the gravel road leading out of the parking lot. See the article in the 1994/95 winter edition of the Michigan Cyclist for more information.

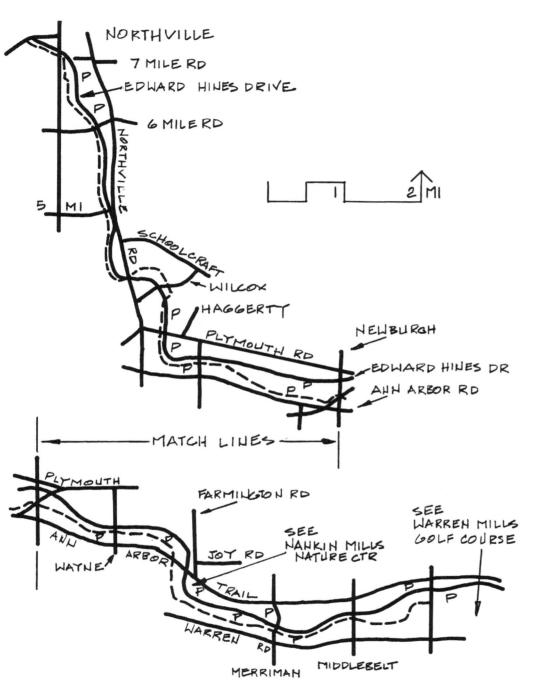

Wayne County, Division of Parks
33175 Ann Arbor Trail
Westland, MI 48185

313-261-2034

Michigan Atlas & Gazetteer Location: 33AB67

County Location: Wayne

Directions To Trailhead:
From Sheldon Rd in Northville to Outer Drive in Dearborn along the Rouge River and Edward Hines Drive

Trail Type: Hiking/Walking, Cross Country Skiing
Trail Distance: 17 mi   Loops: NA   Shortest: NA   Longest: NA
Trail Surface: Asphalt
Trail Use Fee: None
Method Of Ski Trail Grooming: None
Skiing Ability Suggested: Novice
Hiking Trail Difficulty: Easy
Mountain Biking Ability Suggested: NA
Terrain: Flat to rolling
Camping: None

Maintained by the Wayne County, Division of Parks.
Currently under construction, to be completed in 1995.
Warren Valley Golf Course and Nankin Mills (see other listings) are along this trail.
Many recreation areas all along this trail.
Horses may use the parkway from Northville to Wilcox in Plymouth.

MIDDLE ROUGE PARKWAY

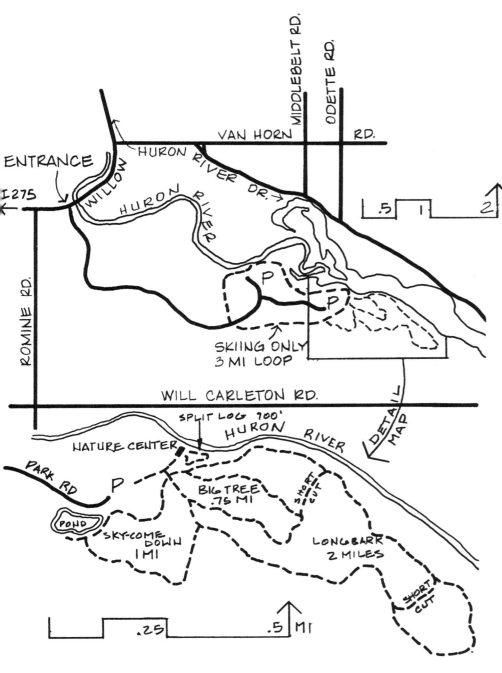

Oakwoods Metropark
PO Box 332
Flat Rock, MI 48134

313-697-9181
800-47-PARKS

Huron-Clinton Metropolitan Authority
13000 High Ridge Drive, PO Box 2001
Brighton, MI 48116-8001

810-227-2757

Michigan Atlas & Gazetteer Location: 33D7

County Location: Wayne

Directions To Trailhead:
From I-275 exit 11 at S. Huron, west to Bell Rd., south to Willow, east on Willow
Rd .75 mile to the park (past the entrance to Willow Metropark)

Trail Type: Hiking/Walking, Cross Country Skiing, Interpretive
Trail Distance: 4 mi   Loops: 5   Shortest: .25 mi Longest: 3 mi
Trail Surface: Natural
Trail Use Fee: None, but vehicle entry fee required
Method Of Ski Trail Grooming: Track set
Skiing Ability Suggested: Novice
Hiking Trail Difficulty: Easy
Mountain Biking Ability Suggested: NA
Terrain: Steep 0%, Hilly 0%, Moderate 30%, Flat 70%
Camping: None

Operated by the Huron-Clinton Metropolitan Authority
Warming area, picnic grounds, nature center and nature study area available.
Hiking / nature trail is different then the ski trail.
The 700' long Splitlog trail is paved for handicappers.
 Adjacent to Willow Metropark.
Call or write for their Metropark Guide, published each year.

OAKWOODS METROPARK

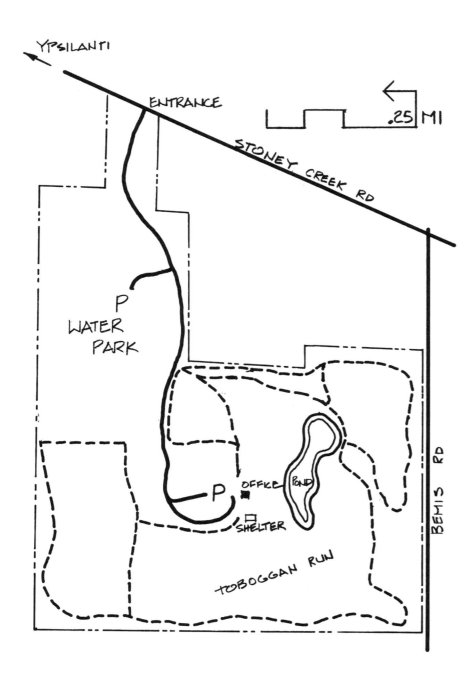

ROLLING HILLS COUNTY PARK

Rolling Hills County Park
7660 Stony Creek Rd.   313-484-3870
Ypsilanti, MI 48197

Washtenaw County Parks and Recreation Commission
PO Box 8645   313-971-6337
Ann Arbor, MI 48107

Michigan Atlas & Gazetteer Location: 33C4

County Location: Washtenaw

Directions To Trailhead:
From I-94, use the Huron Street exit (183) and proceed south to Stony Creek
Rd., then turn right and go 5 miles on Stony Creek Road. The park entrance is
on the right side of the road. The entrance is .5 mile north of Bemis Road.
Follow brown park directional signs.

Trail Type: Hiking/Walking, Cross Country Skiing, Interpretive
Trail Distance: 3 mi   Loops: Several   Shortest: .5 mi   Longest: 3 mi
Trail Surface: Gravel and natural
Trail Use Fee: None, but entrance fee required
Method Of Ski Trail Grooming: Track set
Skiing Ability Suggested: Novice to intermediate
Hiking Trail Difficulty: Easy
Mountain Biking Ability Suggested: NA
Terrain: Flat to rolling
Camping: None

Maintained by the Washtenaw County Parks and Recreation Commission
Ski rentals, toboggan rentals, toboggan run, lighted ski trails, ice skating,
warming shelter, picnic area, water park, fishing pond, ball fields and much
more make for a complete year-around recreational facility.
Skiing permitted on all trails except the nature trail (.5 mile)

Washtenaw Audubon Society
1733 Jackson Ave   313-994-3569
Ann Arbor, MI 48103   313-994-6287

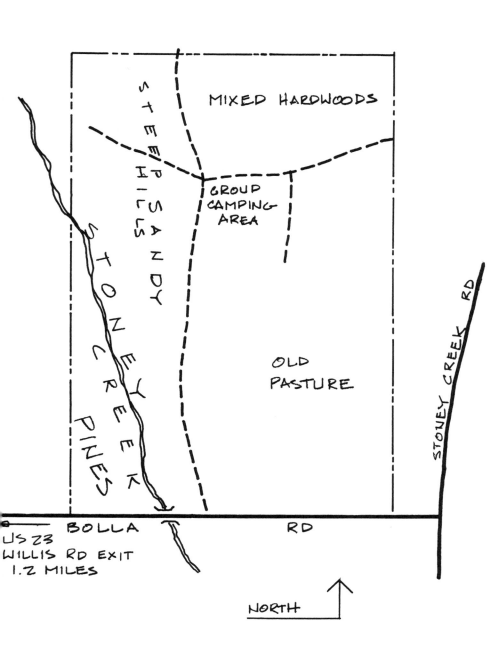

Michigan Atlas & Gazetteer Location: 33C4

County Location: Washtenaw

Directions To Trailhead:
Take US23 south from Ann Arbor to Willis Rd exit 31, then east about 1.25 miles, then continue east on Bolla Rd due east as Willis turns south, continue east .4 miles on Willis to the Preserve. Gate and sign designate the entrance.

Trail Type: Hiking/Walking, Cross Country Skiing, Interpretive
Trail Distance: 1 mi   Loops: Shortest: Longest:
Trail Surface: Natural
Trail Use Fee: None
Method Of Ski Trail Grooming: None
Skiing Ability Suggested: Novice
Hiking Trail Difficulty: Easy
Mountain Biking Ability Suggested: NA
Terrain: Steep 0%, Hilly 0%, Moderate 30%, Flat 70%
Camping: Camgground about 4 miles north.

Owned by the Washtenaw Audubon Society.
A 50 parcel that is full of plants and yes, birds.
Trails are not marked but are easy to locate.

SEARLES AUDUBON NATURE PRESERVE

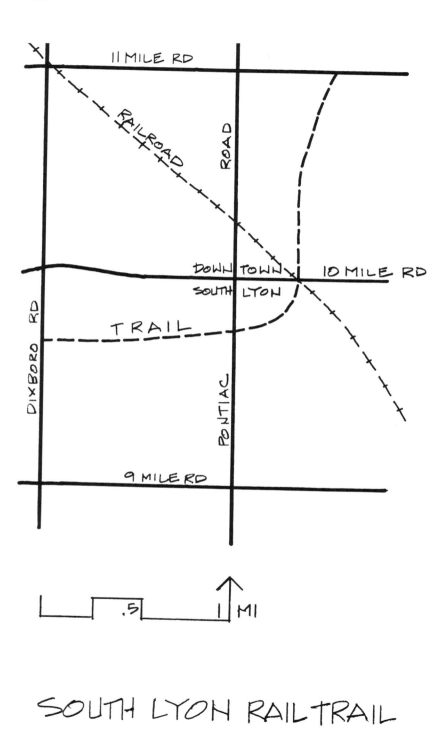

City of South Lyon
214 West Lake St.
South Lyon, MI 48178

810-437-1735

Michigan Atlas & Gazetteer Location: 33A4

County Location: Oakland

Directions To Trailhead:
In the City of South Lyon, from Dixboro on the southwest to11Mile Rd on the northeast

Trail Type: Hiking/Walking, Cross Country Skiing
Trail Distance: 2.7 mi   Loops: NA   Shortest: NA   Longest: NA
Trail Surface: Paved
Trail Use Fee: None
Method Of Ski Trail Grooming: None
Skiing Ability Suggested: Novice
Hiking Trail Difficulty: Easy
Mountain Biking Ability Suggested: NA
Terrain: 100%Flat
Camping: None

Owned by the City of South Lyon

SOUTH LYON RAILTRAIL

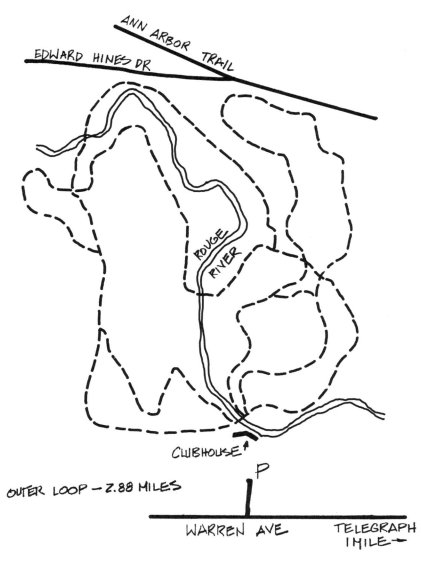

ANN ARBOR TRAIL

EDWARD HINES DR

ROUGE RIVER

CLUBHOUSE

P

OUTER LOOP — 2.88 MILES

WARREN AVE

TELEGRAPH
1 MILE →

.25 MI

WARREN VALLEY GOLF COURSE

Wayne County, Division of Parks
33175 Ann Arbor Trail   313-261-1990
Westland, MI 48135

Warren Valley Golf Course
26116 West Warren   313-561-1040
Dearborn, MI 48127

Michigan Atlas & Gazetteer Location: 33B7

County Location: Wayne

Directions To Trailhead:
In Dearborn Heights on Warren Rd. just east of Beech Daly Rd.

Trail Type: Cross Country Skiing
Trail Distance: 5 mi   Loops: Many   Shortest: Longest:
Trail Surface: Natural
Trail Use Fee: None
Method Of Ski Trail Grooming: Track set
Skiing Ability Suggested: Novice
Hiking Trail Difficulty: NA
Mountain Biking Ability Suggested: NA
Terrain: Flat to rolling
Camping: None

Operated by the Wayne County, Division of Parks
Warming area, rentals, lessons, restaurant, lounge and snack bar.
All trails are on a golf course.

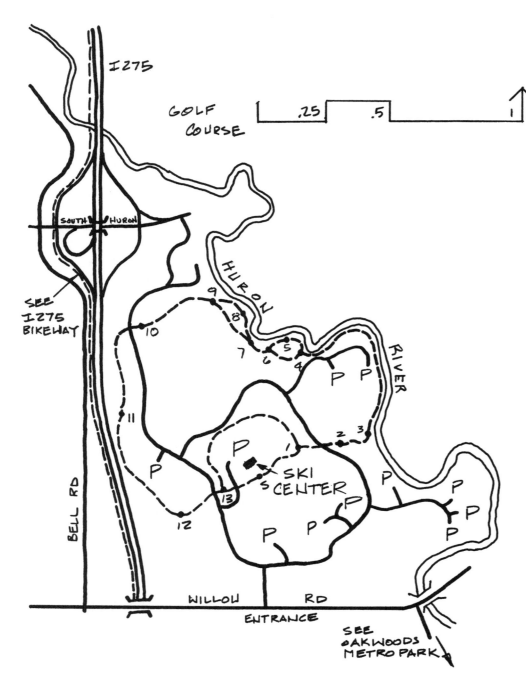

Willow Metropark
17845 Savage Rd.
Belleville, MI 48111

313-697-9181
800-47-PARKS

Huron-Clinton Metropolitan Authority
13000 High Ridge Drive, PO Box 2001
Brighton, MI 48116-8001

313-227-2757

Michigan Atlas & Gazetteer Location: 33D7

County Location: Wayne

Directions To Trailhead:
Off I-275 south of I-94 interchange at South Huron Rd exit.

Trail Type: Cross Country Skiing
Trail Distance: 4.8 mi   Loops: 1   Shortest: 4.8 mi Longest: 4.8 mi
Trail Surface: Natural
Trail Use Fee: None, but vehicle entry fee required.
Method Of Ski Trail Grooming: Track set when snow depth permits
Skiing Ability Suggested: Novice
Hiking Trail Difficulty: NA
Mountain Biking Ability Suggested: NA
Terrain: Steep 0%, Hilly 10%, Moderate 35%, Flat 55%
Camping: None

Operated by the Huron-Clinton Metropolitan Authority.
Warming area, sledding hill and picnic grounds, ski rentals and snack bar.
Adjacent to Oakwoods Metropark on the south and Lower Huron Metropark to the north.
Call or write for their Metropark Guide, published each year.

WILLOW METROPARK

U of M, Natural Areas Department
4901 Evergreen
Dearborn, MI 48128

313-593-5338

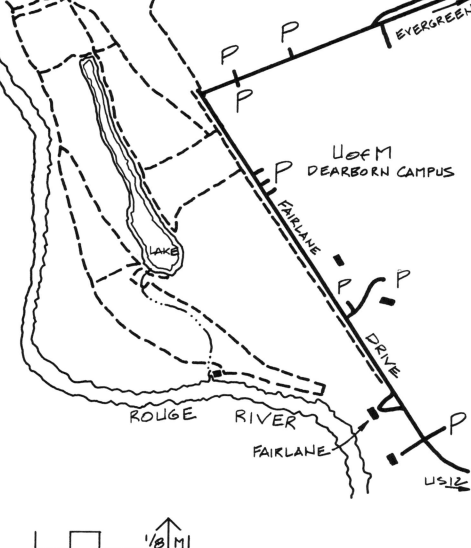

Michigan Atlas & Gazetteer Location: 34B1

County Location: Wayne

Directions To Trailhead:
Adjacent to Fairlane Manor in the University of Michigan - Dearborn Campus. Also near Fairlane Mall and Greenfield Village. North of Michigan Ave off Monteith Blvd via Evergreen Rd or Fairlane Drive.

Trail Type: Hiking/Walking, Interpretive
Trail Distance: 5 mi   Loops: Many   Shortest: .25 mi Longest: 2 mi
Trail Surface: Paved and natural
Trail Use Fee: None
Method Of Ski Trail Grooming: NA
Skiing Ability Suggested: NA
Hiking Trail Difficulty: Easy
Mountain Biking Ability Suggested: NA
Terrain: Steep 0%, Hilly 0%, Moderate 5%, Flat 95%
Camping: None

Owned by the University of Michigan - Dearborn Campus
This natural area is the grounds of the Henry Ford estate home on the Rouge River.
NO motor vehicles, bicycles, jogging, swimming, fishing, pets or picnicking.
Call or write for brochure.

UNIVERSITY of MICHIGAN
DEARBORN ENVIRONMENTAL STUDY AREA

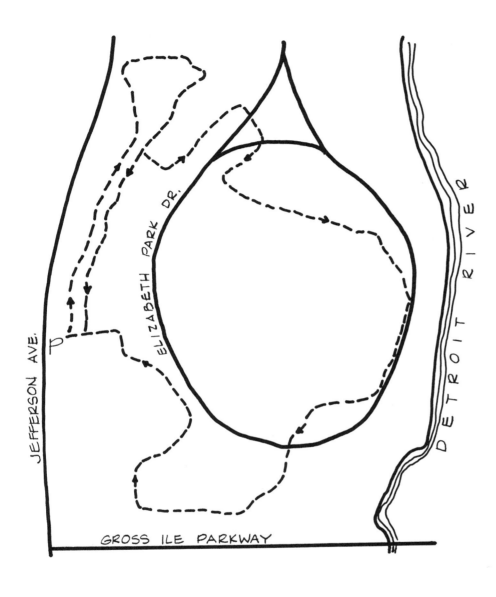

Elizabeth Park

Wayne County , Division of Parks
33175 Ann Arbor Trail   313-261-1990
Westland, MI 48135

Elizabeth Park
4250 Elizabeth Park Drive   313-675-8037
Trenton, MI 48183

Michigan Atlas & Gazetteer Location: 34C1

County Location: Wayne

Directions To Trailhead:
I-75 to eastbound West Rd., then 3.5 miles to southbound Jefferson, then to
3873 W. Jefferson.
Trailhead is at the first recreation building on the left side past Solcum St.

Trail Type: Hiking/Walking, Cross Country Skiing
Trail Distance: 2 mi   Loops: 1   Shortest: Longest:
Trail Surface: Natural
Trail Use Fee: None
Method Of Ski Trail Grooming: None
Skiing Ability Suggested: Novice
Hiking Trail Difficulty: Easy
Mountain Biking Ability Suggested: NA
Terrain: Steep 0%, Hilly 0%, Moderate 40%, Flat 60%
Camping: None

Operated by the Wayne County Department of Parks and Recreation
Scenic views of the Detroit River from along the trail.

NO SCALE

ELIZABETH PARK

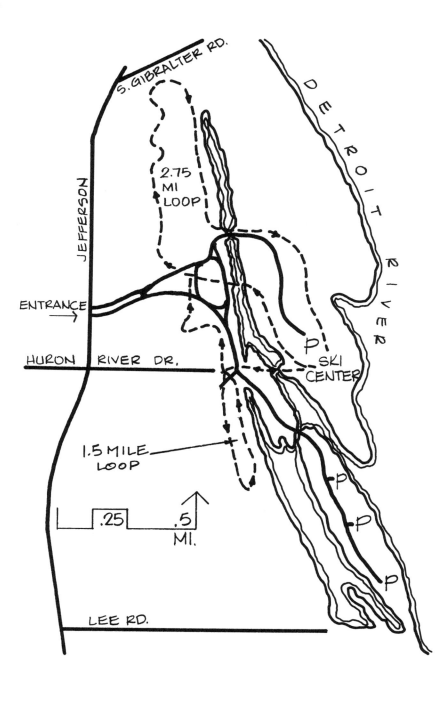

LAKE ERIE METROPARK

Lake Erie Metropark
32481 West Jefferson, PO Box 120
Rockwood , MI 48173

313-379-5020
800-24-PARKS

Huron-Clinton Metropolitan Authority
13000 High Ridge Drive, PO Box 2001
Brighton, MI 48116-8001

810-227-2757

Michigan Atlas & Gazetteer Location: 34D1

County Location: Wayne

Directions To Trailhead:
South of Gibraltar on Jefferson Ave along the shore of Lake Erie. Just north of Huron River Drive east of Jefferson Ave

Trail Type: Cross Country Skiing, Interpretive
Trail Distance: 4.25 mi   Loops: 2   Shortest: 1.5 mi Longest: 2.75 mi
Trail Surface: Natural
Trail Use Fee: None, but vehicle entry fee required
Method Of Ski Trail Grooming: Track set
Skiing Ability Suggested: Novice
Hiking Trail Difficulty: NA
Mountain Biking Ability Suggested: NA
Terrain: Steep 0%, Hilly 0%, Moderate 20%, Flat 80%
Camping: None

Operated by the Huron-Clinton Metropolitan Authority.
Nature trail planned for completion in late 1994 or early 1995.
Rentals and snack bar available.
Great Wave Pool, picnic area, golf course(under construction) and marina available.
Call or write for their Metropark Guide, published each year.

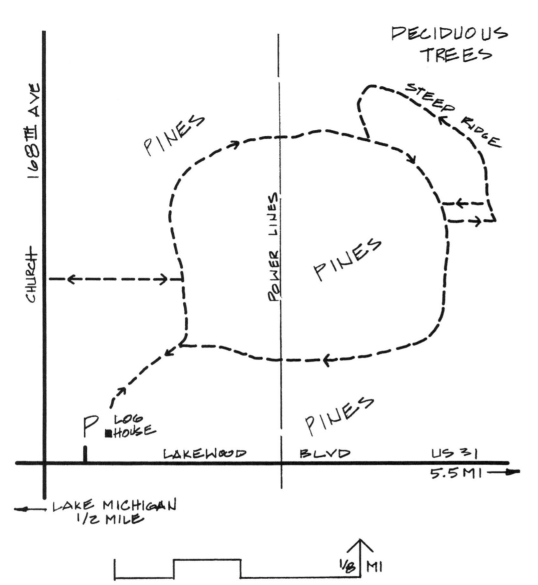

DECIDUOUS TREES

PINES

STEEP RIDGE

POWER LINES

PINES

PINES

168TH AVE

CHURCH

P LOG HOUSE

LAKEWOOD BLVD   US 31

5.5 MI →

← LAKE MICHIGAN 1/2 MILE

1/8 MI

Park Township
52 152nd Ave
Holland, MI 49424

616-399-4520

Michigan Atlas & Gazetteer Location: 35B5

County Location: Ottawa

Directions To Trailhead:
Northwest of Holland. From Holland go north to Lakewood Blvd, then west 4 miles to parking lot.

Trail Type: Hiking/Walking, Cross Country Skiing, Mountain Biking, Interpretive
Trail Distance: 1.5 mi   Loops: 2   Shortest: Longest:
Trail Surface: Natural
Trail Use Fee: None
Method Of Ski Trail Grooming: None
Skiing Ability Suggested: Novice
Hiking Trail Difficulty: Easy
Mountain Biking Ability Suggested: Novice
Terrain: Steep 0%, Hilly 0%, Moderate 10%, Flat 90%
Camping: Holland State Park nearby

Owned by Park Township
A small 40 acre park with limited trail opportunities.
No motorized vehicles permitted.

ALBERT C KEPPEL FOREST PRESERVE

TRAIL NOTES

Allegan State Game Area
4590 118th Ave   616-673-2430
Allegan, MI 49010   616-788-5055

DNR Wildlife Division

                                                        517-373-1263

Michigan Atlas & Gazetteer Location: 35D67

County Location: Allegan

Directions To Trailhead:
7 miles west of Allegan on Monroe Rd. (118th Ave)

SEE MAPS ON NEXT PAGE

Trail Type: Hiking/Walking, Cross Country Skiing, Mountain Biking, Interpretive
Trail Distance: 22 mi   Loops: Many   Shortest: 2.5 mi Longest: 13 mi
Trail Surface: Natural
Trail Use Fee: None
Method Of Ski Trail Grooming: None
Skiing Ability Suggested: Novice to intermediate
Hiking Trail Difficulty: Easy
Mountain Biking Ability Suggested: Novice
Terrain: Steep 0%, Hilly 1%, Moderate 9%, Flat 90%
Camping: Campground available on the east side of Swan Creek Pond

Maintained by the DNR Wildlife Division.
Trail specifications are for the ski/mountain biking trail system.
Skiing not permitted until January 1st. Ski trails and hiking trails are not all
identical. The trails are well marked. Cross country ski trailhead is located 1/10
mile north of 118th Ave. on 46th St.
Swan Creek Foot Trail is not suitable for skiing or mountain biking.
Swan Creek Foot Trail: Hilly 5%, Moderate 15%, and Flat 80%.
Swan Creek Foot Trail starting point is at the parking area north of Swan Creek
Pond and just west of the dam.
Trail users are the guests of the hunters. Wear bright clothing during the
hunting season .

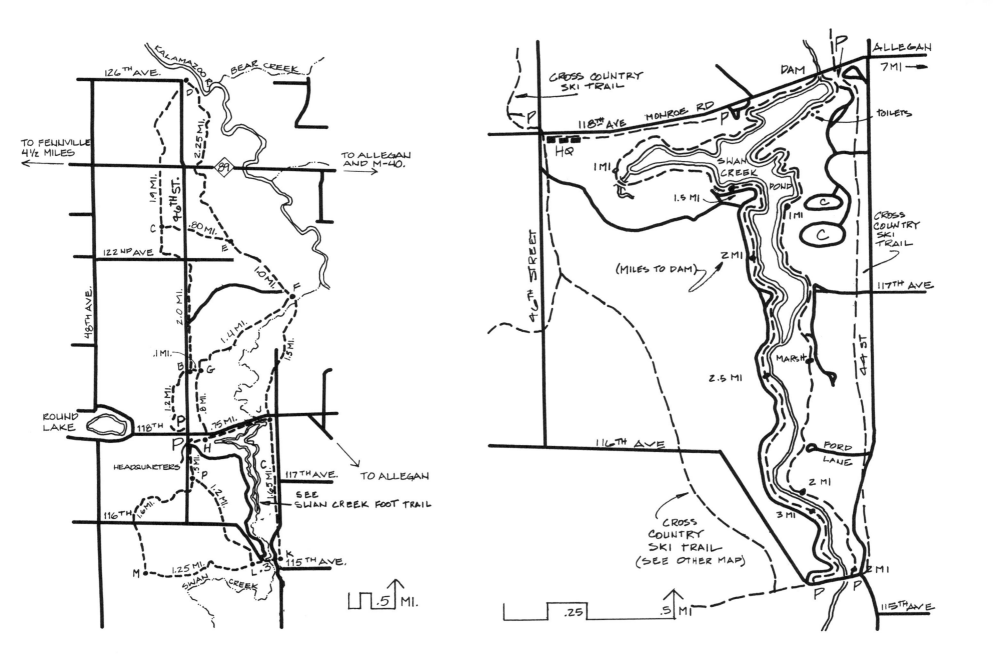

CROSS COUNTRY SKI TRAIL
ALLEGAN STATE GAME AREA

SWAN CREEK FOOT TRAIL
ALLEGAN STATE GAME AREA

79

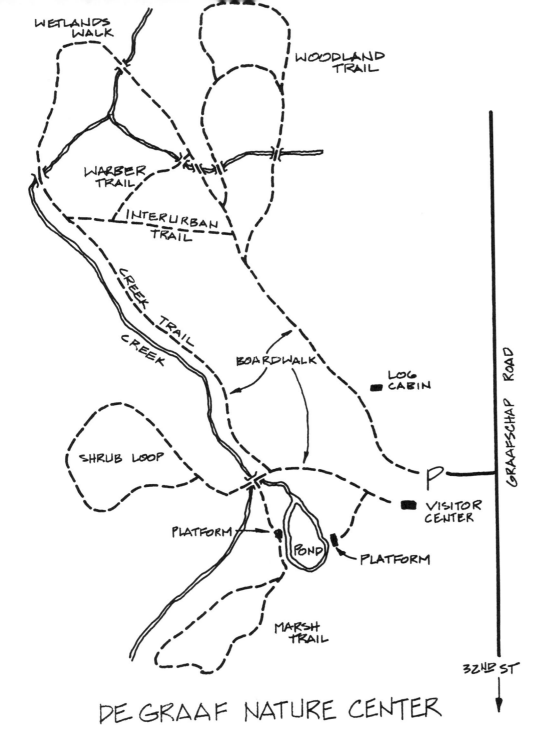

DE GRAAF NATURE CENTER

De Graaf Nature Center
600 Graafschap Rd
Holland, Mi 49423-4549

616-396-2739

City Of Holland, Cultural & Leisure Serivces Dept
150 West 8th St
Holland, MI 49423

616-392-9044

Michigan Atlas & Gazetteer Location: 35B5

County Location: Ottawa

Directions To Trailhead:
In Holland, from US31, take 32nd St west about 2.6 miles to Graafschap Rd.,
then north(right) to nature center about .2 mile on Graafschap Rd to the nature
center.
Or from US31 take 16th St. west to the end, then continue on South Shore Dr.
about .2 miles to Graafschap Rd., then south to the nature center.

Trail Type: Hiking/Walking, Cross Country Skiing, Interpretive
Trail Distance: 1.5 mi   Loops: Several   Shortest: Longest:
Trail Surface: Paved and natural
Trail Use Fee: None
Method Of Ski Trail Grooming: Not known
Skiing Ability Suggested: Novice
Hiking Trail Difficulty: Easy
Mountain Biking Ability Suggested: NA
Terrain: Steep 0%, Hilly 0%, Moderate 15%, Flat %85%
Camping: None

Maintained by the City of Holland, Cultural and Leisure Services Department.
This small 15 acre nature center is located within the city limits.
A 26 station nature trail is provided and trail guide is available.
Nature center building at trailhead.
Many activities take place at the nature center.

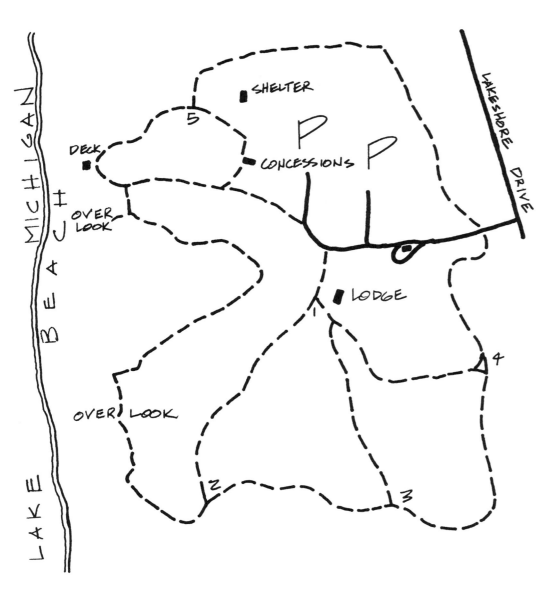

MICHIGAN BEACH

LAKE

DECK

5

SHELTER

OVER LOOK

CONCESSIONS

P

P

LAKESHORE DRIVE

LODGE

OVER LOOK

1

2

3

4

└──┐ ┌──┐ ↑
│   └─┘ │ 1/8 MI

KIRK COUNTY PARK

Ottawa County Parks and Recreation Commission
414 Washington St
Grand Haven, MI 49417

616-846-8117

Michigan Atlas & Gazetteer Location: 35A5

County Location: Ottawa

Directions To Trailhead:
Take US31 south of Grand Haven for 8 miles to Stanton Rd, then west 2 miles
to Lakeshore Drive, then north .5 miles to the park entrance

Trail Type: Hiking/Walking, Cross Country Skiing
Trail Distance: 2 mi   Loops: 3   Shortest: .4 mi   Longest: 1 mi
Trail Surface: Natural
Trail Use Fee: None
Method Of Ski Trail Grooming: None
Skiing Ability Suggested: Intermediate t o advanced
Hiking Trail Difficulty: Moderate
Mountain Biking Ability Suggested: NA
Terrain: Steep 10%, Hilly 40%, Moderate 20%, Flat 30%
Camping: None

Owned by the Ottawa County Parks and Recreation Commission
This area is a sensitive primary dune area with overlooks and established trails.
Help preserve this enviornment by not leaving these trails.
Trails designed for hiking an cross country skiing only.

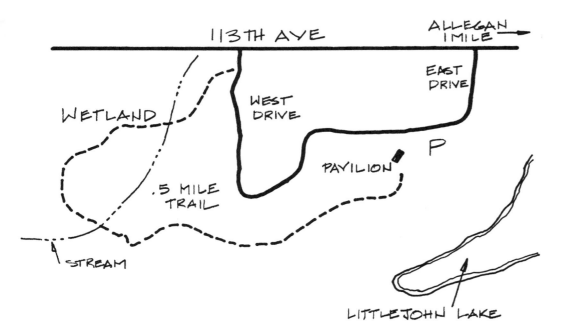

113TH AVE

ALLEGAN
I MILE →

EAST
DRIVE

WETLAND

WEST
DRIVE

.5 MILE
TRAIL

PAVILION

P

STREAM

LITTLEJOHN LAKE

NORTH

Allegan Country Parks and Recreation Commission
108 Chestnut Street
Allegan, MI 49010

616-673-0376

Michigan Atlas & Gazetteer Location: 35D7

County Location: Allegan

Directions To Trailhead:
Take M40 south from Allegan, then west on Thomas St, then south on Ely St, then just past 34th St is the park entrance. The trailhead is just south of the volleyball court

Trail Type: Hiking/Walking
Trail Distance: .5 mi   Loops: 1   Shortest: NA   Longest: .5 mi
Trail Surface: Natural
Trail Use Fee: None
Method Of Ski Trail Grooming: None
Skiing Ability Suggested: Novice
Hiking Trail Difficulty: Easy
Mountain Biking Ability Suggested: NA
Terrain: Not known
Camping: None

Maintained by the Allegan County Parks and Recreation Commission
Small county park just outside Allegan.

LITTLEJOHN LAKE
COUNTY PARK

Ottawa County Parks and Recreation Commission
414 Washington St.   616-846-8295
Grand Haven, MI 49417

Michigan Atlas & Gazetteer Location: 35A6

County Location: Ottawa

Directions To Trailhead:
Take US31 south of Grand Haven 8 miles to Stanton Rd, then east 3 miles to the park.

Trail Type: Hiking/Walking, Cross Country Skiing
Trail Distance: 1.2 mi   Loops: 2   Shortest: .4 mi   Longest: 1 mi
Trail Surface: Natural
Trail Use Fee: None
Method Of Ski Trail Grooming: None
Skiing Ability Suggested: Novice
Hiking Trail Difficulty: Easy
Mountain Biking Ability Suggested: NA
Terrain: Steep 0%, Hilly 0%, Moderate 50%, Flat 50%
Camping: None

Managed by the Ottawa County Parks and Recreation Commission

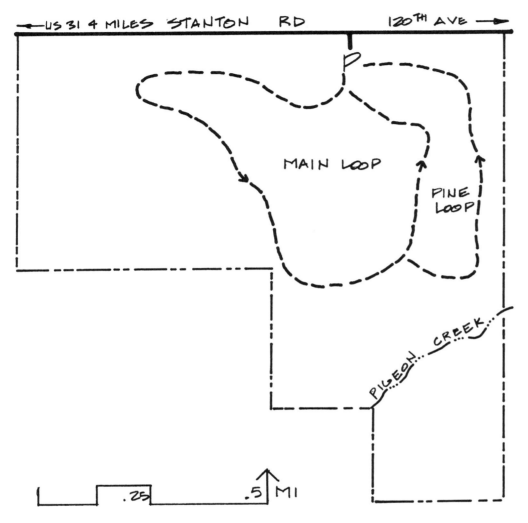

US 31 4 MILES   STANTON   RD   120TH AVE →

MAIN LOOP

PINE LOOP

PIGEON CREEK

.25   .5 MI

PIGEON CREEK PARK

Park Township
52 152nd Ave
Holland, MI 49424

313-399-4520

Michigan Atlas & Gazetteer Location: 35B5

County Location: Ottawa

Directions To Trailhead:
Northwest of Holland about 1 mile from Lake Michigan.
4.7 miles west of US31 on Riley St.
Just west of 160th Ave.

Trail Type: Hiking/Walking, Cross Country Skiing, Mountain Biking
Trail Distance: 5+ mi   Loops: 4   Shortest: .75 mi Longest: 2.25 mi
Trail Surface: Natural
Trail Use Fee: None
Method Of Ski Trail Grooming: Not known
Skiing Ability Suggested: Novice
Hiking Trail Difficulty: Easy
Mountain Biking Ability Suggested: Novice to advanced
Terrain: Steep 0%, Hilly 10%, Moderate 25%, Flat 65%
Camping: None

Owned by Park Township, Ottawa County.
Multi use recreational area for hiking, mountain biking and cross country skiing.
Popular mountain biking area for local riders.
Wooded trails throughout.
Trail map is usually posted in the parking area at the trailhead.

160TH AVE

RILEY ST

.4 MILE

B

B

LANDFILL
(KEEP OUT)

P

C

A

A

A
C

HILLS

SAND

HILL

A

C
&
V

HILL

C & V

TRAILS
A. .75 MILE
B. .75 MILE
C. 1.25 MILES
V. 2.25 MILES

RILEY TRAILS

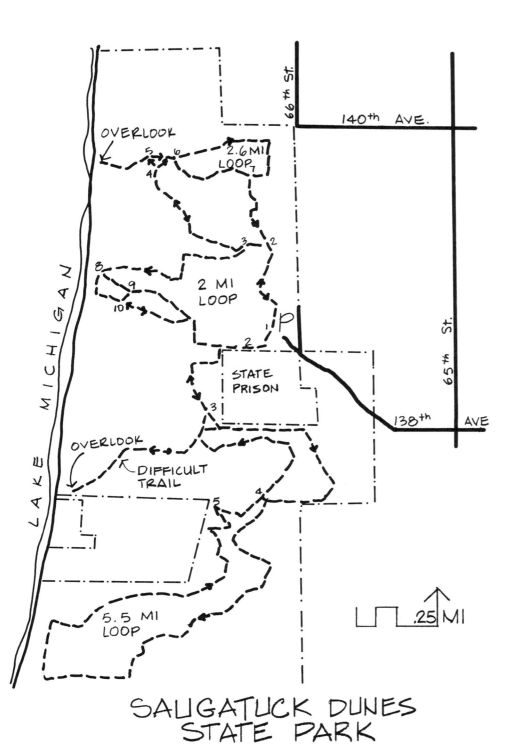

SAUGATUCK DUNES STATE PARK

Van Buren State Park
23960 Ruggles Rd.
South Haven , MI 49090

616-637-2788

DNR Parks and Recreation Division

517-373-1270

Michigan Atlas & Gazetteer Location: 35C5

County Location: Allegan

Directions To Trailhead:
1 mile north of Saugatuck via north on A2 to 64th St., then north 1 mile to 138th St, then west 1 mile to the park entrance .

Trail Type: Hiking/Walking, Cross Country Skiing
Trail Distance: 13.5 mi   Loops: 7   Shortest: 2 mi   Longest: 5.5 mi
Trail Surface: Natural and granular surface
Trail Use Fee: None, but vehicle entry fee required $2/day, $10/year
Method Of Ski Trail Grooming: Track set
Skiing Ability Suggested: Novice (limited) & advanced
Hiking Trail Difficulty: Moderate
Mountain Biking Ability Suggested: NA
Terrain: Steep 10%, Hilly 90%, Moderate 0%, Flat 0%
Camping: None

Maintained by the DNR Parks and Recreation Division
Scenic view of Lake Michigan and the dunes.
Over 1000 acres of hardwoods, pine forests and sand dunes.
Sand dunes raise up to 180 feet above Lake Michigan.
Beach and picnic grounds are provided.

Allegan County Parks and Recreation Commission
108 Chestnut St.
Allegan, MI 49010

616-673-8471
ext. 375

Michigan Atlas & Gazetteer Location: 35C7

County Location: Allegan

Directions To Trailhead:
M40 south of Hamilton, then east on 134th Ave 4 miles to the park

Trail Type: Hiking/Walking, Cross Country Skiing, Mountain Biking, Interpretive
Trail Distance: 3 mi   Loops: 2   Shortest: 1 mi   Longest: 2 mi
Trail Surface: Natural
Trail Use Fee: None
Method Of Ski Trail Grooming: Not known
Skiing Ability Suggested: Novice
Hiking Trail Difficulty: Easy
Mountain Biking Ability Suggested: Novice
Terrain: Steep 0%, Hilly 10%, Moderate 10%, Flat 80%
Camping: Campground in the park

Owned by the Allegan County Parks and Recreation Commission
Adjacent to Allegan State Game Area (See other listing for more trails.)

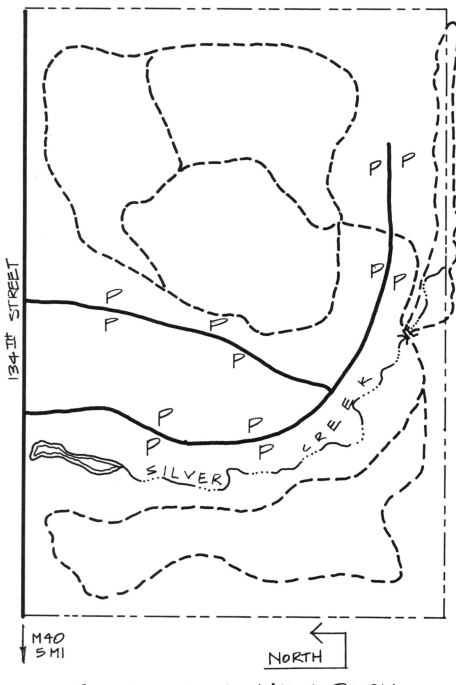

SILVER CREEK COUNTY PARK

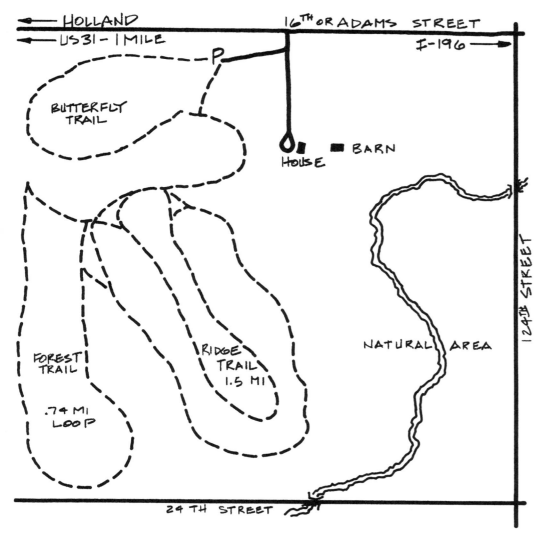

HOLLAND ←
← US31 - 1 MILE

16TH OR ADAMS STREET
I-196 →

P

BUTTERFLY TRAIL

HOUSE ■ ■ BARN

BUTTERFLY TRAIL

NATURAL AREA

124TH STREET

FOREST TRAIL

.74 MI LOOP

RIDGE TRAIL 1.5 MI

24TH STREET

City of Holland
150 West 8th Street
Holland, MI 49423

616-392-9044

Michigan Atlas & Gazetteer Location: 35B56

County Location: Ottawa

Directions To Trailhead:
From US31 in Holland, turn east on Adams or 16th Street, go 1 mile to the farm entrance or
from I-196, exit on Adams or 16th St., then west about 2 miles to the farm entrance.

Trail Type: Hiking/Walking, Interpretive
Trail Distance: 3 mi   Loops: 3   Shortest: .5 mi   Longest: 1 mi
Trail Surface: Natural
Trail Use Fee: None
Method Of Ski Trail Grooming: NA
Skiing Ability Suggested: NA
Hiking Trail Difficulty: Easy
Mountain Biking Ability Suggested: NA
Terrain: Steep 0%, Hilly 25%, Moderate 25%, Flat 50%
Camping: None

Owned and maintained by the City of Holland
Historical farm exhibit.

.25 MI

VAN RAALTE
HISTORICAL FARM & RECREATION AREA

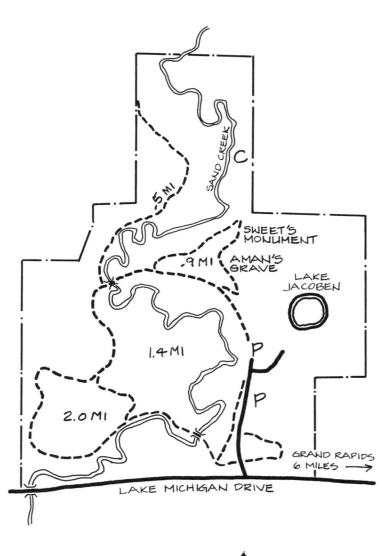

Grand Rapids Department of Parks
201 Market St SW
Grand Rapids, MI 49503

616-456-3216

Michigan Atlas & Gazetteer Location: 36A1

County Location: Ottawa

Directions To Trailhead:
6 miles west olf Grand Rapids on Lake Michigan Drive (M-45)

Trail Type: Hiking/Walking, Cross Country Skiing, Mountain Biking
Trail Distance: 3 mi   Loops: 3   Shortest: .9 mi   Longest: 2 mi
Trail Surface: Natural
Trail Use Fee: None
Method Of Ski Trail Grooming: Snowmobile packed after 2" snowfall
Skiing Ability Suggested: Novice to intermediate
Hiking Trail Difficulty: Easy
Mountain Biking Ability Suggested: Novice
Terrain: Steep 0%, Hilly 10%, Moderate 30%, Flat 60%
Camping: None

Maintained by the Grand Rapids Department of Parks.
Trail follows the Sand Creek.
Mature Beech-Maple forest.
Variety of wildflowerspresent. Please leave flowers for others to enjoy.
Mountain biking continues on a trial basis. Do not abuse the trail system by
riding carelessly and damaging the trail surface.

AMAN PARK

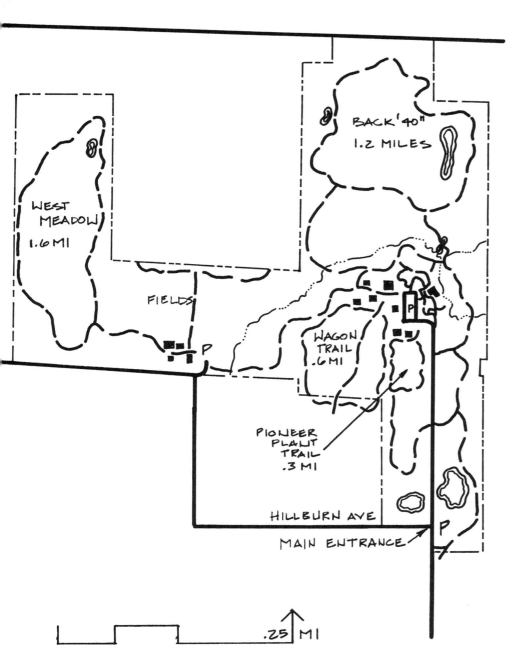

Public Museum of Grand Rapids
1715 Hillburn NW
Grand Rapids, MI 49504

616-453-6192

Michigan Atlas & Gazetteer Location: 36A2

County Location: Kent

Directions To Trailhead:
Exit 131 at Leonard St, then west 3 miles to Hillburn, then right to parking lot .5 miles ahead.

Trail Type: Hiking/Walking, Cross Country Skiing, Interpretive
Trail Distance: 4 mi   Loops: 9   Shortest: .1 mi   Longest: 1.6 mi
Trail Surface: Paved and natural
Trail Use Fee: None
Method Of Ski Trail Grooming: None
Skiing Ability Suggested: Novice
Hiking Trail Difficulty: Easy to moderate
Mountain Biking Ability Suggested: NA
Terrain: Steep 5%, Hilly 20%, Moderate 50%, Flat 25%
Camping: None

Owned by the Public Museum of Grand Rapids
Heritage settlement and farmstead are part of the complex
Trails cover a diverse habitat.
Visitor Center houses exhibits and the Wildlife Care Center.
Open daily except major holidays.
Trails are open from dawn to dusk.

BLANDFORD NATURE CENTER

Ottawa County Parks and Recreation Department
414 Washington
Grand Haven, MI 49417

616-846-8117

NO MAP

Michigan Atlas & Gazetteer Location: 35A1

County Location: Ottawa

Directions To Trailhead:
Corner of 28th Ave an Bauer Rd in Jenison

Trail Type: Hiking/Walking, Cross Country Skiing, Interpretive
Trail Distance: 2 mi   Loops: 5   Shortest: .25 mi Longest: 1 mi
Trail Surface: Natrual
Trail Use Fee: None
Method Of Ski Trail Grooming: None
Skiing Ability Suggested: Novice
Hiking Trail Difficulty: Easy
Mountain Biking Ability Suggested: NA
Terrain: 100% Flat
Camping: None

Owned by Ottawa County
Trails are not well marked and no map is avaiable.
Future plans call for marked trail system with a trail map.

Grand Rapids Department of Parks
201 Market St. SW
Grand Rapids, MI 49503

616-456-3211

Michigan Atlas & Gazetteer Location: 36A4

County Location: Kent

Directions To Trailhead:
On Kalamazoo Ave, 2.5 miles west of East Beltline, just north of 28th Street in Grand Rapids.

Trail Type: Cross Country Skiing
Trail Distance: 6 km   Loops: 2   Shortest: 3 km   Longest: 5 km
Trail Surface: Natural
Trail Use Fee: Yes
Method Of Ski Trail Grooming: Track set
Skiing Ability Suggested: Novice
Hiking Trail Difficulty: NA
Mountain Biking Ability Suggested: NA
Terrain: Flat to rolling on a golf course
Camping: None

Maintained by the Grand Rapids Department of Parks
Warming area, snack bar, and rentals available in the golf course lodge

INDIAN TRAILS

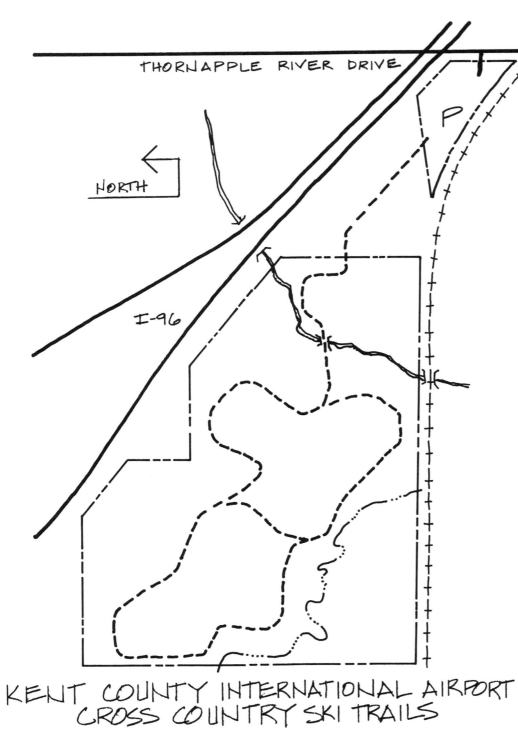

Kent County Parks Department
1500 Scribner Ave, NW
Grand Rapids, MI 49504

616-242-6948
616-774-3697

Michigan Atlas & Gazetteer Location: 36A3

County Location: Kent

Directions To Trailhead:
Thornapple Drive south of I-96

Trail Type: Cross Country Skiing
Trail Distance: 1.25 mi   Loops: 2   Shortest: .7 mi   Longest: 1.1 mi
Trail Surface: Natural
Trail Use Fee: None
Method Of Ski Trail Grooming: Track set
Skiing Ability Suggested: Novice
Hiking Trail Difficulty: Easy
Mountain Biking Ability Suggested: Novice
Terrain: Steep 0%, Hilly 0%, Moderate 10%, Flat 90%
Camping: None

Maintained by the Kent County Parks Department

KENT COUNTY INTERNATIONAL AIRPORT
CROSS COUNTRY SKI TRAILS

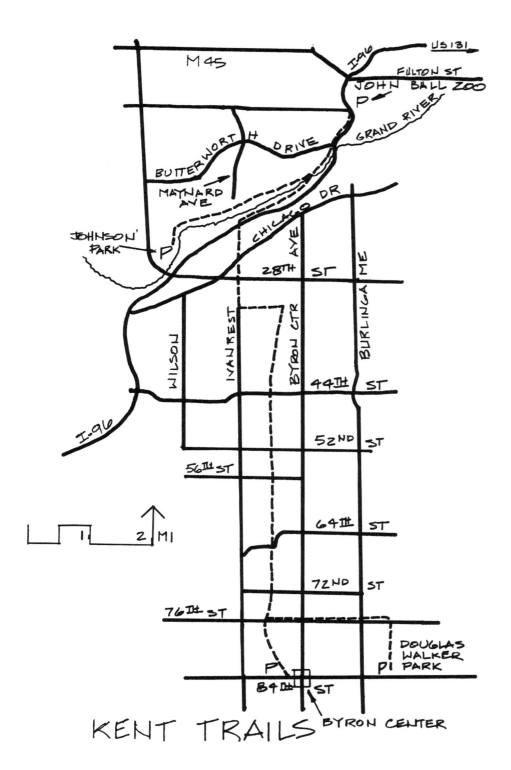

Kent Trails

Kent County Parks Department
1500 Scribner Ave, NW
Grand Rapids, MI 49504

616-242-6948
616-774-3697

Michigan Atlas & Gazetteer Location: 36AB12

County Location: Kent

Directions To Trailhead:
North trailhead - John Ball Park Zoo at Fulton St and I-96
South trailhead - Byron Center or Douglas Walker Park on 84th St

Trail Type: Hiking/Walking, Cross Country Skiing,
Trail Distance: 13 mi   Loops: NA   Shortest: NA   Longest: NA
Trail Surface: Paved
Trail Use Fee: None
Method Of Ski Trail Grooming: None
Skiing Ability Suggested: Novice
Hiking Trail Difficulty: Easy
Mountain Biking Ability Suggested: NA
Terrain: Steep 0%, Hilly 0%, Moderate 10%, Flat 90%
Camping: None

Maintained by the Kent County Parks Department
Part of the trail is rail-trail conversion
Some of the trail is on city sidewalks.

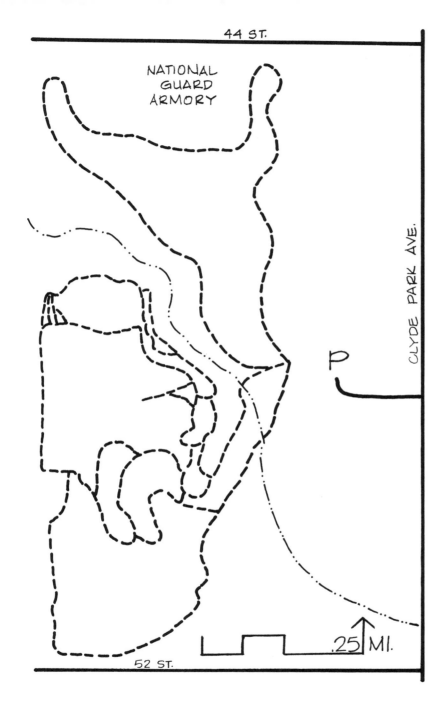

44 ST.

NATIONAL
GUARD
ARMORY

CLYDE PARK AVE.

P

.25 MI.

52 ST.

PALMER PARK

Kent County Park Department
1500 Scribner Ave. NW
Grand Rapids, MI 49504

616-774-3697
616-224-6948

Michigan Atlas & Gazetteer Location: 36AB2

County Location: Kent

Directions To Trailhead:
In Wyoming (Grand Rapids), at 52nd St and Clyde Park Ave.

Trail Type: Hiking/Walking, Cross Country Skiing
Trail Distance: 5 mi   Loops: Several   Shortest: Longest:
Trail Surface: Natural
Trail Use Fee: Fee for skiing only
Method Of Ski Trail Grooming: Track set occasionally
Skiing Ability Suggested: Novice
Hiking Trail Difficulty: Easy
Mountain Biking Ability Suggested: NA
Terrain: Flat to rolling
Camping: Camping not permitted

Maintained by the Kent County Park Commission
Warming building, rentals, snacks and lighted practice area available.
Trails on a golf course.

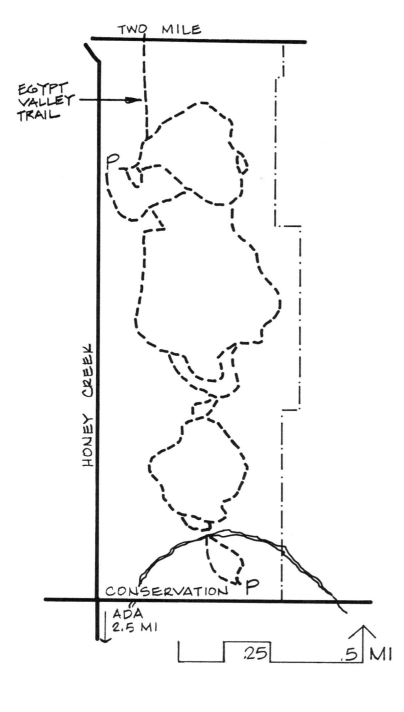

TWO MILE

EGYPT
VALLEY
TRAIL

P

HONEY CREEK

CONSERVATION P

ADA
2.5 MI

.25   .5 MI

SEIDMAN PARK

Seidman Park

Kent County Park Commission
1500 Scribner Ave. NW
Grand Rapids, MI 49504-3299

616-774-6968
616-242-6948

Michigan Atlas & Gazetteer Location: 36A4

County Location: Kent

Directions To Trailhead:
Honey Creek Ave between 2 Mile Rd and Conservation Rd

Trail Type: Hiking/Walking, Cross Country Skiing
Trail Distance: 4.5 mi   Loops: 3   Shortest: Longest:
Trail Surface: Natural
Trail Use Fee: None
Method Of Ski Trail Grooming: None
Skiing Ability Suggested: Novice to intermediate
Hiking Trail Difficulty: Easy
Mountain Biking Ability Suggested: NA
Terrain: ?
Camping: None

Maintained by the Kent County Park Commission

Rails to Trails Conservancy
913 W. Holmes Rd, Suite 145
Lansing, MI 48901

517-393-6022

Friends of the Trail
PO Box 393
Middleville, MI 49333

616-795-3385

Michigan Atlas & Gazetteer Location: 36ABC34,37C4

County Location: Kent, Barry

Directions To Trailhead:
Northwest trailhead - Southeast of Kentwood, 2 miles west of M37 at 60th St and Patterson Rd.
Southwest trailhead - Irving Rd on the south side of the Thornapple River. Take M37 west from Hastings about 5 miles to Irving Rd, then north on Irving about 1 mile to the trailhead near a private campground.

Trail Type: Hiking/Walking, Cross Country Skiing, Mountain Biking
Trail Distance: 18 mi   Loops: NA   Shortest: NA   Longest: NA
Trail Surface: Ballast and natural
Trail Use Fee:
Method Of Ski Trail Grooming:
Skiing Ability Suggested:
Hiking Trail Difficulty:
Mountain Biking Ability Suggested:
Terrain: 100% Flat
Camping: Private campground at the east trailhead

Owned by the Rails to Trails Conservancy
Recently purchased(1994)a significant length of the trail. Additional purchases are planned.
Development planned for near future. Contact above organizations for current status
The Friends of the Trail welcome you to join and take part in the development of this trail.
The phone number listed is the Village of Middleville. They should have information on the current officers of the Friends of the Trail.
Trail name is unofficial. Official trail name has yet to be established

THORNAPPLE RAIL TRAIL

TRAIL NOTES

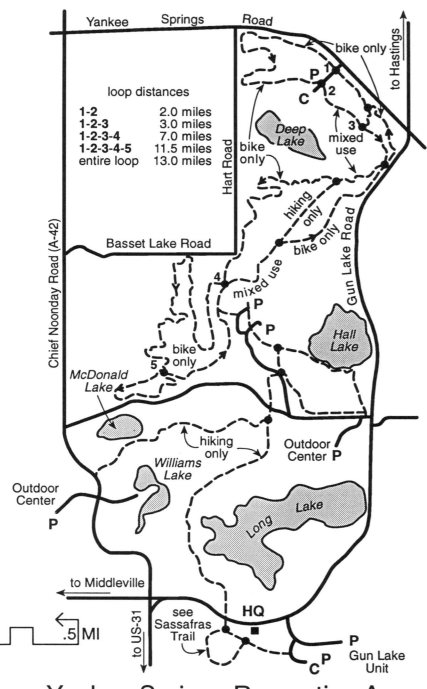

Yankee Springs Recreation Area

loop distances

1-2	2.0 miles
1-2-3	3.0 miles
1-2-3-4	7.0 miles
1-2-3-4-5	11.5 miles
entire loop	13.0 miles

Yankee Springs Recreation Area
2140 Gun Lake Rd.
Middleville, MI 49333

616-795-9081
517-322-1300

DNR Parks and Recreation Division

517-373-1270

Michigan Atlas & Gazetteer Location: 36BC34

County Location: Barry

Directions To Trailhead:
9 miles west of Hastings on Co Rd A42. Skiing trailhead - Long Lake Outdoor Center on Gun Lake Rd.
Hiking trailheads - Park Hdqs, Long Lake Outdoor Center, near Chief Noonday Outdoor Center and and Beach CG. Mountain biking trailhead - Deep Lake Campground Contact Station.

Trail Type: Hiking/Walking, Cross Country Skiing, Mountain Biking, Interpretive
Trail Distance: 20+ mi   Loops: Many   Shortest: .5 mi   Longest: 13 mi
Trail Surface: Natural
Trail Use Fee: None, but vehicle entry fee required
Method Of Ski Trail Grooming: Track set as needed
Skiing Ability Suggested: Novice to advanced
Hiking Trail Difficulty: Easy to moderate
Mountain Biking Ability Suggested: Intermediate to advanced
Terrain: Varies depending on trail system
Camping: Campgrounds in the recreation area

Maintained by the DNR Parks and Recreation Division.
Recreation area with many facilities. Call or write for information.
Separate maps of each trail type.
Hiking, mountain biking and cross-country ski trails are overlapping systems.
Hiking/walking: 11 mi.; 4 trails; 2 to 5 mile loops; S5%, H35%, M30%, F30%
X-C skiing: 7 mi; 6 loops; .5 to 5 mile loops; S5%, H35%, M50%; F10%
Mountain biking: 13 mi; 5 loops; 2 to 13 mile loops; S10%, H45%, M30%; F15%
Nature trail: 1/2 mile; 1 loop; F100%
Popular ski area due to reliable lake effect snow off Lake Michigan. Warming shelter at the Long Lake Outdoor Center. Open weekends and holidays.
Popular mountain bike trail (part of hiking trail). Part of trail developed by the Michigan Mountain Biking Association members.
Great swimming and boating on Gunn Lake and Deep Lake.
North Country Trail passes through this recreation area.

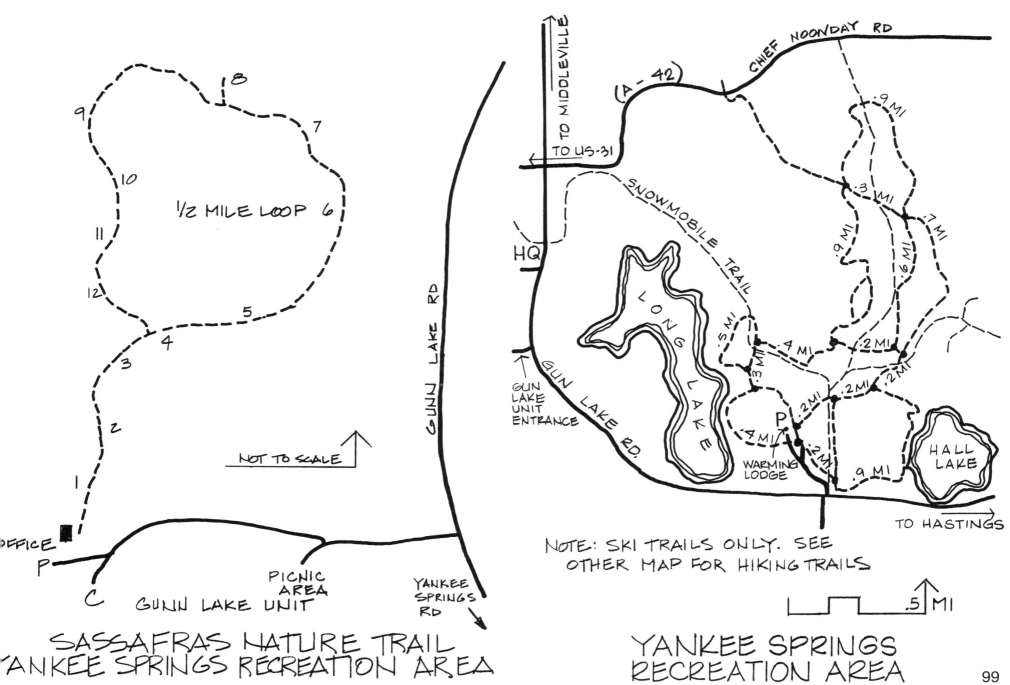

SASSAFRAS NATURE TRAIL
YANKEE SPRINGS RECREATION AREA

1/2 MILE LOOP

8
9
7
10
6
11
5
12
4
3
2
1

OFFICE
P
C

GUNN LAKE UNIT

PICNIC AREA

GUNN LAKE RD

YANKEE SPRINGS RD

NOT TO SCALE

YANKEE SPRINGS
RECREATION AREA

TO MIDDLEVILLE

(A-42)

CHIEF NOONDAY RD

TO US-31

.9 MI

HQ

SNOWMOBILE TRAIL

.3 MI

.7 MI

.9 MI

.6 MI

LONG LAKE

.5 MI

.4 MI

.2 MI

.3 MI

.2 MI

GUN LAKE UNIT ENTRANCE

GUN LAKE RD.

.7 MI

P

.2 MI

.2 MI

.2 MI

.2 MI

WARMING LODGE

.9 MI

HALL LAKE

TO HASTINGS

NOTE: SKI TRAILS ONLY. SEE OTHER MAP FOR HIKING TRAILS

.5 MI

99

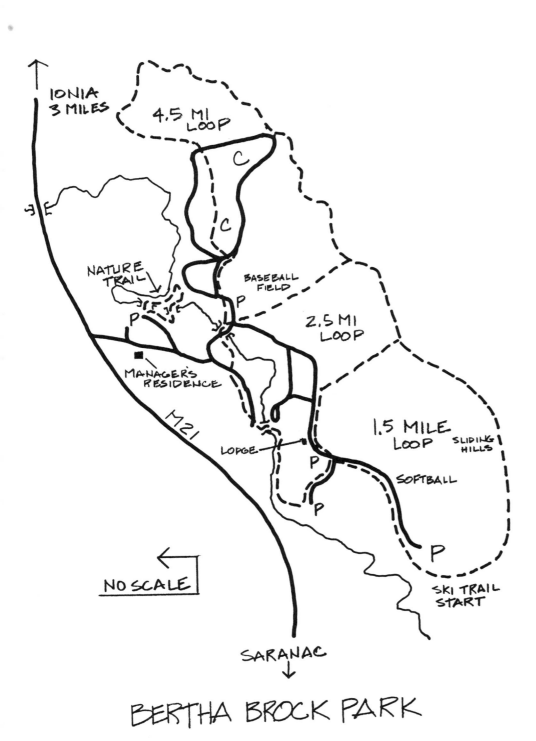

IONIA
3 MILES

4.5 MI LOOP

C
C

NATURE TRAIL

BASEBALL FIELD

P

2.5 MI LOOP

P
P

MANAGER'S RESIDENCE

M21

LODGE

P

1.5 MILE LOOP

SLIDING HILLS

P

SOFTBALL

P

P

NO SCALE

SKI TRAIL START

SARANAC

BERTHA BROCK PARK

Ionia County Parks Department
2311 W Bluewater Hwy, Rte 3
Ionia, MI 48846

616-527-0478

Michigan Atlas & Gazetteer Location: 37A6

County Location: Ionia

Directions To Trailhead:
3 miles west of Ionia on M21

Trail Type: Hiking/Walking, Cross Country Skiing, Interpretive
Trail Distance: 8.5 mi   Loops: 4   Shortest: 1.5 mi Longest: 4.5 mi
Trail Surface: Natural including gravel
Trail Use Fee: None
Method Of Ski Trail Grooming: None
Skiing Ability Suggested: Novice to intermediate
Hiking Trail Difficulty: Easy to moderate
Mountain Biking Ability Suggested: NA
Terrain: Flat to rolling
Camping: Rustic campground in the park

Operated by the Ionia County Parks Department.
Warming shelter, sledding and tubing hill on site.
Interpretive trail is not for skiing
Tennis courts, ball fields and playground provided on site.
Rustic lodge available for rent.

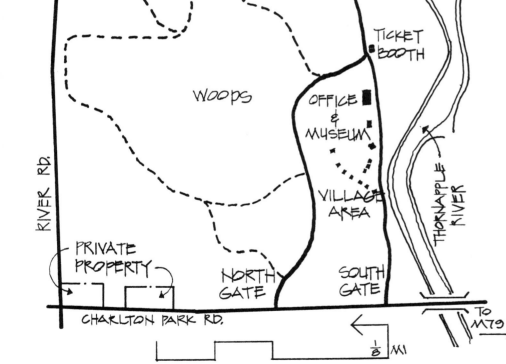

THORNAPPLE LAKE

BEACH

PRIVATE PROPERTY

P

BOAT LAUNCH

P

BALL DIAMOND

TICKET BOOTH

WOODS

OFFICE & MUSEUM

VILLAGE AREA

RIVER RD.

PRIVATE PROPERTY

NORTH GATE

SOUTH GATE

THORNAPPLE RIVER

CHARLTON PARK RD.

TO M79

$\frac{1}{8}$ MI

CHARLTON PARK

Charlton Park
2545 S. Charlton Park Rd
Hastings, MI 49058

616-945-3775

Michigan Atlas & Gazetteer Location: 37D6

County Location: Barry

Directions To Trailhead:
1/10 mile north of M79 between Nashville and Hastings on Charlton Park Rd.

Trail Type: Hiking/Walking, Cross Country Skiing, Mountain Biking, Interpretive
Trail Distance: 5 km   Loops: Several   Shortest: Longest:
Trail Surface: Natural
Trail Use Fee: Yes
Method Of Ski Trail Grooming: NA
Skiing Ability Suggested: Novice
Hiking Trail Difficulty: Easy
Mountain Biking Ability Suggested: Novice
Terrain: Steep 0%, Hilly 0%, Moderate 80%, Flat 20%
Camping: None

Owned by a non-profit organization
Historical village re-creation.
Special events held throughout the year.

Ionia Recreation Area
2880 David Highway
Ionia, MI 48846

616-527-3750
517-322-1300

DNR Parks and Recreation Division

517-372-1270

Michigan Atlas & Gazetteer Location: 37A67

County Location: Ionia

Directions To Trailhead:
South from Ionia 5 miles on M66 to David Hwy, then west 3 miles to Recreation Area entrance. Trailheads at Beechwood Picnic Area, Point Picnic Area and Riverside Picnic Area

Trail Type: Hiking/Walking, Cross Country Skiing, Mountain Biking
Trail Distance: 13+ mi   Loops: 5   Shortest: Longest:
Trail Surface: Natural
Trail Use Fee: None, but vehicle entry fee required
Method Of Ski Trail Grooming: None
Skiing Ability Suggested: Novice to advanced
Hiking Trail Difficulty: Easy to difficult
Mountain Biking Ability Suggested: Novice
Terrain: Steep 2%, Hilly 5%, Moderate 30%, Flat 63%
Camping: Campground on site

Maintained by the DNR Parks and Recreation Division
Greatly varied terrain with woods, lakes, fields, streams, rivers and numerous scenic views. Separate equestrain trails are also in the park
New mountain biking trails underdevelopment.

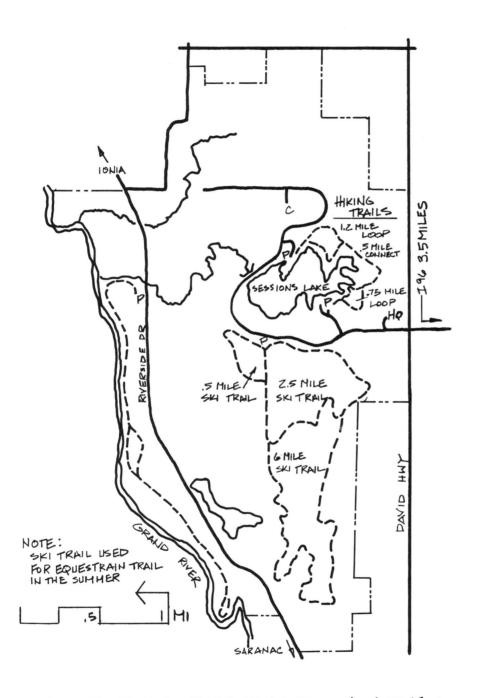

IONIA STATE RECREATION AREA

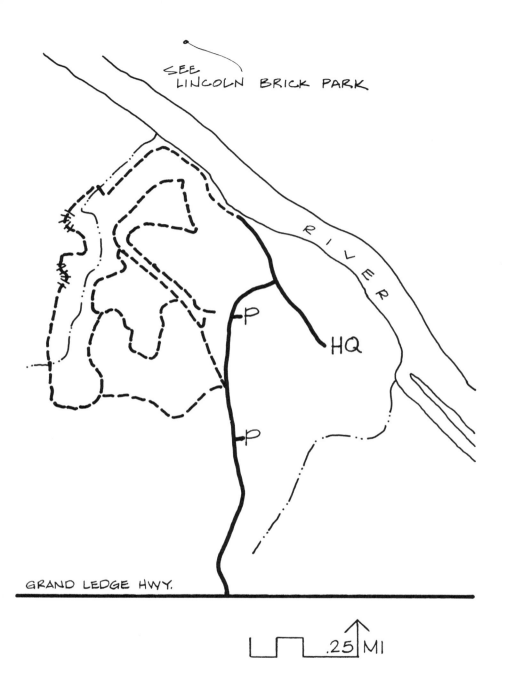

SEE LINCOLN BRICK PARK

RIVER

P

HQ

P

GRAND LEDGE HWY.

.25 MI

FITZGERALD PARK

Eaton County Parks and Recreation Department
3808 Grand Ledge Highway
Grand Ledge, MI 48837

517-627-7351

Michigan Atlas & Gazetteer Location: 38B2

County Location: Eaton

Directions To Trailhead:
I-96 to exit 93A (M-43 Saginaw Hwy West), then west on M-43 to Grand Ledge, then east on Jefferson.St to park entrance.

Trail Type: Hiking/Walking, Cross Country Skiing, Interpretive
Trail Distance: 3 mi   Loops: 3   Shortest: .25 mi Longest: 1 mi
Trail Surface: Gravel and natural
Trail Use Fee: None but vehicle entry permit is required (in season)
Method Of Ski Trail Grooming: Track set when snow depth permits
Skiing Ability Suggested: Novice to advanced
Hiking Trail Difficulty: Easy to moderate
Mountain Biking Ability Suggested: NA
Terrain: Steep 0%, Hilly 2%, Moderate 80%, Flat 28%
Camping: None

Operated by the Eaton County Parks and Recreation Commission.
This park is famous for its sedimentary rock outcrops.
Popular location for local rock climbers.
Ski rentals available and warming shelter open on winter weekends.
Night skiing on selected winter weekends.
Naturalist programs provided free with advance arrangements.
Nature center and 1/2 mile self guided interpretive trail.
Picnic facilities, canoe rentals and game fields available.

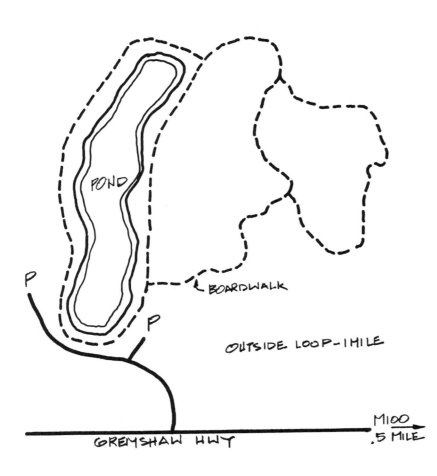

POND

P

P

BOARDWALK

OUTSIDE LOOP - 1 MILE

M100
.5 MILE

GRENSHAW HWY

NO SCALE

FOX PARK

Eaton County Parks & Recreation Department
3808 Grand Ledge Hwy
Grand Ledge, MI 48837

517-627-7351

Michigan Atlas & Gazetteer Location: 38C3

County Location: Eaton

Directions To Trailhead:
I-96 to exit 66, Potterville, M-100, then north on M-100 to Gresham Hwy, then west on Gresham Hwy to the park entrance.

Trail Type: Hiking/Walking, Cross Country Skiing, Interpretive
Trail Distance: 2 mi   Loops: 3   Shortest: .5 mi   Longest: 1 mi
Trail Surface: Natural
Trail Use Fee: None, but vehicle fee during summer months
Method Of Ski Trail Grooming: None
Skiing Ability Suggested: Novice
Hiking Trail Difficulty: Easy
Mountain Biking Ability Suggested: NA
Terrain: Steep 0%, Hilly 0%, Moderate 2%, Flat 98%
Camping: None

Operated by the Eaton County Parks and Recreation Commission.
Picnic facilities and concession stand available.
Trails around several ponds and through wooded areas.
Swimming, fishing, Ice fishing, ice skating available seasonally.

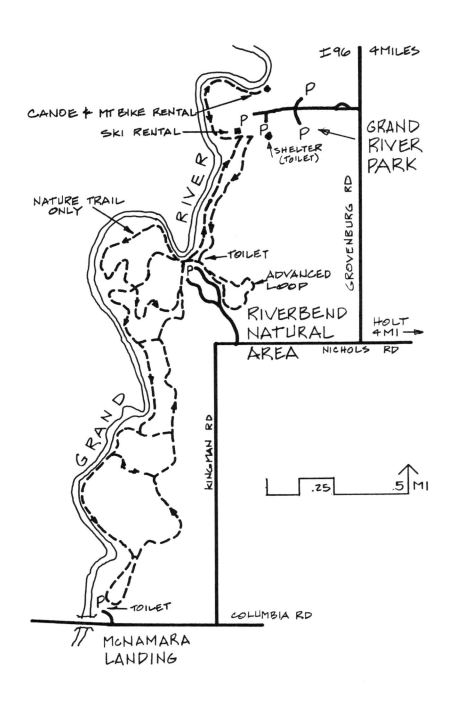

Ingham County Parks Department
PO Box 38
Mason, MI 48854

517-676-2233

Michigan Atlas & Gazetteer Location: 38D4

County Location: Ingham

Directions To Trailhead:
SW of Lansing on Grovenburg Rd, just north of Nichols Rd. Use Logan St exit south off I-96, then turn left on Bishop Rd. east to Grovenburg Rd., then south to the park past Holt Rd..

Trail Type: Hiking/Walking, Cross Country Skiing, Mountain Biking
Trail Distance: 4.5 mi   Loops: 5   Shortest: .8 mi   Longest: 4.5 mi
Trail Surface: Natural
Trail Use Fee: None, but vehicle entry fee charged
Method Of Ski Trail Grooming: Track set as snow condition permits.
Skiing Ability Suggested: Novice to intermediate
Hiking Trail Difficulty: Easy to moderate
Mountain Biking Ability Suggested: Novice
Terrain: Steep 5%, Hilly 30%, Moderate 45%, Flat 20%
Camping: None

Operated by the Ingham County Parks Department.
Marked 4.5 mile mountain bike trail is provided.
Ski rentals, canoe rentals, snack bar, tobogganing, ice skating, sledding, swimming, softball diamond and picnic grounds are provided seasonally.
Additional services are provided seasonally.

GRAND RIVER PARK

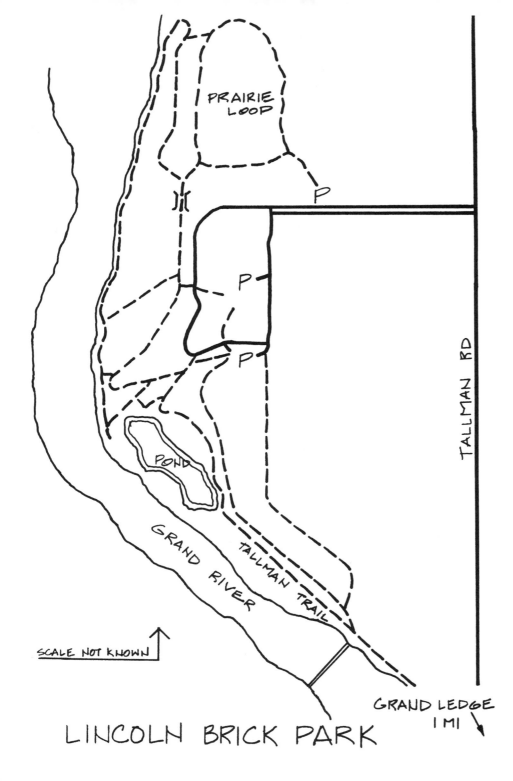

LINCOLN BRICK PARK

PRAIRIE LOOP

P

P

P

POND

GRAND RIVER

TALLMAN TRAIL

TALLMAN RD

SCALE NOT KNOWN

GRAND LEDGE
1 MI

Lincoln Brick Park

Eaton County Parks and Recreation Commission
3808 Grand Ledge Hwy   517-627-7351
Grand Ledge, MI 48837

Michigan Atlas & Gazetteer Location: 38B2

County Location: Eaton

Directions To Trailhead:
I-96 to Grand Ledge exit, M43 west to M100, then north to Main Street, then north to Tallman Rd, then west to park entrance.

Trail Type: Hiking/Walking, Cross Country Skiing
Trail Distance: 3 mi   Loops: 8   Shortest: .5 mi   Longest: 2 mi
Trail Surface: Natural
Trail Use Fee: None, but vehicle entry fee charged from April through October
Method Of Ski Trail Grooming: None
Skiing Ability Suggested: Novice to intermediate
Hiking Trail Difficulty: Easy to moderate
Mountain Biking Ability Suggested: NA
Terrain: Steep 0%, Hilly 25%, Moderate 40%, Flat 35%
Camping: None

Owned by the Eaton County Parks and Recreaton Commission
County park with picnic area, pavilions, playgrounds, fishing, archery, and much more
Ski trails marked with orange flags

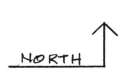

City of Portland
259 Kent St
Portland, MI 48875

517-647-7985

Michigan Atlas & Gazetteer Location: 38AB1

County Location: Ionia

Directions To Trailhead:
In downtown Portland along the Grand River.

Trail Type: Hiking/Walking, Cross Country Skiing, Interpretive
Trail Distance: 3.5 mi   Loops: NA   Shortest: NA   Longest: NA
Trail Surface: Paved
Trail Use Fee: None
Method Of Ski Trail Grooming: None
Skiing Ability Suggested: Novice
Hiking Trail Difficulty: Easy
Mountain Biking Ability Suggested: Paved
Terrain: 100%Flat
Camping: None

Owned by the City of Portland
The trail connects two city parks and has several bridges.

PORTLAND RIVERTRAIL PARK

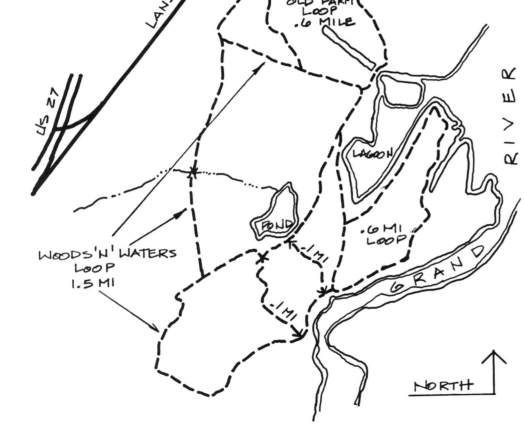

LANSING
4 MILES

LANSING RD

US 27

P

INTERPRETATIVE CENTER
LOG HOUSE

BARN

OLD FARM LOOP .6 MILE

LAGOON

POND

.6 MI LOOP

WOODS'N' WATERS LOOP 1.5 MI

.1 MI

.1 MI

GRAND RIVER

NORTH

WOLDUMAR NATURE CENTER

Nature Way Association
5539 Lansing Rd.
Lansing, MI 48917

517-322-0030

Michigan Atlas & Gazetteer Location: 38C34

County Location: Eaton

Directions To Trailhead:
SW of Lansing on Lansing Rd off BR US27, just NE of I-96 exit 98B

Trail Type: Hiking/Walking, Cross Country Skiing, Interpretive
Trail Distance: 2.75 mi   Loops: 5   Shortest: .25 mi Longest: 1.5 mi
Trail Surface: Natural
Trail Use Fee: Yes
Method Of Ski Trail Grooming: Skied in by naturalist after each snowfall
Skiing Ability Suggested: Novice to advanced
Hiking Trail Difficulty: Easy to moderate
Mountain Biking Ability Suggested: NA
Terrain: Steep 5%, Hilly 15%, Moderate 70%, Flat 10%
Camping: None

A non-profit nature center with nature trails
Some hiking trails may not be suitable for skiing because of steps.
Area borders the Grand River for one mile.
Very scenic area with a wide selection of forest cover.
Warming shelter that serves snacks is open Tuesday - Friday from 9am to 5pm
and weekends from 1 to 5.
Very nice moderate sized trail system.
Write for brochure.

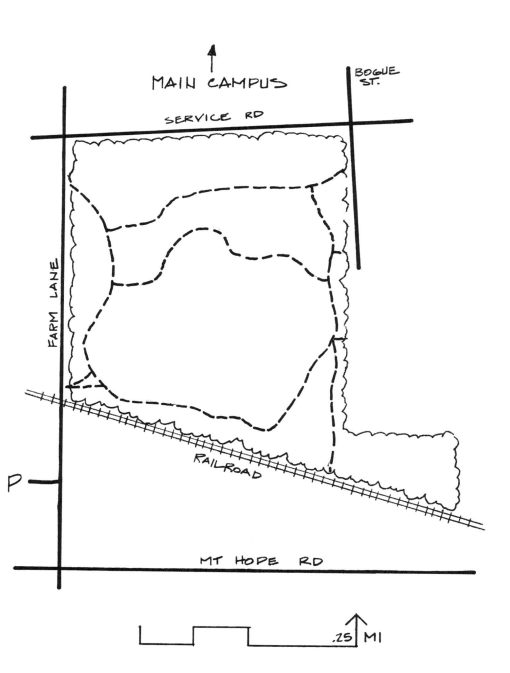

BAKER WOODLOT

Secretary, Natural Areas Committee, M.S.U.
Div. of Campus Park and Planning, 412 Olds Hall   517-355-9582
East Lansing, MI 48824

Michigan Atlas & Gazetteer Location: 39C5

County Location: Ingham

Directions To Trailhead:
On the Michigan State University Campus. Bordered by Service Rd on the
north, Farm Lane on the west and Bogue St. on the east

Trail Type: Hiking/Walking, Interpretive
Trail Distance: 2.5+ mi   Loops: Several   Shortest: Longest:
Trail Surface: Natural
Trail Use Fee: None
Method Of Ski Trail Grooming: NA
Skiing Ability Suggested: Novice
Hiking Trail Difficulty: Easy
Mountain Biking Ability Suggested: NA
Terrain: 100% Flat
Camping: None

Owned by Michigan State University.
One of many natural areas managed for research and preservation.
Access to woodlot from one of several gates along Farm Lane and Bogue St.
This 78 acres woodlot is heavily used for research and recreational walking by
the campus community.

Meridian Township Park Commission
5151 Marsh Rd.
Okemos, MI 48864

517-349-1200

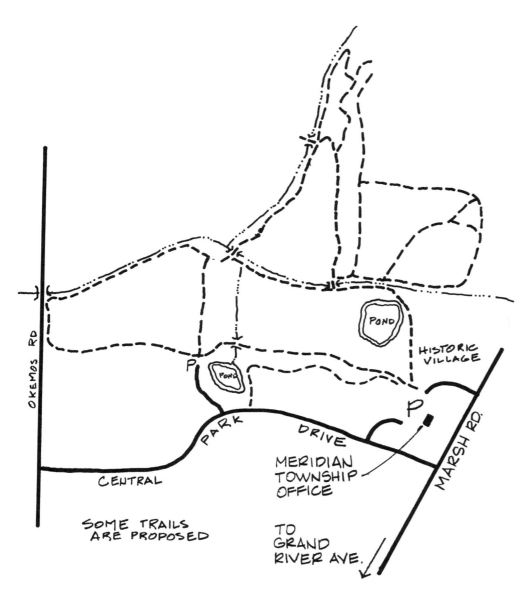

OKEMOS RD

POND

HISTORIC VILLAGE

P

POND

P

PARK DRIVE

CENTRAL

MARSH RD.

MERIDIAN TOWNSHIP OFFICE

SOME TRAILS ARE PROPOSED

TO GRAND RIVER AVE.

.25 MI.

CENTRAL PARK

Michigan Atlas & Gazetteer Location: 39C5

County Location: Ingham

Directions To Trailhead:
From Grand River Ave (M-43) and Marsh Rd intersection, .25 mile north of Grand River Ave on the west side of Marsh Rd., behind the township offices. Immediately north of the Meridian Mall.

Trail Type: Hiking/Walking, Cross Country Skiing, Interpretive
Trail Distance: 5 mi   Loops: 6   Shortest: .75 mi Longest: 1.5 mi
Trail Surface: Natural
Trail Use Fee: None
Method Of Ski Trail Grooming: None
Skiing Ability Suggested: Novice
Hiking Trail Difficulty: Easy
Mountain Biking Ability Suggested: NA
Terrain: Steep 0%, Hilly 0%, Moderate 5%, Flat 95%
Camping: None

Maintained by the Meridian Township Park Commission
Trails start at the Meridian Historical Village located behind the township offices and from a parking lot on the north side of Central Park Drive.
The park contains over 230 acres with ball fields picnic area, ponds and creeks.

Eastgate Park

Meridian Township Park Commission
5151 Marsh Rd
Okemos, Mi 48864

517-349-1200

Michigan Atlas & Gazetteer Location: 39C5

County Location: Ingham

Directions To Trailhead:
From the intersection of Grand River Ave and Okemos Rd in Okemos, take Grand River (M43) east for 4.5 miles to Meridian Rd, turn right(south) on Meridian Rd to the park entrance which is on the west side.

Trail Type: Hiking/Walking, Cross Country Skiing, Interpretive
Trail Distance: 1.2 mi   Loops: 2   Shortest: .35 mi Longest: .85 mi
Trail Surface: Natural
Trail Use Fee: None
Method Of Ski Trail Grooming: None
Skiing Ability Suggested: Novice
Hiking Trail Difficulty: Easy
Mountain Biking Ability Suggested: NA
Terrain: Steep 0%, Hilly 25%, Moderate 55%, Flat 20%
Camping: None

Maintained by the Meridian Township Park Commission.
Property follows the Red Cedar River.
Beautiful river enviornment.
Connects with the Harris Center Park which connects to Legg Park.

Map

GRAND RIVER AVE .5 MI

RED CEDAR RIVER

PLAY FIELDS

MERIDIAN ROAD

P

BEECH TREE LOOP

SEE HARRIS CENTER

.25 MI

EAST GATE PARK

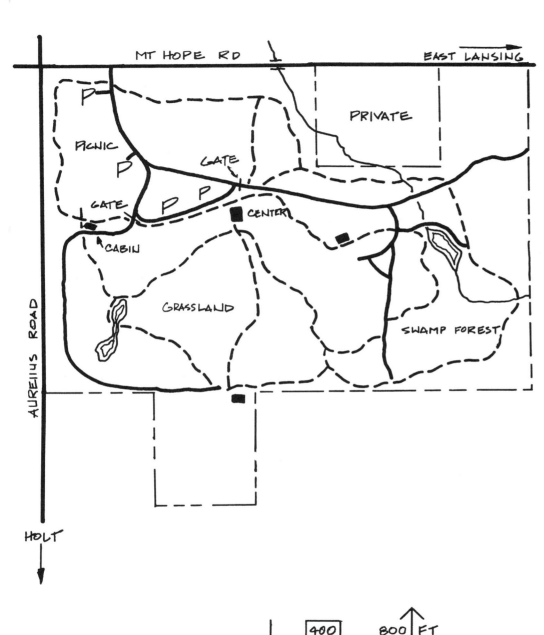

Fenner Arboretum
2020 E. Mt. Hope Rd
Lansing, MI 48910

517-483-4224

Lansing Park and Recreation Department

517-483-4277

Michigan Atlas & Gazetteer Location: 39C5

County Location: Ingham

Directions To Trailhead:
On the east side of Lansing at the corner of Aurelius Rd and Mt Hope Rd.
About 1.5 miles south of Michigan Ave.

Trail Type: Hiking/Walking, Interpretive
Trail Distance: 4.5 mi   Loops: 6+   Shortest: .5 mi   Longest: 1 mi
Trail Surface: Paved, gravel and natural
Trail Use Fee: None
Method Of Ski Trail Grooming: NA
Skiing Ability Suggested: NA
Hiking Trail Difficulty: Easy
Mountain Biking Ability Suggested: NA
Terrain: Steep 0%, Hilly 0%, Moderate 10%, Flat 90%
Camping: Group campground on site

Owned by the City of Lansing.
Features include a multi-purpose visitor center, pioneer cabin, picnic grounds, ponds and bison exhibit.

FENNER ARBORETUM

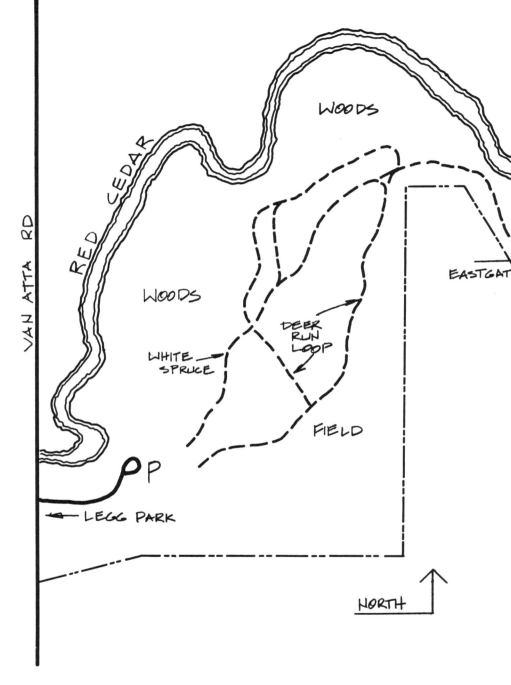

Meridian Township Parks Commission
5151 Marsh Rd
Okemos, MI 48864

517-349-1200

Michigan Atlas & Gazetteer Location: 39C5

County Location: Ingham

Directions To Trailhead:
Take Okemos Rd north to Jolly Rd, then east about 3.5 miles to Van Atta Rd, then north 1 mile to park.

Trail Type: Hiking/Walking, Cross Country Skiing, Interpretive
Trail Distance: 1.5 mi   Loops: 3   Shortest: .35 mi Longest: .65 mi
Trail Surface: Natural
Trail Use Fee: None
Method Of Ski Trail Grooming: None
Skiing Ability Suggested: Novice
Hiking Trail Difficulty: Easy
Mountain Biking Ability Suggested: NA
Terrain: Steep 0%, Hilly 0%, Moderate 10%, Flat 90%
Camping: None

Owned by the Charter Township of Meridian
Adjacent to East Gate and Legg Parks along the Red Cedar River.

HARRIS CENTER

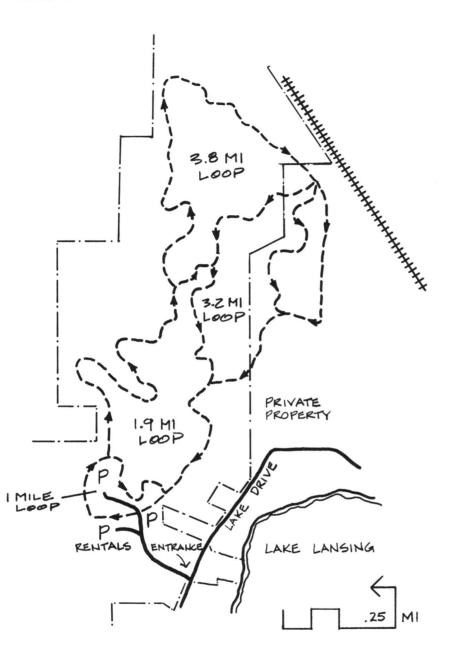

Ingham County Parks Department
PO Box 38
Mason, MI 48854

517-676-2233

Michigan Atlas & Gazetteer Location: 39B5

County Location: Ingham

Directions To Trailhead:
Northeast of Lansing on the north shore of Lake Lansing near Haslett. Take Saginaw Hwy to Haslett Rd., then left on Marsh Rd. about 1.5 miles to North Lake Drive (bear to the right), follow for about 1.5 miles, the park is on the left side of the road.

Trail Type: Hiking/Walking, Cross Country Skiing
Trail Distance: 4.5 mi   Loops: 3   Shortest: 1 mi   Longest: 3.8 mi
Trail Surface: Natural
Trail Use Fee: None
Method Of Ski Trail Grooming: Track set
Skiing Ability Suggested: Novice to intermediate
Hiking Trail Difficulty: Easy
Mountain Biking Ability Suggested: NA
Terrain: Flat to rolling
Camping: None

Operated by the Ingham County Parks Department
Ski rentals and warming building are available.
Picnic grounds and ball fields are available.
Mountain bikes are not permitted on the trails in this park.

LAKE LANSING PARK-NORTH

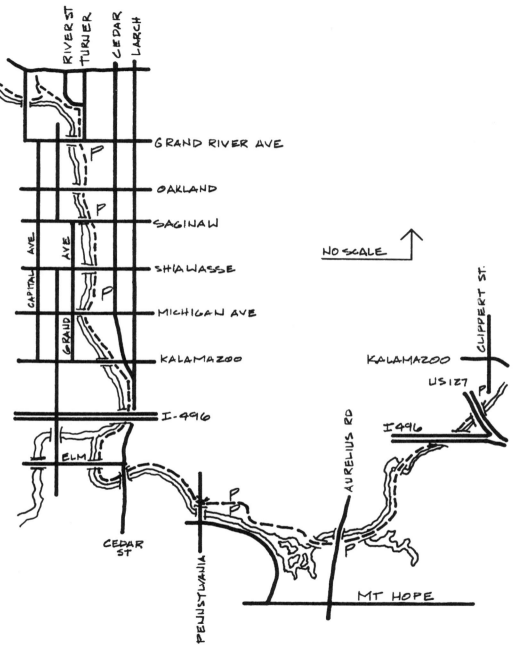

Lansing Parks & Recreation Department
124 W . Michigan Ave. 4th Floor
Lansing, MI 48933

517-483-4277

Michigan Atlas & Gazetteer Location: 39C45

County Location: Ingham

Directions To Trailhead:
Along the Red Cedar and Grand Rivers in Lansing.
East trailhead - South end of Clippert St. just west of the MSU campus, south of Kalamazoo St.
West trailhead - Grand River Ave at the Grand River.

Trail Type: Hiking/Walking
Trail Distance: 6 mi   Loops: NA   Shortest: NA   Longest: NA
Trail Surface: Asphalt
Trail Use Fee: None
Method Of Ski Trail Grooming: NA
Skiing Ability Suggested: NA
Hiking Trail Difficulty: Easy
Mountain Biking Ability Suggested: NA
Terrain: Steep 0%, Hilly 0%, Moderate 10%, Flat 90%
Camping: None

Owned by the City of Lansing
Trail parallels the Red Cedar and Grand Rivers. It passes by the Potter Park Zoo, several neighborhood parks, Lansing Community College, Impressions Five and R.E. Olds Museums and under Michigan Ave and the Lansing Center. Mountain biking on paved trail only.

LANSING RIVER TRAIL

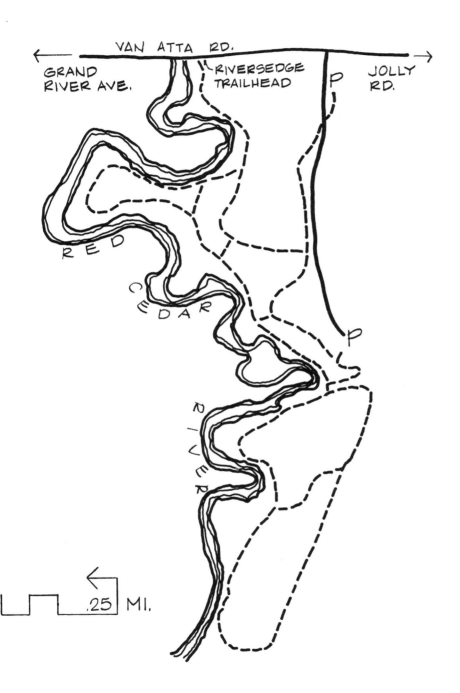

Meridian Township Park Commission
5151 Marsh Rd.
Okemos, MI 48864

517-349-1200

Michigan Atlas & Gazetteer Location: 39C5

County Location: Ingham

Directions To Trailhead:
East of Okemos on Grand River Ave to Van Atta Rd., then south 1 mile across the Red Cedar River to the park entrance on the right (west) side of the road. There is a trailhead on Van Atta Rd. at the Red Cedar River at the bridge but parking is very limited.

Trail Type: Hiking/Walking, Cross Country Skiing, Interpretive
Trail Distance: 2.25 mi   Loops: 3   Shortest: .5 mi   Longest: 1 mi
Trail Surface: Natural
Trail Use Fee: None
Method Of Ski Trail Grooming: None
Skiing Ability Suggested: Novice to intermediate
Hiking Trail Difficulty: Easy
Mountain Biking Ability Suggested: NA
Terrain: Flat with some rolling terrain
Camping: None

Maintained by Meridain Charter Township
Trail along the Red Cedar River.
The area is designated as a riverfront natural area.
Toilets provided at the trailhead.
Terrian has both floodpain and upland enviornments represented.

LEGG PARK

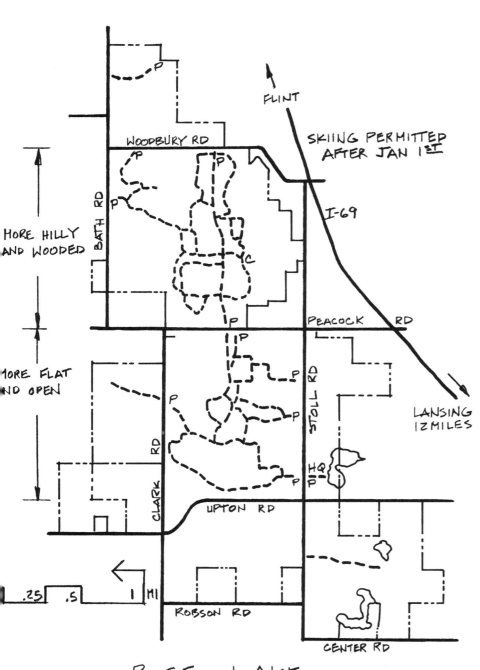

MORE HILLY AND WOODED

MORE FLAT AND OPEN

FLINT

SKIING PERMITTED AFTER JAN 1ST

I-69

WOODBURY RD

BATH RD

PEACOCK RD

STOLL RD

CLARK RD

LANSING 12 MILES

HQ P

UPTON RD

.25 .5 I MI

ROBSON RD

CENTER RD

ROSE LAKE
WILDLIFE RESEARCH AREA

Rose Lake Wildlife Research Area
8562 East Stoll Rd.
East Lansing, MI 48823

517-373-9358

DNR Wildlife Division Office

517-373-1263

Michigan Atlas & Gazetteer Location: 39B56

County Location: Clinton

Directions To Trailhead:
12 miles NE of Lansing off I-69 From I-69 north on Upton, Peacock or Woodbury Rds to parking areas.

Trail Type: Hiking/Walking, Cross Country Skiing, Mountain Biking
Trail Distance: 10+ mi   Loops: Many   Shortest: Longest:
Trail Surface: Natural
Trail Use Fee: None
Method Of Ski Trail Grooming: None
Skiing Ability Suggested: Novice to intermediate
Hiking Trail Difficulty: Easy to moderate
Mountain Biking Ability Suggested: Novice to intermediate
Terrain: Steep 5%, Hilly 10%, Moderate 30%, Flat 55%
Camping: Youth group campground available, with reservations only

Maintained by the DNR Wildlife Division.
Skiing not permitted until January 2nd.
Very popular area for Lansing area residents and MSU students.
The best terrain with the most wooded trails are between Woodbury and Peacock Roads. This land was purchased with hunting licenses.
Please respect the rights of the hunters when in this area. Use of the area for non hunting purposes is discouraged during the firearm hunting season.
If you must use the trails during the hunting season, it is strongly suggested that hunter orange should be worn.

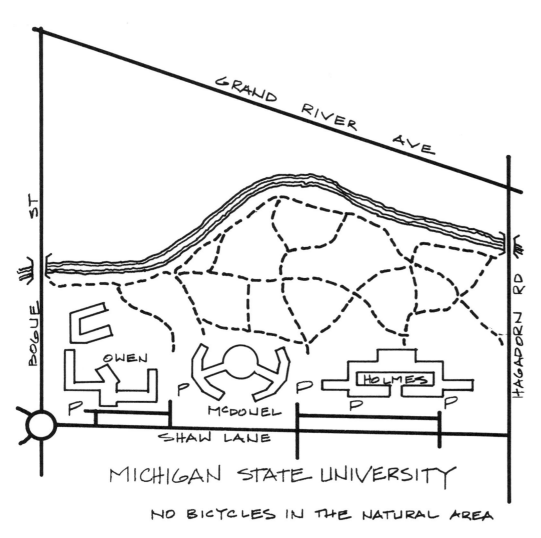

MICHIGAN STATE UNIVERSITY

NO BICYCLES IN THE NATURAL AREA

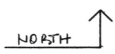

NORTH

Secretary, Natural Areas Committee
Div. of Campus Park and Planning, 412 Olds Hall   517-355-9582
MSU, East Lansing, MI 48824

Michigan Atlas & Gazetteer Location: 39C5

County Location: Ingham

Directions To Trailhead:
On the Michigan State University campus. Bordered by the Red Cedar River on the north, Hagadorn Rd on the east , Bogue St on the west and just north of Shaw Lane on the south.

Trail Type: Hiking/Walking, Cross Country Skiing, Interpretive
Trail Distance: 11 mi   Loops: Many   Shortest: Longest:
Trail Surface: Natural
Trail Use Fee: None
Method Of Ski Trail Grooming: None
Skiing Ability Suggested: Novice
Hiking Trail Difficulty: Easy
Mountain Biking Ability Suggested: NA
Terrain: 100% Flat
Camping: None

Owned by Michigan State University
Managed as a research and natural area.
This 34 acres forest is heavily used by MSU students since several residence hall border the natural area on the south.
Bicycles area strictly prohibited in this area.

SANFORD NATURAL AREA

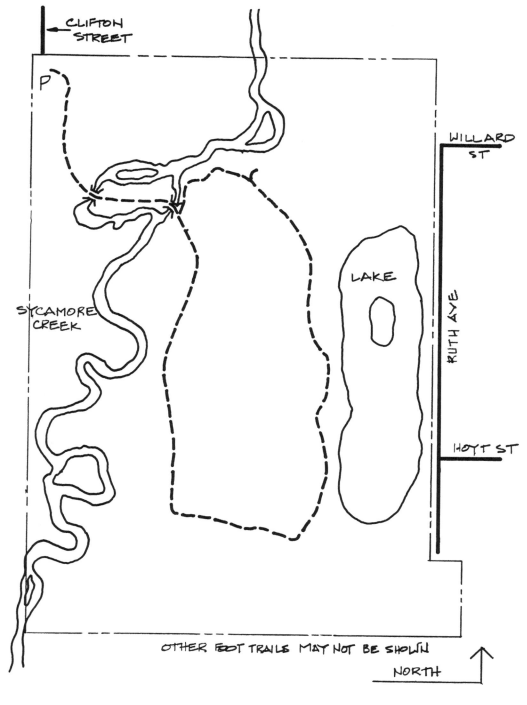

CLIFTON STREET

P

WILLARD ST

SYCAMORE CREEK

LAKE

RUTH AVE

HOYT ST

OTHER FOOT TRAILS MAY NOT BE SHOWN

NORTH

SCOTT WOODS

Scotts Woods Park

Lansing Parks and Recreation Department
124 West Michigan Ave, 4th Floor
Lansing, MI 48933

517-483-4277

Michigan Atlas & Gazetteer Location: 39C5

County Location: Ingham

Directions To Trailhead:
South of Pennsylvania Ave to Mt Hope, then east on Mt Hope to Clifton, then south on Clifton to end of street which is the entrance to Scotts Woods

Trail Type: Hiking/Walking, Cross Country Skiing
Trail Distance: 1.25 mi   Loops: 1   Shortest: NA   Longest: 1.25 mi
Trail Surface: Natural
Trail Use Fee: None
Method Of Ski Trail Grooming: None
Skiing Ability Suggested: Novice
Hiking Trail Difficulty: Easy
Mountain Biking Ability Suggested: NA
Terrain: 100% Flat
Camping: None

Owned by the City of Lansing

Sleepy Hollow State Park
7835 Price Rd.
Lainsburg, MI 48848

517-651-6217
616-527-3750

DNR Parks and Recreation Division

517-373-1270
517-322-1300

Michigan Atlas & Gazetteer Location: 39A5

County Location: Clinton

Directions To Trailhead:
15 miles NE of Lansing From US27 take Price Rd. east 6 miles to park entrance.

Trail Type: Hiking/Walking, Cross Country Skiing, Mountain Biking
Trail Distance: 15.75 mi   Loops: Several   Shortest: 1.7 mi Longest: 12.6 mi
Trail Surface: Natural
Trail Use Fee: None, but vehicle entry fee required
Method Of Ski Trail Grooming: Track set with sufficient snow depth
Skiing Ability Suggested: Novice to intermediate
Hiking Trail Difficulty: Easy to moderate
Mountain Biking Ability Suggested: Novice
Terrain: Steep 2%, Hilly 4%, Moderate 20%, Flat 74%
Camping: Modern campground in park

Maintained by the DNR Parks and Recreation Division
Park has campground, swimming and great fishing.
Cross country ski trail maps are available at the park office.
Cross country ski trail system is less extensive than the hiking trail system shown.

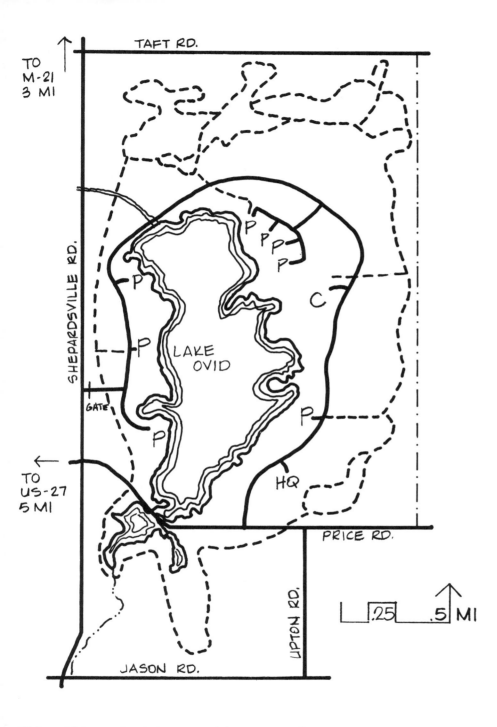

SLEEPY HOLLOW STATE PARK

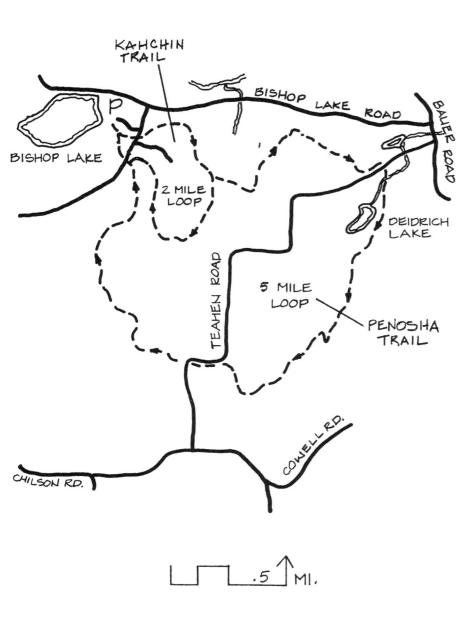

KAHCHIN TRAIL

BISHOP LAKE ROAD

BAUER ROAD

P

BISHOP LAKE

2 MILE LOOP

DEIDRICH LAKE

TEAHEN ROAD

5 MILE LOOP

PENOSHA TRAIL

COWELL RD.

CHILSON RD.

.5 MI.

BRIGHTON RECREATION AREA

Brighton Recreation Area
6360 Chilson Rd., Rte 3
Howell , MI 48843

313-229-6566

DNR Parks and Recreation Division

517-373-1270
517-322-1300

Michigan Atlas & Gazetteer Location: 40D3

County Location: Livingston

Directions To Trailhead:
West from Brighton on Brighton Rd. about 4 miles to Chilson Rd., then south 1.5 miles to Bishop Lake Rd., then east 1.5 miles to Bishop Lake picnic area. Trailhead is located at the south end of the east Bishiop Lake parking lot.

Trail Type: Hiking/Walking, Cross Country Skiing, Mountain Biking
Trail Distance: 7 mi   Loops: 2   Shortest: 2 mi   Longest: 5 mi
Trail Surface: Natural
Trail Use Fee: None, but vehicle entry fee required
Method Of Ski Trail Grooming: None
Skiing Ability Suggested: Novice
Hiking Trail Difficulty: Easy to moderate
Mountain Biking Ability Suggested: Novice to intermediate
Terrain: Steep 5%, Hilly 25%, Moderate 40%, Flat 30%
Camping: Campground available at Bishop Lake and Appleton Lake.

Maintained by the DNR Parks and Recreation Division.
The long trail is the Penosha and the short trail is the Kahchin.
Trails not specifically designed for skiing but are generally skiable.
May not be signed at all intersections but because the trails are well used, it is usually easy to determine the designated trail. For those who like to explore, there are additional unmarked trails in the recreation area.
The two loops although rather short are very popular for mountain biking. Ride clockwise.
This nearly 5,000 acre recreation area has numerous lakes for fishing.

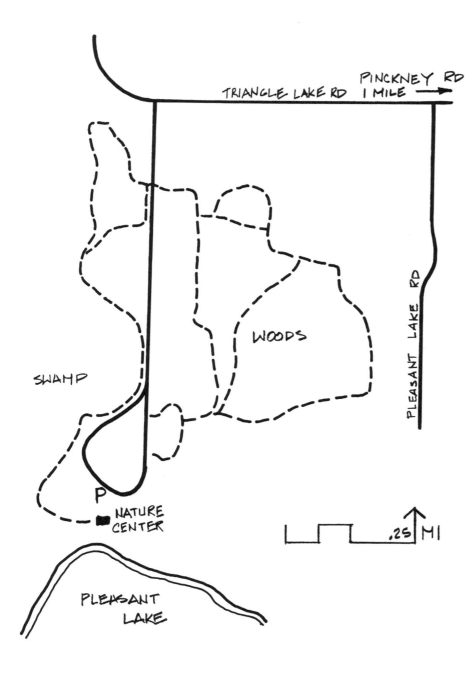

PINCKNEY RD
TRIANGLE LAKE RD   1 MILE →

WOODS

PLEASANT LAKE RD

SWAMP

P

NATURE CENTER

.25 MI

PLEASANT LAKE

HOWELL NATURE CENTER

Howell Nature Center Attn. Dick Grant
1005 Triangle Rd.   517-546-0249
Howell, MI 48843

Michigan Atlas & Gazetteer Location: 40D2

County Location: Livingston

Directions To Trailhead:
South of Howell, 4.5 miles on Pinckney Rd., then west on Triangle Rd. for about
1.5 miles to the nature center entrance

Trail Type: Hiking/Walking, Cross Country Skiing, Interpretive
Trail Distance: 3 mi   Loops: 4   Shortest: .25 mi Longest: 2 mi
Trail Surface: Natural
Trail Use Fee: Yes
Method Of Ski Trail Grooming: None
Skiing Ability Suggested: Novice to intermediate
Hiking Trail Difficulty: Easy to moderate
Mountain Biking Ability Suggested: NA
Terrain: Steep 5%, Hilly 65%, Moderate 20%, Flat 10%
Camping: None

Operated by the Presbytery of Detroit.
Available to any organized group for day or overnight use.
Ski rentals and lodge available for groups with advance reservations.

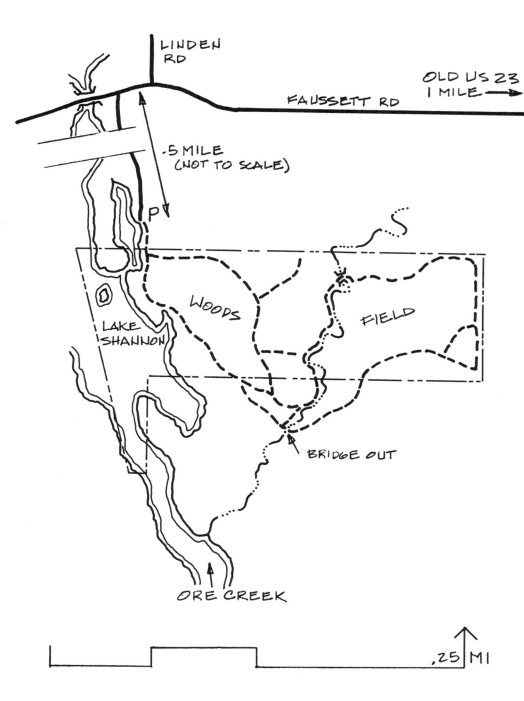

Michigan Nature Association
PO Box 102
Avoca, MI 48006

810-324-2626

Michigan Atlas & Gazetteer Location: 40C3

County Location: Livingston

Directions To Trailhead:
From US23/M59 , go north 3 miles on US23 to Clyde Rd.exit, then west and turn north on Old US23, then north 2 miles to Faussett Rd., then one mile west to the 2 track access road, which goes south. It is about 200 feet west of Linden Rd. Drive through unlocked plastic gate about .5 mile south to a mowed parking area. Follow 2 track to the sanctuary entrance gate.

Trail Type: Hiking/Walking, Interpretive
Trail Distance: .75 mi   Loops: 2   Shortest: .3 mi   Longest: .75 mi
Trail Surface: Natural
Trail Use Fee: None
Method Of Ski Trail Grooming: NA
Skiing Ability Suggested: NA
Hiking Trail Difficulty: Easy
Mountain Biking Ability Suggested: NA
Terrain: Steep 0%, Hilly 0%, Moderate 20%, Flat 80%
Camping: None

Maintained by the Michigan Nature Association
Small but full of interesting plants.
Many birds nest in the area.

SHANNON NATURE SANCTUARY

Bald Mountain Recreation Area
1330 Greenshield Rd., Rte 1   810-693-6767
Lake Orion, MI 48060

DNR Parks and Recreation Division

                                                      517-373-1270
                                                      517=322-1300

Michigan Atlas & Gazetteer Location: 41BC7,42B1

County Location: Oakland

Directions To Trailhead:
9 miles north of Rochester and 4 miles east of Lake Orion on West Romeo Rd.
Headquarters-Northbound M24 from I-75 3 miles to Greenshield Rd. Turn right
(east) and proceed for 1.5 miles to HQ.
Trailhead parking areas along Greenshield Rd, Stoney Creek Rd, Harmon Rd,
Miller Rd and Predmore Rd.

Trail Type: Hiking/Walking, Cross Country Skiing, Mountain Biking
Trail Distance: 15.1 mi   Loops: 5   Shortest: 2.1 mi Longest: 4.8 mi
Trail Surface: Natural
Trail Use Fee: None, but vehicle entry fee required.
Method Of Ski Trail Grooming: Skied-in trails only
Skiing Ability Suggested: Intermediate to advanced
Hiking Trail Difficulty: Easy but with some hills
Mountain Biking Ability Suggested: Novice to intermediate
Terrain: Steep 5%, Hilly 40%, Moderate 50%, Flat 5%
Camping: Group campground only but rustic cabins may be rented

Maintained by the DNR Parks and Recreation Division.
Mostly wooded trails that are well signed and marked with some road crossings.
Scenic trails with vistas and many lakes make this trail system a pleasent
experience. Water pumps are located at the rustic cabins on Tamarack Lake
and the group campground on Kern Rd. Wildflowers are plentiful in the spring.
Insects can be plentiful during the summer months. Sledding available on
Stoney Creek Rd.
Mountain biking opportunities are excellent for cyclists of all skill levels, since the
terrian is not very demanding but is enjoyable for the more skilled riders. The
south unit can be very wet and slippery in the spring for mountain biking.
Cross country skiing is recommended only in the North Unit since snowmobiling
is allowed on the South Unit trails.
Since hunting is permitted, wear bright clothing during the hunting season.

SEE MAPS ON NEXT PAGE

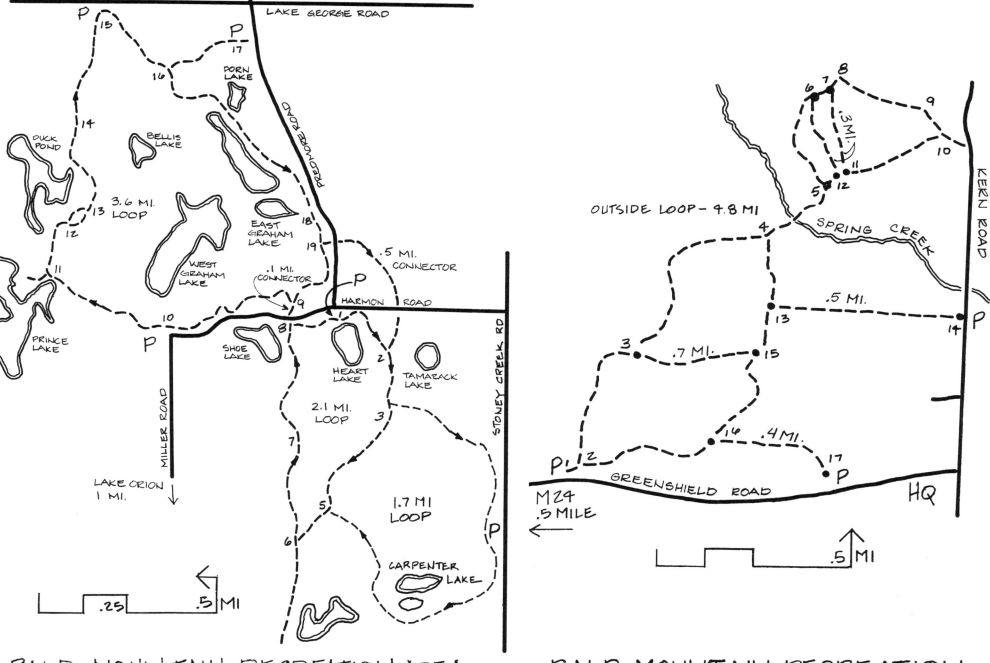

BALD MOUNTAIN RECREATION AREA
NORTH UNIT

BALD MOUNTAIN RECREATION
AREA - SOUTH UNIT

125

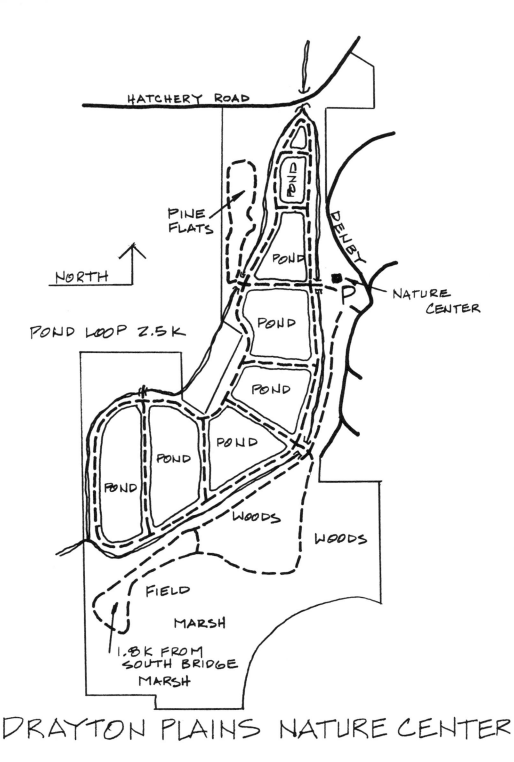

POND LOOP 2.5K

DRAYTON PLAINS NATURE CENTER

Drayton Plains Nature Center, Inc.
2125 Denby Drive
Waterford, MI 48329

810-674-2119

Michigan Atlas & Gazetteer Location: 41C67

County Location: Oakland

Directions To Trailhead:
North on US24 from Pontiac about 5 miles to Hatchery Rd., then west 3/4 mile, then south on Edmore and follow signs to the center.

Trail Type: Hiking/Walking, Cross Country Skiing, Interpretive
Trail Distance: 6 km   Loops: Several   Shortest: .5 km   Longest: 2.5 km
Trail Surface: Natural and gravel
Trail Use Fee: Donations requsted
Method Of Ski Trail Grooming: None
Skiing Ability Suggested: Novice
Hiking Trail Difficulty: Easy
Mountain Biking Ability Suggested: NA
Terrain: Steep 0%, Hilly 0%, Moderate 40%, Flat 60%
Camping: None

A profit non profit nature center.
Formerly the second oldest fish hatchery (1903 to 1960) in Michigan.
Large (137 acres) nature center within an urban area.

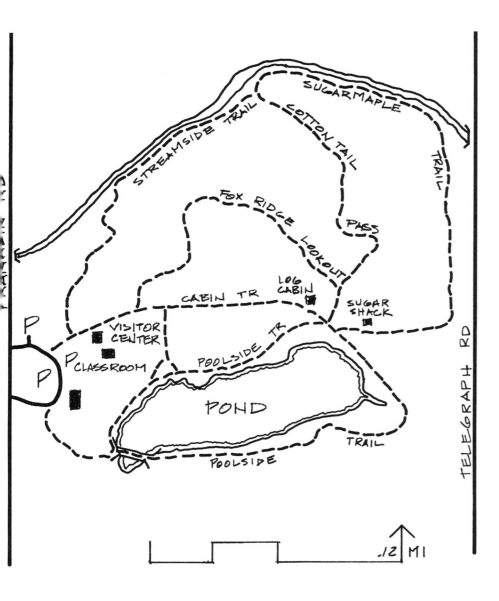

Bloomfield Hills Public Schools
3325 Franklin Rd
Bloomfield Hills, MI 48302

810-339-3497

Michigan Atlas & Gazetteer Location: 41D7

County Location: Oakland

Directions To Trailhead:
On Franklin Rd Between Long Lake Rd and Square Lake Rd, .25 mile west of Telegraph Rd

Trail Type: Hiking/Walking, Interpretive
Trail Distance: 1.7 mi   Loops: 4   Shortest: .2 mi   Longest: .9 mi
Trail Surface: Natural
Trail Use Fee: None
Method Of Ski Trail Grooming: NA
Skiing Ability Suggested: NA
Hiking Trail Difficulty: Easy
Mountain Biking Ability Suggested: NA
Terrain: Steep 0%, Hilly 15%, Moderate 15%, Flat 70%
Camping: None

Owned by the Bloomfield Hills Public Schools
Trail guide available.
Open to the public with special event throughout the year.

E.J. JOHNSON
NATURE CENTER

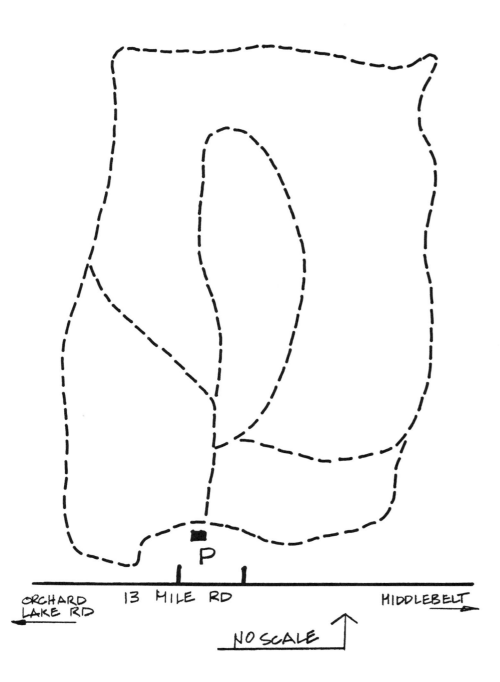

GLEN OAKS GOLF COURSE

ORCHARD
LAKE RD

13 MILE RD

MIDDLEBELT

P

NO SCALE

Glen Oaks County Park
30500 West 13 Mile Rd.   810-851-8356
Farmington Hills, MI 48018

Oakland County Parks & Recreation Commission
2800 Watkins Lake Rd.   810-858-0906
Pontiac, MI 48054-1697

Michigan Atlas & Gazetteer Location: 41D7

County Location: Oakland

Directions To Trailhead:
Between Orchard Lake and Middlebelt Rds on 13 Mile Rd.

Trail Type: Cross Country Skiing
Trail Distance: 5.7 km   Loops: 3   Shortest: Longest:
Trail Surface: Natural
Trail Use Fee: None
Method Of Ski Trail Grooming: Packed
Skiing Ability Suggested: Novice
Hiking Trail Difficulty: NA
Mountain Biking Ability Suggested: NA
Terrain: Steep 0%, Hilly 0%, Moderate 80%, Flat 20%
Camping: None

Operated by the Oakland County Parks and Recreation Commission.
Warming area, snack bar and ski rental available.
Trails on a golf course.

Highland Recreation Area
5200 East Highland Rd.
Milford, MI 48042

810-887-5135

DNR Parks and Recreation Division

517-373-1270
517-322-1300

Michigan Atlas & Gazetteer Location: 41C5

County Location: Oakland

Directions To Trailhead:
NE of Milford off M59 1 mile east of Duck Lake Rd.

Trail Type: Hiking/Walking, Cross Country Skiing, Mountain Biking
Trail Distance: 10 mi   Loops: 3   Shortest: 1   Longest: 5
Trail Surface: Natural
Trail Use Fee: None, but vehicle entry fee required
Method Of Ski Trail Grooming: Track set
Skiing Ability Suggested: Novice to intermediate
Hiking Trail Difficulty: Easy to moderate
Mountain Biking Ability Suggested: In planning stages
Terrain: Rolling to moderate
Camping: Campground within the recreation area

Maintained by the DNR Parks and Recreation Division
Warming area, downhill slopes, rentals and snack bar on weekends.
Trail uses may overlap seasonally.
Bridle trails exist in this recreation area.

A mountain bike trail is in the planning stages by the Michigan Mountain Biking
Association. Contact the Park Manager or the Michigan Mountain Biking
Association for current status (1994)

HIGHLAND RECREATION AREA

Holly Recreation Area
8100 Grange Hall Rd.   810-634-8811
Holly , MI 48442

DNR Parks and Recreation Division
                                                                 517-373-1270

Michigan Atlas & Gazetteer Location: 41B56

County Location: Oakland

Directions To Trailhead:
Main Entrance:Exit I-75 at Grange Hall Rd. (east of Holly), then east 2.5 miles to
the recreation area entrance .
Mountain Bike Trail Entrance: Exit I-75 at Grange Hall Rd, then west to Hess
Rd., then north on Hess Rd to the trailhead.

Trail Type: Hiking/Walking, Cross Country Skiing, Mountain Biking, Interpretive
Trail Distance: 25+ mi   Loops: Many   Shortest: .8 mi   Longest: 5 mi
Trail Surface: Natural and wood decking
Trail Use Fee: None, but vehicle entry fee required
Method Of Ski Trail Grooming: None
Skiing Ability Suggested: Novice to advanced
Hiking Trail Difficulty: Easy to difficult
Mountain Biking Ability Suggested: Novice to intermediate
Terrain: Steep 5%, Hilly 15%, Moderate 60%, Flat 20%
Camping: Campground available on site

Maintained by the DNR Parks and Recreation Division
Hiking, skiing and mountain biking trails are not all identical.
Map 1 shows the entire RA with some hiking/skiing trails.
Map 2 shows detailed hiking/skiing trails in the McGinnis/Heron/Wildwood Lakes
area.
Map 3 Shows the general mountain bike area with new and proposed loops west
of I-75 in the Holdridge Lakes area.
Map 4 shows the completed mountain bike loops (1994) developed by the
Holly/Flint Chapter of the Michigan Mountian Biking Association.

SEE MAPS ON NEXT 2 PAGES

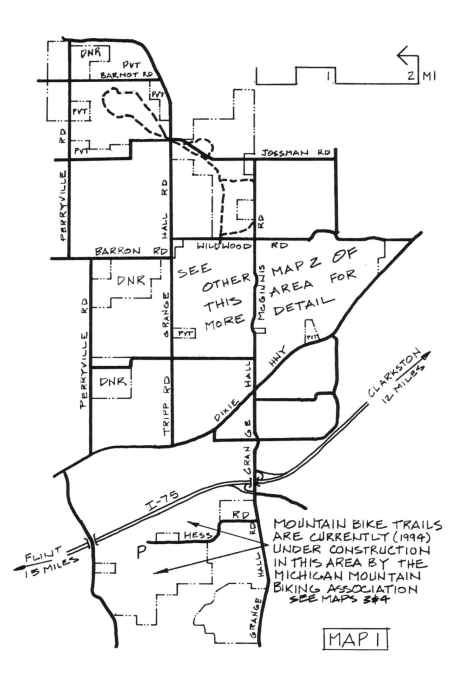

MAP 1

DNR

PVT
BARHOT RD

PERRYVILLE RD

PVT

PVT

PVT

JOSSMAN RD

HALL RD

MCGINNIS RD

WILDWOOD RD

BARRON RD

DNR

GRANGE RD

PVT

SEE OTHER MAP 2 OF AREA FOR THIS MORE DETAIL

PERRYVILLE RD

DNR

TRIPP RD

DIXIE HALL HWY

CLARKSTON 12 MILES

GRANGE HALL RD

I-75

FLINT 15 MILES

P

HESS RD

RD

MOUNTAIN BIKE TRAILS ARE CURRENTLY (1994) UNDER CONSTRUCTION IN THIS AREA BY THE MICHIGAN MOUNTAIN BIKING ASSOCIATION SEE MAPS 3 & 4

1   2 MI

HOLLY RECREATION AREA

MAP 2

GRANGE HALL RD   TOWNSHIP HALL

7 P

3

.35   .65

.8   .5

.4

.6

C   C   C

.2

C   C

1.0

.4

McGINNIS LAKE

.8

.35   9

VAN RD

8

.5

SEE OTHER MAP FOR MORE TRAILS

McGINNIS   RD

.15   .25   .3
14   10

13   .25
12   11

.2
16   .5

RAMP BEACH   P

P

OVERLOOK
17 P
18
19

HERON LAKE

WILDWOOD RD

P   24

P

P

WILDWOOD LAKE

VALLEY LAKE

.4   20
P

.5

P   24
22   .35   21   P
P

DIXIE HWY

.5 MI

HOLLY RECREATION AREA   131

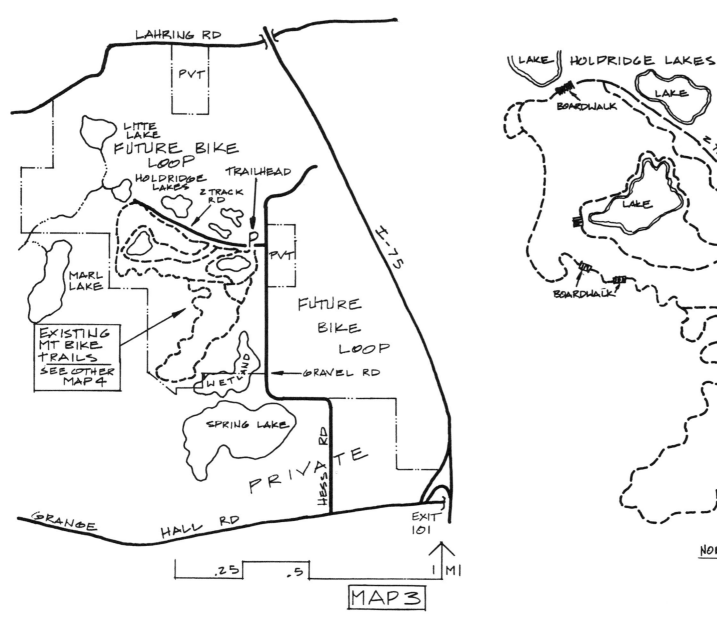

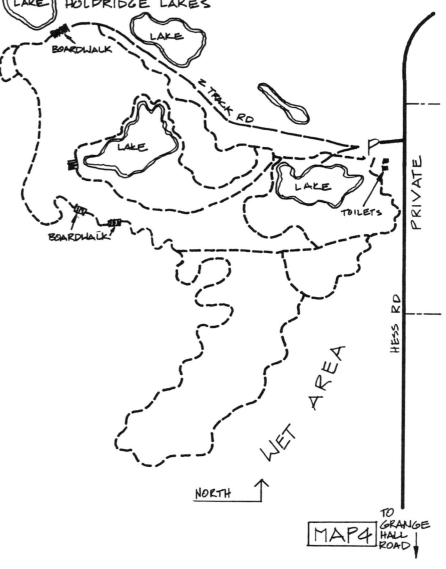

HOLLY RECREATION AREA
MOUNTAIN BIKE AREA

HOLLY RECREATION AREA
MOUNTAIN BIKE TRAIL

132

Independence Oaks County Park
9501 Sashabaw Rd.   810-625-0877
Clarkston, MI 48016   810-625-6473

Oakland County Parks and Recreation Commission
2800 Watkins Lake Rd.   810-858-0906
Waterford, MI 48328

Michigan Atlas & Gazetteer Location: 41B6

County Location: Oakland

Directions To Trailhead:
North of Pontiac off I-75 at Sashabaw Rd. exit 89, then north 2.5 miles to the park entrance

Trail Type: Hiking/Walking, Cross Country Skiing, Interpretive
Trail Distance: 6.8 mi   Loops: Many   Shortest: 2.5 mi Longest: 3.2 mi
Trail Surface: Paved and natural
Trail Use Fee: None, but vehicle entry fee required
Method Of Ski Trail Grooming: Double track set
Skiing Ability Suggested: Novice to advanced
Hiking Trail Difficulty: Easy to moderate
Mountain Biking Ability Suggested: NA
Terrain: Steep 2%, Hilly 45%, Moderate 15%, Flat 38%
Camping: Youth group camping only

Operated by the Oakland County Parks and Recreation Commission
The complex trail system provides many different route options. Using different sections, over 10 miles of ski trails and 12 miles of hiking trail routes are available.
Ski rentals, warming area, snack bar, picnic grounds, fishing, boating, Rubach Sensory Garden, swimming, nature trail and center and ice skating. Some of the best cross country trails in SE Michigan. Open 8am to sunset daily (Closed Christmas Day) Fishing and ice skating available.
A .3 mile "All Visitors Trail" is available for visitors with disabilities.

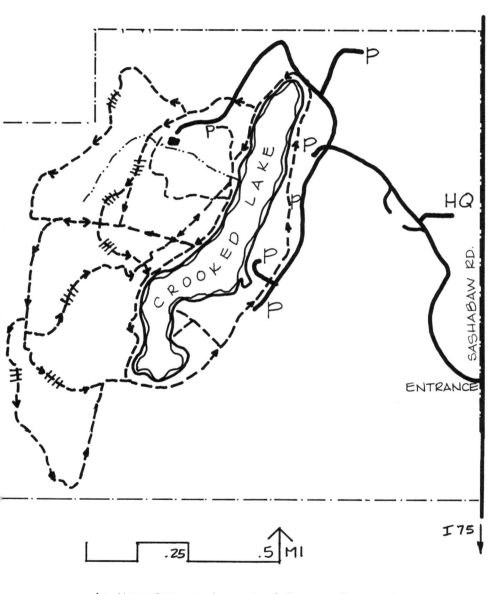

CROOKED LAKE

HQ

SASHABAW RD.

ENTRANCE

I 75

.25   .5 MI

INDEPENDENCE OAKS
COUNTY PARK

Indian Springs Metropark
5200 Indian Trail   810-625-7280
Clarkston, MI 48016   800-47-PARKS

Huron-Clinton Metropolitan Authority
13000 High Ridge Drive, PO Box 2001   810-227-2757
Brighton, MI 48116-8001

Michigan Atlas & Gazetteer Location: 41C56

County Location: Oakland

Directions To Trailhead:
Just north of Pontaic Lake Recreation Area and south of Clarkston on White Lake Rd, between Cuthbert and Teggerdine Roads.

Trail Type: Hiking/Walking, Cross Country Skiing, Interpretive
Trail Distance: 11 mi   Loops: Many   Shortest: .3 mi   Longest: 4.2 mi
Trail Surface: Paved and natural
Trail Use Fee: None, but vehicle entry fee required
Method Of Ski Trail Grooming: Track set
Skiing Ability Suggested: Novice
Hiking Trail Difficulty: Easy
Mountain Biking Ability Suggested: NA
Terrain: Steep 0%, Hilly 5%, Moderate 35%, Flat 60%
Camping: None

Operated by the Huron-Clinton Metropolitan Authority.
Year around regional recreation area with a variety of facilities.
Hiking trail terrain is listed above.
Mountan bikes are restricted to the paved hike/bike trail.
Cross country ski trail terrain is 5% steep, 25% hilly, 35% moderate and 35% flat. Ski rentals on weekends only.
Nature Center building is open on a limited schedule during the school year weekdays and 10AM to 5PM during the summer. The weekend schedule all year is 10AM to 5PM. Trails for skiing and hiking/biking are not identical.
Call or write for their Metropark Guide, published each year.

SEE MAPS ON NEXT PAGE

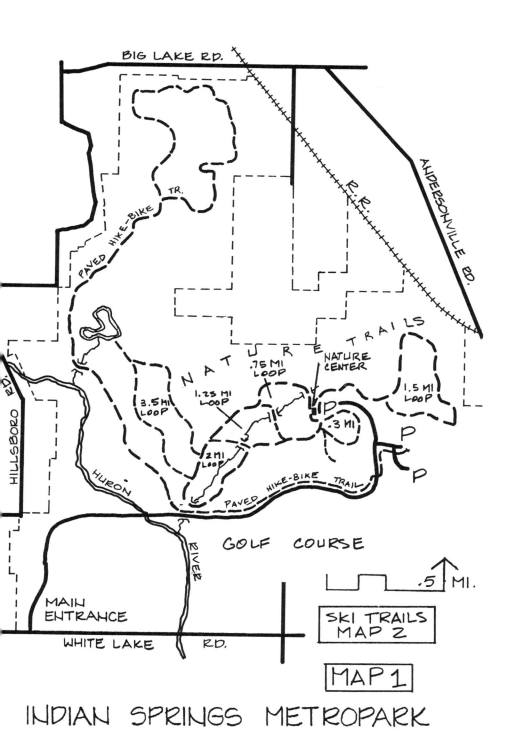

BIG LAKE RD.

ANDERSONVILLE RD.

R.R.

PAVED HIKE-BIKE TR.

N A T U R E   T R A I L S

NATURE CENTER

.75 MI LOOP

1.25 MI LOOP

3.5 MI LOOP

1.5 MI LOOP

.3 MI

P

P

.2 MI LOOP

HURON

PAVED HIKE-BIKE TRAIL

HILLSBORO RD.

RIVER

GOLF COURSE

MAIN ENTRANCE

WHITE LAKE RD.

.5 MI.

SKI TRAILS MAP 2

MAP 1

INDIAN SPRINGS METROPARK

BIG LAKE RD   ANDERSONVILLE

ANDERSONVILLE RD

1.1 MI

.11

.1 MI

10

SEE MICHIGAN NATURE ASSOCIATION

1.5 MI

P

6

7

8

P

.1 MI

.8 MI

HILLSBORO RD

1.1 MI

9

P

SKI CENTER

3

5

.7 MI

4

.7 MI

.7 MI

.8 MI

2

CUTHBERT RD

WHITE LK RD

TEGGERDINE RD

MAP 2

.5

1 MI

SKI TRAILS
INDIAN SPRINGS METROPARK

135

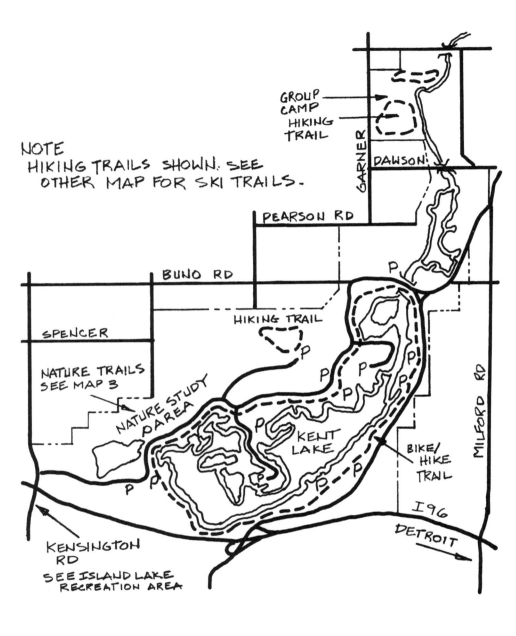

NOTE
HIKING TRAILS SHOWN. SEE
OTHER MAP FOR SKI TRAILS.

GROUP
CAMP
HIKING
TRAIL

GARNER

DAWSON

PEARSON RD

BUNO RD

SPENCER

HIKING TRAIL

NATURE TRAILS
SEE MAP 3

NATURE STUDY AREA

KENT LAKE

MILFORD RD

BIKE/
HIKE
TRAIL

I 96

DETROIT

KENSINGTON RD

SEE ISLAND LAKE
RECREATION AREA

.5   1   2 MI   MAP 1

KENSINGTON METROPARK

Kensington Metropark
2240 West Buno Rd.
Milford , MI 48042-9725

810-685-1561
800-47-PARKS

Huron-Clinton Metropolitan Authority
1300 High Ridge Drive, PO Box 2001
Brighton, MI 48116-8001

810-227-2757

Michigan Atlas & Gazetteer Location: 41D4

County Location: Oakland & Livingston

Directions To Trailhead:
SW of Milford toward Brighton, just north of I96 Exit I96 at Milford Rd., Kent Lake Rd. (exit153) or Kensington Rd.   (exit 151) and turn north toward park

Trail Type: Hiking/Walking, Cross Country Skiing, Interpretive
Trail Distance: 24 mi   Loops: 12+   Shortest: .5 mi   Longest: 6 mi
Trail Surface: Paved, gravel and natural
Trail Use Fee: None, but vehicle entry fee required
Method Of Ski Trail Grooming: Track set as needed
Skiing Ability Suggested: Novice to intermediate
Hiking Trail Difficulty: Easy
Mountain Biking Ability Suggested: NA
Terrain: Steep 10%, Hilly 40%, Moderate 30%, Flat 20%
Camping: Youth group campground only, reservations required

Operated by the Huron-Clinton Metropolitan Authority
Warming area, rentals, lessons, snack bar, fishing, ice skating, boating, golf, nature center with trails, group camping and sledding are available in the park.
The main hiking/biking trail is paved and follows the shore of Kensington Lake.
Biking limited to the paved trail in non skiing months.
Some ski trails on the golf course.
Bike/hike trail distance is 8.2 miles. Terrain listed above.
Nature Trails: 6 loops from .5 to 3 mi; Steep 0%, Hilly 25%, Moderate 30%, Flat 45%.
Bike/hike and ski trails overlap.
Call or write for their Metropark Guide, published each year.

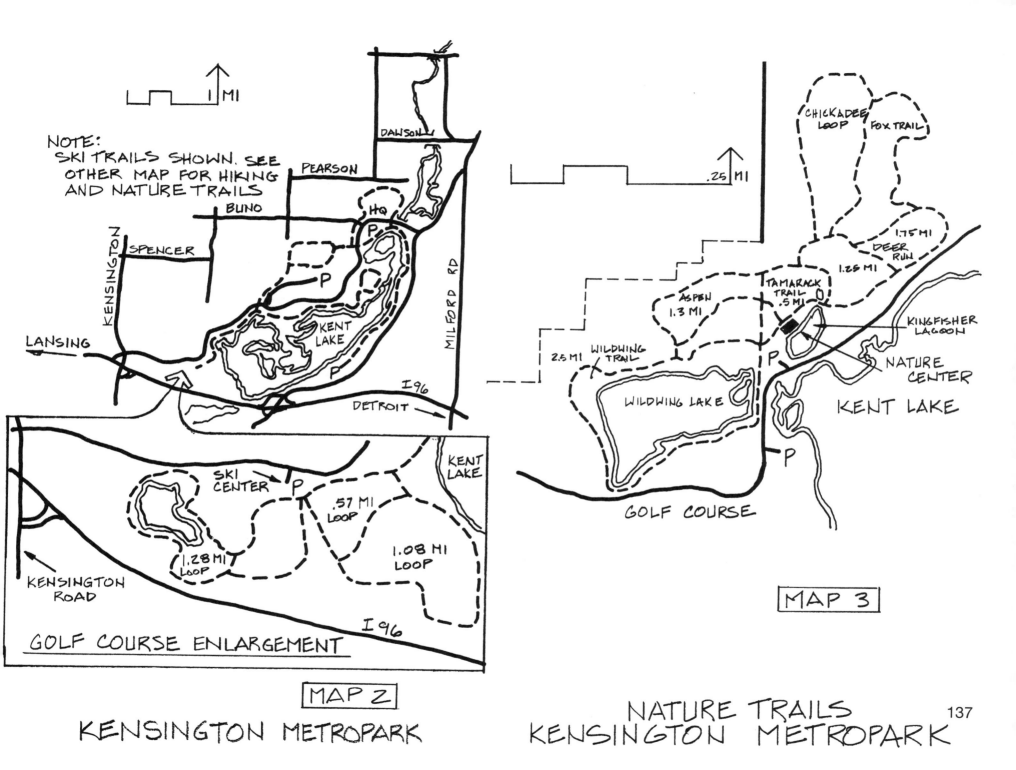

↑ 1 MI

NOTE:
SKI TRAILS SHOWN. SEE
OTHER MAP FOR HIKING
AND NATURE TRAILS

DAWSON

PEARSON

BUNO

HQ
P

KENSINGTON

SPENCER

P

P

KENT
LAKE

MILFORD RD

LANSING

DETROIT →

I 96

KENT
LAKE

SKI
CENTER
P

.57 MI
LOOP

1.08 MI
LOOP

1.28 MI
LOOP

KENSINGTON
ROAD

I 96

GOLF COURSE ENLARGEMENT

MAP 2

KENSINGTON METROPARK

↑ .25 MI

CHICKADEE
LOOP   FOX TRAIL

1.75 MI
DEER
RUN

1.25 MI

ASPEN
1.3 MI

TAMARACK
TRAIL
.5 MI

KINGFISHER
LAGOON

WILDWING
TRAIL

2.5 MI

P

NATURE
CENTER

WILDWING LAKE

KENT LAKE

P

GOLF COURSE

MAP 3

NATURE TRAILS
KENSINGTON METROPARK

137

Metamora-Hadley Recreation Area
3871 Hurd Rd.   810-797-4439
Metamora, MI 48455

DNR Parks and Recreation Division

                           517-373-1270

Michigan Atlas & Gazetteer Location: 41A7

County Location: Lapeer

Directions To Trailhead:
South from Lapeer on M24 to Pratt Rd., then west 2 miles to Herd Rd., then south .7 mile to recreation area entrance. Trailheads at campground office and beach area.

Trail Type: Hiking/Walking, Cross Country Skiing, Interpretive
Trail Distance: 6 mi   Loops: 2   Shortest: 1.3 mi   Longest: 2.5 mi
Trail Surface: Natural
Trail Use Fee: None, but vehicle entry fee required
Method Of Ski Trail Grooming: None
Skiing Ability Suggested: Novice to intermediate
Hiking Trail Difficulty: Easy
Mountain Biking Ability Suggested: NA
Terrain: Steep 1%, Hilly 30%, Moderate 40%, Flat 29%
Camping: Campground in recreation area

Maintained by the DNR Parks and Recreation Division.
Trails were designed for hiking but are skiable when snow depth permits.

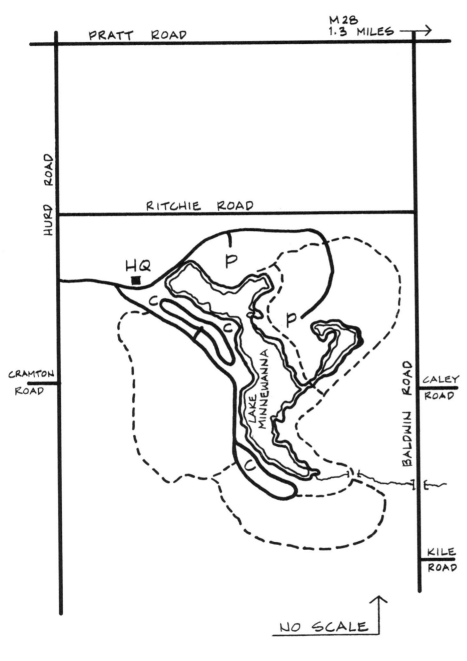

METAMORA - HADLEY RECREATION AREA

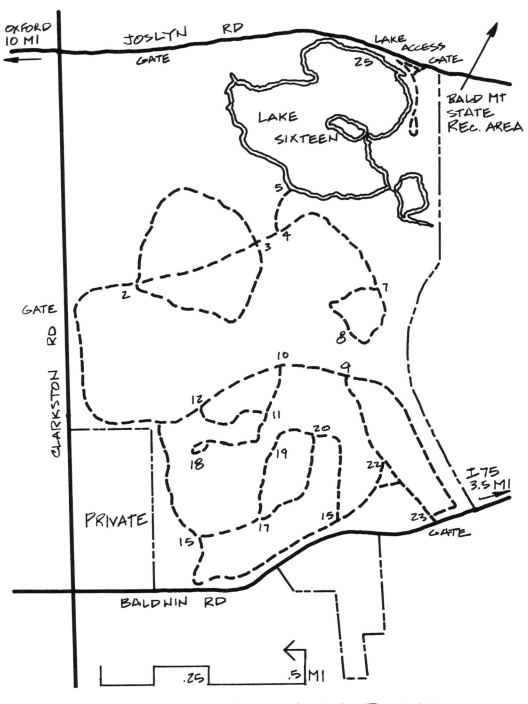

Orion Oaks County Park
2301 Clarkston Rd   810-625-0877
Lake Orion, MI 48360

Oakland County Parks and Recreation Commission
2800 Watkins Lake Rd   810-858-0906
Waterford, MI 48328

Michigan Atlas & Gazetteer Location: 41B7

County Location: Oakland

Directions To Trailhead:
Clarkston Rd between Baldwin and Joslyn Rds north of Pontiac.

Trail Type: Hiking/Walking, Cross Country Skiing
Trail Distance: 5 mi   Loops: Many   Shortest: Longest:
Trail Surface: Natural
Trail Use Fee: None but vehicle permit is required
Method Of Ski Trail Grooming: None
Skiing Ability Suggested: Novice
Hiking Trail Difficulty: Easy
Mountain Biking Ability Suggested: NA
Terrain: Steep 10%, Hilly 25%, Moderate 45%, Flat 20%
Camping: None

Maintained by Oakland County Parks
Park is underdevelopment

ORION OAKS COUNTY PARK

Ortonville Recreation Area
5779 Hadley Rd.
Ortonville, MI 48462

810-627-3828

DNR Parks and Recreation Division

517-373-1270

Michigan Atlas & Gazetteer Location: 41AB6

County Location: Oakland & Lapeer

Directions To Trailhead:
SE of Flint, north of Clarkston and east of M15.
Big Fish Unit - 1.5 miles NE of Ortonville 1.25 miles north of Oakwood Rd on Hadley Rd.
Bloomer Unit - .5 mile east of Sands Rd. on State Park Rd.

Trail Type: Hiking/Walking, Cross Country Skiing, Mountain Biking
Trail Distance: 4.25 mi   Loops: 2   Shortest: 1.5 mi Longest: 2.75 mi
Trail Surface: Natural
Trail Use Fee: None, but vehicle entry fee required
Method Of Ski Trail Grooming: None
Skiing Ability Suggested: Intermediate to advanced
Hiking Trail Difficulty: Moderate
Mountain Biking Ability Suggested: Novice
Terrain: Steep 10%, Hilly 30%, Moderate 30%, Flat 30%
Camping: Group campground available

Maintained by the DNR Parks and Recreation Division.
Cabins available for rent in the Bloomer Unit.

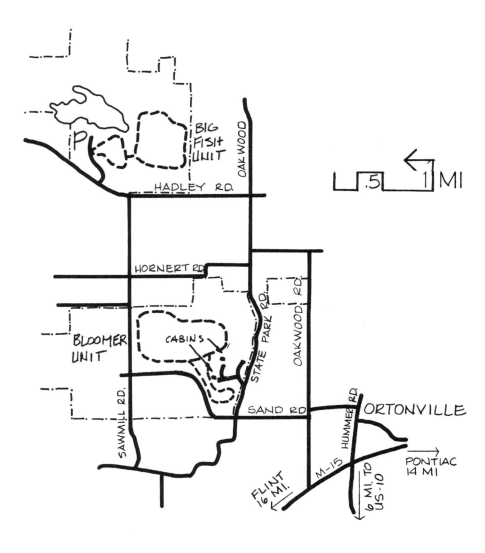

ORTONVILLE RECREATION AREA

TRAIL NOTES

Pontiac Lake Recreation Area
7800 Gale Rd
Waterford, MI 48327

810-666-1020

DNR Parks and Recreation Division

517-322-1300
517-373-1270

Michigan Atlas & Gazetteer Location: 41C56

County Location: Oakland

Directions To Trailhead:
11 miles west of the Pontiac Silverdome on M-59. M-59 (west of Pontiac) to
Williams Lake Rd, then north to Gale Rd, then left(west) to beach parking lot..

SEE MAPS ON NEXT PAGE

Trail Type: Hiking/Walking, Cross Country Skiing, Mountain Biking, Interpretive
Trail Distance: 17 mi   Loops: Many   Shortest: .25 mi Longest: 6 mi
Trail Surface: Natural and gravel
Trail Use Fee: None, but vehicle entry permit required
Method Of Ski Trail Grooming: None
Skiing Ability Suggested: Novice to advanced
Hiking Trail Difficulty: Moderate to difficult
Mountain Biking Ability Suggested: Intermediate to advanced
Terrain: Steep 15%, Hilly 45%, Moderate 25%, Flat 20
Camping: Campground in the recreation area.

Maintained by the DNR Parks and Recreation Divsion
Trail distances vary and some may overlap.
          Mountain biking trails - 8.6 miles
          Hiking trails - Both trails above are used for hiking trails
          Skiing trails - Trails above are used for skiing.
          (Horse trails throughout the park)
Large modern campground located along trail system.
Bike trail designed and maintained by the Michigan Mountain Biking Association.
Snowmobiles are permitted in the park and may find their way onto the trails.

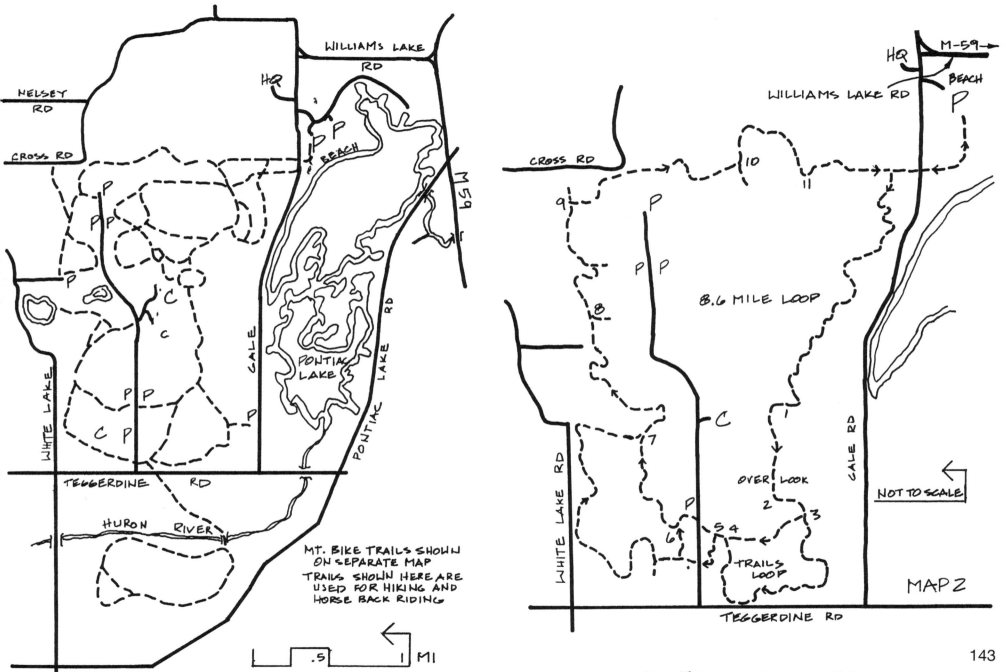

WILLIAMS LAKE RD

HQ

NELSEY RD

CROSS RD

BEACH

M59

C T

c

PONTIAC LAKE

GALE RD

PONTIAC LAKE RD

WHITE LAKE

P P

C P

P

TEGGERDINE RD

HURON RIVER

MT. BIKE TRAILS SHOWN ON SEPARATE MAP
TRAILS SHOWN HERE ARE USED FOR HIKING AND HORSE BACK RIDING

.5   1 MI

MAP1
PONTIAC LAKE RECREATION AREA

HQ   M-59 →

WILLIAMS LAKE RD   BEACH
P

CROSS RD   10   11

9

P

8   8.6 MILE LOOP

P P

C

7

OVER LOOK

P   2   3

5 4

6   TRAILS LOOP

WHITE LAKE RD

GALE RD

NOT TO SCALE

MAP 2

TEGGERDINE RD

MOUNTAIN BIKE TRAIL
PONTIAC LAKE RECREATION AREA

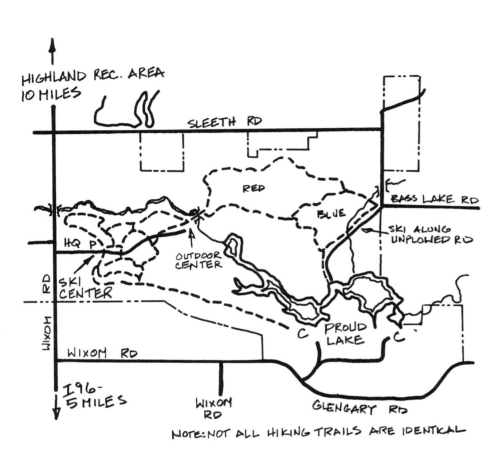

HIGHLAND REC. AREA
10 MILES

SLEETH RD

RED

BLUE

BASS LAKE RD

SKI ALONG UNPLOWED RD

HQ P

OUTDOOR CENTER

SKI CENTER

NIXOM RD

WIXOM RD

I96- 5 MILES

WIXOM RD

C

PROUD LAKE

C

GLENGARY RD

NOTE: NOT ALL HIKING TRAILS ARE IDENTICAL

.5   1 MI

Proud Lake Recreation Area
3500 Wixom Rd., Rte 3   810-685-2433
Milford, MI 48042

DNR Parks and Recreation Division

517-373-1270

Michigan Atlas & Gazetteer Location: 41D5

County Location: Oakland

Directions To Trailhead:
3 miles SE of Milford on Wixom Rd. or From I-96 take Wixom Rd. north 6 miles

Trail Type: Hiking/Walking, Cross Country Skiing, Mountain Biking, Interpretive
Trail Distance: 8 mi   Loops: Several   Shortest: 1 mi   Longest: 5 mi
Trail Surface: Natural
Trail Use Fee: None, but vehicle entry fee required
Method Of Ski Trail Grooming: None
Skiing Ability Suggested: Novice
Hiking Trail Difficulty: East
Mountain Biking Ability Suggested: Novice
Terrain: Steep 0%, Hilly 0%, Moderate 40%, Flat 60%
Camping: Campground with heated restroom open all year

Maintained by the DNR Parks and Recreation Division
Nature and hiking trails provided.
Ski center located at trailhead, operated by Heavner Concessions.
Rentals, lessons, ski shop, refreshments and warming shelter .
Horse back riding trails (not shown on map) west of Nixon Rd are sometimes
use by hikers and mountain bikers.
Lodging available for groups 685-2433

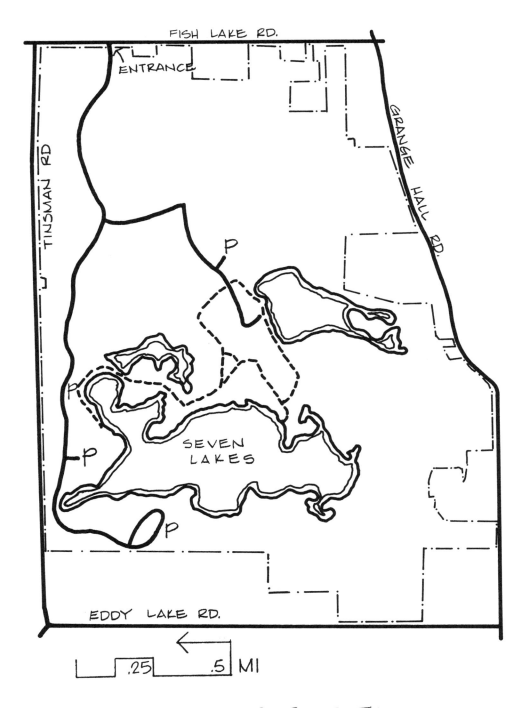

Seven Lakes State Park
2220 Tinsman Rd.
Fenton , MI 48430

810-634-7271
810-634-8811

DNR Parks and Recreation Division

517-373-1270

Michigan Atlas & Gazetteer Location: 41B45

County Location: Oakland

Directions To Trailhead:
Exit I-75 at Grange Hall Rd, then go 6 miles west to Fish Lake Rd., then north on Fish Lake Rd 1 mile to park entrance. Trailheads at boat launch and north picnic area .

Trail Type: Hiking/Walking, Cross Country Skiing, Mountain Biking, Interpretive
Trail Distance: 3.5 mi   Loops: Several   Shortest: Longest:
Trail Surface: Natural
Trail Use Fee: None, but vehicle entry fee required
Method Of Ski Trail Grooming: None
Skiing Ability Suggested: Novice
Hiking Trail Difficulty: Easy
Mountain Biking Ability Suggested: Novice
Terrain: Steep 2%, Hilly 20%, Moderate 50%, Flat 28%
Camping: On site

Maintained by the DNR Parks and Recreation Division
8 miles west of the Holly Recreation Area
All 1,400 acres are open for cross-country skiing.
Trails not designed for skiing but are skiable.

SEVEN LAKES STATE PARK

Springfield Oaks County Park
12450 Andersonville Rd.   810-625-2540
Davisburg, MI 48019

Oakland County Parks and Recreation Commission
2800 Watkins Lake Rd.   810-858-0906
Pontiac , MI 48056

Michigan Atlas & Gazetteer Location: 41C5

County Location: Oakland

Directions To Trailhead:
Just west of I-75 at Andersonville Rd. and Davisburg Rd.. in Davisburg

Trail Type: Cross Country Skiing
Trail Distance: 8.5 km   Loops: 3   Shortest: Longest:
Trail Surface: Natural
Trail Use Fee: None
Method Of Ski Trail Grooming: None
Skiing Ability Suggested: Novice to intermediate
Hiking Trail Difficulty: NA
Mountain Biking Ability Suggested: NA
Terrain: Steep 0%, Hilly 0%, Moderate 40%, Flat 60%
Camping: None

Maintained by the Oakland County Parks & Recreation Commission
Warming building available.
Trails on a golf course.

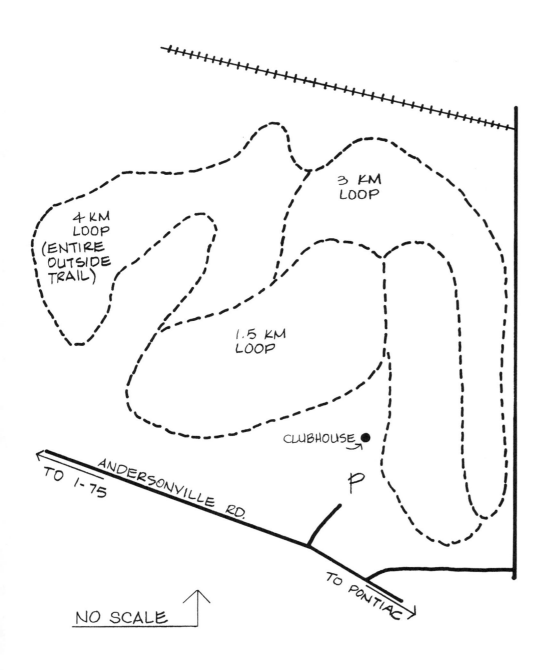

SPRINGFIELD OAKS
GOLF COURSE

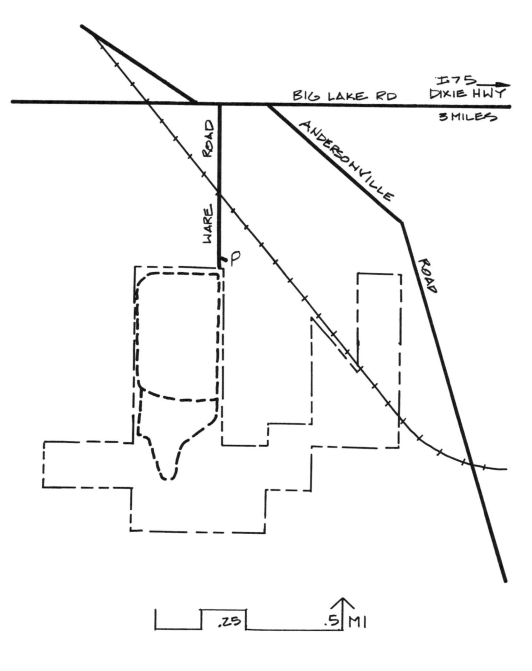

Michigan Nature Association
PO Box 102
Avoca, MI 48006

810-324-2626

Michigan Atlas & Gazetteer Location: 41C56

County Location: Oakland

Directions To Trailhead:
On the north side of Indian Hills Metropark off Big Lake Rd just west of
Andersonville Rd. Take Ware Rd south to the trailhead.

Trail Type: Hiking/Walking, Interpretive
Trail Distance: 2.5 mi   Loops: 2   Shortest: 1.5 mi Longest: 2 mi
Trail Surface: Natural
Trail Use Fee: None
Method Of Ski Trail Grooming: NA
Skiing Ability Suggested: NA
Hiking Trail Difficulty: Moderate
Mountain Biking Ability Suggested: NA
Terrain: 100% Flat
Camping: None

Maintained by the Michigan Nature Association
A unique 245 acre sanctuary that is the Michigan Nature Association's
showplace.   Other than logged, the sanctuary has never been disturbed
including tilling for farmland.
Every season provides the visitor with new things to see and experience.

BIG LAKE RD

I75
DIXIE HWY

3 MILES

ANDERSONVILLE

ROAD

WARE   ROAD

P

.25   .5 MI

TIMBERLAND SWAMP
NATURE SANCTUARY

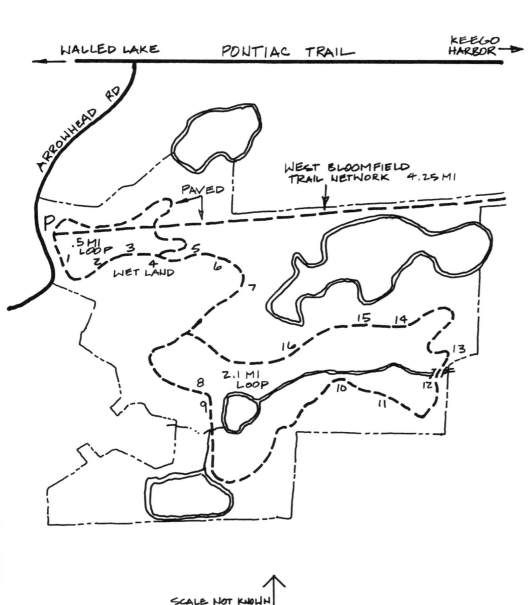

WALLED LAKE ← PONTIAC TRAIL → KEEGO HARBOR

ARROWHEAD RD

WEST BLOOMFIELD TRAIL NETWORK 4.25 MI

PAVED

P

.5 MI LOOP

2   3   4   5
WET LAND   6
7

15   14
16   13
2.1 MI LOOP   8   10   12
9   11

SCALE NOT KNOWN

WEST BLOOMFIELD WOODS
NATURE PRESERVE

West Bloomfield Woods Nature Preserve

West Bloomfield Parks and Recreation Commission
3325 Middlebelt Road
West Bloomfield, MI 48323

810-334-5660

Michigan Atlas & Gazetteer Location: 41D6

County Location: Oakland

Directions To Trailhead:
North on Orchard Lake Rd to Pontiac Trail, then west on Pontiac Trail to
Arrowhead Rd, then south on Arrowhead to trailhead parking

Trail Type: Hiking/Walking, Cross Country Skiing, Interpretive
Trail Distance: 2.6 mi   Loops: 2   Shortest: .5 mi   Longest: 2.1 mi
Trail Surface: Natural and paved(.5 mi)
Trail Use Fee: None
Method Of Ski Trail Grooming: None
Skiing Ability Suggested: Novice to intermediate
Hiking Trail Difficulty: Easy to moderate
Mountain Biking Ability Suggested: NA
Terrain: Steep 0%, Hilly 15%, Moderate 60%, Flat 20%
Camping: None

Maintained by the West Bloomfield Parks and Recreation Commission
A 16 station interpretive trail along ponds and a creek.
Adjacent to the West Bloomfield Trail Network (see other listing)

West Bloomfield Parks and Recreation Commission
3325 Middlebelt Road   810-334-5660
West Bloomfield, MI 48323

Michigan Atlas & Gazetteer Location: 41D67

County Location: Oakland

Directions To Trailhead:
North on Orchard Lake Rd to Pontiac Trail, then left(west) on Pontiac Trail to
Arrowhead Rd, then left(south) on Arrowhead to trailhead.

Trail Type: Hiking/Walking, Cross Country Skiing, Mountain Biking, Interpretive
Trail Distance: 4.25 mi   Loops: NA   Shortest: NA   Longest: NA
Trail Surface: Crushed limestone
Trail Use Fee: None
Method Of Ski Trail Grooming: None
Skiing Ability Suggested: Novice
Hiking Trail Difficulty: Easy
Mountain Biking Ability Suggested: Novice
Terrain: 100% Flat
Camping: None

Maintained by the West Bloomfield Parks and Recreation Commission
Trail has 21 interpreted stations from end to end.
West Bloomfield Nature Preserve is located along this trail. (see other listing)

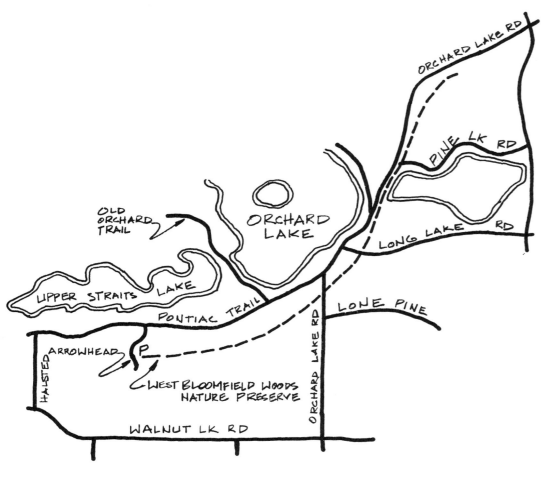

White Lake Oaks County Park
991 S. Williams Lake Rd.   810-698-2700
Pontiac, MI 48054

Oakland County Parks & Recreation Commission
2800 Watkins Lake Rd.   810-858-0906
Pontiac, MI 48054-1697

Michigan Atlas & Gazetteer Location: 41C6

County Location: Oakland

Directions To Trailhead:
On Williams Lake Rd., just south of Highland Rd. (M59) and Pontiac Lake Rd.

Trail Type: Cross Country Skiing
Trail Distance: 6.6 km   Loops: 3   Shortest: Longest:
Trail Surface: Natural
Trail Use Fee: None
Method Of Ski Trail Grooming: Packed
Skiing Ability Suggested: Novice
Hiking Trail Difficulty: NA
Mountain Biking Ability Suggested: NA
Terrain: Flat to rolling
Camping: None

Maintained by the Oakland County Parks & Recreation Commission
Warming area, snack bar, lessons and rentals available.
Trails are on a golf course

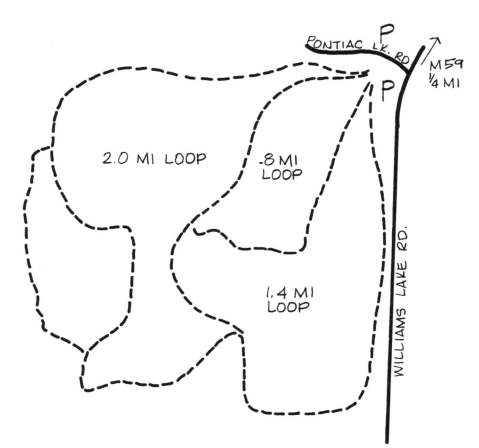

WHITE LAKE OAKS
GOLF COURSE

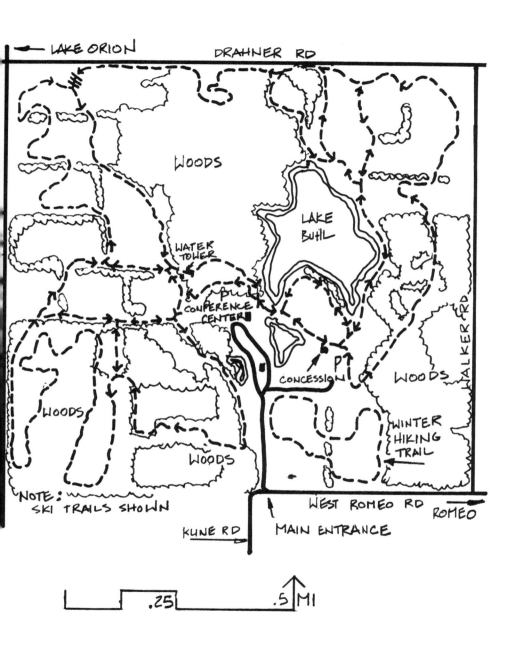

Addison Oaks County Park
1480 W Romeo Rd.
Leonard, MI 48367

810-693-2432

Oakland County Parks and Recreation Commission
2800 Watkins Lake Rd.
Pontiac, MI 48056

810-858-0906

Michigan Atlas & Gazetteer Location: 42B1

County Location: Oakland

Directions To Trailhead:
North on Rochester Rd. from Rochester, then west on West Romeo Rd. about 2 miles to the park entrance which is on the right.

Trail Type: Hiking/Walking, Cross Country Skiing, Mountain Biking
Trail Distance: 10.75 mi   Loops: Many   Shortest: .1 mi   Longest: 5.3 mi
Trail Surface: Paved and natural
Trail Use Fee: None, but vehicle entry fee required.
Method Of Ski Trail Grooming: Track set when snow depth permits
Skiing Ability Suggested: Novice to intermediate
Hiking Trail Difficulty: Easy to moderate
Mountain Biking Ability Suggested: Novice to advanced
Terrain: Steep 8%, Hilly 15%, Moderate 57%, Flat 20%
Camping: Modern, primitive and group camping facilities in the park

Operated by the Oakland County Parks and Recreation Commission.
A complete year-round recreation area. Call for information and brochure.
Excellent trail system with a wide variety of terrain and many wooded trails.
Trail distance listed above is a combined distance for all trails.
Mountain bike trail distance is about 5 miles.
Cross country ski trail distance is about 9.75 miles.
Cross country ski trails use both the hiking trail and mountain bike trail systems.
Both cross country ski and mountain bike events held seasonally. Lighted ski trail, cross country ski lessons and ski rentals available.   There is an open slope available for telemarking.
One hiking trail remains available throughout the winter months.

ADDISON OAKS COUNTY PARK

City of Rochester Hills
1000 Rocherster Hills Drive
Rochester Hills, MI 48309

810-652-1321

Michigan Atlas & Gazetteer Location: 42C12

County Location: Oakland

Directions To Trailhead:
Take John R Rd north to park. About 3 miles north of M59

Trail Type: Hiking/Walking, Cross Country Skiing, Mountain Biking, Interpretive
Trail Distance: 6 mi   Loops: 6   Shortest: 1.2 mi Longest: 1.6 mi
Trail Surface: Natural
Trail Use Fee: Yes, daily or annual vehicle entry permit required
Method Of Ski Trail Grooming: None
Skiing Ability Suggested: Novice
Hiking Trail Difficulty: Easy
Mountain Biking Ability Suggested: Novice
Terrain: Steep 2%, Hilly 18%, Moderate 45%, Flat 35%
Camping: None

Owned by the City of Rochester Hills
Previously the Bloomer Unit, Rochester -Utica State Recreation Area
Continues under development by the city.

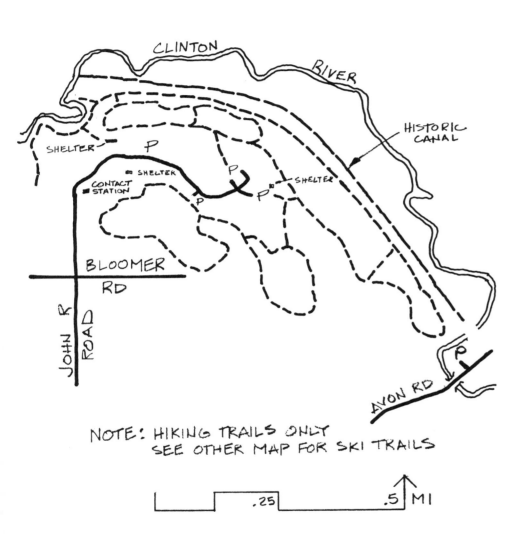

NOTE: HIKING TRAILS ONLY
SEE OTHER MAP FOR SKI TRAILS

BLOOMER PARK

Dinosaur Hill Nature Preserve
333 North Hill Circle
Rochester, MI 48307

810-656-0999

Michigan Atlas & Gazetteer Location: 42C1

County Location: Oakland

Directions To Trailhead:
From Rochester Rd, take Tienken 2 blocks to Winry, then 2 blocks south to Axford, then 1 block to North Hill Circle and the preserve.

Trail Type: Hiking/Walking, Interpretive
Trail Distance: 2 mi   Loops: Several   Shortest: Longest:
Trail Surface: Natural
Trail Use Fee: None
Method Of Ski Trail Grooming: None
Skiing Ability Suggested: Novice
Hiking Trail Difficulty: Easy
Mountain Biking Ability Suggested: NA
Terrain: Steep 0%, Hilly 0%, Moderate 15%, Flat 85%
Camping: None

A small (17 acre) but active nature preserve in the center of Rochester
Guided walks and all types of programs available.
Adjacent to the Paint Creek Trail (see other listing)
Call for brochure and further information

NORTH

DINOSAUR TRAIL

NINEBARK TRAIL

PAINT

OLD HICKORY TRAIL

TREE TREE TRAIL

PAINT CREEK TRAIL

FERN MEADOW

LOG CABIN

AXFORD PLACE

N. HILL CIRCLE

NATURE CENTER

N. OAK ST

CREEK

SEE OTHER LISTING

DINOSAUR HILL NATURE PRESERVE

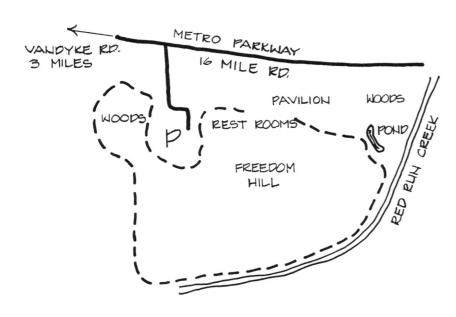

VANDYKE RD.
3 MILES

METRO PARKWAY

16 MILE RD.

WOODS

P

REST ROOMS

PAVILION

WOODS

POND

FREEDOM HILL

RED RUN CREEK

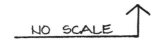

NO SCALE

FREEDOM HILL COUNTY PARK

Freedom Hill County Park
15000 Metro Parkway   810-979-7010
Sterling Heights, MI 48077   810-979-8750

Michigan Atlas & Gazetteer Location: 42D23

County Location: Macomb

Directions To Trailhead:
1.5 miles east of Schoenherr Rd on Metropolitan Parkway (16 Mile Rd.).

Trail Type: Cross Country Skiing
Trail Distance: 2 km   Loops: 1   Shortest: Longest:
Trail Surface: Natural
Trail Use Fee: None
Method Of Ski Trail Grooming: Track set
Skiing Ability Suggested: Novice
Hiking Trail Difficulty: Easy
Mountain Biking Ability Suggested: NA
Terrain: Steep 0%, Hilly 0%, Moderate 95%, Flat 5%
Camping: None

Operated by the Macomb County Park Parks and Recreation Commission.
Picnic area, restrooms, tot lot, multi-use building and amphitheater available.
Heated building available in winter.

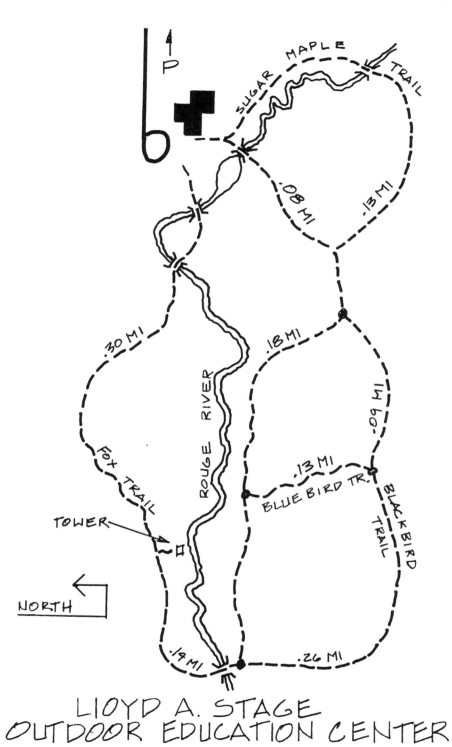

LIOYD A. STAGE
OUTDOOR EDUCATION CENTER

City of Troy
6685 Collidge Rd
Troy, MI 48098

810-524-3567

Michigan Atlas & Gazetteer Location: 42D1

County Location: Oakland

Directions To Trailhead:
Exit I-75 at Crooks Rd, then north to Square Lake Rd, then west to Coolidge Rd, then north .74 mile to entrance on the west side of the road.

Trail Type: Hiking/Walking, Interpretive
Trail Distance: 1.3 mi   Loops: 4   Shortest: .4 mi   Longest: 1 mi
Trail Surface: Natrual
Trail Use Fee: None
Method Of Ski Trail Grooming: NA
Skiing Ability Suggested: NA
Hiking Trail Difficulty: Easy
Mountain Biking Ability Suggested: NA
Terrain: Steep 2%, Hilly 10%, Moderate 75%, Flat 13%
Camping: None

Owned by the City of Troy
An outdoor education center with a nature center building.

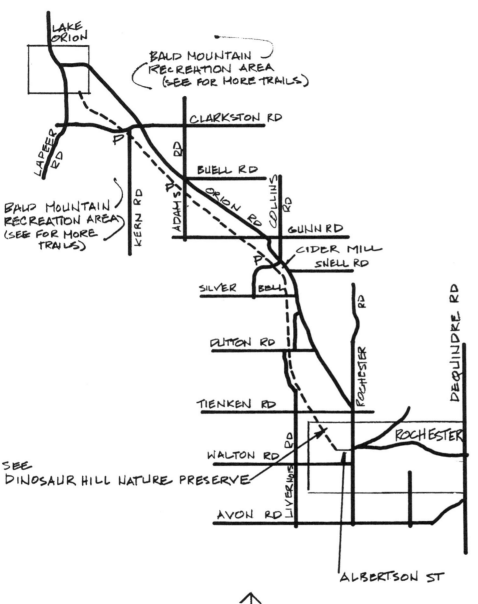

SEE
DINOSAUR HILL NATURE PRESERVE

PAINT CREEK TRAIL

Paint Creek Trailways Commission
4393 Collins Rd.
Rochester, MI 48064

810-651-9260

Michigan Atlas & Gazetteer Location: 42BC1

County Location: Oakland

Directions To Trailhead:
Between Lake Orion and Utica along the Paint Creek and the City of Rochester.
Trailheads- Located at many road crossings. Some with parking lots.

Trail Type: Hiking/Walking, Cross Country Skiing, Mountain Biking, Interpretive
Trail Distance: 10.5 mi   Loops: NA   Shortest: NA   Longest: NA
Trail Surface: Paved and granular surfaces
Trail Use Fee: None
Method Of Ski Trail Grooming: None
Skiing Ability Suggested: Novice
Hiking Trail Difficulty: Easy
Mountain Biking Ability Suggested: Novice
Terrain: Steep 0%, Hilly 0%, Moderate 10%, Flat 90%
Camping: None, but camping is available nearby

Maintained by the Paint Creek Trailways Commission whos members are the
Oakland Township, Rochester Hills, Rochester and Orion Township.
Trail follows the route of a former railroad track. Development of trail facilities
continues.
Two cider mills are located along the trail.
Restaurants are located at each end of the trail.
See also the Dinosaur Hill Nature Preserve.
Only paved sections are in Rochester.
Listed as a mountain bike trail, since most is limestone surfaced. No speical
single track trail provided.

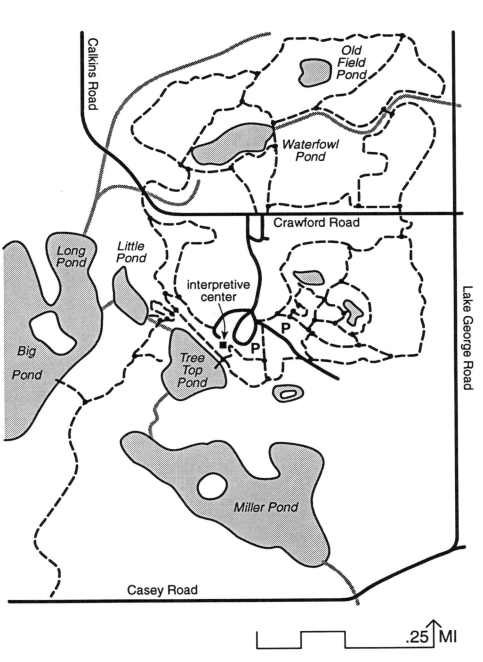

Calkins Road

Old Field Pond

Waterfowl Pond

Crawford Road

Long Pond

Little Pond

interpretive center

Big Pond

Tree Top Pond

Miller Pond

Lake George Road

Casey Road

.25 ⬆ MI

Seven Ponds Nature Center

Seven Ponds Nature Center
3854 Crawford Road
Dryden, MI 48428

810-796-3200

Michigan Atlas & Gazetteer Location: 42A1

County Location: Lapeer

Directions To Trailhead:
I-96 to M24, then south to Dryden Rd, then east 7 miles to Calkins Rd, then 1 mile south to the nature center.

Trail Type: Hiking/Walking, Cross Country Skiing, Interpretive
Trail Distance: 5 mi   Loops: 10   Shortest: .25 mi Longest: 1 mi
Trail Surface: Natural
Trail Use Fee: Yes, an entry fee is charged and memberships are available
Method Of Ski Trail Grooming: None
Skiing Ability Suggested: Novice to intermediate
Hiking Trail Difficulty: Easy
Mountain Biking Ability Suggested: NA
Terrain: Steep 0%, Hilly 25%, Moderate 25%, Flat 50%
Camping: None

Owned by the Michigan Audubon Society
An intensively used 250 acre nature center with much to offer and many programs throughout the year.
Seven Ponds was written about in the Fall 1989 issue of the "Great Lakes Skier" as an excellent place to ski.
Write or call for their brochure

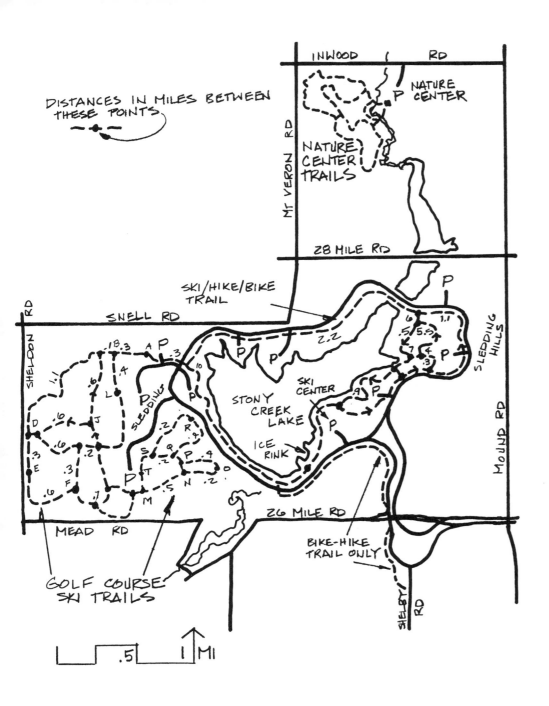

DISTANCES IN MILES BETWEEN THESE POINTS

INWOOD RD

NATURE CENTER

MT VERON RD

NATURE CENTER TRAILS

28 MILE RD

SKI/HIKE/BIKE TRAIL

SNELL RD

SHELDON RD

SLEDDING HILLS

STONY CREEK LAKE

SKI CENTER

ICE RINK

MOUND RD

GOLF COURSE SKI TRAILS

MEAD RD

26 MILE RD

BIKE-HIKE TRAIL ONLY

SHELBY RD

.5 1 MI

STONY CREEK METROPARK

Stony Creek Metropark
4300 Main Park Rd.
Washington , MI 48094-9763

810-781-4242
800-47-PARKS

Huron-Clinton Metropolitan Authority
1300 High Ridge Drive, PO Box 2001
Brighton, MI 48116-8001

810-227-2757

Michigan Atlas & Gazetteer Location: 42C2

County Location: Oakland & Macomb

Directions To Trailhead:
NE of Rochester, north of Utica off of Van Dyke Expressway (M53). From M53, take 26 Mile Rd. west 1.5 miles to park entrance

Trail Type: Hiking/Walking, Cross Country Skiing, Interpretive
Trail Distance: 20+ mi   Loops: Many   Shortest: .5 mi   Longest: 6.2 mi
Trail Surface: Paved, gravel and natural
Trail Use Fee: None, but vehicle entry fee required
Method Of Ski Trail Grooming: Track set
Skiing Ability Suggested: Novice to advanced
Hiking Trail Difficulty: Easy
Mountain Biking Ability Suggested: NA
Terrain: Below
Camping: Group campground available, reservations required

Operated by the Huron-Clinton Metropolitan Authority
Complete outdoor recreation area with almost every activity available.
Hike/bike trails overlap on some ski trails. During the winter the use of the trails is limited for skiing only. The hike/bike trail loop is about 6.2 miles long and is limited to a route around the lake. (No off pavement mountain bike trails provided) Terrain: Generally moderate to flat.
Cross country ski trail network is about 15 miles with 6 loops. Terrain for the ski trails is 30% hilly, 20% moderate, 50% flat.
Nature trials are 3 loops in 4.25 mile system with loops of .5, 1.25 and 2.5 mile loops. Terrain:
Hilly 10%,Moderate 40%, Flat 50%
Campground is for organized youth group only.
Call or write for their Metropark Guide, published each year.

← M53 1¼ MILES   26 MILE RD

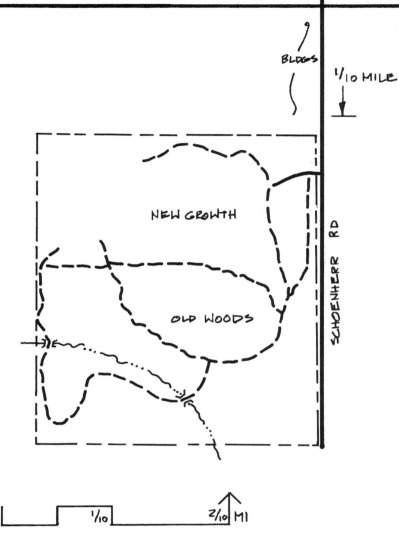

BLDGS

1/10 MILE

NEW GROWTH

OLD WOODS

SCHOENHERR RD

←||E

1/10   2/10 MI

Michigan Nature Association
Box 102
Avoca, MI 48006

810-324-2626

Michigan Atlas & Gazetteer Location: 42C23

County Location: Macomb

Directions To Trailhead:
From M53 north of Utica, take exit for 26 Mile Rd(Marine City Hwy), then 1.5 miles east to Schoenherr Rd, then south less than .2 mile to sanctuary sign on west side of the road.

Trail Type: Hiking/Walking, Interpretive
Trail Distance: 1 mi   Loops: 1   Shortest: .5 mi   Longest: .75 mi
Trail Surface: Natural
Trail Use Fee: None
Method Of Ski Trail Grooming: NA
Skiing Ability Suggested: NA
Hiking Trail Difficulty: Easy
Mountain Biking Ability Suggested: NA
Terrain: 100% Flat
Camping: None

Maintained by the Michigan Nature Association
Over 365 vegetative species have been inventoried on the property including over 500 tuliptrees of all ages.
Property given by relative of original land grant owner who acquired the property in 1833.

WILCOX-WARNES
MEMORIAL NATURE SANCTUARY

Algonac State Park
8732 River Road
Marine City, MI 48039

810-765-5605
810-327-6765

DNR Parks and Recreation Division

517-373-1270
517-322-1300

Michigan Atlas & Gazetteer Location: 43C6

County Location: St. Clair

Directions To Trailhead:
On M29 between Algonac an Marine City on the St. Clair River.

Trail Type: Hiking/Walking, Cross Country Skiing
Trail Distance: 2.5 mi   Loops: 1   Shortest: NA   Longest: 2.5 mi
Trail Surface: Natural
Trail Use Fee: None, except vehicle entry permit required
Method Of Ski Trail Grooming: None
Skiing Ability Suggested: Novice
Hiking Trail Difficulty: Easy
Mountain Biking Ability Suggested: NA
Terrain: 100% Flat
Camping: Campgrounds on site for both individuals and groups

Maintained by the DNR Parks and Recreation Division
Though relatively small with only 63 acres the park supports many varieties of plant life.

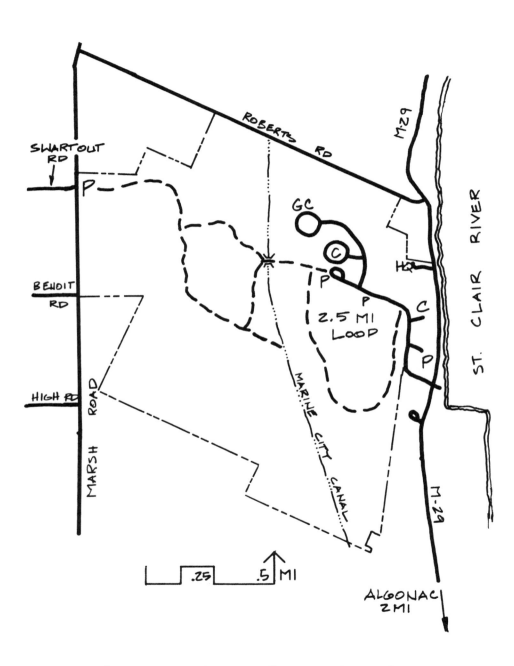

ALGONAC STATE PARK

Michigan Nature Association
PO Box 102
Avoca, MI 48006

810-324-2626

Michigan Atlas & Gazetteer Location: 43B67

County Location: St Clair

Directions To Trailhead:
On the north city limits of St Clair

Trail Type: Hiking/Walking, Interpretive
Trail Distance: 1.5 mi   Loops: 1   Shortest: NA   Longest: 1.5 mi
Trail Surface: Natural
Trail Use Fee: None
Method Of Ski Trail Grooming: NA
Skiing Ability Suggested: NA
Hiking Trail Difficulty: Easy
Mountain Biking Ability Suggested: NA
Terrain: 100 % Flat
Camping: None

Owned by the Michigan Nature Association
Virgin oak-hickory forest. Some tree trunks are 3' in diameter.
Sanctuary publication available from the association

PIPELINE

DOG POND

SIXTH ST.

MELDRUM CIRCLE

HAWTHORN

STRATFORD

M-29

ST. CLAIR

.25 MI

ALICE W. MOORE WOODS NATURE SANCTUARY

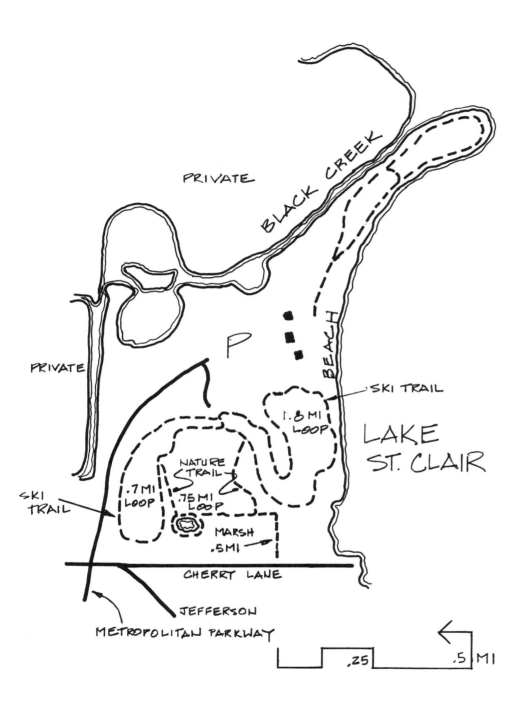

Metro Beach Metropark
13000 High Ridge Rd
Brighton, MI 48116-8001

810-227-2757
800-47-PARKS

Huron-Clinton Metropolitan Authority
1300 High Ridge Drive, PO Box 2001
Brighton, MI 48116-8001

810-227-2757

Michigan Atlas & Gazetteer Location: 43D4

County Location: Macomb

Directions To Trailhead:
At the east end of the Metro Parkway in Mt Clemens on Lake St. Clair
Trailhead - At the Center Plaza

Trail Type: Hiking/Walking, Cross Country Skiing, Interpretive
Trail Distance: 3.75 mi   Loops: 2   Shortest: 1.25 mi Longest: 2.5 mi
Trail Surface: Natural
Trail Use Fee: None, but vehicle entry fee required
Method Of Ski Trail Grooming: Track set
Skiing Ability Suggested: Novice
Hiking Trail Difficulty: NA
Mountain Biking Ability Suggested: NA
Terrain: 100% Flat
Camping: None

Operated by the Huron-Clinton Metropolitan Authority
Warming shelter, ski rentals and snack bar available. Special group rate for ski rentals during the week. Complete summer recreation center with beach, par 3 golf, tennis, nature study area, picnic grounds and much more.
Nature Trail is 1.25 miles long
Cross Country Ski Trail is 2.5 miles long
Call or write for their Metropark Guide, published each year.

METRO BEACH METROPARK

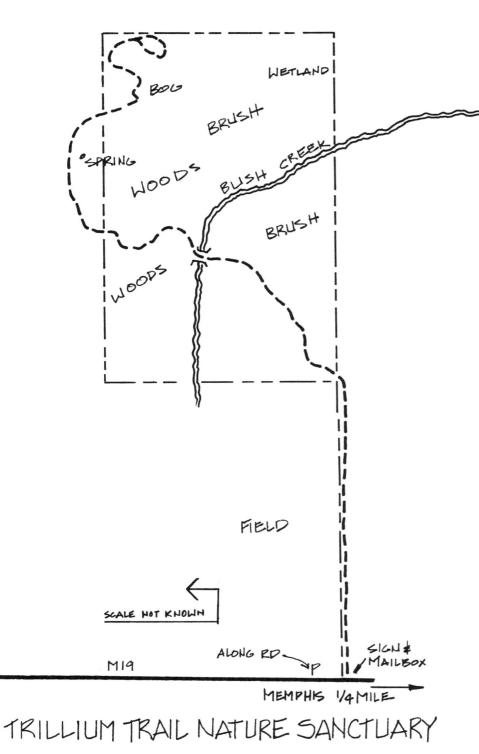

Michigan Nature Association
PO Box 102
Avoca, MI 48006

810-324-2626

Michigan Atlas & Gazetteer Location: 43A45

County Location: St. Clair

Directions To Trailhead:
From Memphis, go .25 mile north on city limits on M19, then look for sign on east side of the road.   Park on road shoulder. Walk east on 1/4 mile long easement between farmers field and neighbors yard to sanctuary.

Trail Type: Hiking/Walking, Interpretive
Trail Distance: .5 mi   Loops: NA   Shortest: NA   Longest: NA
Trail Surface: Natural
Trail Use Fee: None
Method Of Ski Trail Grooming: NA
Skiing Ability Suggested: NA
Hiking Trail Difficulty: Easy
Mountain Biking Ability Suggested: NA
Terrain: Steep 5%, Hilly 45%, Moderate 20%, Flat 30%
Camping: None

Maintained by the Michigan Nature Association
Sanctuary of mixed hardwoods with extensive areas of white trillium.
Trail is well established and should be easy to find.

TRILLIUM TRAIL NATURE SANCTUARY

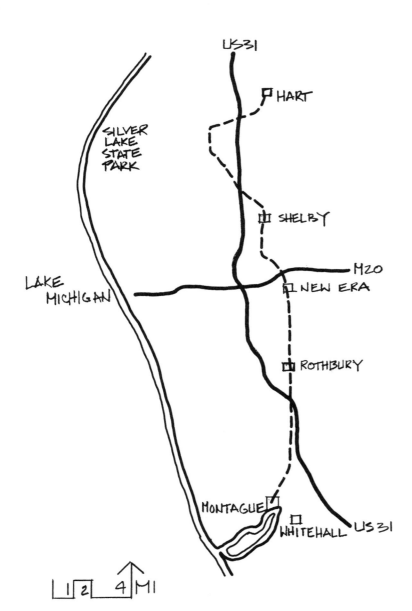

HART-MONTAGUE BICYCLE TRAIL STATE PARK

Silver Lake State Park
Rte 1, Box 254
Mears, MI 49436   616-873-3083

DNR Parks and Recreation Division

517-373-1270
517-322-1300

Michigan Atlas & Gazetteer Location: 44A4,54CD34

County Location: Oceana & Muskegon

Directions To Trailhead:
Between Hart and Montague parallel to US-31. Trail passes through the communities of New Era, Shelby and Mears.

Trail Type: Hiking/Walking, Cross Country Skiing, Interpretive
Trail Distance: 22.5 mi   Loops: NA   Shortest: NA   Longest: NA
Trail Surface: Paved
Trail Use Fee: Yes,
Method Of Ski Trail Grooming: Not groomed
Skiing Ability Suggested: Novice
Hiking Trail Difficulty: Easy
Mountain Biking Ability Suggested: NA
Terrain: Steep 0%, Hilly 0%, Moderate 5%, Flat 95%
Camping: Campgrounds are in the area

Maintained by the DNR Parks Division and the Oceana-Muskegon Trailways Commission
Food, lodging, bike shops, picnic shelters, restrooms and water are available along the trail.
The trail is all asphalt paved. Right of Way width varies from 30 to 100 wide.
Ski and bike rental equipment is available in the area.
There are no special dirt mountain bike trails .
Ski shops are located in Pentwater and Whitehall.
A bike shop is located at the southern end of the trail in Montague
Detailed map guide book is available from White Lake C of C at 616-893-4585, Hart/Silver Lake C of C at 616-873-2247, Silver Lake Tourist Association at 616-873-5048

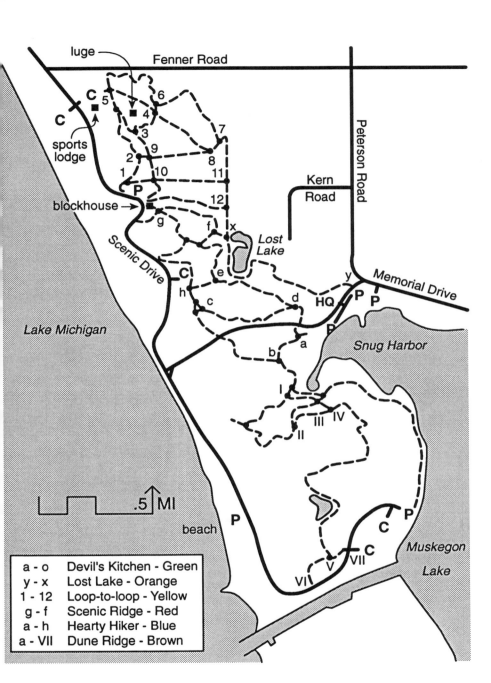

a - o	Devil's Kitchen - Green
y - x	Lost Lake - Orange
1 - 12	Loop-to-loop - Yellow
g - f	Scenic Ridge - Red
a - h	Hearty Hiker - Blue
a - VII	Dune Ridge - Brown

Muskegon State Park

Muskegon State Park
3560 Memorial Drive
North Muskegon, MI 49445

616-744-3480

DNR Parks and Recreation Division

517-373-1270

Michigan Atlas & Gazetteer Location: 44BC4

County Location: Muskegon

Directions To Trailhead:
NW side of Muskegon. Take US31 to North Muskegon and follow signs to the state park. on Lake Michigan off Memorial Drive.

Trail Type: Hiking/Walking, Cross Country Skiing
Trail Distance: 10.5 mi   Loops: 6+   Shortest: .75 mi   Longest: 5 mi
Trail Surface: Natural
Trail Use Fee: None, but vehicle entry fee required
Method Of Ski Trail Grooming: Track set
Skiing Ability Suggested: Novice to intermediate
Hiking Trail Difficulty: Moderate
Mountain Biking Ability Suggested: NA
Terrain: Steep 20%, Hilly 50%, Moderate 20%, Flat 10%
Camping: Campground in the park

Maintained by the DNR Parks and Recreation Division
Typical state park with beaches, campgounds and trails. Luge run, biathalon range, ski rentals, lessons and the customary summer facilities are available. The luge is one of only 4 luge runs in the United States.
Large complex of trails for both hiking and cross country skiing.
The designated ski trails are a portion of the hiking trail system.
A detailed descriptive brochure of the hiking trails and a separated ski trail map are available.

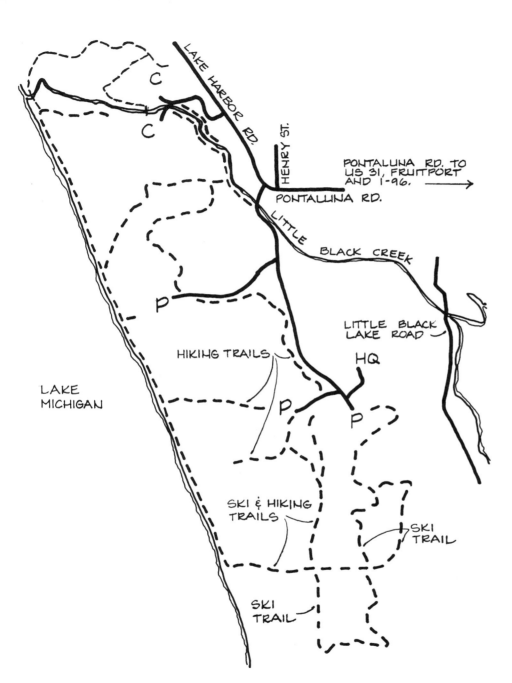

Hoffmaster State Park
6585 Lake Harbor Rd.
Muskegon, MI 49441

616-798-3573

DNR Parks and Recreation Division

517-373-1270

Michigan Atlas & Gazetteer Location: 45CD5

County Location: Muskegon

Directions To Trailhead:
South of Muskegon on Lake Michigan Take US31 south from I-69 to Pontaluna Rd., then west 3 miles to the park .

Trail Type: Hiking/Walking, Cross Country Skiing, Interpretive
Trail Distance: 10 mi   Loops: Many   Shortest: Longest:
Trail Surface: Natural - sand and some paved
Trail Use Fee: None, but vehicle entry fee required
Method Of Ski Trail Grooming: None
Skiing Ability Suggested: Novice to advanced
Hiking Trail Difficulty: Easy to moderate
Mountain Biking Ability Suggested: NA
Terrain: Rolling to hilly
Camping: Campgound in park

Maintained by the DNR Parks and Recreation Division
Ski trails are 2.5 miles long. Extensive hiking trail system throughout the park and along the shore of Lake Michigan.
The Gillette Nature Center (accessible) in the park is open daily 8am to 10pm.
For additional information contact the Gillette Nature Center at 616-798-3573

HOFFMASTER STATE PARK

Hofma Park

Grand Haven Township
13300 168th Ave
Grand Haven, MI 49417

616-842-3515

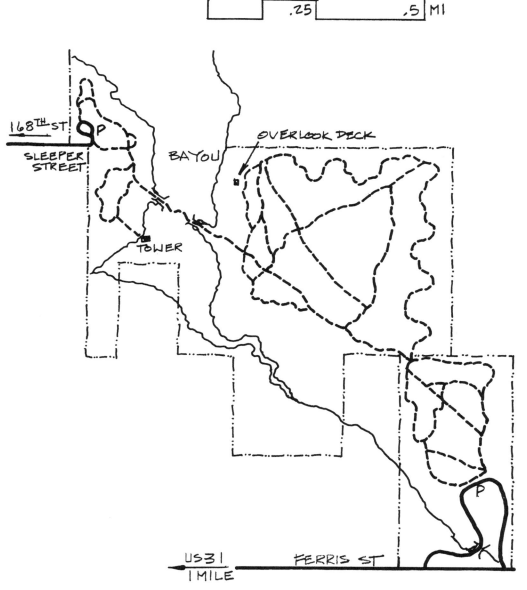

Michigan Atlas & Gazetteer Location: 45D5

County Location: Ottawa

Directions To Trailhead:
US31 south from Grand Haven 2.6 miles to Ferris St., then east on Ferris 1.5 miles to the entrance

Trail Type: Hiking/Walking, Cross Country Skiing, Mountain Biking
Trail Distance: 4.5 mi   Loops: Many   Shortest: .25 mi Longest: 1 mi
Trail Surface: Natural
Trail Use Fee: None
Method Of Ski Trail Grooming: None
Skiing Ability Suggested: Novice to intermediate
Hiking Trail Difficulty: Easy to moderate
Mountain Biking Ability Suggested: Novice to intermediate
Terrain: Steep 1%, Hilly 4%, Moderate 10%, Flat 80%
Camping: None

Owned by Grand Haven Township
Managed as a community park.

HOFMA PARK

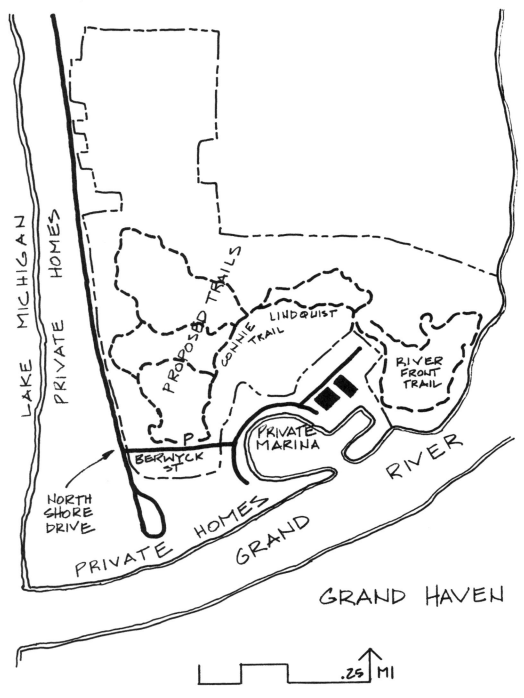

City Manager, City of Ferrysburg
408 Fifth St., PO Box 38
Ferrysburg, MI 49409

616-842-5950
616-842-5803

Michigan Atlas & Gazetteer Location: 45D5

County Location: Ottawa

Directions To Trailhead:
On US31 north from Grand Haven across the bridge for a very short distance, take the Ferrysburg exit, then left (west) at the Stop sign at the bottom of the off ramp(3rd St.), go .4 mi. to North Shore Drive(sharp curve to the north), then left (west again) on North Shore Drive, go 1.7 mi to North Beach Park, then south 1.5 mi to Berwyck St., then .2 mi on Berwyck St. to paved parking lot on the north side of the street.

Trail Type: Hiking/Walking, Interpretive
Trail Distance: 1.5 mi   Loops: 2   Shortest: Longest:
Trail Surface: Natural-sand and wood chips
Trail Use Fee: None
Method Of Ski Trail Grooming: NA
Skiing Ability Suggested: NA
Hiking Trail Difficulty: Easy to moderate
Mountain Biking Ability Suggested: NA
Terrain: Steep 0%, Hilly 0%, Moderate 95%, Flat 5%
Camping: Hoffmaster State Park is about 8 miles north on Lake Michigan

Owned by the City of Ferrysburg
This trail covers part of the 51 acre dune preserve along the shore of Lake Michigan .
Do not wander off the established trail because it will deteriorate the fragile landscape.
15 station interpretive signs are along the trail.
Paved handicapper parking and adjacent very short boardwalk at parking lot.
No extensive handicapper trails.

KITCHEL-LINDQUIST DUNES PRESERVE

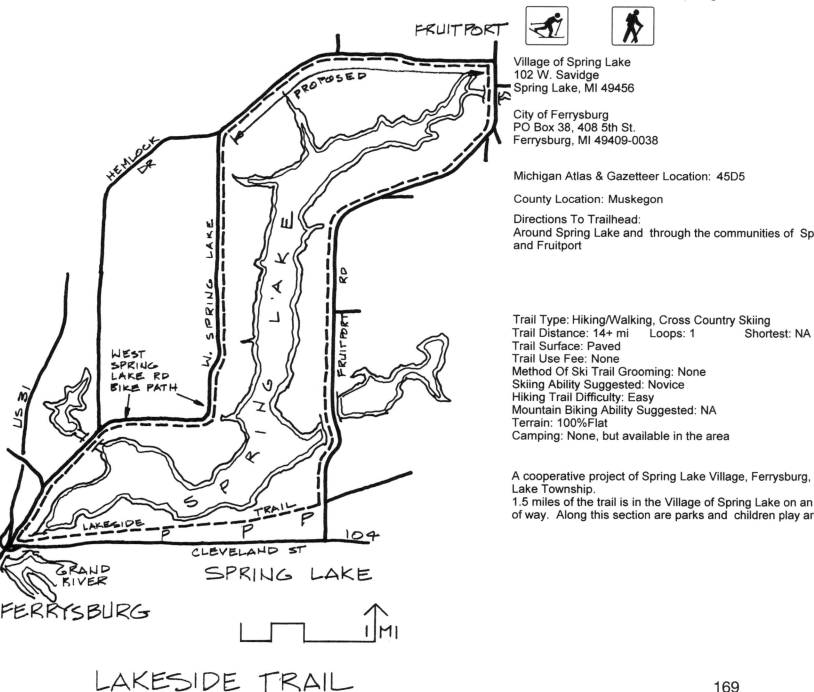

Village of Spring Lake
102 W. Savidge
Spring Lake, MI 49456

616-842-1393

City of Ferrysburg
PO Box 38, 408 5th St.
Ferrysburg, MI 49409-0038

616-842-5950

Michigan Atlas & Gazetteer Location: 45D5

County Location: Muskegon

Directions To Trailhead:
Around Spring Lake and through the communities of Spring Lake, Ferrysburg and Fruitport

Trail Type: Hiking/Walking, Cross Country Skiing
Trail Distance: 14+ mi   Loops: 1   Shortest: NA   Longest: NA
Trail Surface: Paved
Trail Use Fee: None
Method Of Ski Trail Grooming: None
Skiing Ability Suggested: Novice
Hiking Trail Difficulty: Easy
Mountain Biking Ability Suggested: NA
Terrain: 100%Flat
Camping: None, but available in the area

A cooperative project of Spring Lake Village, Ferrysburg, Fruitport and Spring Lake Township.
1.5 miles of the trail is in the Village of Spring Lake on an abandon railroad right of way. Along this section are parks and children play areas.

DNR, Forest Mangement Division, Recreation & Trails Section
PO Box 30452   517-373-9483
Lansing, MI 48909

Michigan Atlas & Gazetteer Location: 45CD567,46D1

County Location: Ottawa

Directions To Trailhead:
North of B72 on the east side of Muskegon Heights through Ravenna then southeast to Herrington which is 2 miles north of Marne.

Trail Type: Hiking/Walking, Cross Country Skiing, Mountain Biking
Trail Distance: 26 mi   Loops: NA   Shortest: NA   Longest: NA
Trail Surface: Ballast and existing surface
Trail Use Fee: None
Method Of Ski Trail Grooming: None
Skiing Ability Suggested: Novice
Hiking Trail Difficulty: Easy
Mountain Biking Ability Suggested: Novice
Terrain: 100% Flat
Camping: None

Managed by the DNR Forest Mangement Division, Recreation and Trails Section Currently under development. To be open to the public in 1995 after basic improvements are made. Surfacing dependent on local support.

16TH AVE

I 96

B72   CONKLIN   FUTURE

RAVENNA   COMPLETED 1995

B35

B72   FUTURE

B31

3   6 MI

I 96

US 31 & I 96

US 31

MUSKEGON

OTTAWA-MUSKEGON RAIL TRAIL

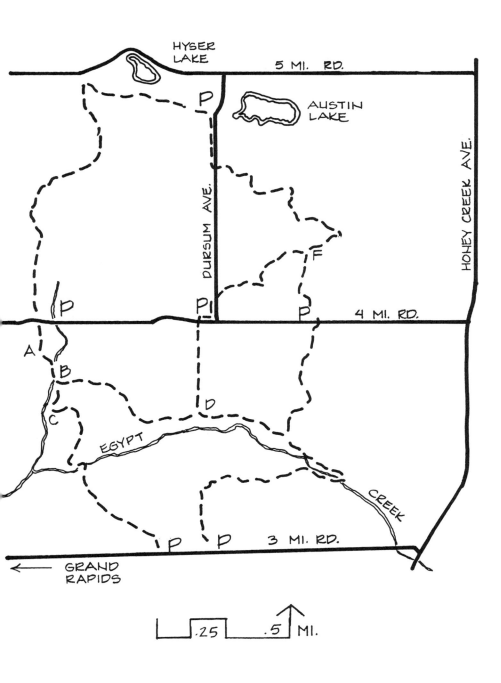

HYSER LAKE

5 MI. RD.

AUSTIN LAKE

P

DURSUM AVE.

HONEY CREEK AVE.

P

F

P

P

4 MI. RD.

A

B

D

C

EGYPT

CREEK

P P 3 MI. RD.

← GRAND RAPIDS

|___|.25|___|.5 | MI.

CANNONSBURG STATE GAME AREA

Cannonsburg State Game Area
350 Ottawa Ave NW
Grand Rapids, MI 49503

616-456-5071

DNR Wildlife Division Office

517-373-1263

Michigan Atlas & Gazetteer Location: 46D34

County Location: Kent

Directions To Trailhead:
8 miles east of Grand Rapids between 3 and 5 Mile Rds and just west of Honey Creek Ave

Trail Type: Hiking/Walking, Cross Country Skiing, Mountain Biking
Trail Distance: 10 mi   Loops: Numerous Shortest: Longest:
Trail Surface: Natural
Trail Use Fee: None
Method Of Ski Trail Grooming: None
Skiing Ability Suggested: Novice to intermediate
Hiking Trail Difficulty: Easy to moderate
Mountain Biking Ability Suggested: Novice
Terrain: Rolling to hilly
Camping: None

Maintained by the DNR Wildlife Division.
Not available for skiing before January 1st . Trail system has a variety of terrain, scenery and habitat. Connects to the Egypt Valley Trail for the winter only. Obey all "No Trespassing" signs since there are privately owned lands within the game area.

VERY IMPORTANT:This area is extremely over used by trail users. Continued additional non-hunting recreational use could close this area to mountain bikers, skiers and hikers.   Consider going to other areas more suited and designed for recreational trail use.   If you must use this area, do so less often than you have in the past.

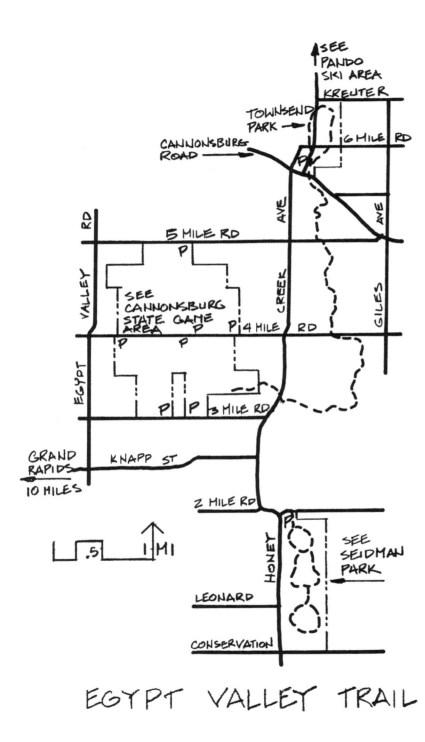

EGYPT VALLEY TRAIL

Egypt Valley Trail

Kent County Park Commission
1500 Scribner NW
Grand Rapids, MI 49504

616-774-3697

Michigan Atlas & Gazetteer Location: 46D4

County Location: Kent

Directions To Trailhead:
9 miles NE of Grand Rapids

Trail Type: Hiking/Walking, Cross Country Skiing
Trail Distance: 5 mi   Loops: None   Shortest: Longest:
Trail Surface: Natural
Trail Use Fee: None
Method Of Ski Trail Grooming: None
Skiing Ability Suggested: Novice to intermediate
Hiking Trail Difficulty: Moderate
Mountain Biking Ability Suggested: NA
Terrain: Flat to hilly
Camping: None

Maintained by the Kent County Park Commission.
Most of the trail is on private property. Please respect the property rights of the owners whos land you are using. Trail open from 12/15 to 4/15 if 2 inches of snow are present .
The state game area section is open for skiing beginning Jan 2nd

Newaygo County Parks Commission
4684 S. Evergreen Drive
Newaygo, MI 49337

616-652-9191

NO MAP

Michigan Atlas & Gazetteer Location: 46A1

County Location: Newaygo

Directions To Trailhead:
From M37 in Newaygo, turn right onto Croton Rd for about .25 mile to park entrance

Trail Type: Hiking/Walking, Interpretive
Trail Distance: 1.5 mi   Loops: 1   Shortest: Longest: 1.5 mi
Trail Surface: Natural
Trail Use Fee: None
Method Of Ski Trail Grooming: NA
Skiing Ability Suggested: NA
Hiking Trail Difficulty: Easy
Mountain Biking Ability Suggested: NA
Terrain: Steep 0%, Hilly 0%, Moderate 10%, Flat 90%
Camping: Campground on site

Owned by the County of Newaygo
Modern campground with all facilities including ball fields, playgrounds and boat ramp

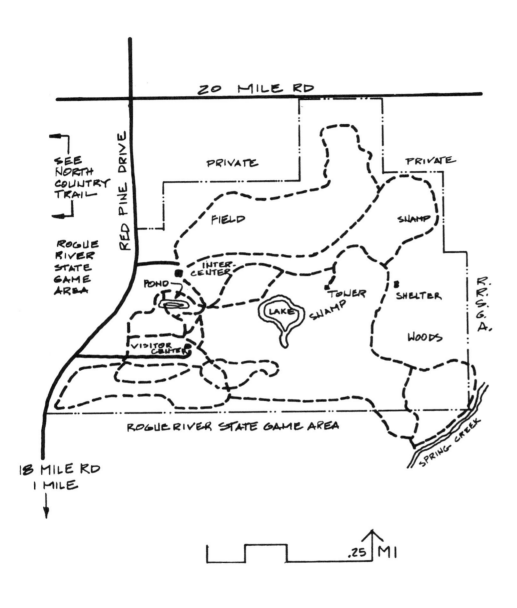

SEE
NORTH
COUNTRY
TRAIL

ROGUE
RIVER
STATE
GAME
AREA

20 MILE RD

RED PINE DRIVE

PRIVATE

PRIVATE

FIELD

SWAMP

INTER-
CENTER

POND

LAKE

TOWER

SWAMP

SHELTER

WOODS

R.
R.
S.
G.
A.

VISITOR
CENTER

ROGUE RIVER STATE GAME AREA

SPRING CREEK

18 MILE RD
1 MILE

.25 MI

HOWARD CHRISTENSEN
NATURE CENTER

Kent Intermediate School District
16160 Red Pine Drive
Kent City, MI 49330

616-887-1852

Michigan Atlas & Gazetteer Location: 46B2

County Location: Muskegon

Directions To Trailhead:
North on M37(Alpine Ave) from Grand Rapids, onto Sparta Ave northbound through Kent City, then right on 17 or 18 Mile Rd to Red Pine, then north to the nature center. The nature center is south of 20 Mile Rd.

Trail Type: Hiking/Walking, Cross Country Skiing, Interpretive
Trail Distance: 5 mi   Loops: 8   Shortest: .25 mi Longest: 1.5 mi
Trail Surface: Paved and natural
Trail Use Fee: None
Method Of Ski Trail Grooming: None
Skiing Ability Suggested: Novice
Hiking Trail Difficulty: Easy
Mountain Biking Ability Suggested: NA
Terrain: Steep 0%, Hilly 5%, Moderate 10%, Flat 85%
Camping: None

Owned by the Kent Intermediate School District
Designed for outdoor education of school groups but the public is invited.

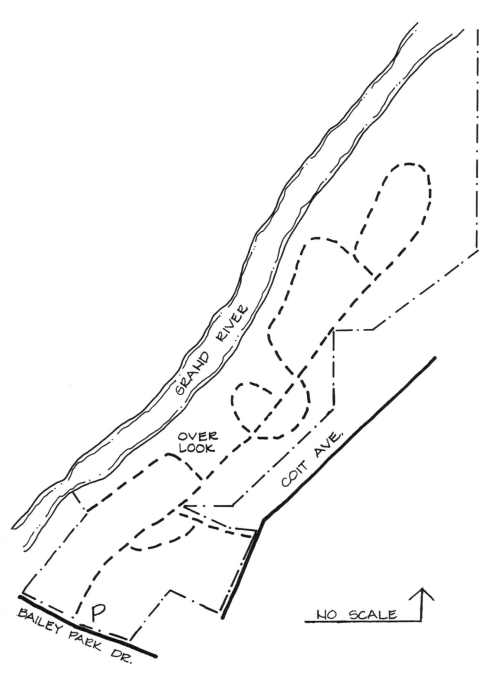

LAMOREAUX PARK

Lamoreaux Park

Kent County Park Commission
1500 Scribner NW
Grand Rapids, MI 49504

616-336-3697

Michigan Atlas & Gazetteer Location: 46D2

County Location: Kent

Directions To Trailhead:
North of the Grand Rapids city limits on Coit Avenue, 1 mile north of 4 Mile Rd

Trail Type: Hiking/Walking, Cross Country Skiing
Trail Distance: 3 mi   Loops: 3   Shortest: Longest:
Trail Surface: Natural
Trail Use Fee: None
Method Of Ski Trail Grooming: Track set occasionally
Skiing Ability Suggested: Novice
Hiking Trail Difficulty: Easy
Mountain Biking Ability Suggested: NA
Terrain: Steep 0%, Hilly 0%, Moderate 15%, Flat 85%
Camping: None

Maintained by the Kent County Park Commission
Parking off Bailey Park Drive and Coit Avenue

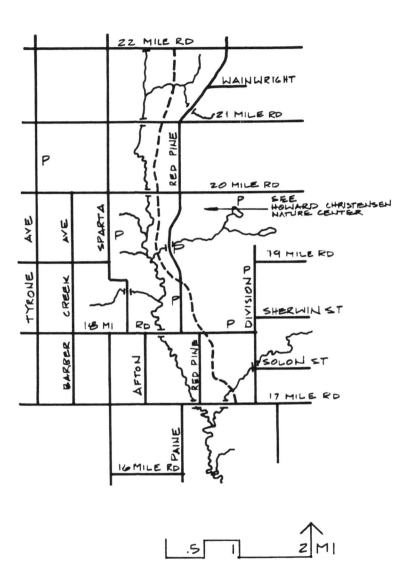

DNR, Wildlife Division, District 9
State Office Bldg, 6th Floor, 350 Ottawa NW   616-456-5071
Grand Rapids, MI 49503

North Country Trail Association
PO Box 311   616-689-1912
White Cloud, MI 49349

Michigan Atlas & Gazetteer Location: 46BC2

County Location: Kent

Directions To Trailhead:
North of Grand Rapids - 7 miles west of Cedar Springs and 5 miles north of Sparta.
South trail head - M46 (17 Mile Rd), between Red Pine and Division
North trail head - 22 Mile Rd, between Sparta and Red Pine

Trail Type: Hiking/Walking, Cross Country Skiing, Mountain Biking
Trail Distance: 5.5 mi   Loops: NA   Shortest: NA   Longest: NA
Trail Surface: Natural
Trail Use Fee: None
Method Of Ski Trail Grooming: None
Skiing Ability Suggested: Novice
Hiking Trail Difficulty: Easy
Mountain Biking Ability Suggested: NA
Terrain: Flat to slightly rolling
Camping: None

Trail in the Rogue River State Game Area
Trail built and maintained by the North Country Trail Association.
See NCT - Michigan Section - Hiker Guide, page 15 available from the NCTA.

Howard Christensen Nature Center nearby on the east side of Red Pine Drive.

NORTH COUNTRY TRAIL
ROGUE RIVER STATE GAME AREA

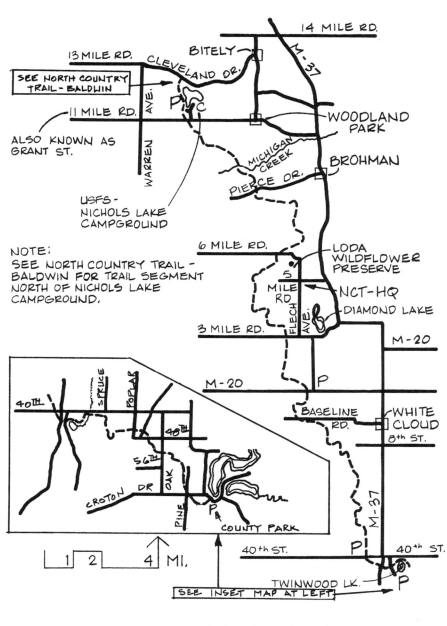

13 MILE RD. CLEVELAND DR. BITELY 14 MILE RD.

M-37

SEE NORTH COUNTRY TRAIL - BALDWIN

11 MILE RD.

WOODLAND PARK

ALSO KNOWN AS GRANT ST.

WARREN AVE.

MICHIGAN CREEK

PIERCE DR. BROHMAN

USFS - NICHOLS LAKE CAMPGROUND

NOTE: SEE NORTH COUNTRY TRAIL - BALDWIN FOR TRAIL SEGMENT NORTH OF NICHOLS LAKE CAMPGROUND.

6 MILE RD. LODA WILDFLOWER PRESERVE

5 MILE RD.

NCT-HQ

FLETCH AVE.

DIAMOND LAKE

3 MILE RD.

M-20

M-20

P

40TH SPRUCE POPLAR

40th

BASELINE RD. WHITE CLOUD 8th ST.

56TH OAK

CROTON DR

PINE

P COUNTY PARK

M-37

1 2   4 MI.

40th ST. P 40th ST.

TWINWOOD LK. P

SEE INSET MAP AT LEFT

NORTH COUNTRY TRAIL - WHITE CLOUD

Baldwin Ranger District, Huron Manistee National Forest
650 N. Michigan Ave, Drawer D
Baldwin, MI 49304

616-745-4631
800-821-6263

White Cloud Ranger District, Huron Manistee National Forest

616-689-6696

White Cloud, MI 49349

800-821-6263

Michigan Atlas & Gazetteer Location: 46A12,55C7,56CD1

County Location: Newaygo

Directions To Trailhead:
South trailhead - E. from White Cloud on Croton Dr. to the Croton Dam. Trailhead just west of Kimble County Park on south side of the road. North trailhead - N. from Brohman 2 miles on M37, then W. on 11 Mile Rd 4.5 miles to entrance of Nichols Lake Rec. Area, then .4 mile to boat launch turnoff, then .1 mile to trailhead on boat launch drive.

Trail Type: Hiking/Walking, Mountain Biking
Trail Distance: 40 mi   Loops: NA   Shortest: NA   Longest: NA
Trail Surface: Gravel and natural
Trail Use Fee: None
Method Of Ski Trail Grooming: None
Skiing Ability Suggested: Advanced
Hiking Trail Difficulty: Easy to moderate
Mountain Biking Ability Suggested: Novice
Terrain: Steep 0%, Hilly 20%, Moderate 50%, Flat 30%
Camping: Nichols Lake Campground and more than 200' from trail

Maintained by the White Cloud Ranger District, Huron-Manistee NF.
For the additional adjacent section of the North Country Trail see North Country Trail - Baldwin.
Varied forest cover and swamp with stream crossings.
Though not very hilly,the rolling terrain makes it very enjoyable for mountain biking.
Detailed trail map sets are available from the NF and the NCTA
For further information about the North Country Trail contact the North Country Trail Association, PO Box 311, White Cloud, MI 49349. 616-689-1912

Pando Ski Area
8076 Belding Rd. NE
Rockford, MI 49341

616-874-8343

SEE MAPS ON NEXT PAGE

Michigan Atlas & Gazetteer Location: 46D4

County Location: Kent

Directions To Trailhead:
12 Miles northeast of Grand Rapids on M44.

Trail Type: Cross Country Skiing, Mountain Biking
Trail Distance: 5 mi   Loops: Many   Shortest: Longest:
Trail Surface: Natural
Trail Use Fee: Yes
Method Of Ski Trail Grooming: Track set when snow conditon permits.
Skiing Ability Suggested: Novice to advanced
Hiking Trail Difficulty: NA
Mountain Biking Ability Suggested: Intermediate to advanced
Terrain: Steep 2%, Hilly 18%, Moderate 50%, Flat 30%
Camping: None

Privately owned all season recreation area.
Total trail distance for mountain bike trails is about 4 miles.
Lodge, ski rentals, snack bar and instruction.
Site of annual mountain bike races.

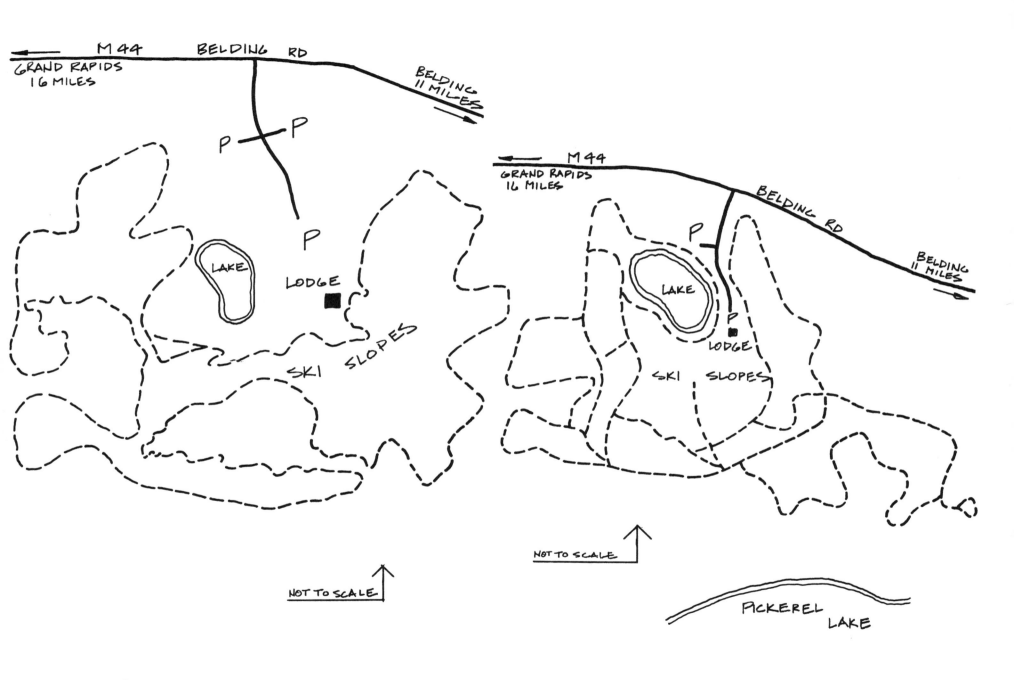

MOUNTAIN BIKE TRAILS
PANDO

SKI TRAILS
PANDO

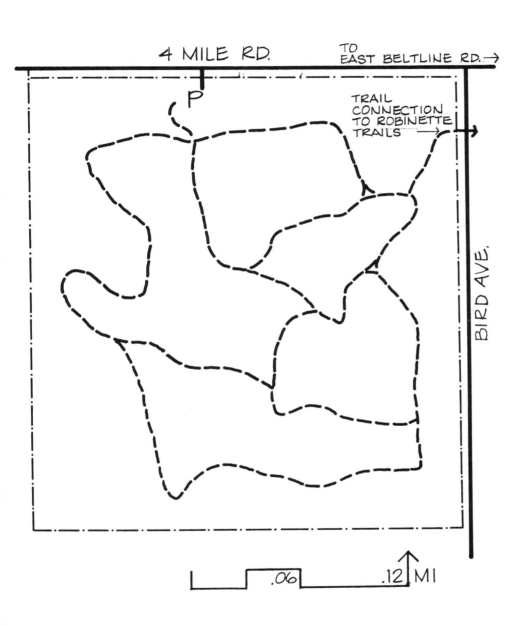

4 MILE RD.

TO EAST BELTLINE RD. →

P

TRAIL CONNECTION TO ROBINETTE TRAILS →

BIRD AVE.

.06 .12 MI

PROVIN TRAILS PARK

Provin Trails Park

Grand Rapids Department of Parks
201 Market St. SW
Grand Rapids, MI 49503

616-456-3211

Kent County Park Commission
1500 Scribner NW
Grand Rapids, MI 49504

616-774-3697

Michigan Atlas & Gazetteer Location: 46D3

County Location: Kent

Directions To Trailhead:
3/4 mile west of East Beltline at the corner of 4 Mile Rd. & Bird Ave

Trail Type: Hiking/Walking, Cross Country Skiing
Trail Distance: 1.7 mi   Loops: Many   Shortest: Longest:
Trail Surface: Natural
Trail Use Fee: None
Method Of Ski Trail Grooming: None
Skiing Ability Suggested: Intermediate to advanced
Hiking Trail Difficulty: Moderate
Mountain Biking Ability Suggested: NA
Terrain: Rolling
Camping: None

Maintained as a joint effort of the Grand Rapids Parks Department, Kent County
Park Commission and Grand Rapids Township
No facilities except restrooms.
Trails connect with Robinette Trails.
Developed as nature trails.
Parking lot is located on 4 Mile Rd.
Extensive mature pine reforestation plantings.
Old farm site visable.

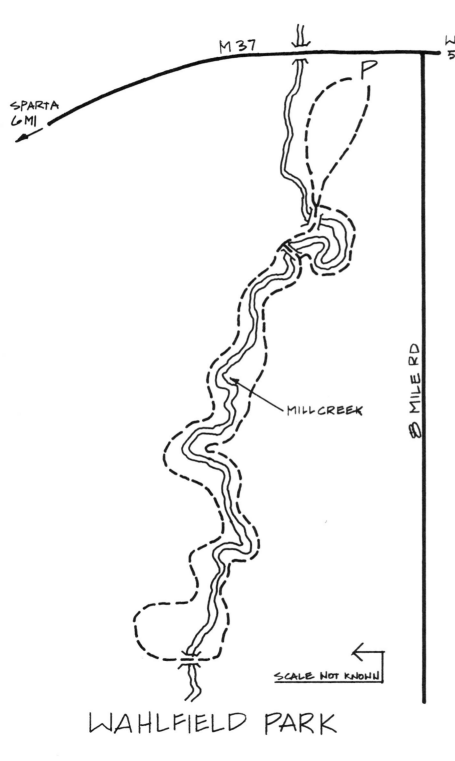

WAHLFIELD PARK

Wahlfield Park

Kent County Parks Commission
1500 Scribner Ave. NW
Grand Rapids, MI 49504-3299

616-774-3697

Michigan Atlas & Gazetteer Location: 46D2

County Location: Kent

Directions To Trailhead:
At M37 and 8 Mile Rd 7 miles north of Grand Rapids

Trail Type: Hiking/Walking, Cross Country Skiing
Trail Distance: 3 mi   Loops: 1   Shortest: NA   Longest: 3 mi
Trail Surface: Natural
Trail Use Fee: None
Method Of Ski Trail Grooming: NA
Skiing Ability Suggested: Novice
Hiking Trail Difficulty: Easy
Mountain Biking Ability Suggested: NA
Terrain: Steep 0%, Hilly 0%, Moderate 25%, Flat 75%
Camping: None

Maintained by the Kent County Park Commission

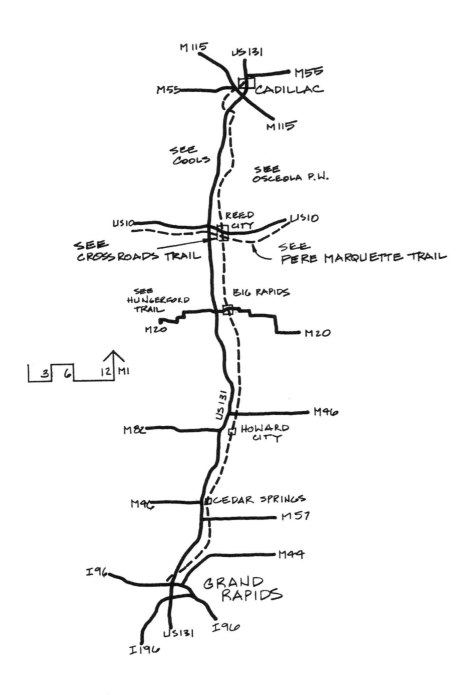

DNR Parks and Recreation Division
PO Box 30257
Lansing, MI 48909

517-373-1270

Michigan Atlas & Gazetteer Location: 46A-D234. 56A-D34,66CD4,67C4

County Location: Wexford, Osceola, Mecosta,Montcalm,Kent

Directions To Trailhead:
South trailhead - Comstock Park near Grand Rapids
North trailhead - Cadillac

Trail Type: Hiking/Walking, Cross Country Skiing, Mountain Biking
Trail Distance: 92 mi   Loops: NA   Shortest: NA   Longest: NA
Trail Surface: Ballast and natural
Trail Use Fee: Not known
Method Of Ski Trail Grooming: None
Skiing Ability Suggested: Novice
Hiking Trail Difficulty: Easy
Mountain Biking Ability Suggested: Novice
Terrain: 100% Flat
Camping: None along trail but nearby

Managed by the DNR, Parks and Recreation Division
Under development. Sections will be opened to the public as basic
improvements are made. Call the DNR to find out current status.

WHITE PINE TRAIL STATE PARK

Rails to Trails Conservancy
913 W. Holmes Rd, Suite 145
Lansing, MI 48901

517-393-6022

Friends of the Heartland Trail
PO Box 233
Sidney, MI 48885

517-427-5589
517-427-3478

Michigan Atlas & Gazetteer Location: 47ABC67,48A123

County Location: Montcalm, Gratiot

Directions To Trailhead:
From just northeast of Greenville on the west to Elwell on the east.
West trailhead - Take M91 north about 2 miles to Peck Rd, then east to Lake Rd, then north to trailhead.
East trailhead - Community of Elwell, about 4 miles west of Alma

Trail Type: Hiking/Walking, Cross Country Skiing, Mountain Biking
Trail Distance: 35 mi   Loops: NA   Shortest: NA   Longest: NA
Trail Surface: Ballast and natural
Trail Use Fee:
Method Of Ski Trail Grooming:
Skiing Ability Suggested:
Hiking Trail Difficulty:
Mountain Biking Ability Suggested:
Terrain: 100%Flat
Camping: None

Owned by the Rails to Trails Conservancy
Being developed the the Friends of the Heartland Trail
This trail was recently purchased (1994) by Fred Meijer and donated to the Rails to Trails Conservancy.
No improvements have been made(1994). Contact above organizations for current status.
The Friends of the Heartland, welcome new members to work on this project.

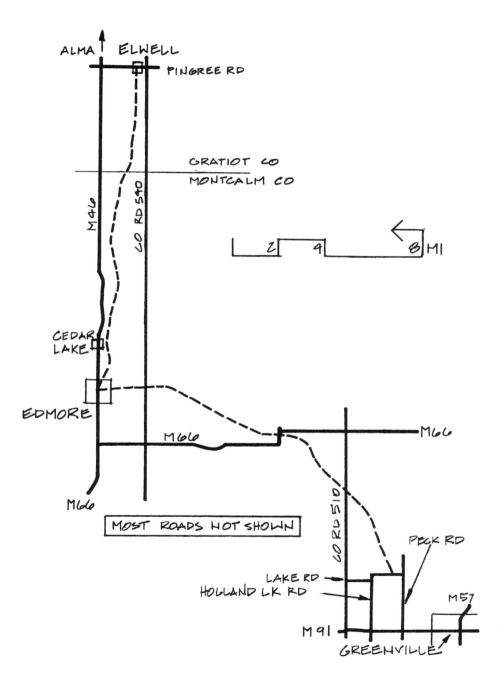

HEARTLAND RAIL TRAIL

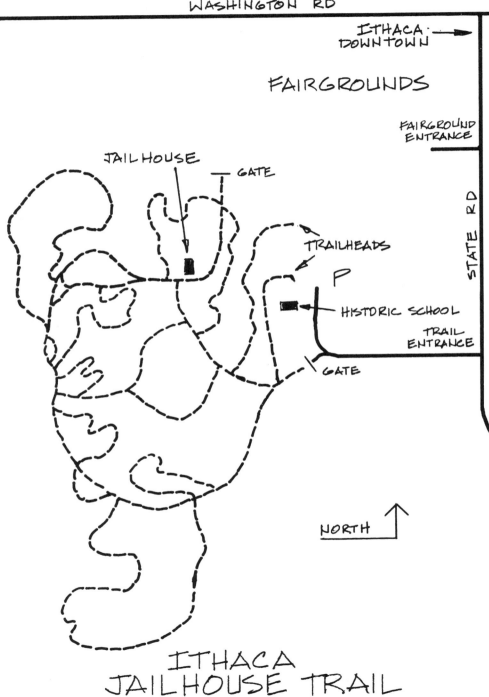

WASHINGTON RD

ITHACA DOWNTOWN →

FAIRGROUNDS

FAIRGROUND ENTRANCE

JAILHOUSE

GATE

STATE RD

TRAILHEADS

P

HISTORIC SCHOOL

TRAIL ENTRANCE

GATE

NORTH ↑

ITHACA JAILHOUSE TRAIL

Ithaca Jailhouse Trail

City of Ithaca
129 West Emerson St
Ithaca, MI 488847

517-875-3200

Michigan Atlas & Gazetteer Location: 48B4

County Location: Gratiot

Directions To Trailhead:
From US27 go west into Ithaca on the main street which is Washington Rd into downtown Ithaca, then south on State Rd to the trailhead.

Trail Type: Hiking/Walking, Cross Country Skiing, Mountain Biking
Trail Distance: 3.2 mi   Loops: 9   Shortest: .36 mi Longest: .75 mi
Trail Surface: Natural, wet in spring
Trail Use Fee: None
Method Of Ski Trail Grooming: None
Skiing Ability Suggested: Novice
Hiking Trail Difficulty: Easy
Mountain Biking Ability Suggested: Novice to intermediate
Terrain: Steep 0%, Hilly 7%, Moderate 30%, Flat 63%
Camping: 20 camping sites near trailhead on fairgrounds

Owned by the City of Ithaca
Developed by volunteers and members of the Michigan Mountain Biking Association
Trail system developed in 1994 as a mountain bike trail. But trails can be used for hiking and cross country skiing.
Site of mountain bike races annually.
Trail expansion is planned for coming years

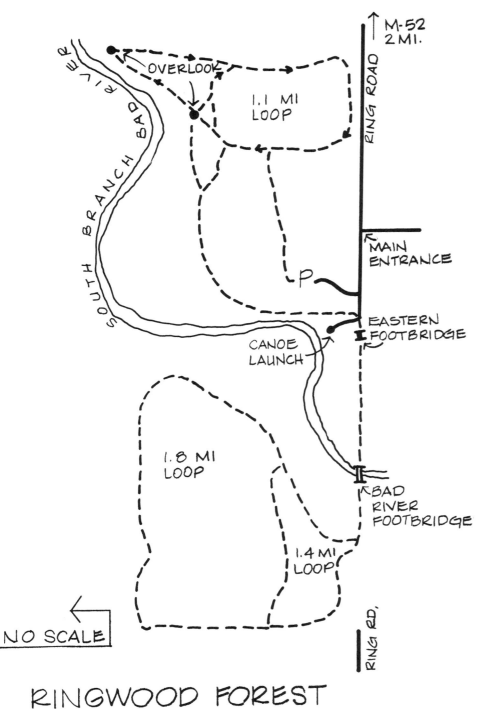

Saginaw County Parks & Recreation Commission
111 S. Michgian Ave
Saginaw, MI 48602

517-790-5280

Michigan Atlas & Gazetteer Location: 49B7

County Location: Saginaw

Directions To Trailhead:
SW of Saginaw near St Charles
Trailhead - From St Charles south on M52, 2 miles to Ring Rd., then west 2 miles to Fordney Road. Park entrance at the corner of Ring Rd. and Fordney Rd.

Trail Type: Hiking/Walking, Cross Country Skiing, Mountain Biking, Interpretive
Trail Distance: 3.5 mi   Loops: 5   Shortest: .9 mi   Longest: 1.8 mi
Trail Surface: Natural
Trail Use Fee: None
Method Of Ski Trail Grooming: Track set
Skiing Ability Suggested: Novice to intermediate
Hiking Trail Difficulty: Easy
Mountain Biking Ability Suggested: Novice
Terrain: Steep 0%, Hilly 5%, Moderate 20%, Flat 75%
Camping: None

Operated by the Saginaw County Parks & Recreation Commission.
Clinics available Park contains the oldest evergreen, a 104 year old spruce.
A 14 station interpretive trail is part of this system.

RINGWOOD FOREST

Bintz Apple Mountain Ski Area
4535 North River Rd.
Freeland , MI 48623

517-781-2550
517-781-2590

Michigan Atlas & Gazetteer Location: 50A1

County Location: Saginaw

Directions To Trailhead:
5 miles south of Freeland and 5 miles NW of Saginaw on North River Rd. I-75 to I-675 and exit at Tittabawassee Rd., then west for 7 miles and across the Tittabawassee River,then first left on River Rd to ski area.

Trail Type: Cross Country Skiing
Trail Distance: 4 mi   Loops: Several   Shortest: Longest:
Trail Surface: Natrual
Trail Use Fee: Yes, daily and annual permits
Method Of Ski Trail Grooming: None
Skiing Ability Suggested: Novice
Hiking Trail Difficulty: NA
Mountain Biking Ability Suggested: NA
Terrain: 100% Flat
Camping: None

Privately operated alpine ski area with cross country skiing.
The first completely man-made ski hill in the United States in 1961.
Lessons, rentals, ski shop, snack bar, restaurant and lounge.
Trails cover 300 acres.

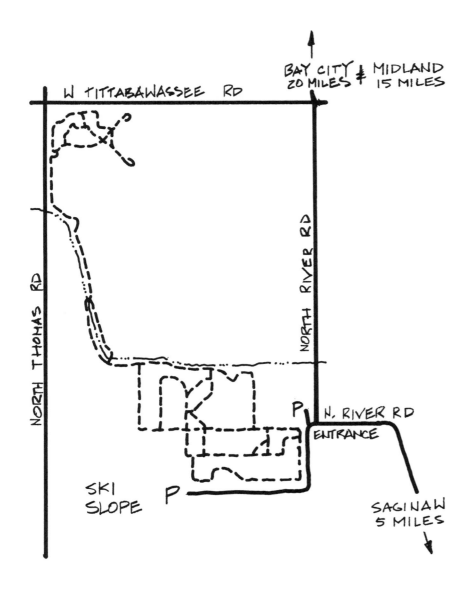

BINTZ APPLE MOUNTAIN

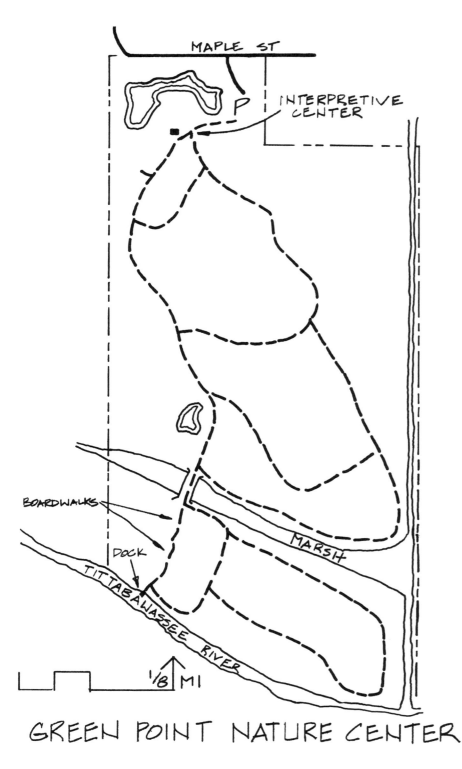

MAPLE ST

INTERPRETIVE
CENTER

P

BOARDWALKS

DOCK

MARSH

TITTABAWASSEE RIVER

1/8 MI

GREEN POINT NATURE CENTER

Green Point Nature Center
3010 Maple St
Saginaw, MI 48630

517-759-1669

Michigan Atlas & Gazetteer Location: 50A2

County Location: Saginaw

Directions To Trailhead:
From I-75 take M46 West Ave(Holland Ave) exit, take M46 through the city and over the Saginaw River, then turn left (south) on Mich. Ave for about 2 blocks west of the bridge, then follow Michigan until there are a set of stop lights on a curve, turn left (south)on Maple St, immediately past the stop lights, look for a brown sign. Follow Maple to the nature center. Germania Golf Course is your right.

Trail Type: Hiking/Walking, Cross Country Skiing, Interpretive
Trail Distance: 2.5 mi   Loops: 6   Shortest: .2 mi   Longest: 1.5 mi
Trail Surface: Gravel and natural
Trail Use Fee: None
Method Of Ski Trail Grooming: None
Skiing Ability Suggested: Novice
Hiking Trail Difficulty: Easy
Mountain Biking Ability Suggested: NA
Terrain: 100% Flat
Camping: None

Owned by trhe city of Saginaw in cooperation with the Fish and Wildlife Service.
Visitor Center is managed and staffed by Fish and Wildlife Service.
Trails open during daylight hours.
No pets or bikes allowed.

Saginaw County Parks & Recreation Commission
111 S. Michigan Ave   517-790-5280
Saginaw, MI 48602

Michigan Atlas & Gazetteer Location: 50A1

County Location: Saginaw

Directions To Trailhead:
5 miles NW of Saginaw on M47 (Midland Rd.)

Trail Type: Hiking/Walking, Cross Country Skiing, Mountain Biking, Interpretive
Trail Distance: 1.5 mi   Loops: 1   Shortest: Longest:
Trail Surface: Natural
Trail Use Fee: None
Method Of Ski Trail Grooming: Track set
Skiing Ability Suggested: Novice
Hiking Trail Difficulty: Easy
Mountain Biking Ability Suggested: Novice
Terrain: 100% Flat
Camping: None

Operated by the Saginaw County Parks & Recreation Commission
Trail follows a scenic section of the Tittabawasse River
8 station interpretative trail. Brochure available
Warming shelter available during clinics
The long trail is a self guided floodplain nature trail
Just south of Bintz Apple Mountain Ski Area

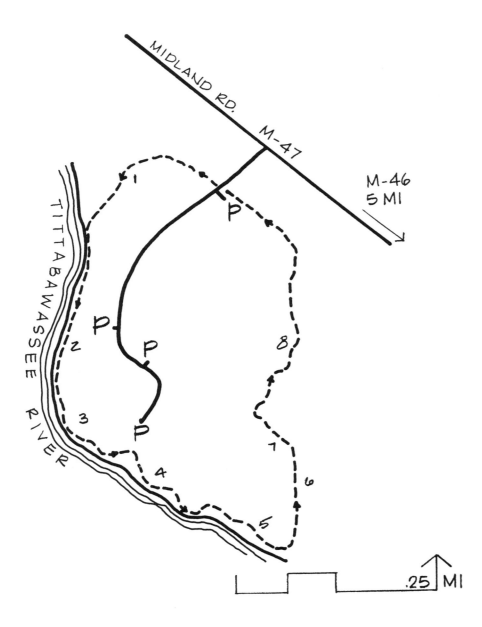

IMERMAN MEMORIAL PARK

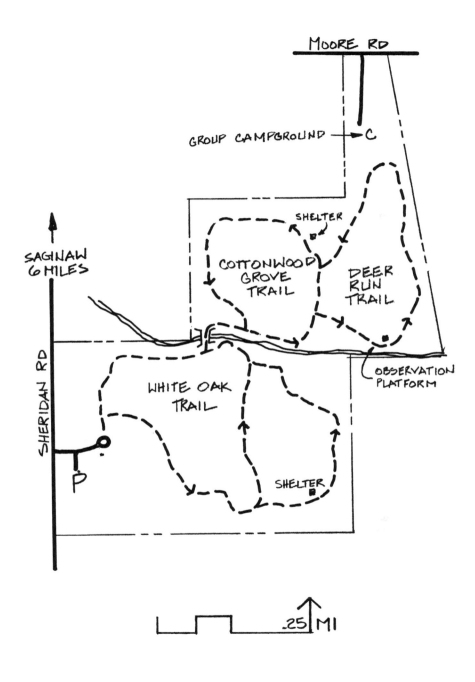

Saginaw County Parks & Recreation Commission
111 S. Michigan Ave
Saginaw, MI 48602

517-790-5280

Michigan Atlas & Gazetteer Location: 50B2

County Location: Saginaw

Directions To Trailhead:
6 miles south of Saginaw on Sheridan Rd (1 mile east of M13), between Moore Rd. and Curtis Rd.

Trail Type: Hiking/Walking, Cross Country Skiing, Interpretive
Trail Distance: 2.7 mi   Loops: 3   Shortest: .7 mi   Longest: 1 mi
Trail Surface: Natural
Trail Use Fee: None
Method Of Ski Trail Grooming: Track set
Skiing Ability Suggested: Novice
Hiking Trail Difficulty: Easy
Mountain Biking Ability Suggested: NA
Terrain: 100% Flat
Camping: Available for organized groups with advance reservation

Operated by the Saginaw County Parks & Recreation Commission
Nature programs and ski clinics available with advance notice 100 year old beech/maple forest
Three loops with individual nature trail guides available
        White Oak Trail - 1 mile
        Cottonwood Grove Trail - 1 mile
        Dear Run - .7 mile

PRICE NATURE CENTER

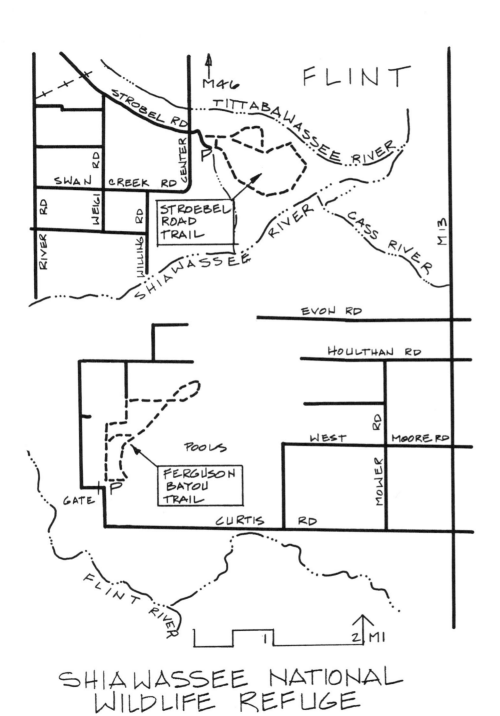

SHIAWASSEE NATIONAL
WILDLIFE REFUGE

Shiawassee National Wildlife Refuge
6975 Mower Rd   517-777-5930
Saginaw, MI 48601

Michigan Atlas & Gazetteer Location: 50B1

County Location: Saginaw

Directions To Trailhead:
Ferguson Bayou Trailhead - 4 miles south of Saginaw and 4 miles west of M13 on Curtis Rd
Stroebel Road Trailhead - Center Rd south of M46(Gratiot Rd), then cross the Tittabawassee River bridge on Center to Stroebel Rd, then turn left(east) for one block to trailhead.

Trail Type: Hiking/Walking, Cross Country Skiing, Mountain Biking, Interpretive
Trail Distance: 9 mi   Loops: 4   Shortest: 1.5 mi Longest: 5 mi
Trail Surface: Natural
Trail Use Fee: None
Method Of Ski Trail Grooming: None
Skiing Ability Suggested: Novice
Hiking Trail Difficulty: Easy
Mountain Biking Ability Suggested: Novice
Terrain: 100% Flat
Camping: None

Maintained by the U.S. Fish and Wildlife Service, Department of Interior
Trails closed during specific hunting periods from October to December
Stroebel Rd Trail: 4 miles long; The trail is subject to spring and fall flooding. Good area for songbird observations; Coal mining took place in this area in the early 1900's.
Feguson Bayou Trail: 5 miles long; The trail is on dikes and well drained most of the year. However the short loop could be wet; The trail passes through bottomland hardwoods and agricultural management areas. At the half way point, there is an observation deck with a 10X spotting scope.
Trails being developed by local volunteers.

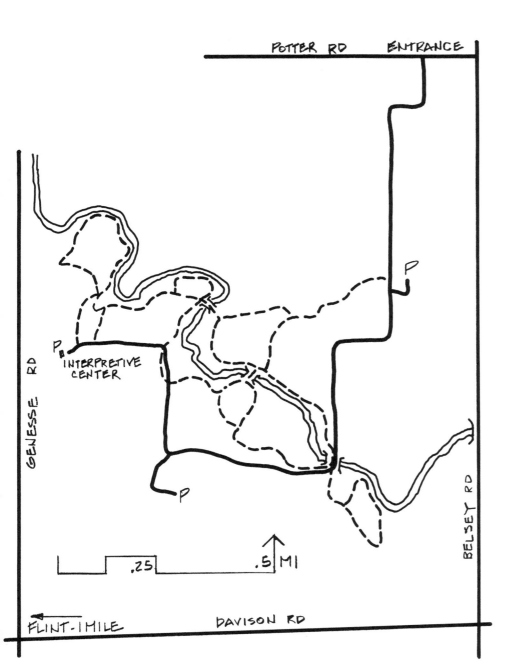

POTTER RD   ENTRANCE

GENESSE RD

INTERPRETIVE
CENTER

P

P

P

BELSEY RD

FLINT - 1 MILE   DAVISON RD

.25   .5 MI

Genesee County Parks and Recreation Commission
G-5055 Branch Rd.   313-736-7100
Flint, MI 48506

For-Mar Nature Preserve
G-5360 E. Potter Rd.   313-763-7100
Flint, MI 48506

Michigan Atlas & Gazetteer Location: 51D5

County Location: Genesse

Directions To Trailhead:
East of Flint 3 miles on I69 to Belsay Rd, north 2 miles to Potter Rd, then west .3
mile to preserve entrance.
Trailhead is at the Interpretive Center.

Trail Type: Hiking/Walking, Cross Country Skiing, Interpretive
Trail Distance: 7 mi   Loops: 8   Shortest: Longest:
Trail Surface: Paved, gravel and natural
Trail Use Fee: None
Method Of Ski Trail Grooming: None
Skiing Ability Suggested: Novice to intermediate
Hiking Trail Difficulty: Easy
Mountain Biking Ability Suggested: NA
Terrain: Flat
Camping: None

Operated by the Genesee County Parks and Recreation Commission.
Hiking trailsare not all be identical to ski trails. Trails start at the DeWaters
Education Center
About 400 acre preserve with many trails. Special trails for visually impared and
wheel chair users.
Call or write for brochure

FOR-MAR NATURE PRESERVE

Genesee County Parks and Recreation Commision
5045 Stanley Rd
Flint, MI 48506

810-736-7100

NO MAP

Michigan Atlas & Gazetteer Location: 51D5

County Location: Genesee

Directions To Trailhead:
On the Flint River in the Genesee Recreation Area northeast of Flint.

Trail Type: Hiking/Walking
Trail Distance: 2.5 mi   Loops: 2   Shortest: .8 mi   Longest: 1.7 mi
Trail Surface: Paved
Trail Use Fee: None, but vehicle entry fee requried
Method Of Ski Trail Grooming: NA
Skiing Ability Suggested: NA
Hiking Trail Difficulty: NA
Mountain Biking Ability Suggested: Easy
Terrain: Steep 0%, Hilly 0%, Moderate 80%, Flat 20%
Camping: None

Owned by the Genesee Coounty Parks and Recreation Commission
Many varied facilities including beaches, boating, Crossroads Village and fishing
sites to name only a few.
Crossroads Village is a turn of the century town complete with pond, main street
and complete steam train ride outside the park.

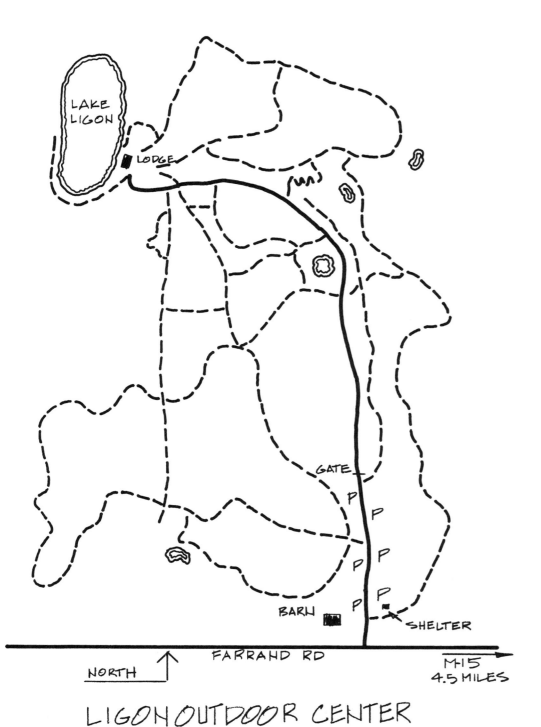

Genesee Intermediate School District
2413 West Maple Rd
Flint, MI 48507

810-687-4270

Michigan Atlas & Gazetteer Location: 51C5

County Location: Genesee

Directions To Trailhead:
From I-75 east on M57 to Genesee Rd, then north 1 mile to Farrand Rd, then east .5 mile to the center

Trail Type: Hiking/Walking, Cross Country Skiing, Interpretive
Trail Distance: 5 mi   Loops: 3   Shortest: 1mi   Longest: 3 mi
Trail Surface: Natural
Trail Use Fee: None
Method Of Ski Trail Grooming: Track set
Skiing Ability Suggested: Novice to intermediate
Hiking Trail Difficulty: Easy
Mountain Biking Ability Suggested: NA
Terrain: Steep 0%, Hilly 80%, Moderate 10%, Flat 10%
Camping: Group camping available

Owned by the Genesee Intermediate School District.
Complete outdoor center with educational programs.

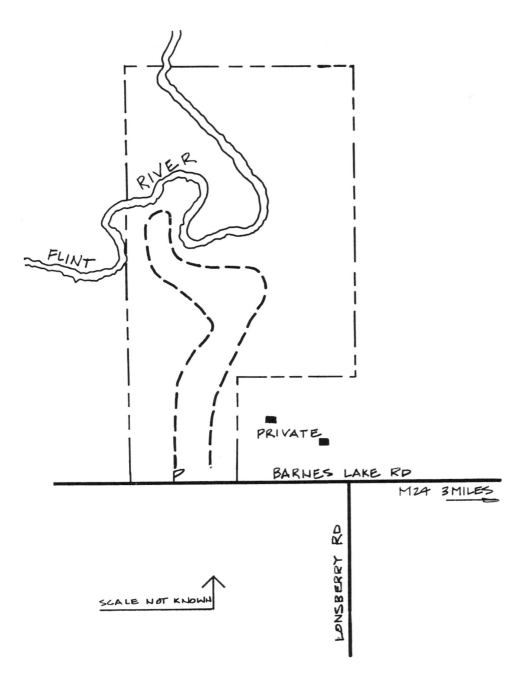

ZUCKER NATURE SANCTUARY

Michigan Nature Association
PO Box 102
Avoca, MI 48006

810-324-2626

Michigan Atlas & Gazetteer Location: 51C67

County Location: Lapeer

Directions To Trailhead:
From Lapeer, go 9.5 miles north on M24 to Barnes Lake Rd, then go 2 miles west to entrance which is just west of Lonsberry Rd. (some maps spell it "Lodsberry")

Trail Type: Hiking/Walking, Interpretive
Trail Distance: 1.5 mi   Loops: 1   Shortest: NA   Longest: 1.5 mi
Trail Surface: Natural
Trail Use Fee: None
Method Of Ski Trail Grooming: NA
Skiing Ability Suggested: NA
Hiking Trail Difficulty: Moderate
Mountain Biking Ability Suggested: NA
Terrain: Steep 10%, Hilly 30%, Moderate 30%, Flat 30%
Camping: None

Maintained by the Michigan Nature Association
This sanctuary is along the North Branch of the Flint River.
A detailed description of all the MNA properties is available from the association.

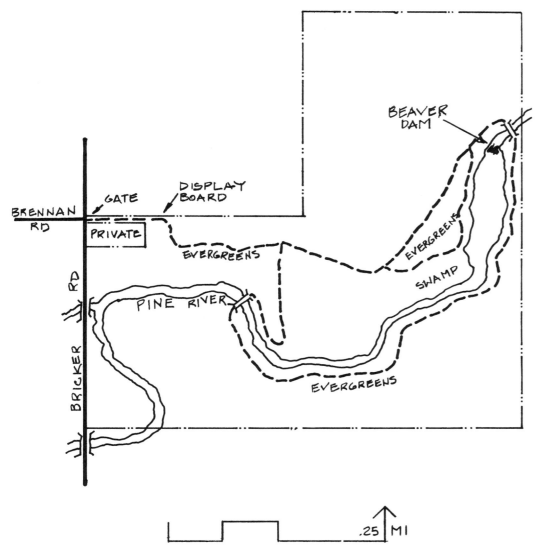

Michigan Nature Sanctuary
PO Box 102
Avoca, MI 48006

810-324-2626

Michigan Atlas & Gazetteer Location: 53D5

County Location: St Clair

Directions To Trailhead:
From Capac, take M21 east about 6.5 miles, where M21 turns southeast
continue east on Bryce Rd about 3 miles to Bricker Rd (second road off M21)
Turn north (left) on Bricker and go .5 mile to Brennan Rd. Turn right at Brennan
Rd. Nature Sanctuary trailhead is on right about 1/8 mile

Trail Type: Hiking/Walking, Interpretive
Trail Distance: 2 mi　　　Loops: 1　　　　Shortest: NA　　Longest:　2 mi
Trail Surface: Natural
Trail Use Fee: None
Method Of Ski Trail Grooming: NA
Skiing Ability Suggested: NA
Hiking Trail Difficulty: Easy
Mountain Biking Ability Suggested: NA
Terrain: Steep 0%, Hilly 0%, Moderate 2%, Flat 98%
Camping: None

Owned by the Michigan Nature Association
Pleasant 118 acre sanctuary along the Pine River.
Write association for their sanctuary guide book.

BRENNAN MEMORIAL
NATURE SANCTUARY

Michigan Nature Association
PO Box 102
Avoca, MI 48006

810-324-2626

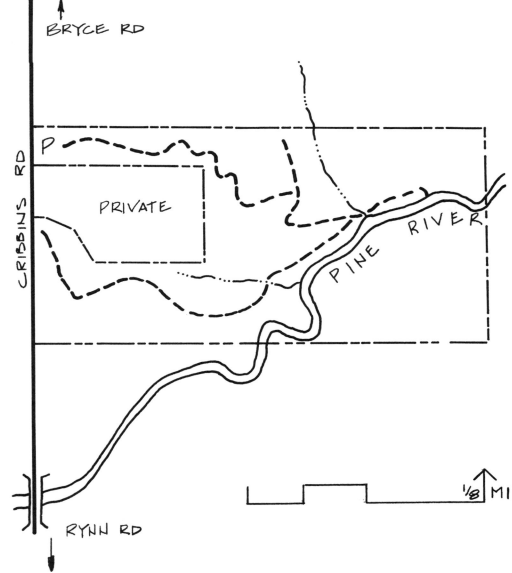

BRYCE RD

CRIBBINS RD

P

PRIVATE

PINE RIVER

RYNN RD

1/8 MI

Michigan Atlas & Gazetteer Location: 53D5

County Location: St. Clair

Directions To Trailhead:
From Port Huron, take I-96 west to Barth Rd exit(about 8 miles), then north on Barth Rd a short distance to Lapeer Rd, then left(west) and go 2.5 miles to Cribbins Rd, then right(north) on Cribbins and go 1.5 miles north to sanctuary entrance sign on your right.

Trail Type: Interpretive
Trail Distance: 1 mi   Loops: 1   Shortest: NA   Longest: 1 mi
Trail Surface: Natural
Trail Use Fee: None
Method Of Ski Trail Grooming: NA
Skiing Ability Suggested: NA
Hiking Trail Difficulty: Easy
Mountain Biking Ability Suggested: NA
Terrain: Steep 20%, Hilly 20%, Moderate 50%, Flat 10%
Camping: None

Maintained by the Michigan Nature Association
1 mile long trail with 44 stations
17.5 acres nature sanctuary

POLOVICH MEMORIAL
NATURE SANCTUARY

TRAIL NOTES

Ludington State Park
Box 709
Ludington , MI 49431

616-843-8671

DNR Parks and Recreation Division

517-373-1270

Michigan Atlas & Gazetteer Location: 54A3,64D23

County Location: Mason

Directions To Trailhead:
North of Ludington at the end of M116 along Lake Michigan

SEE MAPS ON NEXT PAGE

Trail Type: Hiking/Walking, Cross Country Skiing, Interpretive
Trail Distance: 22 mi   Loops: 15   Shortest: .5 mi   Longest: 2.7 mi
Trail Surface: Paved and natural
Trail Use Fee: None, but vehicle entry fee required
Method Of Ski Trail Grooming: Track set as needed
Skiing Ability Suggested: Novice to advanced
Hiking Trail Difficulty: Easy to difficult
Mountain Biking Ability Suggested: NA
Terrain: Steep 0%, Hilly 40%, Moderate 40%, Flat 20%
Camping: Campgrounds in the park

Maintained by the DNR Parks and Recreation Division
Extensive trail system.
Some hiking trails are not suitable for skiing and some ski trails are not available
for hiking In the summer.
Some trails are not well marked.
Be sure to take both hiking and ski trail maps with you in the winter.
Shelters and toilets are available along the trail system.
1,699 acres have been designated as a Wilderness Natural Area. This area
includes the park land from Big Sable Lighthouse to north the boundary (which is
the south boundary of the Nordhouse Dunes, managed by the Forest Service).
Paved trail along the river useable for bikes and handicappers.
Of the distance listed, 4 miles are designated ski trials in 4 trails(loops) from the
visitor center.

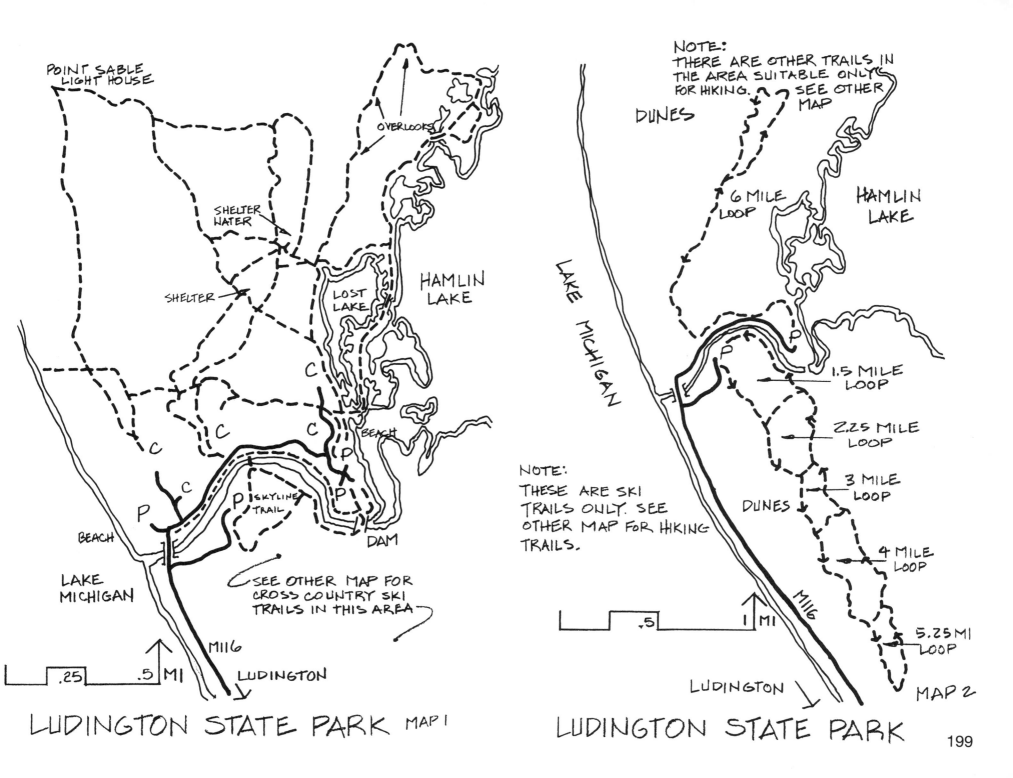

POINT SABLE
LIGHT HOUSE

OVERLOOKS

SHELTER
WATER

SHELTER

LOST
LAKE

HAMLIN
LAKE

C

C   C   C

BEACH

C

P   P

P   SKYLINE
     TRAIL   P

BEACH   P

DAM

LAKE
MICHIGAN

SEE OTHER MAP FOR
CROSS COUNTRY SKI
TRAILS IN THIS AREA

.25   .5 MI

M116

LUDINGTON

LUDINGTON STATE PARK MAP 1

NOTE:
THERE ARE OTHER TRAILS IN
THE AREA SUITABLE ONLY
FOR HIKING. SEE OTHER
MAP

DUNES

6 MILE
LOOP

HAMLIN
LAKE

LAKE MICHIGAN

P

P

1.5 MILE
LOOP

2.25 MILE
LOOP

NOTE:
THESE ARE SKI
TRAILS ONLY. SEE
OTHER MAP FOR HIKING
TRAILS.

3 MILE
LOOP

DUNES

4 MILE
LOOP

.5   1 MI

M116

5.25 MI
LOOP

LUDINGTON

MAP 2

LUDINGTON STATE PARK

199

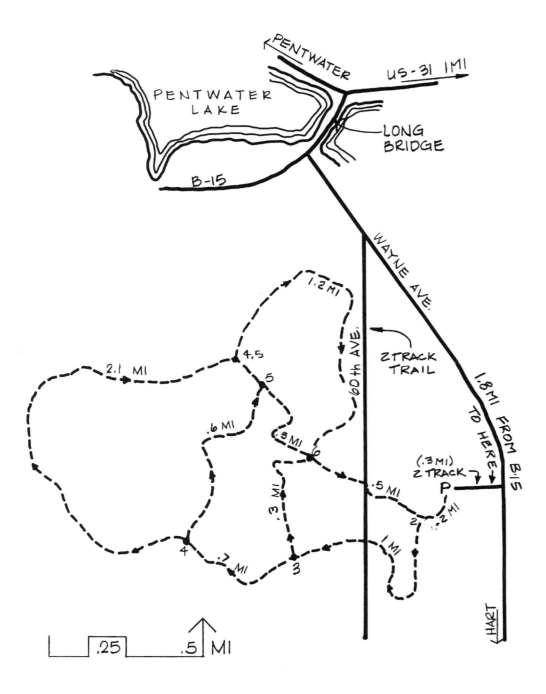

Field Office, Baldwin Forest Area
1757 E. Hayes Rd   616-861-5636
Shelby, MI 49455

Baldwin Area Forest, Pere Marquette State Forest
Rte 2, Box 2810   616-745-4651
Baldwin, MI 49304

Michigan Atlas & Gazetteer Location: 54B3

County Location: Oceana

Directions To Trailhead:
SE of Pentwater on B15 to Wayne Ave., then south on Wayne Ave. to the
Pathway. It is southeast of Pentwater Lake.

Trail Type: Hiking/Walking, Cross Country Skiing, Mountain Biking
Trail Distance: 7.4 mi   Loops: 4   Shortest: 2.3 mi Longest: 6 mi
Trail Surface: Natural
Trail Use Fee: None
Method Of Ski Trail Grooming: None
Skiing Ability Suggested: Novice
Hiking Trail Difficulty: Easy
Mountain Biking Ability Suggested: Novice
Terrain: Flat to rolling with a hilly section.
Camping: None

Managed by the DNR Forest Management Division
Trail maintained by local volunteers.
Other contacts:
        DNR Forest Management Division Office, Lansing, 517-275-1275
        DNR Forest Management Region Office, Roscommon, 517-275-5151

PENTWATER PATHWAY

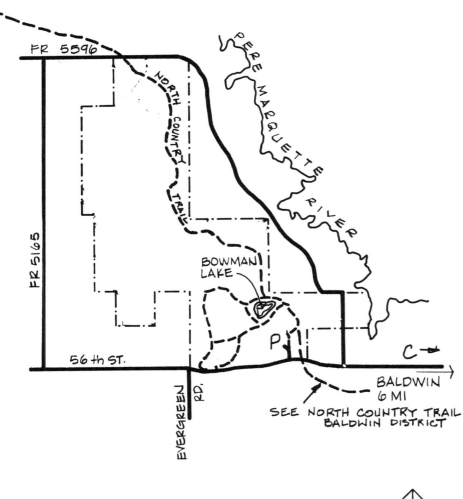

FR 5596

PERE MARQUETTE RIVER

NORTH COUNTRY TRAIL

FR 5165

BOWMAN LAKE

P

56th ST.

EVERGREEN RD.

C →

BALDWIN
6 MI

SEE NORTH COUNTRY TRAIL
BALDWIN DISTRICT

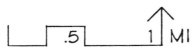

.5   1 MI

BOWMAN LAKE
FOOT TRAVEL AREA

Baldwin Ranger District, Huron-Manistee National Forest
650 N. Michigan Ave, Drawer D   616-745-4631
Baldwin, MI 49304

Forest Supervisor, Huron-Manistee National Forest
421 S. Mitchell St.   616-775-2421
Cadillac, MI 49601   800-999-7677

Michigan Atlas & Gazetteer Location: 55A6

County Location: Lake

Directions To Trailhead:
6 miles west of Baldwin on Carr Rd (56th Street)
Trailhead - Take Carrs Rd. west out of Baldwin about 2.5 miles, then left at fork
to continue on Carrs Rd, proceed across the Pere Marquette River and the road
to the parking lot is on your right about 1.5 miles past the bridge to the trailhead.

Trail Type: Hiking/Walking, Cross Country Skiing
Trail Distance: 2.25 mi   Loops: 2   Shortest: 2 mi   Longest: 2.25 mi
Trail Surface: Natural
Trail Use Fee: None
Method Of Ski Trail Grooming: None
Skiing Ability Suggested: Intermediate
Hiking Trail Difficulty: Moderate
Mountain Biking Ability Suggested:
Terrain: Steep 0%, Hilly 10%, Moderate 80%, Flat 10%
Camping: Campground nearby an primitive camping permitted

Maintained by the Baldwin Ranger District, Huron-Manistee National Forest
Many old unmarked two track roads and paths are available for wilderness skiing
and hiking.
The foot travel area contains over 1,000 acres.
The North Country Trail - Baldwin passes through this tract of land.
If mountain biking on the NCT, stay on the trail and and do not explore the
Bowman Lake trails since mountain biking is prohibited in the foot travel area.

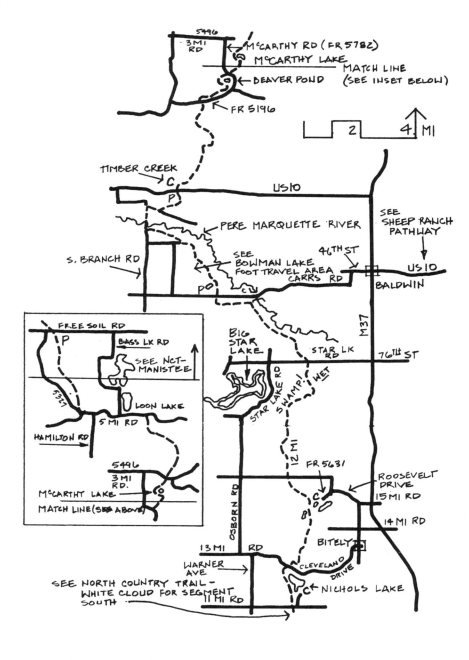

Baldwin Ranger District, Huron-Manistee National Forest
650 North Michigan Ave, Drawer D   616-745-4631
Baldwin, MI 49304

Forest Supervisor, Huron-Manistee National Forest
421 S. Mitchell St.   616-775-2421
Cadillac, MI 49601   800-821-6263

Michigan Atlas & Gazetteer Location: 55ABC7,65D7

County Location: Newaygo & Lake

Directions To Trailhead:
Trailheads - From Baldwin take M37 south 3 miles to Star Lake Rd (76th St), then west 2.5 miles to the trail . Also, From Baldwin take M37 south 8.5 miles to Lilley, then west and south on Bingham Rd to Bitely, then take Cleveland Drive west 3.5 miles to Nichols Lake R.A.. Also, Bowman Lake Foot Travel Area on Carrs Rd, take M37 south from Baldwin about 1 mile, then west on Carrs Rd about 6 miles to Bowman Lake.   Also many others.

Trail Type: Hiking/Walking, Mountain Biking
Trail Distance: 40 mi   Loops: NA   Shortest: NA   Longest: NA
Trail Surface: Natural
Trail Use Fee: None
Method Of Ski Trail Grooming: None
Skiing Ability Suggested: Advanced
Hiking Trail Difficulty: Easy to moderate
Mountain Biking Ability Suggested: Novice
Terrain: Steep 0%, Hilly 35%, Moderate 40%, Flat 25%
Camping: Nichols Lake RA , Bowman Bridge CG , Timber Creek CG and others

Maintained by the Baldwin Ranger District, Huron-Manistee National Forest
A very pleasant segment of the North Country Trail. The trail routing gives the impression of passing through a much more isolated area. Surprisingly little used for being so close to large urban areas. Great trail for easy going mountain biking.
With campgrounds all along this segment, it is ideal trail opportunity.
See the NCT - White Cloud, for the adjacent segment to the south and NCT - Manistee for the adjacent segment to the north.
Camping is also permitted 200' from the trail.
For more information about the North Country Trail, contact the North Country Trail Association, PO Box 311, White Cloud, MI 49349 616-689-1912

NORTH COUNTRY TRAIL- BALDWIN

CAMPGROUND RD

P

BOAT LAUNCH

1 MILE LOOP

WHITE RIVER

SCALE NOT KNOWN

PINES POINT PATHWAY

Trail Coordinator, White Cloud & Baldwin Ranger Dist.
650 N Michigan Ave, Drawer D   616-745-4631
Baldwin, MI 49304

Forest Supervisor, Huron Manistee National Forest
421 S. Mitchell St   800-821-6263
Cadillac, MI 49601

Michigan Atlas & Gazetteer Location: 55D6

County Location: Oceana

Directions To Trailhead:
From Hesperia go west on M20 2 miles to 192nd Ave, then turn right for 3 miles, then follow signs leading to Pines Point Recreation Area

Trail Type: Hiking/Walking
Trail Distance: 1 mi   Loops: 1   Shortest: Longest: 1 mi
Trail Surface: Natural
Trail Use Fee: None
Method Of Ski Trail Grooming: NA
Skiing Ability Suggested: NA
Hiking Trail Difficulty: Easy
Mountain Biking Ability Suggested: NA
Terrain: 100% Flat
Camping: At trailhead

Maintained by the White Cloud Ranger District
Short campground trail.
Actual trail may be at different location than shown on map.

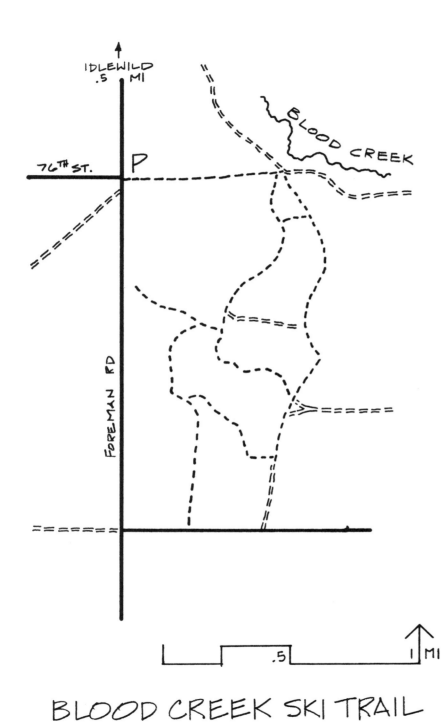

IDLEWILD .5 MI

76TH ST.

P

BLOOD CREEK

FOREMAN RD

.5   1 MI

BLOOD CREEK SKI TRAIL

Baldwin Ranger District, Huron Manistee National Forest
650 N. Michigan Ave, Drawer D   616-745-4631
Baldwin, MI 49304

Forest Supervisior, Huron Manistee National Forest
421 S. Mitchell St   800-821-6263
Cadillac, MI 49601   616-775-2421

Michigan Atlas & Gazetteer Location: 56B1

County Location: Lake

Directions To Trailhead:
South of Baldwin 3.5 miles on M37 to 76th St., then east to Foreman Rd
intersection and trailhead.

Trail Type: Cross Country Skiing
Trail Distance: 4.5 mi   Loops: 3+   Shortest: 1.2 mi Longest: 3.5 mi
Trail Surface: Natural
Trail Use Fee: None
Method Of Ski Trail Grooming: None
Skiing Ability Suggested: None
Hiking Trail Difficulty: NA
Mountain Biking Ability Suggested: NA
Terrain: Steep 0%, Hilly 10%, Moderate 90%, Flat 20%
Camping: None

Maintained by the Baldwin Ranger District, Huron Manistee National Forest
Popular cross country ski area for local skiers.

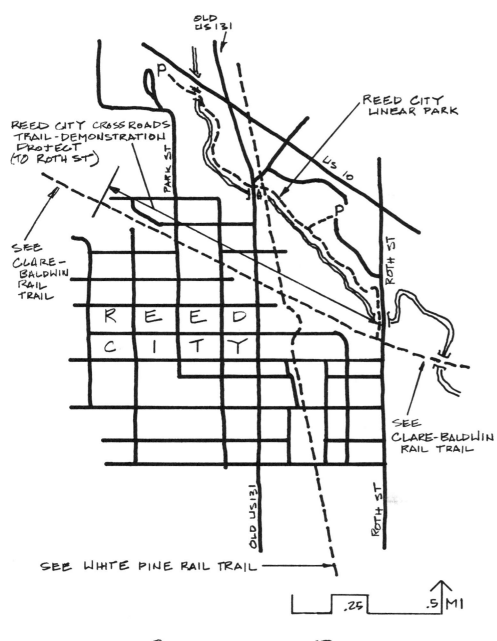

REED CITY CROSSROADS TRAIL-DEMONSTRATION PROJECT (TO ROTH ST)

REED CITY LINEAR PARK

OLD US131

SEE CLARE-BALDWIN RAIL TRAIL

R E E D
C I T Y

PARK ST

US 10

ROTH ST

P

P

SEE CLARE-BALDWIN RAIL TRAIL

OLD US131

ROTH ST

SEE WHITE PINE RAIL TRAIL

.25   .5 MI

CROSSROADS TRAIL
REED CITY LINEAR PARK

Reed City Chamber of Commerce/Cross Roads Trail Committee
780 N. Park St.   616-832-5431
Reed City, MI 49677

DNR, Forest Management Division-Recreation and Trails Section
PO Box 30452   517-373-9483
Lansing, MI 48090

Michigan Atlas & Gazetteer Location: 56AB3

County Location: Osceola

Directions To Trailhead:
In downtown Reed City

Trail Type: Hiking/Walking, Cross Country Skiing,
Trail Distance: 2 mi   Loops: NA   Shortest: NA   Longest: NA
Trail Surface: Paved and wood chips
Trail Use Fee: None
Method Of Ski Trail Grooming: None
Skiing Ability Suggested: Novice
Hiking Trail Difficulty: Easy
Mountain Biking Ability Suggested: Novice
Terrain: Steep 0%, Hilly 0%, Moderate 10%, Flat 90%
Camping: None

Maintained by Reed City
Crossroads Rail Trail is paved. Reed City Linear Park is wood chip surface
Crossroads Rail Trail will become a part of the Pere Marquette Tail (Clare - Baldwin)

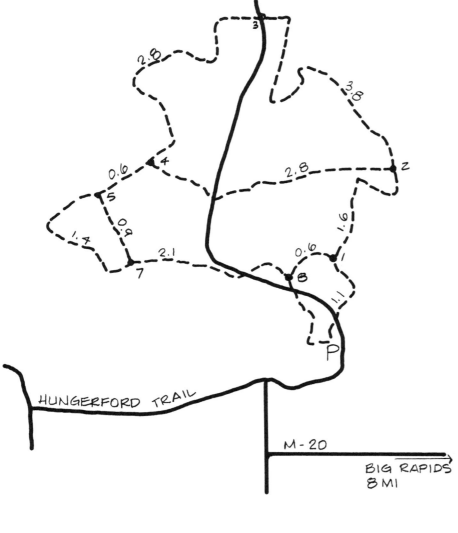

HUNGERFORD TRAIL

Trails Coordinator, Baldwin Ranger District
650 N Michigan Ave, Drawer D   616-745-4631
Baldwin, MI 49304

Forest Supervisor, Huron-Manistee National Forest
421 S. Mitchell Street   616-775-2421
Cadillac, MI 49601

Michigan Atlas & Gazetteer Location: 56C23

County Location: Newaygo

Directions To Trailhead:
West of Big Rapids about 7 miles and NE of White Cloud about 18 miles
Trailhead - West from Big Rapids 8.5 miles to the Norwitch Township Hall turn
north on Cypress Ave. .5 mile to cemetery, then east .5 mile, then north on
FH5134 for .25 mile to the trailhead .

Trail Type: Hiking/Walking, Cross Country Skiing, Mountain Biking
Trail Distance: 20.8 km   Loops: 4   Shortest: 3.1 mi Longest: 13 mi
Trail Surface: Natural
Trail Use Fee: None
Method Of Ski Trail Grooming: None
Skiing Ability Suggested: Novice to intermediate
Hiking Trail Difficulty: Easy
Mountain Biking Ability Suggested: Novice to intermediate
Terrain: Steep 0%, Hilly 35%, Moderate 40%, Flat 25%
Camping: Primitive campground along the trail

Maintained by the White Cloud Ranger District, Huron-Manistee National Forest
Benches are located at some intersections.
Trail maps are located at intersections
Bike and ski shop in Big Rapids.

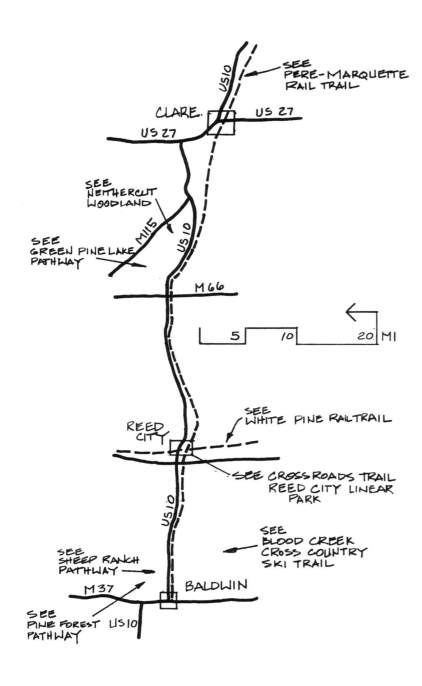

DNR, Forest Mangement Division, Recreation and Trails Section
PO Box 30452
Lansing, MI 48909

517-373-1275

Michigan Atlas & Gazetteer Location: 56B4,57AB4567,58B12

County Location: Clare, Lake, Osceola

Directions To Trailhead:
From Clare to Baldwin. Parallel to US10
West trailhead - M37
East trailhead - Next to Old US10 near Harrison Ave about 3 miles west of Clare

Trail Type: Hiking/Walking, Cross Country Skiing, Mountain Biking
Trail Distance: 55 mi   Loops: NA   Shortest: NA   Longest: NA
Trail Surface: Ballast and natural
Trail Use Fee: None
Method Of Ski Trail Grooming: NA
Skiing Ability Suggested: Novice
Hiking Trail Difficulty: Easy
Mountain Biking Ability Suggested: Novice
Terrain: 100% Flat
Camping: None

Currently under development by the DNR Forest Management Division,
Recreation and Trails Sections
Open for non-motorized uses. Essential improvements expected to be
completed in 1994. Future surfacing is dependent on on local support.
Crossroads Trail in Reed City will become part of this rail trail
In the future, this trail should connect with the Pere Marquette of Mid-Michigan at
Clare.
A 2 mile section of the right of way in Evart is owned by the community.
Inclusion of that section is this trail has yet to be determined.
Name is not official as of 9/94

PERE MARQUETTE TRAIL
(CLARE TO BALDWIN)

Baldwin Forest Area, Pere Marquette State Forest
Rte 2, Box 2810
Baldwin, MI 49304

616-745-4651

District Forest Manager, Pere Marquette State Forest
Rte 1, 8015 South US131
Cadillac, MI 49601

616-775-9727

Michigan Atlas & Gazetteer Location: 56A1

County Location: Lake

Directions To Trailhead:
At the Bray Creek State Forest Campgound NE from Baldwin on Dog Track Rd. for 1.5 miles then east on 40th St. for about .5 mile

Trail Type: Hiking/Walking, Cross Country Skiing
Trail Distance: 1 mi   Loops: 1   Shortest: Longest:
Trail Surface: Natural
Trail Use Fee: None
Method Of Ski Trail Grooming: None
Skiing Ability Suggested: Novice
Hiking Trail Difficulty: Easy
Mountain Biking Ability Suggested: NA
Terrain: Steep 0%, Hilly 0%, Moderate 80%, Flat 20%
Camping: Campgound at trailhead

Maintained by the DNR Forest Management Division
Part of the trail follows the Baldwin River.
Short and pleasant nature trail from the campground.
Sheep Ranch Pathway is just across the river.

Map

40TH ST.

MERRVIllE RD

C

2 TRACK TRAIL

1 MI LOOP

BALDWIN RIVER

BALDWIN ← .5 MI

SCALE NOT KNOWN

PINE FOREST PATHWAY

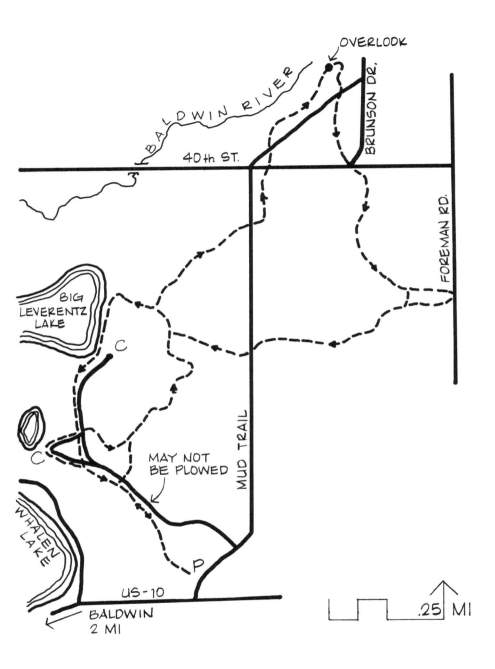

Baldwin Forest Area, Pere Marquette Forest Area
Rte 2, Box 2810   616-745-4651
Baldwin, MI 49304

District Forest Manager, Pere Marquette State Forest
Rte 1, 8015 South US131   616-775-9727
Cadillac, MI 49601

Michigan Atlas & Gazetteer Location: 56A1

County Location: Lake

Directions To Trailhead:
2 miles east of Baldwin on US10, then north on Mud Trail, parking lot
immediately on the left (west).

Trail Type: Hiking/Walking, Cross Country Skiing, Mountain Biking
Trail Distance: 4.5 mi   Loops: 2   Shortest: 1 mi   Longest: 2.3 mi
Trail Surface: Natural
Trail Use Fee: None
Method Of Ski Trail Grooming: None
Skiing Ability Suggested: Novice
Hiking Trail Difficulty: Easy
Mountain Biking Ability Suggested: Novice
Terrain: Steep 0%, Hilly 0%, Moderate 10%, Flat %90%
Camping: Campgrounds along trail but with limited facilities in winter

Maintained by the DNR Forest Management Division
Swamps, low hills, Baldwin River, two lakes and small creeks will be found
along this trail Snowmobilers may be present in the area. Pit toilet at parking lot.
Other contacts:
    DNR Forest Management Division Office, Lansing, 517-373-1275
    DNR Forest Management Region Office, Roscommon, 517-275-5151

SHEEP RANCH PATHWAY

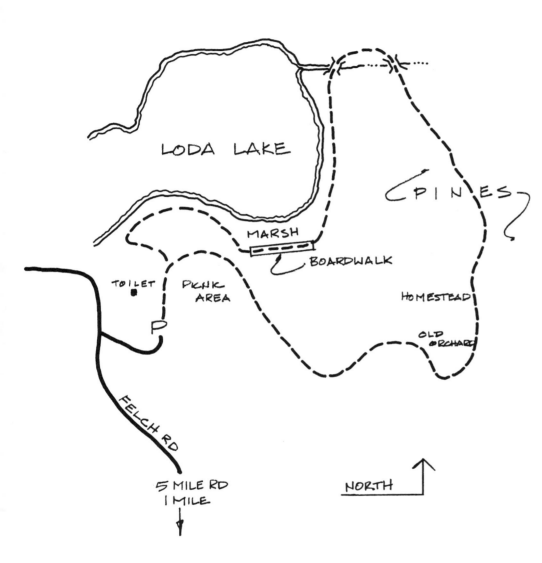

LODA LAKE

(PINES)

MARSH

BOARDWALK

TOILET   PICNIC AREA

HOMESTEAD

OLD ORCHARD

P

FELCH RD

5 MILE RD
1 MILE

NORTH

VOTEY TRAIL

Baldwin Ranger District, Huron Manistee National Forest
650 N. Michigan Ave, Drawer D   616-745-4631
Baldwin, MI 49304

Forest Supervisor, Huron Manistee National Forest
421 S. Mitchell St   616-775-2421
Cadillac, MI 49601   800-821-6263

Michigan Atlas & Gazetteer Location: 56C1

County Location: Newaygo

Directions To Trailhead:
On M37 south of Brohman to 5 Mile Rd, then west 1 mile to Felch, then north to the trailhead.

Trail Type: Hiking/Walking, Interpretive
Trail Distance: 1.5 mi   Loops: 1   Shortest: NA   Longest: 1.5 mi
Trail Surface: Natural and boardwalk
Trail Use Fee: None
Method Of Ski Trail Grooming: NA
Skiing Ability Suggested: NA
Hiking Trail Difficulty: Easy
Mountain Biking Ability Suggested: NA
Terrain: 100% Flat
Camping: Nichols Lake NFCG about 10 miles away

Maintained by the Baldwin Ranger District, Huron Manistee National Forest
Trail through a small wildflower sanctuary.
North Country Trail is about 1 mile to the west.

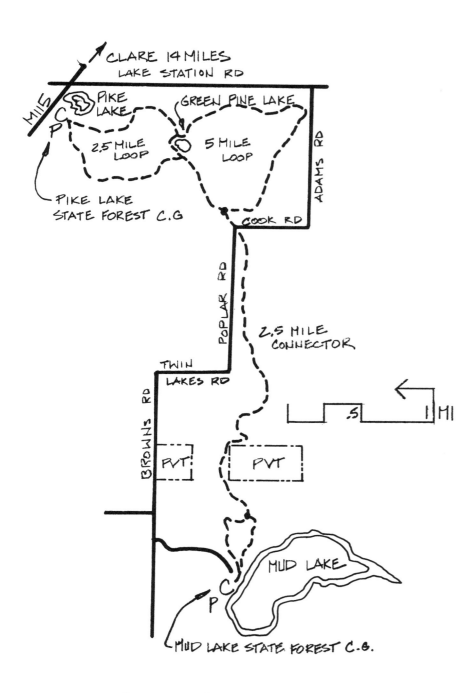

Gladwin Forest Area, Au Sable State Forest
801 N. Silver Leaf, PO Box 337
Gladwin, MI 48624

517-426-9205

District Forest Manager, Au Sable State Forest
191 S. Mt. Tom Rd., PO Box 939
Mio, MI 48647

517-826-3211

Michigan Atlas & Gazetteer Location: 57A7

County Location: Clare

Directions To Trailhead:
14 miles NW of Clare on M115 at the Pike Lake State Forest Campground

Trail Type: Hiking/Walking, Cross Country Skiing, Mountain Biking
Trail Distance: 8.5 mi   Loops: 3   Shortest: 1 mi   Longest: 5 mi
Trail Surface: Natural
Trail Use Fee: None
Method Of Ski Trail Grooming: None
Skiing Ability Suggested: Novice
Hiking Trail Difficulty: Easy
Mountain Biking Ability Suggested: Novice
Terrain: Flat to slightly rolling
Camping: Campground available at trailhead

Maintained by the DNR Forest Management Division
About 4 miles north from the new Pere Marquette Trail (Clare to Baldwin)
Other contacts:
        DNR Forest Management Division Office, Lansing, 517-373-1275
        DNR Forest Management Region Office, Roscommon, 517-275-5151

GREEN PINE LAKE PATHWAY

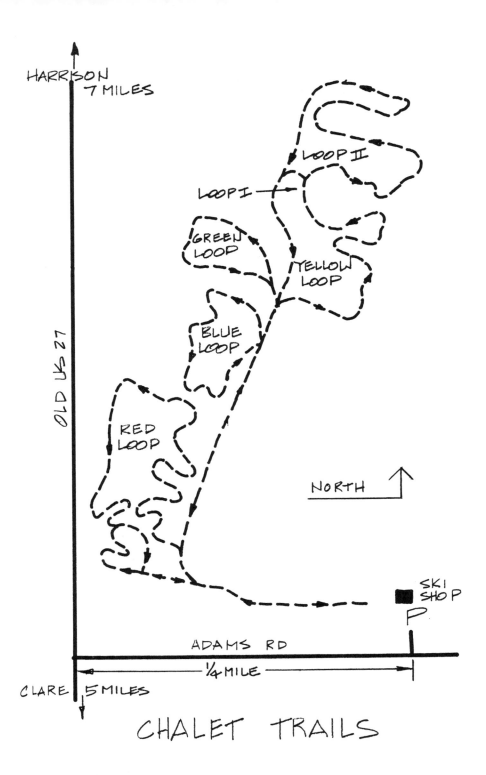

Chalet Cross Country
4275 Adams Rd
Clare, MI 48617

517-386-9697

Michigan Atlas & Gazetteer Location: 58A2

County Location: Clare

Directions To Trailhead:
6 miles north of Clare on old US27. From the north US10/27 Clare exit, take Clare Ave (Old 27) north 5 miles to Adams Rd., then right (east) .25 mile to the trailhead.

Trail Type: Cross Country Skiing
Trail Distance: 10 km   Loops: 4   Shortest: 2.2 km Longest: 2.8 km
Trail Surface: Natural
Trail Use Fee: Yes
Method Of Ski Trail Grooming: Track set with skating trails
Skiing Ability Suggested: Novice to advanced
Hiking Trail Difficulty: NA
Mountain Biking Ability Suggested: NA
Terrain: Steep 5%, Hilly 30%, Moderate 50%, Flat 15%
Camping: None

Privately operated ski touring center
Warming area, lessons, candlelight skiing, rentals and ski shop.
Enjoyable trail system that is certianly worth a visit.
Open weekends from 10 to 6 and Thursday-Friday, but call ahead.

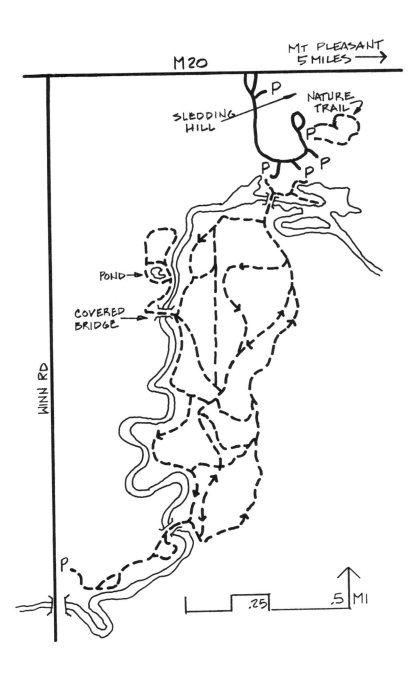

Isabella County Parks Department
200 N. Main St.   517-772-0911
Mt Pleasant , MI 48858   x233

Deerfield County Park
2445 W Remus Rd.   517-772-2879
Mt Pleasant, MI 48858

Michigan Atlas & Gazetteer Location: 58D1

County Location: Isabella

Directions To Trailhead:
5.5 miles west of Mt Pleasant on M-20

Trail Type: Hiking/Walking, Cross Country Skiing, Mountain Biking
Trail Distance: 7.5 mi   Loops: 10   Shortest: .1 mi   Longest: 2.6 mi
Trail Surface: Natrual
Trail Use Fee: None but park entry fee required
Method Of Ski Trail Grooming: Track set
Skiing Ability Suggested: Novice
Hiking Trail Difficulty: Easy
Mountain Biking Ability Suggested: Novice
Terrain: Steep 0%, Hilly 0%, Moderate 5%, Flat 95%
Camping: Ten canoe and hike-in camping sites

Operated by the Isabella County Parks Department
Over 591 acres of all season recreational facilities. Picnic area, ponds for
swimming and fishing, sledding, ice fishing, tubing and field game areas are
available. Two suspension bridges and a wooden covered bridge are in the
park.
Ski trails are always well groomed.
Ski shop with ski rentals available in Mt. Pleasant.

DEERFIELD NATURE PARK

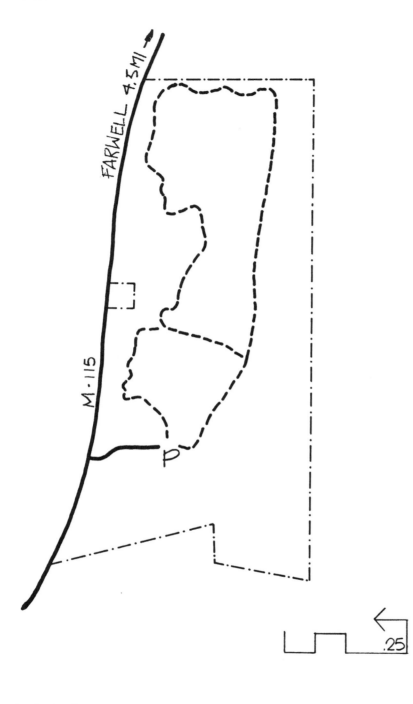

Neithercut Woodland
Department of Biology, Central Michigan University   517-774-3412
Mt. Pleasant, MI 48859

Michigan Atlas & Gazetteer Location: 58A1

County Location: Clare

Directions To Trailhead:
4.5 miles west of Farwell on M115, on the south side of the road Property starts just west of US10/M115 intersection (the west end of the divided section of US10). The entrance is about 1 mile farther west.

Trail Type: Hiking/Walking, Cross Country Skiing
Trail Distance: 2.5 mi   Loops: 3   Shortest: Longest:
Trail Surface: Natural
Trail Use Fee: Donations accepted
Method Of Ski Trail Grooming: None
Skiing Ability Suggested: Novice
Hiking Trail Difficulty: Easy
Mountain Biking Ability Suggested: NA
Terrain: Rolling
Camping: None

Maintained by Central Michigan University, Department of Biology
This is primarily an outdoor classroom with trails for hiking and skiing containing 250 acres

NEITHERCUT WOODLAND

Midland County Parks and Recreation Commission
220 W. Ellsworth   517-832-6870
Midland, MI 48640

Michigan Atlas & Gazetteer Location: 58BC34,59CD4567

County Location: Midland, Isabella

Directions To Trailhead:
East trailhead - Exit US10 at the Eastman Rd exit then take Eastman Rd south.
After it curves to the left, take a right on Ashman and follow it to the trailhead in
downtown Midland.
West trailhead - The east city limit of Coleman. This may move to the west in the
future.

Trail Type: Hiking/Walking, Cross Country Skiing,
Trail Distance: 23 mi   Loops: NA   Shortest: NA   Longest: NA
Trail Surface: Paved, existing ballast, natural
Trail Use Fee: None
Method Of Ski Trail Grooming: None
Skiing Ability Suggested: Novice
Hiking Trail Difficulty: Easy
Mountain Biking Ability Suggested: NA
Terrain: 100%Flat
Camping: None

Maintained by Midland County Parks and Recreation
Asphalt 12' wide for first 3 miles from Midland and 14' wide for the next 20 miles
to Coleman.
Additional parking available at Emerson Park on the west side of Midland
Future expansion to Clare is planned.
The 3 mile section at the east end of the rail trail is owned by the City of Midland.

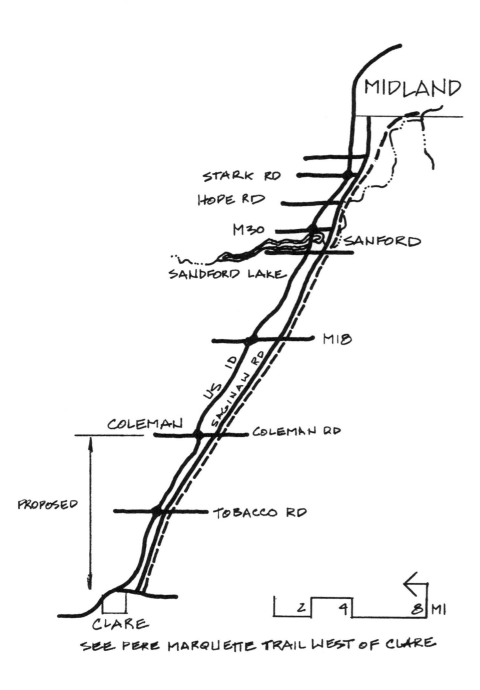

PERE MARQUETTE TRAIL
OF MID-MICHIGAN

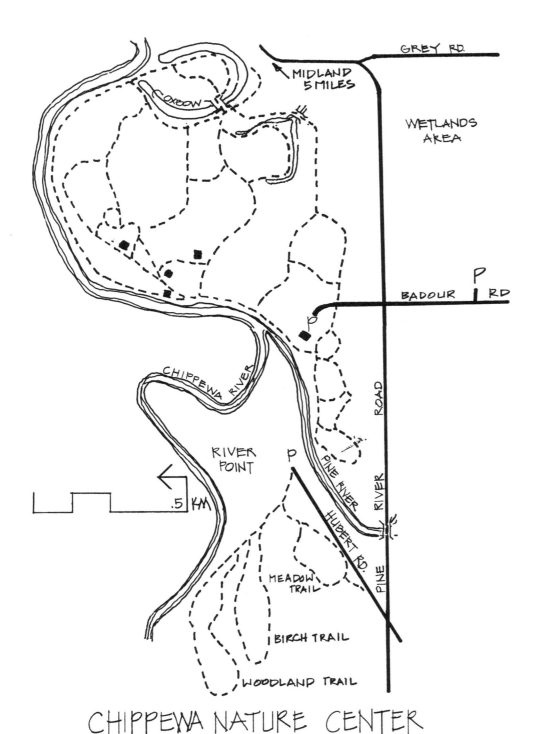

CHIPPEWA NATURE CENTER

Chippewa Nature Center
400 South Badour Rd
Midland, MI 48640

517-631-0830

Michigan Atlas & Gazetteer Location: 59D6

County Location: Midland

Directions To Trailhead:
From M20 west of Midland, south on Homer Rd, East on Prairie Rd to sign at entrance(follow brown/white signs from M20. From Business US10 in Midland, west on Poseyville Rd to St. Charles (cross Tittabawassee River) follow signs.

Trail Type: Hiking/Walking, Cross Country Skiing, Interpretive
Trail Distance: 12 mi   Loops: 8   Shortest: .4 mi   Longest: 3.1 mi
Trail Surface: Paved and natural
Trail Use Fee: None
Method Of Ski Trail Grooming: None
Skiing Ability Suggested: Novice to intermediate
Hiking Trail Difficulty: Easy
Mountain Biking Ability Suggested: NA
Terrain: Steep 0%, Hilly 0%, Moderate 05%, Flat 95%
Camping: None

A private, non-profit educational organization open to the public.
Very popular area for cross country skiing.
Trails are open seven days a week all year long from dawn to dusk..
Only minutes from Midland on the Pine and Chippewa Rivers, this is without a doubt an outstanding nature center.
Historical buildings; a visitor center that houses museums, gift shop, library classrooms; arboretum; enviornmental study area and 900 acres of beautiful land to explore. The visitor center was designed by famous Michigan architect Alden Dow.
Year around programs for the entire family.
Visitor Center is staffed from 8-5 M-F, 9-5 Sat. and 1-5 Sun.
Write or call for information and brochure.
Please - no pets, smoking or bicycles.

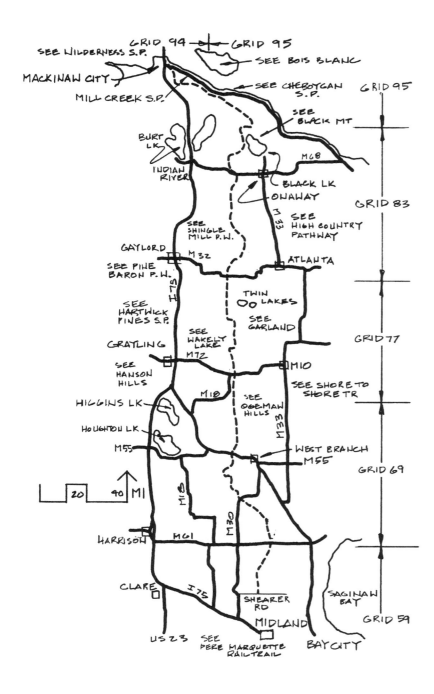

Midland-Mackinac Trail Commission
1211 Kingsbury Court   517-631-5230
Midland, Mi 48640

District Ranger, Mio Ranger District, HMNF
401 Court St   517-826-3252
Mio, MI 48647

Michigan Atlas & Gazetteer Location: 59AB67.69A-D57,77A-D,83A-D56,94BC3
                                     4,95CD56

County Location: Midland, Gladwin, Ogemaw,Oscoda, plus more

Directions To Trailhead:
Southern trailhead - 11 miles north of Midland at the Mills Community Center on
Shearer Rd, 2 miles west of Herner Rd.
Northern trailhead- Mackinaw City

Trail Type: Hiking/Walking, Cross Country Skiing, Mountain Biking
Trail Distance: 200+ mi   Loops: Shortest: Longest:
Trail Surface: Natural
Trail Use Fee: None
Method Of Ski Trail Grooming: None
Skiing Ability Suggested: Intermediate to advanced
Hiking Trail Difficulty: Easy to moderate
Mountain Biking Ability Suggested: Novice to advanced
Terrain: Steep 0%, Hilly 10%, Moderate 10%, Flat 80%
Camping: Many campgounds along the trail

Developed and maintained by the Mackinaw Trail Commission, Boy Scouts of
America and the Huron-Manistee National Forest
Follows the approximate route of the old Saginaw & Mackinaw native american
trail.
12 miles passes through the Huron Manistee National Forest.
Due to the isolated nature of this trail, only experienced skiers with good winter
survial skills should ski this trail.
Other counties: Montmorency, Otsego, Cheboygan, Crawford

MIDLAND-MACKINAC TRAIL

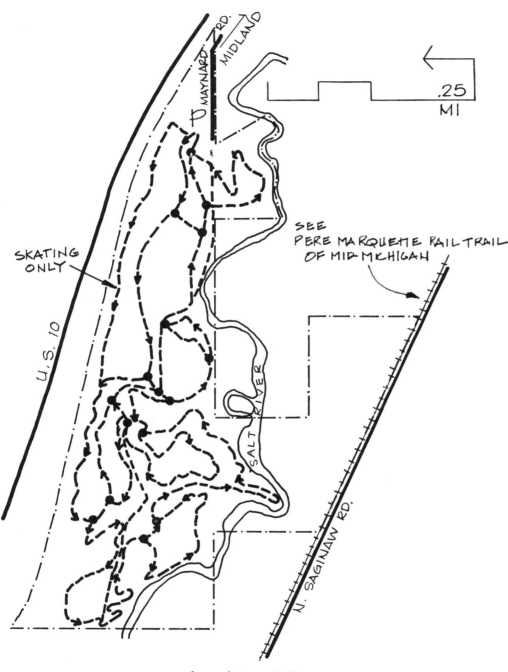

SKATING
ONLY

U.S. 10

MAYNARD RD.

MIDLAND

.25
MI

SEE
PERE MARQUETTE RAIL TRAIL
OF MID-MICHIGAN

SALT RIVER

N. SAGINAW RD.

PINE HAVEN RECREATION AREA

Midland County Parks & Recreation Commission
220 W. Ellsworth   517-832-6870
Midland, MI 48640

Michigan Atlas & Gazetteer Location: 59C5

County Location: Midland

Directions To Trailhead:
NW of Midland and the Village of Sanford, adjacent to and south of US10 Exit at West River Rd., turn south to Maynard Rd., then west on Maynard to the end of the road.

Trail Type: Hiking/Walking, Cross Country Skiing, Mountain Biking, Interpretive
Trail Distance: 8/5 mi   Loops: 9   Shortest: .2 mi   Longest: 2.3 mi
Trail Surface: Natural
Trail Use Fee: None, but donations accepted at trailhead
Method Of Ski Trail Grooming: Track set
Skiing Ability Suggested: Novice to advance
Hiking Trail Difficulty: Easy to moderate
Mountain Biking Ability Suggested: Novice to intermediate
Terrain: Steep 10%, Hilly 10%, Moderate 50%, Flat 30%
Camping: None

Maintained by the Midland County Parks and Recreation Commission
Food concession on site during ski season.
Site of cross country ski races throughout the winter.
A very pleasant wooded trail system designed for cross country skiing.
The Pere Marquette Rail Trail of Mid Michigan is along the south border of the park property.

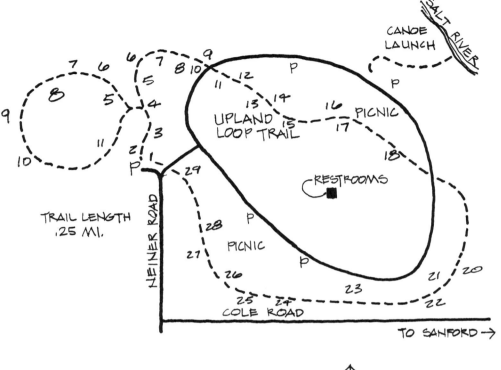

CANOE LAUNCH

SALT RIVER

P

P

7 6 6 7 8 10 9
5 12
8 5 4 11
9 3 13 14
8 2 1 UPLAND 15 16 PICNIC
10 11 LOOP TRAIL 17

P

18

TRAIL LENGTH .25 MI.

HEINER ROAD

29

RESTROOMS

28 P

27 PICNIC

P

26 P 21 20

25 24 23 22

COLE ROAD

TO SANFORD →

NO SCALE

Midland County Parks and Recreation Commission
220 W. Ellsworth   517-832-6870
Midland MI 48640

Michigan Atlas & Gazetteer Location: 59C5

County Location: Midland

Directions To Trailhead:
Take US10 10 miles west of Midland to the west River Rd exit, then left one mile
to Saginaw Rd, then left again and go about .25 mile to M30, then right about
.25 mile to Cole Rd, then right on Cole Rd to the park.

Trail Type: Hiking/Walking, Interpretive
Trail Distance: 1.15 mi   Loops: 2   Shortest: .25 mi Longest: 1 mi
Trail Surface: Natural
Trail Use Fee: None
Method Of Ski Trail Grooming: NA
Skiing Ability Suggested: NA
Hiking Trail Difficulty: Easy
Mountain Biking Ability Suggested: NA
Terrain: Steep 0%, Hilly 0%, Moderate 95%, Flat 5%
Camping: None

Maintained by the Midland Country Parks and Recreation Commission
Two nature trails are in the system.
        Veterans Grove Trail with 12 stations
        Upland Loop Trail with 30 stations.
Additional park property is undeveloped.
Trail brochure is available.

Bay City State Park
3582 State Park Drive
Bay City, MI 48706

517-667-0717
517-684-3020

DNR Parks and Recreation Division
PO Box 30028
Lansing, MI 48909

517-373-1270
517-322-1300

Michigan Atlas & Gazetteer Location: 60C2

County Location: Bay

Directions To Trailhead:
I-75 to exit 168(Beaver Rd), turn east and follow Beaver Rd for 5 miles to the state park.

Trail Type: Hiking/Walking, Cross Country Skiing, Mountain Biking, Interpretive
Trail Distance: 5 mi   Loops: 4   Shortest: .75 mi Longest: 3 mi
Trail Surface: Paved, gravel and natural
Trail Use Fee: None, but vehicle entry permit required
Method Of Ski Trail Grooming: None
Skiing Ability Suggested: Novice
Hiking Trail Difficulty: Easy
Mountain Biking Ability Suggested: NA
Terrain: Steep 0%, Hilly 0%, Moderate 5%, Flat 95%
Camping: Available on site

Maintained by the DNR Parks and Recreation Division
Several nature trails, observation towers, campground and nature center are available in this complex. The trails wind through a decidious forest, cattail marsh and the Lake Huron beach. The Chickadee Trail next to the Jennison Nature Center and Frank D. Andersen Nature Trail provides accessible trails for handicappers. Interpretive signs, benches , toilets and shelter areas are located along the trails. The Jennison Nature Center, constructed in 1949 is the center of nature study for the park and wildlife refuge. The Frank D. Andersen Nature Trail has two specialized areas. One is for bird observation with a covered viewing area and the other is a marsh overlook with another covered viewing area. The Tobico Marsh provides an excellent opportunity to view many varieties of waterfowl from the two 30' observation towers.

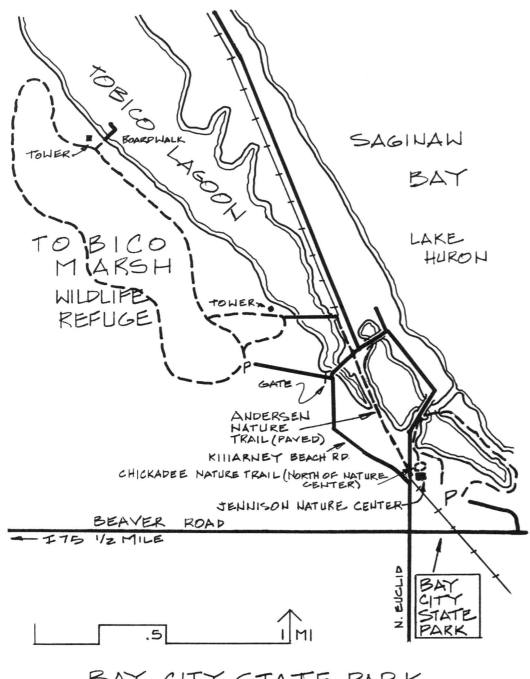

BAY CITY STATE PARK
TOBICO MARSH WILDLIFE REFUGE

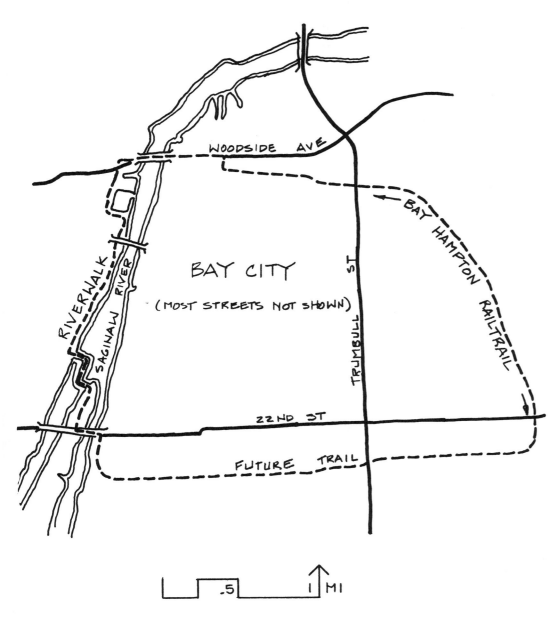

WOODSIDE AVE

RIVERWALK

SAGINAW RIVER

BAY CITY

(MOST STREETS NOT SHOWN)

TRUMBULL ST

BAY HAMPTON RAILTRAIL

22ND ST

FUTURE TRAIL

.5   1 MI

BAY CITY RIVERWALK
BAY HAMPTON RAILTRAIL

Bay County Convention and Visitors Bureau
901 Saginaw St   517-893-1222
Bay City, Mi 48708

Michigan Atlas & Gazetteer Location: 60D23

County Location: Bay

Directions To Trailhead:
Downtown Bay City. Riverwalk is on the west side of the Saginaw River between Salxburg Ave on the south and Midland St. on the north. Bay Hampton Rail Trail is between N. Johnson at 1st St to Youngs Ditch Rd in Hampton Township

Trail Type: Hiking/Walking
Trail Distance: 4.3 mi   Loops: NA   Shortest: NA   Longest: NA
Trail Surface: Paved, gravel and ballast
Trail Use Fee: None
Method Of Ski Trail Grooming: NA
Skiing Ability Suggested: NA
Hiking Trail Difficulty: Easy
Mountain Biking Ability Suggested: Novice
Terrain: 100% Flat
Camping: None

Owned by Bay City
Currently 2 separate trails. Riverwalk is 2 miles and the Bay Hampton Rail Trail is 2.3 miles. Plans call for additional sections to make the two trails a loop trail of over 10 miles.
The Riverwalk is a well developed paved trail along the Saginaw River with many recreational features inlcuding a fishing pier, exercise course and picnic areas
No special mountain bike trail is provided. General biking is allowed.

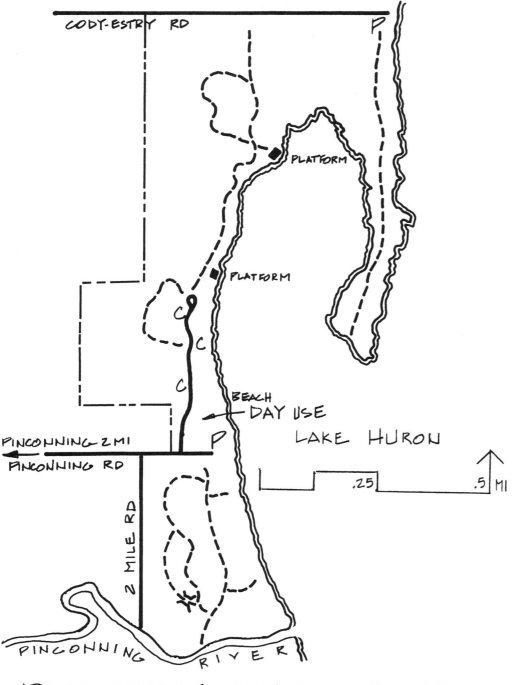

PINCONNING COUNTY PARK

Bay County Recreation Department
800 John F Kennedy Drive
Bay City, MI 48706

517-893-5531

Michigan Atlas & Gazetteer Location: 60B2

County Location: Bay

Directions To Trailhead:
I-75 to the Pinconning exit, then east on Pinconning Rd to the Saginaw Bay and the park.

Trail Type: Hiking/Walking, Cross Country Skiing, Interpretive
Trail Distance: 3.5 mi   Loops: 4   Shortest: .25 mi Longest: .75 mi
Trail Surface: Natural
Trail Use Fee: Yes
Method Of Ski Trail Grooming: None
Skiing Ability Suggested: Novice
Hiking Trail Difficulty: Easy
Mountain Biking Ability Suggested: NA
Terrain: Steep 0%, Hilly 0%, Moderate 30%, Flat 70%
Camping: Campground on the site

Maintained by the Bay County Recreation Department
Boat launch and general recreation facilities are provided
Observation tower along the trail at the bay

FISH
PT
2 MILES

WETLAND

SAGINAW BAY
.5 MILE

P

P

P
HQ

P

KINDER RD

P

GOTHAM RD   P

SEBEWAING
6 MILES

CLARK RD

.25   .5 MI

FISH POINT
STATE WILDLIFE AREA

DNR, Wildlife Division
225 East Spruce St.
St. Charles, MI 48655

517-865-6211

DNR, Wildlife Division

517-373-1263

Michigan Atlas & Gazetteer Location: 61C5

County Location: Tuscola

Directions To Trailhead:
Southeast of Sebewaing on Saginaw Bay. 3.5 miles north of M25 on Ringle Rd

Trail Type: Hiking/Walking, Interpretive
Trail Distance: 1.1 mi   Loops: 1   Shortest: NA   Longest: 1.1 mi
Trail Surface: Gravel and natural
Trail Use Fee: None
Method Of Ski Trail Grooming: NA
Skiing Ability Suggested: NA
Hiking Trail Difficulty: Easy
Mountain Biking Ability Suggested: NA
Terrain: 100% Flat
Camping: None

Managed by the DNR, Wildlife Division
Major waterfowl migration area.

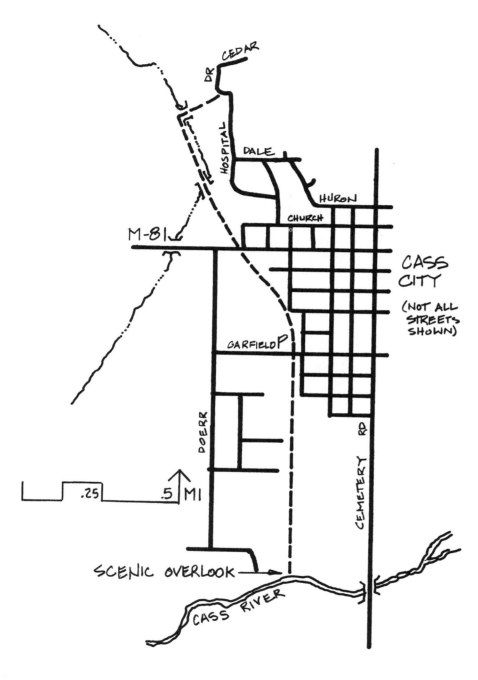

Village of Cass City
6737 Church St.
Cass City, MI 48726

517-872-2911

Michigan Atlas & Gazetteer Location: 62D1

County Location: Tuscola

Directions To Trailhead:
In the village of Cass City. Trail crosses M81

Trail Type: Hiking/Walking, Interpretive
Trail Distance: 1.6 mi   Loops: NA   Shortest: NA   Longest: NA
Trail Surface: Gravel
Trail Use Fee: None
Method Of Ski Trail Grooming: NA
Skiing Ability Suggested: NA
Hiking Trail Difficulty: Easy
Mountain Biking Ability Suggested: NA
Terrain: 100% Flat
Camping: None

Owned by the Village of Cass City
This is a rail trail project.
Scenic overlook at the Cass River end.
Parking at Garfield Ave.

CASS CITY HIKING TRAIL

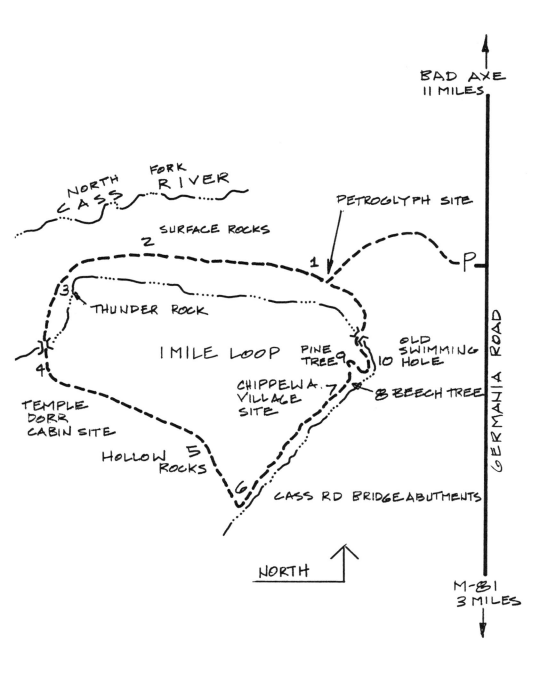

BAD AXE
11 MILES

NORTH CASS FORK RIVER

SURFACE ROCKS

2

PETROGLYPH SITE

1

3

THUNDER ROCK

P

4

1 MILE LOOP

PINE TREE 9

OLD SWIMMING 10 HOLE

GERMANIA ROAD

TEMPLE DORR CABIN SITE

CHIPPEWA VILLAGE SITE 7

8 BEECH TREE

HOLLOW 5 ROCKS

6

CASS RD BRIDGE ABUTMENTS

NORTH

M-81
3 MILES

Michigan Department of State, History Department
717 West Allegan   517-373-1979
Lansing, MI 48919-1847

Michigan Atlas & Gazetteer Location: 62C2

County Location: Sanilac

Directions To Trailhead:
3 miles north of M81 or 11 miles south of Bad Axe on Germania Rd

Trail Type: Interpretive
Trail Distance: 1 mi   Loops: 1   Shortest: NA   Longest: 1 mi
Trail Surface: Natural
Trail Use Fee: None
Method Of Ski Trail Grooming: NA
Skiing Ability Suggested: NA
Hiking Trail Difficulty: Easy
Mountain Biking Ability Suggested: NA
Terrain:
Camping: None

Managed by the History Department, Michigan Department of State
1000 year old prehistoric rock carvings in limestone
Interpretive trail includes 10 stations explaining various historical points along
the trail.

PETROGLYPH PARK NATURE TRAIL

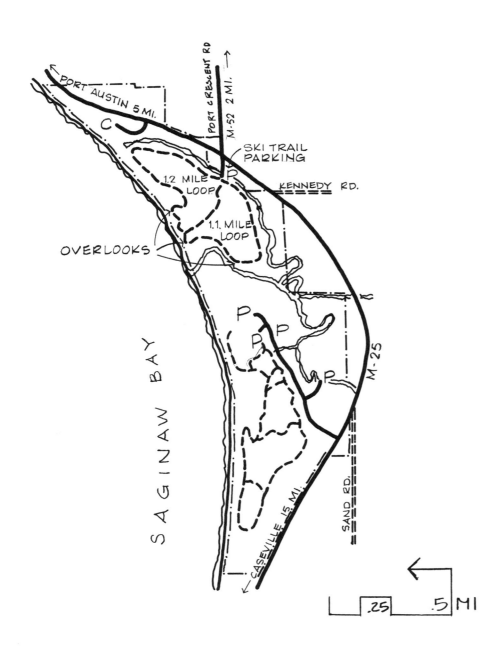

Port Crescent State Park
1776 Port Austin Rd.
Port Austin , MI 48467

517-738-8663

DNR Parks and Recreation Division

517-373-1270

Michigan Atlas & Gazetteer Location: 62A2

County Location: Huron

Directions To Trailhead:
On Saginaw Bay, 5 miles west of Port Austin. Ski trail accessible from the west end of Port Crescent Rd at M25 when gates are open and snow depth is adequate. Hiking/nature trails are accessible from main park day use area.

Trail Type: Hiking/Walking, Cross Country Skiing, Interpretive
Trail Distance: 5.3 mi   Loops: 7   Shortest: 2.3 mi Longest: 3 mi
Trail Surface: Naatural
Trail Use Fee: None, but vehicle entry fee required
Method Of Ski Trail Grooming: Not known
Skiing Ability Suggested: Novice
Hiking Trail Difficulty: Easy
Mountain Biking Ability Suggested: NA
Terrain: Steep 0%, Hilly 0%, Moderate 10%, Flat 90%
Camping: Campground available in the park

Maintained by the DNR Parks and Recreation Division.
Separate trails for hiking and skiing.
Overlooks of Saginaw Bay from trail.
Ski trails are accessable from the west end of Port Crescent Rd at M25, when gates are open and snow depth is adequate for skiiing. Candlelight ski tours scheduled throughout the winter. Ski rentals available locally.
Very popular campground in the summer requiring reservation or arrive during the early weekdays.

PORT CRESCENT STATE PARK

Sleeper State Park
6573 State Park Rd.
Caseville, MI 48725

517-856-4411

DNR Parks and Recreation Division

517-373-1270

Michigan Atlas & Gazetteer Location: 62A1

County Location: Huron

Directions To Trailhead:
4 miles east of Caseville on M25 at the north tip of the thumb
Ski trailhead - Headqarters building on State Park Rd., just east of main park entrance
Summer trailheads - From campground

Trail Type: Hiking/Walking, Cross Country Skiing, Mountain Biking, Interpretive
Trail Distance: 4 mi   Loops: 2   Shortest: 1.5 mi Longest: 2.5 mi
Trail Surface: Natural
Trail Use Fee: None, but vehicle entry fee required
Method Of Ski Trail Grooming: Track set
Skiing Ability Suggested: Novice
Hiking Trail Difficulty: Easy
Mountain Biking Ability Suggested: Novice
Terrain: 100% Flat
Camping: Campground in the park

Maintained by the DNR Parks and Recreation Division
The Ridges Nature Trail has 14 stations that explains various features of both natural and historical interest.

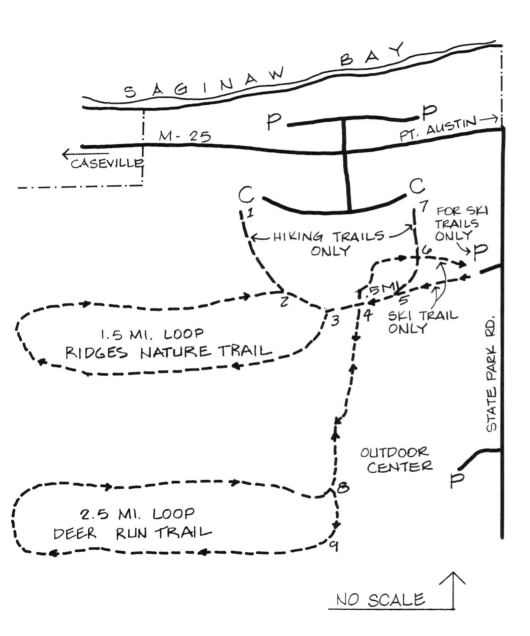

SAGINAW BAY

M-25

CASEVILLE

PT. AUSTIN →

P   P

C   C

HIKING TRAILS
ONLY

FOR SKI
TRAILS
ONLY

P

1.5 MI.

SKI TRAIL
ONLY

1.5 MI. LOOP
RIDGES NATURE TRAIL

STATE PARK RD.

OUTDOOR
CENTER

P

2.5 MI. LOOP
DEER RUN TRAIL

NO SCALE

SLEEPER STATE PARK

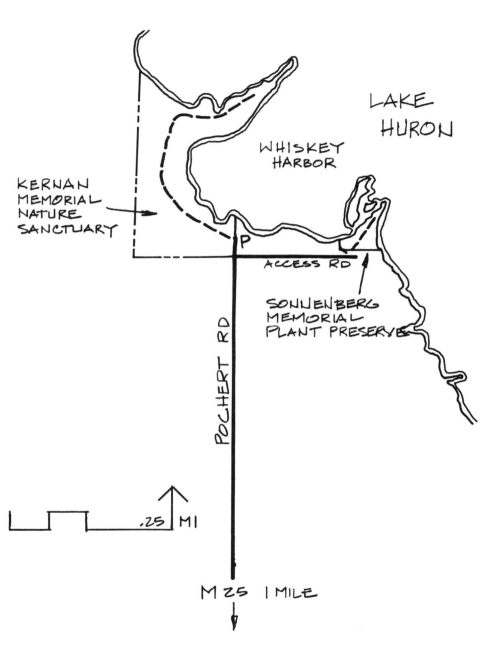

LAKE HURON

WHISKEY HARBOR

KERNAN MEMORIAL NATURE SANCTUARY

P

ACCESS RD

SONNENBERG MEMORIAL PLANT PRESERVE

POCHERT RD

.25 MI

M 25   1 MILE

Michigan Nature Association
PO Box 102
Avoca, MI 48006

810-324-2626

Michigan Atlas & Gazetteer Location: 63A5

County Location: Huron

Directions To Trailhead:
From Port Hope, take US25 north about 2.5 miles, then turn right on Pochert Rd about 1.5 miles to dead end and park. Preserves are east and west of parking location.

Trail Type: Interpretive
Trail Distance: 1.25 mi   Loops: NA   Shortest: NA   Longest: NA
Trail Surface: Natural
Trail Use Fee: None
Method Of Ski Trail Grooming: NA
Skiing Ability Suggested: NA
Hiking Trail Difficulty: Easy
Mountain Biking Ability Suggested: NA
Terrain: Steep 0%, Hilly 0%, Moderate 10%, Flat 90%
Camping: None

Maintained by the Michigan Nature Association
The complete name is Kernan Memorial Sanctuary and Thelma Sonnenberg Memorial Plant Preserve
Access between the two facilities can be on the beach or the access road.
Complete written descriptions of the preserves are available from the MNA.

KERNAN MEMORIAL NATURE SANCTUARY
SONNENBERG MEMORIAL PLANT PRESERVE

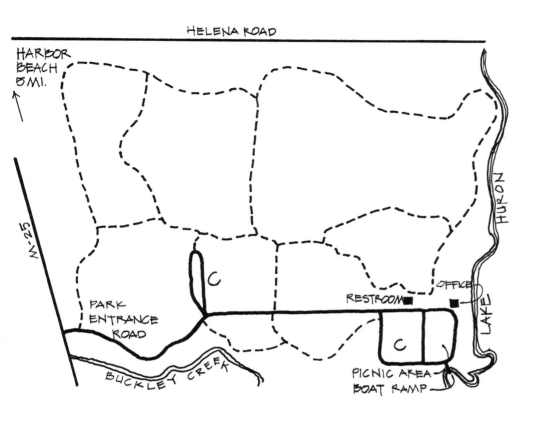

HELENA ROAD

HARBOR BEACH 5 MI.

M-25

PARK ENTRANCE ROAD

C

BUCKLEY CREEK

RESTROOM

OFFICE

C

PICNIC AREA

BOAT RAMP

LAKE HURON

NO SCALE

WAGENER COUNTY PARK

Wagener County Park
2671 Lakeshore (M-25)
Harbor Beach, MI 48441

517-479-9131

Huron County Road Commission
417 S. Hanselman St.
Bad Axe, MI 48413

517-269-6404

Michigan Atlas & Gazetteer Location: 63B5

County Location: Huron

Directions To Trailhead:
5 miles south of Harbor Beach on Lake Huron

Trail Type: Hiking/Walking, Cross Country Skiing, Interpretive
Trail Distance: 5 mi   Loops: 4   Shortest: .2 mi   Longest: 1.5 mi
Trail Surface: Natural
Trail Use Fee: None
Method Of Ski Trail Grooming: none
Skiing Ability Suggested: Novice
Hiking Trail Difficulty: Easy
Mountain Biking Ability Suggested: NA
Terrain: 100% Flat
Camping: Modern campground available in the park

Maintained by the Huron County Road Commission
A seasonal (May 1st to Oct. 1st) campground with trails.
The campground is full service Skiing permitted during the winter but, no
facilities except pit toilets are available.
The park contains 139 acres

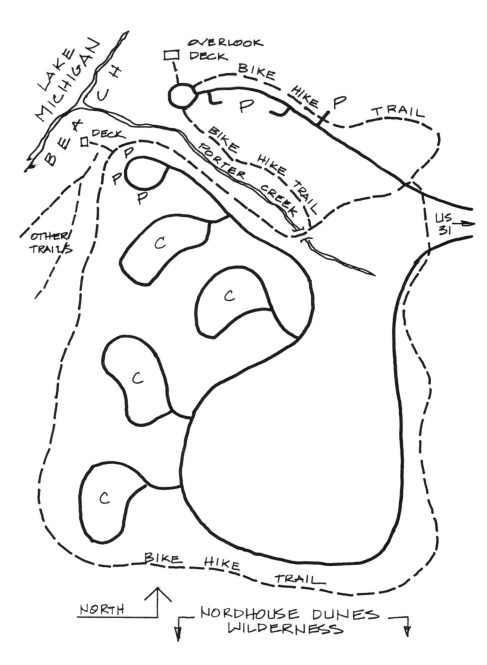

Manistee Ranger District, Huron Manistee National Forest
1658 Manistee Hwy   616-723-2211
Manistee, MI 49660

Forest Supervisor, Huron Manistee National Forest
421 S. Mitchell St.   616-775-2421
Cadillac, Mi 49601   800-821-6263

Michigan Atlas & Gazetteer Location: 64D3

County Location: Manistee

Directions To Trailhead:
Follow signs west from US31 about 8 miles south of Manistee

Trail Type: Hiking/Walking, Mountain Biking
Trail Distance: 3+ mi   Loops: 2   Shortest: .5 mi   Longest: 2.5 mi
Trail Surface: Gravel
Trail Use Fee: None
Method Of Ski Trail Grooming: NA
Skiing Ability Suggested: NA
Hiking Trail Difficulty: Easy
Mountain Biking Ability Suggested: Novice
Terrain: Steep 0%, Hilly 05%, Moderate 20%, Flat 80%
Camping: Campground at trailhead

Maintained by the Manistee Ranger District, Huron Manistee National Forest
Bike/walking trail that is routed around the campground.
Reported that road bicycles can ride on the gravel trail.

LAKE MICHIGAN RECREATION AREA

Filer Township
2107 Red Apple Rd
Manistee, MI 49660

616-723-2073

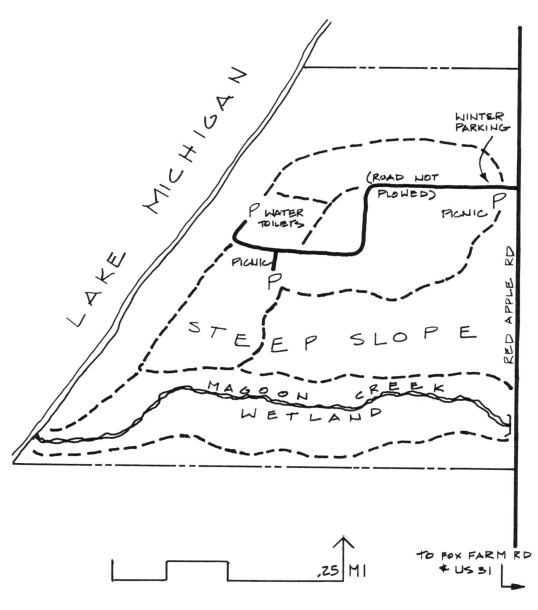

Michigan Atlas & Gazetteer Location: 64C4

County Location: Manistee

Directions To Trailhead:
Take US31 4.5 miles south of Manistee, then 3 miles west on Fox Farm Rd, then .5 mile north on Red Apple Rd to natural area entrance.

Trail Type: Hiking/Walking, Cross Country Skiing, Interpretive
Trail Distance: 2.5 mi   Loops: Several   Shortest: .5 mi   Longest: 2 mi
Trail Surface: Natural
Trail Use Fee: None
Method Of Ski Trail Grooming: None
Skiing Ability Suggested: Novice to intermediate
Hiking Trail Difficulty: Easy
Mountain Biking Ability Suggested: NA
Terrain: Steep 0%, Hilly 25%, Moderate 0%, Flat 75%
Camping: None

Owned by Filer Township
Community recreation and natural area along the shore of Lake Michigan and Magoon Creek.
Plant and animal enthusiasts are attacted to the several eco-systems in less than 100 acres. "It combines 2,300' of Lake Michigan shoreline of young dune formation including the mouth of Magoon Creek. The creek environs are a temperate rain forest bordered by thickets opening to rolling meadows affording each its own distinct flora and fauna. Second growth white pines, a climax beech/maple forest, old orchards and cedar stands afford variety and beauty. This small parcel of rolling hills provides glorious views of Lake Michigan. It is a sheltered valley for evening and winter deer; the quiet of a deep woods and temperate rain forest; the sun of an open meadow; the ripple of a gentle stream and the crash of waves on a sandy beach."

MAGOON CREEK NATURAL AREA

Manistee Ranger District, Huron-Manistee National Forest
1658 Manistee Highway   616-723-2211
Manistee, MI 49660

Forest Supervisor, Huron-Manistee National Forest
421 S. Mitchell St.   616-775-2421
Cadillac, MI 49601   800-999-7677

Michigan Atlas & Gazetteer Location: 64CD3

County Location: Mason

Directions To Trailhead:
Between Ludington and Manistee on Lake Michigan
South trailhead - At west end of Nurnberg Rd., 6 miles west of Quarterline Rd.
North trailhead - Lake Michigan Recreation Area which is at the west end of FH 5629, 7.5 miles from US31 (9 miles south of Manistee)

Trail Type: Hiking/Walking, Cross Country Skiing
Trail Distance: 15 mi   Loops: Many   Shortest: 1 mi   Longest: 3 mi
Trail Surface: Natural
Trail Use Fee: None
Method Of Ski Trail Grooming: None
Skiing Ability Suggested: Intermediate to advanced
Hiking Trail Difficulty: Moderate
Mountain Biking Ability Suggested: NA
Terrain: Steep 5%, Hilly 60%, Moderate 20%, Flat 15%
Camping: Campground available at Lake Michigan Recreation Area

Maintained by Manistee Ranger District, Huron-Manistee National Forest
Trails not designed for skiing but are skiable for experience skiers only. Some trails in dune area along Lake Michigan shore. Lake Michigan Recreation Area is located at the north trailhead off FR 5629, 7.5 miles west of US31. FR 5629 is not plowed. Access must be gained via Nurnberg Rd. The Wilderness is 1200 acres of wooded sand dunes 700 acres of open sand 4 miles of beach on Lake Michigan. Because it is a wilderness area, all trail markings have been removed.

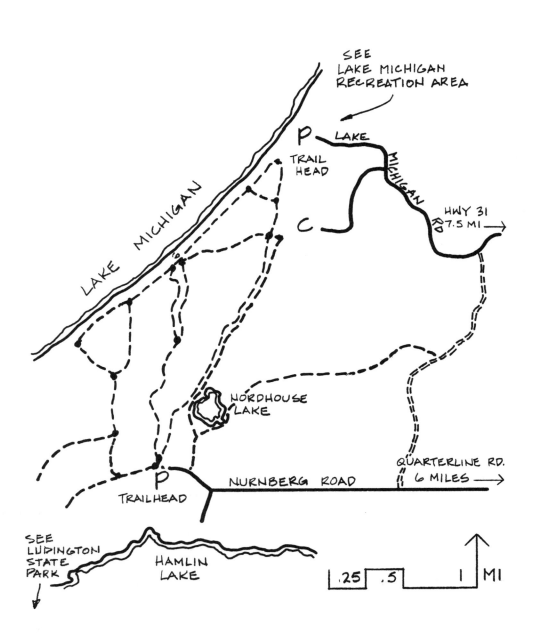

NORDHOUSE DUNES WILDERNESS

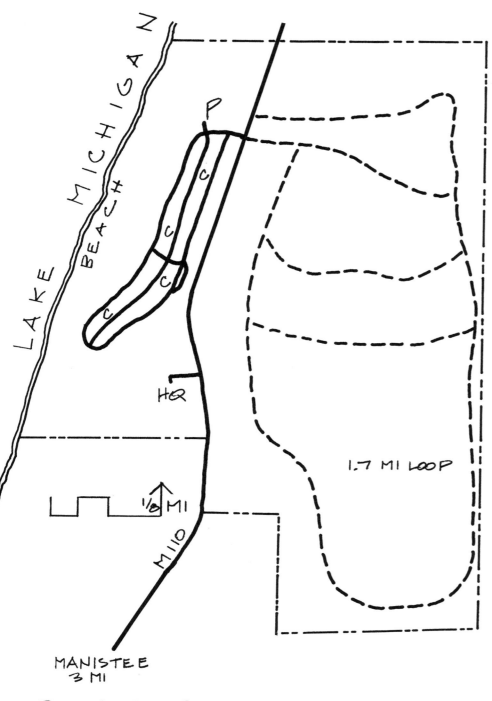

Ludington State Park
PO Box 709
Ludington, MI 49431

616-843-8671

Michigan Atlas & Gazetteer Location: 64B4

County Location: Manistee

Directions To Trailhead:
From Manistee, take M110 west off on US31 2 miles to the Park

Trail Type: Hiking/Walking, Cross Country Skiing, Interpretive
Trail Distance: 2.3 mi   Loops: 4   Shortest: .6 mi   Longest: 1.7 mi
Trail Surface: Natural
Trail Use Fee: None, but vehicle entry fee required
Method Of Ski Trail Grooming: None
Skiing Ability Suggested: Novice
Hiking Trail Difficulty: Easy
Mountain Biking Ability Suggested: NA
Terrain: Steep 0%, Hilly 30%, Moderate 30%, Flat 40%
Camping: Campground on site

Maintained by the DNR Parks and Recreation Divsion
Along Lake Michigan

ORCHARD BEACH STATE PARK

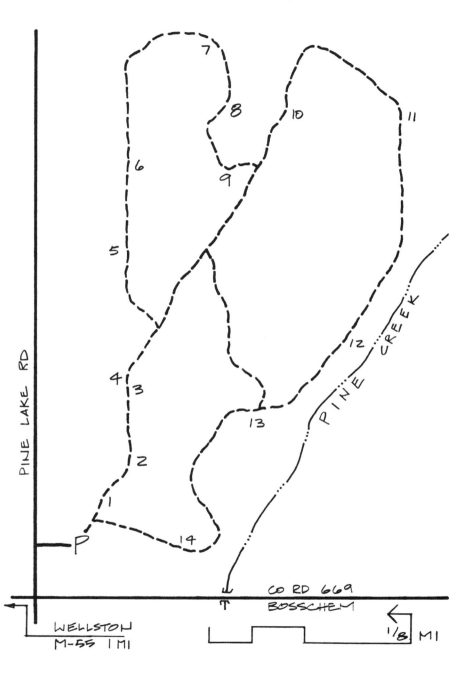

PINE LAKE RD

WELLSTON
M-55 1 MI

CO RD 669
BOSSCHEM

1/8 MI

ARBORETUM TRAIL

Manistee Ranger District, Huron Manistee National Forest
1658 Manistee Hwy   616-732-2211
Manistee, MI 49660

Forest Supervisor, Huron Manistee National Forest
421 S. Mitchell St   616-775-2421
Cadillac, MI 49601   800-821-6263

Michigan Atlas & Gazetteer Location: 65C7

County Location: Manistee

Directions To Trailhead:
From Wellston, go west on M55 1 mile to Bosschem Rd, then south 1 mile to parking lot trailhead

Trail Type: Hiking/Walking, Interpretive
Trail Distance: .84 mi   Loops: 3   Shortest: .2 mi   Longest: .65 mi
Trail Surface: Natural
Trail Use Fee: None
Method Of Ski Trail Grooming: None
Skiing Ability Suggested: NA
Hiking Trail Difficulty: Easy
Mountain Biking Ability Suggested: NA
Terrain: Steep 0%, Hilly 0%, Moderate 10%, Flat 90%
Camping: None nearby

Managed by the Huron Manistee National Forest
This is a demonstration arboretum
The trail passes through trees that were planted in 1940 to test their growth potential in this climate.
Trees from Europe, Asia and variouls parts of the USA are planted here.

Manistee Cross Country Ski Council
PO Box 196   616-723-2575
Manistee, MI 49660   616-723-6062

Manistee Ranger District, Manistee National Forest
1658 Manistee Hwy   616-732-2211
Manistee, MI 49660

Michigan Atlas & Gazetteer Location: 65C6

County Location: Manistee

Directions To Trailhead:
About 18 miles east of Manistee and 7 miles west of Wellston on M55, then south 3.5 miles on Udell Hills Rd.

Trail Type: Cross Country Skiing
Trail Distance: 30 km   Loops: 6   Shortest: 1.3 km Longest: 4+ km
Trail Surface: Natural
Trail Use Fee: Yes; Daily donation, annual and family memberships available
Method Of Ski Trail Grooming: Track set
Skiing Ability Suggested: Novice to advanced
Hiking Trail Difficulty: NA
Mountain Biking Ability Suggested: NA but is being considered
Terrain: Steep 15%, Hilly 40%, Moderate 20%, Flat 25%
Camping: None

Developed and maintained by the Manistee Cross Country Ski Council in cooperation with the Huron-Manistee National Forest.
Expertly designed trails by John Capper. On the site of the former Big M alpine ski area .
A very scenic trail system. Day use cabin on site at the trailhead that is open on weekends. Rentals available in Manistee. Well designed and groomed classic trail system that is very popular by local and state wide skiers alike. Write for brochure which includes list of local accomodations and restaurants that support the trail. Food and lodging in Wellston and   Manistee. The Manistee Cross Country Ski Council is an all volunteer organization of individuals and businesses. New members are always welcome.

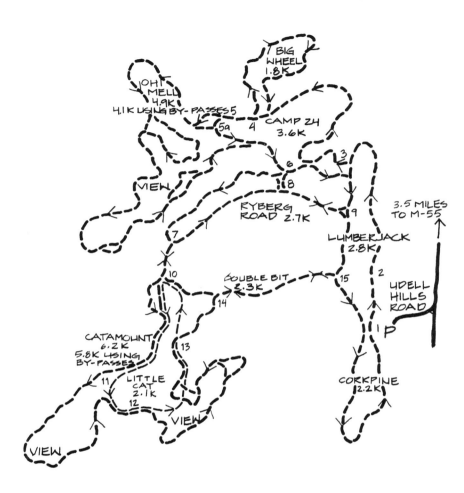

BIG M
CROSS COUNTRY SKI AREA

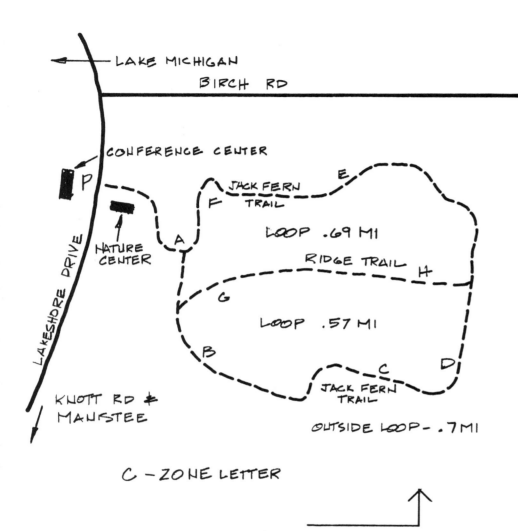

LAKE MICHIGAN

BIRCH RD

CONFERENCE CENTER

P

LAKESHORE DRIVE

NATURE CENTER

JACK FERN TRAIL

LOOP .69 MI

RIDGE TRAIL

LOOP .57 MI

JACK FERN TRAIL

OUTSIDE LOOP - .7 MI

KNOTT RD & MANISTEE

C - ZONE LETTER

Lake Bluff Audubon Center
4374 W. Fox Farm
Manistee, MI 49660

616-723-2872
616-723-2625

Michigan Atlas & Gazetteer Location: 65B4

County Location: Manistee

Directions To Trailhead:
From US31 north, take M110(Lake Shore Dirve) along the Lake Michigan shoreline past Orchard Beach State Park about 1 mile to the center.

Trail Type: Hiking/Walking, Interpretive
Trail Distance: 1 mi   Loops: 2   Shortest: .57 mi Longest: .7 mi
Trail Surface: Natural (wood chips)
Trail Use Fee: None
Method Of Ski Trail Grooming: NA
Skiing Ability Suggested: NA
Hiking Trail Difficulty: Easy
Mountain Biking Ability Suggested: NA
Terrain: Steep 0%, Hilly 25%, Moderate 40%, Flat 35%
Camping: None

Owned by the Michigan Audubon Society
Small but very interesting interpretive trail.

LAKE BLUFF AUDUBON CENTER

TRAIL NOTES

Manistee Ranger District, Huron-Manistee National Forest
1658 Manistee Highway   616-723-2211
Manistee, MI 49660

Forest Supervisor, Huron-Manistee National Forest
421 S. Mitchell St.   616-775-2421
Cadillac, MI 49601   800-821-6263

Michigan Atlas & Gazetteer Location: 65BCD567,66AB1

County Location: Manistee

Directions To Trailhead:
From Marilla go north .5 mile to Beers Rd., then east 2 miles to trailhead.
From Brethren go east on Coats Hwy 7 miles to trail. From Brethren go east on
Coats Hwy 2.5 miles, then south 1.75 miles on Drilling Rd. to the trail.
From Brethren go south 2.5 miles to the bridge and trailhead.

Trail Type: Hiking/Walking, Mountain Biking
Trail Distance: 43   Loops: NA   Shortest: NA   Longest: NA
Trail Surface: Natural
Trail Use Fee: None
Method Of Ski Trail Grooming: None
Skiing Ability Suggested: Advanced
Hiking Trail Difficulty: Moderate
Mountain Biking Ability Suggested: Novice
Terrain: Steep 10%, Hilly 30%, Moderate 40%, Flat 20%
Camping: Camping is permitted 200' from trail

Maintained by Manistee Ranger District, Huron-Manistee National Forest.
Part of the trail follows a ridge that parallels the Manistee River. Excellent scenic
views of the Hodenpyl Pond, Manistee River valley and the Udell Hills in the
spring and fall.
Trail is marked with gray diamond blazes.
Detailed trail maps are available from the national forest.
For further information about the North Country Trail, contact the North Country
Trail Association, PO Box 311, White Cloud, MI 49349 616-689-1912

SEE MAPS ON NEXT PAGE

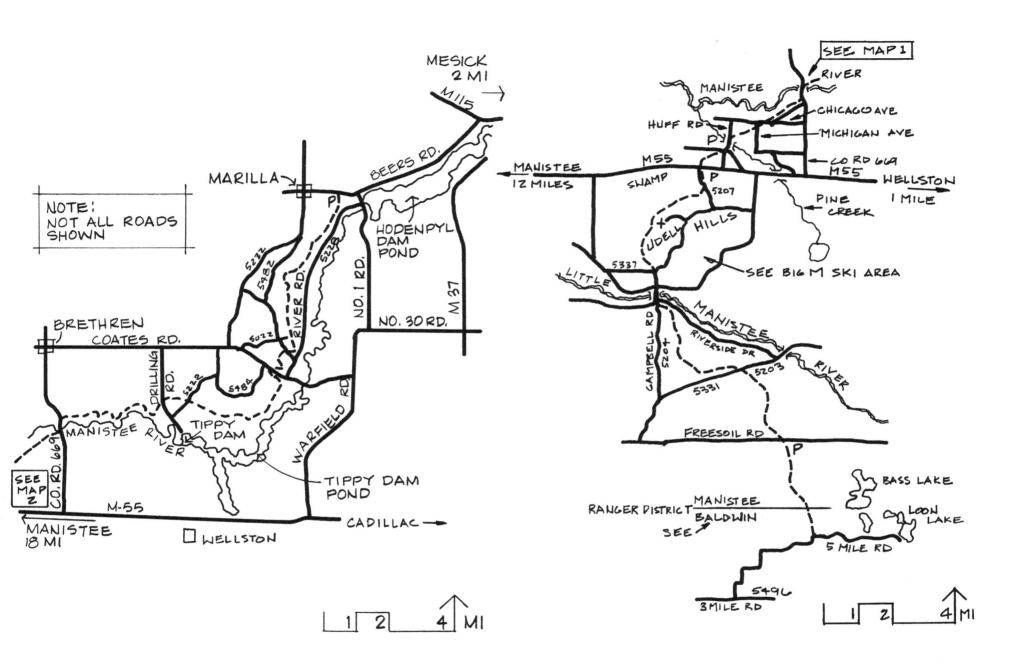

MESICK
2 MI →

M 115

BEERS RD.

MARILLA

NOTE:
NOT ALL ROADS
SHOWN

P

HODENPYL
DAM
POND

5232

5482

5228

RIVER RD.

NO. 1 RD.

NO. 30 RD.

M 37

BRETHREN
COATES RD.

5022

5484

5222

DRILLING RD.

5222

WARFIELD RD.

TIPPY
DAM

TIPPY DAM
POND

MANISTEE RIVER

CO. RD. 669

SEE MAP 2

M-55

□ WELLSTON

MANISTEE
18 MI

CADILLAC →

1 2 4 MI

NORTH COUNTRY TRAIL-
MANISTEE (MAP 1)

SEE MAP 1

MANISTEE

RIVER

CHICAGO AVE

HUFF RD.

MICHIGAN AVE

P y

M 55

CO RD 669

M 55

MANISTEE
12 MILES

SWAMP

P
5207

PINE
CREEK

WELLSTON
1 MILE →

UDELL HILLS

SEE BIG M SKI AREA

LITTLE

5337

MANISTEE

CAMPBELL RD.

5207

RIVERSIDE DR

RIVER

5203

5331

FREESOIL RD.

P

BASS LAKE

RANGER DISTRICT

MANISTEE

BALDWIN

SEE →

LOON
LAKE

5 MILE RD

5496

3 MILE RD

1 2 4 MI

NORTH COUNTRY TRAIL
MANISTEE (MAP 2)

239

Manistee Soil and Water Conservaton District
8840 Chippewa Hwy
Bear Lake, MI 49614

616-889-4761

Michigan Atlas & Gazetteer Location: 65A6

County Location: Manistee

Directions To Trailhead:
Take US31 about 5 miles north of Bear Lake to Norkonk Rd, then east 1 mile to trailhead parking lot.

Trail Type: Interpretive
Trail Distance: .75 mi   Loops: 1   Shortest: NA   Longest: .75 mi
Trail Surface: Natural
Trail Use Fee: None
Method Of Ski Trail Grooming: NA
Skiing Ability Suggested: NA
Hiking Trail Difficulty: Easy
Mountain Biking Ability Suggested: NA
Terrain: Moderate
Camping: None

A cooperative project of the Manistee Soil Conservation Service District, Michigan Youth Corp, USDA Forest Service-NE Area, State and PRivate Forestry and the DNR Forest Management Division
A 19 station interpretive trail of woodland mangement techniques.

.75 MILE LOOP

NORTH

US31 1 MILE

NORKONK RD

WOODLAND MANAGEMENT TRAIL

Cool Cross Country Ski Area
5557 N 210th Ave
Le Roy, MI 49655

616-768-4624

Michigan Atlas & Gazetteer Location: 66D34

County Location: Osceola

Directions To Trailhead:
16 miles south of Cadillac and 8 miles north of Reed City east of US131. Exit US131 at exit 162, then west t o 210th St., then north 2.5 miles to the ski area.

Trail Type: Hiking/Walking, Cross Country Skiing, Mountain Biking, Interpretive
Trail Distance: 40 km   Loops: Many   Shortest: 1 mi   Longest: 6 mi
Trail Surface: Natural
Trail Use Fee: Yes
Method Of Ski Trail Grooming: Track set with skating lanes
Skiing Ability Suggested: Novice to advanced
Hiking Trail Difficulty: Easy to moderate
Mountain Biking Ability Suggested: Novice to advanced
Terrain: Steep 15%, Hilly 25%, Moderate 40%, Flat 25%
Camping: Camping area available on site

Family owned touring center since 1976. One of the best touring centers in the state, with something for everyone. Mountain biking added several years ago. Mountain bike and ski races held annually. Lodging of all kinds from cabins to a bunk house and lakeside camping. Pro shop, rentals, restaurant, warming house, lessons, moonlight & guided tours, snowshoe rental, ice skating pond and clinics. The trails are delightful with ammenities of benches, fire pits and a portion of the trail is lighted. Trails pass through a variety of terrain and vegatation. Some trails are double tracked and all are continually well groomed. Write or call for brochure and reservations.

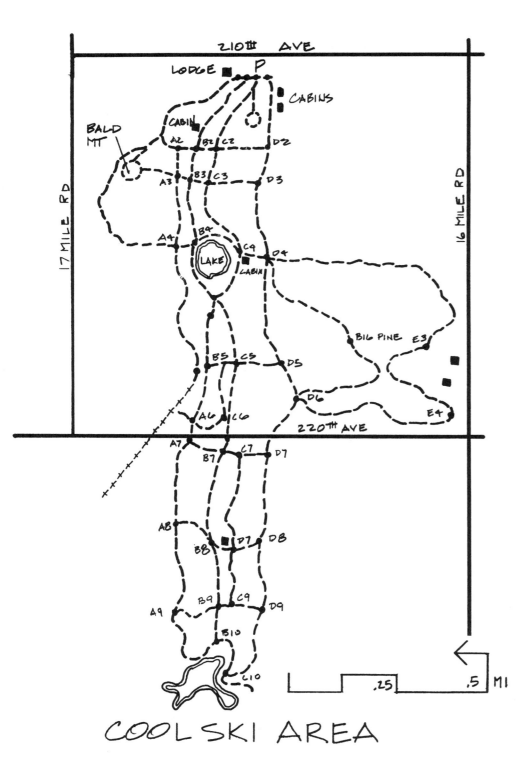

COOL SKI AREA

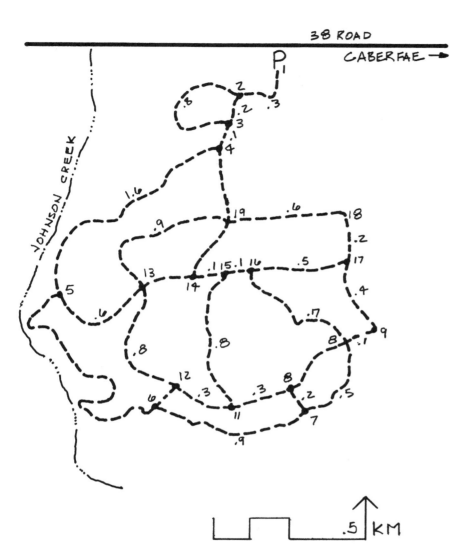

38 ROAD

CABERFAE →

JOHNSON CREEK

P

.5 KM

DISTANCES IN KILOMETERS

MACKENZIE TRAIL

Cadillac Ranger District, Huron-Manistee National Forest
1800 West M55
Cadillac, MI 49601

616-775-8539

Forest Supervisor, Huron-Manistee National Forest
421 S. Mitchell St.
Cadillac , MI 49601

616-774-2421
800-821-6263

Michigan Atlas & Gazetteer Location: 66C2

County Location: Wexford

Directions To Trailhead:
From M55/115 junction take M55 west 13 miles to Caberfae Rd., then north 2 miles to trailhead
Trailhead - About 1 mile west of the downhill ski area on 38 Rd to parking lot on the south side of the road.

Trail Type: Hiking/Walking, Cross Country Skiing, Mountain Biking
Trail Distance: 18 km   Loops: Many   Shortest: 1.8 km Longest:
Trail Surface: Natural
Trail Use Fee: None
Method Of Ski Trail Grooming: Some loops double track set
Skiing Ability Suggested: Novice to intermediate
Hiking Trail Difficulty: Easy
Mountain Biking Ability Suggested: Novice to intermediate
Terrain: Steep 3%, Hilly 15%, Moderate 50%, Flat 32%
Camping: Backcountry camping permitted along trail

Maintained by Cadillac Ranger District, Huron-Manistee National Forest
Ski shop, first aid, rentals and lodging at the adjacent Caberfae Ski Area. Interesting trails that are well worth the time to ski. Trail system is good for intermediate skiers and novice mountain bikers. Some trails are not groomed. But since this trail is very popular, usually those trails not groomed are well skied in by others.

Manistee Ranger District, Huron Manistee National Forest
1800 West M55   616-775-8539
Cadillac, MI 49601

Forest Supervisior, Huron Manistee National Forest
421 S. Mitchell St.   616-775-2421
Cadillac, MI 49601

Michigan Atlas & Gazetteer Location: 66B1

County Location: Manistee

Directions To Trailhead:
From the north: From Mesick, take M37 south 6 miles to 26 Rd., then west on 26 Rd for 3 miles to FR 5993 (stay to the right fork), then right on FR 5993 for about 1 mile to Seaton Creek Campground.
From the south: From junction of M37 and M55, follow M37 north 9 miles to 26 Rd, then left on 26 Rd and follow instructions above

Trail Type: Hiking/Walking
Trail Distance: 11 mi   Loops: NA   Shortest: NA   Longest: NA
Trail Surface: Natural
Trail Use Fee: None
Method Of Ski Trail Grooming: NA
Skiing Ability Suggested: NA
Hiking Trail Difficulty: Moderate
Mountain Biking Ability Suggested: NA
Terrain:
Camping: At north trailhead

Maintained by the Manistee Ranger District, Huron Manistee National Forest.
This hiking trail was built in 1991along the east side of the Manistee River just below Hodenpyl Dam and north of Red Bridge, connecting to the North Country Trail on the south end. The trail offers hikers the opportunity to experience the riverlands along the beautiful Manistee River, which is a nationally designated Wild and Scenic River. The trail meanders through native hardwoods and pine and low areas along the river. Overlooks are abundant for viewing wildlife along the trail. The trail is marked with gray colored diamonds. There is a 60' bridge over Stagle Creek that was built in 1992. Near the trail is fragile water fall formed by clay and gravel. Please do not climb around on the waterfall, since any activity could accelerate erosion and distroy the falls. Future plans call for a bridge across the Manistee River just below the dam, making a 26 mile loop with the North Country Trail.
THIS TRAIL IS NOT TO BE USED FOR MOUNTAIN BIKING.

MANISTEE RIVER TRAIL

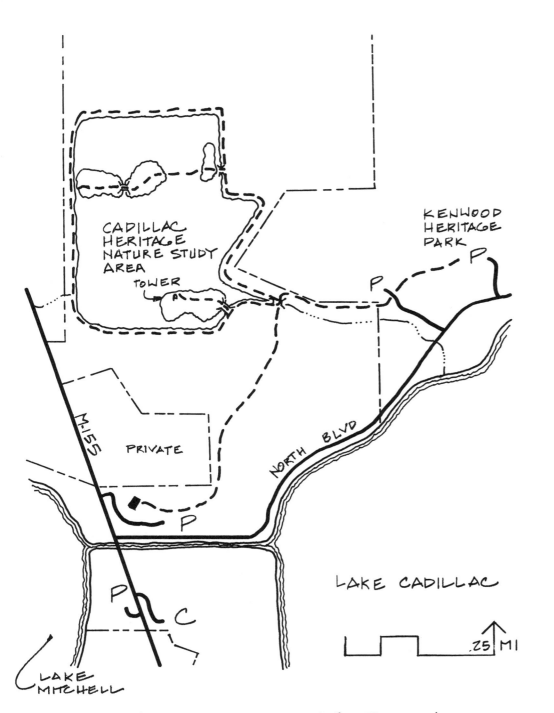

LAKE CADILLAC

.25 MI

MITCHELL STATE PARK

Mitchell State Park
6093 E. M115
Cadillac, MI 49601

616-775-7911

DNR Parks and Recreation Division

517-373-1270

Michigan Atlas & Gazetteer Location: 66B4

County Location: Wexford

Directions To Trailhead:
South trailhead - Just north of main campground on M115 between Lake Mitchell and Lake Cadillac.
East trailheads - On North Boulevard .75 mile east of M 115 and a short time farther at the Kenwood Heritage Park

Trail Type: Hiking/Walking, Cross Country Skiing, Interpretive
Trail Distance: 2.25 mi   Loops: 2   Shortest: 1.75 mi Longest: 2 mi
Trail Surface: Paved and natural
Trail Use Fee: None but the Fishing & Hunting Center has an admission fee
Method Of Ski Trail Grooming: None
Skiing Ability Suggested: Novice
Hiking Trail Difficulty: Easy
Mountain Biking Ability Suggested: NA
Terrain: 100% Flat
Camping: On site

Maintained by the DNR Parks and Recreation Divsion
Adjacent to the Johnson Hunting & Fishing Center.

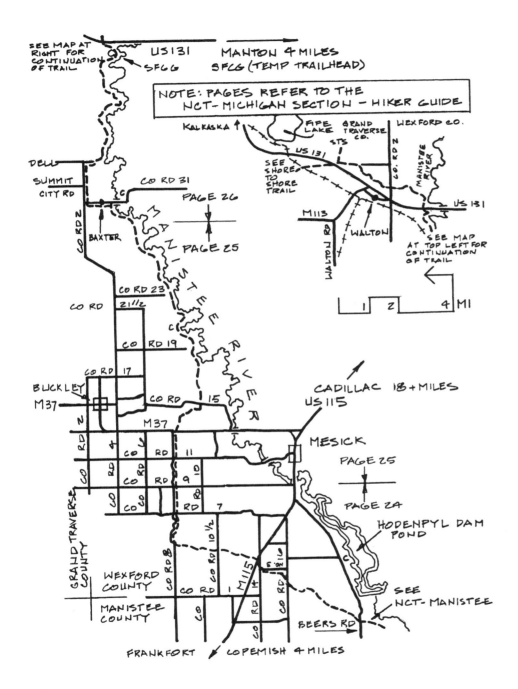

District Forest Manager, Pere Marquette State Forest
8015 Mackinaw Trail   616-775-9727
Cadillac, MI 49601

North Country Trail Association
PO Box 311   616-689-1912
White Cloud, MI 49349

Michigan Atlas & Gazetteer Location: 66AB1-5,67A4,74D34,75D4

County Location: Wexford, Grand Traverse

Directions To Trailhead:
Southwest trailhead - Beers Rd, just west of the Hodenpyl Dam east of Mesick
East trailhead - About 1.5 miles north of the M113/US131 intersection

Trail Type: Hiking/Walking, Mountain Biking
Trail Distance: 45.15   Loops: NA   Shortest: NA   Longest: NA
Trail Surface: Natural
Trail Use Fee: None
Method Of Ski Trail Grooming: NA
Skiing Ability Suggested: NA
Hiking Trail Difficulty: Moderate to difficult
Mountain Biking Ability Suggested: Intermediate to advanced
Terrain: Rolling to steep
Camping: Some campgrounds nearby

Trail located in the Pere Marquette State Forest
Trail built and maintained by members of the North Country Trail Association
Very scenic views of the Manistee River Valley and surrounding area.
Varied forest cover.
Trail follows old ORV trails, two-tracks and constructed single track trails
Contact the North Country Trail Association for the detailed map book of the
entire Michigan Section which is updated periodically. See pages 24,25 & 26
Trail marked with blue blazes
Campgrounds:
        Private campground on Hodenpyl Dam Pond at No.3 1/2 Rd
        Baxter Bridge SFCG at Co Rd 31 just south of the Manistee River
        Old US131 SFCG just west of US131 at the Manistee River

NORTH COUNTRY TRAIL-PERE MARQUETTE SF 1

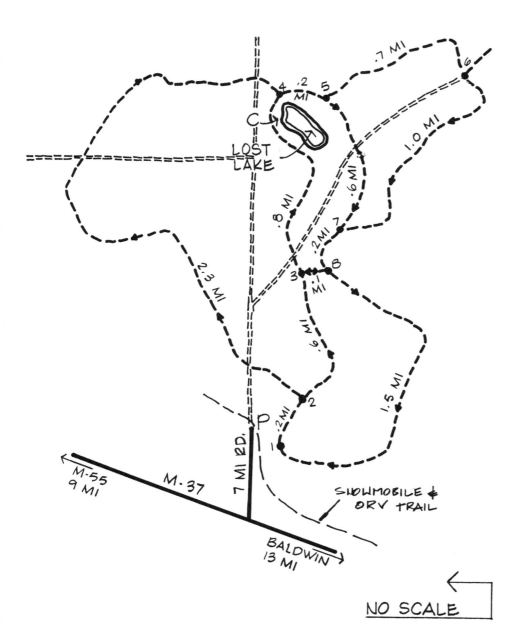

Baldwin Forest Area, Pere Marquette State Forest
Rte 2, Box 2810   616-745-4651
Baldwin, MI 49304

District Forest Manager, Pere Marquette State Forest
Rte 1, 8015 South US131   616-775-9727
Cadillac, MI 49601

Michigan Atlas & Gazetteer Location: 66D1

County Location: Clare

Directions To Trailhead:
Between Baldwin and M55 on M37 17 miles north of Baldwin and 9 miles south
of M55, then east on 7 Mile Rd   .2 mile to parking lot

Trail Type: Hiking/Walking, Cross Country Skiing, Mountain Biking
Trail Distance: 8.2 mi   Loops: 4   Shortest: 1.8 mi Longest: 6.1 mi
Trail Surface: Natural
Trail Use Fee: None
Method Of Ski Trail Grooming: None
Skiing Ability Suggested: Novice
Hiking Trail Difficulty: Easy
Mountain Biking Ability Suggested: Novice
Terrain: Steep 0%, Hilly 10%, Moderate 40%, Flat 50%
Camping: None

Maintained by the DNR Forest Management Division
The southern loops are more interesting than the northern loop that passes
through a recent clear cut area
ORV and horse trails nearby and crossing this trail system
Popular cross country ski trail.
Other contacts:
        DNR Forest Management Division Office, Lansing, 517-373-1275
        DNR Forest Management Region Office, Roscommon, 517-275-5151

PINE VALLEYS PATHWAY

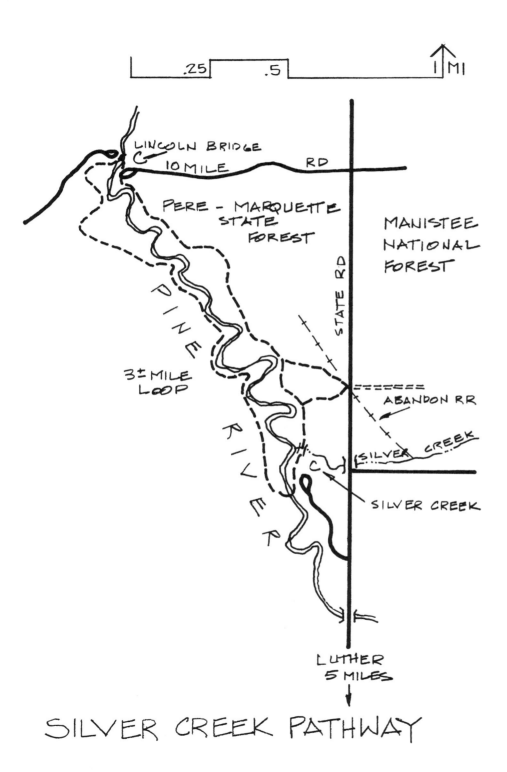

SILVER CREEK PATHWAY

Baldwin Forest Area, Pere Marquette State Forest
Rte 2, Box 2810   616-745-4651
Baldwin, MI 49304

District Forest Manager, Pere Marquette State Forest
8015 Mackinaw Trail   616-775-9727
Cadillac, MI 49601

Michigan Atlas & Gazetteer Location: 66C2

County Location: Lake

Directions To Trailhead:
5.5 miles north of Luther via State Rd to SFCG

Trail Type: Hiking/Walking, Cross Country Skiing, Mountain Biking
Trail Distance: 3+ mi   Loops: 1   Shortest: NA   Longest: 3+ mi
Trail Surface: Natural
Trail Use Fee: None
Method Of Ski Trail Grooming: None
Skiing Ability Suggested: Novice
Hiking Trail Difficulty: Easy
Mountain Biking Ability Suggested: Novice
Terrain: Steep 0%, Hilly 0%, Moderate 40%, Flat 60%
Camping: At Lincoln Bridge and Silver Creek SFCG's

Maintained by the DNR Forest Management Division
Trail loops both sides of Silver Creek with a SFCG at the half way point.

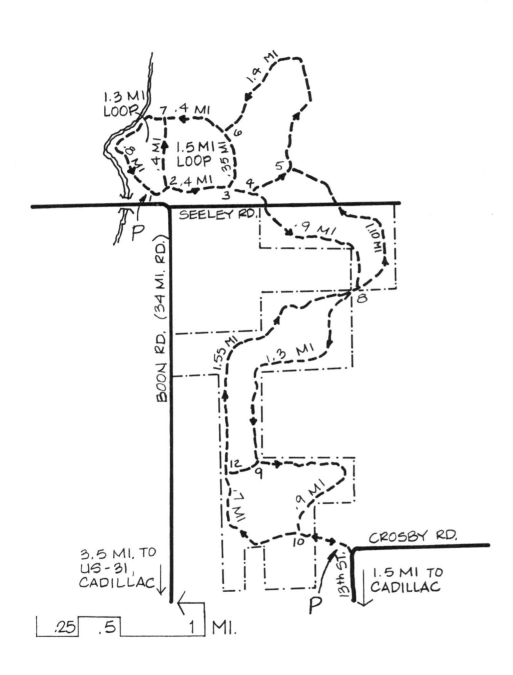

Kalkaska Forest Area, Pere Marquette State Forest
2089 N. Birch   616-258-2711
Kalkaska, MI 49464

District Forest Manager, Pere Marquette State Forest
Rte 1, 8015 South US131   616-775-9727
Cadillac, MI 49601

Michigan Atlas & Gazetteer Location: 67B5

County Location: Wexford

Directions To Trailhead:
Trailhead - North from Cadillac on US131, then right on 13th St. for 1.5 miles to the point where the road turns south (at playground) Trailhead at edge of the playground.
Trailhead - North from Cadillac on US131, then right on 34 Mile Rd.(Boon Rd.) 3.5 miles to Seeley Rd (the road turns north) and the parking lot will be found just past the turn on the right.

Trail Type: Hiking/Walking, Cross Country Skiing, Mountain Biking
Trail Distance: 11.3 mi   Loops: 6   Shortest: 1.2 mi Longest: 9.75 mi
Trail Surface: Natural
Trail Use Fee: None
Method Of Ski Trail Grooming: Track set
Skiing Ability Suggested: Novice to intermediate
Hiking Trail Difficulty: Easy
Mountain Biking Ability Suggested: Novice
Terrain: Steep 0%, Hilly 10%, Moderate 60%, Flat 30%
Camping: Campgrounds in the Cadillac area

Maintained by the DNR Forest Management Division
The west loops are more challenging then the east loops. The east loops off Boon Rd are over more level terrain. Parking for access to the trailhead for the west loops is on 13th St is at the Wexford-Missaukee Intermediate School District building. The trailhead is at the edge of the playground.
A rather good ski trail.   A very enjoyable trail that I usually try to ski every year.
Other contacts:
        DNR Forest Management Division Office, Lansing, 517-373-1275
        DNR Forest Management Region Office, Roscommon, 517-275-5151

CADILLAC PATHWAY

City of Cadillac
200 Lake St
Cadillac, MI 49601

616-775-0181

Michigan Atlas & Gazetteer Location: 67C4

County Location: Wexford

Directions To Trailhead:
Along Lake Cadillac on the northeast shore in Cadillac

Trail Type: Hiking/Walking
Trail Distance: 1 mi   Loops: NA   Shortest: NA   Longest: NA
Trail Surface: Paved
Trail Use Fee: None
Method Of Ski Trail Grooming: NA
Skiing Ability Suggested: NA
Hiking Trail Difficulty: Easy
Mountain Biking Ability Suggested: NA
Terrain: 100% Flat
Camping: Campground nearby

Owned by the City of Cadillac
The trail follows the shoreline.

CADILLAC

CASS ST

P

HARRIS ST

LAKE ST

CHESTNUT ST.

P

LAKE CADILLAC

SCALE NOT KNOWN

P

McKELLOP WALKWAY

McGuires Resort
7880 Mackinaw Trail
Cadillac, MI 49601

616-775-9947
800-632-7302

NO MAP

Michigan Atlas & Gazetteer Location: 67C4

County Location: Wexford

Directions To Trailhead:
Southeast of Cadillac via US131 and west on the Mackinaw Trail

Trail Type: Cross Country Skiing
Trail Distance: 6 km   Loops: 2   Shortest: 3 km   Longest: 3 km
Trail Surface: Natural
Trail Use Fee: None
Method Of Ski Trail Grooming: Track set
Skiing Ability Suggested: Novice
Hiking Trail Difficulty: NA
Mountain Biking Ability Suggested: NA
Terrain: Steep 0%, Hilly 0%, Moderate 30%, Flat 70%
Camping: Campground nearby

Private 4 season resort with golf course.
Ski trails on a golf course.

SUNRISE LAKE

P

15 MILE RD

M115

15 MI→

FOREST TRAIL

P

BOG

SCALE NOT KNOWN

OSCEOLA PATHWAY

Osceola Pathway

Baldwin Forest Area, Pere Marquette State Forest
Rte 2, Box 2810
Baldwin, MI 49304   616-745-4651

District Forest Manager, Pere Marquette State Forest
8015 Mackinaw Trail   616-775-9727
Cadillac, MI 49601

Michigan Atlas & Gazetteer Location: 67D5

County Location: Osceola

Directions To Trailhead:
6 miles east of LeRoy via Sunrise Lake Rd and 15 Mile Rd south Cadillac at Sunrise Lake SFCG

Trail Type: Hiking/Walking
Trail Distance: .5 mi   Loops: 1   Shortest: Longest: .5 mi
Trail Surface: Natural
Trail Use Fee: None
Method Of Ski Trail Grooming: NA
Skiing Ability Suggested: NA
Hiking Trail Difficulty: Easy
Mountain Biking Ability Suggested: NA
Terrain:
Camping: Campground at trailhead

Maintained by the DNR Forest Management Divsion

Michigan Trail Riders Association Inc
Chamber of Commerce   616-947-5075
Traverse City, MI 49684

DNR Forest Management Division, Recreation and Trails Section
PO Box 30452   517-373-9483
Lansing, MI 48909

Michigan Atlas & Gazetteer Location: 67,70,71,73,74,75,76,77,78

County Location: Many

Directions To Trailhead:
Extends from Empire to Oscoda with spurs north from Frederick to M33 and south from Mayfield to Cadillac

Trail Type: Hiking/Walking, Mountain Biking
Trail Distance: 302 mi   Loops: NA   Shortest: NA   Longest: NA
Trail Surface: Natural with lots of sand
Trail Use Fee: None
Method Of Ski Trail Grooming: NA
Skiing Ability Suggested: NA
Hiking Trail Difficulty: Easy to difficult
Mountain Biking Ability Suggested: Intermediate
Terrain: Steep 2%, Hilly 10%, Moderate 50%, Flat 38%
Camping: Campgounds along trail(see map)

Maintained by the DNR Forest Management and Parks and Recreation Division and the Michigan Trail Riders Association(horseback riders user group). Connects with sections maintained by the Huron-Manistee National Forest in the Oscoda to Mio area. See other listings for more detail. Used heavily by horseback riders. Some sections may not be suitable for hiking because of extensive loose sand. Other trails near or along this trail: Mackinaw Trail, Mason Tract Pathway, Muncie Lakes Pathway Wakeley Lake Non-Motorized Area, Corsair Trail, Highbanks Trail, Sand Lakes Quiet Area and Loud Creek Pathway. This is a point to point trail across the state from Lake Michigan to   Lake Huron with spurs north and south. Part used for the North Country Trail.
Detailed trail maps available from the Michigan Trail Riders Association, 1650 Ormond Rd, White Lake, MI 48383-2344. Memberships also available.

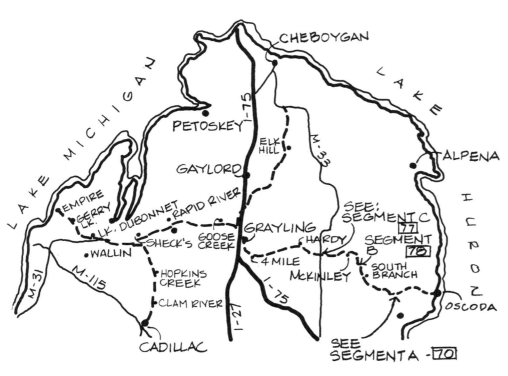

NOTE:
SEE SEGMENTS IN MORE
DETAIL ELSEWHERE IN
ATLAS.

• CAMGROUNDS

SHORE TO SHORE TRAIL

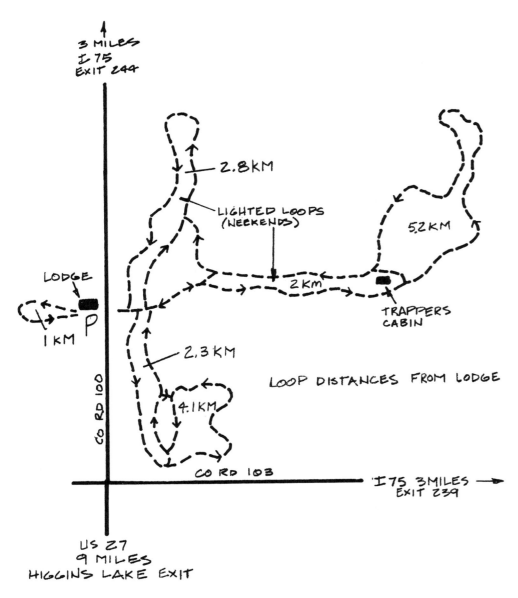

Cross Country Ski Headquarters
9435 Co Rd 100, Higgins Lake
Roscommon, MI 48653

517-821-6661

Michigan Atlas & Gazetteer Location: 68A3

County Location: Roscommon

Directions To Trailhead:
On the east side of Higgins Lake on Co Rd 100 From NB I75 take exit 239, turn left over overpass, then right on Co Rd 103. Continue 3.5 miles to stop and blinker, then right .5 mile to shop From US27 take Higgins Lake Rd. exit, go towards Higgins Lake 3.5 miles past the South Park(9.1 miles from US27)

Trail Type: Hiking/Walking, Cross Country Skiing, Interpretive
Trail Distance: 17.4 km   Loops: 8   Shortest: 1 km   Longest: 8 km
Trail Surface: Natural
Trail Use Fee: None, but donations accepted*
Method Of Ski Trail Grooming: Track set with skating lanes
Skiing Ability Suggested: Novice to advanced
Hiking Trail Difficulty: Easy
Mountain Biking Ability Suggested: NA
Terrain: Steep 0% Hilly 15%, Moderate 40%, Flat 45%
Camping: None

Privately operated touring center.
Ski shop, lodge with sundeck, snack bar and restrooms.
Owners, Bob and Lynne Frye are very knowledgeable in the proper selection of ski equipment for every level of skier.
Trails are constantly groomed very well.
Lighted trail.
Races and events held throughout the ski season.
Newsletter available.

CROSS COUNTRY SKI HEADQUARTERS

Roscommon Forest Area, Au Sable State Forest
Box 158   517-422-5522
Houghton Lake Heights, MI 48630

District Forest Manager, Au Sable State Forest
1919 S. Mt. Tom Rd.   517-826-3211
Mio, MI 48647

Michigan Atlas & Gazetteer Location: 68C3

County Location: Roscommon

Directions To Trailhead:
7 miles south of M55 (Houghton Lake) on Reserve Rd. (Co Rd 400)
(McDonalds's is on the corner of M55 and Reserve Rd.) Trailhead is not well
marked.

Trail Type: Hiking/Walking, Cross Country Skiing, Mountain Biking
Trail Distance: 3 mi   Loops: 1   Shortest: NA   Longest: 1 mi
Trail Surface: Natrual
Trail Use Fee: None
Method Of Ski Trail Grooming: None
Skiing Ability Suggested: Intermediate to advanced
Hiking Trail Difficulty: Moderate to difficult
Mountain Biking Ability Suggested: Novice
Terrain: Very hilly
Camping: None

Maintained by the DNR Forest Management Division
Other contacts:
         DNR Forest Manggement Division Office, Lansing, 517-373-1275
         DNR Forest Management Region Office, Roscommon, 517-275-5151

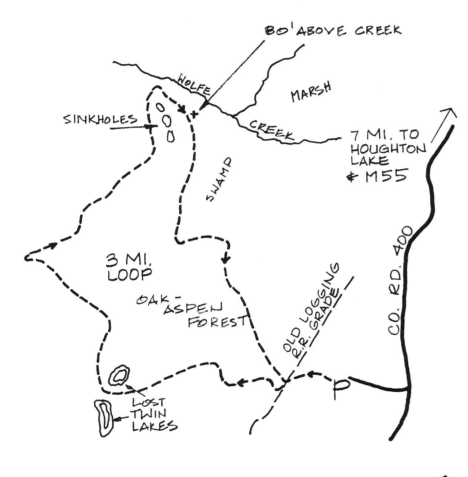

LOST TWIN LAKES PATHWAY

South Higgins Lake State Park
106 State Park Drive
Roscommon , MI 48653

517-821-6374

DNR Parks and Recreation Division

517-373-1270

Michigan Atlas & Gazetteer Location: 68A3

County Location: Roscommon

Directions To Trailhead:
On the south end of Higgins Lake on Co Rd 100

Trail Type: Hiking/Walking, Cross Country Skiing, Mountain Biking
Trail Distance: 5.8 mi   Loops: 3   Shortest: 2 mi   Longest: 5.5 mi
Trail Surface: Natural
Trail Use Fee: None, but vehicle entry fee required
Method Of Ski Trail Grooming: Track set
Skiing Ability Suggested: Novice to intermediate
Hiking Trail Difficulty: Easy
Mountain Biking Ability Suggested: Novice
Terrain: Steep 0%, Hilly 0%, Moderate 20%, Flat 80%
Camping: Campground in the park open throughout the year

Maintained by the DNR Parks and Recreation Division
Trails designed for skiing
Rentals available from nearby private ski shops.

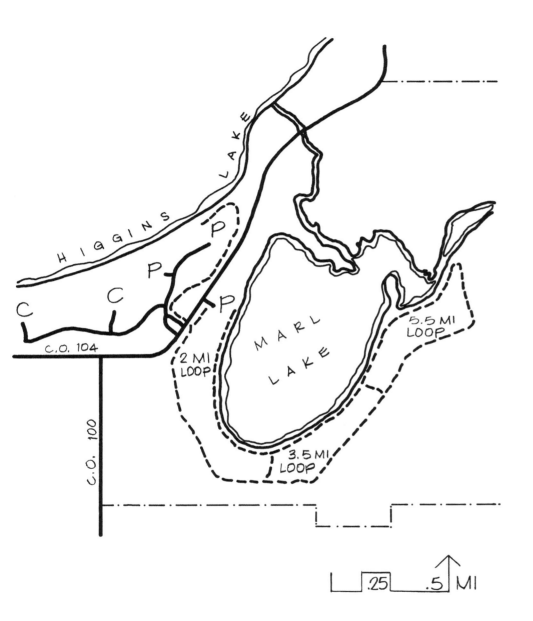

HIGGINS LAKE

MARL LAKE

C.O. 104

C.O. 100

2 MI LOOP

3.5 MI LOOP

5.5 MI LOOP

.25   .5 MI

SOUTH HIGGINS LAKE
STATE PARK

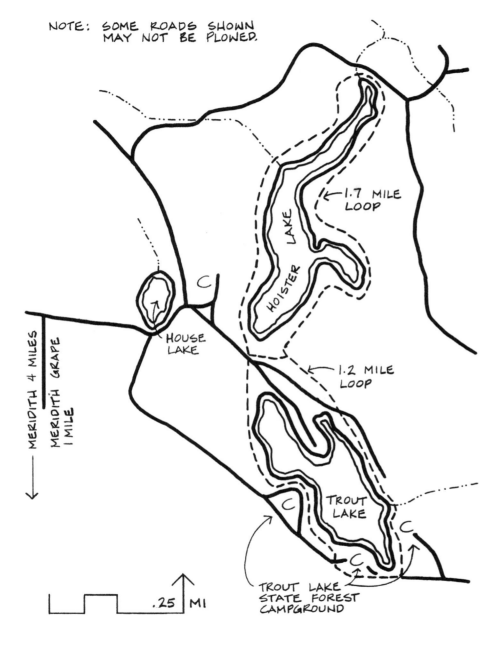

NOTE: SOME ROADS SHOWN MAY NOT BE PLOWED.

1.7 MILE LOOP

HOISTER LAKE

HOUSE LAKE

MERIDITH 4 MILES

MERIDITH GRAPE 1 MILE

1.2 MILE LOOP

TROUT LAKE

TROUT LAKE STATE FOREST CAMPGROUND

.25 | MI

TROUT LAKE PATHWAY

Gladwin Forest Area, Au Sable State Forest
801 North Silverleaf   517-426-9205
Gladwin, MI 48624

District Forest Manager, Au Sable State Forest
191 S. Mt. Tom Rd., PO Box 939   517-826-3211
Mio, MI 48647

Michigan Atlas & Gazetteer Location: 68C4,69C4

County Location: Gladwin

Directions To Trailhead:
In the NW corner of Gladwin County, 2 miles east of Meridith 1 mile north of M18 off the Meridith Grade

Trail Type: Hiking/Walking, Cross Country Skiing, Mountain Biking
Trail Distance: 2.7 mi   Loops: 2   Shortest: 1.2 mi Longest: 1.7 mi
Trail Surface: Natural
Trail Use Fee: None
Method Of Ski Trail Grooming: None
Skiing Ability Suggested: Novice
Hiking Trail Difficulty: Easy
Mountain Biking Ability Suggested: Novice
Terrain: 100% Flat
Camping: Available along the trail

Maintained by the DNR Forest Management Division
A nice easy day hike for families.
The trail connects several state forest campgrounds.

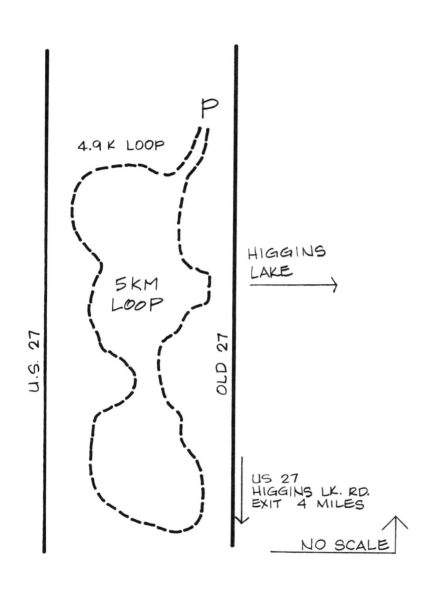

4.9 K LOOP

P

HIGGINS LAKE →

5 KM LOOP

U.S. 27

OLD 27

US 27 HIGGINS LK. RD. EXIT 4 MILES

NO SCALE

WEST HIGGINS LAKE TRAIL

Au Sable Valley Nordic Ski Club

Cross Country Ski Headquarters
9435 Co Rd 100, Higgins Lake
Roscommon, MI 48653

517-821-6661

Michigan Atlas & Gazetteer Location: 68A2

County Location: Roscommon

Directions To Trailhead:
Exit US27 northbound at Higgins Lake Rd. (South Higgins Lake State Park), then east .25 mile to Old 27, then north about 4 miles to a parking lot on the west side of the road .

Trail Type: Cross Country Skiing
Trail Distance: 3 mi   Loops: 1   Shortest: 3mi   Longest: 3 mi
Trail Surface: Natural
Trail Use Fee: Donation accepted
Method Of Ski Trail Grooming: Track set as needed
Skiing Ability Suggested: Novice to intermediate
Hiking Trail Difficulty: NA
Mountain Biking Ability Suggested: NA
Terrain: Steep 0%, Hilly 15%, Moderate 40%, Flat 45%
Camping: None

Developed and maintained by the Au Sable Valley Nordic Ski Club
Trail maintained strictly on a volunteer basis with volunteer equipment and labor. Only gas and oil are paid for by the club from memberships, donations and profits from the Beaver Creek Challenge Ski Race held the 1st Sunday in February at the nearby North Higgins Lake State Park.

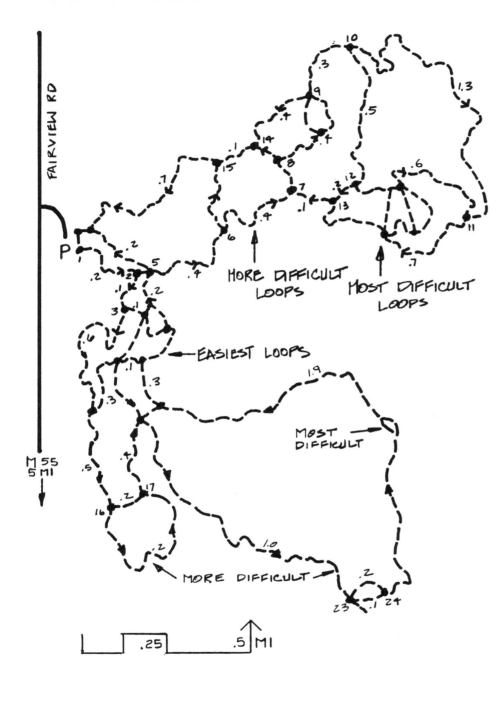

West Branch Area Chamber of Commerce
422 W. Houghton Ave   517-345-2821
West Branch, MI 48661

Roscommon Forest Area, Au Sable State Forest
Box 218, 8717 N. Roscommon Rd.   517-275-5151
Roscommon , MI 48653

Michigan Atlas & Gazetteer Location: 69B7

County Location: Ogemaw

Directions To Trailhead:
5.5 miles north of West Branch on Fairview Rd. (F7) Use exit 212 off I-75

Trail Type: Hiking/Walking, Cross Country Skiing, Mountain Biking
Trail Distance: 13.6 mi   Loops: 12   Shortest: .5 mi   Longest: 5 mi
Trail Surface: Natural
Trail Use Fee: None, but donations accepted
Method Of Ski Trail Grooming: Track set weekly
Skiing Ability Suggested: Intermediate to advanced
Hiking Trail Difficulty: Moderate
Mountain Biking Ability Suggested: Intermediate
Terrain: Hilly
Camping: Available in the area seasonally

Developed by the West Branch Kiwanis and Optimist Clubs, Michigan Youth
Corps, DNR, Ogemaw Ski Council and many local volunteers
Maintained by the Ogemaw Ski Council.
Well designed, marked and groomed trail system.
Good trail for mountain biking.
Rentals available in West Branch.

OGEMAW HILLS PATHWAY

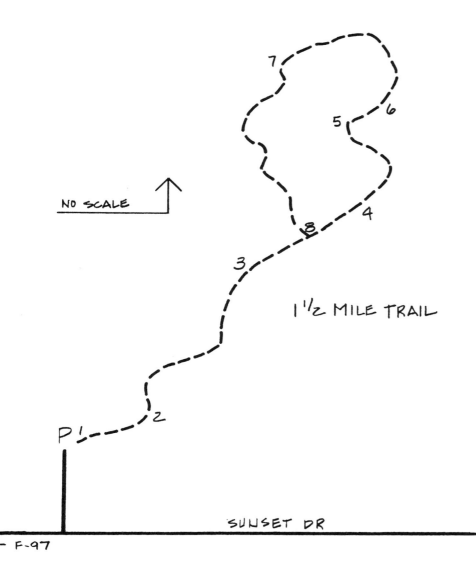

NO SCALE

1½ MILE TRAIL

7

5   6

8   4

3

2

P 1

SUNSET DR

F-97

Roscommon Forest Area, Au Sable State Forest
Box 218   616-275-8512
Roscommon, MI 48653

District Forest Manger, Au Sable State Forest
191 S. Mt. Tom, PO Box 939   517-826-3211
Mio, MI 48947

Michigan Atlas & Gazetteer Location: 69A5

County Location: Roscommon

Directions To Trailhead:
8 miles north of St. Helen on Co Rd F97 then east on Sunset Drive about 1 mile
to trailhead

Trail Type: Hiking/Walking, Interpretive
Trail Distance: 1.5 mi   Loops: 1   Shortest: NA   Longest: 1.5 mi
Trail Surface: Natural
Trail Use Fee: None
Method Of Ski Trail Grooming: NA
Skiing Ability Suggested: NA
Hiking Trail Difficulty: Easy
Mountain Biking Ability Suggested: NA
Terrain: 100% Flat
Camping: None

Maintained by the DNR Forest Management Division
Site of former largest Red Pine in Michigan(died around 1982)
8 station interpretative trail, Brochure available from Area office only

RED PINE NATURAL AREA   259

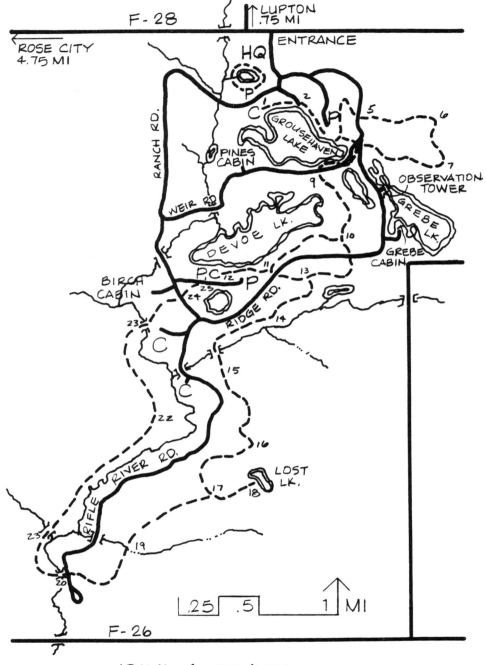

Rifle River Recreation Area
2550 East Rose City Rd
Lupton, MI 48635

517-437-2258

DNR Parks and Recreation Division

517-373-1270
517-322-1300

Michigan Atlas & Gazetteer Location: 70AB12

County Location: Ogemaw

Directions To Trailhead:
4.75 miles east of Rose City on F28 (Rose City Rd)

Trail Type: Hiking/Walking, Cross Country Skiing, Mountain Biking, Interpretive
Trail Distance: 13. 5 mi   Loops: 2   Shortest: Longest: 13.5 mi
Trail Surface: Natural
Trail Use Fee: None, but vehicle entry fee required
Method Of Ski Trail Grooming: None
Skiing Ability Suggested: Novice
Hiking Trail Difficulty: Easy to moderate
Mountain Biking Ability Suggested: Novice
Terrain: Steep 0%, Hilly 25%, Moderate 25%, Flat 50%
Camping: Campground in recreation area

Maintained by the DNR Parks and Recreation Division
Extensive trail system.
Trails south of Ridge Rd(south half of the park) are flat. Trails east of
Grousenhaven and Devoe Lake are hilly.
Excellent for wildlife observations

RIFLE RIVER RECREATION AREA

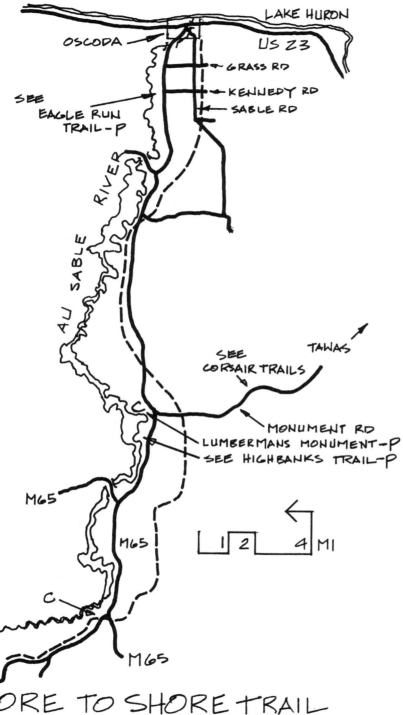

SHORE TO SHORE TRAIL SEGMENT A

Tawas Ranger District, Huron-Manistee National Forest
326 Newman St.   517-362-4477
East Tawas, MI 48730

Forest Supervisor, Huron-Manistee National Forest
421 S. Mitchell St.   616-775-2421
Cadillac, MI 49601   800-999-7677

Michigan Atlas & Gazetteer Location: 70A34, 71A567, 78D3

County Location: Iosco

Directions To Trailhead:
East trailhead - South edge of Au Sable (adjacent to the south side of Oscoda).
West trailhead - Iosco/ Alcona county line on Curtisville Rd. About 2.5 north of
the South Branch Trail Camp.

Trail Type: Hiking/Walking, Mountain Biking
Trail Distance: 45 mi   Loops: No   Shortest: NA   Longest: NA
Trail Surface: Natural
Trail Use Fee: None
Method Of Ski Trail Grooming: None
Skiing Ability Suggested: NA
Hiking Trail Difficulty: Easy to moderate
Mountain Biking Ability Suggested: Novice but sand present
Terrain: Steep 0%, Hilly 0%, Moderate 50%, Flat 50%
Camping: Campgrounds along the trail

Maintained by the Tawas Ranger District, Huron-Manistee National Forest
Primarily a equestrian trail.
Campgrounds at Rollways and South Branch with wilderness camping pemitted
more than 200' from the trail.
Drinking water available at the campgrounds and Rollways Picnic Areas. For
detailed maps of the entire trail contact: Michigan Trail Riders Association, 1650
Ormond Rd, White Lake, MI 48383
Mountain biking is difficult because of loose sand conditions on much of the trail.

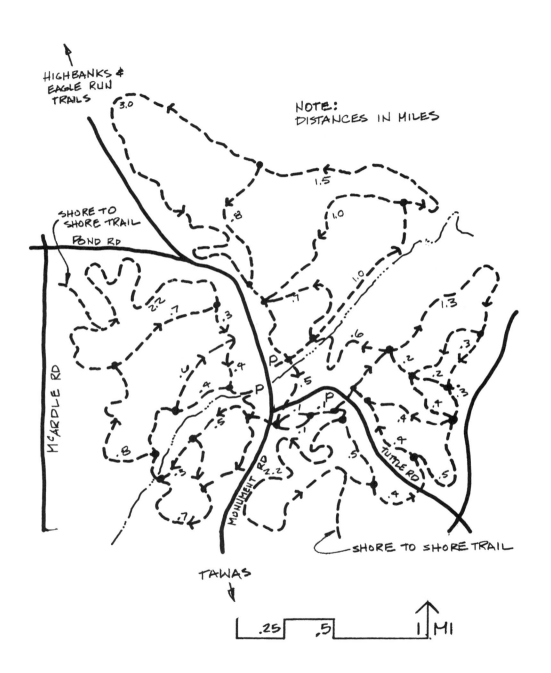

Corsair Trail Council
PO Box 608
Tawas City, MI 48763

800-558-2927
517-362-2001

Tawas Ranger District, Huron-Manistee National Forest
Federal Building
East Tawas, MI 48730

517-362-4477

Michigan Atlas & Gazetteer Location: 71A5

County Location: Iosco

Directions To Trailhead:
From M55 & US23 intersection take M55 west about .8 mile to Wilbur Rd, then north on Wilbur Rd to 1.2 miles to Monument Rd, then NW on Monument Rd about 7 miles to trails. Trailheads on both sides of the road for the 3 systems, Corsair, Wright's Lake and Silver Valley .

Trail Type: Hiking/Walking, Cross Country Skiing, Interpretive
Trail Distance: 26.2 mi   Loops: 19   Shortest: 1.3 mi Longest: 7.2 mi
Trail Surface: Natural
Trail Use Fee: None
Method Of Ski Trail Grooming: Track set with 10 km for skating
Skiing Ability Suggested: Novice to advanced
Hiking Trail Difficulty: Easy to moderate
Mountain Biking Ability Suggested: NA
Terrain: Steep 15%, Hilly 35%, Moderate 30%, Flat 20%
Camping: Many campgrounds in the general area

Developed by the local community in cooperation with the Huron-Manistee National Forest
A well goomed excellent trail system for all skill levels.
The Silver Valley section is the site of an old toboggan and alpine ski area of the 1940's. Site of the annual Silver Creek Challenge citizen race held the last Saturday of January each year.
Excellent lodging packages are available from the local motels. Ski rentals and ski equipment are available from Nordic Sports in East Tawas at 218 West Bay St., 517-362-2001.
Write or call the tourist bureau for lodging information and reservations
Many other trails in the area.

CORSAIR TRAILS

Tawas Ranger District, Huron-Manistee National Forest
326 Newman St
East Tawas, MI 48730

517-362-4477

Oscoda Chamber of Commerce
100 W Michigan
Oscoda, MI 48750

800-235-4625

Michigan Atlas & Gazetteer Location: 71A6

County Location: Iosco

Directions To Trailhead:
NW from East Tawas on Monument Rd. to River Rd., then east 13 miles, or west from Oscoda 2 1/2 miles on River Rd. to the trail.

Trail Type: Hiking/Walking, Cross Country Skiing, Mountain Biking
Trail Distance: 7 mi   Loops: 4   Shortest: 2.5 mi Longest: 5 mi
Trail Surface: Natural
Trail Use Fee: None
Method Of Ski Trail Grooming: Track set
Skiing Ability Suggested: Novice
Hiking Trail Difficulty: Easy
Mountain Biking Ability Suggested: Novice
Terrain: 100% Flat
Camping: Campgrounds nearby

Maintained by the Huron-Manistee National Forest with community support
Scenic views of the Au Sable River from the trail
Local ski shop - Nordic Sports Ski Shop, 218 West Bay St., East Tawas, 362-2001
For information contact the Oscoda Chamber of Commerce.

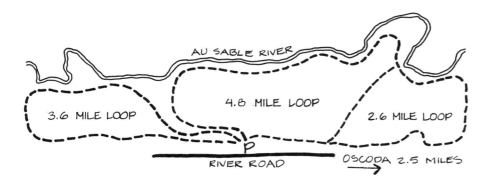

AU SABLE RIVER

4.8 MILE LOOP

3.6 MILE LOOP

2.6 MILE LOOP

RIVER ROAD

OSCODA 2.5 MILES

NO SCALE

EAGLE RUN

Corsair Ski Council
PO Box 608
Tawas City , MI 48763

800-558-2927
517-362-2001

Tawas Ranger District, Huron-Manistee National Forest
Federal Building
East Tawas , MI 48730

517-362-4477

Michigan Atlas & Gazetteer Location: 71A45

County Location: Iosco

Directions To Trailhead:
Take Monument Rd. past the Corsair Trails north until it ends at River Rd. The trailhead is in the parking lot directly across from that intersection.

Trail Type: Hiking/Walking, Cross Country Skiing, Interpretive
Trail Distance: 10 km   Loops: NA   Shortest: NA   Longest: NA
Trail Surface: Natural
Trail Use Fee: None
Method Of Ski Trail Grooming: None
Skiing Ability Suggested: Novice to intermediate
Hiking Trail Difficulty: Easy to moderate
Mountain Biking Ability Suggested: NA
Terrain: Steep 0%, Hilly 0%, Moderate 30%, Flat 70%
Camping: None

Developed by the local community in cooperation with the Huron-Manistee National Forest The trail is rather flat but the scenery of the Au Sable River is outstanding
The Lumbermans Monument is located at the trailhead. Recently renovated the monument now as a pavilion, interpretive center and historical displays and bathrooms. A deck over the "Highbanks" 120' above the river affords an outstanding view of the area.
largo Springs (the west end of the trail) has been completely renovated. Cantlevered deck over the Highbanks provides another view of the AuSable River valley.
River Road, the road that parallels the ski trail is designated a National Scenic Byway.

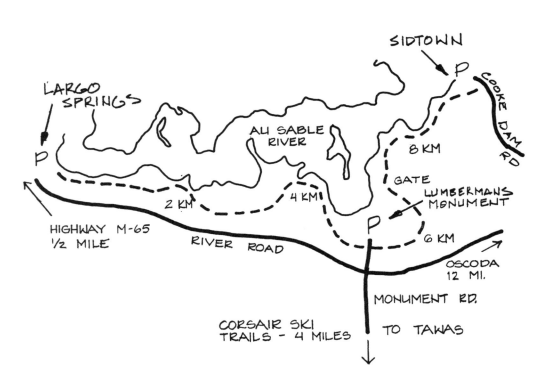

HIGHBANKS TRAIL

TAWAS BAY

TAWAS
6 MILES
US 23

HQ

C

COAST
GUARD

P P
P P
P

BEACH

LAKE
HURON

SANDY
HOOK
NATURE
TRAIL

Tawas Point State Park
686 Tawas Beach Rd
East Tawas, MI 48730

517-362-5041

DNR Parks and Recreation Division

517-373-1270
517-275-5151

Michigan Atlas & Gazetteer Location: 71B6

County Location: Iosco

Directions To Trailhead:
Trailhead - Picnic area located 2.5 miles east of US23 on Tawas Beach Rd

Trail Type: Interpretive
Trail Distance: 1.5 mi   Loops: 1   Shortest: NA   Longest: 1.5 mi
Trail Surface: Natural
Trail Use Fee: None, but vehicle entry permit required
Method Of Ski Trail Grooming: NA
Skiing Ability Suggested: NA
Hiking Trail Difficulty: NA
Mountain Biking Ability Suggested: NA
Terrain: 100% Flat
Camping: On site

Maintained by the DNR Parks and Recreation Division
The Sandy Hook Nature Trail has 21 stations. A trail guide is available.

.25   .5 MI

TAWAS POINT STATE PARK

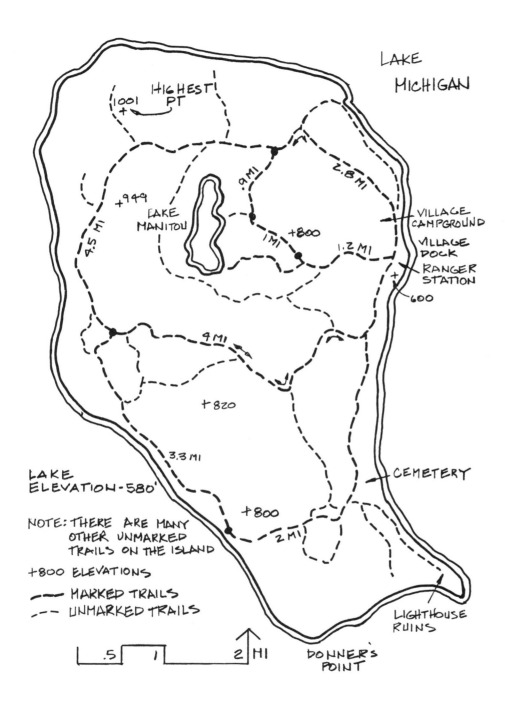

LAKE
MICHIGAN

HIGHEST PT
1001 +

+949

LAKE MANITOU

4.5 MI

.9 MI

2.8 MI

1 MI   +800

1.2 MI

VILLAGE CAMPGROUND

VILLAGE DOCK

RANGER STATION

600

9 MI

+820

3.3 MI

LAKE ELEVATION - 580'

+800

2 MI

CEMETERY

NOTE: THERE ARE MANY OTHER UNMARKED TRAILS ON THE ISLAND

+800 ELEVATIONS

- - - MARKED TRAILS
- -- UNMARKED TRAILS

.5   1   2 MI

DONNER'S POINT

LIGHTHOUSE RUINS

NORTH MANITOU ISLAND

Sleeping Bear Dunes National Lakeshore
PO Box 277, 9922 Front St. (M72)   616-326-5134
Empire, MI 49630

Michigan Atlas & Gazetteer Location: 72A2

County Location: Leelanau

Directions To Trailhead:
In Lake Michigan, west of Leland, 12 miles offshore

Trail Type: Hiking/Walking, Interpretive
Trail Distance: 50+ mi   Loops: Many   Shortest: Longest:
Trail Surface: Natural
Trail Use Fee: None
Method Of Ski Trail Grooming: NA
Skiing Ability Suggested: NA
Hiking Trail Difficulty: Easy to difficult
Mountain Biking Ability Suggested: NA
Terrain: Steep 0%, Hilly 5%, Moderate 40%, Flat 55%
Camping: One developed campground with wilderness camping permitted

Maintained by Sleeping Bear Dunes National Lakeshore
A wilderness area with very minimal developed facilities. Recommended for campers with some backcountry experience. Season 5/30 to 11/15 Since there are a minimum of marked trails and available maps do not show all trails and roads, backcountry hiking experience is required. A very unique island that is worth the effort to reach. This island is rich in history of the late 1800's to the 1940's. All campers must register at the Ranger Station on the island There is a special deer hunt from 10/15 - 11/15 Write for brochure and more detailed map needed for hiking. Low impact camping methods are required to protect this fragile environment. Cooking must be done on portable stoves. Daily ferry service is available from Leland at 10am returning to Leland by 5pm. Call 616-256-9061 or 616-271-4217 for information and reservations.

Sleeping Bear Dunes National Lakeshore
PO Box 277, 9922 Front St.(M72)   616-326-5134
Empire, MI 49630

Michigan Atlas & Gazetteer Location: 72B1

County Location: Leelanau

Directions To Trailhead:
In Lake Michigan, west of Leland, 17 miles off shore

Trail Type: Hiking/Walking, Interpretive
Trail Distance: 15 mi   Loops: Many   Shortest: Longest:
Trail Surface: Gravel roads and natural
Trail Use Fee: None
Method Of Ski Trail Grooming: NA
Skiing Ability Suggested: NA
Hiking Trail Difficulty: Easy to moderate
Mountain Biking Ability Suggested: NA
Terrain: Steep 0%, Hilly 0%, Moderate 20%, Flat 80%
Camping: Some campgrounds on the island with designated site camping

Maintained by the Sleeping Bear Dunes National Lakeshore
Two track roads are used for hiking trails, as well as many miles of foot paths
that form a network that reaches every corner of the island. A very unique island
with a very fragile ecosystem that should be experienced with great care.
Outstanding spring wildflower displays. All campers must register at the Ranger
Station located at the Visitor Center .
Low impact camping methods are required to protect this fragile enviornment..
Season - Memorial Day through 10/15. Daily ferry service available from Leland
at 10am returning back to Leland by 5:30pm call 616-256-9061 for information
and reservations.

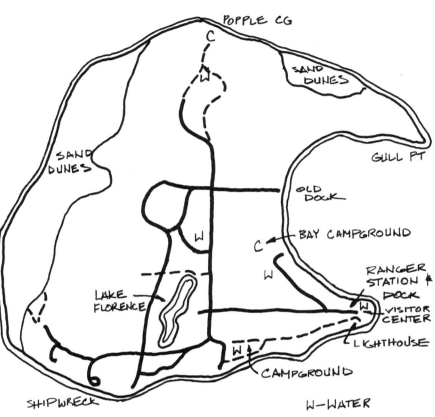

POPPLE CG

C

W

SAND
DUNES

GULL PT

SAND
DUNES

OLD
DOCK

W

C ← BAY CAMPGROUND

W

RANGER
STATION &
DOCK

W VISITOR
CENTER

LAKE
FLORENCE

LIGHTHOUSE

W

SHIPWRECK

CAMPGROUND

W - WATER

NOTE: PLEASE RESPECT RIGHTS OF
PRIVATE PROPERTY OWNERS

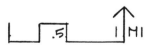
.5   1 MI

SOUTH MANITOU ISLAND

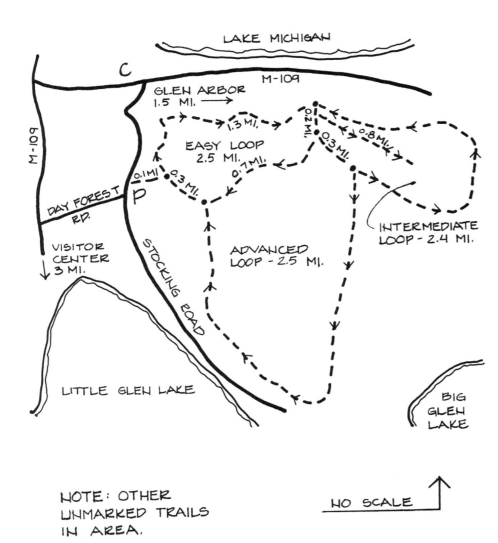

NOTE: OTHER
UNMARKED TRAILS
IN AREA.

NO SCALE

ALLIGATOR HILL TRAIL

Sleeping Bear Dunes National Lakeshore
PO Box 277, 9922 Front St. (M72)   616-326-5134
Empire, MI 49630

Michigan Atlas & Gazetteer Location: 73A67

County Location: Leelanau

Directions To Trailhead:
Between Glen Haven and Glen Arbor, just south of M109 on Lake Michigan.
Trailhead - 1 mile east of M109 on Day Forest Rd, where Day Forest Rd
intersects Stocking Rd or take Stocking Rd south from M109 just east of the DH
Day campground entrance.

Trail Type: Hiking/Walking, Cross Country Skiing
Trail Distance: 8.6 mi   Loops: 3   Shortest: 2.5 mi Longest: 6.7 mi
Trail Surface: Natural
Trail Use Fee: None
Method Of Ski Trail Grooming: None
Skiing Ability Suggested: Novice to advanced
Hiking Trail Difficulty: Moderate
Mountain Biking Ability Suggested: NA
Terrain: Steep 0%, Hilly 30%, Moderate 55%, Flat 15%
Camping: Camping at 2 locations in the park and backcountry camping
permitted

Maintained by the Sleeping Bear Dunes National Lakeshore.
Very scenic overlooks of Glen Haven, Lake Michigan and Glen Lake.
Trail has gradual but long climbs end in long downhill runs.
The wide trails attest to the fact that this site was originally planned as a
subdivision before it was rescued for public recreation.
Hunting in season: 9/15 to 12/15, please wear bright clothing.
Many other trails in the Sleeping Bear Dunes National Lakeshore.

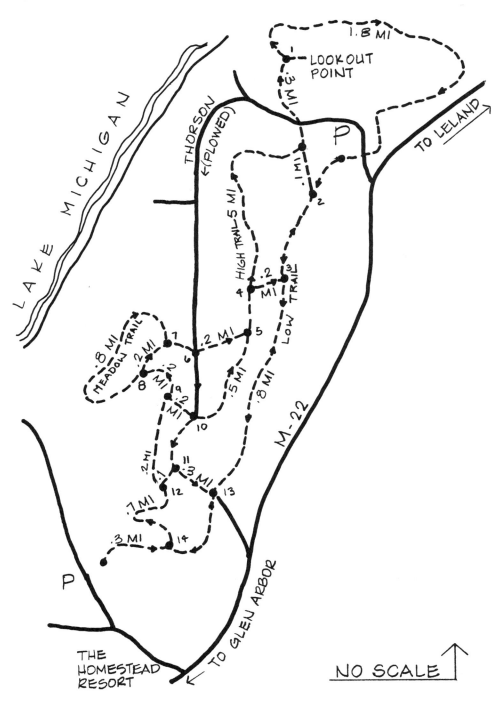

BAYVIEW TRAIL

Sleeping Bear Dunes National Lakeshore
PO Box 277, 9922 Front St. (M72)   616-326-5134
Empire, MI 49630   616-334-3756

Homestead
Wood Ridge Rd.   616-334-5000
Glen Arbor, MI 49636

Michigan Atlas & Gazetteer Location: 73A7

County Location: Leelanau

Directions To Trailhead:
Trailhead - About .5 mile west of M22 on Thorson Rd between Glen Arbor and Leland, just north of the Homestead .
Trailhead - Just inside the main entrance of the Homestead on the right near the reception center.

Trail Type: Hiking/Walking, Cross Country Skiing
Trail Distance: 15 km   Loops: 8   Shortest: 1km   Longest: 15 km
Trail Surface: Natural
Trail Use Fee: Fri., Sat. & Sun. when groomed
Method Of Ski Trail Grooming: Track set Fridays and weekends
Skiing Ability Suggested: Novice to advanced
Hiking Trail Difficulty: Moderate
Mountain Biking Ability Suggested: NA
Terrain: Steep 23%, Hilly 34%, Moderate 25%, Flat 18%
Camping: Campground available in park at 2 locations

Maintained by the Homestead under permit from the Sleeping Bear Dunes National Lakeshore.
Varied and interesting trail for the intermediate and above skier. Novice skiers will find the trail quite challenging.
From the lookout, a panoramic view of both Manitou islands, South Fox Island, and Pyramid Point are visable.

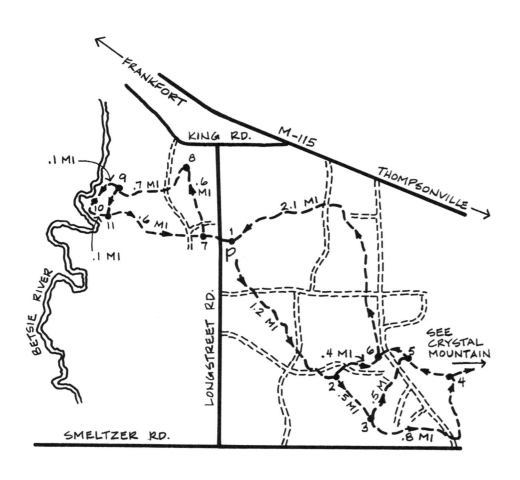

SMELTZER RD.

BETSIE RIVER
PATHWAY

Traverse City Forest Area, Pere Marquette State Forest
404 W 14th St.   616-964-4920
Traverse City, MI 49684

District Forest Manager, Pere Marquette State Forest
Rte 1, 8015 South US131   616-775-9727
Cadillac, MI 49601

Michigan Atlas & Gazetteer Location: 73D6

County Location: Benzie

Directions To Trailhead:
Between Frankfort and Thompsonville on M115
Trailhead - West from Thompsonville 5 miles (just beyond Crystal Mt), then bear
left(south) on King Rd. .5 mile to Longstreet Rd., then left again for .75 miles to
parking lot.

Trail Type: Hiking/Walking, Cross Country Skiing, Mountain Biking
Trail Distance: 10 mi   Loops: 5   Shortest: Longest:
Trail Surface: Natural
Trail Use Fee: None
Method Of Ski Trail Grooming: None
Skiing Ability Suggested: Novice to intermediate
Hiking Trail Difficulty: Easy to moderate
Mountain Biking Ability Suggested: Novice to intermediate
Terrain: Steep 0%, Hilly 20%, Moderate 30%, Flat 50%
Camping: None, but campgrounds available 16 miles away at Platte River

Maintained by the DNR Forest Management Division.
Trails west of the parking lot are more difficult than the loops toward the east.
Trails connect to Crystal Mountain Resort (trail use fee area). See other entry.
The combination of the DNR and Crystal Mountain trails makes for a very
enjoyable day of skiing. The connecting trail may not be signed.
Other contacts:
    DNR Forest Management Division Office, Lansing, 517-373-1275
    DNR Forest Management Region Office, Roscommon, 517-275-5151

SAND DUNES

8 7

9

6

5

4

LAKE
MICHIGAN

3

2

P 1

P DUNE
OVERLOOK

P

PICNIC
MOUNTAIN
PICNIC
AREA

NORTH

PIERCE
STOCKING
SCENIC
DRIVE

SEE DUNES TRAIL

DUNE
CLIMB P

GREAT
LAKES P
PICNIC
AREA

M-109

GLEN
LAKE

COTTONWOOD TRAIL

Sleeping Bear Dunes National Lakeshore
PO Box 277, 9922 Front St   616-326-5134
Empire, MI 49630

Michigan Atlas & Gazetteer Location: 73AB6

County Location: Leelanau

Directions To Trailhead:
Along the Pierce Stocking Scenic Drive south of Glen Haven off M109

Trail Type: Hiking/Walking
Trail Distance: 1.5 mi   Loops: 1   Shortest: NA   Longest: 1.5 mi
Trail Surface: Natural and boardwalk
Trail Use Fee: None
Method Of Ski Trail Grooming: NA
Skiing Ability Suggested: NA
Hiking Trail Difficulty: Moderate
Mountain Biking Ability Suggested: NA
Terrain: Moderate
Camping: Nearby in the National Lakeshore

Managed by the Sleeping Bear Dunes National Lakeshore
A 9 station dune interpretive trail.
A trail guide is available.

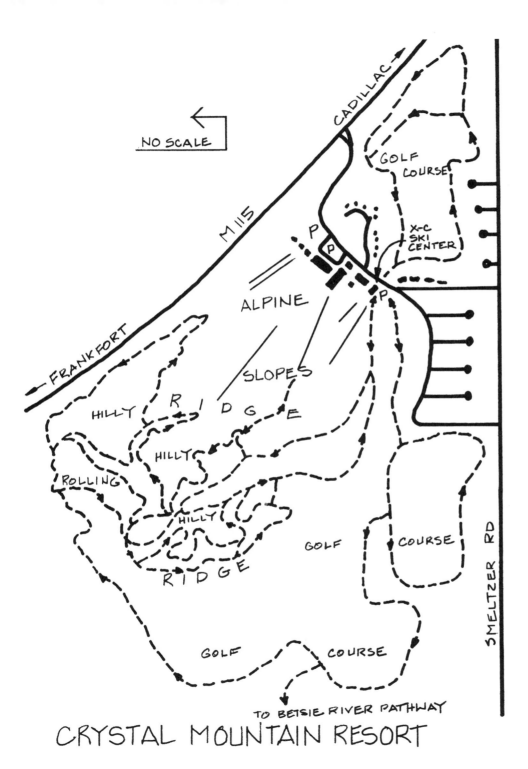

NO SCALE

CRYSTAL MOUNTAIN RESORT

Crystal Mountain Resort

Thompsonville, MI 49683

616-378-2911
800-321-4637

Michigan Atlas & Gazetteer Location: 73D67

County Location: Benzie

Directions To Trailhead:
On M115, 36 miles NW of Cadillac 28 miles SW of Traverse City via county roads

Trail Type: Hiking/Walking, Cross Country Skiing, Mountain Biking
Trail Distance: 26 km   Loops: 12   Shortest: 1 km   Longest: 7 km
Trail Surface: Natural
Trail Use Fee: Yes, $5.00 with lift ticket privileges
Method Of Ski Trail Grooming: Double track set with skating lanes
Skiing Ability Suggested: Novice to advanced
Hiking Trail Difficulty: NA
Mountain Biking Ability Suggested: Novice to advanced
Terrain: Steep 15%, Hilly 25%, Moderate 40%, Flat 20%
Camping: None

Privately operated 4 season alpine ski area with extensive cross country trail system.
Lodging, restaurant, instruction, rentals, ski shop, entertainment and an outdoor pool.
Trails were expertly designed by John Capper.
Trail system connects to the Betsie River Pathway to the west.
Very scenic views westward from the trail.
10 km lighted trails.
Quality skating and classic ski rentals available.
Trail access can be gained from the Cheers Chairlift.
The cross country ski center is at the golf course clubhouse.
An exceptional nordic center with terrific trails and expert grooming.

Sleeping Bear Dunes National Lakeshore
PO Box 277, 9922 Front St. (M72)   616-326-5134
Empire, MI 49630

Michigan Atlas & Gazetteer Location: 73A6

County Location: Leelanau

Directions To Trailhead:
South trailhead - On M109 near the Dune Climb, south of Glen Haven
North trailhead - Near Sleeping Bear Dunes Point Coast Guard Station west of
Glen Haven

Trail Type: Hiking/Walking
Trail Distance: 3.6 mi   Loops: 2   Shortest: 2.8 mi Longest: 3.5 mi
Trail Surface: Natural sand
Trail Use Fee: None
Method Of Ski Trail Grooming: NA
Skiing Ability Suggested: NA
Hiking Trail Difficulty: Difficult
Mountain Biking Ability Suggested: NA
Terrain: Varies
Camping: Available at 2 locations in the park

Maintained by the Sleeping Bear Dunes National Lakeshore.
South trail is a point to point trail of 3.5 miles round trip leading to the Lake
Michigan shoreline from the Dune Climb.
North trail is a 2.8 mile loop with a point to point spur of .4 mile just west of the
Maritime Museum west of Glen Haven.
Groups and families are strongly cautioned to stay togather since distances on
the dunes are deceiving and its easy to become disoriented and lost.
Wear bright clothing during the hunting season 9/15 to 12/15

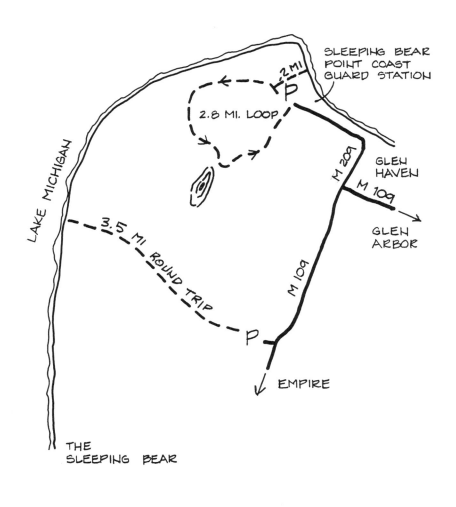

DUNES TRAIL

Sleeping Bear Dunes National Lakeshore
PO Box 277, 9922 Front St. (M72)   616-326-5134
Empire, MI 49630

Michigan Atlas & Gazetteer Location: 73B6

County Location: Leelanau

Directions To Trailhead:
1 mile south of Empire on Wilco Rd. along Lake Michigan

Trail Type: Hiking/Walking, Cross Country Skiing, Interpretive
Trail Distance: .75 mi   Loops: NA   Shortest: NA   Longest: NA
Trail Surface: Natural
Trail Use Fee: None
Method Of Ski Trail Grooming: None
Skiing Ability Suggested: Intermediate to advanced
Hiking Trail Difficulty: Moderate
Mountain Biking Ability Suggested: NA
Terrain: Steep 0%, Hilly 10%, Moderate 85%, Flat 5%
Camping: Available at two locations in the park

Maintained by the Sleeping Bear Dunes National Lakeshore
This is a point to point trail.
Brochure available explaining the 6 stations of this trail.
Very impressive overlook of Lake Michigan from the end of the trail.
Wear bright clothing during hunting season 9/15 - 12/15.
The trail has some challenging sections.

LAKE MICHIGAN

EMPIRE BLUFF

EMPIRE

6 5 4 3 2 P

M-22

WILCO RD.

FRANKFORT
AND HONOR

NO SCALE

EMPIRE BLUFF TRAIL

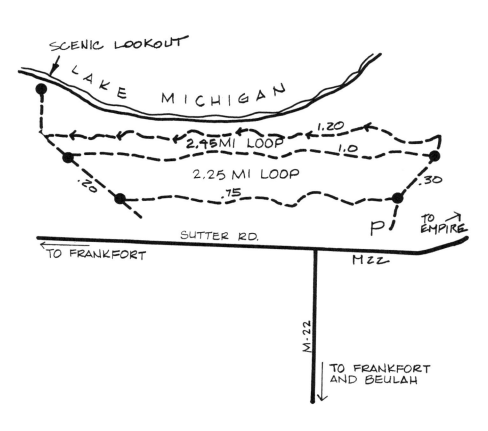

SCENIC LOOKOUT

LAKE MICHIGAN

2.45 MI LOOP

2.25 MI LOOP

1.20

1.0

.30

.75

.20

SUTTER RD.

P

TO EMPIRE

TO FRANKFORT

M22

M-22

TO FRANKFORT AND BEULAH

NO SCALE

OLD INDIAN TRAIL

Sleeping Bear Dunes National Lakeshore
PO Box 277, 9922 Front St. (M72)   616-326-5134
Empire, MI 49630

Michigan Atlas & Gazetteer Location: 73C5

County Location: Benzie

Directions To Trailhead:
Between Frankfort and Empire on the north side of Crystal Lake near the west end of Long Lake
Trailhead - At the intersection of M22 and Sutter Rd.

Trail Type: Hiking/Walking, Cross Country Skiing
Trail Distance: 3.55 mi   Loops: 2   Shortest: 2.25 mi Longest: 2.3 mi
Trail Surface: Natural
Trail Use Fee: None
Method Of Ski Trail Grooming: None
Skiing Ability Suggested: Novice
Hiking Trail Difficulty: Easy
Mountain Biking Ability Suggested: NA
Terrain: Flat to rolling with one steep hill
Camping: Available at two locations in the park

Maintained by the Sleeping Bear Dunes National Lakeshore.
Scenic view of Lake Michigan along the trail.
Wear bright clothing during hunting season 9/15 - 12/15

Platte Plains Trail

Sleeping Bear Dunes National Lakeshore
PO Box 277, 9922 Front St.(M72)
Empire, MI 49630

616-326-5134

Michigan Atlas & Gazetteer Location: 73C6

County Location: Benzie

Directions To Trailhead:
North of Platte Lake off M22
South trailhead - At Platte River Campground
North trailhead - At the west end of Esch Rd., 1 mile west of M22 and 3.5 miles south of Empire
Central trailhead - Just south of Trails End Rd. and M22 intersection

Trail Type: Hiking/Walking, Cross Country Skiing
Trail Distance: 18.3 mi   Loops: 3   Shortest: 3.5 mi Longest: 6.6 mi
Trail Surface: Gravel and natural
Trail Use Fee: None
Method Of Ski Trail Grooming: None
Skiing Ability Suggested: Novice to intermediate
Hiking Trail Difficulty: Easy to moderate
Mountain Biking Ability Suggested: NA
Terrain: Steep 0%, Hilly 10%, Moderate 50%, Flat 40%
Camping: Campground at south trailhead and along trail on Lake Michigan

Maintained by the Sleeping Bear Dunes National Lakeshore
Several overlooks of Lake Michigan Extensive trail system of diverse habitat.
Wear bright clothing during hunting season 9/15 - 12/15.
Skiing on unplowed roads provides additional trail length not listed above.
Detailed trail maps available from Sleeping Bear Dunes National Lakeshore.

Map Labels

EMPIRE

ESCH RD

LAKE MICHIGAN

M 22

4.6 MI OTTER CREEK LOOP

SUMMER

OTTER LAKE

VISTA

C

HILLS

1.2 MI VISTA

.8 MI

1.1 MI

P

.5 MI

3.5 MI BASS LAKE LOOP

NOT PLOWED

6.6 MI LASSO LOOP

LASSO RD (NOT PLOWED)

1 MI

.9 MI

DEER LAKE

.3

NOT PLOWED

NOT PLOWED

1.1 MI

P

WINTER

C

HQ

2 MI

M 22

FRANKFORT

HONOR

SCALE NOT KNOWN

PLATTE PLAINS TRAIL

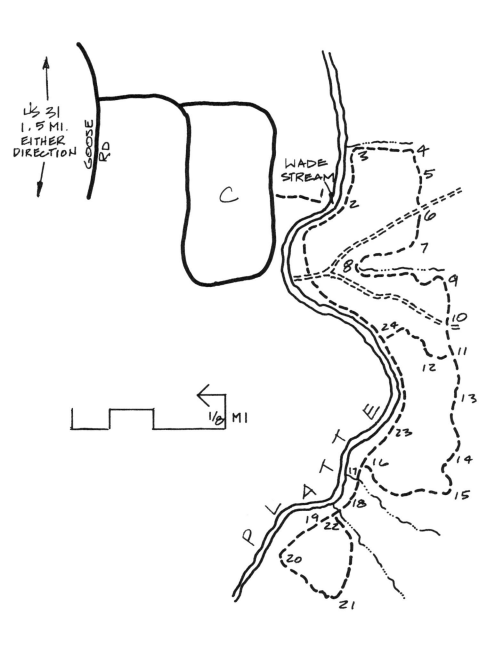

Traverse City Forest Area, Pere Marquette State Forest
404 West 14th Street   616-922-5280
Traverse City, MI 49684

District Forest Manager, Pere Marquette State Forest
8015 Mackinaw Trail   616-775-9727
Cadillac, MI 49601

Michigan Atlas & Gazetteer Location: 73C7

County Location: Benzie

Directions To Trailhead:
2.5 miles southeast of Honor via US31 and Goose Rd. (MUST WADE RIVER TO GET TO PATHWAY)

Trail Type: Hiking/Walking, Interpretive
Trail Distance: 2.5 mi   Loops: 3   Shortest: .5 mi   Longest: 2.5 mi
Trail Surface: Natural and water
Trail Use Fee: None
Method Of Ski Trail Grooming: NA
Skiing Ability Suggested: NA
Hiking Trail Difficulty: Easy
Mountain Biking Ability Suggested: NA
Terrain: Steep 0%, Hilly 70%, Moderate 20%, Flat 10%
Camping: At trailhead

Maintained by the DNR Forest Management Division
This is a 26 station interpretive trail.
Brochure available

PLATTE SPRINGS PATHWAY

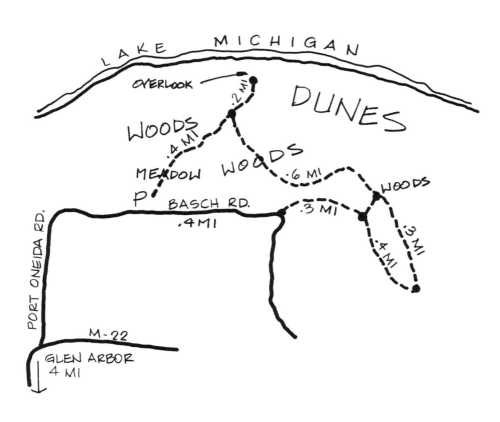

Sleeping Bear Dunes National Lakeshore
PO Box 277, 9922 Front St. (M72)   616-326-5134
Empire, MI 49630

Michigan Atlas & Gazetteer Location: 73A7

County Location: Leelanau

Directions To Trailhead:
Between Glen Arbor and Leland, north of M22 on Lake Michigan
Trailhead - 5 miles north of Glen Arbor, turn north on Port Oneida Rd., parking area is on the north side of the road, about .5 mile after Point Oneida Rd. turns east..

Trail Type: Hiking/Walking
Trail Distance: 2.8 mi   Loops: 1   Shortest: NA   Longest: 2.7 mi
Trail Surface: Natural and gavel road
Trail Use Fee: None
Method Of Ski Trail Grooming: NA
Skiing Ability Suggested: NA
Hiking Trail Difficulty: Moderate
Mountain Biking Ability Suggested: NA
Terrain: Hilly
Camping: Available at 2 locations in the park

Maintained by the Sleeping Bear Dunes National Lakeshore
Quite varied environments along the trail, including a meadow, beech-maple forest, an open sand dune and an outstanding vista of Lake Michigan.
Part of the loop trail is on a vehicle road.
Trail can be hiked in either direction.
Wear bright clothing during hunting season 9/15 - 12/15.

PYRAMID POINT TRAIL

Sleeping Bear Dunes National Lakeshore
PO Box 277, 9922 Front St. (M72)   616-326-5134
Empire, MI 49630

Michigan Atlas & Gazetteer Location: 73AB6

County Location: Leelanau

Directions To Trailhead:
SW of Glen Lake on M109 Trailhead - 3 miles north of Empire on M109 just
south of Welch Rd. then a short distance to the trailhead parking lot on the west
side of the road .

Trail Type: Cross Country Skiing
Trail Distance: 7.2 mi   Loops: 5+   Shortest: 2.1 mi Longest: 6 mi
Trail Surface: Natural
Trail Use Fee: None
Method Of Ski Trail Grooming: None
Skiing Ability Suggested: Novice and advanced
Hiking Trail Difficulty: Moderate to difficult
Mountain Biking Ability Suggested: NA
Terrain: Steep 5%, Hilly 40%, Moderate 40%, Flat 15%
Camping: Available at two locations in the park

Maintained by the Sleeping Bear Dunes National Lakeshore
An advanced return trail is very difficult and should only be attempted by
experienced skiers . Spectacular scenic overlook of the shore of Lake Michigan
and the dunes.
Across the road from the Windy Moraine Trail.
Sandy snow may be encountered near overlooks. Previously this trail was known
as the Shauger Hill Trail. Scenic views of Glen Lake, Lake Michigan and the
dunes. Parts of the trail are the Pierce Stocking Scenic Drive used in the
snowless months. These sections can be skied in both directions.
The downhill sections of the drive are great for telemarking.
Wear bright clothing during hunting season 9/15 - 12/15.

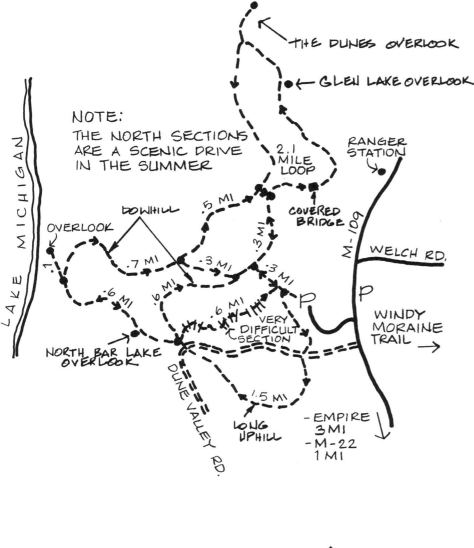

SCENIC DRIVE CROSS COUNTRY SKI TRAIL

Sleeping Bear Dunes National Lakeshore
PO Box 277, 9922 Front St.   616-326-5134
Empire, MI 49630

Michigan Atlas & Gazetteer Location: 73B6

County Location: Leelanau

Directions To Trailhead:
Between Empire and Glen Haven on M109. Trailhead at the first parking lot on the Stocking Scenic Drive

Trail Type: Hiking/Walking
Trail Distance: 2.4 mi   Loops: 1   Shortest: NA   Longest: 2.4 mi
Trail Surface: Natural
Trail Use Fee: None
Method Of Ski Trail Grooming: NA
Skiing Ability Suggested: NA
Hiking Trail Difficulty: Moderate
Mountain Biking Ability Suggested: NA
Terrain: Steep 30%, Hilly 30%, Moderate 25%, Flat 15%
Camping: Campgrounds in the National Lakeshore and surrounding area

Maintained by the Sleeping Bear Dunes National Lakeshore
This is part of the Scenic Drive Cross Country Ski Trail system

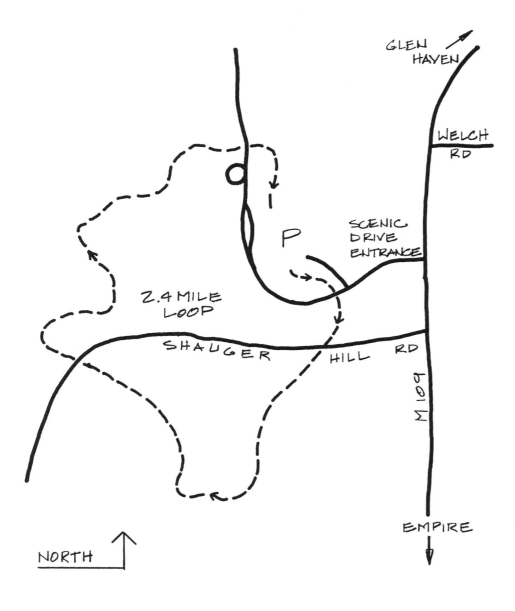

GLEN HAVEN

WELCH RD

SCENIC DRIVE ENTRANCE

P

2.4 MILE LOOP

SHAUGER HILL RD

M109

EMPIRE

NORTH

SHAUGER HILL HIKING TRAIL

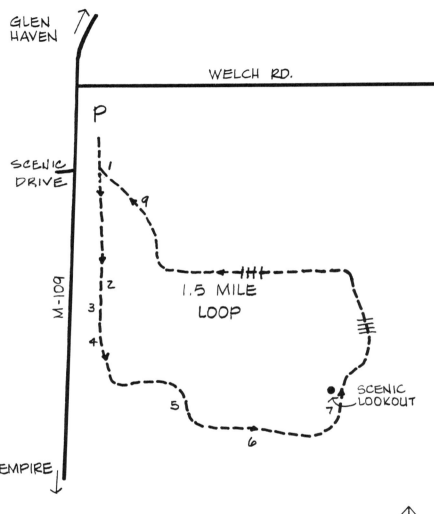

GLEN
HAVEN

WELCH RD.

P

SCENIC
DRIVE

M-109

1
9
2
3
4
5
6
7

1.5 MILE
LOOP

SCENIC
LOOKOUT

EMPIRE

NO SCALE

ON SCENIC DRIVE SEE:
- SCENIC DRIVE SKI TRAIL
- COTTONWOOD TRAIL (FOOT TRAIL)
SEE MANY OTHER TRAILS IN THE S.B.D.N.L.

WINDY MORAINE TRAIL

Sleeping Bear Dunes National Lakeshore
PO Box 277, 9922 Front St. (M72)   616-326-5134
Empire, MI 49630

Michigan Atlas & Gazetteer Location: 73B6

County Location: Leelanau

Directions To Trailhead:
SW of Glen Lake on M109
Trailhead - 3 miles north of Empire on Welch Rd. just east of M109.

Trail Type: Hiking/Walking, Interpretive
Trail Distance: 1.5 mi   Loops: 1   Shortest: Longest: 1.5 mi
Trail Surface: Natural
Trail Use Fee: None
Method Of Ski Trail Grooming: None
Skiing Ability Suggested: Novice
Hiking Trail Difficulty: Easy
Mountain Biking Ability Suggested: NA
Terrain: Rolling
Camping: Available at two locations in the park

Maintained by the Sleeping Bear Dunes National Lakeshore
Across M109 from the Scenic Drive Cross Country Ski Trail.
The trail consists of 1/3 downhill, 1/3 flat and 1/3 uphill.
Wear bright clothing during hunting season 9/15 - 12/15.

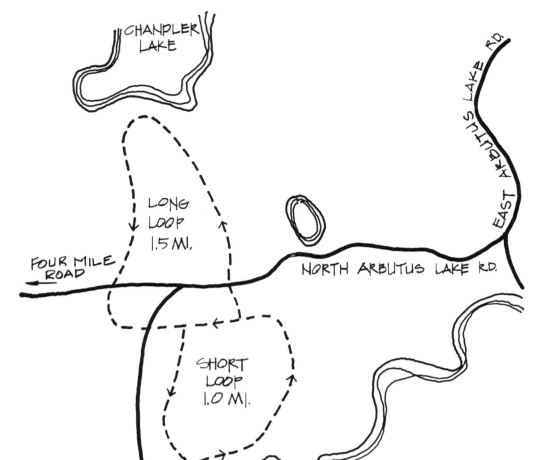

CHANDLER LAKE
PATHWAY

NO SCALE

Traverse City Forest Area, Pere Marquette State Forest
404 W. 14th St   616-922-5280
Traverse City, MI 49684

District Forest Manger, Pere Marquette State Forest
8015 Mackinaw Trail   616-775-9727
Cadillac, MI 49601

Michigan Atlas & Gazetteer Location: 74C3

County Location: Grand Traverse

Directions To Trailhead:
10 miles southeast of Traverse City via Garfield Rd, east on Potter Rd, south on
4 Mile Rd, east on N. Arbutus Rd

Trail Type: Hiking/Walking, Cross Country Skiing, Mountain Biking
Trail Distance: 2.5 mi   Loops: 2   Shortest: 1 mi   Longest: 1.5 mi
Trail Surface: Natural
Trail Use Fee: None
Method Of Ski Trail Grooming: None
Skiing Ability Suggested: Novice
Hiking Trail Difficulty: Easy
Mountain Biking Ability Suggested: Novice
Terrain: Steep 0%, Hilly 0%, Moderate 20%, Flat 80%
Camping: State Forest Campground at trailhead

Maintained by the DNR Forest Management Division

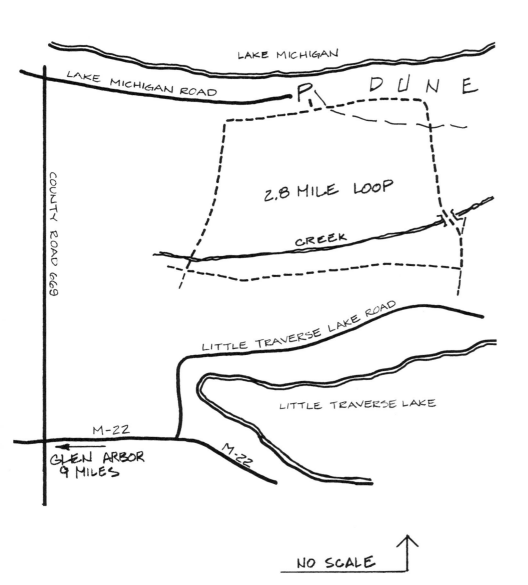

Sleeping Bear Dunes National Lakeshore
PO Box 277, 9922 Front St. (M72)   616-326-5134
Empire, MI 49630

Michigan Atlas & Gazetteer Location: 74A1

County Location: Leelanau

Directions To Trailhead:
Between Glen Arbor and Leland, north of M22 on Lake Michigan.
Trailhead - On M22 between Little Traverse Lake and Bass Lake, take Co Rd 669 to Lake Michigan and turn right and proceed to end of the road

Trail Type: Hiking/Walking, Cross Country Skiing
Trail Distance: 2.8 mi   Loops: 1   Shortest: NA   Longest: 2.8 mi
Trail Surface: Natural
Trail Use Fee: None
Method Of Ski Trail Grooming: None
Skiing Ability Suggested: Novice
Hiking Trail Difficulty: Easy
Mountain Biking Ability Suggested: NA
Terrain: Flat
Camping: Available at 2 locations in the park

Maintained by the Sleeping Bear Dunes National Lakeshore
Trailhead along the shore of Lake Michigan

GOOD HARBOR BAY SKI TRAIL

Map

MUNSON AVE   US 31 & M 72

GARFIELD AVE

IN ONLY

COURTS

SHOP

OFFICE

ICE RINK

PROBATE COURT OFFICE

BALL

FIELDS

P

P

P

BALL   FIELDS

FAIR ST

P

P

BAND SHELL

P

■ RESTROOM

MAIN ENTRANCE   TITUS ST

NORTH ↑

GRAND TRAVERSE COUNTY
CIVIC CENTER

Information

Grand Traverse County Parks and Recreation Department.
1125 W. Civic Center Drive   616-922-4818
Traverse City, MI 49684

Michigan Atlas & Gazetteer Location: 74B3

County Location: Grand Traverse

Directions To Trailhead:
In downtown Traverse City at the county Civic Center

Trail Type: Hiking/Walking, Cross Country Skiing
Trail Distance: 1 mi   Loops: 1   Shortest: NA   Longest: 1 mi
Trail Surface: Paved 8' wide
Trail Use Fee: None
Method Of Ski Trail Grooming: Yes
Skiing Ability Suggested: Novice
Hiking Trail Difficulty: Easy
Mountain Biking Ability Suggested: NA
Terrain: Steep 0%, Hilly 0%, Moderate 5%, Flat 95%
Camping: None

Maintained by the Grand Traverse County Parks and Recreation Department
Part of a multi recreational facility complex .

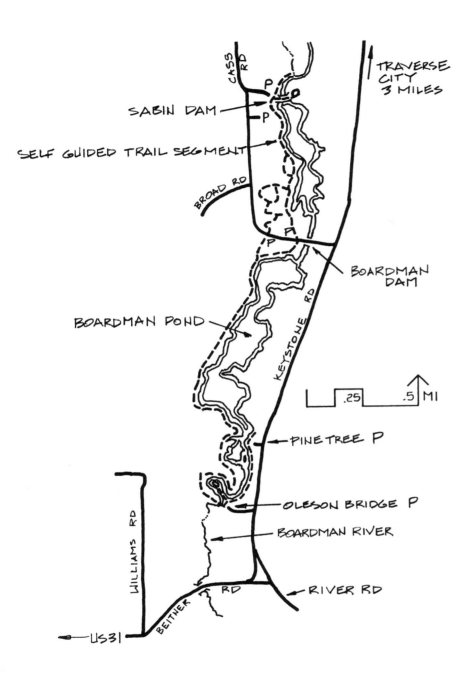

Grand Traverse County Parks and Recreation Department
1125 W. Civic Center Drive
Traverse City, MI 49684

616-922-4818

Michigan Atlas & Gazetteer Location: 74C23

County Location: Grand Traverse

Directions To Trailhead:
South of Traverse City on the Boardman River at Sabin and Boardman Dams.
Trailheads off Cass Rd and Keystone Road at Sabin Dam, Boardman Dam,
Pine Tree and Oleson Bridge.

Trail Type: Hiking/Walking, Cross Country Skiing, Interpretive
Trail Distance: 6 mi   Loops: Many   Shortest: .25 mi   Longest: 2 mi
Trail Surface: Wood chips
Trail Use Fee: None
Method Of Ski Trail Grooming: None
Skiing Ability Suggested: Novice
Hiking Trail Difficulty: Easy
Mountain Biking Ability Suggested: NA
Terrain: Steep 0%, Hilly 40%, Moderate 40%, Flat 20%
Camping: None

Owned by Grand Traverse County as a park and teaching facility
374 acres along the Boardman River
The self guided nature trail off Cass Rd has 9 stations.
Trail guide is available.
Surprisingly secluded area very close to Traverse City.

GRAND TRAVERSE
NATURAL EDUCATION PRESERVE

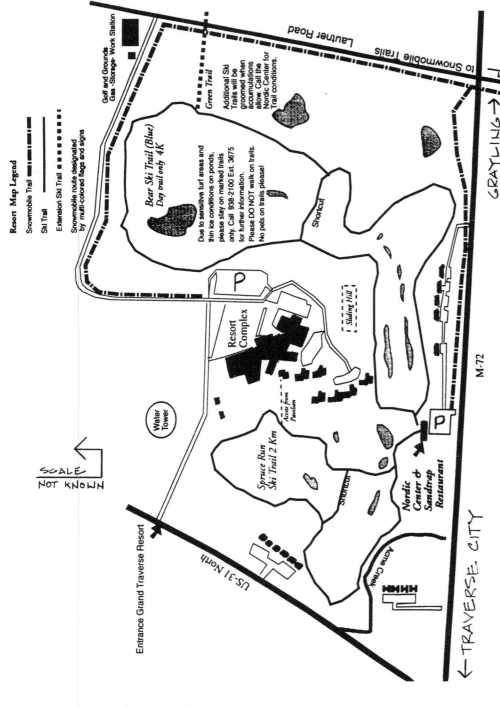

Grand Traverse Resort Village
PO Box 404
Acme, MI 49610-0404

616-938-2100
800-748-0303

Michigan Atlas & Gazetteer Location: 74B4

County Location: Grand Traverse

Directions To Trailhead:
Ski trailhead - About .5 mile west of the M72 and US31 intersection 6 miles NE of Traverse City

Trail Type: Hiking/Walking, Cross Country Skiing
Trail Distance: 5 mi   Loops: 4   Shortest: .5 mi   Longest: 2 mi
Trail Surface: Paved, gravel and natural
Trail Use Fee: Yes
Method Of Ski Trail Grooming: Track set
Skiing Ability Suggested: Novice to intermediate
Hiking Trail Difficulty: NA
Mountain Biking Ability Suggested: NA
Terrain: Steep 0%, Hilly 15%, Moderate 60%, Flat 25%
Camping: Campground available at Traverse City State Park

A complete 4 seasons resort with all facilities including golf course, pool, tennis courts, racket ball courts and everything else .
Ski center is at the golf course started building on M72.
Lighted ski trail available.
Walking/jogging trail is 2 miles long.

GRAND TRAVERSE RESORT

Traverse City Recreation Department
625 Woodmere St.
Traverse City, MI 49684

616-922-4910
616-947-8566

NO MAP

Michigan Atlas & Gazetteer Location: 74B2

County Location: Grand Traverse

Directions To Trailhead:
One mile west of the Traverse City city limit, at the end of Randolph St. in the hills overlooking Traverse City

Trail Type: Hiking/Walking, Cross Country Skiing
Trail Distance: 2.5 km   Loops: 2   Shortest: 1 km   Longest: 1.5 km
Trail Surface: Natural
Trail Use Fee: Yes,
Method Of Ski Trail Grooming: Track set daily
Skiing Ability Suggested: Novice to advanced
Hiking Trail Difficulty: NA
Mountain Biking Ability Suggested: NA
Terrain: Steep 0%, Hilly 20%, Moderate 20%, Flat 60%
Camping: None

Downhill ski area operated by Traverse City Recreation Department
Warming area, rentals and snack bar
Loops are relatively short but most are very challenging
Lighted for cross country ski trails and downhill slopes

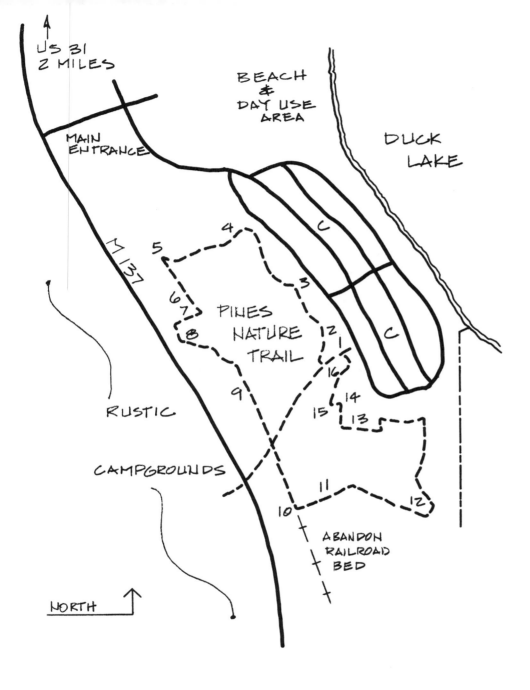

Interlochen State Park
M137
Interlochen, Mi 49643

616-276-9511

DNR Parks and Recreation Division

616-992-5270
517-275-5151

Michigan Atlas & Gazetteer Location: 74C1

County Location: Grand Traverse

Directions To Trailhead:
Interlochen is located southwest of Traverse City via US31, then south at Interlochen Corners for 2 miles to the park.

Trail Type: Hiking/Walking, Cross Country Skiing, Interpretive
Trail Distance: 3 mi   Loops: Several   Shortest: Longest:
Trail Surface: Natural and gravel
Trail Use Fee: None, but vehicle entry permit required
Method Of Ski Trail Grooming: None
Skiing Ability Suggested: Novice
Hiking Trail Difficulty: Easy
Mountain Biking Ability Suggested: NA
Terrain: Steep 0%, Hilly 0%, Moderate 20%, Flat 80%
Camping: On site

Maintained by the DNR Parks and Recreation Division
A popular state park with swimming and boating.
This is a interpretive trail of the history and nature of the area.
A trail guide is available for the 16 station trail.

PINES NATURE TRAIL
INTERLOCHEN STATE PARK

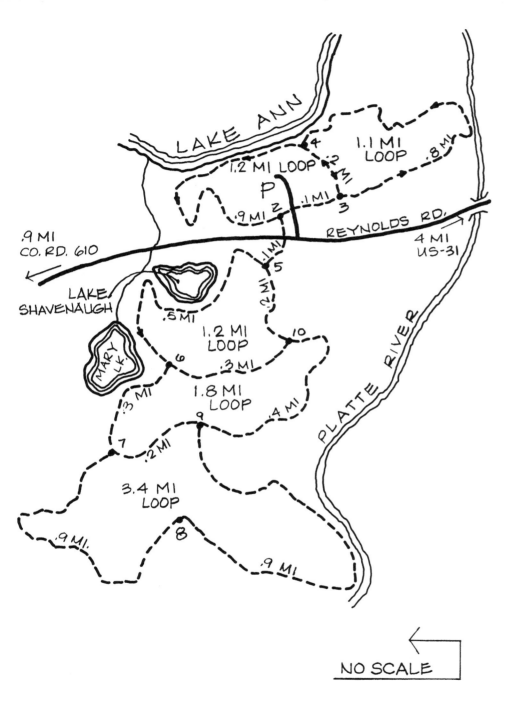

LAKE ANN PATHWAY

Lake Ann Pathway

Traverse City Forest Area, Pere Marquette State Forest
404 W 14th St.   616-922-5280
Traverse City, MI 49684

District Forest Manager, Pere Marquette State Forest
Rte. 1, 8015 South US131   616-775-9727
Cadillac, MI 49601

Michigan Atlas & Gazetteer Location: 74C1

County Location: Benzie

Directions To Trailhead:
West of Traverse City between M72 and US31 near Lake Ann
Trailhead - From Lake Ann west on Almira Rd. to Reynolds Rd., then south 2.5
miles to Lake Ann State Forest   Campground

Trail Type: Hiking/Walking, Cross Country Skiing, Mountain Biking
Trail Distance: 5.8 mi   Loops: 5   Shortest: 1 mi   Longest: 3 mi
Trail Surface: Natural
Trail Use Fee: None
Method Of Ski Trail Grooming: Track set
Skiing Ability Suggested: Novice to advanced
Hiking Trail Difficulty: Easy to moderate
Mountain Biking Ability Suggested: Novice to intermediate
Terrain: Steep 0%, Hilly 10%, Moderate 40%, Flat 50%
Camping: Campground at trailhead

Maintained by the DNR Forest Management Division
Loops provide interesting skiing for skiers of all skill levels.
The loops west of Reynolds Rd are some of the best designed in the DNR
system. Simply a joy to ski!!!
Other contacts:
        DNR Forest Management Division Office, Lansing, 517-373-1275
        DNR Forest Management Region Office, Roscommon, 517-275-5151

Traverse City Area Forest, Pere Marquette State Forest
404 14th St.   616-946-4920
Traverse City, MI 49684

District Forest Manager, Pere Marquette State Forest
Rte 1, 8015 South US131   616-775-9727
Cadillac, MI 49601

Michigan Atlas & Gazetteer Location: 74C1

County Location: Grand Traverse

Directions To Trailhead:
12 miles SW of Traverse City on US31 at near Interlochen
Trailhead - West 1.5 miles from Interlochen on US31 to Wildwood Rd., then
north 1 mile to state forest campground

Trail Type: Hiking/Walking, Cross Country Skiing, Mountain Biking, Interpretive
Trail Distance: 6.3 mi   Loops: 3   Shortest: 2.4 mi Longest: 6.15 mi
Trail Surface: Natural
Trail Use Fee: None
Method Of Ski Trail Grooming: Track Set
Skiing Ability Suggested: Novice
Hiking Trail Difficulty: Easy
Mountain Biking Ability Suggested: Novice to intermediate
Terrain: Steep 0%, Hilly 0%, Moderate 50%, Flat 50%
Camping: Campground available at trailhead

Maintained by the DNR Forest Management Division
Lake DuBonnet is an artifical lake with a floating island.
21 station interpretive trail
Trail reviewed in the Great Lakes Skier, fall 1989.
Other contacts:
        DNR Forest Management Division Office, Lansing, 517-373-1275
        DNR Forest Management Region Office, Roscommon, 517-275-5151

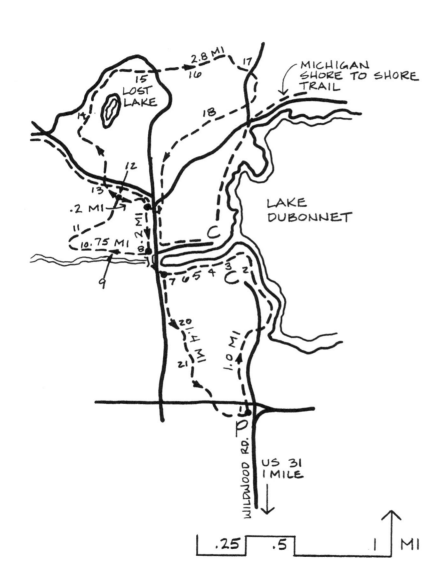

LOST LAKE PATHWAY

Traverse City Forest Area, Pere Marquette State Forest
404 W 14th St.   616-946-4920
Traverse City, MI 49684

District Forest Manager, Pere Marquette State Forest
Rte 1, 8015 South US131   616-775-9727
Cadillac, MI 49601

Michigan Atlas & Gazetteer Location: 74C4,75C4

County Location: Grand Traverse

Directions To Trailhead:
SE of Traverse City about 13 miles near Ranch Rudolf resort. From Traverse City take Garfield Ave south to Hammond Rd., then east on Hammond Rd to High Lake Rd, south .5 mile to Supply Rd., then east on Supply Rd. about 3 miles to Rennie Lake Rd., then turn south until it dead ends, turn left and the parking lot is about 2 miles away .

Trail Type: Hiking/Walking, Cross Country Skiing, Mountain Biking
Trail Distance: 11.5 mi   Loops: 5   Shortest: .95 mi Longest: 5.35 mi
Trail Surface: Natural
Trail Use Fee: None
Method Of Ski Trail Grooming: Track set
Skiing Ability Suggested: Novice
Hiking Trail Difficulty: Easy
Mountain Biking Ability Suggested: Novice
Terrain: Steep 0%, Hilly 5%, Moderate 60%, Flat 35%
Camping: State forest CG are nearby and Jellystone Campground on 5 Mile Rd

Maintained by the DNR Forest Management Division
The first cross country ski trail developed by the DNR in the early 1970's.
Numerous refinements have been made since that time to make this a delightful trail that passes by the beautiful Boardman River.
A trail connects to Ranch Rudolf with its food and lodging facilities.
Many hills throughout the system makes for a very popular trail for local skiers.
Sand Lakes Quiet Area is only a few miles to the east.
Other contacts:
        DNR Forest Management Division Office, Lansing, 517-373-1275
        DNR Forest Management Region Office, Roscommon, 517-275-5151

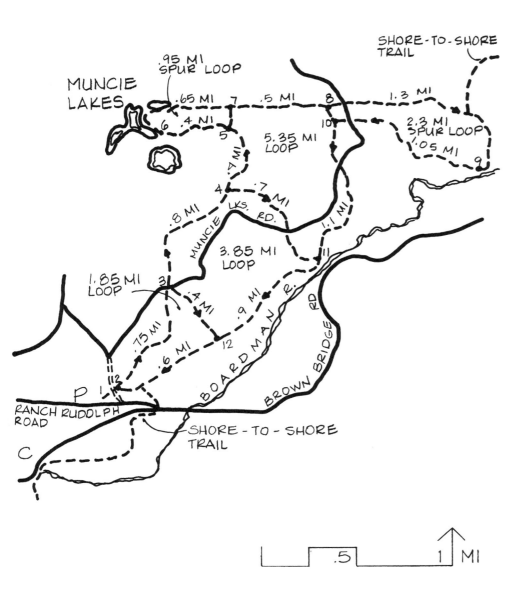

MUNCIE LAKES PATHWAY

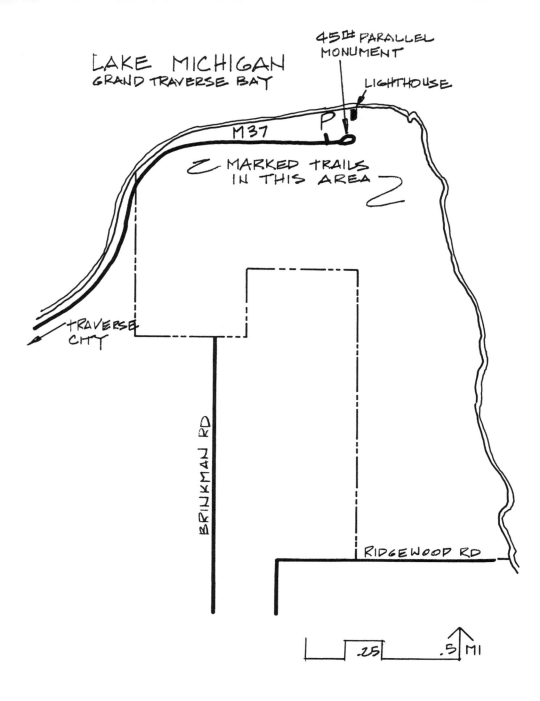

LAKE MICHIGAN
GRAND TRAVERSE BAY

45ᵗʰ PARALLEL MONUMENT

LIGHTHOUSE

M37

⊂ MARKED TRAILS IN THIS AREA ⊃

TRAVERSE CITY

BRINKMAN RD

RIDGEWOOD RD

.25   .5 MI

OLD MISSION STATE PARK

DNR Parks and Recreation Division
PO Box 30028
Lansing, MI 48909

517-373-1270

Michigan Atlas & Gazetteer Location: 74A4

County Location: Grand Traverse

Directions To Trailhead:
North end of Old Mission peninsula on M37.

Trail Type: Hiking/Walking, Cross Country Skiing
Trail Distance: 3 mi?   Loops: Shortest: Longest:
Trail Surface: Natural
Trail Use Fee: None
Method Of Ski Trail Grooming: None
Skiing Ability Suggested: Novice
Hiking Trail Difficulty: Easy
Mountain Biking Ability Suggested: NA
Terrain: Steep 0%, Hilly 0%, Moderate 15%, Flat 85%
Camping: None

Owned by the state of Michigan
Managed by the DNR Parks and Recreation Division
Northern portion - Leased to Peninsula Township for park purposes
Southern portion - DNR plans to lease remainder of land to the township for park purposes.

Some trails exist around the tip near the lighthouse. Some casual trail marking has been done but may not be marked well.

LAKE MICHIGAN

EAST GRAND TRAVERSE BAY

BASSETT
ISLAND
(CAMPING)

SHALLOW

NORTH BEACH

EAGLES
NEST
LOOKOUT

HIGH RIDGE

RANGER
RESIDENCE

PUBLIC DOCK

HIGH
POINT

PICNIC
BEACH

T

T

T

SOUTH BEACH

T-TOILET

SAND
POINT

LAKE MICHIGAN

POWER ISLAND WILDERNESS PARK

Grand Traverse County Parks and Recreation Departme Department
1125 W.Civic Center Drive   616-922-4818
Traverse City, MI 49684

Michigan Atlas & Gazetteer Location: 74B3

County Location: Grand Traverse

Directions To Trailhead:
In Grand Traverse Bay (west arm), just off shore near Bowers Harbor

Trail Type: Hiking/Walking
Trail Distance: 5 mi   Loops: Many   Shortest: Longest:
Trail Surface: Natural
Trail Use Fee: None
Method Of Ski Trail Grooming: NA
Skiing Ability Suggested: NA
Hiking Trail Difficulty: Easy to difficult
Mountain Biking Ability Suggested: NA
Terrain: Steep 5%, Hilly 10%, Moderate 35%, Flat 50%
Camping: Campground on the island

Maintained by the Grand Traverse County Parks and Recreation Department
The island is also known as Marion Island.
Power Island has a beach, toilets and picnic area.
A campground is located on the adjacent Bassett Island which is connected to
Power Island by a narrow Isthmus. Depending on the water level of Grand
Traverse Bay the isthmus may be above or just below water level.
The two islands have a colorful past. Bassett Island was named after a hermit of
the same name that lived on the island in the 1890's.
Henry Ford bought both islands in 1917 for the site of a future summer home
that was never built. He may have camped on the island in August of 1923 with
Thomas Edison and Harvey Firestone. In the 1960's the island was bought by
Eugene Power of Ann Arbor and given to Grand Traverse County for a public
park.

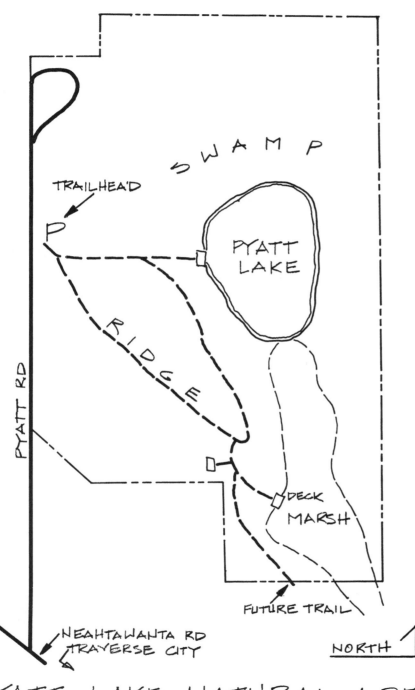

PYATT LAKE NATURAL AREA

Grand Traverse Regional Land Conservancy
624 Third Street
Traverse City, MI 49684

616-929-7911

Michigan Atlas & Gazetteer Location: 74A3

County Location: Grand Traverse

Directions To Trailhead:
Take Peninsula Drive north out of Traverse City on Old Mission Peninsula about 10 miles to Neahtawanta Rd, then west .25 mile to Pyatt Rd(seasonal), then north .25 mile to trailhead parking lot.

Trail Type: Hiking/Walking, Cross Country Skiing, Interpretive
Trail Distance: 1 mi   Loops: 1   Shortest: NA   Longest: 1 mi
Trail Surface: Natural
Trail Use Fee: None
Method Of Ski Trail Grooming: None
Skiing Ability Suggested: Novice
Hiking Trail Difficulty: Easy
Mountain Biking Ability Suggested: NA
Terrain: 100%Flat
Camping: None

Owned by the Grand Traverse Regional Land Conservancy
Trail is to be completed by 6/1/95
Trail not designed for skiing but permitted.
Trail has two observation decks.
The natural area contains 135 acres

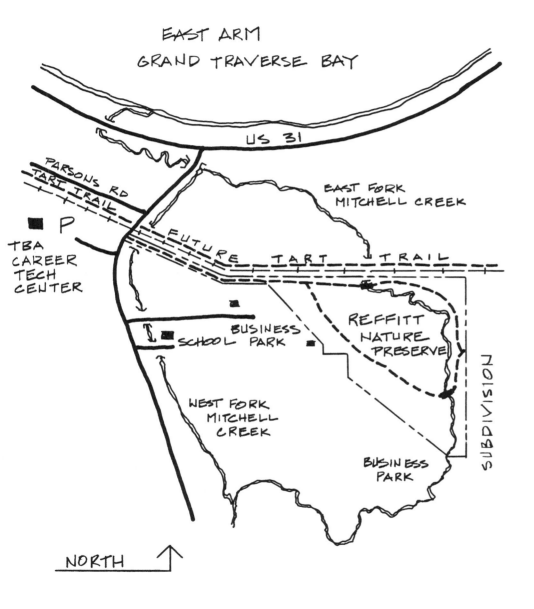

EAST ARM
GRAND TRAVERSE BAY

US 31

PARSONS RD
TART TRAIL

P

TBA
CAREER
TECH
CENTER

EAST FORK
MITCHELL CREEK

FUTURE   TART   TRAIL

BUSINESS
SCHOOL PARK

WEST FORK
MITCHELL
CREEK

REFFITT
NATURE
PRESERVE

SUBDIVISION

BUSINESS
PARK

NORTH

Reffitt Nature Preserve

Grand Traverse Regional Land Conservancy
624 Third St.
Traverse City, MI 49684

616-929-7911

Michigan Atlas & Gazetteer Location: 74C3

County Location: Grand Traverse

Directions To Trailhead:
Take 3 Mile south from US31 off East Grand Traverse Bay, to Parsons Rd., turn west (right) into the Traverse Bay Area Vocational Center parking lot. Park there. Pick up the TART trail located on the north side of the parking lot and take the trail east across 3 Mile Rd., then cross the railroad tracks to the preserve sign at the trailhead.

Trail Type: Hiking/Walking, Cross Country Skiing, Interpretive
Trail Distance: ! mi   Loops: 1   Shortest: NA   Longest: 1 mi
Trail Surface: Natural and boardwalk
Trail Use Fee: None
Method Of Ski Trail Grooming: None
Skiing Ability Suggested: Novice
Hiking Trail Difficulty: Easy
Mountain Biking Ability Suggested: NA
Terrain: 100% Flat
Camping: State Park nearby

Owned by the Grand Traverse Regional Land Conservancy
Located along the Mitchell Creek, a state designated trout stream.
The preserve was acquired in 1992.
The trail including boardwalks are scheduled for installation by 6/1/95.
The trail is not designed for skiing but is permitted.

REFFITT NATURE PRESERVE

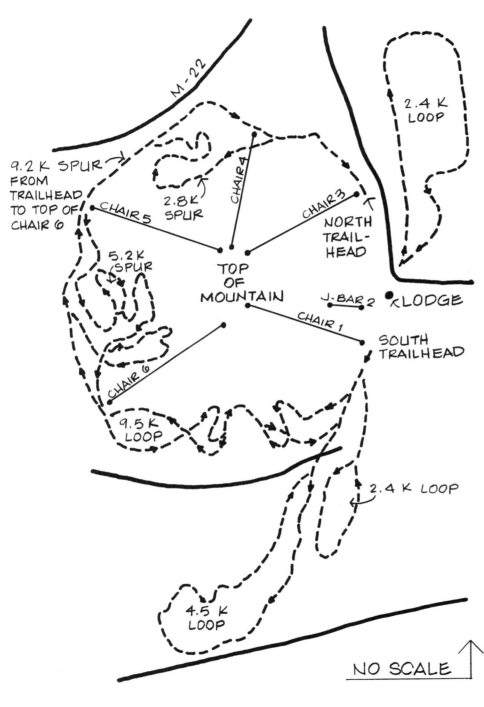

Sugar Loaf Resort

Sugar Loaf Resort
Route 1
Cedar, MI 49621

616-228-5461
800-632-9802

Michigan Atlas & Gazetteer Location: 74A1

County Location: Leelanau

Directions To Trailhead:
From Traverse City, take M72 west for 7 miles, then turn right (north) on Co Rd 651and follow the signs

Trail Type: Hiking/Walking, Cross Country Skiing, Mountain Biking
Trail Distance: 26 km   Loops: 8   Shortest: 1 km   Longest: 5.6 km
Trail Surface: Natural
Trail Use Fee: Yes, for skiing
Method Of Ski Trail Grooming: Double track set daily with skating lane
Skiing Ability Suggested: Novice to advanced
Hiking Trail Difficulty: Easy to moderate
Mountain Biking Ability Suggested: Intermediate to advanced
Terrain: Flat to very hilly
Camping: Available in the nearby Sleeping Bear Dunes National Lakeshore

Privately operated 4 season alpine ski resort with an extensive well designed and maintained trail system. Lodging, ski shop, lessons, restaurants to name only a few features Expertly designed trails by John Capper. Breathtaking views of Lake Michigan, off shore islands and surrounding landscape from the top of Sugar Loaf.

SUGAR LOAF RESORT

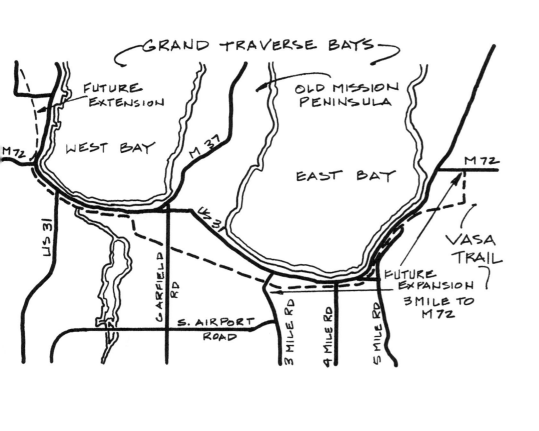

TART
PO Box 252
Traverse City, MI 49685-0252

616-941-2453

Michigan Atlas & Gazetteer Location: 74B234

County Location: Grand Traverse

Directions To Trailhead:
From Acme on the east to the west side of West Bay on the west.

Trail Type: Hiking/Walking
Trail Distance: 12 mi   Loops: Shortest: Longest:
Trail Surface: Paved and ballast
Trail Use Fee: None
Method Of Ski Trail Grooming: None
Skiing Ability Suggested: NA
Hiking Trail Difficulty: Easy
Mountain Biking Ability Suggested: NA
Terrain: 100% Flat
Camping: Traverse City State Park

Maintained by TART
Bike and roller blade rentals and repairs are available in Traverse City
Trail is 8' wide asphalt pavement.
Trail is within view of the West Bay of Grand Traverse Bay

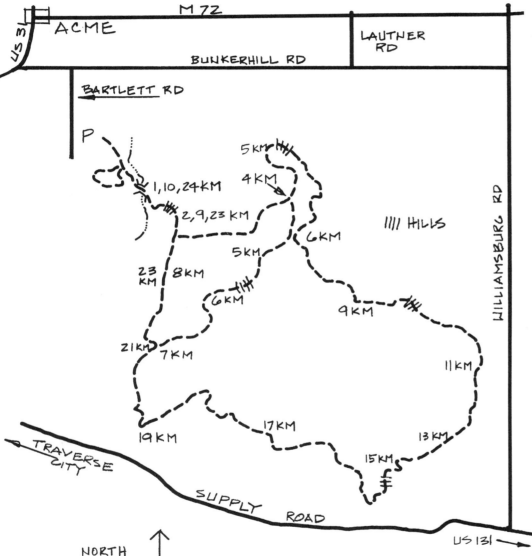

M 72

ACME

US 31

LAUTHER RD

BUNKERHILL RD

BARTLETT RD

P

1,10,24 KM

5 KM

4 KM

2,9,23 KM

HILLS

6 KM

5 KM

23 KM

8 KM

6 KM

9 KM

21 KM

7 KM

11 KM

WILLIAMSBURG RD

19 KM

17 KM

13 KM

15 KM

TRAVERSE CITY

SUPPLY ROAD

US 131

NORTH

North American Vasa, Inc.
PO Box 581
Traverse City, MI 49685

616-946-8272

Michigan Atlas & Gazetteer Location: 74C4,75C4

County Location: Grand Traverse

Directions To Trailhead:
M72 south from Acme to Bunker Hill Rd, then to Bartlett Rd, then south on Bartlett to trailhead on left (east) side of the road.

Trail Type: Hiking/Walking, Cross Country Skiing, Mountain Biking
Trail Distance: 30 km   Loops: 3   Shortest: 3 km   Longest: 26 km
Trail Surface: Natural
Trail Use Fee: None, but donations accepted at the trailhead
Method Of Ski Trail Grooming: Track set with skating lane
Skiing Ability Suggested: Novice to intermediate
Hiking Trail Difficulty: Easy but long
Mountain Biking Ability Suggested: Novice
Terrain: Steep 5%, Hilly 25%, Moderate 50%, Flat 20%
Camping: SFCG nearby and Jellystone Campground seasonally (summer)

Maintained by the North American Vasa, Inc a non-profit organization
Site of the annual North American Vasa race held in February
Heated restrooms at the trailhead.
The Vasa course and many other forest roads and trails are used for mountain biking.

VASA TRAIL

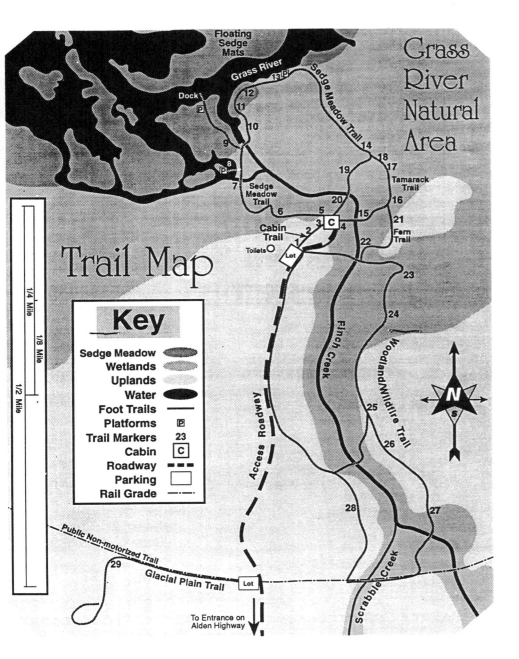

Floating Sedge Mats

Grass River

Dock

Trail Map

Key

Sedge Meadow	⬭
Wetlands	⬭
Uplands	⬭
Water	⬭
Foot Trails	—
Platforms	P
Trail Markers	23
Cabin	C
Roadway	- - -
Parking	☐
Rail Grade	-·-·-

1/4 Mile
1/8 Mile
1/2 Mile

Sedge Meadow Trail

Cabin Trail

Toilets

Lot

Sedge Meadow Trail

Tamarack Trail

Fern Trail

Finch Creek

Woodland/Wildlife Trail

Access Roadway

Public Non-motorized Trail

Glacial Plain Trail

Lot

To Entrance on Alden Highway

Scrabble Creek

N

Grass River Natural Area

GRASS RIVER NATURAL AREA

Grass River Natural Area, Inc
PO Box 231
Bellaire, MI 49615-0231

616-533-8576
616-533-8314

Michigan Atlas & Gazetteer Location: 75A6

County Location: Antrim

Directions To Trailhead:
Between Lake Bellaire and Clam Lake, 8.5 miles west of Mancelona via M88 and Co Rd 618 (Alden Hwy) 1.5 miles east of Crystal Springs Rd. and .5 mile west of Comfort Rd. on Co Rd 618 (Alden Hwy).

Trail Type: Hiking/Walking, Cross Country Skiing, Interpretive
Trail Distance: 3 mi   Loops: 5   Shortest: .25 mi Longest: 2.25 mi
Trail Surface: Natural and boardwalks
Trail Use Fee: None, donations accepted (tax deductible)
Method Of Ski Trail Grooming: None
Skiing Ability Suggested: Novice
Hiking Trail Difficulty: Easy
Mountain Biking Ability Suggested: NA
Terrain: 100% flat
Camping: Not permitted

Maintained by Grass River Natural Area, Inc a non profit corporation
The Natural Area covers over 1,000 acres.
Interpretive Center phone answered in the summer only.
Limited skiing because of narrow boardwalks.
Additional 5 miles of old railroad right-of-way from Crystal Springs Rd to Brake Rd. is available for skiing and hiking (closed to motorized vehicles).
A 3/4 mile long access road from Co Rd 618 is not plowed.
Please leave your smoking, pets and food at home when visiting this natural area.
Call or write for the Trail Guide.

Traverse City Forest Area, Pere Marquette State Forest
404 W. 14th St.   616-946-4920
Traverse City, MI 49684

District Forest Manager, Pere Marquette State Forest
8015 Mackinaw Trail   616-775-9727
Cadillac, MI 49601

Michigan Atlas & Gazetteer Location: 75C5

County Location: Grand Traverse and Kalkaska

Directions To Trailhead:
Between Kalkaska and Traverse City, south of M72. Trailhead - (For skiers) 1.5 miles east of Williamsburg on M72 take Broomhead Rd. south for about 4 miles to parking lot on the left. Trailhead -(For hikers) Take Island Lake Rd. west from Kalkaska for about 9 miles to Guernsey Lake State Forest Campground (follow signs).

Trail Type: Hiking/Walking, Cross Country Skiing, Mountain Biking
Trail Distance: 10.98+ mi Loops: Several   Shortest: Longest: 8.6 mi
Trail Surface: Natural
Trail Use Fee: None
Method Of Ski Trail Grooming: None, but well skied all of the time
Skiing Ability Suggested: Novice
Hiking Trail Difficulty: Easy to moderate
Mountain Biking Ability Suggested: NA
Terrain: Flat to very hilly
Camping: Campground in the quiet area is open during snowless months

Maintained by the DNR Forest Management Division
This 2,800 acre quiet area is closed to motorized vehicles, making it a very delightful ski, hiking and mountain bikel area.
The Shore to Shore Trail passes through the area.
The circular route around the quiet area is best for biking and skiing since the EW and NS trails are on section lines and ignore the difficult terrain that is very difficult to ski and ride.
A hike-in camping site is provided on the interior of the area with pit toilets and a water well . This area is a favorite of the local skiers.

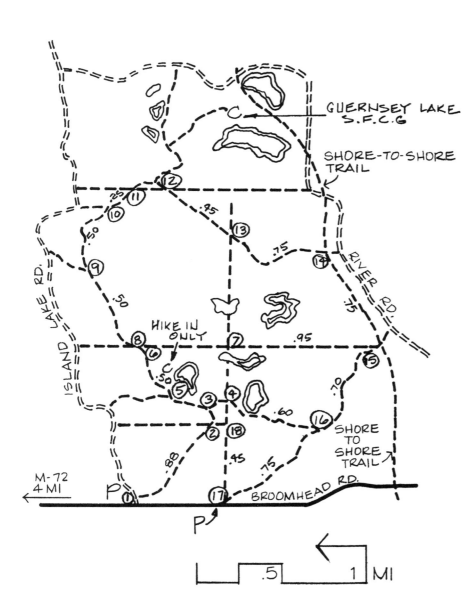

SAND LAKES
QUIET AREA

TRAIL NOTES

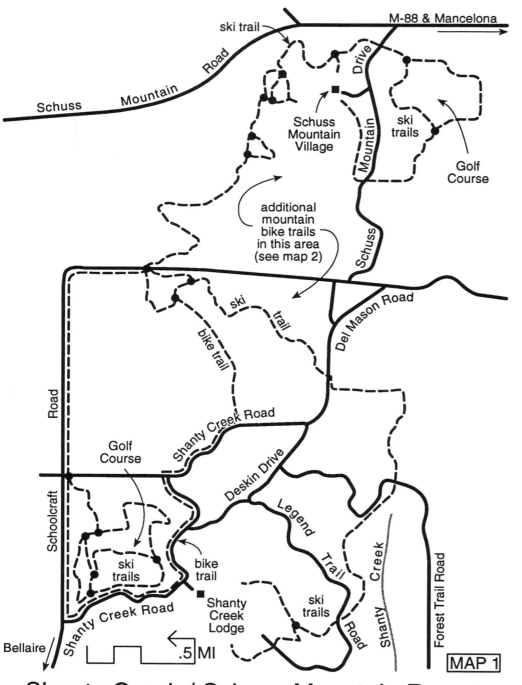

Shanty Creek/Schuss Mountain Resorts
Shanty Creek
Bellaire, MI 49615

616-533-8621
800-678-4111

Michigan Atlas & Gazetteer Location: 75A67

County Location: Antrim

Directions To Trailhead:
Between Mancelona and Bellaire north and east of M88 (follow signs) Shuss Mountain Resort is just west of Mancelona and Shanty Creek Lodge is Just southeast of Bellaire.

Trail Type: Hiking/Walking, Cross Country Skiing, Mountain Biking
Trail Distance: 25+ mi   Loops: Many   Shortest: .75 mi Longest: 15 mi
Trail Surface: Paved, gravel, natural
Trail Use Fee: Yes, varies with season and trail use
Method Of Ski Trail Grooming: Track set
Skiing Ability Suggested: Novice to advanced
Hiking Trail Difficulty: Easy to difficult
Mountain Biking Ability Suggested: Novice to advanced
Terrain: Steep 15%, Hilly 40%, Moderate 40%, Flat 5%
Camping: Campgrounds nearby

Privately operated 2 lodge, 4 season resort complex with all amenities SKIING-Site of the annual White Pine Stampede held the first Saturday of February . This unique 2 lodge trail system allows for some very unique trail opportunities with an interconnecting trail between the lodges. Lighted ski trail. Some trails on golf courses. Trail fee includes shuttle bus service between resorts. Long downhill ski runs on the ski trail from Schuss Mt to Shanty Creek. MOUNTAIN BIKING-Site of the NORBA Nationals held in June each year. The Course uses some of the ski trails and additional single track trails used for the annual NORBA race.   The NORBA course has Beginner (11 mi), Sport(13.8 mi) and Pro(5.5 mi) loops. Smaller loops are possible because of the trail layout. Intermediate or better riders should enjoy all three courses. Resort trails (mostly 2 tracks between the resorts)are for beginners.

Shanty Creek / Schuss Mountain Resort

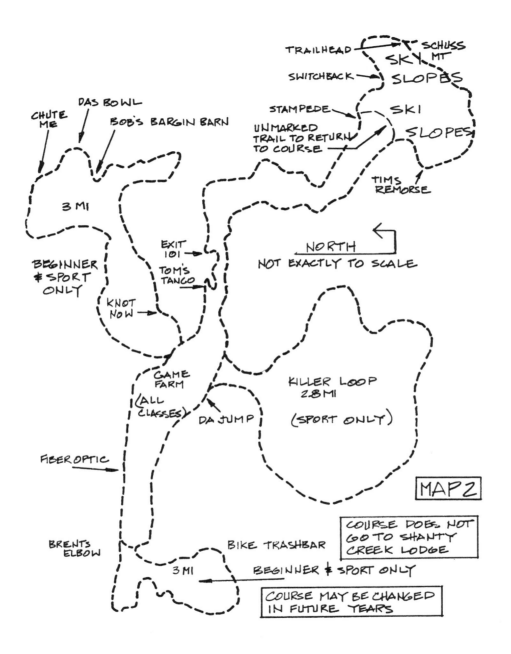

TRAILHEAD
SCHUSS MT
SKY
SLOPES
SWITCHBACK
STAMPEDE
SKI
UNMARKED TRAIL TO RETURN TO COURSE
SLOPES
CHUTE ME
DAS BOWL
BOB'S BARGIN BARN
TIMS REMORSE
3 MI
BEGINNER & SPORT ONLY
EXIT 101
NORTH
NOT EXACTLY TO SCALE
TOM'S TANGO
KNOT NOW
GAME FARM
(ALL CLASSES)
DA JUMP
KILLER LOOP 2.8 MI
(SPORT ONLY)
FIBER OPTIC
MAP 2
COURSE DOES NOT GO TO SHANTY CREEK LODGE
BRENTS ELBOW
BIKE TRASHBAR
3 MI
BEGINNER & SPORT ONLY
COURSE MAY BE CHANGED IN FUTURE YEARS

SHANTY CREEK/SCHUSS MT. RESORT
1994 NORBA COURSE

Kalkaska Forest Area, Pere Marquette State Forest
2089 N. Birch   616-258-2711
Kalkaska, MI 49646

District Forest Manager, Pere Marquette State Forest
8015 Mackinaw Trail   616-775-9727
Cadillac, MI 49601

Michigan Atlas & Gazetteer Location: 75B5

County Location: Antrim

Directions To Trailhead:
From Kalkaska take M72 west about 4.5 miles, then north on Co. Rd. 597
(Rapid City Rd) about 5 miles to trail head. Trailhead - On west side just after a
bend in the road.

Trail Type: Hiking/Walking, Cross Country Skiing, Mountain Biking, Interpretive
Trail Distance: 1.75 mi   Loops: NA   Shortest: NA   Longest: NA
Trail Surface: Natural
Trail Use Fee: None
Method Of Ski Trail Grooming: None
Skiing Ability Suggested: Novice
Hiking Trail Difficulty: Easy
Mountain Biking Ability Suggested: Novice
Terrain: 100% Flat
Camping: None

Maintained by the DNR Forest Management Division
Part of the trail is on an abandon railroad bed.
Viewing platform at end of trail overlooking Skegemog Lake shoreline

RAPID CITY
1 MILE

.25   .5 MI

P

CO RD 597

PRIVATE

PRIVATE

SKEGEMOG
LAKE

VIEWING
PLATFORM

ABANDON
RAILROAD
GRADE

SKEGEMOG LAKE PATHWAY

Whitewater Township Park
9500 Park Rd.
Williamsburg, MI 49690

616-267-9321

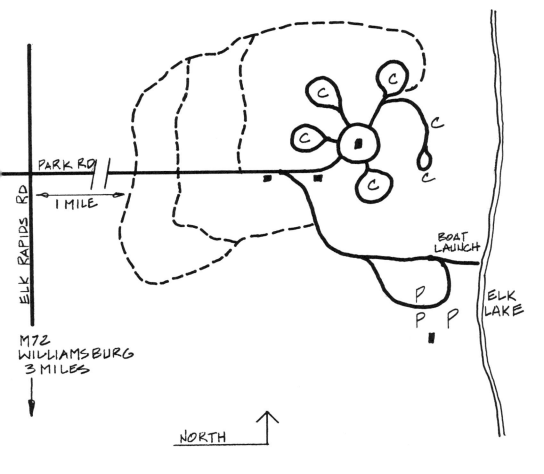

PARK RD

ELK RAPIDS RD

1 MILE

M72
WILLIAMSBURG
3 MILES

NORTH

BOAT
LAUNCH

ELK
LAKE

Michigan Atlas & Gazetteer Location: 75B4

County Location: Grand Traverse

Directions To Trailhead:
M72, 10 miles east from Traverse City to Williamsburg, north on Elk Lake Rd 3 miles to Park Rd., then east on Park Rd to the park.

Trail Type: Hiking/Walking, Cross Country Skiing, Interpretive
Trail Distance: 1.5 mi   Loops: 2   Shortest: .5 mi   Longest: 1 mi
Trail Surface: Wood chips and natural
Trail Use Fee: None
Method Of Ski Trail Grooming: None
Skiing Ability Suggested: Novice to intermediate
Hiking Trail Difficulty: Easy
Mountain Biking Ability Suggested: NA
Terrain: Steep 0%, Hilly 0%, Moderate 80%, Flat 20%
Camping: Campground at trailhead

Owned by Whitewater Township
Very nice campground with boat launch on the shore of Elk Lake.
Total park is 117 acres.

WHITEWATER PARK

Cross Country Ski Shop
PO Box 745
Grayling, MI 49738

517-348-8558
517-821-6559

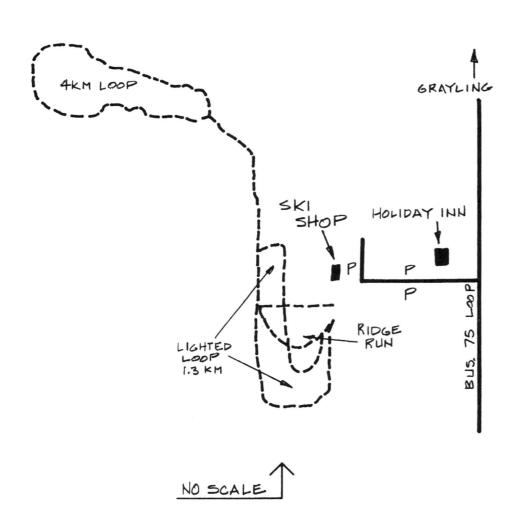

Michigan Atlas & Gazetteer Location: 76C3

County Location: Roscommon

Directions To Trailhead:
On I-75 Business Loop behind the Holiday Inn on the south side of Grayling

Trail Type: Cross Country Skiing
Trail Distance: 2.5 mi   Loops: 3   Shortest: .3 mi   Longest: 2.5 mi
Trail Surface: Natural
Trail Use Fee: None
Method Of Ski Trail Grooming: Track set with skating lanes
Skiing Ability Suggested: Novice
Hiking Trail Difficulty: NA
Mountain Biking Ability Suggested: NA
Terrain: Steep 0%, Hilly 0%, Moderate 5%, Flat 95
Camping: None

Complete ski shop with rentals.
Owned and staffed by expert nordic skiers.
Excellent place to try out equipment before purchasing.
One of the most knowledgeable shops for racing and touring equipment in the state.
A .8 mile lighted trail on site.

CROSS COUNTRY SKI SHOP

Dave Forbush
4971 Co. Rd. 612, PO Box 327   517-348-5989
Frederic , MI 49733

I·75
EXIT 264 .5MI (FREDERIC-LEWISTON)

DAYSKIERS LODGE

P

NIGHT TRAIL

GREEN
LOOP
3.5 KM

ROLLERCOASTER LOOP
8 KM

MOST DIFFICULT

BLUE LOOP
5.1 KM

SCALE NOT KNOWN

PINES
LOOP
11.5KM

SEE
HARTWICK
PINES
STATE
PARK FOR MORE TRAILS

FORBUSH CORNER

Michigan Atlas & Gazetteer Location: 76B3

County Location: Crawford

Directions To Trailhead:
9 miles north of Grayling on I-75, then .25 mile east of exit 264
(Lewiston/Fredric) to the ski area

Trail Type: Cross Country Skiing
Trail Distance: 36+ km   Loops: 5   Shortest: 1 km   Longest: 11.5 km
Trail Surface: Natural
Trail Use Fee: Yes
Method Of Ski Trail Grooming: Expertly track set and groomed space for skating
Skiing Ability Suggested: Novice to advanced
Hiking Trail Difficulty: NA
Mountain Biking Ability Suggested: NA
Terrain: Steep 5%, Hilly 45%, Moderate 35%, Flat 15%
Camping: Campground available at Hartwick Pines State Park

A privately operated touring center.
Brown bag eating area, limited food service(weekends only), lessons, lodging,
quality ski shop with rentals.
Owner, Dave Forbush prides himself in the expertly goomed trails accomplished
by three Snowcat grooming machines.
Lighted trail available. Trails connect with Hartwick Pines State Park.
Scheduled ski instruction with Scott Hartwig.
Ski clinics held by Olympic Gold Medalist, Nikolai Anikin, former head coach of
the Soviet team.
Write for a free brochure.

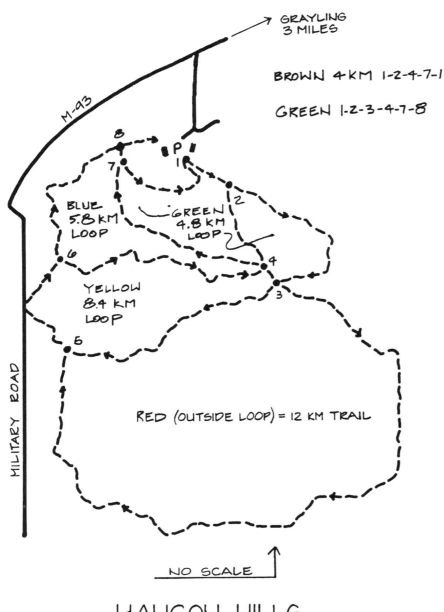

GRAYLING
3 MILES

BROWN 4 KM 1-2-4-7-1

GREEN 1-2-3-4-7-8

M-93

8

7

P

1

2

BLUE
5.8 KM
LOOP

GREEN
4.8 KM
LOOP

6

4

3

YELLOW
8.4 KM
LOOP

5

RED (OUTSIDE LOOP) = 12 KM TRAIL

MILITARY ROAD

NO SCALE

HANSON HILLS
RECREATION AREA

Hanson Hills Recreation Park
PO Box 361
Grayling, MI 49738

517-348-9266

Michigan Atlas & Gazetteer Location: 76CD23

County Location: Crawford

Directions To Trailhead:
Takes M72/M93 west 1.5 miles to the M93 cutoff, then south on M93 to the park 1.5 miles west of Grayling

Trail Type: Hiking/Walking, Cross Country Skiing, Mountain Biking
Trail Distance: 35 km   Loops: 5   Shortest: 4 km   Longest: 12 km
Trail Surface: Natural
Trail Use Fee: Yes, daily and seasonal passes available
Method Of Ski Trail Grooming: Track set
Skiing Ability Suggested: Novice to intermediate
Hiking Trail Difficulty: Easy to moderate
Mountain Biking Ability Suggested: Novice to intermediate
Terrain: Steep 0%, Hilly 60%, Moderate 30%, Flat 10%
Camping: None

Maintained by a local community group on the Hanson State Game Refuge
Ski rentals, snack bar, warming area and alpine skiing.
Orginally developed in the 1930's for cross-country skiing.
Some of the original trail signs are still visable.
All trails completely redone in 1986.
Site of races held annually.
Skating trail available.
Write for the brochure.

TRAIL NOTES

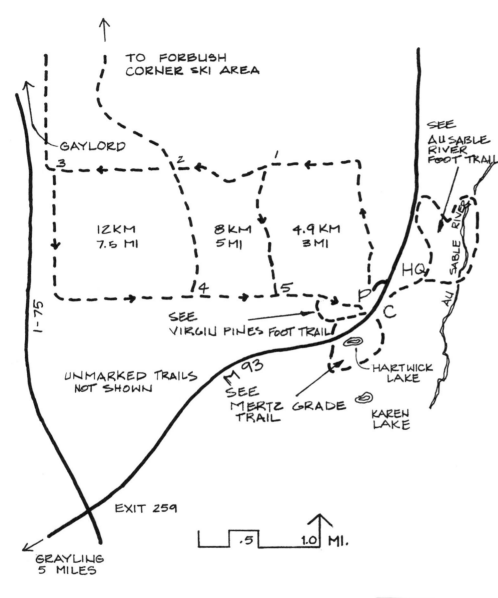

TO FORBUSH
CORNER SKI AREA

SEE
AUSABLE
RIVER
FOOT TRAIL

GAYLORD

3   2   1

12 KM
7.5 MI

8 KM
5 MI

4.9 KM
3 MI

HQ

I-75

4   5

P

C

SEE
VIRGIN PINES FOOT TRAIL

UNMARKED TRAILS
NOT SHOWN

M 93

SEE
MERTZ GRADE
TRAIL

HARTWICK
LAKE

KAREN
LAKE

EXIT 259

.5   1.0 MI.

GRAYLING
5 MILES

MAP 1

SKI TRAILS
HARTWICK PINES STATE PARK

Hartwick Pines State Park

Hartwick Pines State Park
Rte 3, Box 3840
Grayling, MI 49738

517-348-7068

DNR Park and Recreation Division

517-373-1270
517-275-5151

Michigan Atlas & Gazetteer Location: 76BC3

County Location: Crawford

Directions To Trailhead:
7.5 miles NE of Grayling on M93 just east of I75 about 3 miles

Trail Type: Hiking/Walking, Cross Country Skiing, Mountain Biking, Interpretive
Trail Distance: 18+ mi   Loops: Many   Shortest: 1 mi   Longest: 7.5+ mi
Trail Surface: Natural
Trail Use Fee: None, but vehicle entry fee required
Method Of Ski Trail Grooming: Designated ski trails are track set
Skiing Ability Suggested: Novice to intermediate
Hiking Trail Difficulty: Easy to moderate
Mountain Biking Ability Suggested: Easy to moderate
Terrain: Steep 3%, Hilly 7%, Moderate 60%, Flat 30%
Camping: Campground in park year open all year

Maintained by the DNR Parks and Recreation Division
A unique state park with a stand of virgin White Pine, one over 300 years old.
Site of the Logging Museum.
Some trails connect with Forbush Corner cross country ski area on the north.
Marked Nature Trails:
      Virgin Pines Nature Trail -1 mile loop
      Mertz Grande Nature Trail -2 mile loop
      AuSable River Foot (nature) Trail - 3 mile loop
Marked Hiking Trails: All in one trail system
      Aspen   3 mile loop
      Deer Run 5 mile loop
      Weary Legs 7.5 mile
Many additional non marked trails in the park.

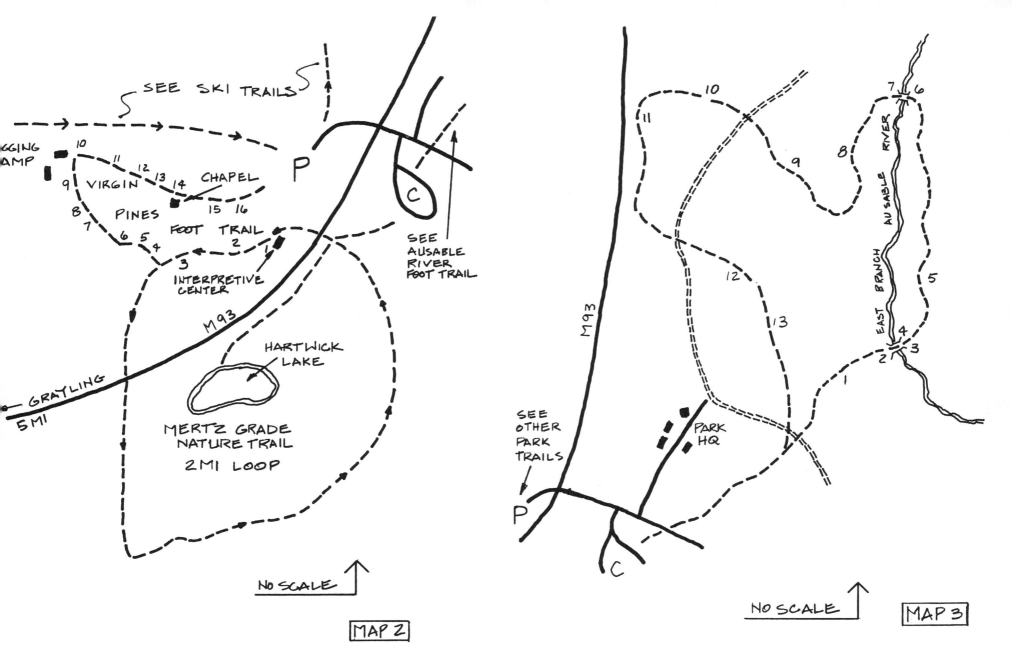

SEE SKI TRAILS

P

C

SEE
AUSABLE
RIVER
FOOT TRAIL

GGING
AMP

10

11
12
13 14   CHAPEL
9   VIRGIN
8   PINES   15 16
7   6 5   FOOT TRAIL
4   2
3   INTERPRETIVE
CENTER

M 93

HARTWICK
LAKE

GRAYLING
5 MI

MERTZ GRADE
NATURE TRAIL
2 MI LOOP

NO SCALE

MAP 2

VIRGIN PINES FOOT TRAIL
MERTZ GRADE NATURE TRAIL
HARTWICK PINES STATE PARK

10
11
9
8
12
13
7 6
5
4
2 3
1

EAST BRANCH AU SABLE RIVER

M 93

SEE
OTHER
PARK
TRAILS

PARK
HQ

P

C

NO SCALE

MAP 3

AU SABLE RIVER FOOT TRAIL
HARTWICK PINES STATE PARK

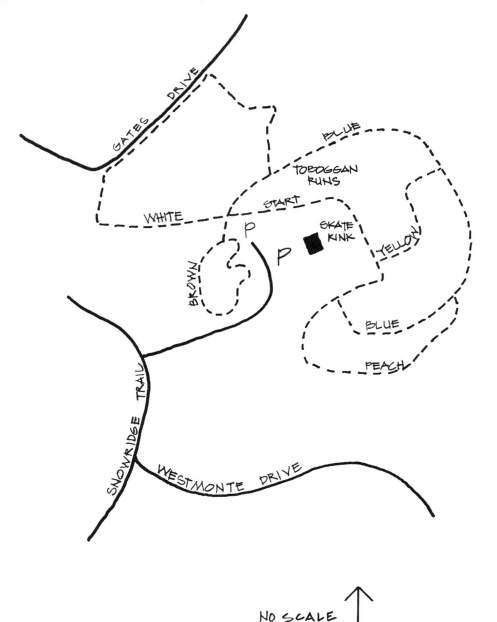

Lakes of the North
541 Skytrails Court
Mancelona, MI 49656

616-585-6155
616-585-6000

Michigan Atlas & Gazetteer Location: 76A2

County Location: Otsego

Directions To Trailhead:
4 miles west of Alba on C42, then 2 miles on Olds Rd to winter sports area

Trail Type: Cross Country Skiing
Trail Distance: 15 km   Loops: 7   Shortest: Longest:
Trail Surface: Natural
Trail Use Fee: Yes
Method Of Ski Trail Grooming:
Skiing Ability Suggested: Novice
Hiking Trail Difficulty: NA
Mountain Biking Ability Suggested: NA
Terrain: Flat to rolling
Camping: On site

Privately operated cross country ski area in a planned recreational community.

LAKES OF THE NORTH

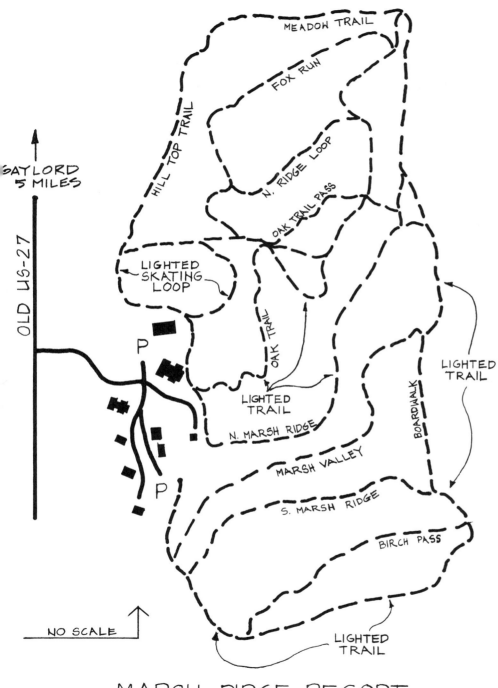

MARSH RIDGE RESORT

Marsh Ridge

Marsh Ridge
4815 Historic 27, PO Box 623
Gaylord, MI 49735

800-624-7518
517-732-6794

Michigan Atlas & Gazetteer Location: 76A3

County Location: Otsego

Directions To Trailhead:
5 miles south of Gaylord I-75 to exit 279, then south on Old 27 about 1.5 miles to the entrance on the east side of the highway.

Trail Type: Cross Country Skiing
Trail Distance: 28 km   Loops: 10   Shortest: 3 km   Longest: 10 km
Trail Surface: Nastural
Trail Use Fee: Yes, guests are free
Method Of Ski Trail Grooming: Track set
Skiing Ability Suggested: Novice to advanced
Hiking Trail Difficulty: NA
Mountain Biking Ability Suggested: NA
Terrain: Steep 10%, Hilly 20%, Moderate 30%, Flat 40%
Camping: None

Privately operated resort and conference center
The resort includes 32 jacuzzi suites, pool, sauna, whirlpool, exerise and tanning facilities.
Eight double jacuzzi theme suites available.
This trail system is small but never the less a delight to ski.
All trails are well groomed with 3.5 km are lighted.
Lodges are elaborately decorated with theme decorating . Four Diamond and AAA rated. Breakfast included with each room.
Golf and ski packages available as well as group rates .

Michaywe Resort
1535 Opal Lake Rd.
Gaylord, MI 49735

517-939-8919
517-939-8800

Michigan Atlas & Gazetteer Location: 76A3

County Location: Otsego

Directions To Trailhead:
7 miles south of Gaylord on old US27, then east on Charles Brink Rd to Michaywe main entrance, then follow signs to Ski Center at the base of the alpine slopes.

Trail Type: Hiking/Walking, Cross Country Skiing
Trail Distance: 11 mi   Loops: 6   Shortest: 1 mi   Longest: 2 mi
Trail Surface: Natural
Trail Use Fee: None
Method Of Ski Trail Grooming: Double track set
Skiing Ability Suggested: Novice to advanced
Hiking Trail Difficulty: NA
Mountain Biking Ability Suggested: NA
Terrain: Steep 20%, Hilly 20%, Moderate 30%, Flat 30%
Camping: Available on site and at a nearby KOA

Privately operated alpine and nordic resort
Lessons, rentals, lodging, restaurant, snack bar, entertainment and bar.
Telemark area with lifts and lessons available.
Very nice well groomed beginner trail system.
Light trail on weekends.

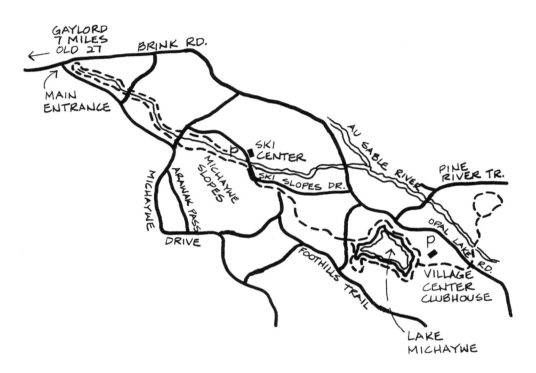

NO SCALE

MICHAYWE RESORT

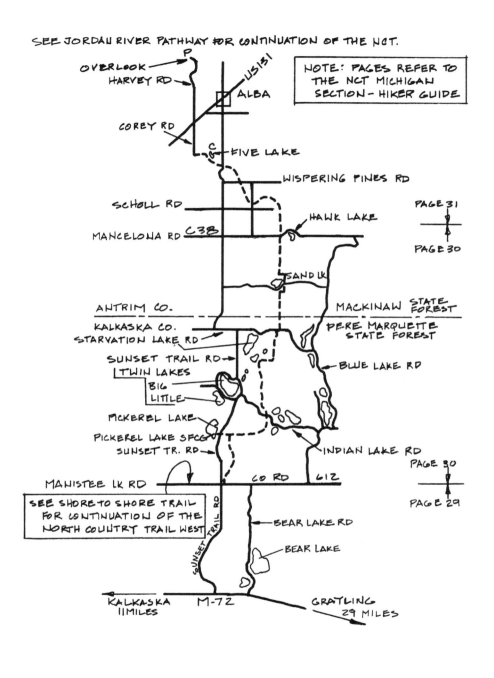

Kalkaska Forest Area, Pere Marquette State Forest
2089 North Birch St   616-258-2711
Kalkaska, MI 49646

Gaylord Forest Area, Mackinaw State Forest
1732 West M32, Box 667   517-732-3541
Gaylord, MI 49735

Michigan Atlas & Gazetteer Location: 76AB1

County Location: Kalkaska, Antrim

Directions To Trailhead:
South Trailhead - Co. Rd. 612 about 100 yards east of Sunrise Trail
North Trailhead - Landside Overlook of the Jordan River Valley on the north
end of Harvey Rd (overlook located 1 mile west of Alba on Co. Rd. 620, then
1.5 miles north on Harvey Rd.)

Trail Type: Hiking/Walking, Mountain Biking
Trail Distance: 21.7 mi   Loops: NA   Shortest: NA   Longest: NA
Trail Surface: Natural
Trail Use Fee: None
Method Of Ski Trail Grooming: NA
Skiing Ability Suggested: NA
Hiking Trail Difficulty: Easy
Mountain Biking Ability Suggested: Easy
Terrain: Rolling to hilly
Camping: Pickerel Lake, Five Lake and Pinney Bridge SFCG's

Trail located in the Pere Marquette and Mackinaw State Forest
Built and maintained by North Country Trail Association members and
volunteers
Contact the North Country Trail Association for the Hiker Guide at PO Box 311,
White Cloud, MI 49349 616-689-1912
Trail marked with blue blazes
See NCNST - Michigan Section - Hiker Guide, pages 30 and 31.

NORTH COUNTRY TRAIL-
PERE MARQUETTE 2/MACKINAW 1 STATE FORESTS

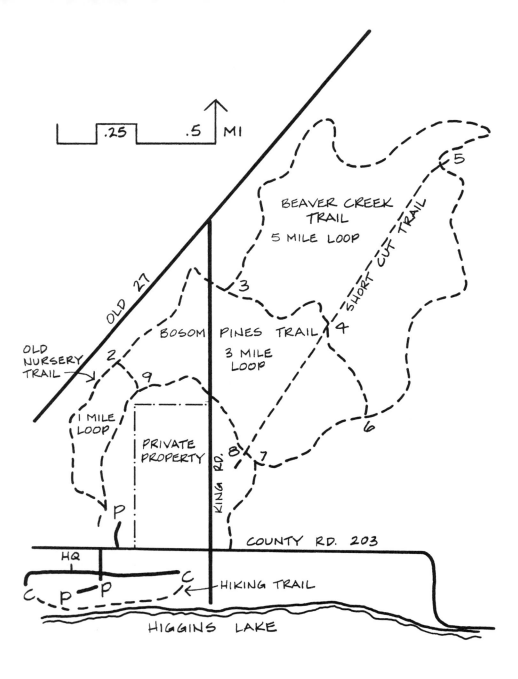

NORTH HIGGINS LAKE STATE PARK

North Higgins Lake State Park
11511 W. Higgins Lake Drive
Roscommon, MI 48653

517-821-6125

DNR Parks and Recreation Division

517-373-1270

Michigan Atlas & Gazetteer Location: 76D23

County Location: Crawford

Directions To Trailhead:
1.5 miles east of US27 or 4.5 miles west of I75 on Co Rd 200 (Roscommon Rd.)
at the north end of Higgins Lake .
Trailhead - Parking lot of CCC Museum and historical exhibit on the north side
of the road.

Trail Type: Hiking/Walking, Cross Country Skiing, Mountain Biking, Interpretive
Trail Distance: 7.5 mi   Loops: 3   Shortest: 1 mi   Longest: 6 mi
Trail Surface: Natural
Trail Use Fee: None, but vehicle entry fee required
Method Of Ski Trail Grooming: Track set
Skiing Ability Suggested: Novice to intermediate
Hiking Trail Difficulty: Easy
Mountain Biking Ability Suggested: Novice
Terrain: Steep 0%, Hilly 20%, Moderate 30%, Flat 50%
Camping: Available in the park

Maintained by the DNR Parks and Recreation Division
Site of the Beaver Creek Challenge held in February
Hanson Hill, Cross Country Ski Headquarters and Tisdale Triangle are other
trails nearby . Most trails are double width. Some are single with a skating lane.
The 1 and 3 mile loops have the most hills.
A nature and fitness trail are also part of the system.

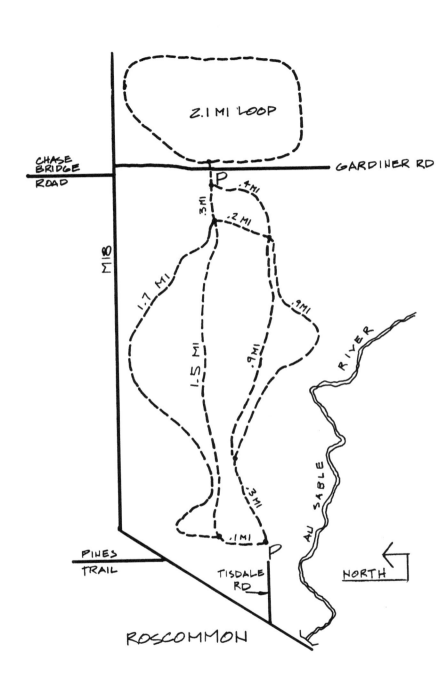

CHASE
BRIDGE
ROAD

GARDINER RD

2.1 MI LOOP

M18

.4 MI

.3 MI

.2 MI

1.7 MI

1.5 MI

.9 MI

.9 MI

.3 MI

.1 MI

PINES
TRAIL

TISDALE
RD

P

RIVER

AU SABLE

NORTH

ROSCOMMON

TISDALE TRIANGLE PATHWAY

Roscommon Forest Area, Au Sable State Forest
Box 218, 8717 N. Roscommon Rd.   517-275-5151
Roscommon, MI 48635

District Forest Manager, Au Sable State Forest
191 S. Mt. Tom Rd.   517-826-3211
Mio, MI 48647

Michigan Atlas & Gazetteer Location: 76D4, 77D4

County Location: Roscommon

Directions To Trailhead:
Trailhead - At the east end of Tisdale Rd. .5 mile east of Roscommon on M18.
Trailhead - .5 mile south of M18, on Gardiner Rd .

Trail Type: Hiking/Walking, Cross Country Skiing, Mountain Biking
Trail Distance: 8.4 mi   Loops: 4   Shortest: 3 mi   Longest: 6 mi
Trail Surface: Natural
Trail Use Fee: None
Method Of Ski Trail Grooming: Track set
Skiing Ability Suggested: Novice to intermediate
Hiking Trail Difficulty: Easy
Mountain Biking Ability Suggested: Novice
Terrain: Steep 0%, Hilly 0%, Moderate 80%, Flat 20%
Camping: None along the trail but public and private campgrounds in the area

Maintained by the DNR Forest Management Division
Popular with local residents of Roscommon and the surrounding area
Other contacts:
        DNR Forest Management Division Office, Lansing, 517-373-1275
        DNR Forest Management Region Office, Roscommon, 517-275-5151

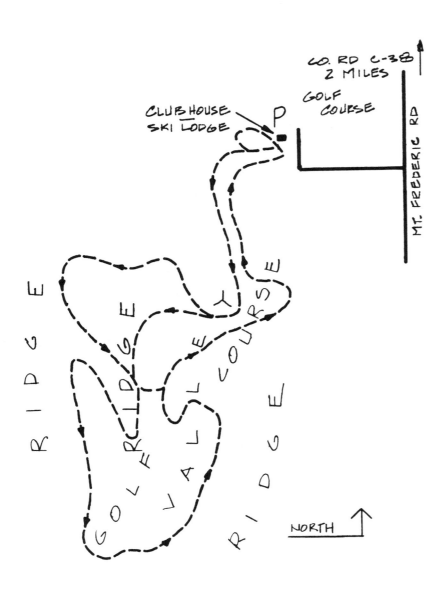

CO. RD C-38
2 MILES

GOLF
COURSE

CLUBHOUSE
SKI LODGE

P

MT. FREDERIC RD

RIDGE

RIDGE

GOLFRIDGE

GOLF VALE COURSE

RIDGE

NORTH

WILDERNESS VALLEY
CROSS COUNTRY SKI CENTER

Wilderness Valley   Attn. Dave Smith
7519 Mancelona Rd.   616-585-7090
Gaylord, MI 49735

Michigan Atlas & Gazetteer Location: 76A2

County Location: Otsego

Directions To Trailhead:
10 miles SW of Gaylord via Old US27 to the south end of Otsego Lake, then west on C-38(Mancelona Rd) 5 miles then south on Mt. Fredrick Rd about 2 miles, then west a short distance to the trailhead lodge (golf course clubhouse).

Trail Type: Cross Country Skiing
Trail Distance: 18 km   Loops: 6   Shortest: 1km   Longest: 18 km
Trail Surface: Natural
Trail Use Fee: Yes
Method Of Ski Trail Grooming: Double track set daily with skating lane
Skiing Ability Suggested: Novice to expert
Hiking Trail Difficulty: Easy to moderate
Mountain Biking Ability Suggested: NA
Terrain: Steep 20%, Hilly 60%, Moderate 15%, Flat 5%
Camping: None

Privately operated ski touring center.
Ski lodge, rentals, ski shop, restaurant and lodging are available on site.
Completely new trail system for 1994 on the 36 hole Black Forest championship golf course south of Co Rd C38. Expansion of the 18km course will take place in coming years.
The golf course club house is used as the ski lodge in the winter.
Consistantly well groomed trails, a reputation for outstanding trail design and reliable snow should continue to make this touring center one of the best in the state.

Gaylord Forest Area, Mackinaw State Forest
West M32, PO Box 667   517-732-3541
Gaylord, Mi 49735

District Forest Manger, Mackinaw State Forest
West M32, PO Box 667   517-732-3541
Gaylord, MI 49725

Michigan Atlas & Gazetteer Location: 77A6

County Location: Otsego

Directions To Trailhead:
From Gaylord take M32 east to Co Rd 495(Meridian Line Rd), then south 1.5 miles to the Bear Lake SFCG or,
3 miles south of Veinna Corners to Bear Lake Rd, then west 2 miles to Bear Lake SFCG
Trailheads are between site 36 and the Day Use Area and at across the road from the main entrance

Trail Type: Hiking/Walking, Interpretive
Trail Distance: 2.5 mi   Loops: 2   Shortest: .6   Longest: 2.2 mi
Trail Surface: Natural
Trail Use Fee: None
Method Of Ski Trail Grooming: NA
Skiing Ability Suggested: NA
Hiking Trail Difficulty: Easy
Mountain Biking Ability Suggested: NA
Terrain: Steep 0%, Hilly 5%, Moderate 80%, Flat 20%
Camping: Campground on site

Maintained by the DNR Forest Management Division
Part of the trail was the AuSable and Northwest Railroad that hauled logs to Lewiston and Oscoda in the late 1800's.
The trail passes through a wide variety of flora including upland hardwoods, pines, aspen and others. Also the trail passes a pond used by beavers.
Trail brochure is available.

Map

TO M-32

POWER LINES

BEAVER LODGE LOOP

BEAVER POND

LITTLE BEAR LAKE RD.

C

EAGLES ROOST LOOP

MERIDIAN LINE RD.

MINK POND

C

BIG BEAR LAKE

.25   .5 MI

BIG BEAR LAKE
NATURE PATHWAY

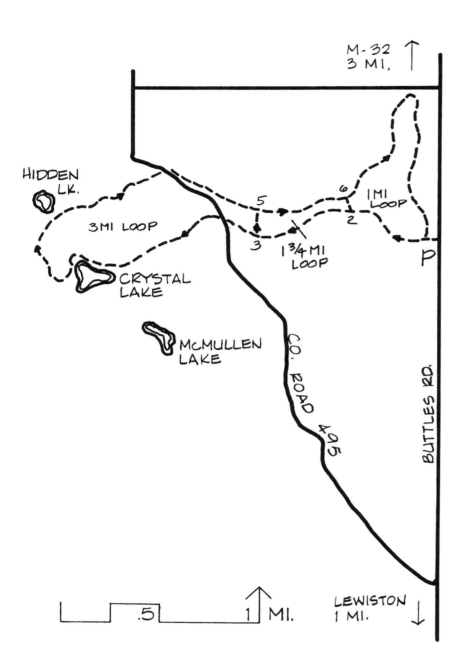

Atlanta Area Forest, Mackinaw State Forest
HCR 74, Box 30   517-785-4251
Atlanta, MI 49709

District Forest Manager, Mackinaw State Forest
Box 667, 1732 West M32   517-732-3541
Gaylord, MI 49735

Michigan Atlas & Gazetteer Location: 77A6

County Location: Montmorency

Directions To Trailhead:
Between Lewiston and M32 on Buttles Rd.(1 mile west of Co Rd 491) Take
Buttles Rd., north about 3 miles to the parking lot at the trailhead on the west
side of the road. Ellsworth Rd. is about 1 mile north of the trailhead.

Trail Type: Hiking/Walking, Cross Country Skiing, Mountain Biking
Trail Distance: 6 mi   Loops: 3   Shortest: 1.2 mi Longest: 3 mi
Trail Surface: Natural
Trail Use Fee: None
Method Of Ski Trail Grooming: None
Skiing Ability Suggested: Novice to intermediate
Hiking Trail Difficulty: Easy
Mountain Biking Ability Suggested: Novice
Terrain: Steep 0%, Hilly 2%, Moderate 30%, Flat 68%
Camping: None

Maintained by the DNR Forest Management Division
An good trail for the beginning skier.
Since much of the trail is in open terrian, this trail should be avoided on windy
winter days.
Other contacts:
          DNR Forest Management Division Office, Lansing, 517-373-1275
          DNR Forest Management Region Office, Roscommon, 517-275-5151

BUTTLES ROAD PATHWAY

Garland
HCR-1, Box 364-M
Lewiston, MI 49756

517-786-2211
800-968-0042

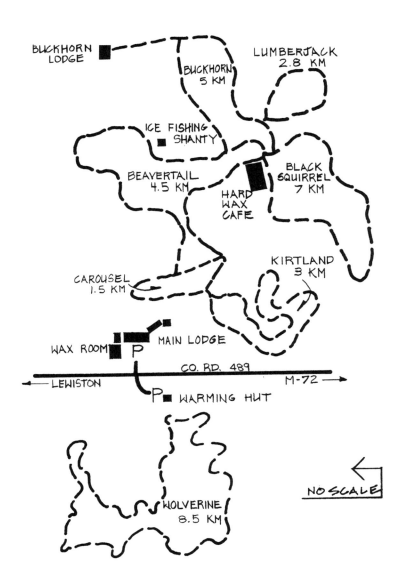

Michigan Atlas & Gazetteer Location: 77B6

County Location: Oscoda

Directions To Trailhead:
On Co Rd 489, 4.5 miles south of Lewiston and 12 miles north of Luzerne.

Trail Type: Cross Country Skiing
Trail Distance: 32.3 km   Loops: 7   Shortest: 1.5 km Longest: 8.5 km
Trail Surface: Natural
Trail Use Fee: Yes
Method Of Ski Trail Grooming: Track set
Skiing Ability Suggested: Novice to intermediate
Hiking Trail Difficulty: NA
Mountain Biking Ability Suggested: NA
Terrain: Steep 0%, Hilly 0%, Moderate 30%, Flat 70%
Camping: None

Privately operated 3,000 acre, four seasons resort
Ski shop, rentals, lodging, lessons, skating rink, restaurant, sauna, pool and jacuzzi are available. 5000 foot airstrip is on the property with charter air service available.
Very elegant lodge with other accomodations available.
Trails are on the golf course and rolling hills of the surrounding area.

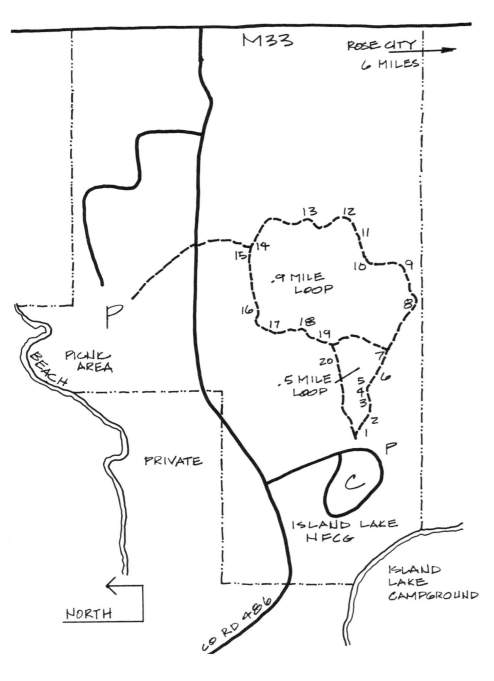

Mio Ranger District, Huron Manistee National Forest
401 Court St   517-826-3252
Mio, MI 48647

Forest Supervisor, Huron Manistee National Forest
421 S. Mitchell St.   616-775-2421
Cadillac, MI 49691   800-821-6263

Michigan Atlas & Gazetteer Location: 77D7

County Location: Oscoda

Directions To Trailhead:
North of M33 about 6 miles from Rose City, then west on Co Rd 486 about .7 mile to the campground where the trailhead is located. The main trailhead is not located at the day use area, but there is a feeder trail to the main loop from the day use area.

Trail Type: Hiking/Walking, Interpretive
Trail Distance: 1.4 mi   Loops: 2   Shortest: .5 mi   Longest: .9 mi
Trail Surface: Natural
Trail Use Fee: None
Method Of Ski Trail Grooming: NA
Skiing Ability Suggested: NA
Hiking Trail Difficulty: Easy
Mountain Biking Ability Suggested: NA
Terrain: Steep 5%, Hilly 85%, Moderate 10%, Flat 0%
Camping: At trailhead

Maintained by the Mio Ranger District, Huron Manistee National Forest
The Island Lake Nature Trail is a self guided 20 station interpretive trail.
A trail guide is available.

ISLAND LAKE NATURE TRAIL

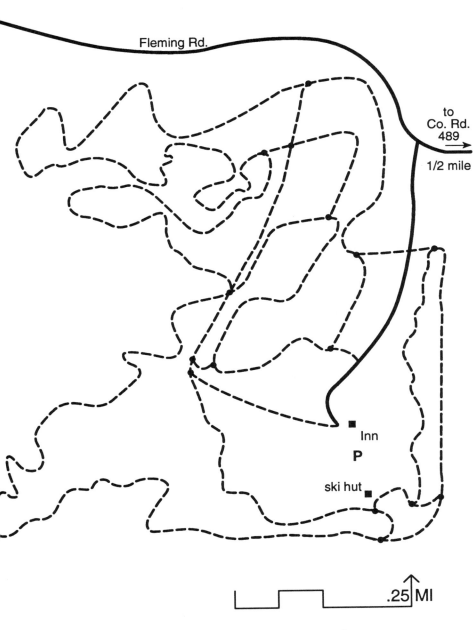

Fleming Rd.

to
Co. Rd.
489
→

1/2 mile

.25 MI

Lakeview Hills Country Inn
Nordic Ski Center

Inn

P

ski hut

LakeView Hills Country Inn and Nordic Ski Center
PO Box 365
Lewiston, MI 49756

517-786-2000
517-786-3445

Michigan Atlas & Gazetteer Location: 77B6

County Location: Oscoda

Directions To Trailhead:
3 miles south of Lewiston on Co Rd 489, then west on Fleming Rd to resort

Trail Type: Hiking/Walking, Cross Country Skiing, Mountain Biking, Interpretive
Trail Distance: 20 km   Loops: Many   Shortest: Longest:
Trail Surface: Gravel and natural
Trail Use Fee: Yes, free to guests
Method Of Ski Trail Grooming: Track set
Skiing Ability Suggested: Novice to advanced
Hiking Trail Difficulty: Easy to difficult
Mountain Biking Ability Suggested: Novice to Advanced
Terrain: Steep 45%, Hilly 10%, Moderate 30%, Flat 15%
Camping: None

Privately operated bed and breakfast with additional lake front resort nearby.
A beautiful hill top bed and breakfast with very challenging trails
The trails are open to the public without being overnight guests.
Site of nordic ski race annually.

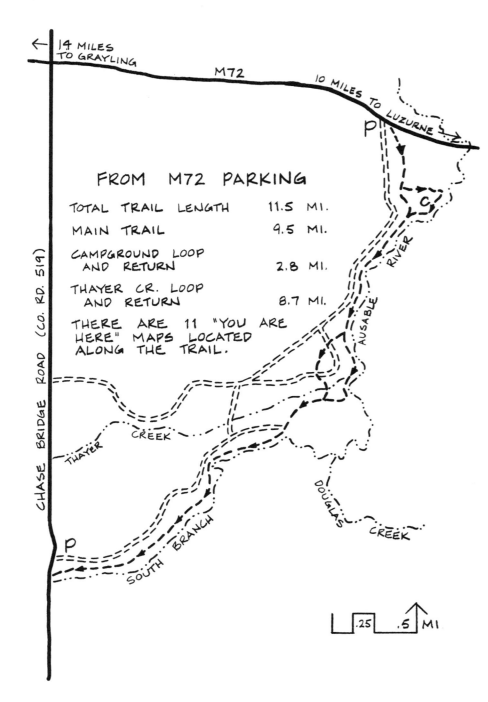

← 14 MILES TO GRAYLING

M72

10 MILES TO LUZURNE

P

C

AUSABLE RIVER

CHASE BRIDGE ROAD (CO. RD. 519)

FROM M72 PARKING

TOTAL TRAIL LENGTH 11.5 MI.

MAIN TRAIL 9.5 MI.

CAMPGROUND LOOP
AND RETURN 2.8 MI.

THAYER CR. LOOP
AND RETURN 8.7 MI.

THERE ARE 11 "YOU ARE
HERE" MAPS LOCATED
ALONG THE TRAIL.

THAYER CREEK

DOUGLAS CREEK

P

SOUTH BRANCH

|__.25__|__.5__| MI

MASON TRACT PATHWAY

Roscommon Forest Area, Au Sable State Forest
Box 218, 8717 N. Roscommon Rd   517-275-5151
Roscommon, MI 48635

District Forest Manager, Au Sable State Forest
191 S. Mt. Tom Rd.   517-826-3211
Mio, MI 48647

Michigan Atlas & Gazetteer Location: 77D45

County Location: Crawford

Directions To Trailhead:
North trailhead - On M72 about 15 miles east of Grayling
South trailhead - 15 miles east of Grayling turn south on Chase Bridge Rd., then continue about 10 miles to South Branch Au Sable River bridge. Trailhead is on the north side of the bridge.

Trail Type: Hiking/Walking, Cross Country Skiing
Trail Distance: 11.3 mi   Loops: NA   Shortest: NA   Longest: NA
Trail Surface: Natural
Trail Use Fee: None
Method Of Ski Trail Grooming: Track set
Skiing Ability Suggested: Novice to intermediate
Hiking Trail Difficulty: Easy
Mountain Biking Ability Suggested: NA
Terrain: Steep 0%, Hilly 5%, Moderate 85%, Flat 10%
Camping: Campground on Au Sable River along trail at Canoe Harbor

Maintained by the DNR Forest Mananagment Division
This is a point to point trail along the east side of the scenic South Branch, Au Sable River.
There are many summer trailheads since a county road passes within sight of the pathway. However, in the winter the road is not plowed and therefore the only trailheads are listed above.
Other contacts:
        DNR Forest Management Division Office, Lansing, 517-373-1275
        DNR Forest Management Region Office, Roscommon, 517-275-5151

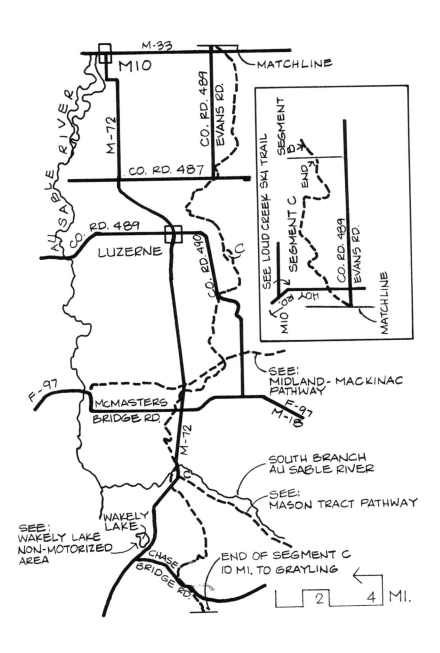

SHORE TO SHORE TRAIL SEGMENT C

Mio Ranger District, Huron-Manistee National Forest
401 Court St.   517-826-3252
Mio, MI 48647

Forest Supervisor, Huron-Manistee National Forest
421 S. Mitchell St.   616-775-2421
Cadillac, MI 49601   800-821-6263

Michigan Atlas & Gazetteer Location: 77D4567

County Location: Oscoda/Crawford

Directions To Trailhead:
From a point 6 miles SE of Mio to about 8 miles SE of Grayling.
Luzerne Trail Camp-Mio west on M72 8 miles to Luzerne, then south on Co Rd 490 for 2 miles, then continue south on Durfree (FR 4153) for about 1 mile to the camp.

Trail Type: Hiking/Walking, Mountain Biking
Trail Distance: 41 mi   Loops: No   Shortest: Longest:
Trail Surface: Natural
Trail Use Fee: None
Method Of Ski Trail Grooming: None
Skiing Ability Suggested: NA
Hiking Trail Difficulty: Moderate
Mountain Biking Ability Suggested: Novice but sand present
Terrain: Steep 0%, Hilly 20%, Moderate 20%, Flat 60%
Camping: Campground at Luzerne Trail Camp and backcountry camping permitted

Maintained by the Mio Ranger District, Huron-Manistee National Forest and the Michigan Trail Riders Association.
Trail is primarily for horse back riding.
For maps of the entire trail contact: Michigan Trail Riders Association, 1650 Ormond Rd, White Lake, MI 48383.

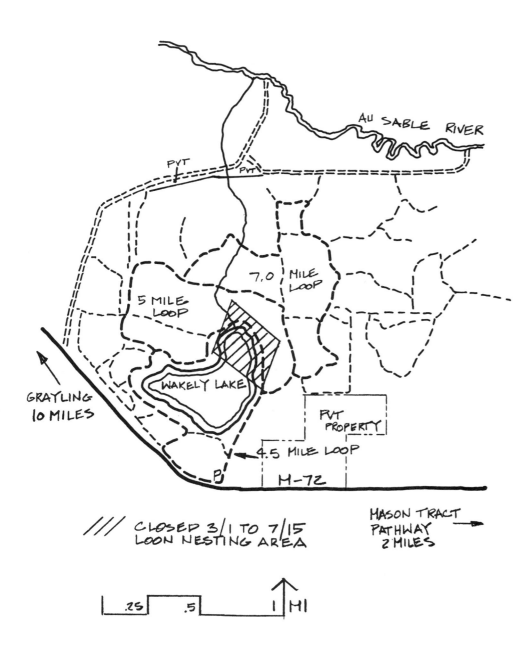

AU SABLE RIVER

PVT

PVT

7.0 MILE LOOP

5 MILE LOOP

WAKELY LAKE

GRAYLING 10 MILES

PVT PROPERTY

4.5 MILE LOOP

M-72

/// CLOSED 3/1 TO 7/15 LOON NESTING AREA

MASON TRACT PATHWAY 2 MILES →

.25 | .5 | 1 MI

Mio Ranger District, Huron Manistee National Forest
401 Court St.   517-826-3252
Mio, MI 48647

Forest Supervisor, Huron-Manistee National Forest
421 S. Mitchell St.   616-775-2421
Cadillac, MI 49601   800-821-6263

Michigan Atlas & Gazetteer Location: 77C45

County Location: Crawford

Directions To Trailhead:
10 miles east Grayling and 22 miles west of Mio on M72

Trail Type: Hiking/Walking, Cross Country Skiing, Mountain Biking
Trail Distance: 16.5 mi   Loops: 3   Shortest: 4.5 mi Longest: 7 mi
Trail Surface: Natural
Trail Use Fee: None
Method Of Ski Trail Grooming: None
Skiing Ability Suggested: Novice to advanced
Hiking Trail Difficulty: Easy to moderate
Mountain Biking Ability Suggested: Novice
Terrain: Steep 0%, Hilly 25%, Moderate 55%, Flat 20%
Camping: Permitted but no developed campgrounds in area

Maintained by the Mio Ranger District, Huron-Manistee National Forest
Part of the area is closed from March 1 -July 1 for Loon Nesting

WAKELY LAKE NON-MOTORIZED AREA

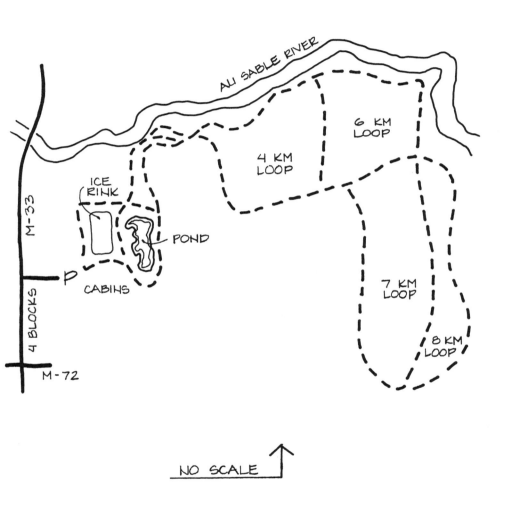

Hinchman Acres Resort

Hinchman Acres Resort
702 N. Morenci (M33), PO Box 220
Mio, MI 48647

517-826-3267
800-438-0203

Michigan Atlas & Gazetteer Location: 78D1

County Location: Oscoda

Directions To Trailhead:
North end of Mio, just south of the Au Sable River on the east side of M33

Trail Type: Hiking/Walking, Cross Country Skiing, Mountain Biking
Trail Distance: 20+ km   Loops: 4   Shortest: 4 km   Longest: 8 km
Trail Surface: Natural
Trail Use Fee: Yes, free for guests of the resort
Method Of Ski Trail Grooming: Double track set
Skiing Ability Suggested: Novice
Hiking Trail Difficulty: Easy
Mountain Biking Ability Suggested: Novice
Terrain: Steep 0%, Hilly 0%, Moderate 40%, Flat 60%
Camping: None

Privately operated 4 season resort since 1933.
Warming area, snack bar, lodging, rentals, ski shop and night skiing Ice skating rink on the property.
Lodging available - 13 cottages, 6 with fireplaces.
Scenic trails in the Huron National Forest with views of the Au Sable River.
Free ski rental, no trail fee and free instruction when staying at the resort.
Great family ski resort.
TRAILS FOR HIKING AND MOUNTAIN BIKING AVAILABLE ONLY FOR GUESTS.
Call for more information on these "special packages" AAA approved resort

HINCHMAN ACRES RESORT

Map

F32 (FR 45/6)

2¼ MI.

2¼ MI.

4

1¾ MI.

3

M 72/65

5

¼ MI.

½ MI.

7

6

P

8

WATER

1 MI.

½ MI. 11

NO HAME LK.

12

PENOYER LK.

WATER

¾ MI.

2

M 72

¾ MI.

9 10

BYRON LAKE

1¾ MI.

N. HOIST LK.

1 MI.

14

1½ MI.

1

2½ MI.

13

W. HOIST LK.

S. HOIST LK.

HARRISVILLE 22 MILES ON M72

GLENNIE 7 MILES

1 MI

FR 4119

HOIST LAKE FOOT TRAVEL AREA

Hoist Lakes Foot Travel Area

78

Harrisville Ranger District, Huron Manistee National Forest
PO Box 289
Harrisville , MI 48740

517-724-6471

Forest Supervisor, Huron-Manistee National Forest
421 S. Mitchell St.
Cadillac, MI 49601

616-775-2421
800-999-7677

Michigan Atlas & Gazetteer Location: 78C34

County Location: Alcona

Directions To Trailhead:
22 miles west of Harrisville on M72 at M65 Jct.
East trailhead - .25 mile south of Jct on M65
West trailhead - On F32(FR4516) just north of the Au Sable Rd intersection

Trail Type: Hiking/Walking, Cross Country Skiing
Trail Distance: 20 mi   Loops: Many   Shortest: 1 mi   Longest: 18 mi
Trail Surface: Natural
Trail Use Fee: None
Method Of Ski Trail Grooming: None
Skiing Ability Suggested: Intermediate to advanced
Hiking Trail Difficulty: Moderate to difficult
Mountain Biking Ability Suggested: NA
Terrain: Rolling to hilly
Camping: Off trail camping permitted

Maintained by the Harrisville Ranger District, Huron-Manistee National Forest
An extensive area of 10,600 acres restricted for use by hikers, skiers and snowshoers only
Tow hand pumps are along the trails at each end of the area and useable year around.
Write for brochure

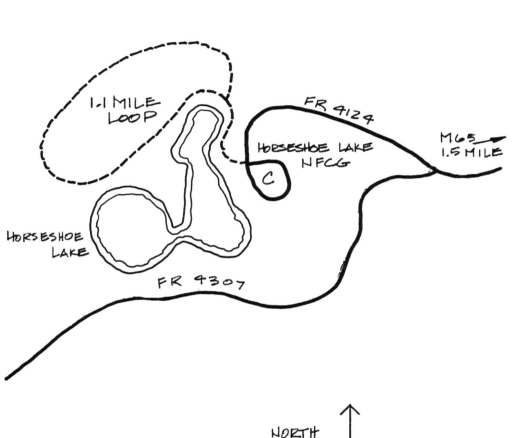

Harrisville Ranger District, Huron Manistee National Forest
PO Box 289   517-724-6471
Harrisville, MI 48740

Forest Supervisor, Huron Manistee National Forest
421 S. Mitchell St.   616-775-2421
Cadillac, MI 49601   800-821-6263

Michigan Atlas & Gazetteer Location: 78D4

County Location: Alcona

Directions To Trailhead:
From the intersection of M72 and M65 go south 3.3 miles to FR 4124, then right
1 mile to campground and trailhead

Trail Type: Hiking/Walking, Interpretive
Trail Distance: 1 MI   Loops: 1   Shortest: NA   Longest: 1 mi
Trail Surface: Natural
Trail Use Fee: None
Method Of Ski Trail Grooming: None
Skiing Ability Suggested: Novice
Hiking Trail Difficulty: Easy
Mountain Biking Ability Suggested: NA
Terrain: Steep 0%, Hilly 0%, Moderate 95%, Flat 5%
Camping: At trailhead

Maintained by the Harrisville Ranger District, Huron Manistee National Forest
Short campground hiking trail along the shore of Horseshoe Lake

HORSESHOE LAKE NATURE TRAIL

MIO 3 MILES   CAUCHY RD

2.2K

EASY LOOPS

HOY RD

1.4 K

1.4 K

MORE DIFFICULT LOOPS

TOILET

1.6 K

1.3 K

2.2 K

PONDS

MOST DIFFICULT LOOPS

L___⌐_____↑ KM
1   2

LOUD CREEK
CROSS COUNTRY SKI TRAIL

Mio Ranger District, Huron-Manistee National Forest
401 Court St.   517-826-3252
Mio, MI 48647

Forest Supervisor, Huron-Manistee National Forest
421 S. Mitchell St.   616-775-2421
Cadillac, MI 49601   800-999-7677

Michigan Atlas & Gazetteer Location: 78CD1

County Location: Ogemaw

Directions To Trailhead:
From East 14th St. in Mio, south 1 mile on Hoy Rd., then east .5 mile on Cauchy Rd. to parking lot

Trail Type: Hiking/Walking, Cross Country Skiing
Trail Distance: 9.8 km   Loops: 6   Shortest: 1.3 km Longest: 2.2 km
Trail Surface: Natural
Trail Use Fee: None
Method Of Ski Trail Grooming: Packed
Skiing Ability Suggested: Intermediate
Hiking Trail Difficulty: Easy
Mountain Biking Ability Suggested: NA
Terrain: Steep 0%, Hilly 40%, Moderate 40%, Flat 20%
Camping: Backcountry camping permitted

Maintained by the Mio Ranger District, Huron-Manistee National Forest
A total of 12 miles of ski loops are planned for this system in coming years
The trail system will be designed for the intermediate to advanced skier
Strong local support from the Loud Creek Nordic Club built and maintains this trail system.
For information about the club, contact the district ranger for the name and address of the current club president.

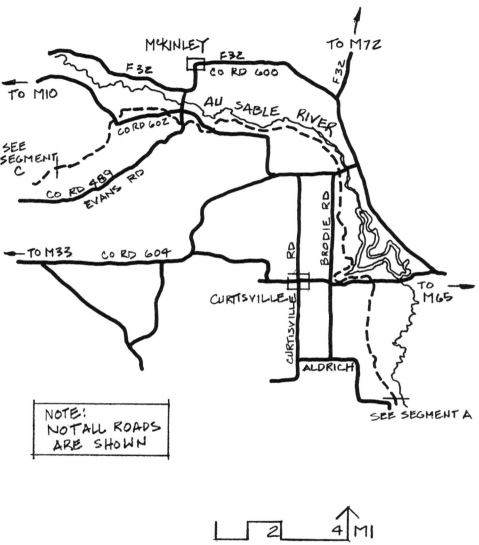

NOTE:
NOT ALL ROADS
ARE SHOWN

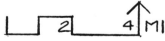

SHORE TO SHORE TRAIL
SEGMENT B

Harrisville Ranger District, Huron-Manistee National Forest
PO Box 289   517-724-6471
Harrisville, MI 48740

Forest Supervisor, Huron-Manistee National Forest
421 S. Mitchell St.   616-775-2421
Cadillac, MI 49601   800-999-7677

Michigan Atlas & Gazetteer Location: 78D123

County Location: Alcona

Directions To Trailhead:
From the Iosco Co line near the Au Sable River west to a point about 4 miles SW of McKinley near Co Rd 602.
West trailhead - McKinley Trail Camp-From Mio east on Co Rd 602 for 9 miles to the camp
Trail access-From M65 in Glennie, take Bamfield Rd west 6 miles to the Curtisville Store. The trail is across the road from the store

Trail Type: Hiking/Walking, Mountain Biking
Trail Distance: 25 mi   Loops: No   Shortest: NA   Longest: NA
Trail Surface: Natural
Trail Use Fee: None
Method Of Ski Trail Grooming: None
Skiing Ability Suggested: NA
Hiking Trail Difficulty: Moderate
Mountain Biking Ability Suggested: Novice but sand present
Terrain: Steep 0%, Hilly 0%, Moderate 70%, Flat 30%
Camping: McKinley Trail Camp and wilderness camping permitted

Maintained by the Harrisville Ranger District, Huron-Manistee National Forest and the Michigan Trail Riders Association
Primarily a horse back riding trail.
Can be used for backcountry skiing for experienced skiers with good winter survival skills
A portion of the trail follows the ridge along the Au Sable River.
Several wood bridges cross streams along the trail.
For detailed maps of the entire trail contact: Michigan Trail Riders Association, 1650 Ormond Rd. White Lake, MI 48383

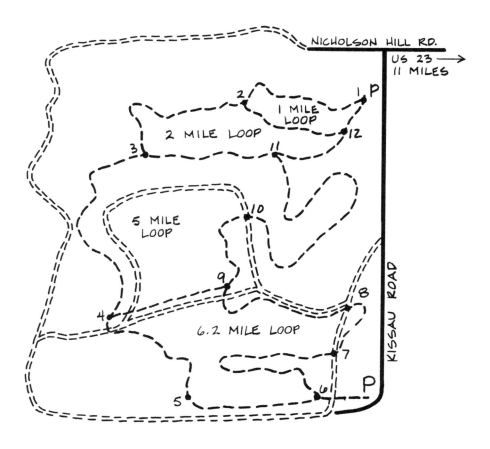

NICHOLSON HILL RD.

US 23 →
11 MILES

1 MILE LOOP

2 MILE LOOP

5 MILE LOOP

6.2 MILE LOOP

KISSAU ROAD

.25   .5 MI

Atlanta Forest Area, Mackinaw State Forest
HCR 74, Box 30   517-785-4252
Atlanta, MI 49709

District Forest Manager, Mackinaw State Forest
Box 667, 1732 West M32   517-732-3541
Gaylord, MI 49735

Michigan Atlas & Gazetteer Location: 79A4

County Location: Alpena

Directions To Trailhead:
Between Harrisville and Alpena, 11 miles west of Ossineke (US23) on Nicholson Hill Rd. Trailhead - Just south of Nicholson Hill Rd. on Kissau Rd. Overflow parking available on Nicholson Hill Rd., just west of Kissau Rd.

Trail Type: Hiking/Walking, Cross Country Skiing, Mountain Biking
Trail Distance: 8 mi   Loops: 4   Shortest: 1 mi   Longest: 2.9 mi
Trail Surface: Natural
Trail Use Fee: None
Method Of Ski Trail Grooming: Track set
Skiing Ability Suggested: Novice to intermediate
Hiking Trail Difficulty: Easy
Mountain Biking Ability Suggested: Novice to intermediate
Terrain: Steep 3%, Hilly 5%, Moderate 60%, Flat 32%
Camping: None

Maintained by the DNR Forest Management Division
Waxing and sitting benches provided along trail.
Trail maps and directional arrows are at all intersections.
Scenic overlook along trail.
Popular local ski trail.
Other contacts:
        DNR Forest Management Division Office, Lansing, 517-373-1275
        DNR Forest Management Region Office, Roscommon, 517-275-5151

CHIPPEWA HILLS
PATHWAY

Tawas Point State Park
686 Tawas Point State Park   517-362-5041
East Tawas, MI 48730

Harrisville State Park
PO Box 326   517-724-5126
Harrrisville, MI 48740

Michigan Atlas & Gazetteer Location: 79C7

County Location: Alcona

Directions To Trailhead:
Along Lake Huron off US23 on the south edge of Harrisville

Trail Type: Interpretive
Trail Distance: 1 mi   Loops: 1   Shortest: NA   Longest: 1 mi
Trail Surface: Natrual
Trail Use Fee: None, except vehicle permit required
Method Of Ski Trail Grooming: NA
Skiing Ability Suggested: NA
Hiking Trail Difficulty: NA
Mountain Biking Ability Suggested: NA
Terrain: Flat 100%
Camping: Modern campground on site

Maintained by the DNR Parks and Recreation Division.
The Cedar Run Nature Trail has 14 interpretated stations.

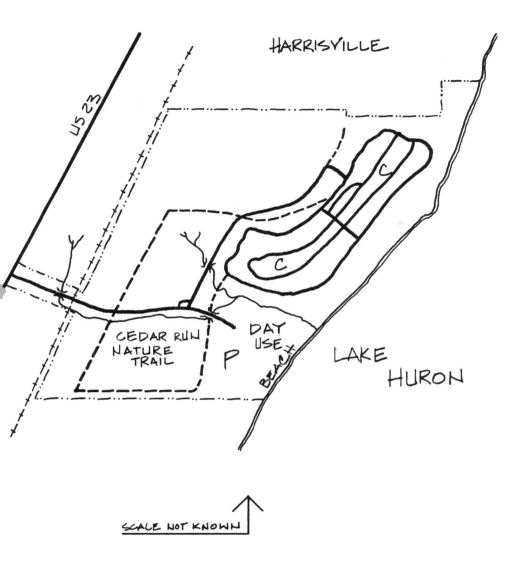

HARRISVILLE

US 23

C
C

CEDAR RUN
NATURE
TRAIL

P

DAY
USE

BEACH

LAKE
HURON

SCALE NOT KNOWN

HARRISVILLE STATE PARK

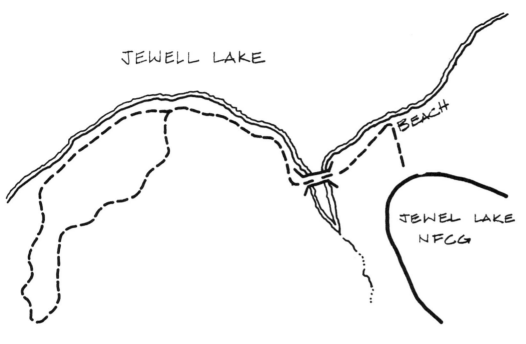

JEWELL LAKE

BEACH

JEWEL LAKE
NFCG

.25 MI

Jewell Lake Trail

Harrisville Ranger District, Huron Manistee National Forest
PO Box 289   517-724-6471
Harrisville, MI 48740

Forest Supervisor, Huron Manistee National Forest
421 S. Mitchell St.   616-775-2421
Cadillac, MI 49601   800-821-6263

Michigan Atlas & Gazetteer Location: 79C5

County Location: Alcona

Directions To Trailhead:
14.5 miles west of Harrisville on M72 then north 1.7 miles on Sanborn Rd, then left on Trask Lake Rd for .7 mile, then left on FR 4601 to campground and trailhead

Trail Type: Hiking/Walking, Cross Country Skiing
Trail Distance: 1 mi   Loops: 1   Shortest: NA   Longest: 1 mi
Trail Surface: Natural
Trail Use Fee: None
Method Of Ski Trail Grooming: None
Skiing Ability Suggested: Novice
Hiking Trail Difficulty: Easy
Mountain Biking Ability Suggested: NA
Terrain: 100%Flat
Camping: Campground at trailhead

Maintained by the Harrisville Ranger District, Huron Manistee National Forest
The trail winds through a variety of vegetation types and interesting forest features. The topography is generally flat for a leisurely walk.

JEWELL LAKE TRAIL

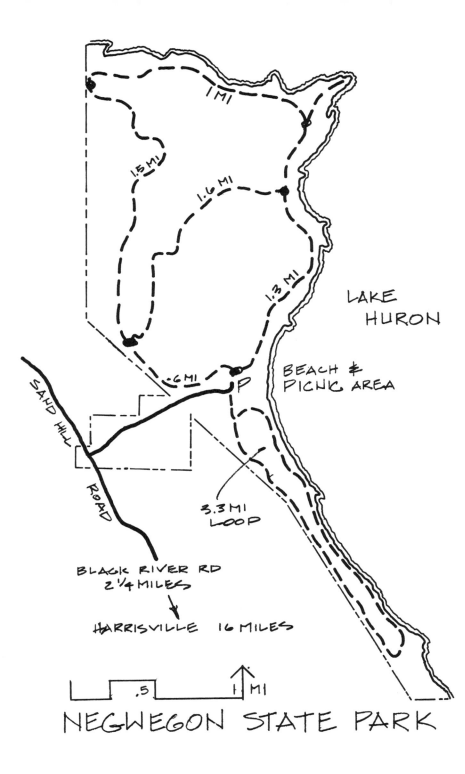

Tawas Point State Park
686 Tawas Beach Rd   517-362-5041
East Tawas, MI 48730

Michigan Atlas & Gazetteer Location: 79AB67

County Location: Alcona

Directions To Trailhead:
12 miles north on US23 from Harrisville to Black River Rd., then east (right) on
Black River Rd about 1.5 miles to Sand Hill Rd, then turn left and go 2.5 miles to
a gravel road, travel east about 1.25 miles to a parking lot.

Trail Type: Hiking/Walking, Mountain Biking
Trail Distance: 10 mi   Loops: 3   Shortest: 3.3 mi Longest: 5.2 mi
Trail Surface: Natural including sand
Trail Use Fee: None
Method Of Ski Trail Grooming: NA
Skiing Ability Suggested: NA
Hiking Trail Difficulty: Easy
Mountain Biking Ability Suggested: Easy
Terrain: 100% Flat
Camping: At Harrisville State Park

Maintained by the DNR Parks and Recreation Division
Relatively new and undeveloped park. Park development is in the planning
stages.
Along the shore of Lake Huron
Very isolated area.

LAKE HURON

BEACH & PICNIC AREA

1 MI

1.5 MI

1.6 MI

1.3 MI

.6 MI

P

SAND HILL ROAD

3.3 MI LOOP

BLACK RIVER RD
2 1/4 MILES

HARRISVILLE 16 MILES

.5   1 MI

NEGWEGON STATE PARK

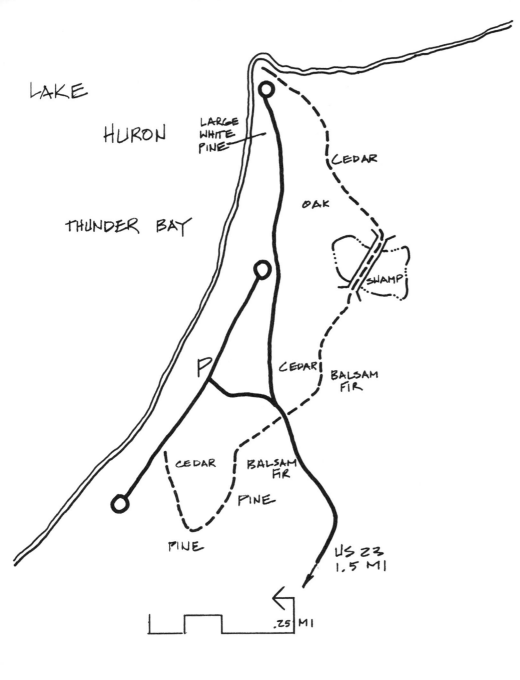

LAKE

HURON

THUNDER BAY

LARGE
WHITE
PINE

CEDAR

OAK

SWAMP

P

CEDAR   BALSAM
         FIR

CEDAR

BALSAM
FIR

PINE

PINE

US 23
1.5 MI

.25 MI

OSSINEKE PATHWAY

Atlanta Forest Area, Mackinaw State Forest
4343 M32 West   517-354-2209
Alpena, MI 49707

District Forest Manager, Mackinaw State Forest
1732 West M32 PO Box 667   517-732-3541
Gaylord, MI 49735

Michigan Atlas & Gazetteer Location: 79A6

County Location: Alpena

Directions To Trailhead:
South of Alpena on Lake Huron at Ossineke SFCG

Trail Type: Hiking/Walking, Cross Country Skiing, Interpretive
Trail Distance: 1 mi   Loops: 1   Shortest: NA   Longest: NA
Trail Surface: Natural
Trail Use Fee: None
Method Of Ski Trail Grooming: None
Skiing Ability Suggested: Novice
Hiking Trail Difficulty: Easy
Mountain Biking Ability Suggested: NA
Terrain: 100% Flat
Camping: Campground at the trailhead

Maintained by the DNR Forest Management Division
Trail along the Lake Huron shoreline.

Harrisville Ranger District, Huron-Manistee National Forest
PO Box 289   517-724-6471
Harrisville, MI 48740

Forest Supervisor, Huron-Manistee National Forest
421 S. Mitchell St.   616-775-2421
Cadillac, MI 49601   800-821-6263

Michigan Atlas & Gazetteer Location: 79C4

County Location: Alcona

Directions To Trailhead:
19 miles west of Harrisville on M72 Trailhead is located on the south side of the road

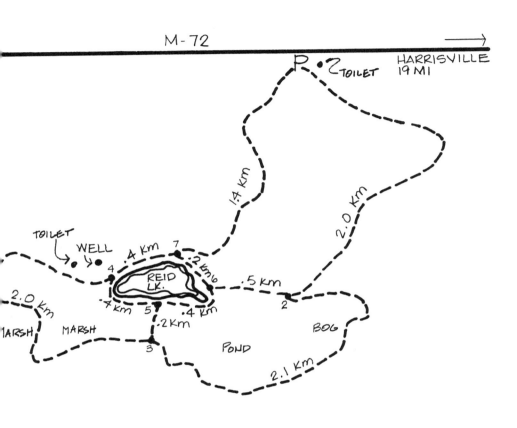

Trail Type: Hiking/Walking, Cross Country Skiing
Trail Distance: 6 mi   Loops: 4   Shortest: 3 mi   Longest: 5.6 mi
Trail Surface: Natural
Trail Use Fee: None
Method Of Ski Trail Grooming: None
Skiing Ability Suggested: Novice to intermediate
Hiking Trail Difficulty: Moderate
Mountain Biking Ability Suggested: NA
Terrain: Steep 0%, Hilly 0%, Moderate 25%, Flat 75%
Camping: Primitive campground available

Maintained by the Harrisville Ranger District, Huron-Manistee National Forest
Pleasant area for back country skiing and hiking.
Near the Hoist Lakes Foot Travel Area.
Mountain biking is prohibited in this area.

REID LAKE FOOT TRAVEL AREA

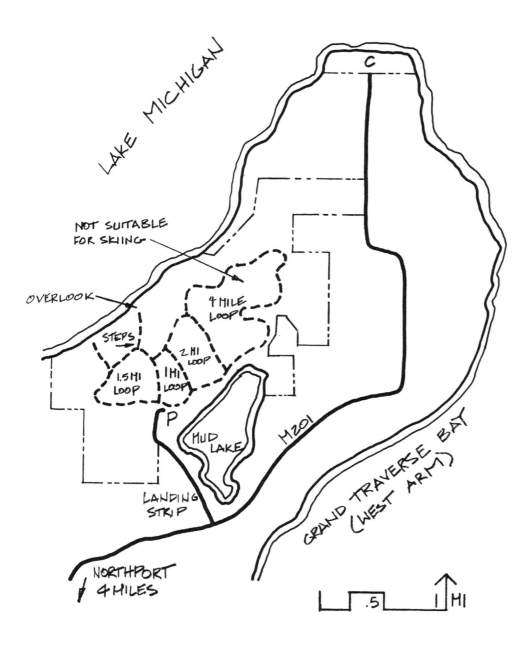

Leelanau State Park
Rte 1 Box 49
Northport, Mi 49670

616-386-5422

Traverse City State Park
1132 US31 North
Traverse City, MI 49684

616-947-7193

Michigan Atlas & Gazetteer Location: 80C3

County Location: Leelanau

Directions To Trailhead:
At the north end of the Leelanau Peninsula, 36 miles north of Traverse City.
Take Co Rd 629 north out of Northport 3 miles to Densmore Rd (Airport Rd),
then left to the parking lot.

Trail Type: Hiking/Walking, Cross Country Skiing, Interpretive
Trail Distance: 8.5 mi   Loops: 6   Shortest: 1.2 mi Longest: 3.5 mi
Trail Surface: Natural
Trail Use Fee: None, but vehicle entry fee required
Method Of Ski Trail Grooming: None
Skiing Ability Suggested: Intermediate to advanced
Hiking Trail Difficulty: Easy to moderate
Mountain Biking Ability Suggested: NA
Terrain: Steep 10%, Hilly 45%, Moderate 35%, Flat 10%
Camping: Campground available 4 miles north of trailhead

Maintained by the DNR Parks and Recreation Division
Scenic views of Lake Michigan are provided from an overlook and beach.
The trail passes through a dune area, hardwoods, pines and along the shore of
an inland lake to provide plenty of variety.
A pleasant trail system for both hiking and skiing.
The 4 mile loop is not suitable for skiing.

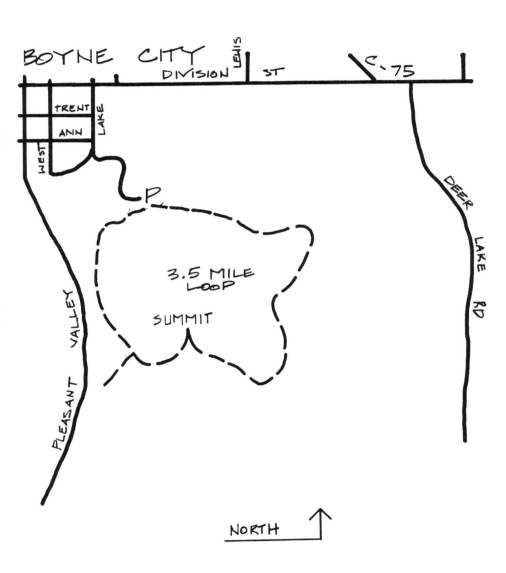

BOYNE CITY

LEWIS

DIVISION ST

C-75

TRENT

LAKE

ANN

WEST

P

3.5 MILE LOOP

SUMMIT

PLEASANT VALLEY

DEER LAKE RD

NORTH ↑

AVALANCHE PRESERVE

Boyne City Chamber of Commerce
28 S. Lake St.
Boyne City, Mi 49712

616-582-6222

Michigan Atlas & Gazetteer Location: 81C7

County Location: Charlevoix

Directions To Trailhead:
In Boyne City, turn south on Lake St. and proceed to end of the road.

Trail Type: Hiking/Walking, Cross Country Skiing, Mountain Biking, Interpretive
Trail Distance: 4.5 mi   Loops: 2   Shortest: 1.5 mi Longest: 3 mi
Trail Surface: Gravel and natural surfaces
Trail Use Fee: None
Method Of Ski Trail Grooming: Track set
Skiing Ability Suggested: Intermediate
Hiking Trail Difficulty: Moderate
Mountain Biking Ability Suggested: Intermediate to advanced
Terrain: Steep 0%, Hilly 80%, Moderate 15%, Flat 5%
Camping: None

Maintained by the City of Boyne City
Spectacular view of Lake Charlevoix and Boyne City from the trail.
Moderately challenging trail for mountain biking and skiing.
Trail map is approximate only.

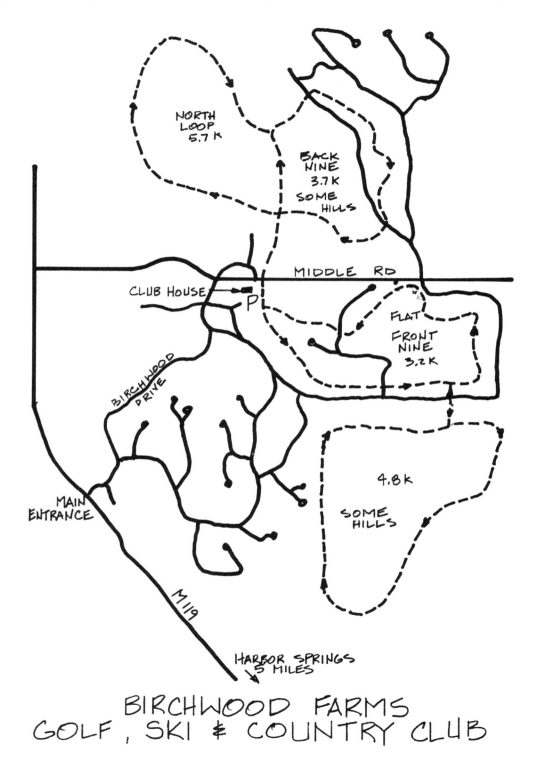

Birchwood Farms Golf and Country Club
600 Birchwood Drive
Harbor Springs, MI 49740

616-526-2166

Michigan Atlas & Gazetteer Location: 81A7

County Location: Emmet

Directions To Trailhead:
East of Harbor Springs on M119

Trail Type: Cross Country Skiing
Trail Distance: 3.5 mi   Loops: 4   Shortest: 3.2 km Longest: 5.7 km
Trail Surface: Natural
Trail Use Fee: None
Method Of Ski Trail Grooming: ?
Skiing Ability Suggested: ?
Hiking Trail Difficulty: NA
Mountain Biking Ability Suggested: NA
Terrain: ?
Camping: None

Privately owned residential resort community with trails open to the public.

BIRCHWOOD FARMS GOLF, SKI & COUNTRY CLUB

Little Traverse Conservancy
3264 Powell Rd
Harbor Springs, MI 49740

616-347-0991

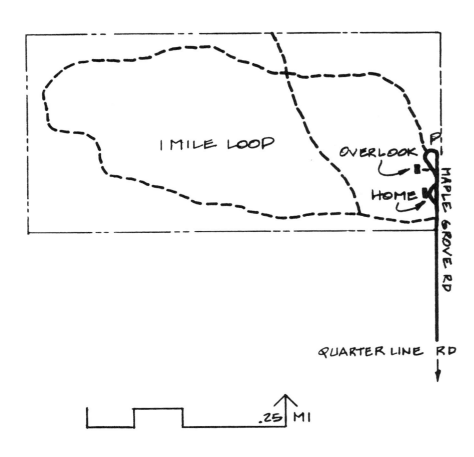

Michigan Atlas & Gazetteer Location: 81B6

County Location: Charlevoix

Directions To Trailhead:
From US31 between Charlevoix and Petoskey, take Burgess Rd 3.5 miles to Quarterline, then left 1 mile east to Maple Grove Rd., then left on Maple Grove and continue about .75 mile to parking area and trailhead.

Trail Type: Hiking/Walking, Cross Country Skiing, Interpretive
Trail Distance: 1.8 mi   Loops: 2   Shortest: .3 mi   Longest: 1.5 mi
Trail Surface: Natural
Trail Use Fee: None
Method Of Ski Trail Grooming: None
Skiing Ability Suggested: Novice to intermediate
Hiking Trail Difficulty: Moderate
Mountain Biking Ability Suggested: NA
Terrain: Steep 0%, Hilly 35%, Moderate 35%, Flat 30%
Camping: None on site but Fisherman's Island State Park south of Charlevoix

Owned by the Little Traverse Conservancy
Though it is a small parcel of 80 acres since is located over 300 above Lake Michigan, it has a panoramic view of the Leelanau Peninsula and Beaver Island. A brochure is available for the self guided nature trail.

CHARLES RANSOM NATURE PRESERVE

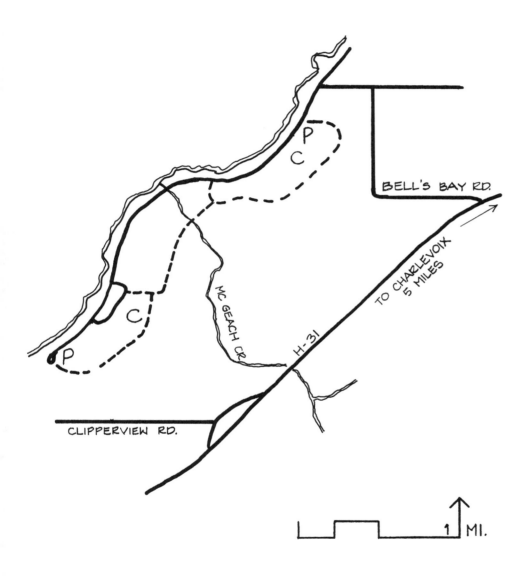

Fisherman's Island State Park
PO Box 456
Charlevoix, MI 49720   616-547-6641

DNR Parks and Recreation Division

517-373-1270
517-275-5151

Michigan Atlas & Gazetteer Location: 81B5

County Location: Charlevoix

Directions To Trailhead:
2 miles SW of Charlevoix on US31, turn west on Bell's Bay Rd. for about 1 mile
to park entrance

Trail Type: Hiking/Walking, Cross Country Skiing, Mountain Biking, Interpretive
Trail Distance: 5 mi   Loops: 2   Shortest: 2 mi   Longest: 4.5 mi
Trail Surface: Natural
Trail Use Fee: None, but vehicle entry fee required $2/day, $10/year
Method Of Ski Trail Grooming: None
Skiing Ability Suggested: Novice to intermediate
Hiking Trail Difficulty: Easy
Mountain Biking Ability Suggested: Novice to intermediate
Terrain: Steep 15%, Hilly 15%, Moderate 50%, Flat 20%
Camping: Rustic campground available in park

Maintained by the DNR Parks Division On the shore of Lake Michigan
Also many miles of unmarked two track roads and trails in this 2,763 acres park
are available for use.

FISHERMAN'S ISLAND
STATE PARK

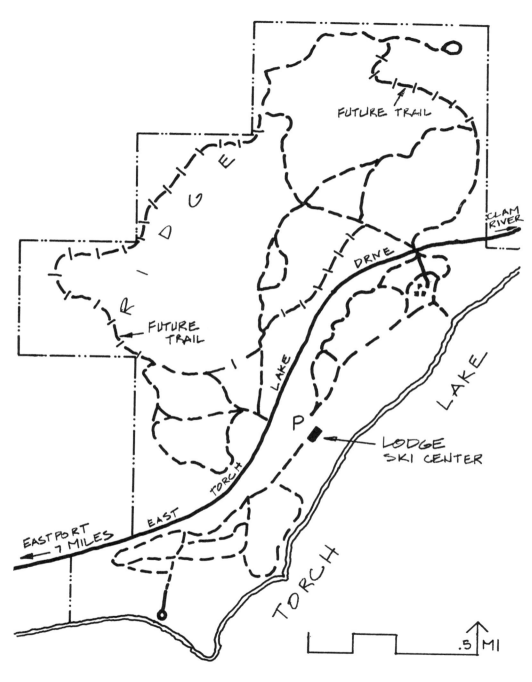

Hayo-Went-Ha Nordic Ski Center

Hayo-Went-Ha
RR1 Box 30
Central Lake, MI 49622

616-544-5915
616-544-2916

81

Michigan Atlas & Gazetteer Location: 81D5

County Location: Antrim

Directions To Trailhead:
5 miles south of Eastport on East Torch Lake Drive or 5 miles west of Central Lake on East Torch Lake Drive

Trail Type: Cross Country Skiing
Trail Distance: 18 km   Loops: 5   Shortest: 1 mi   Longest: 3.5 mi
Trail Surface: Natural and gravel
Trail Use Fee: Yes, day, annual, senior and childrens special rates
Method Of Ski Trail Grooming: Track set
Skiing Ability Suggested: Novice to advanced
Hiking Trail Difficulty: NA
Mountain Biking Ability Suggested: NA
Terrain: Steep 5%, Hilly 25%, Moderate 40%, Flat 30%
Camping: None

Owned by the State YMCA of Michigan
Ski rentals, lodge and instruction available.
Modern camp lodge available for overnight groups during the fall, winter and spring seasons.
Scenic views of Torch Lake from the trail.

HAYO-WENT-HA

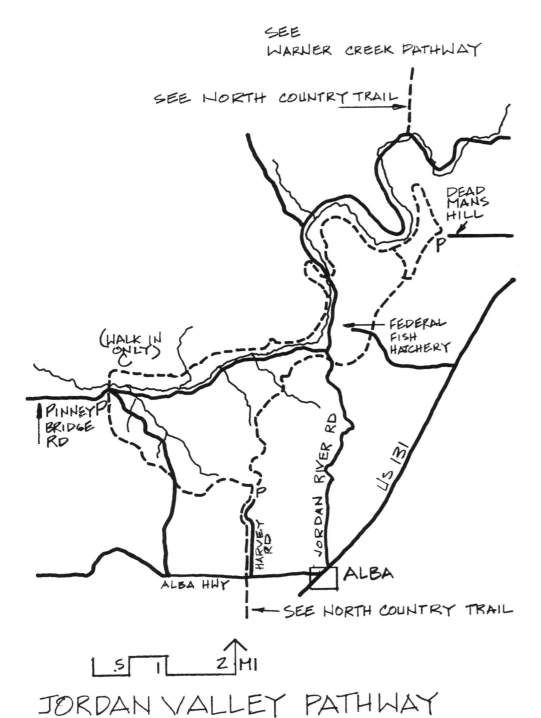

SEE
WARNER CREEK PATHWAY

SEE NORTH COUNTRY TRAIL →

DEAD MANS HILL

P

(WALK IN ONLY)

FEDERAL FISH HATCHERY

PINNEY BRIDGE RD

JORDAN RIVER RD

US 131

HARVEY RD

P

ALBA

ALBA HWY

← SEE NORTH COUNTRY TRAIL

.5 1 2 MI

JORDAN VALLEY PATHWAY

Gaylord Forest Area, Mackinaw State Forest
1732 West M32, PO Box 667   517-732-3541
Gaylord, MI 49735

District Forest Manager, Mackinaw State Forest
 1732 West M32, PO Box 667   517-732-3541
Gaylord, MI 49735

Michigan Atlas & Gazetteer Location: 81D7, 82D7

County Location: Antrim

Directions To Trailhead:
West of US131; 6 miles north of Mancelona; 9 miles south of Boyne Falls
Trailhead 1 - 1 mile west of Alba on Alba Rd, then north to trail. and valley overlook.
Trailhead 2 - 1.5 miles south of the intersection of M32 and US131, turn west on Deadmans Hill Rd. to overlook .
Trailhead 3 - 2 miles west from M66 on Pinney Bridge Rd. to SFCG

Trail Type: Hiking/Walking, Interpretive
Trail Distance: 18.2 mi   Loops: 2   Shortest: 3 mi   Longest: 18 mi
Trail Surface: Natural
Trail Use Fee: None
Method Of Ski Trail Grooming: NA
Skiing Ability Suggested: NA
Hiking Trail Difficulty: Moderate to difficult
Mountain Biking Ability Suggested: NA
Terrain: Steep 5%, Hilly 70%, Moderate 20%, Flat 5%
Camping: At Pinney Bridge hike in campground only

Maintained by the DNR Forest Management Division
Not suitable for skiing because there are no outruns and sharp turns in the trail.
Not recommended for mountain biking because of the sensitive flora in the river valley.
One of the most scenic river valley's in the state.
The loop is most rewarding with an overnight stay at the hike-in campground which is sited nicely on the edge of a clearing which was once the site of a CCC camp.
Portions of the trail are designated as the North Country Trail.
Much of the trail on the north side of the river usually wet.
On the south side of river the trail follows a course that is much higher up the valley wall which. makes the trail much drier and with more scenic views.
The north-south portion of the route to Trailhead 1 is part of the North Country Trail.

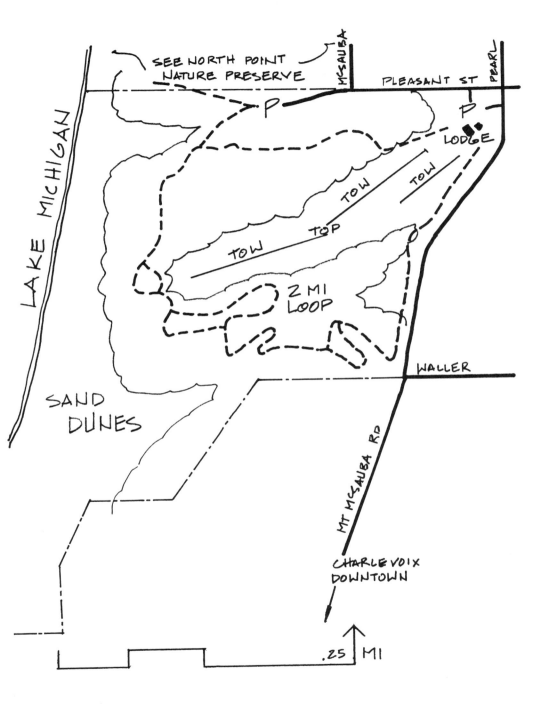

City of Charlevoix, Mt. McSauba Ski Area,
210 State St.   616-547-3267
Charlevoix, MI 49720

City of Charlevoix, Recreation Department
210 State St.   616-547-3253
Charlevoix, Mi 49720

Michigan Atlas & Gazetteer Location: 81B5

County Location: Charlevoix

Directions To Trailhead:
1 mile north of Charlevoix, west of US31 near Lake Michigan. Take Mercer St. north from US31 to Pleasant St. then west on Pleasant to the ski hill lodge or further west to the parking lot at the end of the street in the Mt. McSauba Recreation Area.

Trail Type: Hiking/Walking, Cross Country Skiing
Trail Distance: 2 mi   Loops: 1   Shortest: Longest: 2 mi
Trail Surface: Natural
Trail Use Fee: None
Method Of Ski Trail Grooming: Track set
Skiing Ability Suggested: Novice to intermediate
Hiking Trail Difficulty: Easy to moderate
Mountain Biking Ability Suggested: NA
Terrain: Rolling to hilly
Camping: None

Owned by the City of Charlevoix
Downhill and cross country ski area and summer recreation program take place here.
Warming area and snack bar at base lodge.
Trails connect to the North Point Nature Preserve (see other listing)
The entire trail is lighted for night skiing.

MT McSAUBA RECREATION AREA

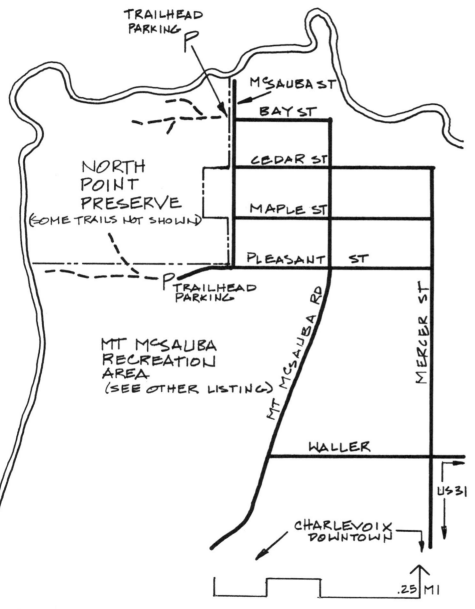

LAKE MICHIGAN

TRAILHEAD PARKING

McSAUBA ST

BAY ST

CEDAR ST

NORTH POINT PRESERVE
(SOME TRAILS NOT SHOWN)

MAPLE ST

PLEASANT ST

TRAILHEAD PARKING

MT McSAUBA RD

MERCER ST

MT McSAUBA RECREATION AREA
(SEE OTHER LISTING)

WALLER

US31

CHARLEVOIX DOWNTOWN

.25 MI

NORTH POINT NATURE PRESERVE

Little Traverse Conservancy
3264 Powell Rd
Harbor Springs, MI 49740

616-347-0991

Charlevoix Township

Michigan Atlas & Gazetteer Location: 81B6

County Location: Charlevoix

Directions To Trailhead:
From US31 in Charlevois, takeMercer Rd north to Pleasant St.,then left to the preserve

Trail Type: Hiking/Walking, Cross Country Skiing, Interpretive
Trail Distance: 1.5 mi   Loops: 1   Shortest: NA   Longest: 1.5 mi
Trail Surface: Natural
Trail Use Fee: None
Method Of Ski Trail Grooming: Track set (planned for 1994/95)
Skiing Ability Suggested: Novice
Hiking Trail Difficulty: Easy to moderate
Mountain Biking Ability Suggested: Novice
Terrain: Steep 0%, Hilly 0%, Moderate 35%, Flat 65%
Camping: None

Owned by the Little Traverse Converancy
Adjacent to Mt. McSauba Recreation Area.
2,800 lf of shoreline and 28 acres.
Many trails lace the preserve.
Groomed ski trails connect with the Mt. McSauba Recreation Area trails.

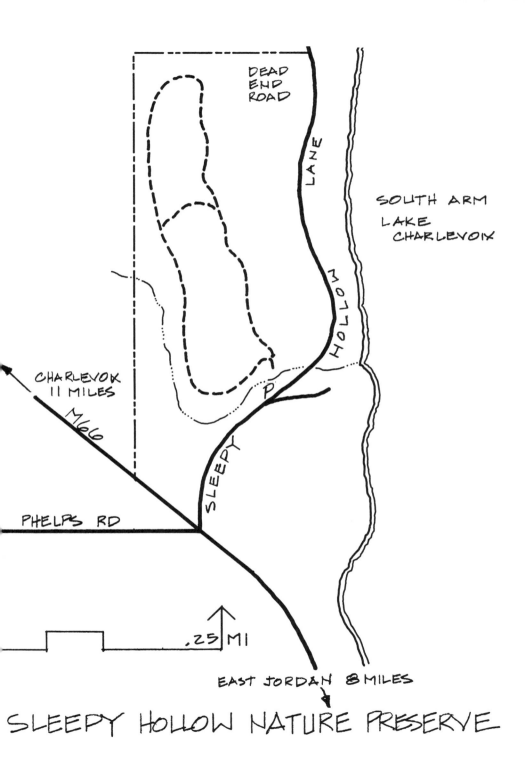

Little Traverse Conservancy
3264 Powell Rd   616-347-0991
Harbor Springs, MI 49740

Michigan Atlas & Gazetteer Location: 81C6

County Location: Charlevoix

Directions To Trailhead:
M66 south of Charlevoix about 11 miles, then left on Sleepy Hollow Lane
(across from Phelps Rd),then park about .12 miles on left side of road.

Trail Type: Hiking/Walking, Cross Country Skiing, Interpretive
Trail Distance: 1+mi   Loops: 2   Shortest: Longest:
Trail Surface: Natural
Trail Use Fee: None
Method Of Ski Trail Grooming: None
Skiing Ability Suggested: Novice
Hiking Trail Difficulty: Easy
Mountain Biking Ability Suggested: NA
Terrain: Steep 0%, Hilly 3%, Moderate 70%, Flat 27%
Camping: None

Owned by the Little Traverse Conservancy
A fifty acre parcel with a dense mature forest and spring fed stream.

SLEEPY HOLLOW NATURE PRESERVE

Thorne Swift Nature Preserve
6696 Lower Shore Drive
Harbor Springs, MI 49740

616-526-6401

Michigan Atlas & Gazetteer Location: 81A7

County Location: Emmet

Directions To Trailhead:
4 miles west of Harbor Springs on Lower Shore Drive via M119

Trail Type: Interpretive
Trail Distance: 1.25 mi   Loops: 2   Shortest: Longest:
Trail Surface: Natural
Trail Use Fee: None, but parking fee for non-township residents
Method Of Ski Trail Grooming: None
Skiing Ability Suggested: NA
Hiking Trail Difficulty: NA
Mountain Biking Ability Suggested: NA
Terrain: 100%Flat
Camping: None

Owned by the Little Traverse Conservancy and leased to West Traverse Township.
Nature preserve complete with a nature center building and resident manager with   naturalist staff. Extensive programs provided.
Beautiful (although small) sandy beach on the north shore of Little Traverse Bay available for swimming and sun bathing.
Open daily from Memorial Day to Labor Day.
A trail guide brochure is available.

THORNE SWIFT NATURE PRESERVE

Young State Park
Boyne City Rd, PO Box 3651   616-582-7523
Boyne City , Mi 49712

DNR Parks and Recreation Division

517-373-1270
517-275-5151

Michigan Atlas & Gazetteer Location: 81C7

County Location: Charlevoix

Directions To Trailhead:
3 miles north of Boyne City on the north side of Lake Charlevoix on Boyne City Rd.

Trail Type: Hiking/Walking, Cross Country Skiing, Interpretive
Trail Distance: 7.5 mi   Loops: 2   Shortest: 3.5 mi Longest: 5 mi
Trail Surface: Natural
Trail Use Fee: None, but vehicle entry fee required
Method Of Ski Trail Grooming: Track set
Skiing Ability Suggested: Novice
Hiking Trail Difficulty: Easy
Mountain Biking Ability Suggested: NA
Terrain: Steep 5%, Hilly 5%, Moderate 10%, Flat 80%
Camping: Campground available in park

Maintained by the DNR Parks and Recreation Division
The White Birch Nature Trail is not groomed for skiing.
An additional trail is groomed in the winter to provide two loops.
Although the park is very popular, considerable wildlife and flora can be observed along the trails.

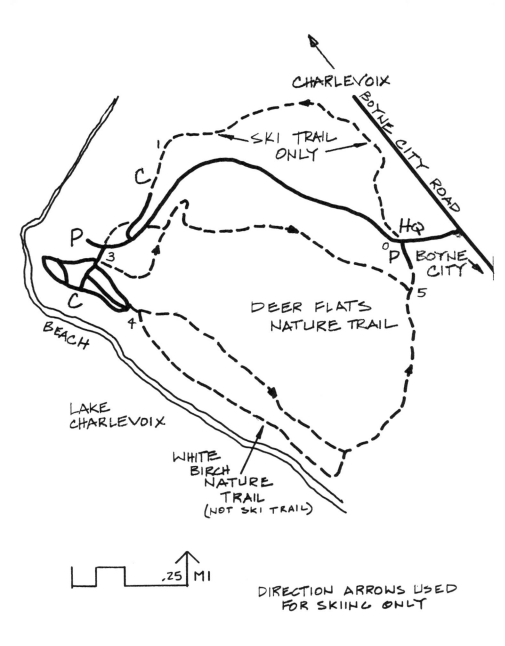

CHARLEVOIX

SKI TRAIL ONLY

BOYNE CITY ROAD

HQ

BOYNE CITY

DEER FLATS NATURE TRAIL

BEACH

LAKE CHARLEVOIX

WHITE BIRCH NATURE TRAIL (NOT SKI TRAIL)

.25 MI

DIRECTION ARROWS USED FOR SKIING ONLY

YOUNG STATE PARK

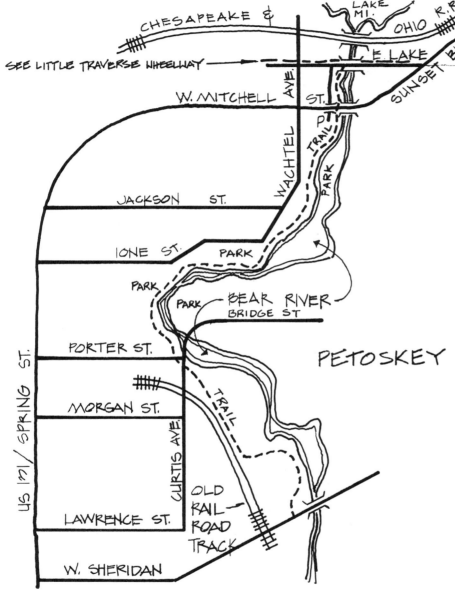

City of Petoskey, Parks and Recreation Department
100 W. Lake St.
Petoskey, MI 49770

616-347-2500

Michigan Atlas & Gazetteer Location: 82AB1

County Location: Emmet

Directions To Trailhead:
From US31, turn on Lake St west to City Hall. Trail across from City Hall.

Trail Type: Hiking/Walking, Cross Country Skiing, Mountain Biking
Trail Distance: 1.75 mi   Loops: NA   Shortest: NA   Longest: NA
Trail Surface: Natural
Trail Use Fee: None
Method Of Ski Trail Grooming: None
Skiing Ability Suggested: Novice to intermediate
Hiking Trail Difficulty: Easy
Mountain Biking Ability Suggested: Novice
Terrain: Steep 0%, Hilly 20%, Moderate 20%, Flat 60%
Camping: Mangus Park in Petoskey

Owned by the City of Petoskey.
In this a city park in the middle of town along the Bear River.
About 1 mile of the trail can be used by mountain bikes.
Trail connects with the Little Traverse Wheelway (see other listing) at Lake St..
There is no sign at the north end of the trail. The trail is just south and across
the street from the fire station on Lake St.

 1/8 MI (APPROX.)

BEAR RIVER PARK

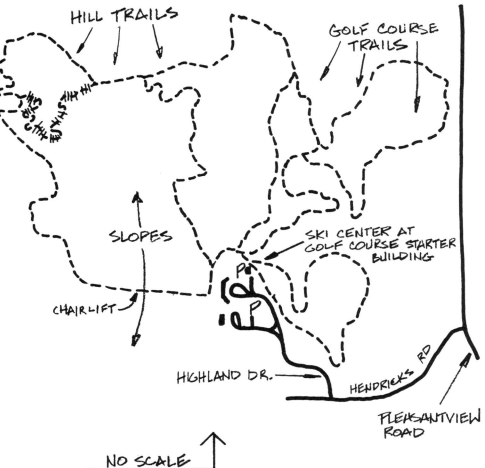

HILL TRAILS

GOLF COURSE TRAILS

SLOPES

SKI CENTER AT GOLF COURSE STARTER BUILDING

CHAIRLIFT

HIGHLAND DR.

HENDRICKS RD

PLEASANTVIEW ROAD

NO SCALE

BOYNE HIGHLANDS

Boyne Highlands

Boyne Highlands

Harbor Springs, MI 49740

616-526-2171
800-562-3899

Michigan Atlas & Gazetteer Location: 82A1

County Location: Emmet

Directions To Trailhead:
Between Harbor Springs and Petoskey on Pleasantview Rd (follow signs).

Trail Type: Cross Country Skiing
Trail Distance: 10 km   Loops: 4   Shortest: Longest:
Trail Surface: Natural
Trail Use Fee: Yes
Method Of Ski Trail Grooming: Track set
Skiing Ability Suggested: Novice to advanced
Hiking Trail Difficulty: NA
Mountain Biking Ability Suggested: NA
Terrain: Steep 0%, Hilly 0%, Moderate 5%, Flat 95%
Camping: Available at Petoskey State Park in summer months only

Privately operated beautiful 4 seasons resort with all facilities.
At press time, only the golf course was assured to be open for cross country skiing this year. Management was hopeful that the mountain loop would be groomed this winter but that was not assured.
Trail specifications listed above are only for the golf course.
Call ahead to confirm the number of trails available and condition of the grooming.

Boyne Mountain
Boyne Mountain
Boyne Falls, MI 49713

616-549-2441
800-632-7174

Cross Country Ski Director
Boyne Mountain
Boyne Falls, MI 49713

same as above

Michigan Atlas & Gazetteer Location: 82C1

County Location: Charlevoix

Directions To Trailhead:
15 miles south of Petoskey at Boyne Falls, just SW of US131and M75
intersection at the south edge of Boyne Falls

Trail Type: Cross Country Skiing, Mountain Biking
Trail Distance: 35 km   Loops: Many   Shortest: .5 km   Longest: 20 km
Trail Surface: Natural
Trail Use Fee: Yes
Method Of Ski Trail Grooming: Track set with skating lanes
Skiing Ability Suggested: Novice to advanced
Hiking Trail Difficulty: Moderate
Mountain Biking Ability Suggested: NA
Terrain: Steep 15%, Hilly 35%, Moderate 25%, Flat 25%
Camping: None

Privately operated 4 season ski resort.
Lodging, restaurant, snack bar, lessons, rentals, pool and shops.
Great trails for cross country skiing and mountain biking.   Site of mountain bike races.
One trail goes to the top of the mountain. Others are in the hills and golf course of the resort.
Special events are planned throughout the winter season, including races, guided picnic tours, nordic demo-days, hot dog roasts and wine & cheeze tours.
Cross country skiing/lodging packages available. Packages include lodging ood, lessons, trail passes, and apres' ski activities.

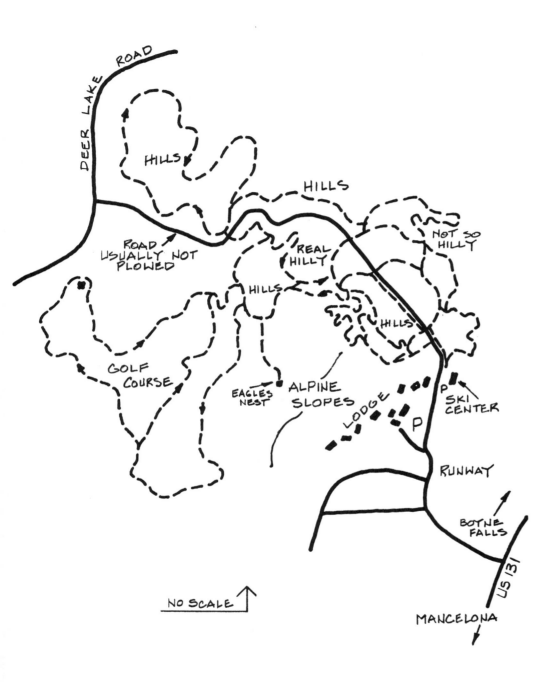

NO SCALE

BOYNE NORDICAN

Burt Lake State Park
6635 State Park Drive
Indian River, MI 49749

616-238-9392

DNR Parks and Recreation Divison

517-373-1270
517-275-5151

Michigan Atlas & Gazetteer Location: 82A4

County Location: Cheboygan

Directions To Trailhead:
1 mile south of Indian River on Old US27

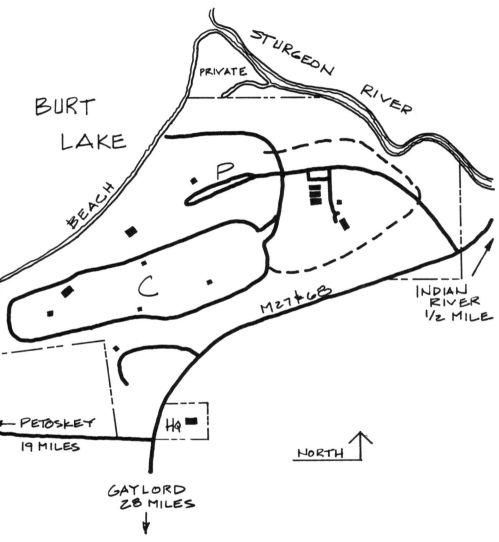

Trail Type: Hiking/Walking, Cross Country Skiing, Interpretive
Trail Distance: 1.5 mi   Loops: 1   Shortest: NA   Longest: 1.5 mi
Trail Surface: Natural
Trail Use Fee: None
Method Of Ski Trail Grooming: None
Skiing Ability Suggested: Novice
Hiking Trail Difficulty: Easy
Mountain Biking Ability Suggested: NA
Terrain: Steep 0%, Hilly 0%, Moderate 20%, Flat 80%
Camping: Campground on site

Maintained by the DNR Parks and Recreation Division
The park has a large sandy beach and is along the shore for a beautiful lake.

BURT LAKE STATE PARK

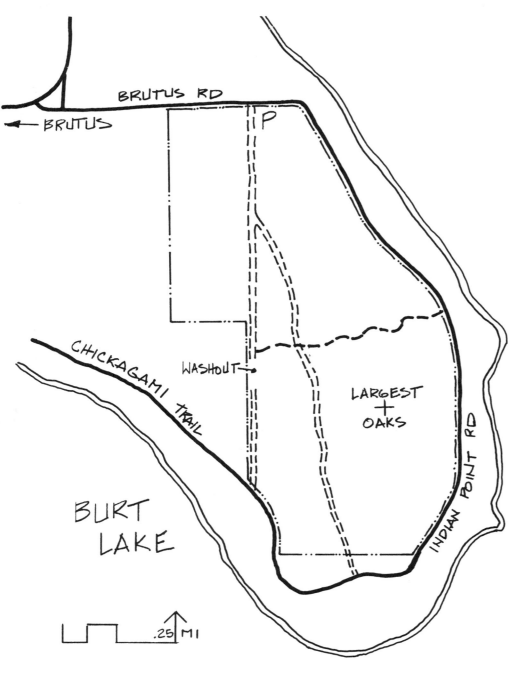

BRUTUS RD

← BRUTUS

P

CHICKAGAMI TRAIL

WASHOUT

LARGEST + OAKS

BURT LAKE

INDIAN POINT RD

.25 MI

COLONIAL POINT MEMORIAL FOREST

Little Traverse Conservancy
3264 Powell Rd
Harbor Springs, MI 49740

616-347-0091

Michigan Atlas & Gazetteer Location: 82A3

County Location: Cheboygan

Directions To Trailhead:
Us 31 north from Petoskey to Brutus Rd, then east on Brutus and continue onto gravel surface. Follow signs to the forest.

Trail Type: Hiking/Walking, Cross Country Skiing, Interpretive
Trail Distance: 2 mi   Loops: Shortest: Longest:
Trail Surface: Natural
Trail Use Fee: None
Method Of Ski Trail Grooming: None
Skiing Ability Suggested: Novice to intermediate
Hiking Trail Difficulty: Easy
Mountain Biking Ability Suggested: MA
Terrain: Steep 0%, Hilly 5%, Moderate 70%, Flat 25%
Camping: Maple Bay SFCG just west of the forest on Burt Lake shoreline.

Owned by the Universtiy of Michigan Biological Station as a gift from the Little Traverse Conservancy and The Nature Conservancy.
The largest stand of old growth Red Oaks in the lower peninsula. Average age is between 100 and 150 years old. Also stands of impressive maple, beech, white pine, basswood, white ash and black cherry are throughout the forest.

Hidden Valley Resort
M32 East, PO Box 556
Gaylord, MI 49735

800-752-5510
517-732-5181

NO MAP

Michigan Atlas & Gazetteer Location: 82D34

County Location: Otsego

Directions To Trailhead:
Just east of Gaylord 1 mile on M32.

Trail Type: Mountain Biking

Trail Surface: Natural
Trail Use Fee: Yes
Method Of Ski Trail Grooming: NA
Skiing Ability Suggested: NA
Hiking Trail Difficulty: NA
Mountain Biking Ability Suggested: Novice to advanced
Terrain:
Camping: None

Privately owned resort open to mountain biking in the summer.
The resort is a private club in the winter and therefore not open to cross country skiing, except on special occasions.

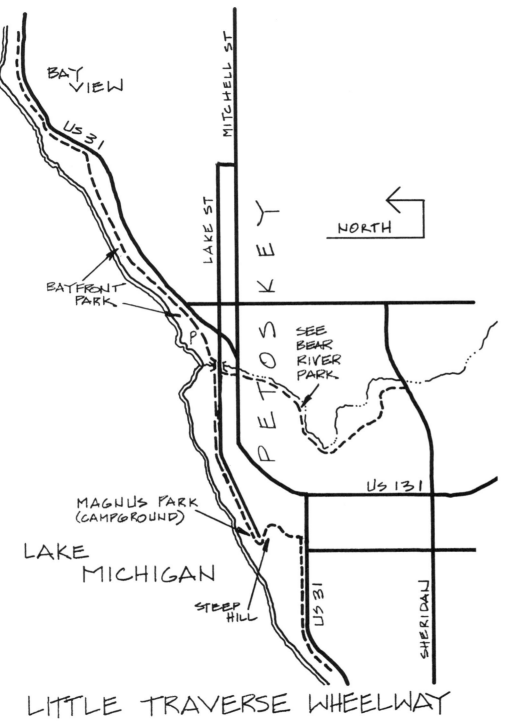

BAY VIEW

US 31

MITCHELL ST

LAKE ST

PETOSKEY

NORTH

BAYFRONT PARK

P

SEE BEAR RIVER PARK

US 131

MAGNUS PARK (CAMPGROUND)

LAKE MICHIGAN

STEEP HILL

US 31

SHERIDAN

LITTLE TRAVERSE WHEELWAY

 Little Traverse Wheelway

City of Petoskey, Parks and Recreation Department
100 West Lake St
Petoskey, MI 49770

616-347-2500

Michigan Atlas & Gazetteer Location: 82AB1

County Location: Emmet

Directions To Trailhead:
Along US 31 in Petoskey between the highway and Lake Michigan. Park at Bayfront Park near the History Museum

Trail Type: Hiking/Walking, Cross Country Skiing
Trail Distance: 1.75 mi   Loops: NA   Shortest: NA   Longest: NA
Trail Surface: Paved
Trail Use Fee: None
Method Of Ski Trail Grooming: None
Skiing Ability Suggested: Novice
Hiking Trail Difficulty: Easy
Mountain Biking Ability Suggested: NA
Terrain: Steep 15%, Hilly 10%, Moderate 0%, Flat 75%
Camping: Mangus Park on the bay in Petoskey

Owned by the City of Petoskey
The trail is along the waterfront on Little Traverse Bay
The Wheelway from Petoskey to Harbor Springs will be a replica of a bikeway that existed in the 1890's.
The Wheelway is connected to the Bear River Park (see other listing)
There are an additional 28 miles of this trail being planned to link Petoskey, Harbor Springs and Charlevoix.

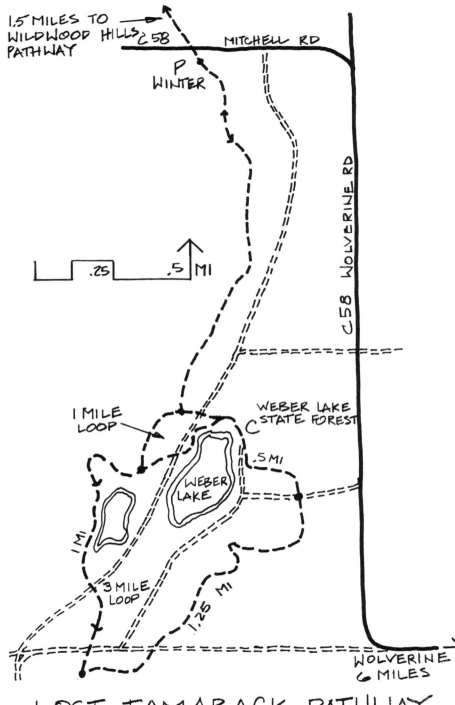

1.5 MILES TO
WILDWOOD HILLS → C58
PATHWAY

MITCHELL RD

P
WINTER

C58 WOLVERINE RD

.25 .5 MI

WEBER LAKE
STATE FOREST

1 MILE
LOOP

C

.5 MI

WEBER
LAKE

1 MI

3 MILE
LOOP

1.25 MI

WOLVERINE →
6 MILES

LOST TAMARACK PATHWAY

Indian River Forest Area, Mackinaw State Forest
6984 M68, PO Box 10   616-238-9313
Indian River, MI 49749

District Forest Manager, Mackinaw State Forest
 1732 West M32, PO Box 667   517-732-3541
Gaylord, MI 49735

Michigan Atlas & Gazetteer Location: 82B3

County Location: Cheboygan

Directions To Trailhead:
6.5 miles west of Wolverine in C58 at Weber Lake State Forest Campground

Trail Type: Hiking/Walking, Cross Country Skiing, Mountain Biking
Trail Distance: 4.75 mi   Loops: 2   Shortest: 1 mi   Longest: 3 mi
Trail Surface: Natural
Trail Use Fee: None
Method Of Ski Trail Grooming: NA
Skiing Ability Suggested: NA
Hiking Trail Difficulty: Easy to moderate
Mountain Biking Ability Suggested: Novice
Terrain: Rolling
Camping: Campground at trailhead

Maintained by the DNR Forest Management Division
Includes a 1.25 mile point to point trail.
The point to point trial is connected to a 1.5 mile trail that connects to to the
Wildwood Hills Pathway.
Not well maintained in recent years. Anyone interested in some volunteer
work?
Other contacts:
        DNR Forest Management Division Office, Lansing, 517-373-1275
        DNR Forest Management Region Office, Roscommon, 517-275-5151

Indian River Forest Area, Mackinaw State Forest
 6984 M68, PO Box 10   616-238-9313
Indian River, MI 49749

District Forest Manger, Mackinaw State Forest
1732 W est M32, PO Box 667   517-732-3541
Gaylord, MI 49735

Michigan Atlas & Gazetteer Location: 82A2, 94BCD23

County Location: Emmet,

Directions To Trailhead:
North trailhead - In Mackinaw City, west of I-75 behind the Chalet House Motel and Shepler's Ferry parking lot.. May park in the Chalet House Motel lot, but check in with them first.
Southern trailhead- Hillside Gardens in Alanson
Suggested southern trailhead at this time(1994) due to overgrown condition of the trail - Levering

Trail Type: Hiking/Walking, Mountain Biking
Trail Distance: 24 mi   Loops: NA   Shortest: NA   Longest: NA
Trail Surface: Gravel, ballast and natural
Trail Use Fee: None
Method Of Ski Trail Grooming: NA
Skiing Ability Suggested: NA
Hiking Trail Difficulty: Easy
Mountain Biking Ability Suggested: Novice
Terrain: 100% Flat
Camping: None

Maintained by the Forest Management Division
Used mostly as a snowmobile trail.
Because of loose surface, this trail may be difficult to ride and hike at his time.
Check conditions of the trail surface before starting.

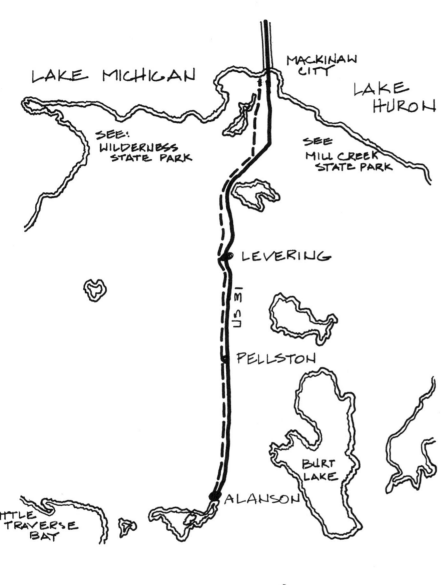

MACKINAW/ALANSON RAIL TRAIL

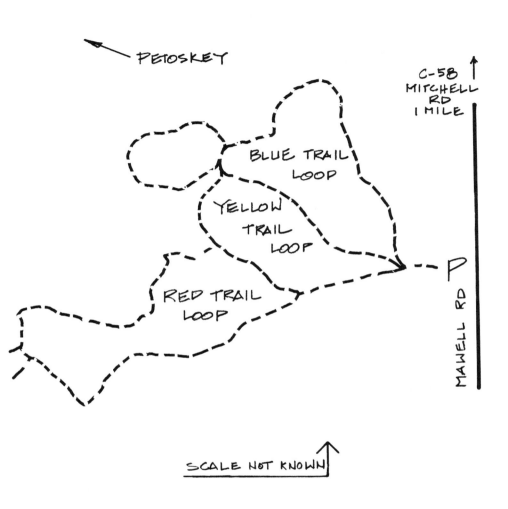

PETOSKEY

C-58
MITCHELL
RD
1 MILE

BLUE TRAIL
LOOP

YELLOW
TRAIL
LOOP

RED TRAIL
LOOP

P

MAWELL RD

SCALE NOT KNOWN

McCUNE NATURE PRESERVE

Little Traverse Conservancy
3264 Powell Rd
Harbor Springs, Mi 49740

616-347-0991

Michigan Atlas & Gazetteer Location: 82B2

County Location: Emmet

Directions To Trailhead:
From US31 east of Petoskey, take Mitchell Rd(C58) east to Maxwell Rd, then right approximately .75 mil to the Preserve. Sign on the west (right) side of the road.

Trail Type: Hiking/Walking, Cross Country Skiing, Interpretive
Trail Distance: 1.5 mi   Loops: 2   Shortest: Longest:
Trail Surface: Natural
Trail Use Fee: None
Method Of Ski Trail Grooming: NA
Skiing Ability Suggested: NA
Hiking Trail Difficulty: Easy
Mountain Biking Ability Suggested: NA
Terrain: Steep 0%, Hilly 5%, Moderate 15%, Flat 80%
Camping: None

Owned by the Little Traverse Conservancy
168 acres donated in 1984
Two branches of the Minnehaha Creek which is spring fed, flow across the property.

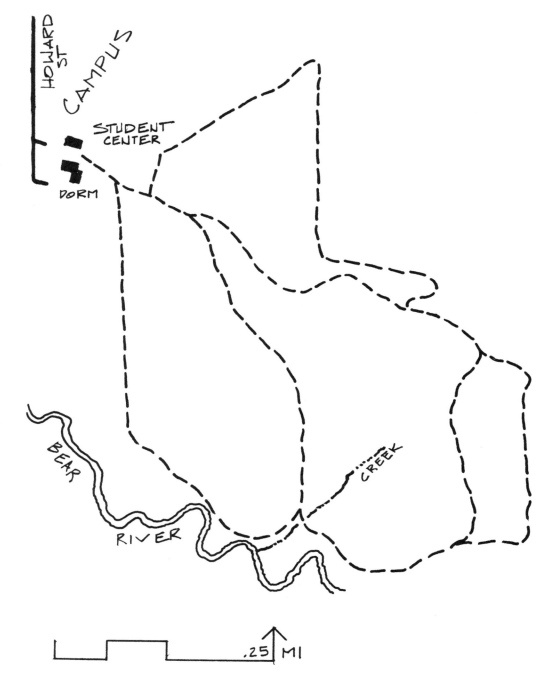

North Central Michigan College
1515 Howard
Petoskey, MI 49770

616-348-6612

Michigan Atlas & Gazetteer Location: 82B1

County Location: Charlevoix

Directions To Trailhead:
Sheridian St to Howard St to the college. Trailhead is behind the Student Center.

Trail Type: Hiking/Walking, Cross Country Skiing, Interpretive
Trail Distance: 5 km   Loops: 3   Shortest: 1.5 km Longest: 4km
Trail Surface: Natural
Trail Use Fee: None
Method Of Ski Trail Grooming: None
Skiing Ability Suggested: Novice
Hiking Trail Difficulty: Easy
Mountain Biking Ability Suggested: NA
Terrain: Steep 0%, Hilly 5%, Moderate 50%, Flat 45%
Camping: None

Owned by North Central Michigan College
Short but pleasant ski trails on the edge of town.

.25 MI

NORTH CENTRAL MICHIGAN COLLEGE

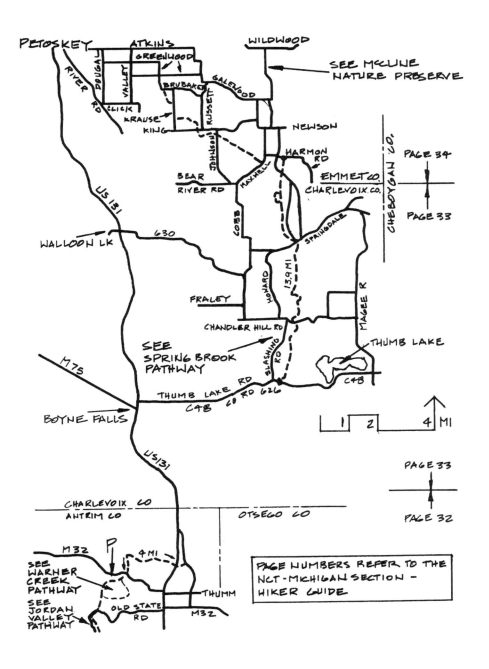

Gaylord Forest Area, Mackinaw State Forest
1732 West M31, PO Box 667   517-732-3541
Gaylord, MI 49735

Indian River Forest Area, Mackinaw State Forest
PO Box 10   616-238-9313
Indian River, MI 49749

Michigan Atlas & Gazetteer Location: 82BCD12

County Location: Antrim, Charlevoix, Emmet

Directions To Trailhead:
Two separate sections are constructed at this time (1994).
Section 1 - North of the Jordan Valley Pathway to the Warner Creek Pathway, continues slightly east of US 131.
Section 2 - Beginning at Thumb Lake Rd (C48 or Co Rd 626) about 5.5 miles east of US131 and heading north to Harmon Rd in Emmet Co. and continuing northwest to Brubaker Rd.(some sections will be rerouted in 1995).

Trail Type: Hiking/Walking, Mountain Biking
Trail Distance: 10+ mi   Loops: NA   Shortest: NA   Longest: NA
Trail Surface: Natural
Trail Use Fee: None
Method Of Ski Trail Grooming: NA
Skiing Ability Suggested: NA
Hiking Trail Difficulty: Moderate to difficult
Mountain Biking Ability Suggested: Intermediate to advanced
Terrain: Hilly to steep for section 2
Camping: No established campgrounds nearby. Off trail camping permitted.

Trail in the Mackinaw State Forest
Section 1 - Rolling to hilly with second growth brush and timber
Section 2 - Hilly to steep with heavily wooded cover
Trail constructed and maintained by the North Country Trail Association members.
Trail construction will continue in this section.
Trail marked with blue blazes.
Mileage is for constructed sections that are NOT part of other trails.
See NCNCT, Michigan Section, Hiker Guide pages 32,33 and 34
Detailed Hiker Guide map book is available from the North Country Trail Associaion , PO Box 311, White Cloud, MI 49349 616-689-1912

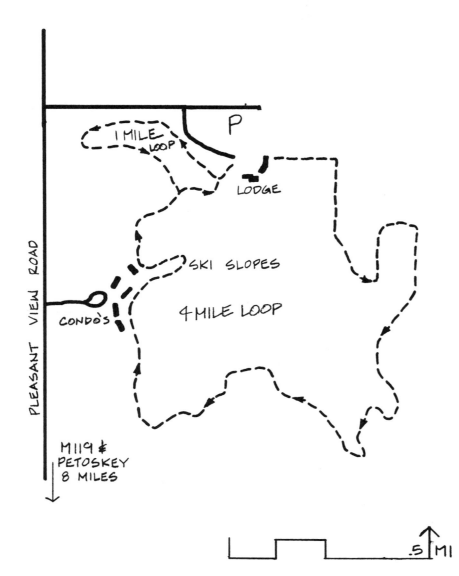

Nub's Nob
4021 Nubs Nob Rd.
Harbor Springs, MI 49740

616-526-2131
800-ski-haus

Michigan Atlas & Gazetteer Location: 82A1

County Location: Emmet

Directions To Trailhead:
Northeast of Harbor Springs on C81. Follow the signs

Trail Type: Cross Country Skiing
Trail Distance: 5 mi   Loops: 2   Shortest: 1 mi   Longest: 4 mi
Trail Surface: Natural
Trail Use Fee: None
Method Of Ski Trail Grooming: None
Skiing Ability Suggested: Novice and advanced
Hiking Trail Difficulty: NA
Mountain Biking Ability Suggested: NA
Terrain: Steep 10%, Hilly 20%, Moderate 30%, Flat 40%
Camping: None

Privately operated downhill ski resort
Restaurant, lodge, and rentals available
Thought not groomed the trail is usually skied in well.
The 4 mile loop should only be attemped by advanced skiers since there is a
400 foot elevation change in the trail.
Follow the blue markers since the trail intersects logging roads often.
Located just east of Boyne Highlands.

NUBS NOB

Petoskey State Park
2475 Harbor-Petoskey Rd.
Petoskey, MI 49770

616-347-2311

DNR Parks and Recreation Division

517-373-1270

Michigan Atlas & Gazetteer Location: 82A1

County Location: Emmet

Directions To Trailhead:
West of Petoskey via US31, then north on M119 (Harbor-Petoskey Rd.) to the park which will be on your left

Trail Type: Hiking/Walking, Cross Country Skiing, Interpretive
Trail Distance: 5 mi   Loops: 2   Shortest: 2 mi   Longest: 4 mi
Trail Surface: Natural
Trail Use Fee: None, but vehicle entry fee required
Method Of Ski Trail Grooming: None
Skiing Ability Suggested: Novice
Hiking Trail Difficulty: Moderate
Mountain Biking Ability Suggested: NA
Terrain: Steep 1%, Hilly 15%, Moderate 40%, Flat 44%
Camping: Campground available in park

Maintained by the DNR Parks and Recreation Division
Beautiful beach on Little Traverse Bay.
The compact trail system is a real joy to ski. It's surprisingly protected from the lake winds.

C

HQ

PARK ENTRANCE

P

C

HIKING TRAIL

M-131

SKI TRAIL

C

M-131

PETOSKEY 3 MI.

LITTLE TRAVERSE BAY

.25 MI.

PETOSKEY STATE PARK

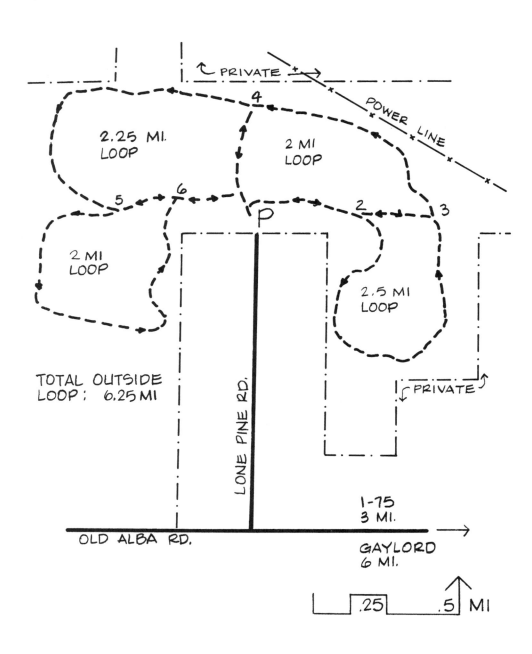

Gaylord Forest Area, Mackinaw State Forest
1732 West M32, PO Box 667   517-732-3541
Gaylord, MI 49735

District Forest Manager, Mackinaw State Forest
1732 West M32, PO Box Box 667   517-732-3541
Gaylord, MI 49735

Michigan Atlas & Gazetteer Location: 82D2

County Location: Otsego

Directions To Trailhead:
West of Gaylord and south of M32
Trailhead - West from I75 at the south Gaylord exit 279 on Alba Rd. 2.4 miles to
Lone Pine Rd., then right (north) to the end of the road.

Trail Type: Hiking/Walking, Cross Country Skiing
Trail Distance: 6.25 mi   Loops: 4   Shortest: 2 mi   Longest: 2.5 mi
Trail Surface: Natural
Trail Use Fee: None, but donations for trail maintenance
Method Of Ski Trail Grooming: Double track set
Skiing Ability Suggested: Novice only
Hiking Trail Difficulty: Easy
Mountain Biking Ability Suggested: NA
Terrain: Steep 0%, Hilly 5%, Moderate 20%, Flat 75%
Camping: Camground available at Otsego Lake State Park and private
campgrounds

Maintained by the DNR Forest Management Division
Forested trail system of second growth trees.
No steep hills on the trail.
Good trail for the beginning skier.
Pit toilet at parking lot
Other contacts:
        DNR Forest Management Division Office, Lansing, 517-373-1275
        DNR Forest Management Region Office, Roscommon, 517-275-5151

PINE BARON PATHWAY

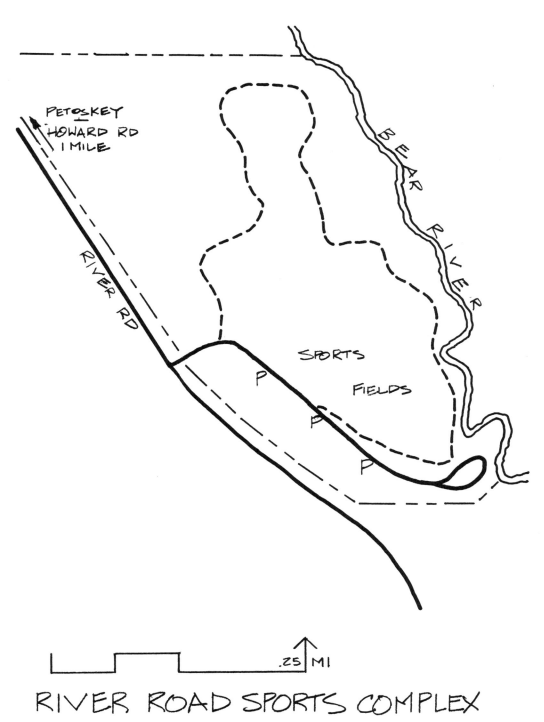

City of Petoskey, Department of Parks and Recreation
100 W. Lake St
Petoskey, MI 49770

616-347-2500

Michigan Atlas & Gazetteer Location: 82AB1

County Location: Charlevoix

Directions To Trailhead:
US131south of Petoskey, turn east on Sheridan to Clarion St., then turn south onClarion to Riverbend Rd. Continue south .5 mile to the complex.

Trail Type: Hiking/Walking, Cross Country Skiing
Trail Distance: 1.5 mi   Loops: 1   Shortest: Longest: 1.5 mi
Trail Surface: Natural
Trail Use Fee: None
Method Of Ski Trail Grooming: Track set
Skiing Ability Suggested: Novice
Hiking Trail Difficulty: Easy
Mountain Biking Ability Suggested: NA
Terrain: 100% Flat
Camping: None

Maintained by the City of Petoskey Department of Parks and Recreation
Ball fields and fishing available.

RIVER ROAD SPORTS COMPLEX

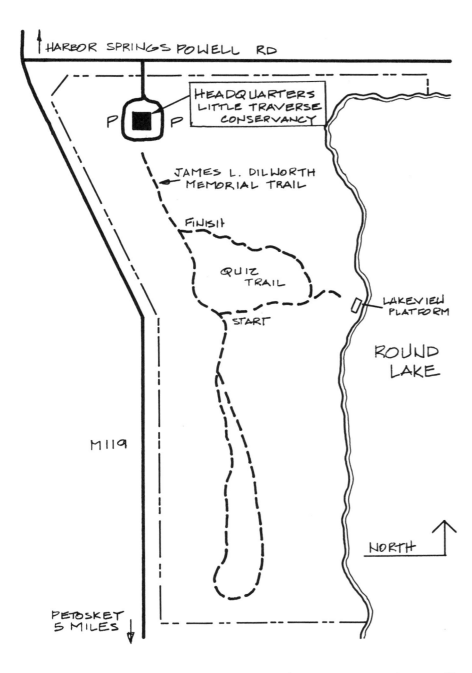

Little Traverse Conservancy
3264 Powell Rd
Harbor Springs, MI 49740

616-347-0991

Michigan Atlas & Gazetteer Location: 82A1

County Location: Emmet

Directions To Trailhead:
From Petoskey take US31 north to M119, then left for about 4 miles to Powell Rd, then right and take first driveway on right into parking lot.

Trail Type: Hiking/Walking, Cross Country Skiing, Interpretive
Trail Distance: 1 mi   Loops: 2   Shortest: Longest:
Trail Surface: Natural
Trail Use Fee: None
Method Of Ski Trail Grooming: None
Skiing Ability Suggested: Novice
Hiking Trail Difficulty: Easy
Mountain Biking Ability Suggested: NA
Terrain: 100%Flat
Camping: None

Owned by the Little Traverse Conservancy
Site of the headquarters building for the organization.
Self guided trail brochure available.

ROUND LAKE NATURE PRESERVE

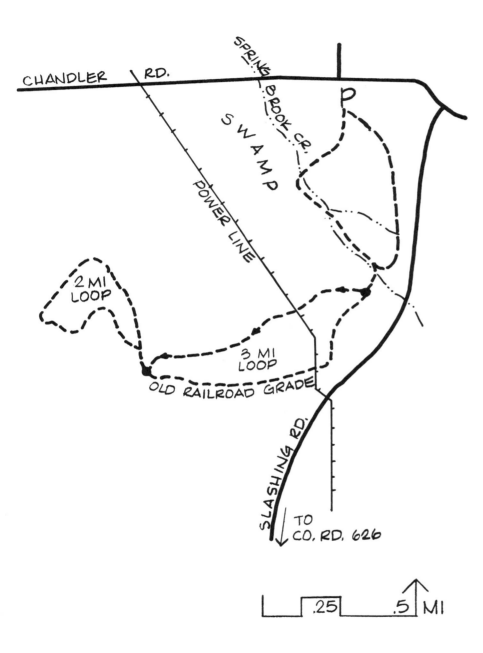

Gaylord Forest Area, Mackinaw State Forest
1732 West M32, PO Box 667   517-732-3541
Gaylord, MI 49735

District Forest Manager, Mackinaw State Forest
 1732 West M32, PO Box 667   517-732-3541
Gaylord, MI 49735

Michigan Atlas & Gazetteer Location: 82C2

County Location: Charlevoix

Directions To Trailhead:
Just east of Boyne Falls on Thumb Lake Rd. (C48) for 5 miles to Slashing Rd.,
then north 2.5 miles to the end of the road, then west on Chandler Rd. .4 miles
to parking lot on the south side (you will pass the old Thunder Mountain ski area
on Slashing Rd.)

Trail Type: Hiking/Walking, Cross Country Skiing, Mountain Biking
Trail Distance: 5 mi   Loops: 3   Shortest: Longest:
Trail Surface: Natural
Trail Use Fee: None
Method Of Ski Trail Grooming: None
Skiing Ability Suggested: Novice to intermediate
Hiking Trail Difficulty: Moderate
Mountain Biking Ability Suggested: Easy
Terrain: Flat to hilly
Camping: None

Maintained by the DNR Forest Management Division
The loops contain more difficult terrain the farther away from the trailhead the
user travels. Habitat varies from cedar lowlands to upland hardwoods.
Other contacts:
        DNR Forest Management Division Office, Lansing, 517-373-1275
        DNR Forest Management Region Office, Roscommon, 517-275-5151

SPRING BROOK PATHWAY

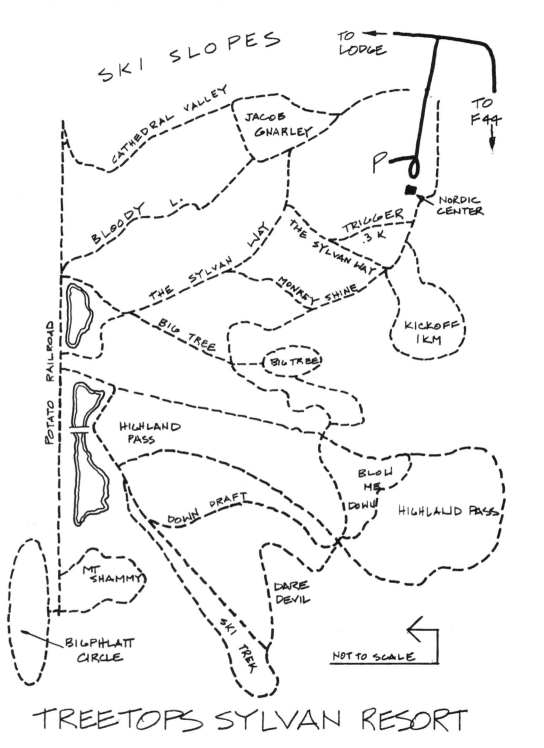

SKI SLOPES

TO LODGE

TO F44

CATHEDRAL VALLEY

JACOB GNARLEY

P

NORDIC CENTER

BLOODY L.

TRIGGER .3 K

THE SYLVAN WAY

THE SYLVAN WAY

MONKEY SHINE

POTATO RAILROAD

THE SYLVAN

BIG TREE

BIG TREE

KICKOFF 1KM

HIGHLAND PASS

BLOW ME DOWN

HIGHLAND PASS

DOWN DRAFT

MT SHAMMY

DARE DEVIL

SKI TREK

BIGPHLATT CIRCLE

NOT TO SCALE

TREETOPS SYLVAN RESORT

Treetops Sylvan Resort

Treetops Sylvan Resort
3962 Wilkinson Rd.
Gaylord, MI 49735

800-444-6711
517-732-6711

Michigan Atlas & Gazetteer Location: 82D4

County Location: Otsego

Directions To Trailhead:
7 miles east of Gaylord via M32 and Wilkinson Rd (follow signs).

Trail Type: Cross Country Skiing
Trail Distance: 20.1 km   Loops: Many   Shortest: 1 km   Longest: 15 km
Trail Surface: Natural
Trail Use Fee: Yes
Method Of Ski Trail Grooming: Single and double track set plus telemark
Skiing Ability Suggested: Novice to advanced
Hiking Trail Difficulty: NA
Mountain Biking Ability Suggested: NA
Terrain: Steep 10%, Hilly 25%, Moderate 35%, Flat 30%
Camping: None

Privately operated full service alpine ski area with cross country ski trails.
All services available including instruction, rentals, ski shop, 128 room hotel, entertainment and complete food service.
Lighted trail available on weekends.
Though most of the trails are on golf course fairways, the terrain is very hilly and many fairways are protected from the wind.
The open steep slopes of the fairways are excellent for telemarking.
There are several hilly wooded trails between the fairways and around the golf course that make for an interesting trail system.
A different kind of trail system that allows for a full variety of techniques including telemarking, classic and skating.
A great place to spend an afternoon on well groomed trails.

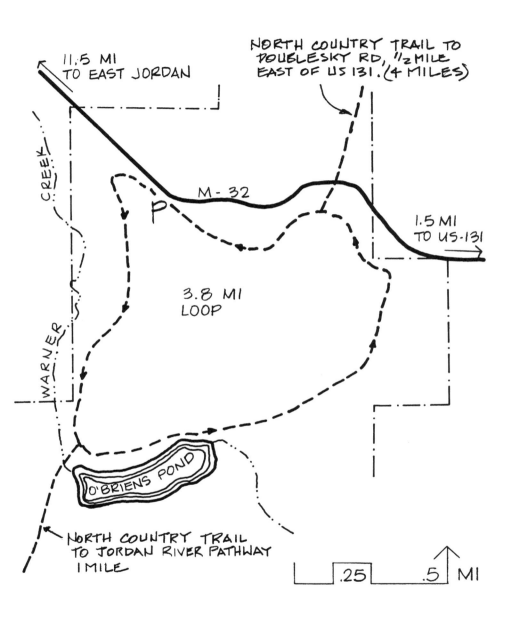

NORTH COUNTRY TRAIL TO DOUBLESKY RD, 1/2 MILE EAST OF US 131. (4 MILES)

11.5 MI TO EAST JORDAN

CREEK

M-32

P

WARNER

1.5 MI TO US-131

3.8 MI LOOP

O'BRIENS POND

NORTH COUNTRY TRAIL TO JORDAN RIVER PATHWAY 1 MILE

.25 .5 MI

WARNER CREEK PATHWAY

Gaylord Forest Area, Mackinaw State Forest
PO Box 667, 1732 West M32
Gaylord, MI 49735

517-732-3541

District Forest Manager, Mackinaw State Forest
PO Box667, 1732 West M32
Gaylord, MI 49735

517-732-3541

Michigan Atlas & Gazetteer Location: 82D1

County Location: Antrim

Directions To Trailhead:
Between US131 and East Jordan on M32
Trailhead - 1.5 miles west of US131 on M32

Trail Type: Hiking/Walking, Cross Country Skiing, Mountain Biking
Trail Distance: 3.8 mi   Loops: 1   Shortest: Longest:
Trail Surface:
Trail Use Fee: None
Method Of Ski Trail Grooming: Track set
Skiing Ability Suggested: Novice to intermediate
Hiking Trail Difficulty: Easy
Mountain Biking Ability Suggested: Novice
Terrain: Steep 0%, Hilly 05%, Moderate 75%, Flat 25%
Camping: None

Maintained by the DNR Forest Management Division
Developed for skiers because the nearby Jordan Valley Pathway is not suitable for skiing
The North Country Trail - Mackinaw 2 uses this pathway for part of its route from the Jordan River Pathway.
Other contacts:
        DNR Forest Management Division Office, Lansing, 517-373-1275
        DNR Forest Management Region Office, Roscommon, 517-275-5151

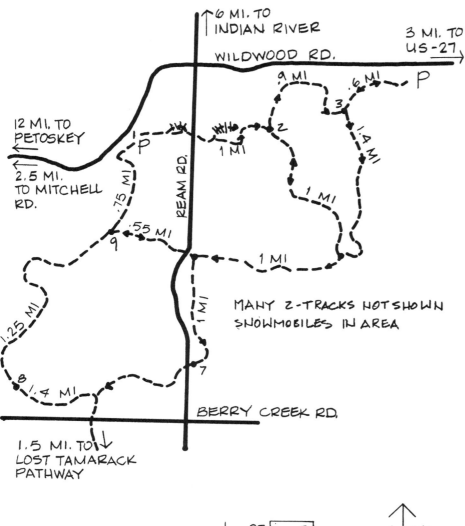

↑ 6 MI. TO
⌐ INDIAN RIVER

WILDWOOD RD.

3 MI. TO
US-27 →

12 MI. TO
PETOSKEY ←

2.5 MI.
TO MITCHELL
RD.

.9 MI

.6 MI

P

3

2

1 MI

.4 MI

1 MI

REAM RD.

P

.75 MI

.55 MI

9

1 MI

MANY 2-TRACKS NOT SHOWN
SNOWMOBILES IN AREA

1 MI

1.25 MI

8 1.4 MI

7

BERRY CREEK RD.

1.5 MI. TO ↓
LOST TAMARACK
PATHWAY

| .25 | .5 | 1 | MI

↑ N

WILDWOOD HILLS PATHWAY

Indian River Forest Area, Mackinaw State Forest
6984 M68, PO Box 10   616-238-9313
Indian River, MI 49749

District Forest Manager, Mackinaw State Forest
1732 West M32, PO Box 667   517-732-3541
Gaylord, MI 49735

Michigan Atlas & Gazetteer Location: 82B3

County Location: Emmet, Cheboygan

Directions To Trailhead:
Between Indian River and Petoskey on Wildwood Rd.
Trailhead - From Indian River on M68 turn south on old US27, then south 2 miles to Wildwood Rd., then west 3 miles to parking lot (south side)
Trailhead - From Petoskey on C58 (Mitchell Rd.) for about 9.5 miles, then pick up Wildwood Rd. (left fork), for 3 miles to parking lot

Trail Type: Hiking/Walking, Cross Country Skiing, Mountain Biking
Trail Distance: 9.3 mi   Loops: 3   Shortest: 4.5 mi Longest: 7 mi
Trail Surface: Natural
Trail Use Fee: None, but donation accepted to groom trail
Method Of Ski Trail Grooming: Track set
Skiing Ability Suggested: Novice to intermediate
Hiking Trail Difficulty: Easy
Mountain Biking Ability Suggested: Novice to intermediate
Terrain: Steep 20%, Hilly 20%, Moderate 40%, Flat 20%
Camping: Available in Alanson and Indian River

Maintained by the DNR Forest Management Division
A very enjoyable trail system for skiers of most skill levels including beginners. Some snowmobiles are in the area but because of the heavy use this trail receives, they seldom if ever cause problems with the trails except for the east parking lot area.
All difficult hills can be by-passed.
One of the better trails developed for skiing by the DNR.
Somewhat difficult trail to locate in the summer because of the open fields that it crosses.
Toilets available at the parking lots.
The Lost Tamarack Pathway(see other listing) connects to the south.
Groomed with donated funds. Please contribute at the parking lot pipes.
Other contacts:
    DNR Forest Management Division Office, Lansing, 517-373-1275
    DNR Forest Management Region Office, Roscommon, 517-275-5151

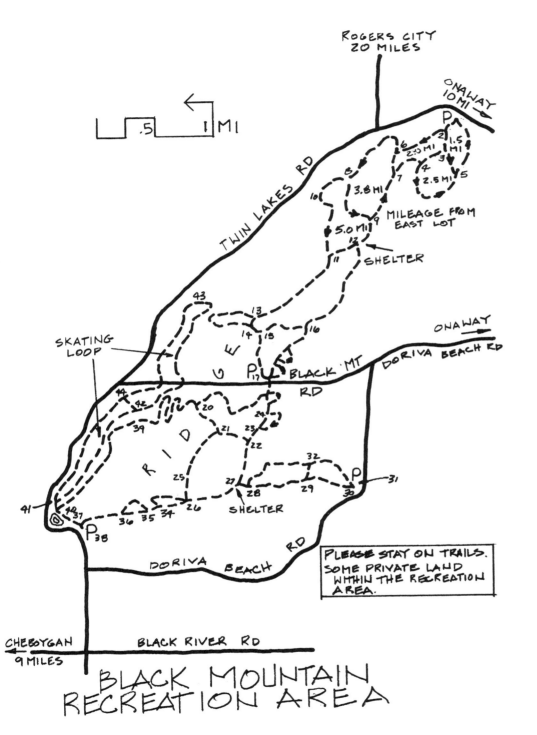

ROGERS CITY
20 MILES

ONAWAY
10 MI

.5 | 1 MI

P

TWIN LAKES RD

2 — 1.5 MI
6 — 2.0 MI
8 — 3
3.8 MI — 7 — 4
10 — 2.5 MI — 5
9 — MILEAGE FROM EAST LOT
5.0 MI
12
11 — SHELTER

43

SKATING LOOP

13

14 — 15 — 16

ONAWAY

R I D G E

P₁₇ — BLACK MT — DORIVA BEACH RD
RD

44
18 — 20
19 — 24
39 — 21 — 23
25 — 22
27 — 32
41 — 28 — 29 — P — 31
40 — 37 — 30
36 — 35 — 34 — 26 — SHELTER
P₃₈

DORIVA BEACH RD

PLEASE STAY ON TRAILS.
SOME PRIVATE LAND
WITHIN THE RECREATION
AREA.

CHEBOYGAN
9 MILES

BLACK RIVER RD

BLACK MOUNTAIN
RECREATION AREA

Atlanta Forest Area, Mackinaw State Forest
HCR 74, Box 30   517-785-4252
Atlanta, MI 49709-9605

District Forest Manager, Mackinaw State Forest
1732 West M32, PO Box 667   517-732-3541
Gaylord, MI 49735

Michigan Atlas & Gazetteer Location: 83A7,95D67

County Location: Cheboygan, Presque Isle

Directions To Trailhead:
North of Onaway on M211 to Co Rd 489 to trailhead.
From Rogers City go north on US23 to Co Rd 646 then west to trailhead

Trail Type: Hiking/Walking, Cross Country Skiing, Mountain Biking, Interpretive
Trail Distance: 30.52 mi   Loops: 12+   Shortest: 1 mi   Longest: 15 mi
Trail Surface: Natural
Trail Use Fee: None
Method Of Ski Trail Grooming: Track set with skating loop
Skiing Ability Suggested: Novice to intermediate
Hiking Trail Difficulty: Easy to moderate
Mountain Biking Ability Suggested: Moderate to advanced
Terrain: Steep 25%, Hilly 30%, Moderate 30%, Flat 15%
Camping: Campgrounds at Black Lake SFCG, Twin Lake SFCG and Bluff
campground

Maintained by the DNR Forest Management Division
Black Mountain is the only significant topography in the area therefore, views
from the trails on the top of the mountain are quite nice.
The trailheads at the east and west end of the complex are in the lower
elevations. The trailhead on Black Mountain Rd is at the top of the mountain.
None of the trails are that difficult, however some grades can be quite long
though not steep. Along the trail there are several short and fast ski loops near
the Black Mountain Rd trailhead. Snowmobile and ORV trails are also in the
area.
The gated trails are only to restrict ORV and snowmobile use and not to stop
non-motorized trail users. Some sand could make mountain biking more difficult
in some sections
Excellent large multi colored trail map is available from the DNR. Unfortunately,
horse back riding is allowed on the skiing/hiking pathway system during the non
snow months.

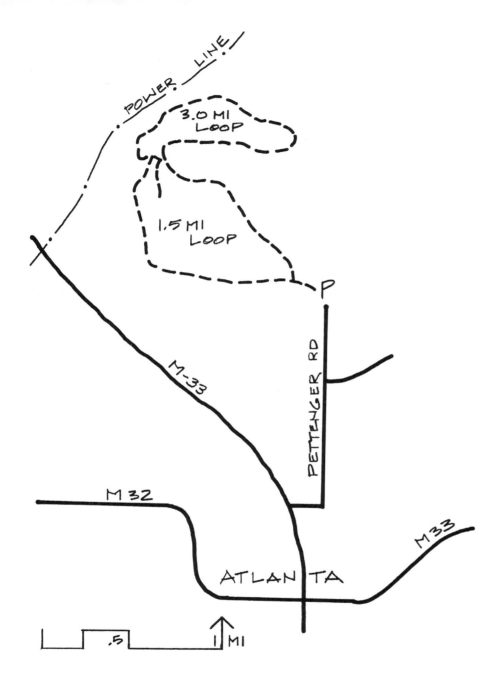

Briley Township Trail

Briley Township
PO Box 207
Atlanta, MI 49709

517-785-4186

Michigan Atlas & Gazetteer Location: 83D7

County Location: Montmorency

Directions To Trailhead:
In Atlanta go north at blinker light, then .5 mile turn right at Pettinger Rd, then about .5 mile ahead is trailhead entrance

Trail Type: Cross Country Skiing
Trail Distance: 3 mi   Loops: 2   Shortest: 1.5 mi Longest: 3 mi
Trail Surface: Natural
Trail Use Fee: None
Method Of Ski Trail Grooming: Track set
Skiing Ability Suggested: Novice to intermediate
Hiking Trail Difficulty: NA
Mountain Biking Ability Suggested: NA
Terrain: Steep 0%, Hilly 50%, Moderate 25%, Flat 25%
Camping: None but Clear Lake SP and state forest campgrounds are nearby

Maintained by Briley Township
Trails in wooded area on the north side of Atlanta.

BRILEY TOWNSHIP TRAIL

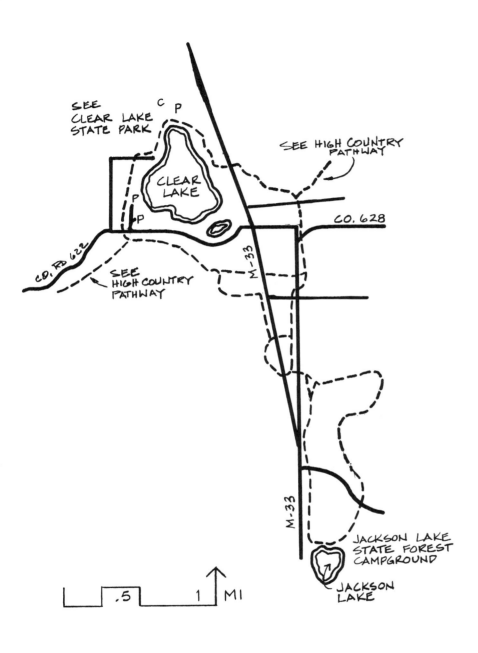

CLEAR LAKE -
JACKSON LAKE PATHWAY

Clear Lake State Park
Rte 1   517-785-4388
Atlanta, MI 49709

Atlanta Forest Area, Mackinaw State Forest
HCR 74, Box 30   517-785-4252
Atlanta, MI 49709

Michigan Atlas & Gazetteer Location: 83CD7

County Location: Presque Isle, Montmorency

Directions To Trailhead:
Trailhead - 10 miles north of Atlanta on M33 at the Clear Lake State Park.
Trailhead - Jackson Lake State Forest Campground, 3 miles south of the state park.

Trail Type: Hiking/Walking, Mountain Biking, Interpretive
Trail Distance: 7.5 mi   Loops: 3   Shortest: 2 mi   Longest: 7 mi
Trail Surface: Natural
Trail Use Fee: None, but vehicle entry permit required
Method Of Ski Trail Grooming: NA
Skiing Ability Suggested: NA
Hiking Trail Difficulty: Easy to moderate
Mountain Biking Ability Suggested: Novice to intermediate
Terrain: Steep 0%, Hilly 25%, Moderate 50%, Flat 25%
Camping: Campground at north trailhead at Clear Lake State Park

Maintained by DNR Parks and Recreation and Forest Management Divisions.
This is a 25 station interpretive trail.
A section is part of the High Country Pathway.
May not always be well maintained due to infrequent use of some sections
Other contacts:
       DNR Parks and Recreation Division Office, Lansing, 517-373-1270
       DNR Forest Management Region Office, Roscommon, 517-275-5151
       DNR Forest Management Division Office, Lansing, 517-373-1275

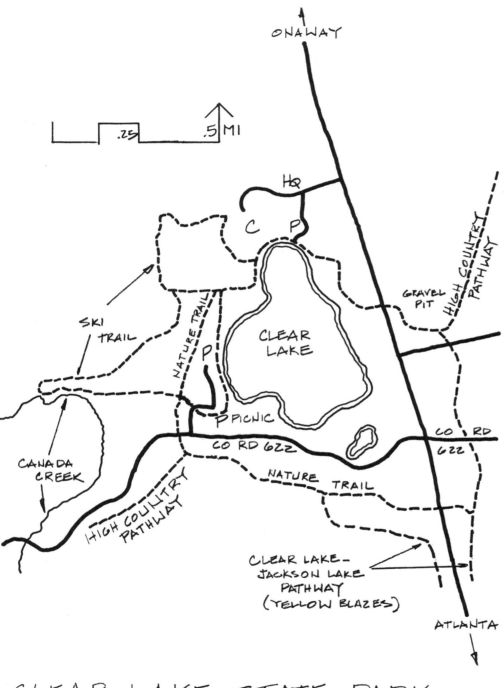

ONAWAY

.25 .5 MI

HQ

C P

SKI TRAIL

NATURE TRAIL

P

CLEAR LAKE

GRAVEL PIT

HIGH COUNTRY PATHWAY

CANADA CREEK

P PICNIC

CO RD 622

CO RD 622

HIGH COUNTRY PATHWAY

NATURE TRAIL

CLEAR LAKE- JACKSON LAKE PATHWAY (YELLOW BLAZES)

ATLANTA

CLEAR LAKE STATE PARK

Clear Lake State Park

Clear Lake State Park
Rte 1, Box 51
Atlanta, MI 49709

517-785-4388

DNR Parks and Recreation Division

517-373-1270
517-275-5151

Michigan Atlas & Gazetteer Location: 83CD7

County Location: Montmorency

Directions To Trailhead:
Between Onaway and Atlanta on M33

Trail Type: Hiking/Walking, Cross Country Skiing, Interpretive
Trail Distance: 4 mi   Loops: 2   Shortest: 1.5 mi Longest: 3.5 mi
Trail Surface: Natural
Trail Use Fee: None, but vehicle entry permit required
Method Of Ski Trail Grooming: Track set
Skiing Ability Suggested: Novice
Hiking Trail Difficulty: Easy to moderate
Mountain Biking Ability Suggested: NA
Terrain: Steep 0%, Hilly 2%, Moderate 3%, Flat 95%
Camping: On site

Maintained by the DNR Parks and Recreation Division
Ski trail is separate from the hiking trail.
The trail has 13 interpreted stations.
Trail guide available.
Hiking trail system connects with the High Country Pathway and the Clear Lake
-Jackson Lake Pathway. (see other trails)

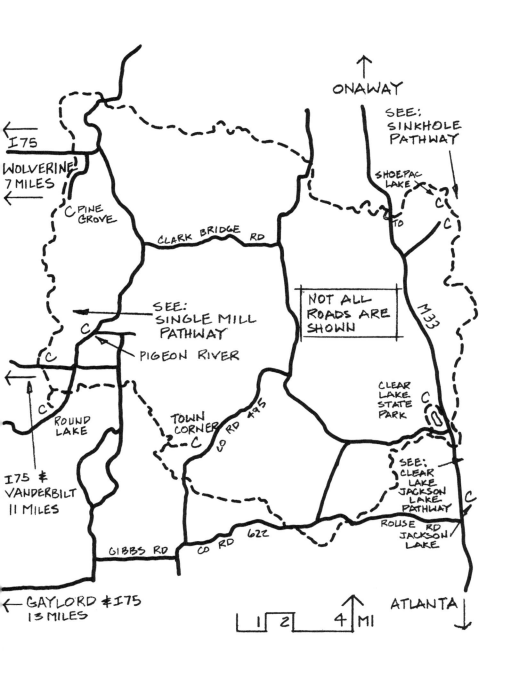

ONAWAY

SEE:
SINKHOLE
PATHWAY

I75

WOLVERINE
7 MILES

C PINE
GROVE

SHOEPAC
LAKE

CLARK BRIDGE RD

SEE:
SINGLE MILL
PATHWAY

NOT ALL
ROADS ARE
SHOWN

M33

PIGEON RIVER

CLEAR
LAKE
STATE
PARK

ROUND
LAKE

TOWN
CORNER

CO RD 495

CO RD 622

SEE:
CLEAR
LAKE
JACKSON
LAKE
PATHWAY

I75 &
VANDERBILT
11 MILES

GIBBS RD

ROUSE RD
JACKSON
LAKE

GAYLORD & I75
13 MILES

1 2   4 MI

ATLANTA

HIGH COUNTRY PATHWAY

Pigeon River Country Forest Area, Mackinaw State Forest
9966 Twin Lakes Rd.   517-983-4101
Vanderbilt, MI 49795

District Forest Manager, Mackinaw State Forest
1732 West M32, PO Box 667   517-732-3541
Gaylord, MI 49735

Michigan Atlas & Gazetteer Location: 83BCD5678

County Location: Cheboygan,Otsego,Montmorency,Presque Isle

Directions To Trailhead:
Northeast of Gaylord,southwest of Onaway and northwest of Atlanta.
Trailheads - West from Vanderbilt about 9 & 12 miles on Sturgeon Valley Rd
Trailhead - Clear Lake State Park on M33 between Onaway and Atlanta
Trailhead - Sinkhole Pathway, 10 miles south of Onaway via M33 and east on Tomahawk Lake Hwy

Trail Type: Hiking/Walking, Mountain Biking
Trail Distance: 70+ mi   Loops: 1   Shortest: NA   Longest: NA
Trail Surface: Natural
Trail Use Fee: None
Method Of Ski Trail Grooming: NA
Skiing Ability Suggested: NA
Hiking Trail Difficulty: Moderate to difficult
Mountain Biking Ability Suggested: Intermediate to advanced ONLY!
Terrain: Steep 2%, Hilly 8%, Moderate 60%, Flat 30%
Camping: Numerous campgrounds along the trail

Maintained by the DNR Forest Management Division
The High Country Pathway is part of the Shingle Mill Pathway and the Clear Lake-Jackson Lake Pathway. It also passes through the Sinkhole Pathway area. See those trails for more detail.
There is as much variety in terrain and habitat as can be found anywhere in the lower peninsula. Several scenic vista's along the trail.
A very descriptive trail guide that is well worth the money is available from the Pigeon River Country Association, PO Box 122, Gaylord, MI 49735. Annual memberships available .,
Other contacts:
     DNR Forest Management Division Office, Lansing, 517-373-1275
     DNR Forest Management Region Office, Roscommon, 517-275-5151

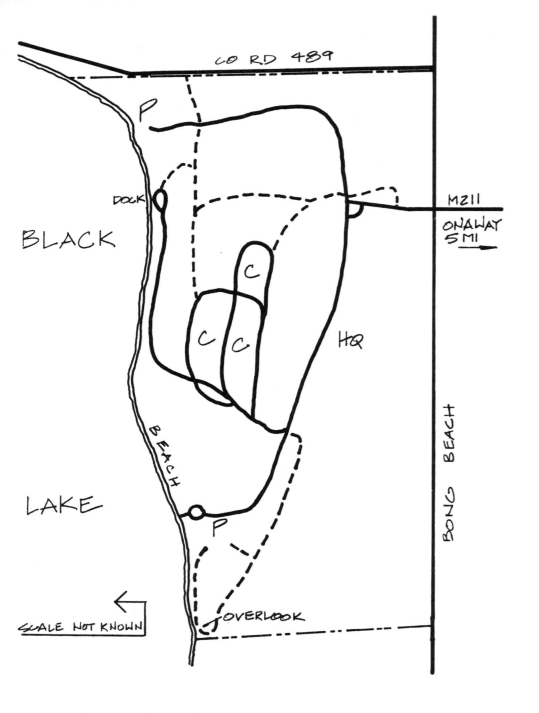

ONAWAY STATE PARK

Onaway State Park
Rte 1, Box 188
Onaway, MI 49765

517-733-8279

Clear Lake State Park
PO Box 51
Atlanta, MI 49709

517-785-4388

Michigan Atlas & Gazetteer Location: 83A7

County Location: Presque Isle

Directions To Trailhead:
Trailhead is located in the campground in the park

Trail Type: Hiking/Walking
Trail Distance: 3 mi   Loops: 2   Shortest: 1 mi   Longest: 2 mi
Trail Surface: Natural
Trail Use Fee: None, but vehicle entry permit required
Method Of Ski Trail Grooming: NA
Skiing Ability Suggested: NA
Hiking Trail Difficulty: Easy to moderate
Mountain Biking Ability Suggested: NA
Terrain: Steep 5%, Hilly 10%, Moderate 65%, Flat 20%
Camping: Campground on site

Maintained by the DNR Parks and Recreation Division
158 acre park

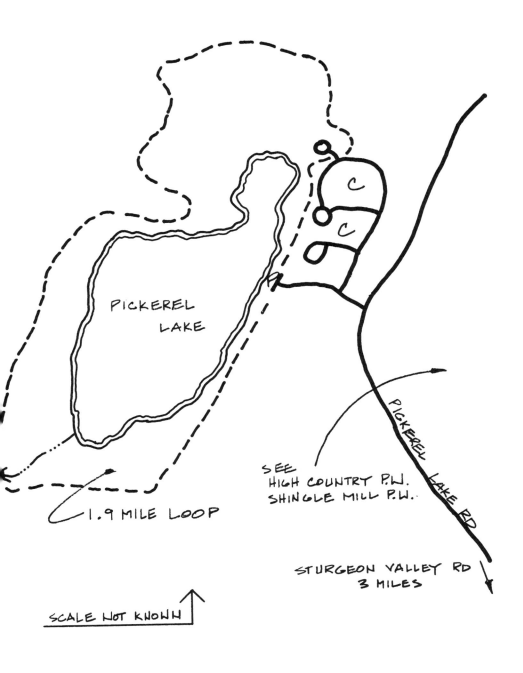

1.9 MILE LOOP

SEE
HIGH COUNTRY P.W.
SHINGLE MILL P.W.

STURGEON VALLEY RD
3 MILES

SCALE NOT KNOWN

PICKEREL LAKE PATHWAY

Pickerel Lake Pathway

Pigeon River Country Forest Area, Mackinaw State Forest
9966 Twin Lakes Road   517-983-4101
Vanderbilt, MI 49795

District Forest Manger, Mackinaw State Forest
1732 West M32, PO Box 667   517-732-3541
Gaylord, MI 49735

Michigan Atlas & Gazetteer Location: 83C4

County Location: Otsego

Directions To Trailhead:
At Pickerel Lake SFCG, east from Vanderbilt 8 miles to Pickerel Lake Rd., then north 2 miles to the day use area in the campground.

Trail Type: Hiking/Walking, Cross Country Skiing,
Trail Distance: 2 mi   Loops: 1   Shortest: NA   Longest: 2 mi
Trail Surface: Natural
Trail Use Fee: None
Method Of Ski Trail Grooming: None
Skiing Ability Suggested: Novice
Hiking Trail Difficulty: Easy
Mountain Biking Ability Suggested: NA
Terrain: Steep 0%, Hilly 0%, Moderate 15%, Flat 85%
Camping: At trailhead

Maintained by the DNR Forest Management Division
The closest campground to the Green Timbers tract.

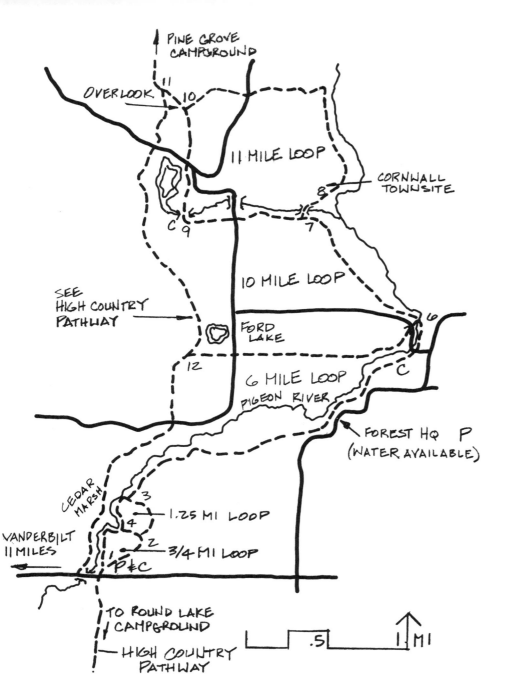

Pigeon River Country Forest Area, Mackinaw State Forest
9966 Twin Lakes Rd.   517-983-4101
Vanderbilt, MI 49759

District Forest Manager, Mackinaw State Forest
1732 West M32, PO Box 667   517-732-3541
Gaylord, MI 48735

Michigan Atlas & Gazetteer Location: 83C5

County Location: Otsego, Cheboygan

Directions To Trailhead:
9 miles east of Vanderbilt on Sturgeon Valley Rd.

Trail Type: Hiking/Walking, Cross Country Skiing, Mountain Biking
Trail Distance: 18 mi   Loops: 5   Shortest: .75 mi Longest: 11 mi
Trail Surface: Natural
Trail Use Fee: None
Method Of Ski Trail Grooming: Track set on occasion
Skiing Ability Suggested: Novice to advanced
Hiking Trail Difficulty: Easy to moderate
Mountain Biking Ability Suggested: Novice to intermediate
Terrain: Steep 2%, Hilly 5%, Moderate 48%, Flat 45%
Camping: Several campgrounds are located along the trail

Maintained by the DNR Forest Management Division
A very popular trail system that can absorb many users without becoming
crowded because of its size.
Pigeon River Country Forest Area HQ with its resident Area Forester, is located
along the trail.
A scenic overlook is along the 10 mile loop.
Drinking water is available all year at the headquarters bldg and seasonally at
the campgrounds
Part of the North Country Pathway which enters the trail at Pigeon Bridge SFCG
from the south and leaves the trail at Point 11 to the north heading to Pine Grove
SFCG
Other contacts:
    DNR Forest Management Division Office, Lansing, 517-373-1275
    DNR Forest Management Region Office, Roscommon, 517-275-5151

Atlanta Forest Area, Mackinaw State Forest
Rte 1, Box 30   517-785-4251
Atlanta, MI 49709

District Forest Manager, Mackinaw State Forest
Box 667, 1732 M32   517-732-3541
Gaylord, MI 49735

Michigan Atlas & Gazetteer Location: 83BC7

County Location: Presque Isle

Directions To Trailhead:
Between Onaway (8 miles) and Atlanta (16 miles) off M33 via Tomahawk Lake
Hwy

Trail Type: Hiking/Walking, Cross Country Skiing, Mountain Biking
Trail Distance: 2.5 mi   Loops: 2   Shortest: .75 mi Longest: 1.5 mi
Trail Surface: Natural
Trail Use Fee: None
Method Of Ski Trail Grooming: None
Skiing Ability Suggested: Novice
Hiking Trail Difficulty: Easy
Mountain Biking Ability Suggested: Novice to intermediate
Terrain: Steep 0%, Hilly 0%, Moderate 80%, Flat 20%
Camping: Shoepac and Thomahawk State Forest Campgounds are nearby

Maintained by the DNR Forest Management Division
The Sinkhole Area contains 2,600 acres that are closed to motorized vehicles.
There are many miles of fire lines within this area that area suitable for skiing &
hiking beyond that which is listed above.
It's recommended that the user take along a compass since there are no maps
or trail makings on the interior of this area.
This area has a unique geological formation from the result of dissolving bed
rock limestone. Shoepac Lake is a result of this dissolving limestone .
Other contacts:
        DNR Forest Management Division Office, Lansing, 517-373-1275
        DNR Forest Management Region Office, Roscommon, 517-275-5151

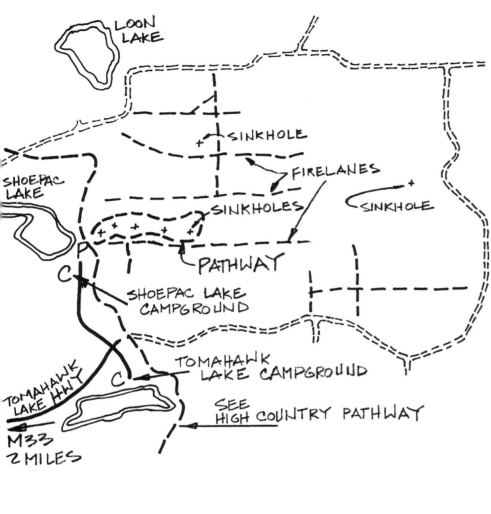

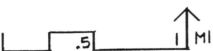

SINKHOLE PATHWAY

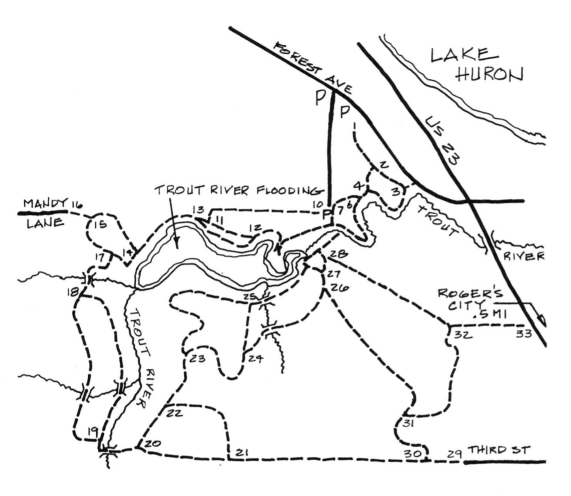

FOREST AVE

LAKE HURON

US 23

TROUT RIVER FLOODING

MANDY LANE 16

TROUT RIVER

ROGER'S CITY .5 MI

THIRD ST

NORTH

HERMAN VOGLER CONSERVATION AREA

Herman Vogler Conservation Area

Presque Isle Soil Conservation District
240 W. Erie St.
Rogers City, MI 49779

517-734-4000

Michigan Atlas & Gazetteer Location: 84A23

County Location: Presque Isle

Directions To Trailhead:
North 1/2 mile from intersection of US 23 and Bus. US23, then west on Forest Ave about .5 mile to parking lot

Trail Type: Hiking/Walking, Cross Country Skiing, Mountain Biking, Interpretive
Trail Distance: 5.25 mi   Loops: Many   Shortest: .75 mi Longest: 2.5 mi
Trail Surface: Natural
Trail Use Fee: None, but donations are accepted
Method Of Ski Trail Grooming: Track set
Skiing Ability Suggested: Novice to intermediate
Hiking Trail Difficulty: Easy to moderate
Mountain Biking Ability Suggested: Novice to intermediate
Terrain: Steep 0%, Hilly 10%, Moderate 20%, Flat 70%
Camping: None

Maintained by the Presque Isle Soil Conservation District
Developed by many individuals and local groups as a conservation education center.

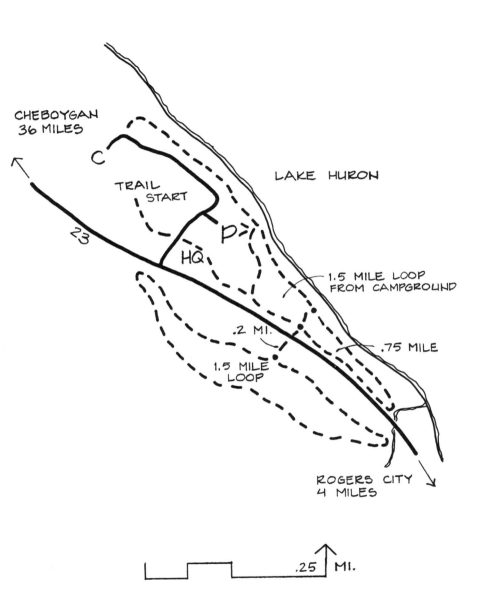

CHEBOYGAN
36 MILES

23

LAKE HURON

C

TRAIL START

P

HQ

1.5 MILE LOOP FROM CAMPGROUND

.2 MI.

.75 MILE

1.5 MILE LOOP

ROGERS CITY
4 MILES

.25 MI.

HOEFT STATE PARK

Hoeft State Park

Hoeft State Park
US23
Rogers City, MI 49779

517-734-2543

DNR Parks and Recreation Division

517-373-1270
517-275-5151

Michigan Atlas & Gazetteer Location: 84A2

County Location: Presque Isle

Directions To Trailhead:
On US23, 5 miles north of Rogers City on Lake Huron

Trail Type: Hiking/Walking, Cross Country Skiing, Interpretive
Trail Distance: 4 mi   Loops: 2   Shortest: .75 mi Longest: 1.5 mi
Trail Surface: Natural
Trail Use Fee: None, but vehicle entry fee required
Method Of Ski Trail Grooming: Track set
Skiing Ability Suggested: Novice
Hiking Trail Difficulty: Easy
Mountain Biking Ability Suggested: NA
Terrain: Flat
Camping: Available in the park (plowed in winter as needed)

Maintained by the DNR Parks and Recreation Division
Trail in the Huron Dunes area.
A portion of the trail passes along Lake Huron.
Food and lodging available in Rogers City.
Ski rental available in Rogers City.

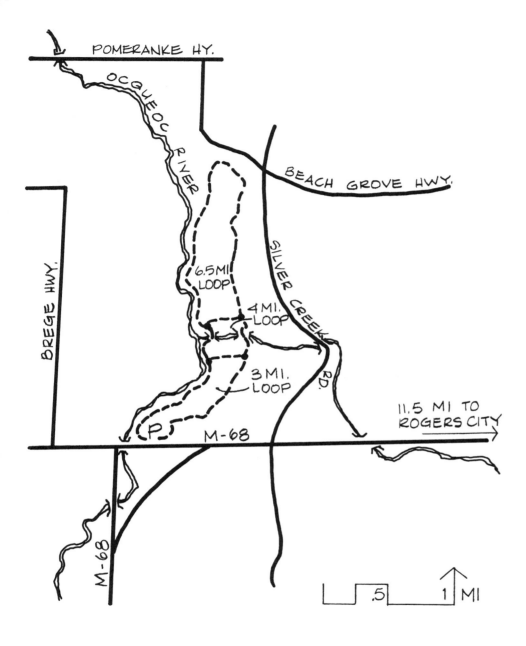

Atlanta Forest Area, Mackinaw State Forest
HCR 74, Box 30   517-785-4251
Atlanta , MI 49709-9605

District Forest Manager, Mackinaw State Forest
1732 West M32, PO Box 667   517-732-3541
Gaylord, MI 49735

Michigan Atlas & Gazetteer Location: 84A1

County Location: Presque Isle

Directions To Trailhead:
On M68, 12 miles west of Rogers City at Ocqueoc Falls Rd. where M68 turns south 11 miles east of Onaway on M68.

Trail Type: Hiking/Walking, Cross Country Skiing, Mountain Biking, Interpretive
Trail Distance: 4 mi   Loops: 3   Shortest: 3 mi   Longest: 6 mi
Trail Surface: Natural
Trail Use Fee: Donation accepted for trail grooming
Method Of Ski Trail Grooming: Track set
Skiing Ability Suggested: Novice to advanced
Hiking Trail Difficulty: Moderate
Mountain Biking Ability Suggested: Intermediate
Terrain: Steep 2%, Hilly 10%, Moderate 88%, Flat 0%
Camping: SF campground at trailhead

Maintained by the DNR Forest Management Division
Falls are at the trailhead Rolling hills in area with scenic overlooks.
Other contacts:
        DNR Forest Management Division Office, Lansing, 517-373-1275
        DNR Forest Management Onaway Field Office, Onaway, 517-733-8775
        DNR Forest Management Region Office, Roscommon, 517-275-5151

OCQUEOC FALLS
BICENTENNIAL PATHWAY

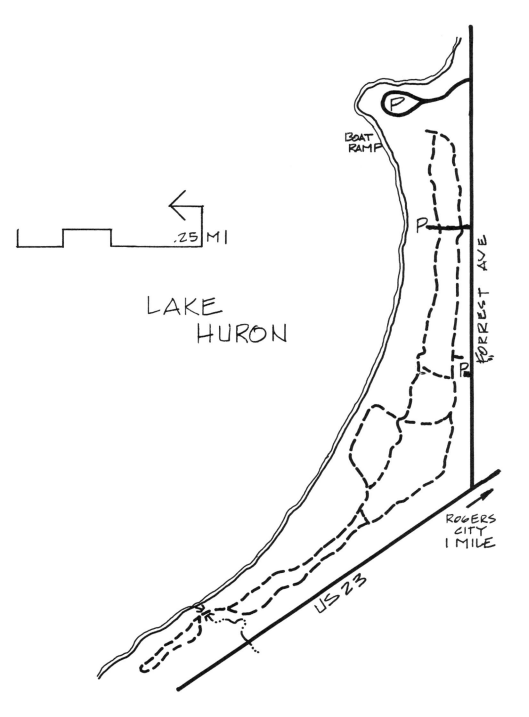

LAKE
HURON

.25 MI

ROGERS
CITY
1 MILE

US 23

Seagull Point Park

City of Rogers City
191 E. Michigan Ave
Rogers City, MI 49779

517-734-2191

Michigan Atlas & Gazetteer Location: 84A23

County Location: Presque Isle

Directions To Trailhead:
Along the shoreline of Lake Huron at the north end of town.

Trail Type: Hiking/Walking, Cross Country Skiing, Interpretive
Trail Distance: 2.25 mi   Loops: 5   Shortest: .25 mi Longest: 2.25 mi
Trail Surface: Wood chips
Trail Use Fee: None
Method Of Ski Trail Grooming: None
Skiing Ability Suggested: Novice
Hiking Trail Difficulty: Easy
Mountain Biking Ability Suggested: NA
Terrain: Steep 0%, Hilly 0%, Moderate 95%, Flat 5%
Camping: Campgrounds nearby

Owned by the City of Rogers City
Beautiful 43 acre lakeside park on the shore of Lake Huron with an extensive
trail system for its size.

SEAGULL POINT PARK

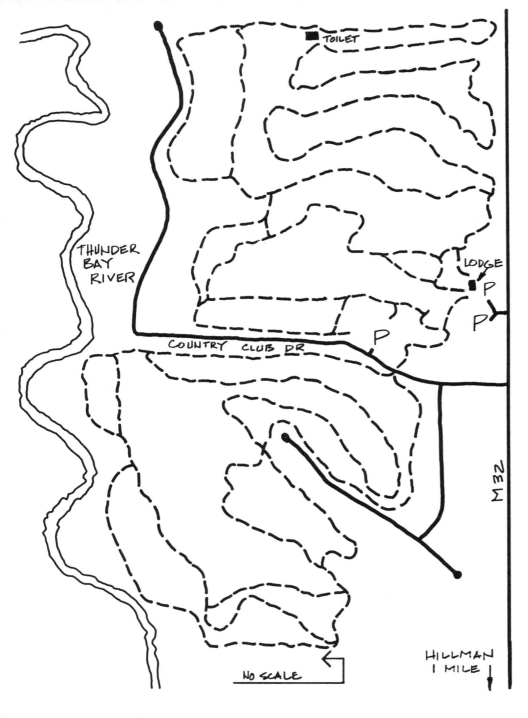

THUNDER BAY RESORT

Thunder Bay Resort

Thunder Bay Resort
One Village Corner
Hillman, MI 49746

800-729-9375
517-742-4732

Michigan Atlas & Gazetteer Location: 84D2

County Location: Montmorency

Directions To Trailhead:
Exit I-75 at exit 202(M33), then take M33 north through Rose City, Mio, Fairview and Comins to M32. At M33 turn east (right) to Hillman. Take M33 east out of Hillman to the resort just past Hillman

Trail Type: Hiking/Walking, Cross Country Skiing
Trail Distance: 15 km   Loops: 10   Shortest: .25 km Longest: 7 km
Trail Surface: Natural
Trail Use Fee: Yes for skiing
Method Of Ski Trail Grooming: Track set
Skiing Ability Suggested: Novice to intermediate
Hiking Trail Difficulty: Easy
Mountain Biking Ability Suggested: NA
Terrain: Steep 0%, Hilly 10%, Moderate 40%, Flat 50%
Camping: None

Privately operated golf resort along Thunder Bay River.
Complete extensive facilities avaiable.
Brochure available.

Atlanta Forest Area, Mackinaw State Forest
Rte 1, Box 30   517-785-4252
Atlanta, MI 49709-9605

District Forest Manager, Mackinaw State Forest
1732 West M32, PO Box 667   517-732-3541
Gaylord, MI 49735

Michigan Atlas & Gazetteer Location: 85BC6

County Location: Presque Isle

Directions To Trailhead:
Between Alpena and Rogers City.
From US23, about 8 miles north of Alpena to Co Rd 405 (Grand Lake Rd.)(near Lakewood) then north on Co Rd 405 to parking lot.

Trail Type: Hiking/Walking, Interpretive
Trail Distance: 1 mi   Loops: 1   Shortest: NA   Longest: 1 mi
Trail Surface: Natural
Trail Use Fee: None
Method Of Ski Trail Grooming: None
Skiing Ability Suggested: NA
Hiking Trail Difficulty: Easy
Mountain Biking Ability Suggested: NA
Terrain: 100% Flat
Camping: None

Maintained by the DNR Forest Management Division
This is a nature with several points of interest
Trail passes near the site of the former village of Bell that once was a logging town of about 100 people.
Other contacts:
       DNR Forest Management Division Office, Lansing, 517-373-1275
       DNR Forest Management Region Office, Roscommon, 517-275-5151

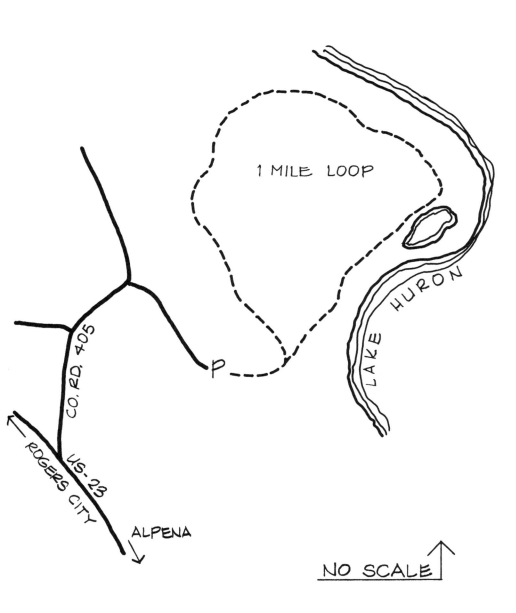

BESSER BELL PATHWAY

City of Alpena
208 N. First
Alpena, MI 49707

800-4-ALPENA

Michigan Atlas & Gazetteer Location: 85D5

County Location: Alpena

Directions To Trailhead:
In Alpena at the corner of US 23 and Johnson St. along the Thunder Bay River.

Trail Type: Hiking/Walking, Interpretive
Trail Distance: 1.5 mi   Loops: 2   Shortest: .5 mi   Longest: 1 mi
Trail Surface: Natural with handicapper viewing deck
Trail Use Fee: None
Method Of Ski Trail Grooming: NA
Skiing Ability Suggested: NA
Hiking Trail Difficulty: Easy
Mountain Biking Ability Suggested: NA
Terrain: Steep 0%, Hilly 0%, Moderate 10%, Flat 90%
Camping: Nearby

Maintained by the City of Alpena
Adjcent to wildlife area.
Viewing platform for handicappers accessible by vehicle. Obtain key from the
Holiday Inn which is located .25 mi north of US23

P

WATERFOWL
FEEDING AREA

US 23 NORTH

GATE

THUNDER BAY
RIVER

STAIRS

WOODS

ALPENA

OPEN

STAIRS

PAVEMENT

HANDICAPPER
VIEWING DECK

STAIRS

NORTH

ISLAND PARK

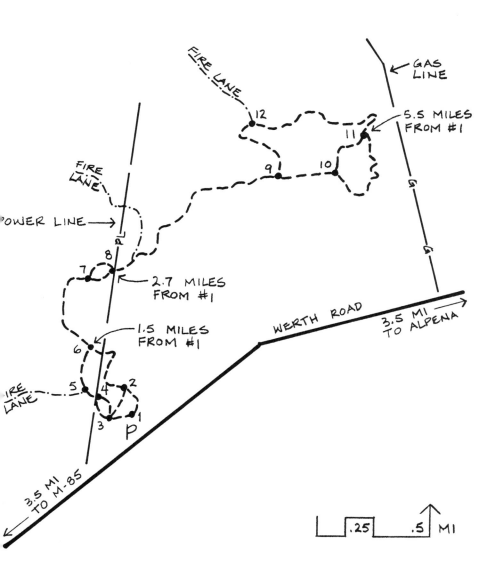

NORWAY RIDGE PATHWAY

Atlanta Forest Area, Mackinaw State Forest
Rte 1, Box 30   517-785-4251
Atlanta, MI 49709

District Forest Manager, Mackinaw State Forest
1732 West M32, PO Box667   517-732-3541
Gaylord, MI 49735

Michigan Atlas & Gazetteer Location: 85D5

County Location: Alpena

Directions To Trailhead:
4.5 miles SW of Alpena on Werth Road

Trail Type: Hiking/Walking, Cross Country Skiing, Mountain Biking
Trail Distance: 3 mi   Loops: 3   Shortest: .5 mi   Longest: 5.5 mi
Trail Surface: Natural
Trail Use Fee: None
Method Of Ski Trail Grooming: Track set
Skiing Ability Suggested: Novice
Hiking Trail Difficulty: Easy
Mountain Biking Ability Suggested: Novice
Terrain: Steep 0%, Hilly 0%, Moderate 20%, Flat 80%
Camping: None

Maintained by the DNR Forest Management Division
A very popular ski trail with the local skiers.

Other contacts:
    DNR Forest Management Division Office, Lansing, 517-373-1275
    DNR Forest Management Region Office, Roscommon, 517-275-5151

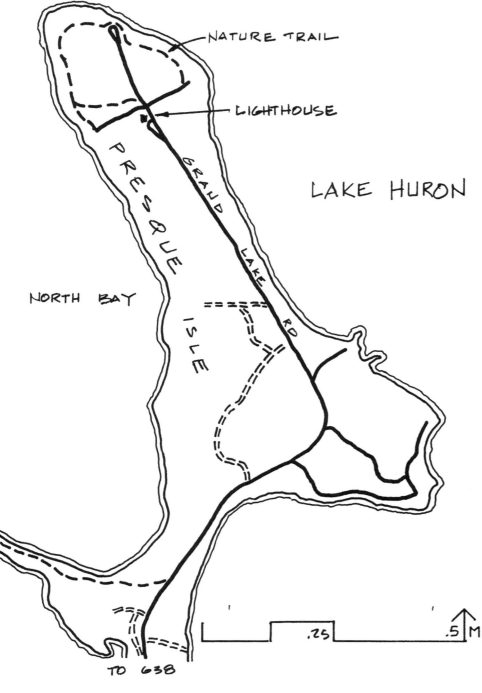

NATURE TRAIL

LIGHTHOUSE

LAKE HURON

PRESQUE ISLE

GRAND LAKE RD

NORTH BAY

.25 .5 MI

TO 638

PRESQUE ISLE LIGHTHOUSE PARK

Presque Isle Area Chamber of Commerce
4500 E. Grand Lake Rd
Presque Isle, MI 49777

517-595-5095
517-595-6970

517-595-2059

Michigan Atlas & Gazetteer Location: 85A5

County Location: Presque Isle

Directions To Trailhead:
US23 between Alpena and Rogers City, then take Co Rd 638 east to Grand Lake Rd, then north to lighthouse

Trail Type: Hiking/Walking, Interpretive
Trail Distance: 1 mi   Loops: 1   Shortest: NA   Longest: 1 mi
Trail Surface: Natural
Trail Use Fee: None
Method Of Ski Trail Grooming: NA
Skiing Ability Suggested: NA
Hiking Trail Difficulty: Easy
Mountain Biking Ability Suggested: NA
Terrain: 100% Flat
Camping: Campground nearby

Lighthouse maintained by the local community
Events held annually.
Trail along shore.

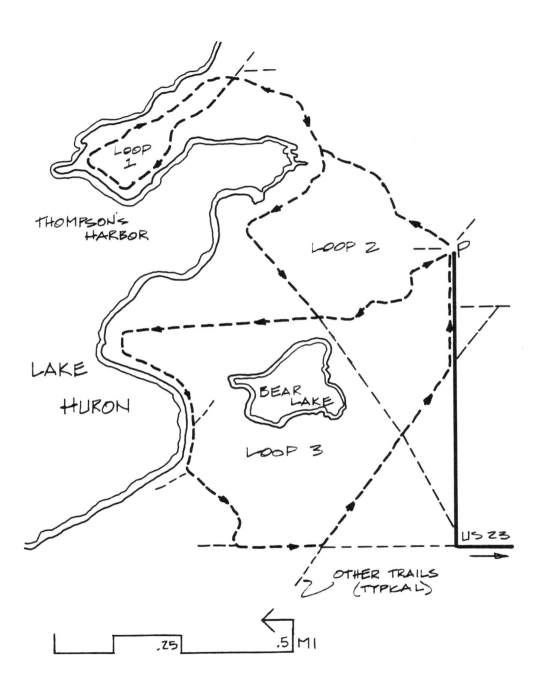

Hoeft State Park
US 23 North
Rogers City, MI 49779

517-734-2543

DNR Parks and Recreation Division

517-373-1263
517-275-5151

Michigan Atlas & Gazetteer Location: 85B45

County Location: Presque Isle

Directions To Trailhead:
12 miles southeast of Rogers City on US 23

Trail Type: Hiking/Walking, Cross Country Skiing, Mountain Biking
Trail Distance: 6 mi   Loops: 3   Shortest: 1.4 mi Longest: 2.6 mi
Trail Surface: Natural
Trail Use Fee: None, but vehicle entry permit required
Method Of Ski Trail Grooming: None
Skiing Ability Suggested: Novice
Hiking Trail Difficulty: Easy
Mountain Biking Ability Suggested: Novice to intermediate
Terrain: Steep 0%, Hilly 0%, Moderate 20%, Flat 80%
Camping: Available at Hoeft State Park

Maintained by the DNR Parks and Recreation Division
Substantially undeveloped park with many 2 tracks and trails.

THOMPSON'S HARBOR STATE PARK

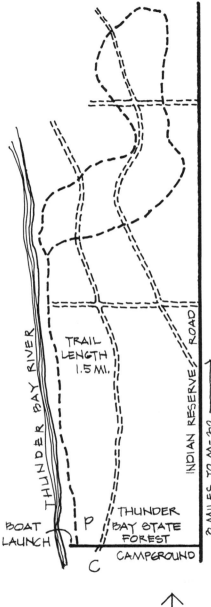

NO SCALE →

WAH-WAH-TAS-SEE PATHWAY

Alpena Field Office, Atlanta Forest Area
4343 M32 West   517-356-2209
Alpena, MI 49707

District Forest Manager, Mackinaw State Forest
1732 West M32, PO Box 667   517-732-3541
Gaylord, MI 49707

Michigan Atlas & Gazetteer Location: 85D5

County Location: Alpena

Directions To Trailhead:
5 miles west of Alpena on M32 to Indian Reserve Rd., then 3 miles south to the
Thunder Bay River SFCG and the trailhead.

Trail Type: Hiking/Walking, Cross Country Skiing, Interpretive
Trail Distance: 1.5 mi   Loops: 1   Shortest: NA   Longest: 1.5 mi
Trail Surface: Natural
Trail Use Fee: None
Method Of Ski Trail Grooming: None
Skiing Ability Suggested: Novice
Hiking Trail Difficulty: Easy
Mountain Biking Ability Suggested: NA
Terrain: 100% Flat
Camping: Campground at the trailhead

Maintained by the DNR Forest Management Division
9 station interpretive trail built in 1976 by the Youth Conservation Corps
Trail brochure is available.

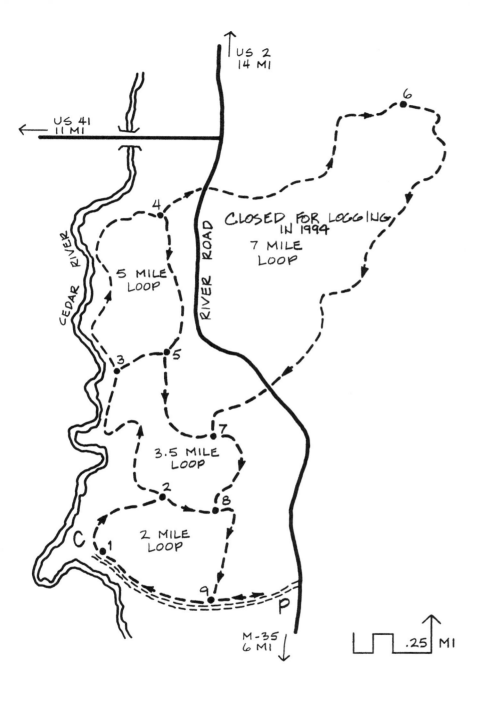

Stephenson Field Office, Escanaba River State Forest
Rte 1, Box 31B   906-753-6317
Stephenson, MI 49987

District Forest Manager, Escanaba River State Forest
6833 US41/2 & M35   906-786-2351
Gladstone, MI 49837

Michigan Atlas & Gazetteer Location: 87A5

County Location: Menominee

Directions To Trailhead:
1.5 miles north of Cedar River (town) on M35. Then north on Co Rd 551(River Rd) for 6 miles to the trailhead.

Trail Type: Hiking/Walking, Cross Country Skiing, Mountain Biking
Trail Distance: 8+ mi   Loops: 4   Shortest: 2 mi   Longest: 7 mi
Trail Surface: Natural
Trail Use Fee: None, but donations accepted for trail grooming
Method Of Ski Trail Grooming: Track set
Skiing Ability Suggested: Novice
Hiking Trail Difficulty: Easy
Mountain Biking Ability Suggested: Novice
Terrain: Steep 0%, Hilly 0%, Moderate 5%, Flat 95%
Camping: Campground along trail (ski-in only)

Managed by the DNR Forest Management Division
Trails touch on the Cedar River at several locations and pass through a variety of forest cover including pine, birch and aspen.
Campgrounds also available at Wells State Park on Lake Michigan near the town of Cedar River.
In 1993 the longest loop was temporarily closed because of a timber sale. Call ahead for current trail status.
Other contacts:
    DNR Forest Management Division Office, Lansing, 517-373-1275
    DNR Forest Management Region Office, Marquette, 906-228-6561

CEDAR RIVER PATHWAY

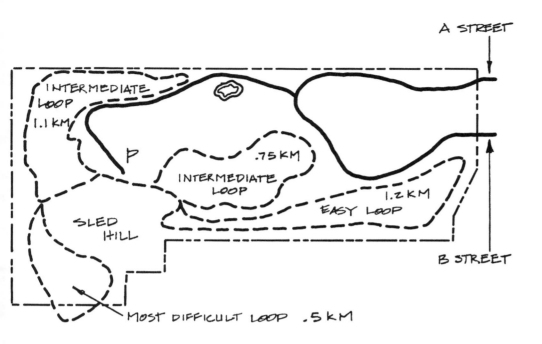

A STREET

INTERMEDIATE LOOP 1.1 KM

P

.75 KM

INTERMEDIATE LOOP

1.2 KM

EASY LOOP

SLED HILL

B STREET

MOST DIFFICULT LOOP .5 KM

NORTH

Iron Mountain City Park

Tourism Association of Dickinson County Area
600 S. Stephenson
Iron Mountain, MI 49801

906-774-2945
800-236-2447

Michigan Atlas & Gazetteer Location: 87B8

County Location: Dickinson

Directions To Trailhead:
From M95 (Carpenter Rd) take A Street west to the end of the street, watch for entrance to the park.

Trail Type: Hiking/Walking, Cross Country Skiing, Mountain Biking
Trail Distance: 3.5 km   Loops: 4   Shortest: .5 km   Longest: 1.2 km
Trail Surface: Natural
Trail Use Fee: None
Method Of Ski Trail Grooming: Track set
Skiing Ability Suggested: Novice
Hiking Trail Difficulty: Easy
Mountain Biking Ability Suggested: Novice
Terrain: Steep 0%, Hilly 10%, Moderate 50%, Flat 40%
Camping: None

Maintained by City of Iron Mountain
Ski rentals available nearby.

IRON MOUNTAIN - CITY PARK

Crystal Fall Forest Area, Copper Country State Forest
1420 East US 2 West   906-875-6622
Crystal Falls, MI 49920

Iron County Road Commission
Fairgrounds   906-265-4622
Iron River, MI 49920

Michigan Atlas & Gazetteer Location: 87A6,98D34,99D56

County Location: Iron

Directions To Trailhead:
South side of Iron River through Crystal Falls and south to Stager near the
Wisconsin/Michigan state line.

Trail Type: Hiking/Walking, Mountain Biking
Trail Distance: 36 mi   Loops: NA   Shortest: NA   Longest: NA
Trail Surface: Ballast, sand and natural
Trail Use Fee: None
Method Of Ski Trail Grooming: NA
Skiing Ability Suggested: NA
Hiking Trail Difficulty: Easy
Mountain Biking Ability Suggested: Intermediate
Terrain: 100% Flat
Camping: Campgrounds nearby

Maintained by the DNR Forest Management Division and the Iron Co. Road
Commission
No development planned in the near future.
Used as a snowmobile trail.
Gates across trail are to restrict motor vehicle access. Non motorized use is not
limited.
Connects to the State Line Rail Trail at two points to form a loop trail system.
Other contacts:
        DNR Forest Management Division 517-373-1275, Lansing
        DNR Forest Management Division 906-353-6651, Baraga
        DNR Forest Management Divsion 906-228-6561, Marquette

Map

CORD 69

US 2 & 141

424

CRYSTAL FALLS

STAGER

US 141

SEE
STATE-LINE
RAIL TRAIL

SEE
BEWABIC STATE PARK

US 2

SEE
GEORGE YOUNG
RECREATION
COMPLEX

189

IRON RIVER

MICHIGAN
WISCONSIN

2   4 MI

IRON RANGE RAIL TRAIL

Pine Mountain Lodge
N3332 Pine Mountain Rd.
Iron Mountain, MI 49801

906-774-2747
800-321-6298

Michigan Atlas & Gazetteer Location: 87B8

County Location: Dickinson

Directions To Trailhead:
2 miles northeast of Iron Mountain on Pine Mountain Rd.

Trail Type: Hiking/Walking, Cross Country Skiing, Mountain Biking
Trail Distance: 4 mi   Loops: 1   Shortest: Longest: 4 mi
Trail Surface: Natural
Trail Use Fee: None
Method Of Ski Trail Grooming: No
Skiing Ability Suggested: Intermediate
Hiking Trail Difficulty: Moderate
Mountain Biking Ability Suggested: NA
Terrain: Steep 0%, Hilly 85%, Moderate 15%, Flat 0%
Camping: Available nearby

Privately operated full facility alpine ski area
Lodging, restaurant, tennis courts, indoor pool, golf course and convention facilities.
90 meter ski jump in view of the trails.

MOUNTAIN BIKE TRAIL
PINE MOUNTAIN SKI & RECREATION

Crystal Falls Forest Area, Copper Country State Forest
1420 US2 West
Crystal Falls, MI 49920   906-875-6622

District Forest Manager, Copper Country State Forest
Box 440, US 41   906-353-6651
Baraga, MI 49908

Michigan Atlas & Gazetteer Location: 87A5,96AB3,97B5678,98CD1234,99D5

County Location: Gogebic, Iron

Directions To Trailhead:
East trailhead - Stager, west of US2, just north of Florence.
West trailhead - Korpela Rd, .4 mile south of US2, 4.7 miles east of Wakefield.

Trail Type: Hiking/Walking, Mountain Biking
Trail Distance: 102.2 mi   Loops: NA   Shortest: NA   Longest: NA
Trail Surface: Natural and original ballast
Trail Use Fee: None
Method Of Ski Trail Grooming: NA
Skiing Ability Suggested: NA
Hiking Trail Difficulty: Easy to moderate
Mountain Biking Ability Suggested: Novice to intermediate
Terrain: 100% Flat
Camping: None on the trail but many nearby

Maintained by the DNR Forest Management Division
Rough and rugged trail for mountain biking but can be done
36 mile section between Watersmeet and Iron River is quite nice with rock
escarpment, bridges, bridges, rivers, beaver ponds
The book "Great Rail Trails" available from the Rail to Trails Conservency is an
excellent resourse for this and other rail trails listed in this atlas.

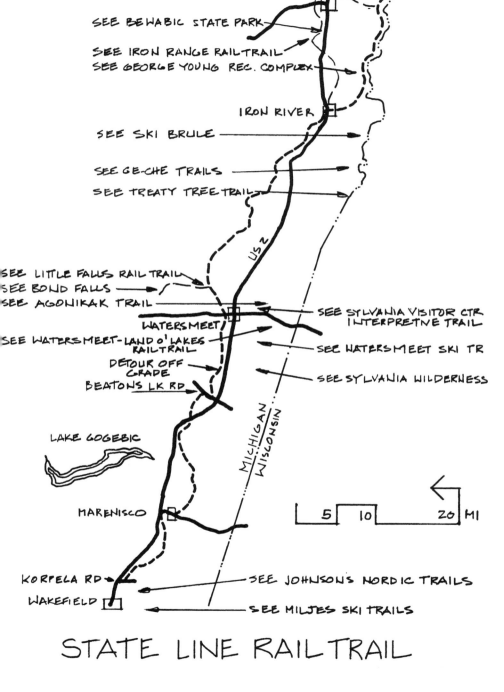

CRYSTAL FALLS   US 2
SEE BEWABIC STATE PARK
SEE IRON RANGE RAILTRAIL
SEE GEORGE YOUNG REC. COMPLEX
IRON RIVER
SEE SKI BRULE
SEE GE-CHE TRAILS
SEE TREATY TREE TRAIL
US 2
SEE LITTLE FALLS RAIL TRAIL
SEE BOND FALLS
SEE AGONIKAK TRAIL
WATERSMEET   SEE SYLVANIA VISITOR CTR INTERPRETIVE TRAIL
SEE WATERSMEET-LAND O'LAKES RAILTRAIL
SEE WATERSMEET SKI TR
DETOUR OFF GRADE
BEATONS LK RD   SEE SYLVANIA WILDERNESS
LAKE GOGEBIC
MICHIGAN
WISCONSIN
5   10   20 MI
MARENISCO
KORPELA RD
WAKEFIELD   SEE JOHNSON'S NORDIC TRAILS
SEE MILJES SKI TRAILS

STATE LINE RAIL TRAIL

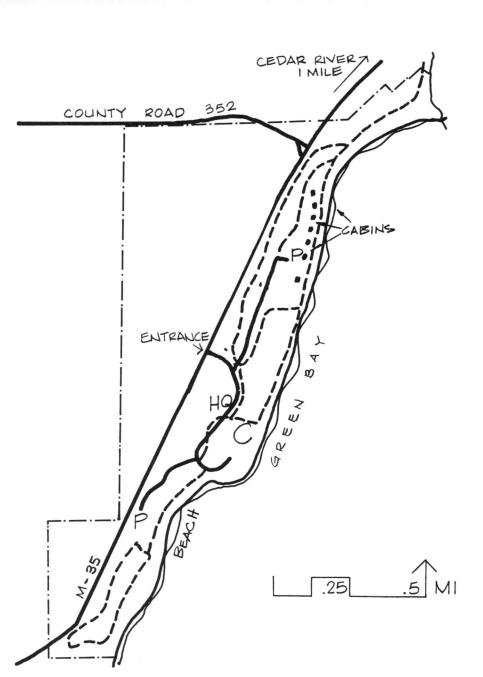

WELLS STATE PARK

Wells State Park
M35
Cedar River, MI 49813

906-863-9747

DNR Parks and Recreation Division

517-373-1270
906-228-6561

Michigan Atlas & Gazetteer Location: 87B5

County Location: Menominee

Directions To Trailhead:
South of Escanaba and 1 mile south of Cedar River on Lake Michigan on M35

Trail Type: Hiking/Walking, Cross Country Skiing
Trail Distance: 5 mi   Loops: 4   Shortest: Longest:
Trail Surface: Natural
Trail Use Fee: None, but vehicle entry fee required
Method Of Ski Trail Grooming: Track set when grooming equipment is provided
Skiing Ability Suggested: Novice to intermediate
Hiking Trail Difficulty: Easy to moderate
Mountain Biking Ability Suggested: NA
Terrain: Steep 0%, Hilly 10%, Moderate 20%, Flat 70%
Camping: Campground in park. Open all year

Maintained by the DNR Parks and Recreation Division
Hiking and ski trails are not be identical.
6 very rustic cabins are available for rent that house up to 16 people.
Snowmobiling permitted in park except on ski trails.
Ski rentals available in Escanaba and Menominee.
Virgin forest throughout park.
3 miles of Lake Michigan shoreline.
Established in 1925 by the children of John Wells, a local lumberman, who donated the land. Many of the buildings were constructed by the CCC in the 1930's & 1940's

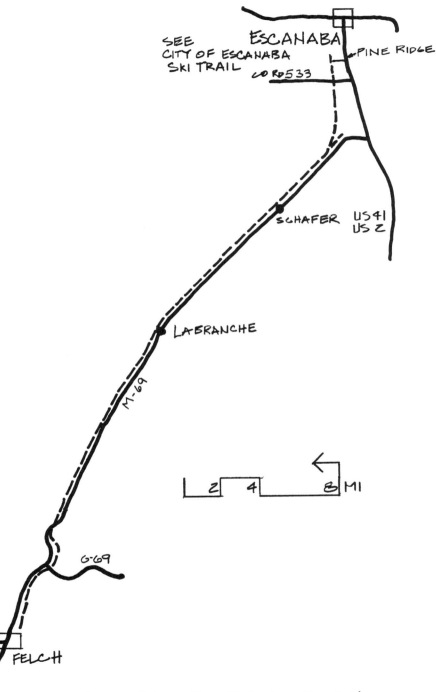

SEE
CITY OF ESCANABA
SKI TRAIL

ESCANABA

PINE RIDGE

CO RD 533

SCHAFER

US 41
US 2

LABRANCHE

M-69

2 4 8 MI

G-69

FELCH

FELCH GRADE RAIL TRAIL

Escanaba Forest Area, Escanaba River State Forest
6833 Hwy US2,41 & M35
Gladstone, MI 49837

906-786-2354

District Forest Manager, Escanaba River State Forest
6833 Hwy2,41 & M35
Gladstone, MI 49837

906-786-2351

Michigan Atlas & Gazetteer Location: 88A234,89BC567

County Location: Delta, Menominee,Dickinson

Directions To Trailhead:
Between Felch and the western edge of Escanaba near Pine Ridge.
West trailhead - Felch Township Community Center on M69. Take Andy's Lane, then turn right on Van Lear Drive, turn left on Old Dump Rd, go 2 blocks, turn left and then make a right onto the trail grade.
East trailhead - From US2, north on Pine Ridge about 1.5 miles to the trail or Co Rd 553 1.75 miles to the trail

Trail Type: Hiking/Walking, Mountain Biking
Trail Distance: 40 mi   Loops: NA   Shortest: NA   Longest: NA
Trail Surface: Natural, ballast and gravel
Trail Use Fee: None
Method Of Ski Trail Grooming: NA
Skiing Ability Suggested: NA
Hiking Trail Difficulty: Easy
Mountain Biking Ability Suggested: Intermediate
Terrain: Steep 0%, Hilly 0%, Moderate 0%, Flat 100%
Camping: None

Managed by the DNR Forest Management Divsion.
Seasonally maintained by local group.
Very rough rail trail. Use M69 when necessary.
A little of everything can be found along this trail. Sand, water, creeks, rivers and a little of everything else.
Along the trail, the Village of LaBranche has a small store and bar and the Village of Schafter has a small store.
No parking at eastern trailheads. Suggest using the park and ride lot at M69 and US2.
ORV's and snowmobiles are permitted use of this trail.

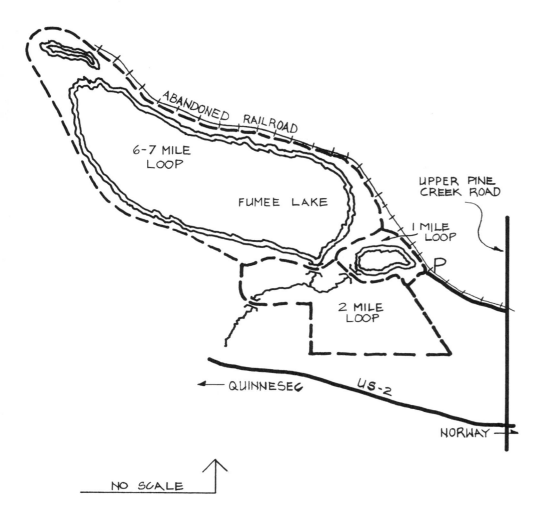

ABANDONED RAILROAD

6-7 MILE LOOP

FUMEE LAKE

UPPER PINE CREEK ROAD

1 MILE LOOP

P

2 MILE LOOP

← QUINNESEC

US-2

NORWAY

NO SCALE

FUMEE LAKE TRAIL

Fumee Lake Trail

Dickinson County Tourism Association
600 S. Stephenson
Iron Mountain, MI 49801

800-236-2447
906-774-2945

Michigan Atlas & Gazetteer Location: 88B1

County Location: Dickinson

Directions To Trailhead:
North of US2 between Norway and Quinnesec, take Upper Pine Creek Rd for 1 mile.

Trail Type: Hiking/Walking, Cross Country Skiing, Mountain Biking, Interpretive
Trail Distance: 8 mi   Loops: 3   Shortest: 1   Longest: 6 mi
Trail Surface: Natural
Trail Use Fee: None
Method Of Ski Trail Grooming: Track set
Skiing Ability Suggested: Novice to intermediate
Hiking Trail Difficulty: Easy
Mountain Biking Ability Suggested: Novice to intermediate
Terrain: Steep 0%, Hilly 15%, Moderate 75%, Flat 10%
Camping: Some camping nearby.

Owned by Dickinson County
Fumee Lake Natural Area has two lakes with 5 miles of undeveloped shoreline. The natural area contains, 270 species of plants, mature trees, 137 species of birds, 7 species of fish, 26 species of mammals, 6 species of anphibians, 6 species of reptiles and historical Indiana Mine.

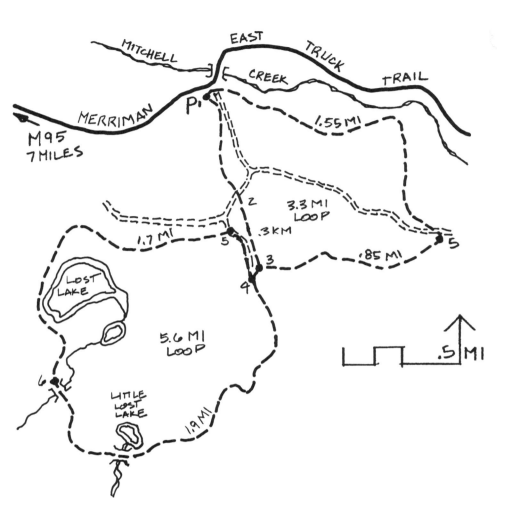

Norway Forest Area, Copper Country State Forest
PO Box 126   906-563-9247
Norway, MI 49870

District Forest Manager, Copper Country State Forest
US41 North, Box 440   906-353-6651
Baraga, MI 49908

Michigan Atlas & Gazetteer Location: 88A1

County Location: Dickinson

Directions To Trailhead:
North of Iron Mountain about 6 miles to the Merriman Truck Trail, then east
about 7 miles to trailhead located just before the Mitchell Creek bridge

Trail Type: Hiking/Walking, Cross Country Skiing, Mountain Biking
Trail Distance: 6.7 mi   Loops: 2   Shortest: 3 mi   Longest: 5.6 mi
Trail Surface: Natural
Trail Use Fee: None
Method Of Ski Trail Grooming: None
Skiing Ability Suggested: Novice to intermediate
Hiking Trail Difficulty: Moderate
Mountain Biking Ability Suggested: Novice
Terrain: Steep 0%, Hilly 20%, Moderate 80%, Flat 0%
Camping: Developed campground not available nearby

Maintained by the DNR Forest Management Division
Skiers should have some winter survival skills since this trail is somewhat
isolated and is not groomed.
Other contacts:
    DNR Forest Management Division Office, Lansing, 517-373-1275
    DNR Forest Management Region Office, Marquette, 906-228-6561

MERRIMAN EAST PATHWAY

City of Escanaba, Department of Recreation
121 S. 11th St.   906-786-4141
Escanaba, MI 49829

Michigan Atlas & Gazetteer Location: 89BC8

County Location: Delta

Directions To Trailhead:
On N. 30th St. (dead end street) in Escanaba, .5 mile north of US2/41 on the west side of town, just before St. Francis Hospital located on US2/41.

Trail Type: Cross Country Skiing
Trail Distance: 4.6 mi   Loops: 3   Shortest: .75 mi Longest: 2.2 mi
Trail Surface: Natural
Trail Use Fee: Yes, daily and annual permits available
Method Of Ski Trail Grooming: Track set daily or as needed
Skiing Ability Suggested: Novice to advanced
Hiking Trail Difficulty: NA
Mountain Biking Ability Suggested: NA
Terrain: Steep 10%, Hilly 40%, Moderate 40%, Flat 10%
Camping: None in area

Maintained by the City of Escanaba
Within the city limits but in a very heavily forested area.
Within 15 miles of 4 other trails; Days River Pathway, Rapid River Cross-Country Ski Trail. Cedar River Pathway and Gladstone Cross Country Ski Trail.

OVERLOOK

6.3 MILES

7.7 MILES

4.5 MILES

30TH STREET

STOP SIGN

STOP SIGN

US2/41

ESCANABA 2 MILES

ST FRANCIS HOSPITAL

NO SCALE

ESCANABA CROSS COUNTRY SKI PATHWAY

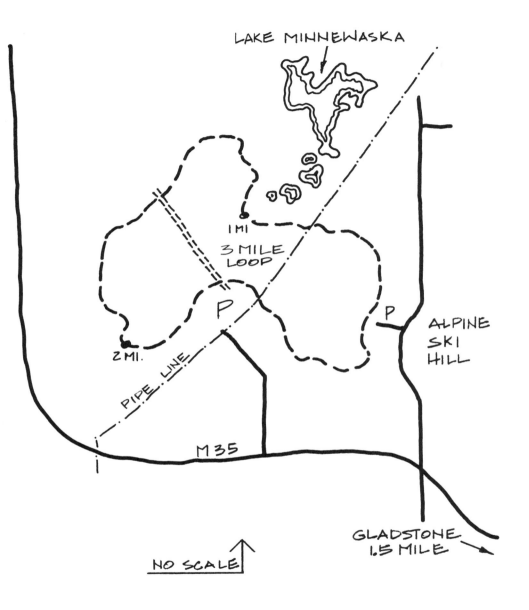

LAKE MINNEWASKA

1 MI

3 MILE LOOP

P

P

ALPINE SKI HILL

2 MI.

PIPE LINE

M 35

GLADSTONE 1.5 MILE

NO SCALE

Gladstone Sports Park
45 North Bluff Drive
Gladstone, MI 49837

906-428-2311

Michigan Atlas & Gazetteer Location: 89B8

County Location: Delta

Directions To Trailhead:
From Gladstone follow US2/41, then north on M35 2 miles, then west 1/4mile on North Bluff Drive.

Trail Type: Hiking/Walking, Cross Country Skiing, Mountain Biking
Trail Distance: 5 km   Loops: 1   Shortest: NA   Longest: NA
Trail Surface: Natural
Trail Use Fee: None
Method Of Ski Trail Grooming: Double track set
Skiing Ability Suggested: Novice tp intermediate
Hiking Trail Difficulty: Easy
Mountain Biking Ability Suggested: Novice
Terrain: Steep 0%, Hilly 0%, Moderate 90%, Flat10%
Camping: Campground available within 3 miles of the park

Municipally operated recreation area by City of Gladstone
Warming area and snack bar, sledding, tubing and downhill ski hills available.

GLADSTONE CROSS COUNTRY SKI TRAIL

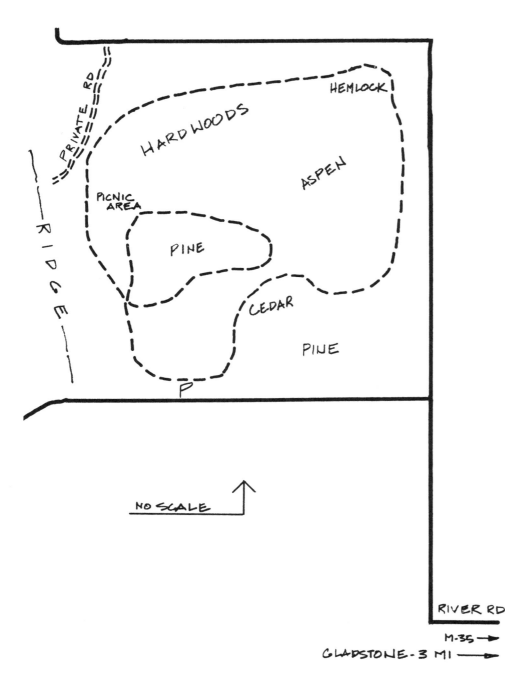

Mead Paper, Woodlands Department
PO Box 1008
Escanaba, MI 49829

906-786-1660
ext 2180

Michigan Atlas & Gazetteer Location: 89B8

County Location: Delta

Directions To Trailhead:
North from Gladstone on M35 to 22st Rd (River Rd)

Trail Type: Hiking/Walking, Cross Country Skiing, Interpretive
Trail Distance: .87 mi   Loops: 2   Shortest: .2 mi   Longest: .75 mi
Trail Surface: Natrual
Trail Use Fee: None
Method Of Ski Trail Grooming: NA
Skiing Ability Suggested: NA
Hiking Trail Difficulty: Easy
Mountain Biking Ability Suggested: NA
Terrain: Not known
Camping: None

Owned by Mead Paper Company
Trail developed by Mead Paper and built by Bay De Noc Naturalists, Audubon
Society and Boy Scouts.
A 38 station interpretive trail.
Trail guide available.

RIVER BLUFF NATURE TRAIL

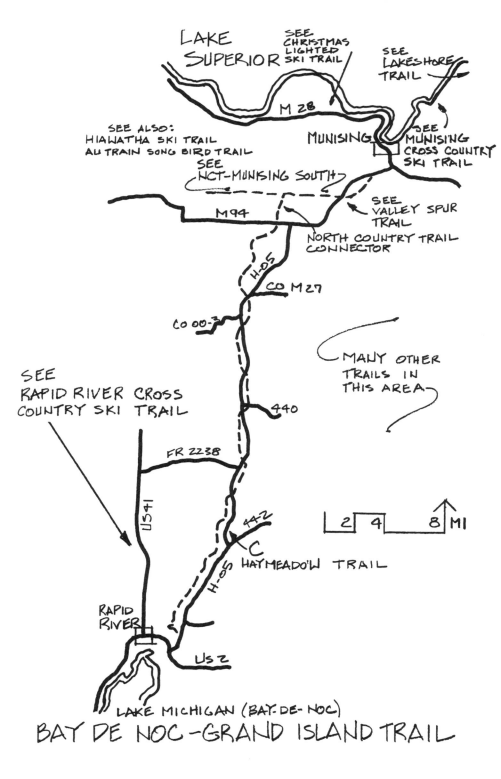

LAKE SUPERIOR

SEE CHRISTMAS LIGHTED SKI TRAIL

SEE LAKESHORE TRAIL

M 28

SEE ALSO:
HIAWATHA SKI TRAIL
AU TRAIN SONG BIRD TRAIL

MUNISING

SEE MUNISING CROSS COUNTRY SKI TRAIL

SEE NCT-MUNISING SOUTH

M 94

SEE VALLEY SPUR TRAIL

NORTH COUNTRY TRAIL CONNECTOR

H-05

CO M 27

CO 00-3

MANY OTHER TRAILS IN THIS AREA

440

SEE RAPID RIVER CROSS COUNTRY SKI TRAIL

FR 2238

US 41

442

C

H-05

HAYMEADOW TRAIL

RAPID RIVER

US 2

2 4 8 MI

LAKE MICHIGAN (BAY-DE-NOC)

BAY DE NOC -GRAND ISLAND TRAIL

Munising Ranger District, Hiawatha National Forest
RR 2, Box 400
Munising, MI 48962

906-387-2512

Rapid River Ranger District, Hiawatha National Forest
8181 US2
Rapid River, MI 49878

906-474-6442

Michigan Atlas & Gazetteer Location: 90A12,102BCD2

County Location: Alger, Delta

Directions To Trailhead:
Between Forest Lake on M94 and Rapid River on US2. From M-28 and M94 intersection 1 mile east of Munising, take M94 9 miles west to trailhead at Ackerman Lake. From Rapid River, take US2 east to Co Rd 509, north on Co Rd 509 for 1.5 miles to trailhead parking lot. Also same direction out of Rapid River but continue north on Co Rd 509 for 16 miles to parking lot on east side of road.

Trail Type: Hiking/Walking, Mountain Biking
Trail Distance: 40 mi   Loops: NA   Shortest: NA   Longest: NA
Trail Surface: Natural with considerable sand
Trail Use Fee: None
Method Of Ski Trail Grooming: NA
Skiing Ability Suggested: NA
Hiking Trail Difficulty: Easy
Mountain Biking Ability Suggested: Intermediate to advanced
Terrain: Steep 10%, Hilly 30%, Moderate 30%, Flat 30%
Camping: Haymeadow NFCG and anywhere more than 200' from the trail

Managed by the Hiawatha National Forest.
Used mostly as a horse back riding trail which makes the trail open to mountain bikes but sections may not be very enjoyable because of loose sand.
Water and toilet facilities available at the three trailhead locations.

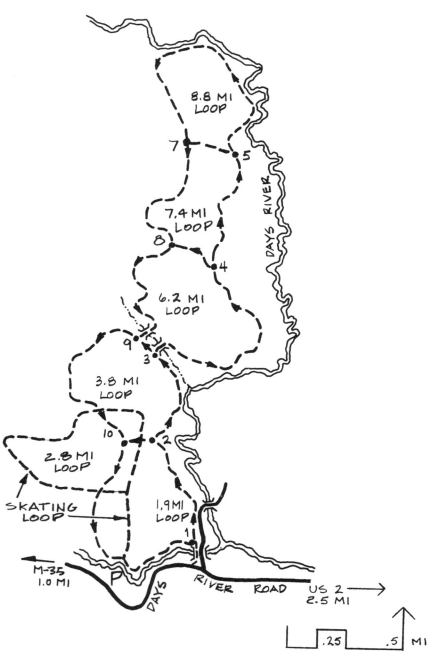

DAYS RIVER PATHWAY

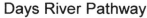

Escanaba Forest Area, Escanaba River State Forest
6833 US2/41 & M35   906-786-2354
Gladstone, MI 49835

District Forest Manager, Escanaba River State Forest
6833 US2/41 & M35   906-786-2351
Gladstone, MI 49835

Michigan Atlas & Gazetteer Location: 90A1, 102D1

County Location: Delta

Directions To Trailhead:
3 miles north of Gladstone on US2/41, then west 2 miles on Days River Rd.

Trail Type: Hiking/Walking, Cross Country Skiing, Mountain Biking
Trail Distance: 9.1 mi   Loops: 5   Shortest: 1.9 mi Longest: 8.8 mi
Trail Surface: Natural
Trail Use Fee: Donations accepted for trail grooming
Method Of Ski Trail Grooming: Track set
Skiing Ability Suggested: Novice to advanced
Hiking Trail Difficulty: Easy to moderate
Mountain Biking Ability Suggested: Novice
Terrain: Steep 5%, Hilly 10%, Moderate 50%, Flat 35%
Camping: None

Maintained by the DNR Forest Management Division
Overlooks the Days River at several locations. Deer usually seen along the trail.
A 2.8 mile skating loop in the system.
Other contacts:
        DNR Forest Management Division Office, Lansing, 517-373-1275
        DNR Forest Management Region Office, Marquette, 906-228-6561

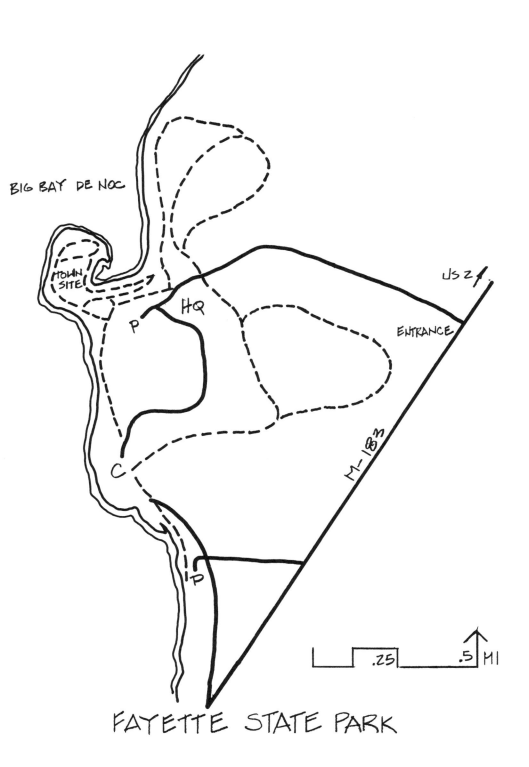

BIG BAY DE NOC

TOWN SITE

HQ

P

ENTRANCE

US 2

M-183

C

P

|___.25___.5| MI

FAYETTE STATE PARK

Fayette State Park
13700 13.25 Lane
Garden, MI 49835

906-644-2603

DNR Parks and Recreation Division

517-373-1270
906-228-6561

Michigan Atlas & Gazetteer Location: 90C3

County Location: Delta

Directions To Trailhead:
SW of Manistique via US2 and M183. On the west shore of the Garden Peninsula near its south end.

Trail Type: Hiking/Walking, Cross Country Skiing, Interpretive
Trail Distance: 7 mi   Loops: Several   Shortest: 1.5 mi   Longest: 4 mi
Trail Surface: Gravel and natural
Trail Use Fee: None, but vehicle entry fee required
Method Of Ski Trail Grooming: Track set
Skiing Ability Suggested: Novice to intermediate
Hiking Trail Difficulty: Easy
Mountain Biking Ability Suggested: NA
Terrain: Steep 0%, Hilly 0%, Moderate 10%, Flat 90%
Camping: Campground is open all year

Maintained by the DNR Parks and Recreation Division
Scenic overlook along trail. A unique restored village of the 1800's, settled to house the iron smelting workers who worked there.
Annual events include:
        The Blessing of the Fleet event is held on the last Saturday in June.
        Heritage Days are held on on the first weekend of August.
Modern visitor center, 15 restored buildings, dock, campground, swimming beach and picnic area.
Self guided tour maps available to tour the townsite.

Rapid River Ranger District, Hiawatha National Forest
8181 US2
Rapid River, MI 49878
906-474-6442

Forest Supervisor, Hiawatha National Forest
2727 N. Lincoln Rd
Escanaba, MI 49829
906-786-4062

Michigan Atlas & Gazetteer Location: 90B1

County Location: Delta

Directions To Trailhead:
East of Rapid River on US2 to Co Rd 513, then 6 miles south to recreation area

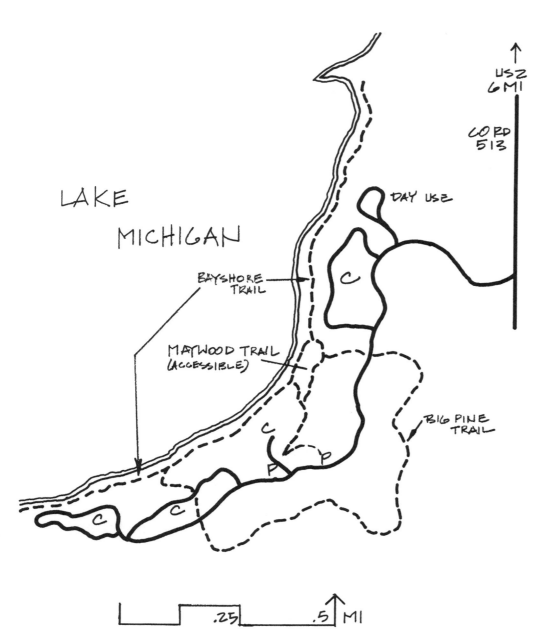

Trail Type: Hiking/Walking, Mountain Biking
Trail Distance: 3.2 mi   Loops: 1   Shortest: NA   Longest: .6 mi
Trail Surface: Paved and natural
Trail Use Fee: A day use fee may be charged in the future
Method Of Ski Trail Grooming: NA
Skiing Ability Suggested: NA
Hiking Trail Difficulty: Easy
Mountain Biking Ability Suggested: NA
Terrain: Note below for each trail
Camping: Campground on site

Maintained by the Rapid River Ranger District, Hiawatha National Forest
Beautiful recreation area on Little Bay De Noc developed in 1990.
Trail Specifications:
        Maywood Trail - fully accessible, .6 miles, interpretive trail, benches, 100% Flat
        Bayshore Trail - point to point, 1.2 miles, 30% moderate, 70% flat
        Big Pines Trail - point to point, 1.3 miles, 10% moderate, 90% flat
Maywood Trail has 200 tall Hemlocks along the trail
A hotel and cottages were located on the site in the 1800's. The area was a popular picnic   area for Glatstone residents at that time.

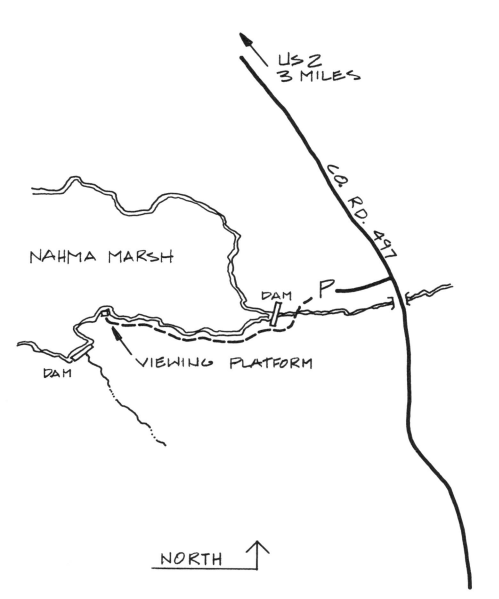

US 2
3 MILES

CO. RD. 497

NAHMA MARSH

DAM
P

DAM

VIEWING PLATFORM

NORTH ↑

Nahma Marsh Hiking Trail

Rapid River Ranger District, Hiawatha National Forest
8181 US 2   906-474-6442
Rapid River, MI 49878

Forest Supervisor, Hiawatha National Forest
2727 N. Lincoln Rd   906-786-4062
Escanaba, MI 49829

Michigan Atlas & Gazetteer Location: 90B3

County Location: Delta

Directions To Trailhead:
From Escanaba, take US2 east about 30 miles to Nahma Junction, then south 3 miles on Co Rd 497 to the trail.

Trail Type: Hiking/Walking, Interpretive

Trail Surface: Hard packed crushed limestone
Trail Use Fee: None
Method Of Ski Trail Grooming: NA
Skiing Ability Suggested: NA
Hiking Trail Difficulty: Easy
Mountain Biking Ability Suggested: NA
Terrain: 100% Flat
Camping: Campground located 6 miles north on FH13 at Flowing Well NFCG

Maintained by the Rapid River Ranger District, Hiawatha National Forest
This trail was designed as a fully accessible hiking trail that ends at a two thired wildlife viewing platform overlooking the Nahma Marsh. One tier is accessible. Rest areas with benches are located every 200 feet along the trail. The maximum grade of the trail is 8%.

NAHMA MARSH HIKING TRAIL

(FAYETTE STATE PARK NEARBY)

4
5
6
7
8
9
3
1.5 MILE LOOP
2
12
1
11
10
13
14
15
LAKE MICHIGAN
PORTAGE BAY S.F.C.G.
C
GARDEN 10 MILES
M183
NORTH

Shingleton Forest Area, Lake Superior State Forest
PO Box 67
Shingleton, MI 49884
906-452-6227

District Forest Manager, Lake Superior State Forest
PO Box 77
Newberry, MI 49868
906-293-5131

Michigan Atlas & Gazetteer Location: 90C4

County Location: Delta

Directions To Trailhead:
10 miles southeast of Garden via M183 on the Garden Peninsula.

Trail Type: Hiking/Walking, Interpretive
Trail Distance: 2 mi   Loops: 2   Shortest: .5 mi   Longest: 1.5 mi
Trail Surface: Natural
Trail Use Fee: None
Method Of Ski Trail Grooming: NA
Skiing Ability Suggested: NA
Hiking Trail Difficulty: Easy
Mountain Biking Ability Suggested: NA
Terrain: Not known
Camping: At trailhead

Maintained by the DNR Forest Management Division
This is a native american interpretive trail of the Ojibwa Indians.

NINGA AKI PATHWAY

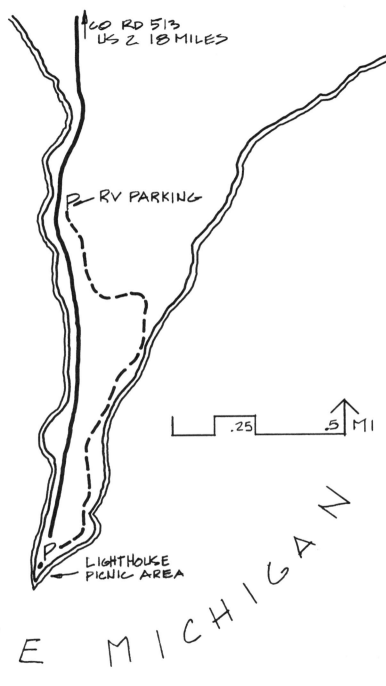

Rapid River Ranger District, Hiawatha National Forest
8181 US2   906-474-6442
Rapid River, MI 49878

Forest Supervisor, Hiawatha National Forest
2727 N. Lincoln Rd   906-786-4062
Escanaba, MI 49829

Michigan Atlas & Gazetteer Location: 90C1

County Location: Delta

Directions To Trailhead:
At the Peninsula Point National Historical Lighthouse. From Rapid River, take US2 east fro 3 miles to Co Rd 513, then south for 18 miles to the trailhead.

Trail Type: Hiking/Walking, Interpretive
Trail Distance: 1 mi   Loops: NA   Shortest: NA   Longest: NA
Trail Surface: Natural
Trail Use Fee: None
Method Of Ski Trail Grooming: NA
Skiing Ability Suggested: NA
Hiking Trail Difficulty: Easy
Mountain Biking Ability Suggested: NA
Terrain: 100% Flat
Camping: Little Bay De Noc Recreation Area

Maintained by the Rapid River Ranger District, Hiawatha National Forest
The focal point of the trail is a historic lighthouse built in 1865.

PENINSULA POINT HIKING TRAIL

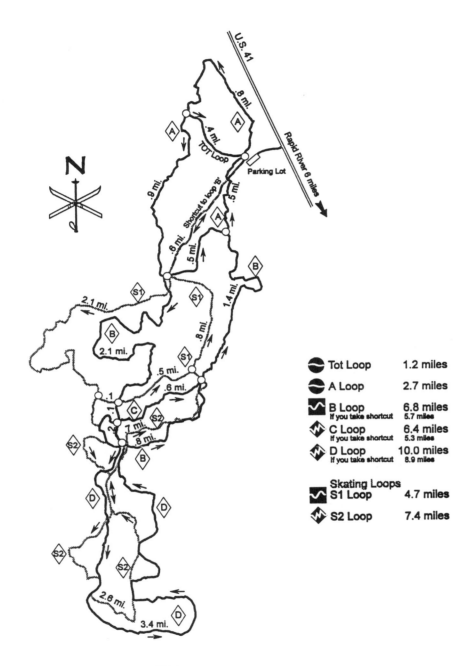

Rapid River Ranger District, Hiawatha National Forest
8181 US 2   906-474-6442
Rapid River, MI 49878

Forest Supervisor, Hiawatha National Forest
2727 N. Lincoln Rd.   906-786-4062
Escanaba, MI 49829

Michigan Atlas & Gazetteer Location: 90A1,102D1

County Location: Delta

Directions To Trailhead:
North of Escanaba and 7 miles north of Rapid River on US41

Trail Type: Hiking/Walking, Cross Country Skiing
Trail Distance: 19.1mi   Loops: 4   Shortest: 1.2 mi Longest: 10 mi
Trail Surface: Natural
Trail Use Fee: None
Method Of Ski Trail Grooming: Track set
Skiing Ability Suggested: Novice to advanced
Hiking Trail Difficulty: NA
Mountain Biking Ability Suggested: NA
Terrain: Steep 27%, Hilly 28%, Moderate 25%, Flat 20%
Camping: None

Maintained by the Rapid River Ranger District, Hiawatha National Forest
Designed for cross country skiing. Well marked and maintained trail.
Loops:

    Tot loop - 1.2 mi - Easy - Classic
    A loop - 2.7 mi - Easy - Classic
    B loop - 6.8 mi - More difficult - Classic
    C loop - 6.4 mi - Most Difficult - Classic
    D loop - 10 mi - Most Difficult - Classic
    S1 loop - 4.7 mi - More difficult - Skating
    S2 loops - 7.4 mi - Most difficult - Skating

Map Legend

◗	Tot Loop	1.2 miles
◗	A Loop	2.7 miles
◩	B Loop (If you take shortcut)	6.8 miles (5.7 miles)
◈	C Loop (If you take shortcut)	6.4 miles (5.3 miles)
◈	D Loop (If you take shortcut)	10.0 miles (8.9 miles)

Skating Loops

◩	S1 Loop	4.7 miles
◈	S2 Loop	7.4 miles

RAPID RIVER
NATIONAL CROSS COUNTRY SKI TRAIL

Munising Ranger District, Hiawatha National Forest
RR 2, Box 400   906-387-2512
Munising, MI 49862

Shingleton Forest Area, Lake Superior State Forest
PO Box 67   906-452-6227`
Shingleton, MI 49884

Michigan Atlas & Gazetteer Location: 91A457,103BCD567

County Location: Alger, Schoolcraft

Directions To Trailhead:
North trailhead - East side of M-94 just south of Shingleton. Take .3 mile access trail to rail trail.
South trailhead - North of Manistique M94 to Riverview Rd. Right (east) on Riverview to parking lot just east of the water intake plant.

Trail Type: Hiking/Walking, Mountain Biking
Trail Distance: 33 mi   Loops: NA   Shortest: NA   Longest: NA
Trail Surface: Ballast, gravel and sand
Trail Use Fee: None
Method Of Ski Trail Grooming: NA
Skiing Ability Suggested: NA
Hiking Trail Difficulty: Easy
Mountain Biking Ability Suggested: Novice to intermediate
Terrain: Flat 100%
Camping: Indian River Camp and Picnic Grounds and wilderness camping

Managed by both the DNR Forest Management Divison and the Hiawatha National Forest
No development has been done to this trail.
Surface is ballast, sand and gravel.
Considerable beaver activity and sand traps will make this a challenge for mountain bikers.
A truely isolated trail with only the village of Steuben along the rail trail to provide a source of drinking water and food.
Most of its use is as a snowmobile and ORV trail.
If you are up for a challenge, try this one.

MUNISING
10 MILES

SHINGLETON
M28

NEWBERRY ➔

P

CLEAR LAKE RD

C

C

CO.RD. 437

STEUBEN

C

M94

2   4 MI

INDIAN LAKE

P

439

RIVERVIEW RD

MANISTIQUE

CO RD 442 ➔

US2

US2

II

LAKE MICHIGAN

HAYWIRE RAIL TRAIL

Shingleton Forest Area, Lake Superior State Forest
M28 West, PO Box 67   906-452-6236
Shingleton, MI 49884   906-341-6917

District Forest Manager, Lake Superior State Forest
South M123, PO Box 77   906-239-5131
Newberry, MI 49868

Michigan Atlas & Gazetteer Location: 91A5, 103D5

County Location: Schoolcraft

Directions To Trailhead:
9 miles NW of Thompson on M149 and 1 mile west of Palms Brook State Park

Trail Type: Hiking/Walking, Cross Country Skiing, Mountain Biking
Trail Distance: 8 mi   Loops: 3   Shortest: 1 mi   Longest: 4.5 mi
Trail Surface: Natural
Trail Use Fee: None
Method Of Ski Trail Grooming: Track set
Skiing Ability Suggested: Novice to advanced
Hiking Trail Difficulty: Moderate
Mountain Biking Ability Suggested: Novice to intermediate
Terrain: Steep 0%, Hilly 25%, Moderate 75%, Flat 0%
Camping: None at trail but available nearby

Maintained by the DNR Forest Management Division
Other contacts:
        DNR Forest Management Division Office, Lansing, 517-373-1275
        DNR Forest Management Region Office, Marquette, 906-228-6561

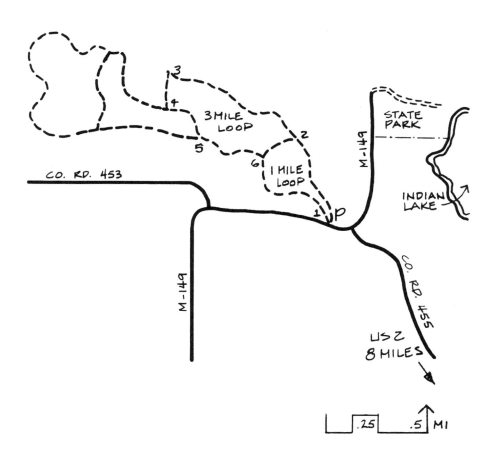

INDIAN LAKE PATHWAY

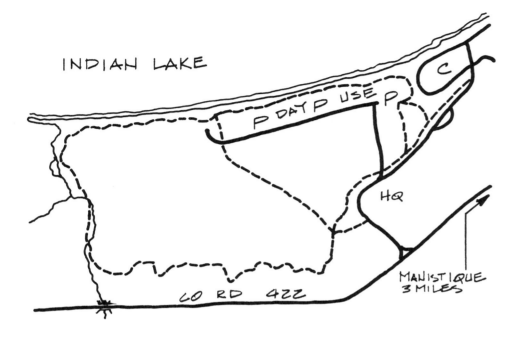

INDIAN LAKE

P DAY P USE P

C

HQ

MANISTIQUE
3 MILES

CO RD 422

NORTH

Indian Lake State Park
Rte 2, Box 2500
Manistique, MI 49854

906-341-2355

DNR Parks and Recreation Divsion

906-228-6561
517-373-1270

Michigan Atlas & Gazetteer Location: 91A6

County Location: Schoolcraft

Directions To Trailhead:
6 miles west of Manistique on US2 to Thompson, then 3 miles north on M149 ,
then .5 mile east on Co Rd 442 to the park

Trail Type: Hiking/Walking, Interpretive
Trail Distance: 4 mi   Loops: 3   Shortest: .25 mi Longest: 2 mi
Trail Surface: Natural
Trail Use Fee: None, but vehicle entry fee required
Method Of Ski Trail Grooming: NA
Skiing Ability Suggested: NA
Hiking Trail Difficulty: Easy
Mountain Biking Ability Suggested: NA
Terrain: 100% Flat
Camping: Campground at trailhead

Maintained by the DNR Parks and Recreation Division
The park contains typical facilities found in Michigan state parks

INDIAN LAKE STATE PARK

MSU Cooperative Extension Service
Schoolcraft County Court House, Rm 218   906-341-5050
Manistique, MI 49854

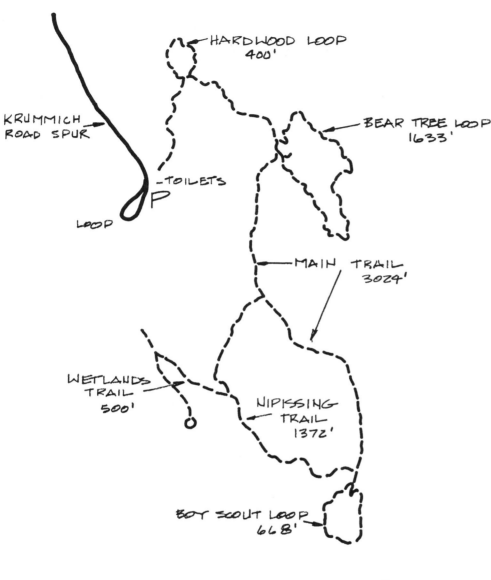

HARDWOOD LOOP
400'

KRUMMICH
ROAD SPUR

BEAR TREE LOOP
1633'

TOILETS
P
LOOP

MAIN TRAIL
3024'

WETLANDS
TRAIL
500'

NIPISSING
TRAIL
1372'

BOY SCOUT LOOP
668'

NORTH

SCHOOLCRAFT COUNTY
ENVIROMENTAL LAB.

Michigan Atlas & Gazetteer Location: 91A7

County Location: Schoolcraft

Directions To Trailhead:
3 miles east of Manistique to Co Rd 433 (River Rd), then north about 2 miles to
Krumich Rd, then west about 2 mile to the trailhead.

Trail Type: Hiking/Walking, Cross Country Skiing, Interpretive
Trail Distance: 1.4 mi   Loops: Shortest: Longest:
Trail Surface: Natural
Trail Use Fee: None
Method Of Ski Trail Grooming: None
Skiing Ability Suggested: Novice
Hiking Trail Difficulty: Easy
Mountain Biking Ability Suggested: NA
Terrain: Steep 0%, Hilly 10%, Moderate 90%, Flat 0%
Camping: None

Managed by the Michigan State University Cooperative Extension Service

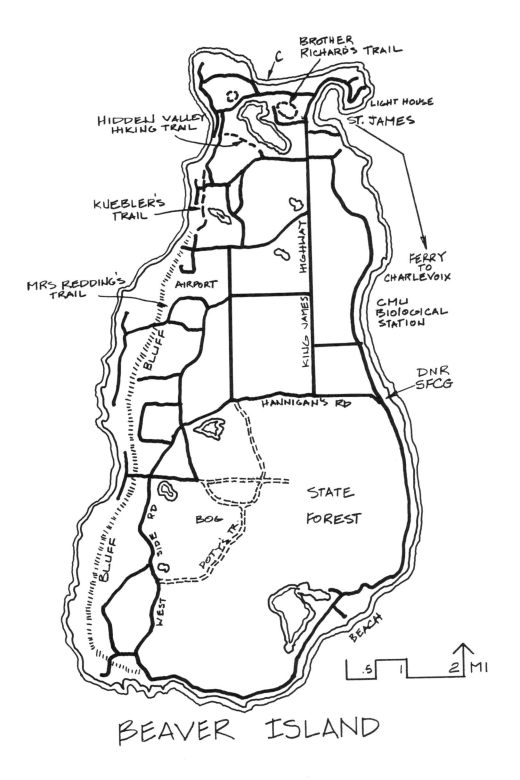

BEAVER ISLAND

Beaver Island Chamber of Commerce
PO Box 153
Beaver Island, MI 49782

616-448-2933
616-448-2396

Michigan Atlas & Gazetteer Location: 92CD4,93CD5

County Location: Charlevoix

Directions To Trailhead:
Offshore in Lake Michigan between Charlevoix and Petoskey. Ferry service from Charlevoix.

Trail Type: Hiking/Walking, Cross Country Skiing, Mountain Biking
Trail Distance: 50+ mi   Loops: Many   Shortest: Short Longest: Long
Trail Surface: Paved, gravel and natural
Trail Use Fee: None
Method Of Ski Trail Grooming: None
Skiing Ability Suggested: Novice to intermediate
Hiking Trail Difficulty: Easy
Mountain Biking Ability Suggested: Novice
Terrain: Steep 0%, Hilly 5%, Moderate 70%, Flat 25%
Camping: Two campgrounds on the island

Ferry service available from the Beaver Island Boat Company, 616-547-2311
A beautiful 53 square mile island with little vehicle traffic.
All roads most of which are gravel surfaced and less developed roads and trails are open to the public.
No trails specifically developed for mountain biking but the island is ideally suited for the activity.
Many miles of isolated shore accessible for hiking.
Camping available at a township campground in St. James and a state forest campground along the east shore.
About 1/3 of the island is state forest.
Write or call for complete information and a large map of the island.

Cheboygan Area Chamber of Commerce
PO Box 69
Cheboygan, MI 49721

616-627-7183

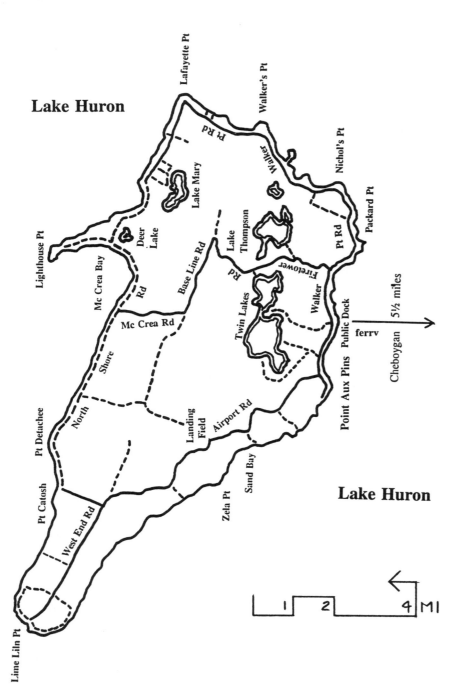

Lake Huron

Lafayette Pt

Walker's Pt

Nichol's Pt

Pt Rd

Walker

Packard Pt

Lake Mary

Pt Rd

Deer Lake

Lake Thompson

Firetower

Walker

Lighthouse Pt

Mc Crea Bay

Base Line Rd

Rd

Lake Thompson Rd

Shore

Mc Crea Rd

Twin Lakes

Public Dock

ferry

Cheboygan 5½ miles

North

Landing Field

Airport Rd

Point Aux Pins

Pt Detache

Sand Bay

Lake Huron

Pt Catosh

Zela Pt

West End Rd

Lime Liln Pt

1 2 4 MI

BOIS BLANC ISLAND

Michigan Atlas & Gazetteer Location: 94B4, 95BC5

County Location: Mackinac

Directions To Trailhead:
In the north end of Lake Huron near Mackinac Island off Cheboygan

Trail Type: Mountain Biking
Trail Distance: 50+ mi   Loops: Many   Shortest: Longest:
Trail Surface: Gravel and natural
Trail Use Fee: None
Method Of Ski Trail Grooming: NA
Skiing Ability Suggested: NA
Hiking Trail Difficulty: Easy
Mountain Biking Ability Suggested: Novice to intermediate
Terrain: Varied
Camping: Primitive campground available.

Somewhat isolated island in the north end of Lake Huron
About 50% of the island is managed by the DNR Forest Management Division.
Numerous gravel and dirt roads along with almost non-existant traffic make this
island excellent for mountain biking. Many miles of roads to explore. Best to
visit before or after bug season, ie April and early May or October.
See Fall 1992 issue of Michigan Cyclist for article about the island
Ferry Services:
        Boblo Islander 616-627-9445
        Plaunt Transportation 616-627-2345/643-7300
Motel and only restaurant (reservations suggested) 616-634-7291

Horseshoe Bay Hiking Trail

St. Ignace Ranger District, Hiawatha National Forest
Rte 2, Box 101
St. Ignace, MI 49781   906-643-7900

Forest Supervisor, Hiawatha National Forest
2727 N. Lincoln Rd   906-786-4062
Escanaba, MI 49826

Michigan Atlas & Gazetteer Location: 94A3

County Location: Mackinac

Directions To Trailhead:
Trailhead located at Foley Creek NFCG on Mackinac Trail about 5 miles north of
St.. Ignace

Trail Type: Hiking/Walking
Trail Distance: 1 mi   Loops: NA   Shortest: NA   Longest: NA
Trail Surface: Natural
Trail Use Fee: None
Method Of Ski Trail Grooming: None
Skiing Ability Suggested: Novice
Hiking Trail Difficulty: Easy
Mountain Biking Ability Suggested: NA
Terrain: 100% Flat
Camping: At trailhead

Maintained by the St. Ignace Ranger District
This is a hiking trail only into the Horseshoe Bay Wilderness that was
established in 1987 to protect the sensitive ecology and secluded character of
this section of the Lake Huron shoreline.
To preserve this wilderness this trail is for walking only.
Camp in dispersed locations, travel in small groups, carry out your trash, be
quiet, use stove instead of wood, move your campsite frequently naturalizing
the area when you leave and do not disturb the area any more than absolutely
necessary.
An information sheet for the trail and area is available.

HORSESHOE BAY HIKING TRAIL

Map labels:
HORSESHOE BAY WILDERNESS
HORSESHOE BAY
LAKE HURON
FOLEY CREEK CNFCG
FOLEY CREEK
I75 * US2
H-63 MACKINAC TRAIL
ST IGNACE 5 MILES

Mackinac Island Chamber of Commerce
Box 451
Mackinac Island, MI 49757

906-847-3783
906-4-lilacs

Mackinac Island State Park Commission
PO Box 30028
Lansing, MI 48909

906-847-3328
517-373-4296

Michigan Atlas & Gazetteer Location: 94AB34

County Location: Mackinac

Directions To Trailhead:
Located in the Straits of Mackniac By ferry from St Ignace or Mackinaw City from March through November By plane from St Ignace year-around

Trail Type: Hiking/Walking, Cross Country Skiing, Mountain Biking, Interpretive
Trail Distance: 50+ mi   Loops: Many   Shortest: Longest:
Trail Surface: Paved, gravel and natural
Trail Use Fee: None
Method Of Ski Trail Grooming: Track set occasionally
Skiing Ability Suggested: Novice to advanced
Hiking Trail Difficulty: Easy to moderate
Mountain Biking Ability Suggested: Novice
Terrain: Steep 0%, Hilly 50%, Moderate 40%, Flat 10%
Camping: None

Maintained by the Mackinac Island State Park Commission
A fabulous ski area. All the trails used in the summer for carriages, horses, bikes and hiking are available for skiing in the winter. Snowmobiles are restricted to the west half of the island, leaving the best trails for the skiers. However, the snowmobiles do an excellent job of grooming the remaining roads for skating. Hiking opportunities are throughout the island. Biking is likewise great on the island. There are several hard surfaced bike trails for road bikes. One takes the shoreline of the island, while two others are more difficult following an interior route. For mountain bike riders, the options are many. I suggest visiting the island in the spring for fall, when the island is less crowded. This way you can explore all the trails the island has to offer. Mountain bikes are limited to paved trails and gravel roads. Hiking and horse trails are not open to mountain bikes. Accomodations are available year around on the island. Always call ahead.

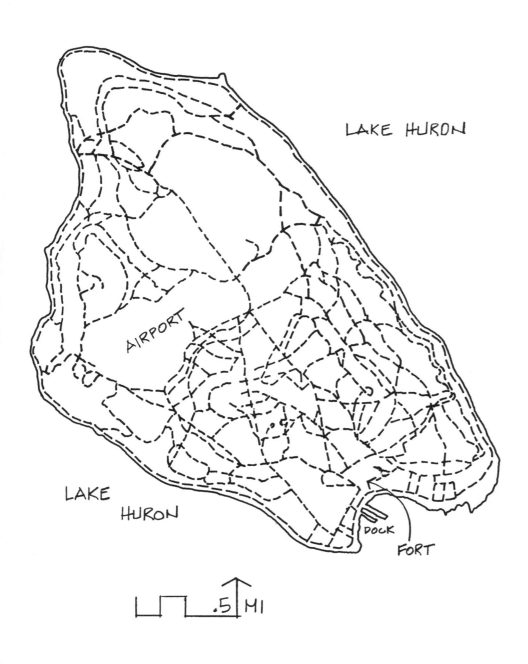

LAKE HURON

AIRPORT

LAKE HURON

DOCK

FORT

.5 MI

MACKINAC ISLAND STATE PARK

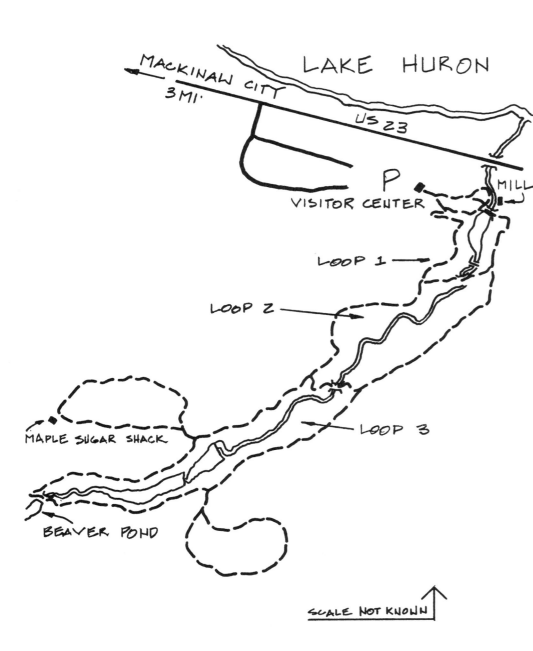

Mill Creek State Historic Park
PO Box 873
Mackinaw City, MI 49701-0873

616-436-5203

DNR Parks and Recreation Division

517-373-1270
517-275-5151

Michigan Atlas & Gazetteer Location: 94B3

County Location: Cheboygan

Directions To Trailhead:
Three miles southeast from Mackinaw City on US23

Trail Type: Hiking/Walking, Cross Country Skiing, Interpretive
Trail Distance: 3+ mi   Loops: 5   Shortest: .3 mi   Longest: 2 mi
Trail Surface: Paved, gravel and natural
Trail Use Fee: Addmission charge
Method Of Ski Trail Grooming: None
Skiing Ability Suggested: Novice
Hiking Trail Difficulty: Easy
Mountain Biking Ability Suggested: NA
Terrain: Steep 0%, Hilly 2%, Moderate 88%, Flat 10%
Camping: Available nearby

Maintained by the Parks and Recreation Divsion
Historical restoration of the a saw mill used from the 1780's to 1873.
Large restoration of the grounds around the sawmill have been developed.
Much of the lumber for structures on Mackinac Island were sawed at this location.
Brochure available.

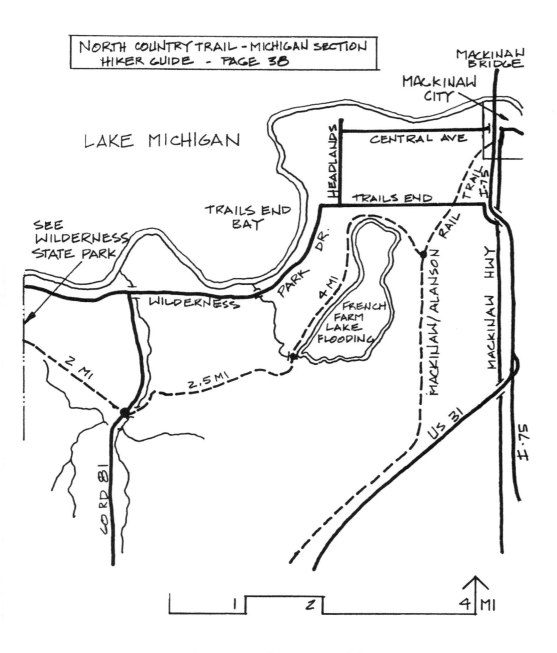

NORTH COUNTRY TRAIL -
MACKINAW STATE FOREST 3

Indian River Forest Area, Mackinaw State Forest
PO Box 10   616-238-9313
Indian River, Mi 49749

North Country Trail Association
PO Box 311   616-689-1912
White Cloud, MI 49349

Michigan Atlas & Gazetteer Location: 94BC2

County Location: Emmet

Directions To Trailhead:
Between the east boundary of Wilderness State Park (see other listing) and the
Mackinaw / Alanson Rail Trail (see other listing)
West trail head - East boundary of Wilderness State Park about 1 mile south of
Wilderness Park Drive
East trail head - Mackinaw / Alanson Rail Trail about 1 mile south of Trails End
Rd, just west of Mackinaw Hwy

Trail Type: Hiking/Walking, Mountain Biking
Trail Distance: 8.5 mi   Loops: NA   Shortest: NA   Longest: NA
Trail Surface: Natural
Trail Use Fee: None
Method Of Ski Trail Grooming: NA
Skiing Ability Suggested: NA
Hiking Trail Difficulty: Easy
Mountain Biking Ability Suggested: Novice
Terrain: Flat to rolling
Camping: Wilderness State Park

Trail in the Mackinaw State Forest
Trail built and maintained by the North Country Trail Association members.
See NCT - Michigan Section - Hiker Guide, page 38 for detailed trail map. Guide
is available from the NCTA.
See Wilderness State Park for NCT section west of this segment. In the park,
NCT uses existing park trails marked as the NCT.
See NCT-St. Ignace for section north of this segment..

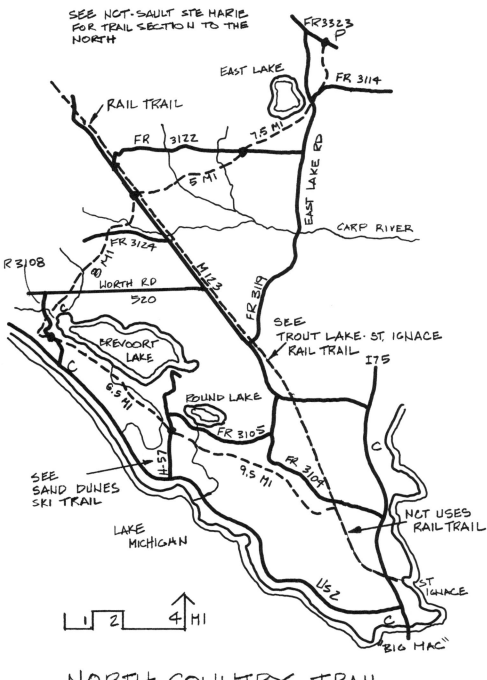

St. Ignace Ranger District, Hiawatha National Forest
1498 West US2   906-643-7900
St. Ignace , MI 49781

Forest Supervisor, Hiawatha National Forest
2727 N. Lincoln Rd.   906-786-4062
Escanaba, MI 49829

Michigan Atlas & Gazetteer Location: 94A123, 106CD12

County Location: Mackinac

Directions To Trailhead:
North and east of St Ignace
South trailhead - Rail trail in St Ignace
North trailhead - Just east of East Lake Rd. (NE of East Lake) on FR 3323
Lake Michigan trailhead - 11 miles west of St Ignace on US2, then 1.8 miles
north on Co Rd H57 (Brevoort Lake Rd.)

Trail Type: Hiking/Walking
Trail Distance: 35 mi   Loops: NA   Shortest: NA   Longest: NA
Trail Surface: Natural
Trail Use Fee: None
Method Of Ski Trail Grooming: NA
Skiing Ability Suggested: NA
Hiking Trail Difficulty: Moderate
Mountain Biking Ability Suggested: NA
Terrain: Rolling
Camping: Campgounds along trail

Maintained by the St. Ignace Ranger District, Hiawatha National Forest
Developed campground is located at Brevort Lake Campground with 70 sites,
toilets and drinking water.
Primitive campgrounds are located on the south side of the trail near the Pt.
Aux Chenes River, on the south side of Lake Brevort and 20 feet from the trail,
1/4 mile east of FR3119.
Wilderness camping is permitted 200' from the trail. Like the entire North
Country Trail, this is a point to point trail.
For more information contact the North Country Trail Association, PO Box 311,
White Cloud, MI 49349 616-689-1912

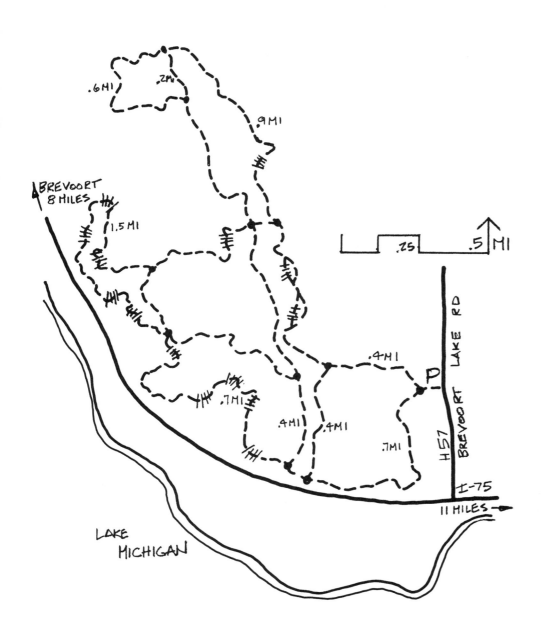

SAND DUNES CROSS COUNTRY SKI TRAIL

St. Ignace Ranger District, Hiawatha National Forest
1498 West US2   906-643-7900
St Ignace, MI 49781

Forest Supervisor, Hiawatha National Forest
2727 North Lincoln Rd   906-786-4062
Escanaba, MI 49829

Michigan Atlas & Gazetteer Location: 94A1

County Location: Mackinac

Directions To Trailhead:
11 miles west of I75 (St. Ignace) on US2, then north on Brevoort Lake Rd.(H57)
.5 miles to parking lot .

Trail Type: Hiking/Walking, Cross Country Skiing
Trail Distance: 15.6 km   Loops: 7   Shortest: 2.4 km Longest: 12.3 km
Trail Surface: Natural
Trail Use Fee: Donations accepted to cover grooming costs
Method Of Ski Trail Grooming: Track set as needed
Skiing Ability Suggested: Novice to advanced
Hiking Trail Difficulty: Easy to moderate
Mountain Biking Ability Suggested: NA
Terrain: Steep 5%, Hilly 20%, Moderate 60%, Flat 15%
Camping: Seasonal camping available at the NF campground 7 miles west

Built by the St. Ignace Ranger District, Hiawatha National Forest, Silver
Mountain Cross Country Ski Club and 12 other local groups.
Excellent ski trail with varied forest cover and well designed loops with scenic
overlooks of Lake Michigan.
The entire trail was contoured to provide for a delightful skiing experience By
passes for difficult sections are provided on the intermediate loops.
The open area at the trailhead was the site of the Round Lake Civilian
Conservation Corps Camp that started in 1935.
Site of the annual Dunes Day Loppet held the first Saturday in March.

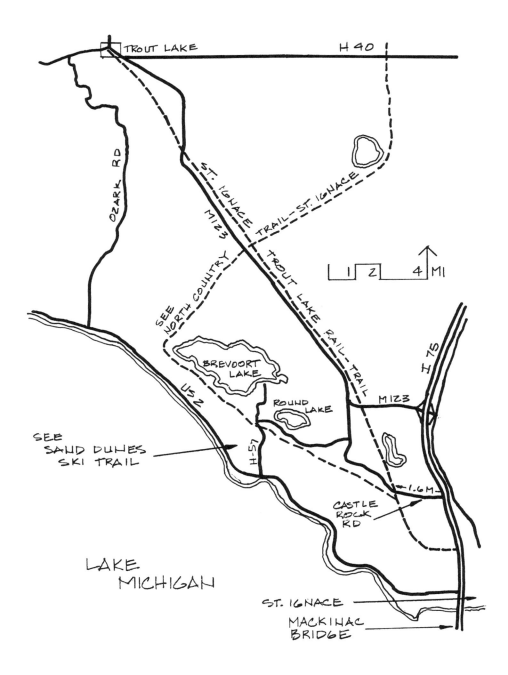

St. Ignace Ranger District, Hiawatha National Forest
1498 West US2   906-643-7900
St. Ignace, MI 49781

Forest Supervisor, Hiawatha National Forest
2727 N. Lincoln Rd   906-786-4062
Escanaba, MI 49829

Michigan Atlas & Gazetteer Location: 94AB23,105C8,106CD12

County Location: Mackinac

Directions To Trailhead:
From St. Ignace on the south to Trout Lake on the north.

Trail Type: Hiking/Walking, Mountain Biking
Trail Distance: 27 mi   Loops: NA   Shortest: NA   Longest: NA
Trail Surface: Natural and ballast
Trail Use Fee: None
Method Of Ski Trail Grooming: NA
Skiing Ability Suggested: NA
Hiking Trail Difficulty: Easy
Mountain Biking Ability Suggested: Intermediate
Terrain: 100% Flat
Camping: Campgrounds nearby

Managed by the St. Ignace Ranger District, Hiawatha National Forest
The south end of the trail is also part of the North Country Trail - St. Ignace

ST. IGNACE/TROUT LAKE RAIL TRAIL

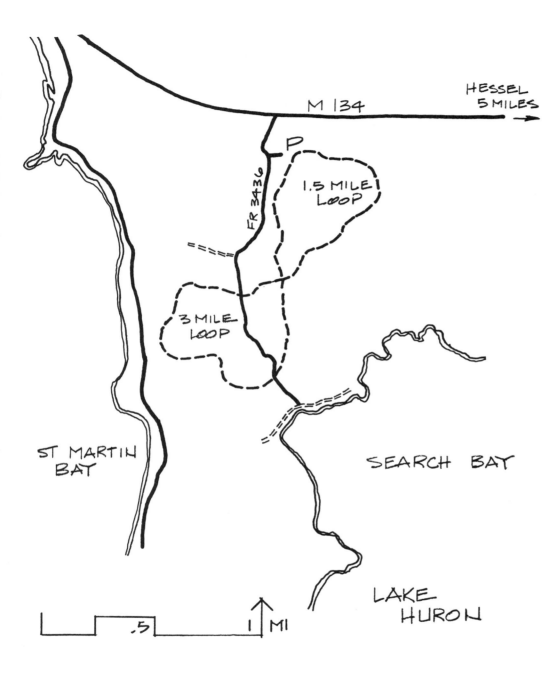

ST MARTIN
CROSS COUNTRY SKI TRAIL

St. Ignace Ranger District, Hiawatha National Forest
Rte 2, Box 101   906-603-7900
St. Ignace, MI 49781

Forest Supervisor, Hiawatha National Forest
2727 N. Lincoln Rd   906-786-4062
Escanaba, MI 49829

Michigan Atlas & Gazetteer Location: 94A4,106D4

County Location: Mackinac

Directions To Trailhead:
6 miles west of Hessel on M134.

Trail Type: Hiking/Walking, Cross Country Skiing
Trail Distance: 3 mi   Loops: 2   Shortest: 1.5 mi Longest: 3 mi
Trail Surface: Natural
Trail Use Fee: None
Method Of Ski Trail Grooming: None
Skiing Ability Suggested: Novice
Hiking Trail Difficulty: Easy
Mountain Biking Ability Suggested: NA
Terrain: Steep 0%, Hilly 0%, Moderate 40%, Flat 60%
Camping: None

Maintained by the St. Ignace Ranger District, Hiawatha National Forest
Hiking the trail could be difficult since it is not maintained in the summer.
Tall grass and no defined treadway makes locating the trail difficult.
Wildlife viewing including eagles, hawks, and dear.

Wilderness State Park

Wilderness State Park
Wilderness Park Drive
Carp Lake, MI 49718

616-436-5381

DNR Parks and Recreation Division

517-373-1270
517-275-5151

Michigan Atlas & Gazetteer Location: 94BC12

County Location: Emmet

Directions To Trailhead:
West of Mackinaw City on C81 and Wilderness Park Drive on Lake Michigan

SEE NCT-MACKINAW 3 FOR TRAIL EAST OF PARK

NUT

EAST BOUNDARY TRAIL

EAST RIDGE TRAIL

MT NEBO

NEBO TRAIL

BIG STONE TRAIL

HEMLOCK TRAIL

RED PINE TRAIL

SOUTH BOUNDARY TR

SWAMP LINE

RD

P C

C

C P

LAKE MICHIGAN

CABIN

CABIN

LITTLE SUCKER CR.

BIG SUCKER CR.

STURGEON BAY TRAIL

NORTH COUNTRY TRAIL
NORTH COUNTY TRAIL -
MICHIGAN SECTION -
HIKER GUIDE - PAGE 37
ABOUT 7.3 MILES IN PARK

NORTH COUNTRY TRAIL

LAKE VIEW RD

P

CABIN

CABIN

LAKE MICHIGAN

ISLANDS NOT SHOWN

.5   1   2 MI

WILDERNESS STATE PARK

Trail Type: Hiking/Walking, Cross Country Skiing, Mountain Biking, Interpretive
Trail Distance: 35 mi   Loops: Many   Shortest: Longest:
Trail Surface: Natural and gravel
Trail Use Fee: None, but vehicle entry fee required
Method Of Ski Trail Grooming: None
Skiing Ability Suggested: Novice to intermediate
Hiking Trail Difficulty: Easy to moderate
Mountain Biking Ability Suggested: Novice to intermediate
Terrain: Steep 0%, Hilly 0%, Moderate 10%, Flat 90%
Camping: Available in park

Maintained by the DNR Parks and Recreation Division
Ski in cabins available for rent on a reservations only basis (bookings for weekends should be made well in advance) Great back country skiing area.
Mountain biking trails limited to: Boundary Trail, Sturgeon Bay Trail, Nebo Trail, Swamp line Rd and Park Drive only.
The North Country Trail passes through this park. To the east see NCT-Mackinaw State Forest 3

Cheboygan State Park
4490 Beach Rd.
Cheboygan, MI 49721

616-627-2811

DNR Parks and Recreation Division

517-373-1270
517-275-5151

Michigan Atlas & Gazetteer Location: 95C5

County Location: Cheboygan

Directions To Trailhead:
5 miles east of Cheboygan on US23, then turn left on Seffern Rd and follow the signs

Trail Type: Hiking/Walking, Cross Country Skiing, Interpretive
Trail Distance: 6 mi   Loops: 3   Shortest: .5 mi   Longest: 2 mi
Trail Surface: Natural
Trail Use Fee: None, but vehicle entry fee required
Method Of Ski Trail Grooming: Track set
Skiing Ability Suggested: Novice
Hiking Trail Difficulty: Easy
Mountain Biking Ability Suggested: NA
Terrain: Steep 0%, Hilly 5%, Moderate 15%, Flat 80%
Camping: Camping on site from April through November

Maintained by the DNR Parks and Recreation Division
Rustic cabins are available for rent all year around.
In the winter cabins can only be reached by skis. Contact the park manager to make reservations, which are required.
Park covers over 1,200 acres
The first lighthouse, the Cheboygan Light, was built in 1857. It was later relocated to the shore and operated until 1930.

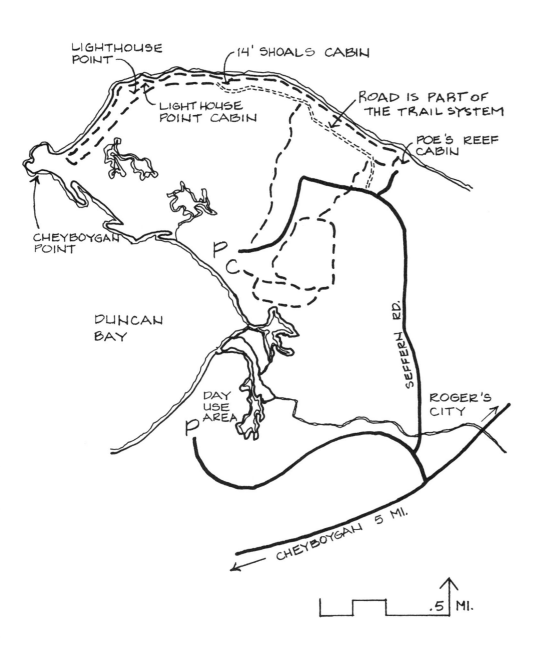

LIGHTHOUSE POINT
14' SHOALS CABIN
LIGHTHOUSE POINT CABIN
ROAD IS PART OF THE TRAIL SYSTEM
POE'S REEF CABIN
CHEYBOYGAN POINT
DUNCAN BAY
P C
SEFFERN RD.
ROGER'S CITY
DAY USE AREA
P
CHEYBOYGAN 5 MI.
.5 MI.

CHEYBOYGAN STATE PARK

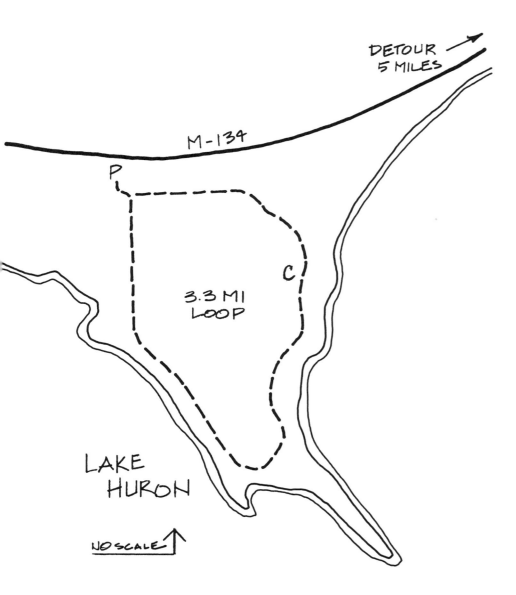

DETOUR
5 MILES

M-134

P

C

3.3 MI
LOOP

LAKE
HURON

NO SCALE

DETOUR AREA
CROSS COUNTRY SKI TRAIL

DeTour Cross Country Ski Trail

DeTour Area Chamber of Commerce
PO Box 161
DeTour, MI 49725

906-297-5987

Michigan Atlas & Gazetteer Location: 95A8,116B1

County Location: Chippewa

Directions To Trailhead:
5 miles west of DeTour off M134 at Detour State Forest Campground

Trail Type: Cross Country Skiing
Trail Distance: 3.3 mi   Loops: 1   Shortest: NA   Longest: 3.3 mi
Trail Surface: Natural
Trail Use Fee: None
Method Of Ski Trail Grooming: None
Skiing Ability Suggested: Novice
Hiking Trail Difficulty: NA
Mountain Biking Ability Suggested: NA
Terrain: Steep 0%, Hilly 0%, Moderate 30%, Flat 70%
Camping: Campground on site in the summer only

Maintained by the local volunteers

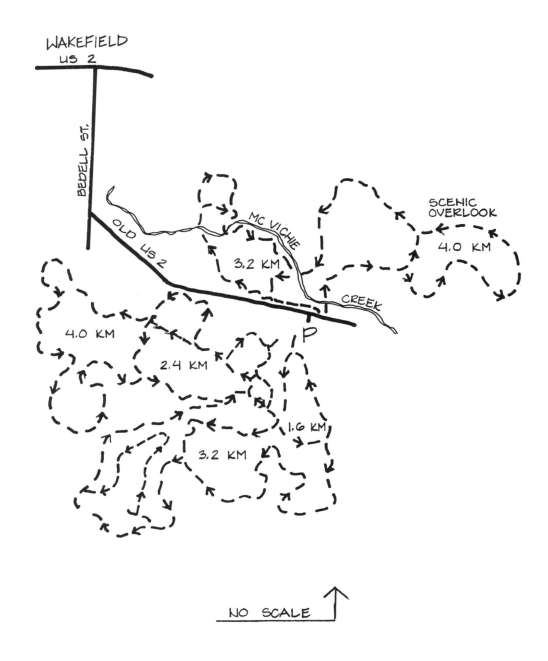

WAKEFIELD
US 2

BEDELL ST.

OLD US 2

MC VICHIE

SCENIC OVERLOOK

4.0 KM

3.2 KM

CREEK

P

4.0 KM

2.4 KM

1.6 KM

3.2 KM

NO SCALE

JOHNSON'S NORDIC SKI TRAILS

Johnson's Nordic Trails
Box 160, Old US2
Wakefield, MI 49968

906-224-4711
906-224-2731

Bessemer Ranger District - Ottawa National Forest
500 N. Moore St.
Bessemer, MI 49911

906-667-0261

Michigan Atlas & Gazetteer Location: 96A1

County Location: Gogebic

Directions To Trailhead:
On the south side of Old US2, 2 miles east of Wakefield Turn right off US2 on Bedell St., then 2 blocks turn left and proceed   1 mile on old US2 to the trailhead

Trail Type: Cross Country Skiing
Trail Distance: 30 km   Loops: 8   Shortest: .4 km   Longest: 4.8 km
Trail Surface: Natural
Trail Use Fee: Yes
Method Of Ski Trail Grooming: Track set with skating lane
Skiing Ability Suggested: Novice to advanced
Hiking Trail Difficulty: NA
Mountain Biking Ability Suggested: NA
Terrain: Steep 0%, Hilly 50%, Moderate 25%, Flat 25%
Camping: None

Outstanding privately operated cross country ski area in the Ottawa National Forest.
Warming area, rentals and ski shop available.
Expertly groomed and track set trails with beautiful scenery.
Site of the annual Early Season Classic 10km Race, held in mid-December.
Many loops are 10 to 12 feet wide for skating.
Guided moonlit ski tours on every full moon during the ski season.
The beginner trails is lit with candles blocked in ice with a bon fire about half way around the trail.
The warming log cabin was built in 1906.
Skiing is usually available from Thanksgiving into April.
Lodging available locally:
Write or call Gogebic Area Convention & Visitor Bureau. (see listing elsewhere)

Porcupine Mountains Wilderness State Park
412 South Boundary Rd.   906-885-5275
Ontonagon, MI 49953

Lake Gogebic State Park
HC 1, Box 139   906-842-3341
Marenisco, MI 48847

Michigan Atlas & Gazetteer Location: 96A4

County Location: Gogebic

Directions To Trailhead:
13 miles NE of Marenisco on the west shore of Lake Gogebic on M64 14 miles
south of Bergland on M64

Trail Type: Hiking/Walking, Interpretive
Trail Distance: 2 mi   Loops: 1   Shortest: NA   Longest: 2 mi
Trail Surface: Natural
Trail Use Fee: None, but vehicle entry fee required
Method Of Ski Trail Grooming: Packed
Skiing Ability Suggested: Intermediate
Hiking Trail Difficulty: Moderate
Mountain Biking Ability Suggested: NA
Terrain: Hilly
Camping: Campground in park. Limited facilities in the winter

Maintained by the DNR Parks and Recreation Division
Trail is a self-guided nature trail.
All types of forest cover is present along trail.

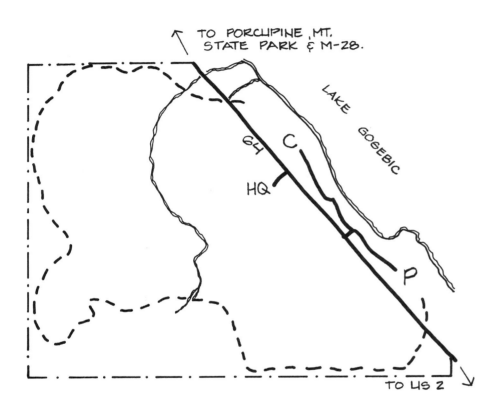

TO PORCUPINE MT.
STATE PARK & M-28.

LAKE GOGEBIC

64

C

HQ

P

TO US 2

NO SCALE

LAKE GOGEBIC STATE PARK

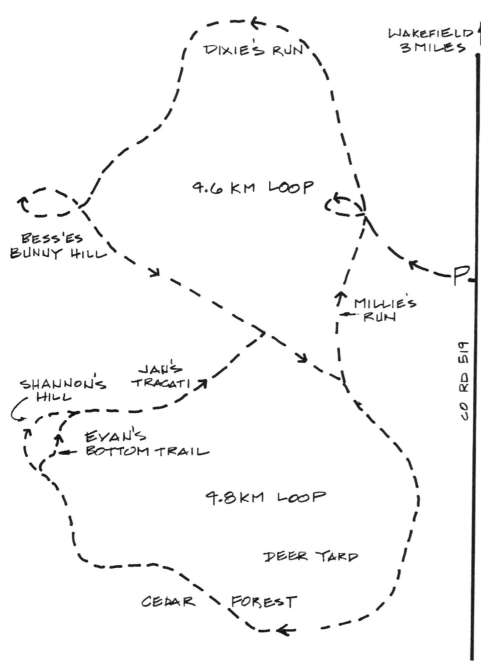

DIXIE'S RUN

4.6 KM LOOP

BESS'ES BUNNY HILL

MILLIE'S RUN

JAN'S TRACATI

SHANNON'S HILL

EVAN'S BOTTOM TRAIL

4.8 KM LOOP

DEER YARD

CEDAR FOREST

CO RD 519

WAKEFIELD 3 MILES

MILJE'S CROSS COUNTY TRAILS

Milje's Cross Country Ski Trails

Rollie Miljevich
205 Smith St.
Wakefield, MI 49968

906-229-5267

Michigan Atlas & Gazetteer Location: 96A1

County Location: Gogebic

Directions To Trailhead:
2 miles south of Wakefield on Co Rd 519

Trail Type: Cross Country Skiing
Trail Distance: 11 km   Loops: 2   Shortest: 5 km   Longest: 6 km
Trail Surface: Natural
Trail Use Fee: Yes, donation
Method Of Ski Trail Grooming: Track set classic only
Skiing Ability Suggested: Novice to advanced
Hiking Trail Difficulty: NA
Mountain Biking Ability Suggested: NA
Terrain: Steep 0%, Hilly 20%, Moderate 60%, Flat 20%
Camping: None

Privately operated ski trail system
Free hot chocolate, hot coffee, hot tea and cookies to skiers.
Deer seen daily along the trails.

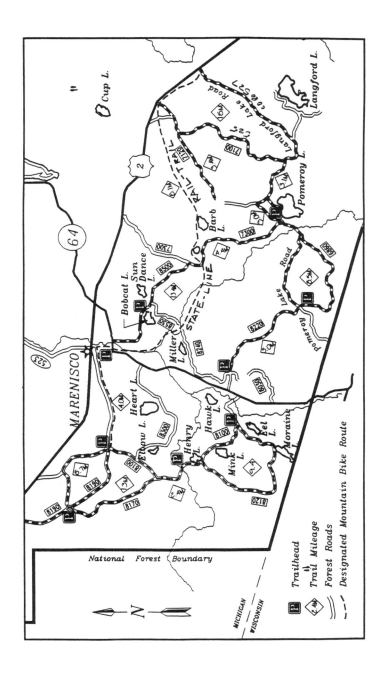

Bessemer Ranger District, Ottawa National Forest
500 N. Moore St.   906-667-0261
Bessemer, MI 49911

Recreation Staff Officer, Ottawa National Forest
2100 E. Cloverland Drive   906-932-1330
Ironwood, MI 49938

Michigan Atlas & Gazetteer Location: 96AB1234, 97B5

County Location: Gogebic

Directions To Trailhead:
South of US2, east and west of Marenisco and south to Wisconsin border.

Trail Type: Mountain Biking
Trail Distance: 50+ mi   Loops: Many   Shortest: Longest:
Trail Surface: Gravel, sand and natural
Trail Use Fee: None
Method Of Ski Trail Grooming: NA
Skiing Ability Suggested: NA
Hiking Trail Difficulty: NA
Mountain Biking Ability Suggested: Novice to advanced
Terrain: Steep 10%, Hilly 25%, Moderate 25%, Flat 40%
Camping: Many campgrounds throughout the area

Maintained by the Ottawa National Forest
Trails designated in 1994. Currently under further development.

POMEROY/ HENRY LAKE
MOUNTAIN BIKE COMPLEX

Porcupine Mountain Wilderness State Park
412 South Boundary Rd
Ontonagon, MI 49953

906-885-5275

DNR Parks and Recreation Division

517-373-1270

Michigan Atlas & Gazetteer Location: 97A8

County Location: Ontonagon

Directions To Trailhead:
4 miles west of Trout Creek on M28.

Trail Type: Hiking/Walking
Trail Distance: 1 mi   Loops: 1   Shortest: NA   Longest: 1 mi
Trail Surface: Natural
Trail Use Fee: None
Method Of Ski Trail Grooming: NA
Skiing Ability Suggested: NA
Hiking Trail Difficulty: Difficult
Mountain Biking Ability Suggested: NA
Terrain: Steep 50%, Hilly 0%, Moderate 0%, Flat 50%
Camping: None

Maintained by the DNR Parks and Recreation Division
Recent purchase.
No plans to develop site at this time.
Short trail to very scenic water falls.
Bond Falls Trail is nearby.

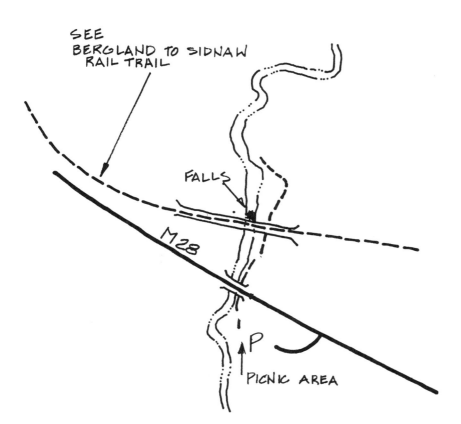

.5 MI

SEE
BERGLAND TO SIDNAW
RAIL TRAIL

FALLS

M28

P

PICNIC AREA

AGATE FALLS

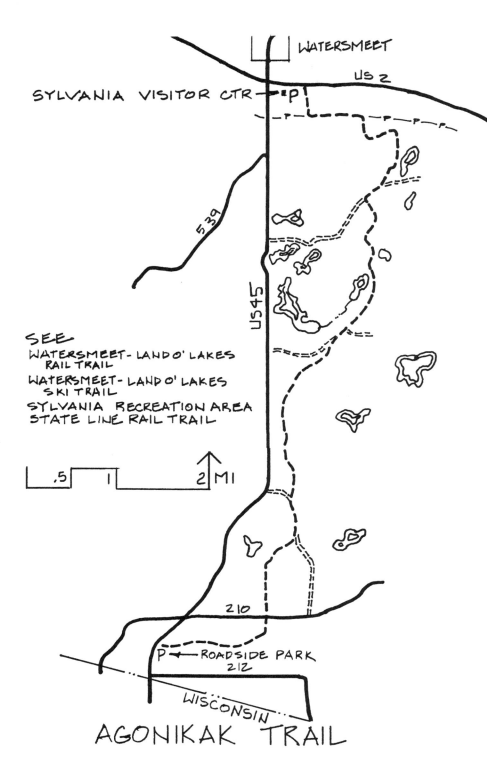

SYLVANIA VISITOR CTR

WATERSMEET

US 2

539

US 45

SEE
WATERSMEET - LAND O' LAKES
RAIL TRAIL
WATERSMEET - LAND O' LAKES
SKI TRAIL
SYLVANIA RECREATION AREA
STATE LINE RAIL TRAIL

.5   1   2 MI

210

P ← ROADSIDE PARK
212

WISCONSIN

AGONIKAK TRAIL

Agonikak Trail

Watersmeet Ranger District, Ottawa National Forest
Box 276   906-358-4551
Watersmeet, MI 49969   906-358-4756

Recreation Staff Officer, Ottawa National Forest
2100 E. Cloverland Drive   906-932-1330
Ironwood, MI 49938

Michigan Atlas & Gazetteer Location: 97BC7

County Location: Gogebic

Directions To Trailhead:
North trailhead is at .5 mile east of the US2 and US45 intersection
South trailhead is on the west side of US45 about .5 mile north of the Wisconsin border.

Trail Type: Hiking/Walking, Cross Country Skiing, Mountain Biking
Trail Distance: 12 mi   Loops: None   Shortest: NA   Longest: NA
Trail Surface: Natural
Trail Use Fee: None
Method Of Ski Trail Grooming: None
Skiing Ability Suggested: Novice to intermediate
Hiking Trail Difficulty: Easy to moderate
Mountain Biking Ability Suggested: Novice to intermediate
Terrain: Steep 0%, Hilly 0%, Moderate 95%, Flat 5%
Camping: Campgrounds within 5 miles in the national forest

Maintained by the Watersmeet Ranger District, Ottawa National Forest
Sections of this trail are shared with motorized trail users.
This point to point trail can be combined with the Watersmeet -Land 0' Lakes Rail Trail to make a 26 mile loop.
The Watersmeet Ski Trail is not suitable as a return route to Watersmeet for mountain biking because of marsh land and beaver dams throughout the area of the ski trail.
The community of Land O' Lakes is just .5 mile south of the south end of the trail.

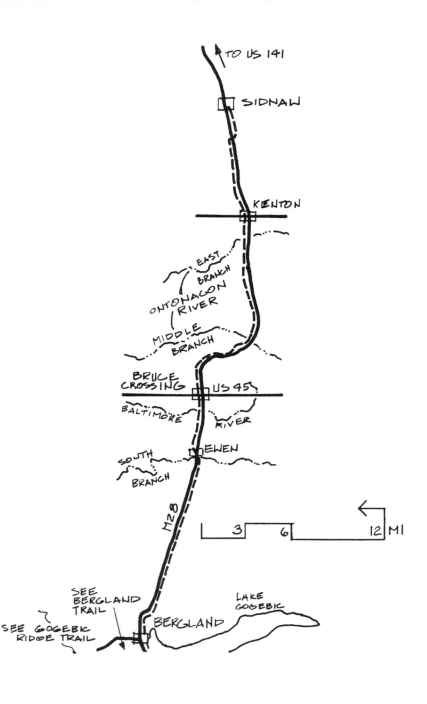

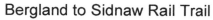

Baraga Forest Area, Copper Country State Forest
PO Box 440
Baraga, MI 49908
906-353-6651

District Forest Manager, Copper Country State Forest
PO Box 440
Baraga, MI 49908
906-353-6651

Michigan Atlas & Gazetteer Location: 97A8,98A12,108D4,109D56,110D2

County Location: Ontonagon, Houghton

Directions To Trailhead:
From Bergland to Sidnaw.
West trailhead - East on M28 from Bergland 2 miles to East Shore Rd.(2 track).
Right(south) .5 miles to the railroad grade. Left on grade (east bound).
East trailhead - Eire St in Sidnaw.

Trail Type: Hiking/Walking, Mountain Biking
Trail Distance: 42.8 mi   Loops: NA   Shortest: NA   Longest: NA
Trail Surface: Gravel, ballast and natural
Trail Use Fee: None
Method Of Ski Trail Grooming: NA
Skiing Ability Suggested: NA
Hiking Trail Difficulty: Moderate
Mountain Biking Ability Suggested: Intermediate
Terrain: 100% Flat
Camping: None on trail but public township campground in Bergland

Maintained by the DNR Forest Mangement Division
Several spectacular bridges along the trail
Agate Falls is within view from the trail. See Agate Falls Trail.

BERGLAND TO SIDNAW RAIL TRAIL

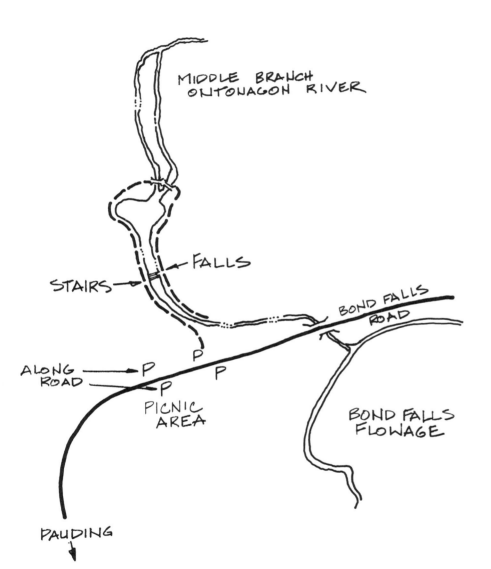

MIDDLE BRANCH
ONTONAGON RIVER

← FALLS

STAIRS →

ALONG → P
ROAD → P

P

P

P

PICNIC
AREA

BOND FALLS
ROAD

BOND FALLS
FLOWAGE

PAUDING

BOND FALLS

Porcupine Mountain Wilderness State Park
412 South Boundary Rd   906-885-5275
Ontonagon, MI 49953

DNR Parks and Recreation Division

517-373-1270

Michigan Atlas & Gazetteer Location: 97A7

County Location: Ontonagon

Directions To Trailhead:
Between Watersmeet and Bruce Crossing on US45, then east from Paulding 4 miles on Bond Falls Rd

Trail Type: Hiking/Walking
Trail Distance: .5 MI   Loops: 1   Shortest: NA   Longest: .5 mi
Trail Surface: Natural
Trail Use Fee: None
Method Of Ski Trail Grooming: NA
Skiing Ability Suggested: NA
Hiking Trail Difficulty: Easy to moderate
Mountain Biking Ability Suggested: NA
Terrain: Steep 0%, Hilly 0%, Moderate 95%, Flat 5%
Camping: Avaialble nearby

Maintained by the DNR Parks and Recreation Division.
Short trail along the creek to the very scenic falls.
No development planned in the near future.

Watersmeet Ranger District, Ottawa National Forest
PO Box 276   906-358-4551
Watersmeet, MI 49969

Recreation Staff Officer, Ottawa National Forest
2100 Cloverland Drive   906-932-1330
Ironwood, Mi 49938

Michigan Atlas & Gazetteer Location: 97B8

County Location: Gogebic, Ontonagon

Directions To Trailhead:
South trailhead - 3 miles east of Watersmeet on the State-Line Rail Trail, then
north on Buck Lake Rd (also known as Peach Lake Rd). The trail veers to the
right from Buck Lake Rd and runs parallel to the road on the east side.   Just
after passing Perch Lake the trail crosses Buck Lake Rd and continues north.
North trailhead - About 2.3 miles east of Paulding on Bond Falls Rd

Trail Type: Hiking/Walking, Mountain Biking
Trail Distance: 12 mi   Loops: NA   Shortest: NA   Longest: NA
Trail Surface: Natural and ballast
Trail Use Fee: None
Method Of Ski Trail Grooming: NA
Skiing Ability Suggested: NA
Hiking Trail Difficulty: Moderate
Mountain Biking Ability Suggested: Advanced
Terrain: Steep 0%, Hilly 0%, Moderate 10%, Flat 90%
Camping: Marion Lake, Bond Falls Flowage and Imp Lake

Managed by the Watersmeet Ranger District, Ottawa National Forest
Rugged rail trail with beaver dam lakes and logging operations.
Used as a snowmobile trail in the winter.
ORV's use this trail as well.

Map labels:

BOND FALLS RD
PAULDING
BOND FALLS FLOWAGE
OTTAWA
LITTLE FALLS
NATIONAL
12 MILES
BEAVER POND
FOREST
US 45
LITTLE FALLS TRAIL
FR 4700
PERCH LAKE
BASS LAKE
STATE-LINE
STATE LINE RAIL TRAIL
RAIL TRAIL
CO RD 208
WATERSMEET
US 2

.5   1   2

LITTLE FALLS TRAIL

Watersmeet Ranger District, Ottawa National Forest
PO Box 276
Watersmeet, MI 49969

906-358-4551
906-358-4756

Recreation Staff Officer, Ottawa National Forest
2100 E. Cloverland Drive
Ironwood, MI 49938

906-932-1330

Michigan Atlas & Gazetteer Location: 97B7

County Location: Gogebic

Directions To Trailhead:
Just southeast of the intersection of US2 and US45

Trail Type: Hiking/Walking, Interpretive
Trail Distance: 1 mi   Loops: 1   Shortest: NA   Longest: 1 mi
Trail Surface: Natural
Trail Use Fee: None
Method Of Ski Trail Grooming: NA
Skiing Ability Suggested: NA
Hiking Trail Difficulty: Easy
Mountain Biking Ability Suggested: NA
Terrain: 100% Flat
Camping: With in 5 miles

Maintained by the Watersmeet Ranger District , Ottawa National Forest
Many other trails nearby.

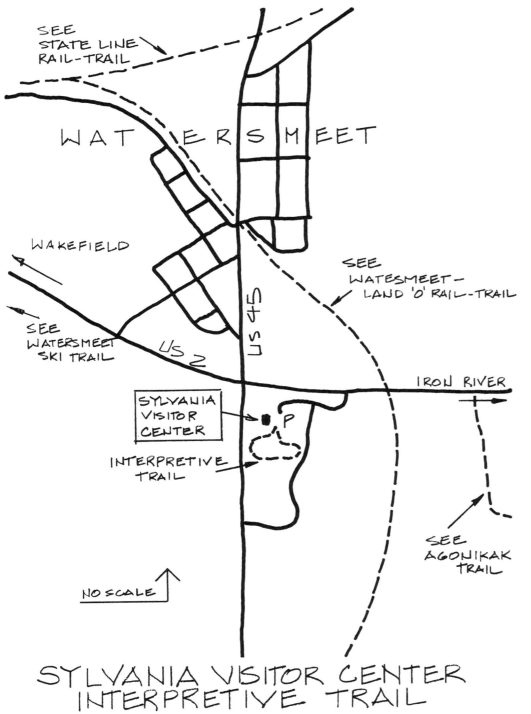

SYLVANIA VISITOR CENTER
INTERPRETIVE TRAIL

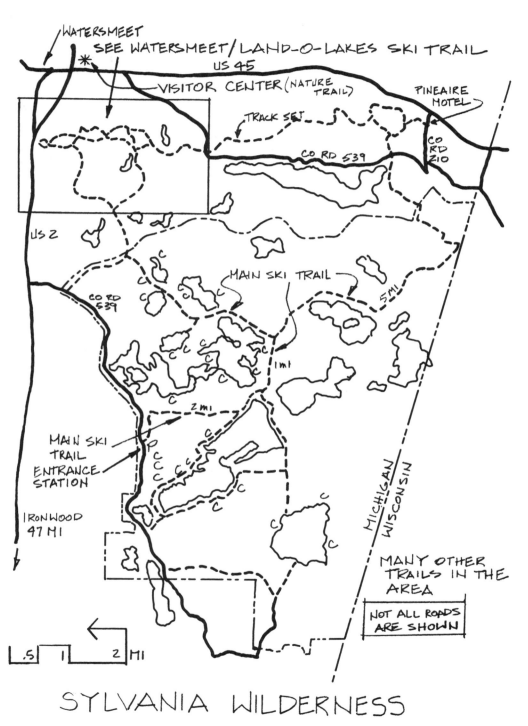

SYLVANIA WILDERNESS

Sylvania Recreation Area
Watersmeet Ranger District, Ottawa National Forest   906-358-4551
Watersmeet , MI 49969

Recreation Staff Officer, Ottawa National Forest
2100 East Cloverland Drive   906-932-1330
Escanaba, MI 49938

Michigan Atlas & Gazetteer Location: 97BC567

County Location: Gogebic

Directions To Trailhead:
4 miles west of Watersmeet to Hwy 535, then south 4 miles(watch for signs) to entrance station where main trailhead is located. Other trailheads further into the Wilderness.

Trail Type: Hiking/Walking, Cross Country Skiing
Trail Distance: 26 mi   Loops: NA   Shortest: NA   Longest: NA
Trail Surface: Natural
Trail Use Fee: None
Method Of Ski Trail Grooming: None
Skiing Ability Suggested: Intermediate to advanced
Hiking Trail Difficulty: Easy to moderate
Mountain Biking Ability Suggested: NA
Terrain: Steep 0%, Hilly 0%, Moderate 80%, Flat 20%
Camping: Available in recreation area. Limited facilites in winter

Maintained by the Watersmeet Ranger District, Ottawa National Forest
Excellent back country skiing.
No ski trail grooming within the wilderness.
Trail connects with the Watersmeet Trail at two locations (skiing only).
Ski shop and lodging in Watersmeet and Land O' Lakes, Wisconsin.
Many lakes in the area provide for excellent canoeing.
Large area of virgin Northern Hardwoods an Hemlock with some Pine.
Excellent area for winter camping.
Winter wildlife include deer, coyote, fisher, martin, squirrels, birds, etc.

Sylvania Outfitters
West US2   906-358-4766
Watersmeet , MI 49969

Watersmeet Ranger District, Ottawa National Forest
PO Box 276   906-358-4551
Watersmeet, MI 49969   906-358-4756

Michigan Atlas & Gazetteer Location: 97BC7

County Location: Gogebic

Directions To Trailhead:
North trailhead - 1 mile west of Watersmeet at Sylvania Outfitters
South trailhead (winter only) - 1 mile north of Land O' Lakes, Wisconsin on US45, then turn west on Co Rd 210, parking on north side near Pineaire Motel.

Trail Type: Hiking/Walking, Cross Country Skiing, Mountain Biking
Trail Distance: 18 mi   Loops: 5   Shortest: 1.7 m i   Longest: 6.2 mi
Trail Surface: Natural
Trail Use Fee: Donations accepted
Method Of Ski Trail Grooming: Track set
Skiing Ability Suggested: Novice to advanced
Hiking Trail Difficulty: Easy to difficult
Mountain Biking Ability Suggested: Intermediate to advanced
Terrain: Steep 0%, Hilly 15%, Moderate 85%, Flat 0%
Camping: Campground available nearby and wilderness camping permitted

Maintained by Sylavnia Outfitters in cooperation with the Ottawa National Forest
Ski shop, warming area, rentals, lessons available at Sylavnia Outfitters.
Two trails connect to the Sylvania Wilderness trail system.
Accomodations and food available in Watersmeet, contact the Chamber of Commerce or Sylvania Outfitters for information.
Generally the southbound travel is uphill with northbound travel being downhill. However, because of the trail layout, the uphill climbs are not difficult and are interrupted with downhill sections.
Danger Hill is 160 feet in elveation above the ski shop.
Trails are marked for skiing only.
Mountain biking is limited to the north 12 miles.
The south 6 miles are very wet during the summer.

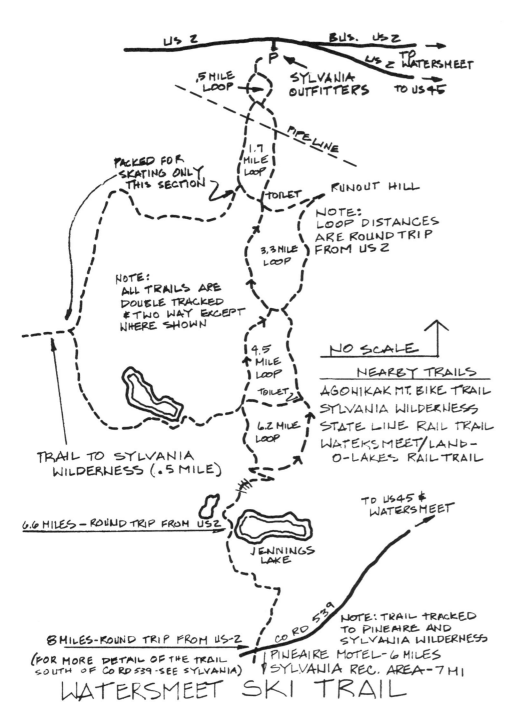

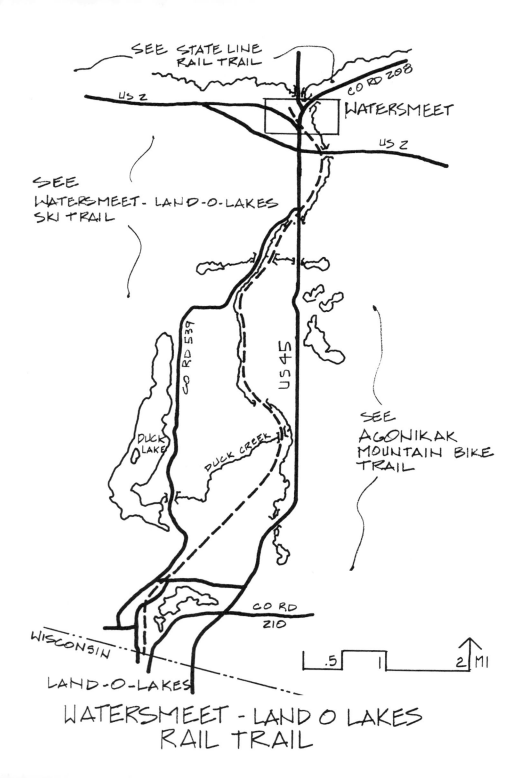

SEE STATE LINE
RAIL TRAIL

US 2

CO RD 208

WATERSMEET

US 2

SEE
WATERSMEET - LAND-O-LAKES
SKI TRAIL

CO RD 539

US 45

DUCK
LAKE

DUCK CREEK

SEE
AGONIKAK
MOUNTAIN BIKE
TRAIL

CO RD
210

WISCONSIN

LAND-O-LAKES

.5   1   2 MI

WATERSMEET - LAND O LAKES
RAIL TRAIL

Watersmeet Ranger District, Ottawa National Forest
PO Box 276   906-358-4551
Watersmeet, MI 49969

Recreation Staff Officer, Ottawa National Forest
2100 E. Cloverland Drive   906-932-1330
Ironwood, MI 49969

Michigan Atlas & Gazetteer Location: 97BC7

County Location: Gogebic

Directions To Trailhead:
From Land O' Lakes Wisconsin to Watersmeet Michigan on the west side of
US45

Trail Type: Hiking/Walking, Mountain Biking
Trail Distance: 8 mi   Loops: NA   Shortest: NA   Longest: NA
Trail Surface: Ballast and natural
Trail Use Fee: None
Method Of Ski Trail Grooming: None
Skiing Ability Suggested: Novice
Hiking Trail Difficulty: Easy
Mountain Biking Ability Suggested: novice
Terrain: 100% Flat
Camping: None along the trail, but neaby

Maintained by the Watersmeet Ranger District, Ottawa National Forest
ORV's and snowmobiles shares this trail
Use in conjunction with the Agonikak Trail to make a loop mountain bike trail

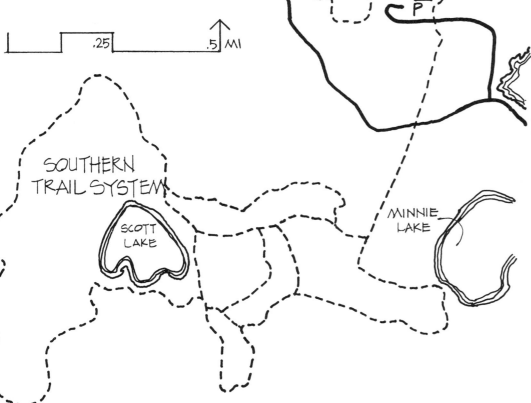

NORTHERN TRAIL SYSTEM

COUNTY ROAD 424

IRON RIVER 0 MILES

.25 .5 MI

SOUTHERN TRAIL SYSTEM

SCOTT LAKE

MINNIE LAKE

P

GEORGE YOUNG RECREATION COMPLEX

George Young Recreation Complex
PO Box 457
Iron River, MI 49935

906-265-3401

Michigan Atlas & Gazetteer Location: 98D4

County Location: Iron

Directions To Trailhead:
Between Iron River and Crystal Falls on Co Rd 424 on Chicagon Lake

Trail Type: Hiking/Walking, Cross Country Skiing, Mountain Biking, Interpretive
Trail Distance: 30 km   Loops: Many   Shortest: Longest:
Trail Surface: Natural
Trail Use Fee: Yes
Method Of Ski Trail Grooming: Track set
Skiing Ability Suggested: Novice to advanced
Hiking Trail Difficulty: Easy to moderate
Mountain Biking Ability Suggested: Novice to advanced
Terrain: Steep 15%, Hilly 15%, Moderate 40%, Flat 30%
Camping: None

Complete recreational complex including 18 hole golf course, ski and mountain
bike trails, indoor pool, sauna and spa and meeting rooms.
Bike and ski rentals available on site.
Write for brochure

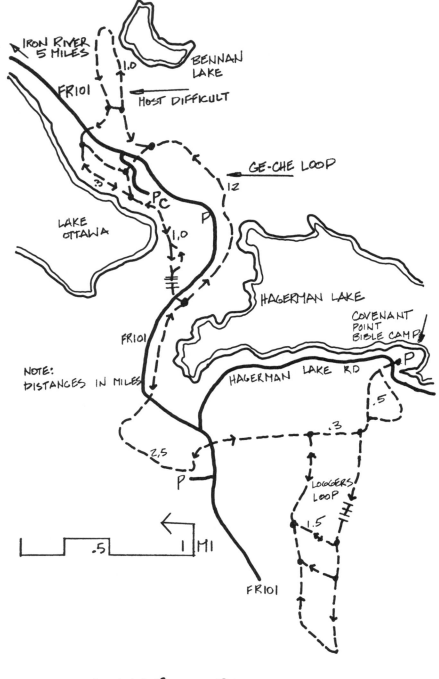

Iron River
5 miles

FR 101

BENNAN LAKE

1.0

MOST DIFFICULT

GE-CHE LOOP

.3

12

PC

P

1.0

LAKE OTTAWA

HAGERMAN LAKE

COVENANT POINT BIBLE CAMP

FR 101

NOTE: DISTANCES IN MILES

HAGERMAN LAKE RD

P

.5

.3

2.5

P

LOGGERS LOOP

1.5

.5   1 MI

FR 101

LAKE OTTAWA RECREATION AREA

Iron River Ranger District, Ottawa National Forest
801 Adams St.   906-265-5139
Iron River, MI 49935

Covenant Point Bible Camp
Hagerman Lake   906-265-2117
Iron River, MI 49935

Michigan Atlas & Gazetteer Location: 98D23

County Location: Iron

Directions To Trailhead:
West trailhead - 8 miles SW of Iron River on US2/M73, then north on Hagerman Lake Rd. to Covenant Point Bible Camp
East trailhead - 3 miles SW of Iron River on US2 M73 to FR 101, then right to Lake Ottawa National Forest campground

Trail Type: Hiking/Walking, Cross Country Skiing
Trail Distance: 10+ mi   Loops: 4   Shortest: Longest:
Trail Surface: Natural
Trail Use Fee: Donations accepted to pay for grooming at trailheads
Method Of Ski Trail Grooming: Track set
Skiing Ability Suggested: Novice to intermediate
Hiking Trail Difficulty: Easy to moderate
Mountain Biking Ability Suggested: NA
Terrain: Steep 5%, Hilly 5%, Moderate 40%, Flat 50%
Camping: Summer camping available at the National Forest campground

Maintained by the Covenant Point Bible Camp in cooperation with the Ottawa National Forest, Iron River Ranger District.
Rentals and group accomodations available from the Covenant Point Bible Camp.
Groomed occasionally but not the entire system all of the time.
Call them if more information is desired.

Ski Brule/Ski Homestead, Att. Bruce Clark
397 Brule Mountain Rd.   906-265-4957
Iron River, MI 49935   800-362-7853

Michigan Atlas & Gazetteer Location: 98D3

County Location: Iron

Directions To Trailhead:
6 miles SW of Iron River between M189 and M73. Follow signs from both M189 and M73 to the ski area. Trailhead is at the Ski Brule Lodge.

Trail Type: Hiking/Walking, Cross Country Skiing
Trail Distance: 23 km   Loops: 5   Shortest: Longest:
Trail Surface: Natural
Trail Use Fee: Yes
Method Of Ski Trail Grooming: Single track set with skating lane
Skiing Ability Suggested: Novice to advance
Hiking Trail Difficulty: Easy to moderate
Mountain Biking Ability Suggested: NA
Terrain: Steep 5%, Hilly 15%, Moderate 30%, Flat 50%
Camping: None

Privately operated alpine and nordic ski resort
Instruction, lodging, restaurant, ski shop and snack bar are available.
A very nice trail system for all levels of skill. Shelters along trails Site of the Brule River Run ski race held in January. Pig roast every Thursday and Saturday nights at the Homestead
Horse back riding, ATB riding and white water rafting trips available in summer months.

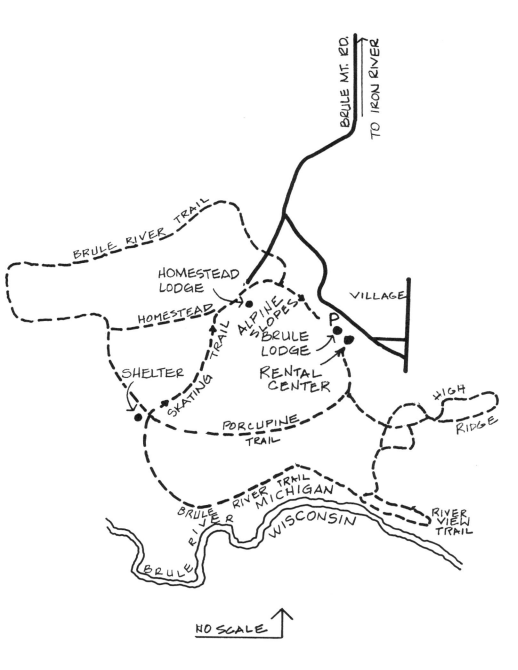

SKI BRULE

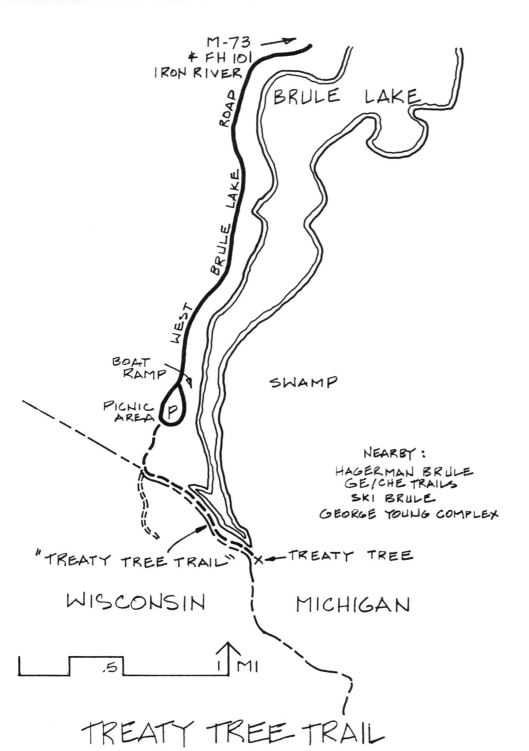

Iron River Ranger District, Ottawa National Forest
801 Adams
Iron River, MI 49935

906-265-5139

Recreation Staff Officer, Ottawa National Forest
2100 E. Cloverland Drive
Ironwood, MI 49938

906-932-1330

Michigan Atlas & Gazetteer Location: 98D2

County Location: Iron

Directions To Trailhead:
West of Iron River M73 to BOttawa Lake Rd to West Brule Lake Rd to Stateline Recreation Area

Trail Type: Hiking/Walking
Trail Distance: .2 mi   Loops: NA   Shortest: NA   Longest: NA
Trail Surface: Natrual
Trail Use Fee: None
Method Of Ski Trail Grooming: None
Skiing Ability Suggested: NA
Hiking Trail Difficulty: Easy
Mountain Biking Ability Suggested: NA
Terrain: Steep 0%, Hilly 0%, Moderate 5%, Flat 95%
Camping: At nearby Lake Ottawa Recreation Area

Maintained by the Iron River Ranger District, Ottawa National Forest

Bewabic State Park
1933 US2 West
Crystal Falls, MI 49920

906-875-3324

DNR Parks and Recreation Division

517-373-1270

Michigan Atlas & Gazetteer Location: 99D5

County Location: Iron

Directions To Trailhead:
4 miles west of Crystal Falls on US2

Trail Type: Hiking/Walking, Cross Country Skiing, Interpretive
Trail Distance: 2 mi   Loops: 1   Shortest: Longest: 2 mi
Trail Surface: Natural
Trail Use Fee: None, but vehicle entry fee required
Method Of Ski Trail Grooming: Packed
Skiing Ability Suggested: Novice
Hiking Trail Difficulty: Easy
Mountain Biking Ability Suggested: NA
Terrain: Rolling to hilly
Camping: Campground available in park from May 15th to October 15th

Maintained by the DNR Parks and Recreation Division
Some ski trail sections use unplowed campground roads
Iron Range and StateLine Rail Trails very nearby.
Ski Brule, Lake Ottawa Recreation Area and Lake Mary Plains Pathway in
vicinity.

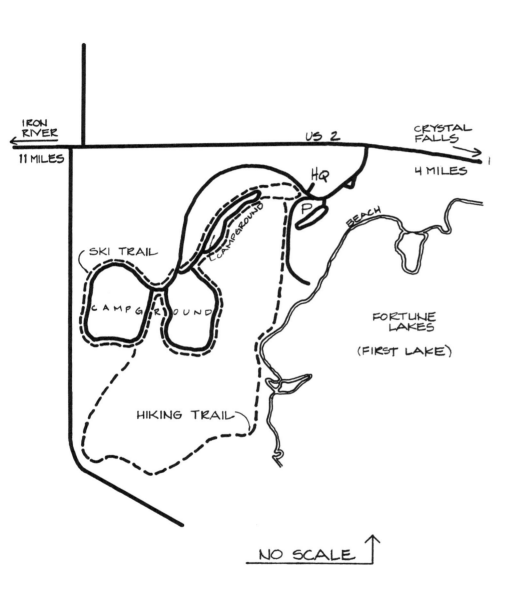

BEWABIC STATE PARK

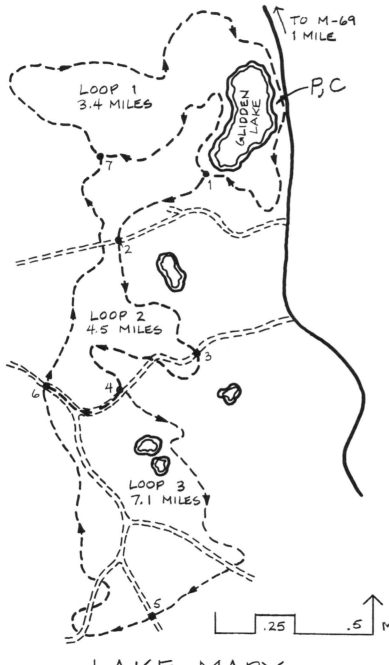

LAKE MARY
PLAINS PATHWAY

Crystal Falls Forest Area, Copper Country State Forest
1420 US2 West
Crystal Falls, MI 49920
906-875-6622

District Forest Manager, Copper Country State Forest
US41 North, PO Box 440
Baraga, MI 49908
906-353-6651

Michigan Atlas & Gazetteer Location: 99D7

County Location: Iron

Directions To Trailhead:
4 miles west of Crystal Falls on M69, then south on Lake Mary Plains Rd. 1 mile to trailhead at Glidden Lake State Forest Campground

Trail Type: Hiking/Walking, Cross Country Skiing, Mountain Biking
Trail Distance: 7+ mi   Loops: 3   Shortest: 3.4 mi Longest: 6.2 mi
Trail Surface: Natural
Trail Use Fee: None
Method Of Ski Trail Grooming: Track set
Skiing Ability Suggested: Novice & expert trails *
Hiking Trail Difficulty: Moderate
Mountain Biking Ability Suggested: Easy to moderate
Terrain: Steep 0%, Hilly 5%, Moderate 45%, Flat 50%
Camping: Campground at trailhead

Maintained by the DNR Forest Management Division
Forest fire occoured in an area that the trail passes through
Because of the hills, none of the trails area rated intermediate
Other contacts:
        DNR Forest Management Division Office, Lansing, 517-373-1275
        DNR Forest Management Region Office, Marquette, 906-228-6561

Silver Lake Trail

Silver Lake Resort, Inc.
N13 195   906-542-7195
Channing, MI 49815

Michigan Atlas & Gazetteer Location: 99C8

County Location: Dickinson

Directions To Trailhead:
On M95, 5 miles north of Channing and north of Iron Mountain

Trail Type: Hiking/Walking, Mountain Biking, Interpretive
Trail Distance: 8 mi   Loops: 2   Shortest: 2 mi   Longest: 6 mi
Trail Surface: Natural
Trail Use Fee: None
Method Of Ski Trail Grooming: Not known
Skiing Ability Suggested: Novice
Hiking Trail Difficulty: Easy
Mountain Biking Ability Suggested: Novice
Terrain: Steep 0%, Hilly 0%, Moderate 20%, Flat 80%
Camping: Campground at the trailhead

Maintained by the Silver Lake Resort, Inc.
30 site campground, 2 cabins, gift shop and gas station on site.

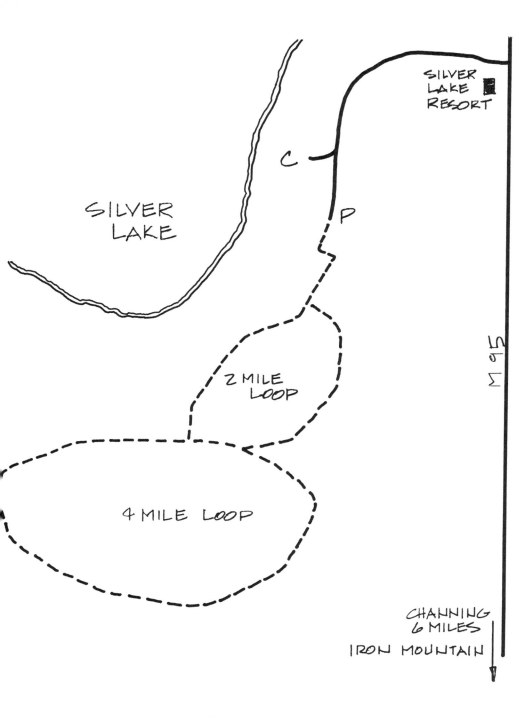

SILVER LAKE RESORT

SILVER LAKE

C

P

M 95

2 MILE LOOP

4 MILE LOOP

CHANNING
6 MILES

IRON MOUNTAIN

SILVER LAKE TRAIL

Ishpeming/Negaunee Chamber of Commerce
661 Palms Ave   906-486-4841
Ishpeming, MI 49849

United States Ski Hall of Fame

Ishpeming, MI 49849

Michigan Atlas & Gazetteer Location: 100A3

County Location: Marquette

Directions To Trailhead:
On the south side of Ishpeming via Jasper St south off Bus M28, then right   on Hill St. to the parking lot. Trailhead is not signed

Trail Type: Cross Country Skiing
Trail Distance: 12.5 km   Loops: 5   Shortest: 3.5 km Longest: 10.5 km
Trail Surface: Natural
Trail Use Fee: Yes, daily and season passes available
Method Of Ski Trail Grooming: Track set   SKATING NOT PERMITTED
Skiing Ability Suggested: Intermediate to expert
Hiking Trail Difficulty: NA
Mountain Biking Ability Suggested: NA
Terrain: Steep 20%, Hilly 60%, Moderate 20%, Flat 0%
Camping: None

Maintained by the Ishpeming Ski Club on Cleveland Cliffs Co. property
Absolutely one of the finest ski trail systems in the state.
Connected to the Suicide Bowl system with two separate 3 km trails.
Originally developed by Norman Juhola of Ishpeming. Connected to the Suicide Bowl Trails to make a 23 km loop. Groomed regularly.

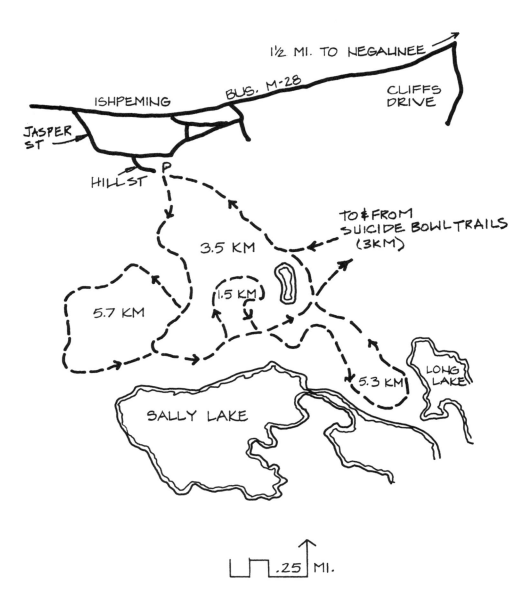

1½ MI. TO NEGAUNEE

ISHPEMING   BUS. M-28   CLIFFS DRIVE

JASPER ST

HILL ST   P

3.5 KM

TO & FROM SUICIDE BOWL TRAILS (3KM)

5.7 KM   1.5 KM

5.3 KM   LONG LAKE

SALLY LAKE

.25 MI.

CLEVELAND CROSS COUNTRY SKI TRAIL

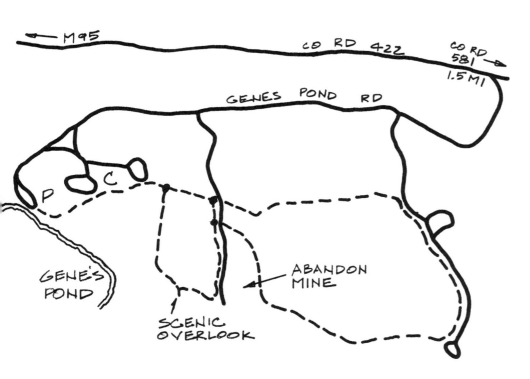

Norway Forest Area, Copper Country State Forest
PO Box 126   906-563-9247
Norway, MI 49870

District Forest Manager, Copper Country State Forest
PO Box 440   906-353-6651
Baraga, MI 49908

Michigan Atlas & Gazetteer Location: 100D12

County Location: Dickinson

Directions To Trailhead:
At Gene's Pond SFCG. 6.5 miles north of Theodore on Co Rd 581 & 422

Trail Type: Hiking/Walking, Interpretive
Trail Distance: 2.3 mi   Loops: 1   Shortest: NA   Longest: 2.3 mi
Trail Surface: Natural
Trail Use Fee: None
Method Of Ski Trail Grooming: NA
Skiing Ability Suggested: NA
Hiking Trail Difficulty: Easy
Mountain Biking Ability Suggested: NA
Terrain: Steep 0%, Hilly 0%, Moderate 95%, Flat 5%
Camping: Campground at the trailhead

Maintained by the DNR Forest Mangement Divsion
Scenic overlook along the trail

GENES POND PATHWAY

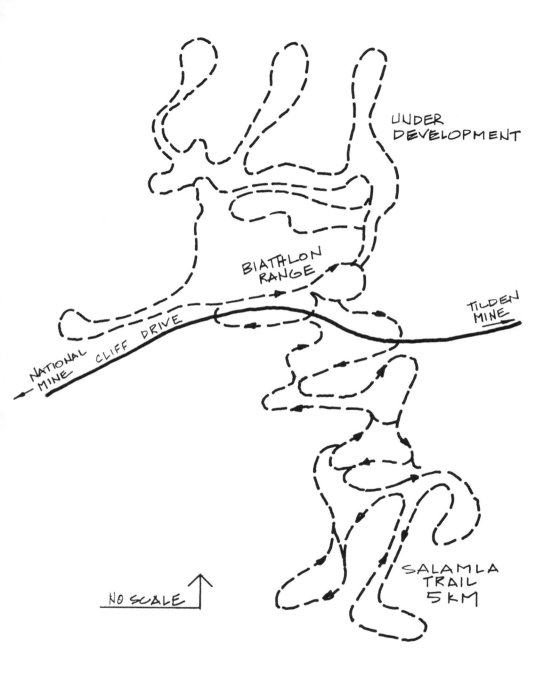

UNDER
DEVELOPMENT

BIATHLON
RANGE

TILDEN
MINE

NATIONAL MINE CLIFF DRIVE

SALAMLA
TRAIL
5 KM

NO SCALE

Michigan Biathlon Association
Rte 3, Box 1024
National Mine, MI 49865

906-486-6706
800-544-4321

Ishpeming Chamber of Commerce
661 Palms Ave
Ishpeming, MI 49849

906-486-4841

Michigan Atlas & Gazetteer Location: 100A3

County Location: Marquette

Directions To Trailhead:
At National Mine on Co. Rd. 476 3 miles south of US41. From westbound US41 in Ishpeming, proceed 1 mile west to yellow blinker, turn south on Lakeshore Dr.,, then proceed .4 mile to Washington St, turn right(west) and proceed 2.7 miles to National Mine (unmarked). Trailhead is 200 feet west on road to Tilden Mine (just south of A-frame)

Trail Type: Hiking/Walking, Cross Country Skiing, Mountain Biking
Trail Distance: 10 km   Loops: 10   Shortest: 1.1 km Longest: 5 km
Trail Surface: Natural
Trail Use Fee: Donations accepted to maintain the trail
Method Of Ski Trail Grooming: Groomed for skating
Skiing Ability Suggested: Novice to advanced
Hiking Trail Difficulty: Moderate
Mountain Biking Ability Suggested: Intermediate to advanced
Terrain: Steep 50%, Hilly 44%, Moderate 51%, Flat 1%
Camping: None in the area

Built and maintained by the Michigan Biathlon Association.
The A-frame is the warming house with showers and toilets.
Very significant elevation changes on trail system.
Few signs to trailhead or on trail.
Ask for directions at A-frame.
Most of the trail is groomed for skating.

NATIONAL MINE SKI AREA

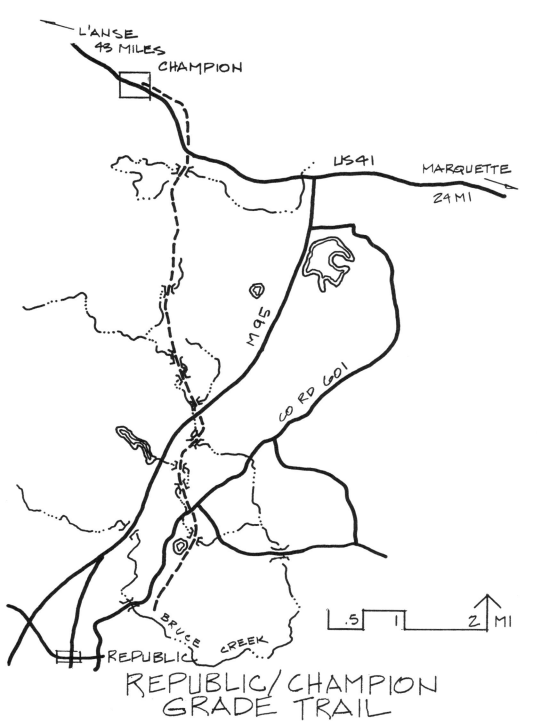

Ishpeming Forest Area, Escanaba River State Forest
1985 US41 West
Ishpeming, MI 49849   906-485-1031

District Forest Manager, Escanaba River State Forest
6833 US2,41 and M35
Gladstone, MI 49837   906-786-2351

Michigan Atlas & Gazetteer Location: 100A1,112D1

County Location: Marquette

Directions To Trailhead:
North trailhead - Behind Mini-Mart in Champion
South trailhead - Bruce Creek Bridge, 1.6 miles south of Co Rd 601. Take Co Rd 601 north out of Republic about 2 miles to the trail crossing

Trail Type: Mountain Biking
Trail Distance: 7.5 mi   Loops: NA   Shortest: NA   Longest: NA
Trail Surface: Natural and ballast
Trail Use Fee: None
Method Of Ski Trail Grooming: NA
Skiing Ability Suggested: NA
Hiking Trail Difficulty: NA
Mountain Biking Ability Suggested: Easy
Terrain: 100% Flat
Camping: None

Maintained by the DNR Forest Management Division
This is a rail trail.
Generally wet with eleven bridges.
Ponds, lakes, creeks, rivers beaver ponds, bogs and other wet features along and on this trail.
Used as a snowmobile trail in the winter.

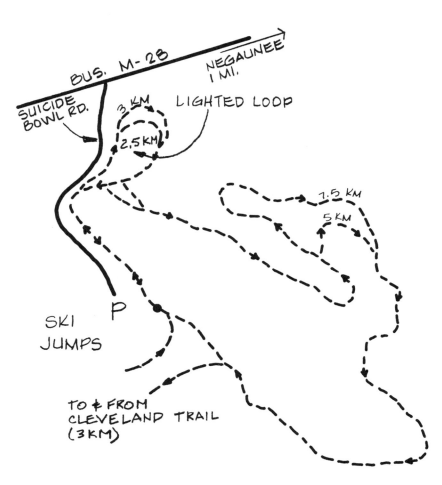

NO SCALE

SUICIDE BOWL

Ishpeming Chamber of Commerce
661 Palms Ave   906-486-4841
Ishpeming, MI 49849

Ski Hall of Fame
                                                   906-485-6323
Ishpeming, MI 49849

Michigan Atlas & Gazetteer Location: 100A4

County Location: Marquette

Directions To Trailhead:
Between Ishpeming and Nagaunee on Business M28

Trail Type: Cross Country Skiing
Trail Distance: 12 km   Loops: 4   Shortest: Longest:
Trail Surface: Natural
Trail Use Fee: Yes, available at the Chamber of Commerce
Method Of Ski Trail Grooming: Track set with skating lane
Skiing Ability Suggested: Novice to advanced
Hiking Trail Difficulty: NA
Mountain Biking Ability Suggested: NA
Terrain: Steep 15%, Hilly 25%, Moderate 35%, Flat 25%
Camping: Available in the area

Maintained by the Ishpeming Ski Club, founded in 1887.
Site of many events for both skiing and jumping.
Connected to Cleveland Trail with two separate one way 3 km trails.
One of the finest ski trail systems in the state.
Originally designed by Norman Juhola of Ishpeming.
Connected to the Cleveland Ski Trail to make a 23 km loop.
Groomed weekly as needed. Individual, family and season memberships available.
Site of 5 ski jumps (10, 20, 30, 50 & 70 meters) 2.5 km lighted trail.

WEST
BRANCH
ESCANABA
RIVER

McGREGOR CREEK

P

C

TRAIL LENGTH
1.4 MI.

COUNTY ROAD 581

← RALPH 6 MI.

.125 .25 MI.

Norway Forest Area, Copper Country State Forest
US2 West, PO Box 126
Norway, MI 49870

906-563-9248

District Forest Manager, Copper Country State Forest
PO Box 440
Baraga, MI 49908

Michigan Atlas & Gazetteer Location: 100C23

County Location: Dickinson

Directions To Trailhead:
At West Branch SFCG.
7 miles north of Ralph on Co Rd 581

Trail Type: Hiking/Walking, Interpretive
Trail Distance: 1.4 mi   Loops: 1   Shortest: NA   Longest: 1.4 mi
Trail Surface: Natural
Trail Use Fee: None
Method Of Ski Trail Grooming: NA
Skiing Ability Suggested: NA
Hiking Trail Difficulty: Easy
Mountain Biking Ability Suggested: NA
Terrain: Steep 0%, Hilly 0%, Moderate 95%, Flat 5%
Camping: Campground at trailhead.

Maintained by the DNR Forest Mangement Division

WEST BRANCH PATHWAY

Gwinn Forest Area, Escanaba River State Forest
410 West M35   906-346-9201
Gwinn, MI 49841

District Forest Manager, Escanaba River State Forest
US2/41 & M35, PO Box 445   906-786-2351
Gladstone, MI 49837

Michigan Atlas & Gazetteer Location: 101C5

County Location: Marquette

Directions To Trailhead:
5 miles SW of Gwinn on Co Rd 557 at the Anderson Lake Campground. From Gwinn take M35 2.5 miles to CR557, then south for 2.5 miles to the pathway

Trail Type: Hiking/Walking, Cross Country Skiing, Mountain Biking, Interpretive
Trail Distance: 6 mi   Loops: 4   Shortest: 2 mi   Longest: 4.3 mi
Trail Surface: Natural
Trail Use Fee: None, donations accepted for ski trail gooming
Method Of Ski Trail Grooming: None
Skiing Ability Suggested: Novice to intermediate
Hiking Trail Difficulty: Easy
Mountain Biking Ability Suggested: Novice to intermediate
Terrain: Steep 10%, Hilly 15%, Moderate 10%, Flat 65%
Camping: Campground at trailhead

Maintained by the DNR Forest Management Division
Ski trails don't include the 2 mile interpretive trail round the two lakes and do require skiing on the access road to the campground.
The 2 mile interpretive trail around Flack Lakes is not suitable for skiing. This trail has 10 interpreted locations.
Other contacts:
        DNR Forest Management Division Office, Lansing, 517-373-1275
        DNR Forest Management Region Office, Marquette, 906-228-6561

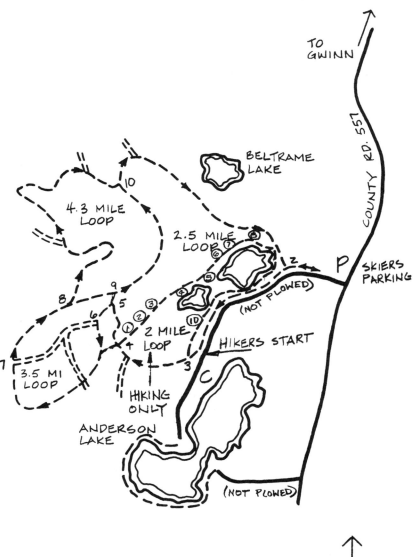

TO GWINN

COUNTY RD. 557

BELTRAME LAKE

4.3 MILE LOOP

2.5 MILE LOOP

10

8   9   5

6   3   4

7   2   1

3.5 MI LOOP

2 MILE LOOP

HIKING ONLY

ANDERSON LAKE

(NOT PLOWED)

SKIERS PARKING

P

HIKERS START

(NOT PLOWED)

NO SCALE

ANDERSON LAKE PATHWAY

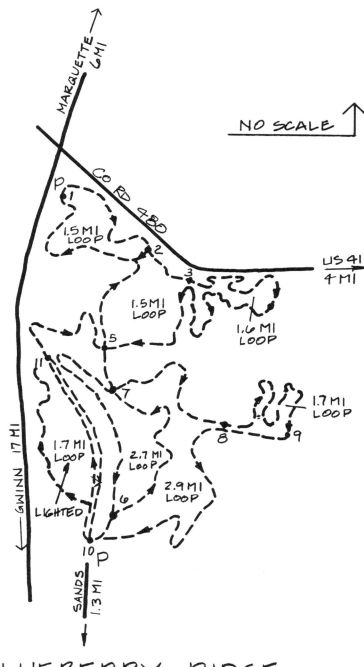

BLUEBERRY RIDGE
PATHWAY

Ishpeming Forest Area, Escanaba River State Forest
Box 632, Teal Lake Road   906-485-1031
Ishpeming, MI 49849

Marquette Field Office, Escanaba River State Forest
110 Ford Rd.   906-249-1497
Marquette, MI 49849

Michigan Atlas & Gazetteer Location: 101A5

County Location: Marquette

Directions To Trailhead:
6 miles south of Marquette on Co Rd 553 at Co Rd 480

Trail Type: Hiking/Walking, Cross Country Skiing, Mountain Biking
Trail Distance: 12 mi   Loops: 5   Shortest: 1.5 mi Longest: 2.9 mi
Trail Surface: Natrual
Trail Use Fee: None, but donations accepted for ski trail grooming
Method Of Ski Trail Grooming: Track set with skating lanes
Skiing Ability Suggested: Novice to advanced
Hiking Trail Difficulty: Easy
Mountain Biking Ability Suggested: Novice to intermediate
Terrain: Steep 20%, Hilly 20%, Moderate 40%, Flat 20%
Camping: Campgrounds available nearby in Marquette area

Maintained by the DNR Forest Management Division
Trail originally designed for skiing, but can be used for hiking and mountain biking.
This trail is always groomed exceptionally well.
Very popular and heavily used Marquette area ski trail.
Used by NMU as a nordic training site.
The northern 2 loops are generally flat with some hills.
The southern 3 loops are generally hilly and used by the racers for training.
Donations are needed to fund the grooming operation.
Many other trails in the area including the North Country Trail and Little Presque Isle Tract trails including several more trails for skiing.

Laughing Whitefish Falls Scenic Site

Van Riper State Park
PO Box 66
Champion, MI 498144

906-339-4461

DNR Parks and Recreation Division

517-373-1270

Michigan Atlas & Gazetteer Location: 101A8

County Location: Alger

Directions To Trailhead:
Between Munising and Marquette north of M94 at Sundell about 3.5 miles to parking lot

Trail Type: Hiking/Walking, Cross Country Skiing
Trail Distance: 1.5 mi   Loops: NA   Shortest: NA   Longest: NA
Trail Surface: Natural
Trail Use Fee: None
Method Of Ski Trail Grooming: None
Skiing Ability Suggested: Intermediate to advanced
Hiking Trail Difficulty: Moderate to difficult
Mountain Biking Ability Suggested: NA
Terrain: Steep 10%, Hilly 30%, Moderate 40%, Flat 20%
Camping: None

Maintained by the DNR Parks and Recreation Division
North end of trail connects with the North Country Trail - Munising
The falls are one of the most picturesque in the state.

NORTH COUNTRY TRAIL
MUNISING

NORTH COUNTRY TRAIL

LAUGHING WHITEFISH RIVER

TRAIL

FALLS

P

M94
3.5 MILES

.5   1 MI

LAUGHING WHITEFALLS SCENIC SITE

Maple Lane Touring Center
124 Kreiger Dr.   906-942-7662
Skandia, MI 49885

Ron Stenfors
PO Box 83   906-942-7230
Skandia, MI 49885

Michigan Atlas & Gazetteer Location: 101A67

County Location: Marquette

Directions To Trailhead:
15 miles south of Marquette via US41 to Skandia, then right on Kreiger Dr. for .2 mile to touring center on the right

Trail Type: Cross Country Skiing
Trail Distance: 11 km   Loops: 4   Shortest: 2 km   Longest: 5 km
Trail Surface: Natural
Trail Use Fee: Yes
Method Of Ski Trail Grooming: Track set as needed
Skiing Ability Suggested: Novice to intermediate
Hiking Trail Difficulty: Easy to moderate
Mountain Biking Ability Suggested: NA
Terrain: Steep 2%, Hilly 18%, Moderate 80%, Flat 20%
Camping: None

Privately operated nordic ski area.
Ski shop, rentals, warming area and snack bar is available.
Snowshoe rentals.
Ski repair and maintenance available and waxing area provided.
A small but well designed and groomed trail system that is a lot of fun Mostly forested trails. Within 10 minutes of fine food and lodging.
Ski school on weekends.
Ski season is from December through March

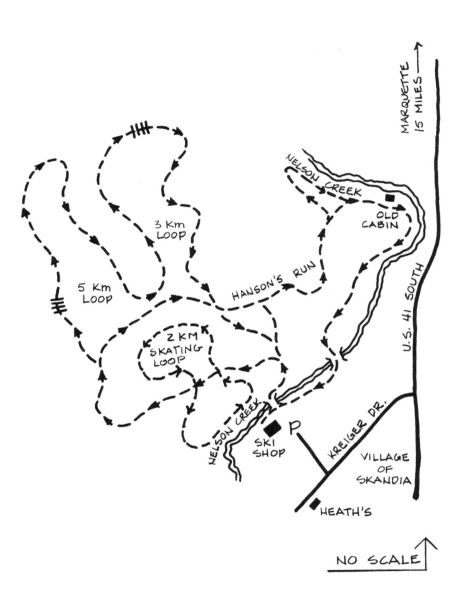

MAPLE LANE TOURING CENTER

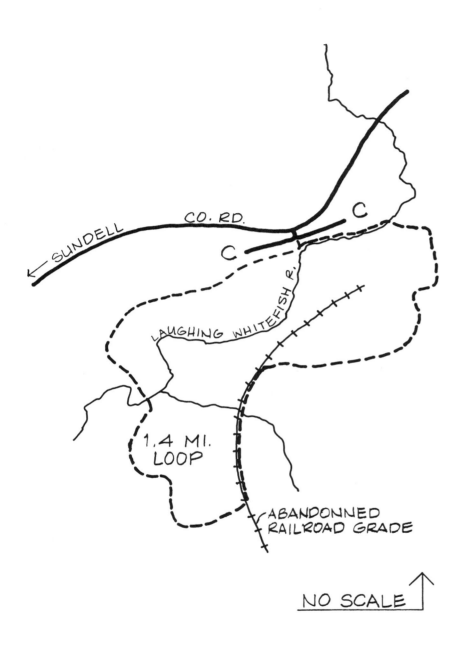

NO SCALE

TYOGA HISTORICAL PATHWAY

Ishpeming Forest Area, Escanaba River State Forest
1985 US 41 West   906-485-1031
Ishpeming, MI 49849

District Forest Manager, Escanaba River State Forest
6833 US41/2 & M35   906-786-2351
Gladstone, MI 49837

Michigan Atlas & Gazetteer Location: 101A8

County Location: Alger

Directions To Trailhead:
Between Marquette and Munising on M28
Trailhead - North on Deerton Rd from M28 toward Laughing Whitefish Falls
State Forest Campground. Pass the Laughing Whitefish Falls State Scenic Site
and continue north several miles to the campground.

Trail Type: Hiking/Walking, Interpretive
Trail Distance: 1.4 mi   Loops: 1   Shortest: Longest:
Trail Surface: Natural
Trail Use Fee: None
Method Of Ski Trail Grooming: NA
Skiing Ability Suggested: NA
Hiking Trail Difficulty: Moderate
Mountain Biking Ability Suggested: NA
Terrain: Steep 0%, Hilly 25%, Moderate 10%, Flat 55%
Camping: Campground at trailhead

Maintained by the DNR Forest Management Division
Developed as a interperative trail with 22 stations explaining the logging days of
the town known as Tyoga and the Tyoga Lumber Company.
Portions of the trail will be wet in the spring and fall.
The North Country Trail, when completed, will pass only a few miles south of the
pathway.
Other contacts:
          DNR Forest Management Region Office, Marquette, 906-228-6561
          DNR Forest Management Division Office, Lansing. 517-373-1275

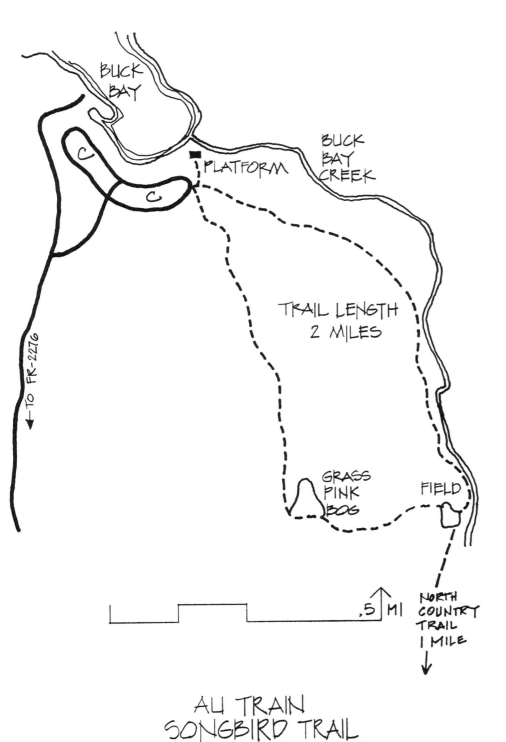

Munising Ranger District, Hiawatha National Forest
RR 2, Box 400   906-387-2512
Munising, MI 49862

Forest Supervisor, Hiawatha National Forest
2727 N. Lincoln Rd   906-786-4062
Escanaba, MI 49829

Michigan Atlas & Gazetteer Location: 102A2

County Location: Alger

Directions To Trailhead:
At the Au Train Lake National Forest Campground located at the south end of
Au Train Lake.
Trailhead - From M28 south 4 miles on H-03 to FR 2276. East on FR 2276 to FR
2596, then north 1 mile to the campground. Trailhead is at the east end of the
campground.

Trail Type: Hiking/Walking
Trail Distance: 2 mi   Loops: 1   Shortest: NA   Longest: 2 mi
Trail Surface: Natural
Trail Use Fee: None
Method Of Ski Trail Grooming: NA
Skiing Ability Suggested: NA
Hiking Trail Difficulty: Easy
Mountain Biking Ability Suggested: NA
Terrain: 100% Flat
Camping: Campground on the site

Maintained by the Hiawatha Nattional Forest
Campground trail along the Buck Bay Creek.
Connector trail to the North Country Trail - Munising
Many other National Forest and National Lakeshore trails in the Munising area.

Munising Ranger District, Hiawatha National Forest
RR 2, Box 400   906-387-2512
Munising, MI 49862

Forest Supervisor, Hiawatha National Forest
2727 N. Lincoln Rd.   906-786-4062
Escanaba, MI 49829

Michigan Atlas & Gazetteer Location: 102C4

County Location: Alger and Schoolcraft

Directions To Trailhead:
Take M28 south from Munising 4 miles to Wetmore, then south 11 miles on H13 (FH13) to the Moccasin Lake Picnic Area where the trailhead is located.

Trail Type: Hiking/Walking, Cross Country Skiing, Mountain Biking
Trail Distance: 11.7 km   Loops: 1   Shortest: NA   Longest: 11.7 km
Trail Surface: Natural
Trail Use Fee: None
Method Of Ski Trail Grooming: Not groomed
Skiing Ability Suggested: Intermediate to advanced
Hiking Trail Difficulty: Easy to moderate
Mountain Biking Ability Suggested: Novice
Terrain: Steep 0%, Hilly 3%, Moderate 40%, Flat 57%
Camping: Pete's Lake and Widewaters NFCG are along the trail

Maintained by the Muising Ranger District, Hiawatha National Forest
Trail is for experienced skiers only since this trail was designed for hiking.
Scenic views, rolling terrain, bridges, lakes and scenic views makes for a very interesting trail. I really enjoyed the trail because of this variety.
This trail is excellent for mountain biking.
See Michigan Cyclist Magazine, winter 1993/94 issue for a review of this trail.
For a nearby trail specially designed for cross country skiing see McKeever Hills Ski Trail which is located adjacent to this trail.

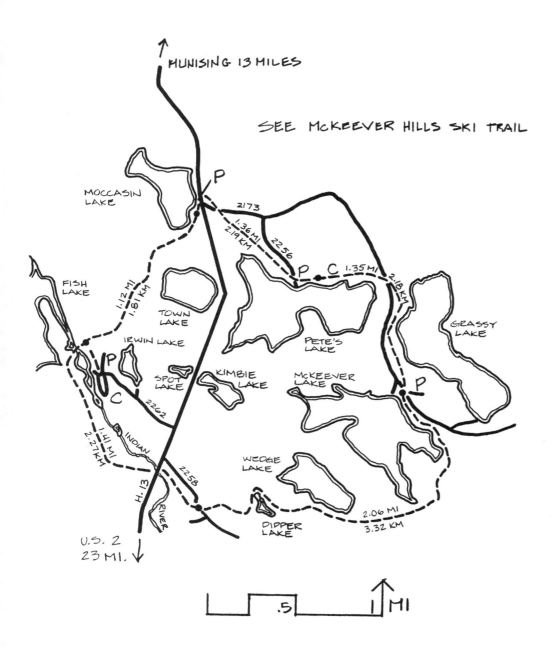

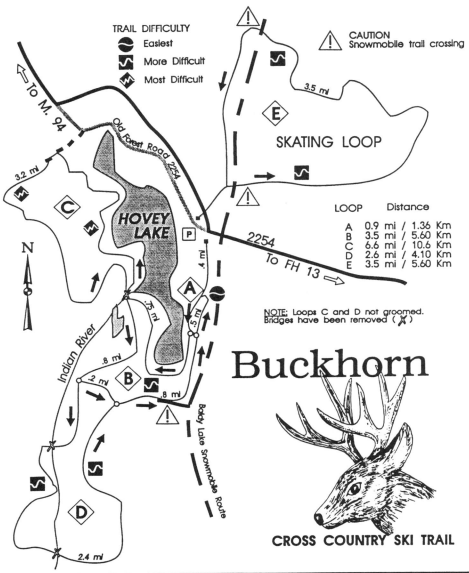

TRAIL DIFFICULTY
- Easiest
- More Difficult
- Most Difficult

CAUTION
Snowmobile trail crossing

SKATING LOOP

HOVEY LAKE

To M. 94

3.2 mi

Old Forest Road 2254

2254

To FH 13

LOOP	Distance
A	0.9 mi / 1.36 Km
B	3.5 mi / 5.60 Km
C	6.6 mi / 10.6 Km
D	2.6 mi / 4.10 Km
E	3.5 mi / 5.60 Km

NOTE: Loops C and D not groomed. Bridges have been removed (X)

3.5 mi

.4 mi

.5 mi

.75 mi

.8 mi

.2 mi

.8 mi

2.4 mi

Indian River

Baby Lake Snowmobile Route

Buckhorn

CROSS COUNTRY SKI TRAIL

HIAWATHA
National Forest

BUCKHORN
CROSS COUNTRY SKI TRAIL

Munising Ranger District, Hiawatha National Forest
RR 2, Box 400
Munising, MI 49862

906-387-2512

Buckhorn Resort and Otter Lake Campground
Buckhorn Rd
Munising, MI 49862

906-387-3559
906-387-4648

Michigan Atlas & Gazetteer Location: 102B3

County Location: Alger

Directions To Trailhead:
At the Buckhorn Resort on FR2254 (Co Rd H-09) between M94 and FH 13 south of Munising on Hovey Lake.

Trail Type: Cross Country Skiing
Trail Distance: 12.55 mi   Loops: 5   Shortest: .9 mi   Longest: 6.6 mmi
Trail Surface: Natural
Trail Use Fee: None
Method Of Ski Trail Grooming: Track set
Skiing Ability Suggested: Novice to advanced
Hiking Trail Difficulty: NA
Mountain Biking Ability Suggested: NA
Terrain: Steep 0%, Hilly 15%, Moderate 25%, Flat 60%
Camping: Private campground at the trailhead and Hovey Lake NFCG .5 mile away

Maintained by the Hiawatha National Forest and the Buckhorn Lodge and Restaurant which is located at the trailhead.
Trail surrounds Hovey Lake and contains loops for all skill levels.

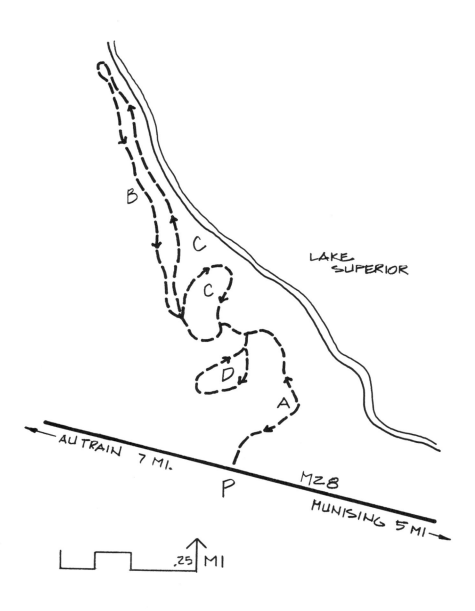

Munising Ranger District, Hiawatha National Forest
RR 2, Box 400   906-387-2512
Munising, MI 49862

Forest Supervisor, Hiawatha National Forest
2727 N. Lincoln Rd   906-786-4062
Escanaba, MI 49829

Michigan Atlas & Gazetteer Location: 102A3

County Location: Alger

Directions To Trailhead:
5 miles west of Munising on M28

Trail Type: Hiking/Walking, Cross Country Skiing
Trail Distance: 3.2 mi   Loops: 3   Shortest: 1.3 mi Longest: 2.3 mi
Trail Surface: Natural in winter
Trail Use Fee: None
Method Of Ski Trail Grooming: None
Skiing Ability Suggested: Novice
Hiking Trail Difficulty: NA
Mountain Biking Ability Suggested: NA
Terrain: Steep 0%, Hilly 0%, Moderate 0%, Flat 100%
Camping: None in winter

Maintained by the Hiawatha Nationa Forest
Trail is the road system of the Bay Furnace National Forest Campground on
Lake Superior.
The campground is not open in the winter.

CHRISTMAS LIGHTED
CROSS COUNTRY SKI TRAIL

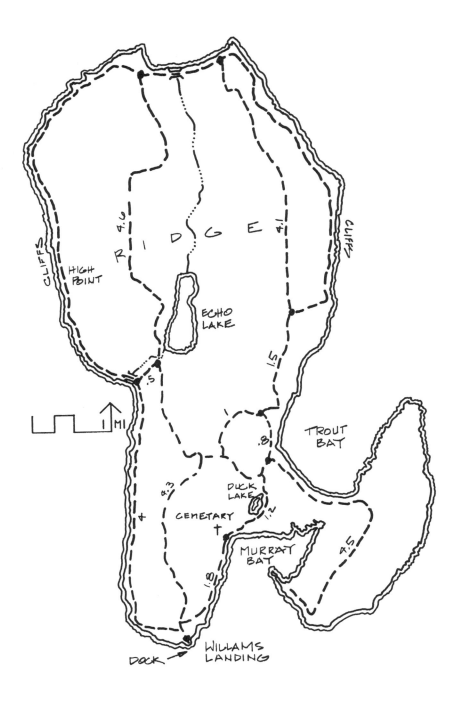

GRAND ISLAND

Munising Ranger District, Hiawatha National Forest
RR 2, Box 400
Munising, MI 49862

906-387-2512

Forest Supervisor, Hiawatha National Forest
2727 N. Lincoln Rd
Escanaba, MI 49829

906-786-4062

Michigan Atlas & Gazetteer Location: 102A34,114D34

County Location: Alger

Directions To Trailhead:
In Lake Superior off shore from Munising. Ferry service from Munising

Trail Type: Hiking/Walking, Cross Country Skiing, Mountain Biking, Interpretive
Trail Distance: 45 km   Loops: Many   Shortest: 2km   Longest: 30 km
Trail Surface: Natural
Trail Use Fee: None
Method Of Ski Trail Grooming: None
Skiing Ability Suggested: Novice to intermediate
Hiking Trail Difficulty: Easy to moderate
Mountain Biking Ability Suggested: Novice
Terrain: Steep 0%, Hilly 0%, Moderate 80%, Flat 20%
Camping: Campgrounds on the island

Maintained by the Munsiing Ranger District, Hiawatha National Forest
A unique island that is well worth the boat ride.
Watch out for bears!
Currently all trails are open to non-motorized trail users. However, the Forest
Service has just completed a development plan for the island. Some trail use
will be restricted. No time table has been established for the implementation of
the plan.

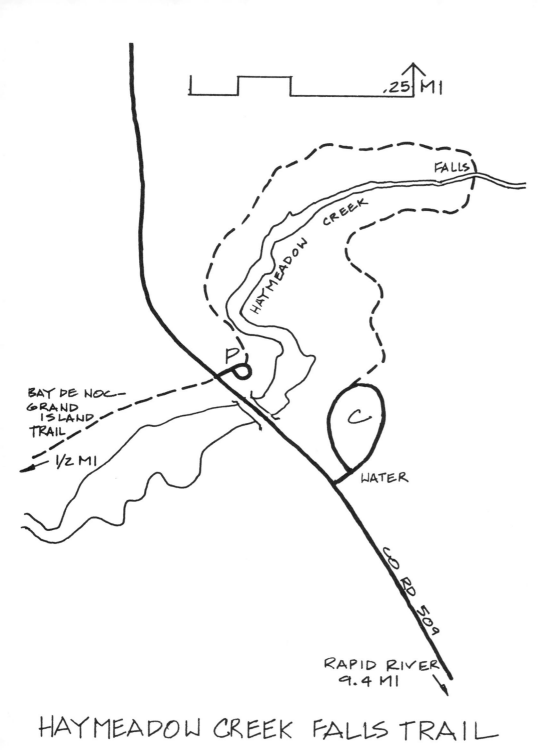

Rapid River Ranger District, Hiawatha National Forest
8181US 2
Rapid River, MI 49878

906-474-6442

Forest Supervisor, Hiawatha National Forest
2727 N. Lincoln Rd
Escanaba, MI 49829

906-786-4062

Michigan Atlas & Gazetteer Location: 102D2

County Location: Delta

Directions To Trailhead:
At the Haymeadow Falls NFCG. From Rapid River take US2 east to Co Rd 509 about 2 miles, then north 9 miles to the campground which will be on the right.

Trail Type: Hiking/Walking
Trail Distance: 1 mi   Loops: 1   Shortest: NA   Longest: 1 mi
Trail Surface: Natural
Trail Use Fee: None
Method Of Ski Trail Grooming: NA
Skiing Ability Suggested: NA
Hiking Trail Difficulty: Easy
Mountain Biking Ability Suggested: NA
Terrain: Steep 0%, Hilly 0%, Moderate 90%, Flat 10%
Camping: Campground at trailhead

Maintained by the Rapid River Ranger District, Hiawatha National Forest
A North Country Spur (.5 mile long) starts near the north trailhead.

HAYMEADOW CREEK FALLS TRAIL

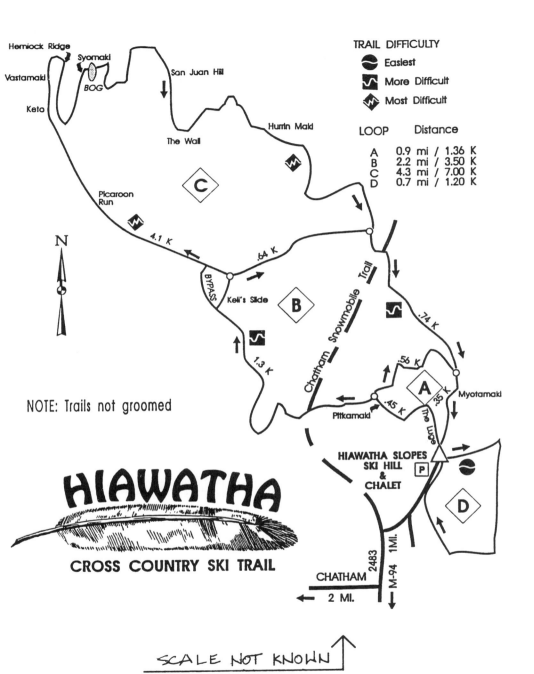

Munising Ranger District, Hiawatha National Forest
RR 2, Box 400
Munising, MI 49862

906-387-3700
906-387-2512

Forest Supervisor, Hiawatha National Forest
2727 N. Lincoln Rd
Escanaba, MI 49829

906-786-4062

Michigan Atlas & Gazetteer Location: 102B1

County Location: Alger

Directions To Trailhead:
Take M28 out of Munising to M94 to FR 2483 (Cemetary Rd), then north 1 mile
to trailhead at small downhill ski area. Trail is 15 miles from Munising.

Trail Type: Hiking/Walking, Cross Country Skiing
Trail Distance: 8.84 mi   Loops: 4   Shortest: .7 mi   Longest: 4.3 mi
Trail Surface: Natural
Trail Use Fee: None
Method Of Ski Trail Grooming: None
Skiing Ability Suggested: Novice to advanced
Hiking Trail Difficulty: Easy to moderate
Mountain Biking Ability Suggested: NA
Terrain: Steep 0%, Hilly 0%, Moderate 50%, Flat 50%
Camping: AuTrain Lake NFCG is 5 miles away

Maintained by the Munising Ranger District, Hiawatha National Forest
Trails may be overgrown in the summer.
At the site of a small local alpine ski area.

Pictured Rocks National Lakeshore
PO Box 40   906-387-3700
Munising, MI 49862

Michigan Atlas & Gazetteer Location: 102A4, 114D4, 115CD5678

County Location: Alger

Directions To Trailhead:
From Munising to Sable Falls west of Grand Marais.
West trailhead - Munising Falls, northeast of Munising.
East trailhead - About 5 miles west of Grand Marais on H58 Other trailheads are all accessible from H58.

Trail Type: Hiking/Walking
Trail Distance: 43 mi   Loops: NA   Shortest: NA   Longest: NA
Trail Surface: Natural
Trail Use Fee: None
Method Of Ski Trail Grooming: NA
Skiing Ability Suggested: NA
Hiking Trail Difficulty: Easy to moderate
Mountain Biking Ability Suggested: NA
Terrain: Steep 0%, Hilly 0%, Moderate 20%, Flat 80%
Camping: 13 backcountry campgounds are along the trail

Maintained by the Pictured Rocks National Lakeshore.
A segment of the North Country Trail.
Permits are required for the backcountry campsites.
30% of the sites are reservable. Only the following locations have drinking water-Munising Falls, Park HQ, Miner's Castle, Miner's Beach, Little Beaver CG,Twelvemile Beach CG, Hurricane River CG and Grand Sable Visitor Center.
Most campgrounds have access to untreated Lake Superior water that must be boiled or treated with a filter.
Some campgrounds have no water available.
Parties of 7 to 20 people must use group backcountry campsites only and must make reservations.
Open fires are prohibited at Chapel and Mosquito CG. Pets are not allowed in the backcountry.
Send for additional information and detailed trail booklet.

SEE NORTH COUNTRY TRAIL-DNR
EAST OF GRAND MARAIS

GRAND MARAIS

M - 77

SEE
GRAND
MARAIS
SKI TRAIL

TRAIL ALONG
ROAD

ADAMS TRAIL

H - 58

SEE
PICTURED ROCKS NATIONAL
LAKESHORE - DAY HIKES

LAKE SUPERIOR

H-58

C

C

C

C

H - 58

H-58

2   4   6 MI

SEE
MUNISING
CROSS COUNTRY
SKI TRAIL

MUNISING

LAKESHORE TRAIL

Munising Ranger District, Hiawatha National Forest
RR 2, Box 400   906-387-3700
Munising, MI 49862

Forest Supervisor, Hiawatha National Forest
2727 N. Lincoln Rd   906-786-4062
Escanaba, MI 49829

Michigan Atlas & Gazetteer Location: 102C4

County Location: Alger

Directions To Trailhead:
Take M28 east from Munising, then south on M94 to FH 13, then south again to the Forest Glen Country Store.
Trail is 13 miles south of Munising.
Park at the country store.

Trail Type: Hiking/Walking, Cross Country Skiing
Trail Distance: 12 km   Loops: 3   Shortest: 1 km   Longest: 7 km
Trail Surface: Natural
Trail Use Fee: None
Method Of Ski Trail Grooming: Track set
Skiing Ability Suggested: Novice to advanced
Hiking Trail Difficulty: Moderate
Mountain Biking Ability Suggested: NA
Terrain: Steep 10%, Hilly 10%, Moderate 50%, Flat 30%
Camping: Neaby at Pete's Lake and Widewaters SFCG

Maintained by the Munising Ranger District, Hiawatha National Forest
Bruno's Run Trail intersects this trail.

LOOP	DISTANCE
A	.3 mi. / .4 km.
B	3.85 mi. / 6.18 km.
C	2.2 mi. / 3.6 km.
Total	6.35 mi. / 10.18 km.

McKEEVER HILLS SKI TRAIL

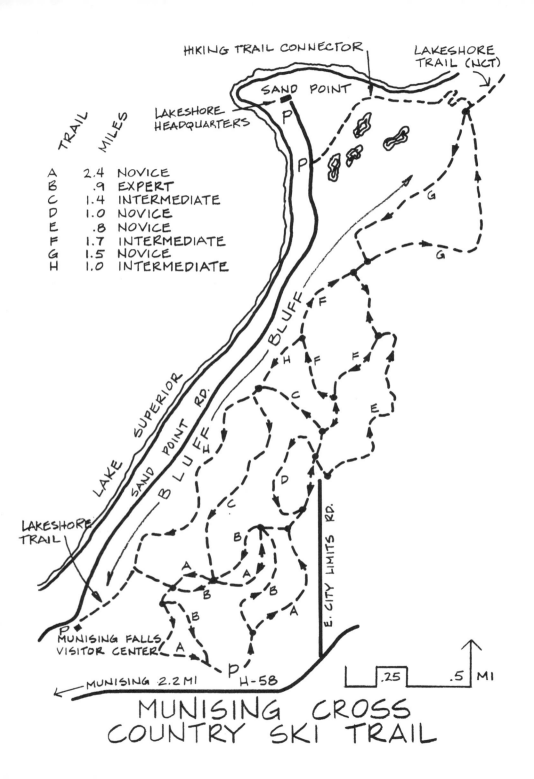

TRAIL MILES

A	2.4	NOVICE
B	.9	EXPERT
C	1.4	INTERMEDIATE
D	1.0	NOVICE
E	.8	NOVICE
F	1.7	INTERMEDIATE
G	1.5	NOVICE
H	1.0	INTERMEDIATE

HIKING TRAIL CONNECTOR

LAKESHORE TRAIL (NCT)

SAND POINT

LAKESHORE HEADQUARTERS

BLUFF

LAKE SUPERIOR

SAND POINT RD.

BLUFF

LAKESHORE TRAIL

E. CITY LIMITS RD.

MUNISING FALLS VISITOR CENTER

MUNISING 2.2 MI   H-58

.25   .5 MI

MUNISING CROSS COUNTRY SKI TRAIL

Pictured Rocks National Lakeshore
PO Box 40   906-387-3700
Munising, MI 49862   906-387-2607

Michigan Atlas & Gazetteer Location: 102A4

County Location: Alger

Directions To Trailhead:
NE of Munising on H58 Trailhead - Take H58 east from the blinking traffic light on M28 in Munising about 2.2 miles to the parking lot on the north side of the road. The left fork is Sand Point Rd. to the the Lakeshore Headquarters.

Trail Type: Hiking/Walking, Cross Country Skiing
Trail Distance: 10.7 mi   Loops: 8   Shortest: Longest:
Trail Surface: Natural
Trail Use Fee: None
Method Of Ski Trail Grooming: Track set twice a week
Skiing Ability Suggested: Novice to advanced
Hiking Trail Difficulty: NA
Mountain Biking Ability Suggested: NA
Terrain: Rolling to hilly
Camping: Campgrounds not open in the winter

Maintained by the Pictured Rocks National Lakeshore
Camping is permitted 200' off the trail Mostly hilly terrain with frozen waterfalls and canyons and some beautiful scenic vistas across Munising Bay to Grand Island.
All trails are well marked and with maps at each intersection Degree of difficulty signs are at the start of each loop.
A well designed and well groomed trail that should not be missed.
A connector trail starts near the Lakeshore Headquarters and ends at the north end of the trail system(not suitable for skiing.
The section of the trail along the cliff is part of the Lakeshore Trail (see separate entry for more detail) which is also part of the North Country Trail.
Pets are not permitted on the trail.
Near the Valley Spur Trail, another great ski trail and many other trails in Alger Co.

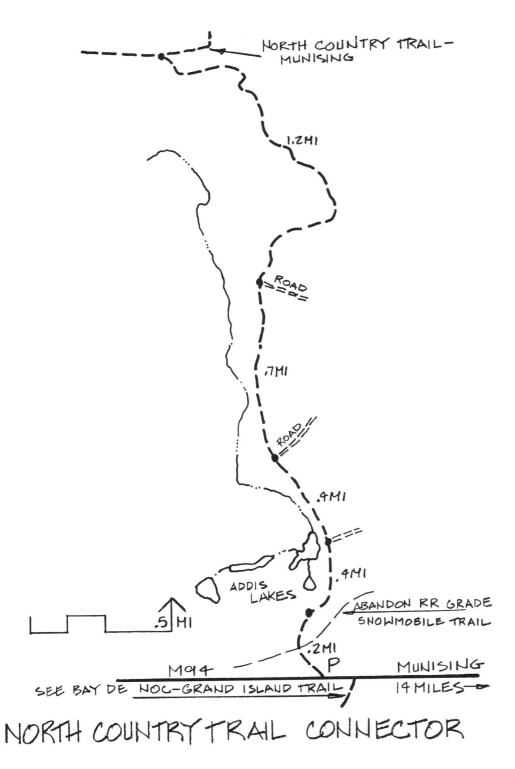

NORTH COUNTRY TRAIL CONNECTOR

Munising Ranger District, Hiawatha National Forest
RR 2, Box 400   906-387-3700
Munising, MI 49862

Forest Supervisor, Hiawatha National Forest
2727 N. Lincoln Rd   906-786-4062
Escanaba, MI 49829

Michigan Atlas & Gazetteer Location: 102B2

County Location: Alger

Directions To Trailhead:
Take M28 east to M94south, then west 9 miles to trailhead at Ackerman Lake

Trail Type: Hiking/Walking
Trail Distance: 5 km   Loops: NA   Shortest: NA   Longest: NA
Trail Surface: Natural
Trail Use Fee: None
Method Of Ski Trail Grooming: NA
Skiing Ability Suggested: NA
Hiking Trail Difficulty: Easy to moderate
Mountain Biking Ability Suggested: NA
Terrain: Steep 0%, Hilly 15%, Moderate 55%, Flat 35%
Camping: Campground at nearby AuTrain Lake NFCG

Maintained by the Munising Ranger District, Hiawatha National Forest
This trail connects the Grand Island -Bay DeNoc Trail to the North Country Trail - Munising.

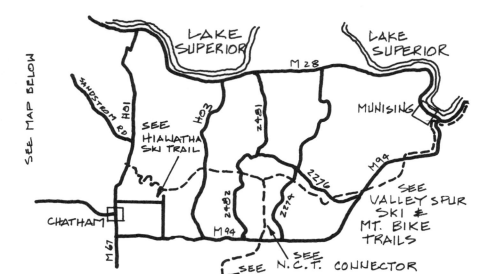

Munising Ranger District, Hiawatha National Forest
RR2, Box 400   906-387-2512
Munising, MI 49862

Forest Supervisor, Hiawatha National Forest
2727 N. Lincoln Rd.   906-786-4062
Escanaba, MI 49829

Michigan Atlas & Gazetteer Location: 102AB123

County Location: Alger

Directions To Trailhead:
Trailhead - SW of Munising 1.5 miles west of M28 on M94, on south side of the road.
Trailhead - On M94 between H05 and H03 at Ackerman Lake.
See North Country Trail Connector.

Trail Type: Hiking/Walking
Trail Distance: 9 mi   Loops: NA   Shortest: NA   Longest: NA
Trail Surface: Natural
Trail Use Fee: None
Method Of Ski Trail Grooming: NA
Skiing Ability Suggested: NA
Hiking Trail Difficulty: Moderate to difficult
Mountain Biking Ability Suggested: NA
Terrain: Steep 0%, Hilly 25%, Moderate 65%, Flat 10%
Camping: Trailside camping is permitted

Maintained by the Munising Ranger District, Hiawatha National Forest Short part of the Valley Spur Ski Trail (2 miles) West end of this section, ends about 3 miles east of H03 road Recommended only for skiers with good winter survival skills.
This trail was not designed for skiing.
Use caution if attempting to ski trail.
Like the entire North Country Trail, is is a point to point trail.
Write the Munising Ranger District for more information
For further information about the North Country Trail, contact the North Country Trail Association, PO Box 311, White Cloud, MI 49349 616-689-1912

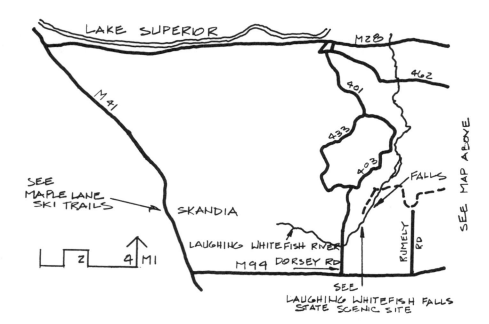

NORTH COUNTRY TRAIL MUNISING

TRAIL NOTES

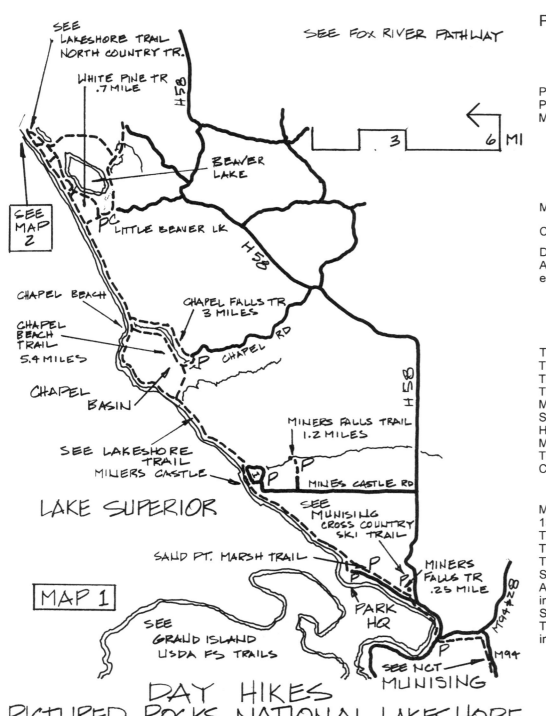

SEE LAKESHORE TRAIL
NORTH COUNTRY TR.

SEE FOX RIVER PATHWAY

WHITE PINE TR
.7 MILE

H 58

BEAVER LAKE

SEE MAP 2

PC
LITTLE BEAVER LK

H 58

CHAPEL BEACH

CHAPEL FALLS TR
3 MILES

CHAPEL
BEACH
TRAIL
5.4 MILES

CHAPEL RD

CHAPEL BASIN

P CHAPEL RD

H 58

MINERS FALLS TRAIL
1.2 MILES

SEE LAKESHORE TRAIL

MINERS CASTLE

P

MINES CASTLE RD

LAKE SUPERIOR

SEE MUNISING CROSS COUNTRY SKI TRAIL

SAND PT. MARSH TRAIL

P

P

MINERS FALLS TR
.25 MILE

MAP 1

SEE GRAND ISLAND USDA FS TRAILS

PARK HQ

M94 & N80

SEE NCT

M94

DAY HIKES
PICTURED ROCKS NATIONAL LAKESHORE

MUNISING

Pictured Rocks National Lakeshore
PO Box 40
Munising, MI 49862

906-387-3700

Michigan Atlas & Gazetteer Location: 102A4,115CD5678

County Location: Alger

Directions To Trailhead:
Along Lake Superior from Munising on the west end to Grand Marais on the east end

Trail Type: Hiking/Walking, Interpretive
Trail Distance: 29.65 mi   Loops: 13   Shortest: .25 mi Longest: .5 mi
Trail Surface: Paved and natural
Trail Use Fee: None
Method Of Ski Trail Grooming: NA
Skiing Ability Suggested: NA
Hiking Trail Difficulty: Easy to moderate
Mountain Biking Ability Suggested: NA
Terrain: Varies with trail
Camping: Several campgrounds are located in the national lakeshore

Maintained by the National Park Service
13 different trails scattered throughout the national lakeshore.
The maps locate the trails and list their trail distances.
The trails are either destination and/or interpretive types.
The two accessible trails are the .25 mile Munising Falls Trail and the .5 mile Sand Point Marsh Trail.
A brochure of describing the day hikes and individual brochures of some individual trails are available from the park.
See also the North Country Trail(Lakeshore Trail), Munising Cross Country Ski Trail, Grand Marais Cross Country Ski Trail, Fox River Pathway and other trails in the area.

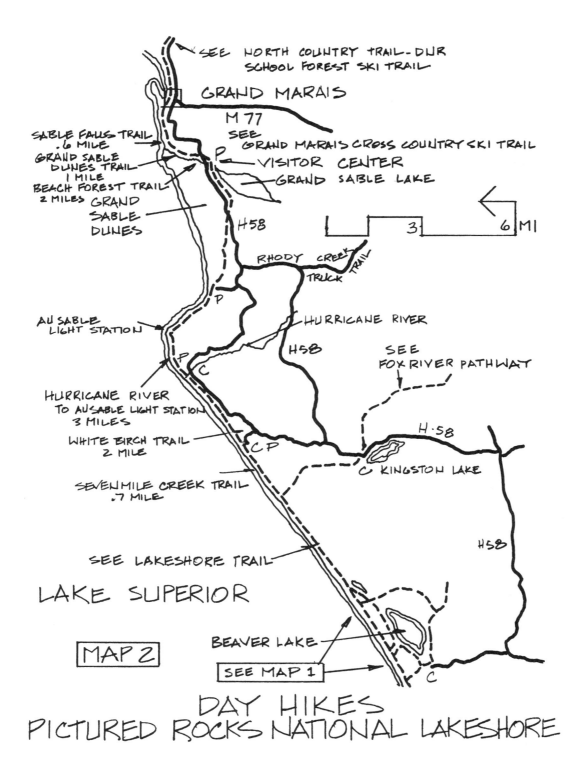

SEE NORTH COUNTRY TRAIL - DNR
SCHOOL FOREST SKI TRAIL

GRAND MARAIS

M 77

SEE
GRAND MARAIS CROSS COUNTRY SKI TRAIL

SABLE FALLS TRAIL
.6 MILE
GRAND SABLE
DUNES TRAIL
1 MILE
BEACH FOREST TRAIL
2 MILES

VISITOR CENTER
GRAND SABLE LAKE

GRAND
SABLE
DUNES

H 58

RHODY CREEK
TRUCK TRAIL

P

AU SABLE
LIGHT STATION

HURRICANE RIVER

H 58

SEE
FOX RIVER PATHWAY

P
C

HURRICANE RIVER
TO AU SABLE LIGHT STATION
3 MILES

WHITE BIRCH TRAIL
2 MILE

H·58

C P

C KINGSTON LAKE

SEVEN MILE CREEK TRAIL
.7 MILE

H 58

SEE LAKESHORE TRAIL

LAKE SUPERIOR

BEAVER LAKE

MAP 2

SEE MAP 1

C

DAY HIKES
PICTURED ROCKS NATIONAL LAKESHORE

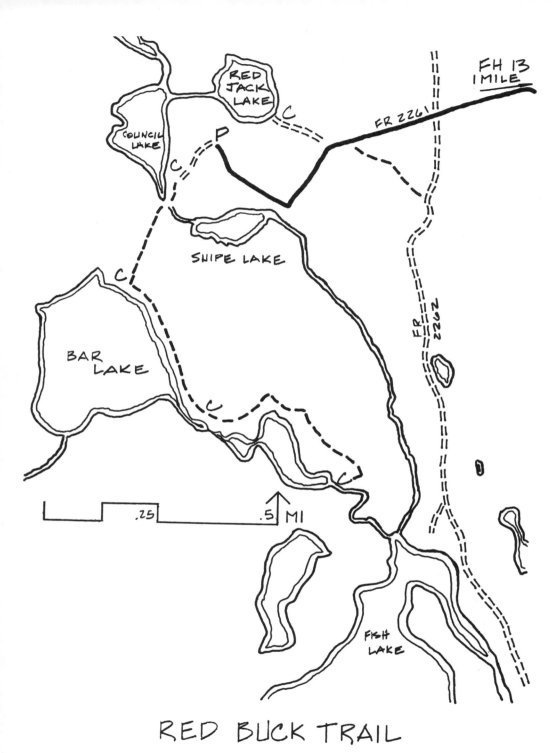

RED BUCK TRAIL

Munising Ranger District, Hiawatha National Forest
RR 2 Box 400   906-387-3700
Munising, Mi 49862   906-387-2512

Forest Supervisor, Hiawatha National Forest
2727 N. Lincoln Rd   906-786-4062
Escanaba, Mi 49829

Michigan Atlas & Gazetteer Location: 102C3

County Location: Alger

Directions To Trailhead:
Take M28 east and FH 13 south 9 miles to Moccasin Lake , then west 1.5 miles
west to Council Lake Primitive Campground. Trailhead is in the campground

Trail Type: Hiking/Walking
Trail Distance: 1.7 km   Loops: NA   Shortest: NA   Longest: NA
Trail Surface: Natural
Trail Use Fee: None
Method Of Ski Trail Grooming: NA
Skiing Ability Suggested: NA
Hiking Trail Difficulty: Easy
Mountain Biking Ability Suggested: NA
Terrain: Steep 0%, Hilly 0%, Moderate 20%, Flat 80%
Camping: At trailhead

Maintained by the Munising Ranger District, Hiawatha National Forest
Bruno's Run Trail and McKeever Hills Trail are very nearby.

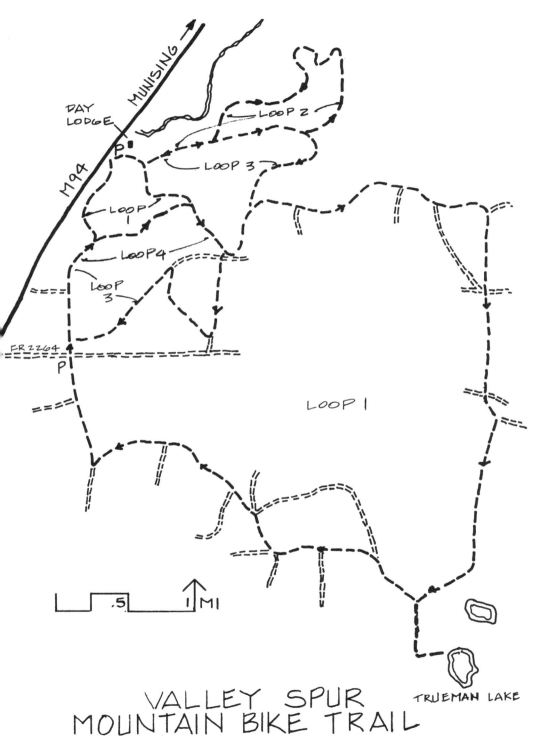

Munising Ranger District, Hiawatha National Forest
RR 2, Box 400
Munising, MI 49862

906-387-3700
906-387-2512

Forest Supervisor, Hiawatha National Forest
2727 N. Lincoln Rd
Escanaba, MI 49829

906-786-4062

Michigan Atlas & Gazetteer Location: 102AB3

County Location: Alger

Directions To Trailhead:
From Munising on M28 to M94 south.
Main trailhead - 5 miles to trailhead at the Valley Spur Ski Trail on the east side of the road.
Second trailhead - about 6.5 miles to FR2264(next to Coalwood Rail Trail), east about .5 mile to trailhead parking.

Trail Type: Hiking/Walking, Mountain Biking
Trail Distance: 15+ mi   Loops: 4   Shortest: 3 mi   Longest: 12 mi
Trail Surface: Natural, single track and 2 track
Trail Use Fee: None
Method Of Ski Trail Grooming: NA
Skiing Ability Suggested: NA
Hiking Trail Difficulty: Easy
Mountain Biking Ability Suggested: Novice to advanced
Terrain: Steep 0%, Hilly 10%, Moderate 50%, Flat 30%
Camping: AuTrain Lake NFCG

Maintained by the Munising Ranger District, Hiawatha National Forest
New trail system developed in 1994.

Route 1 - 12 miles, Novice, gentle grades, mostly woods roads, side trip to Truman Lake
Route 2 - 4 miles, Advanced, very challenging route with steep uphills and downhills
Route 3 - 7.5 miles, Novice, generally flat with one steep hill, last .5 mile is all downhill
Route 4 - 3 miles, Novice, flat, access from second trailhead parking area

These trails are not exclusively for use by mountain bikers. Mountain bikers must share the trail with others.

Open May through November.

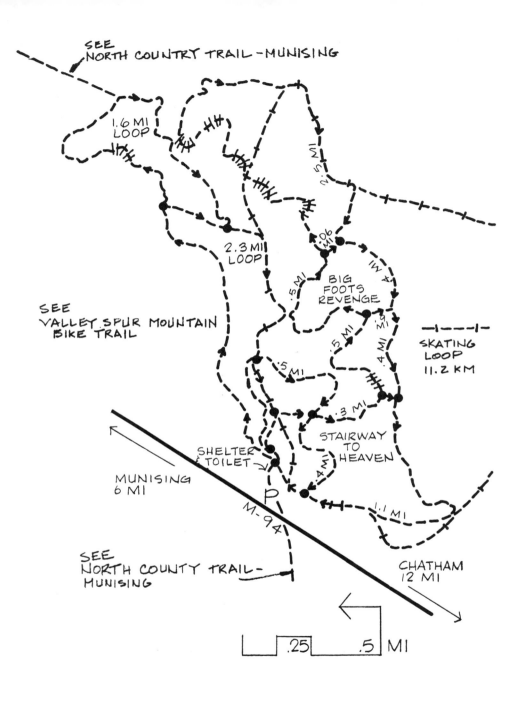

SEE
NORTH COUNTRY TRAIL - MUNISING

1.6 MI
LOOP

2.3 MI
LOOP

.2 MI

SEE
VALLEY SPUR MOUNTAIN
BIKE TRAIL

.06 MI

.4 MI

BIG
FOOTS
REVENGE

.5 MI

.9 MI

.5 MI

.4 MI

SKATING
LOOP
11.2 KM

.5 MI

.3 MI

STAIRWAY
TO
HEAVEN

SHELTER
TOILET

.4 MI

MUNISING
6 MI

P

M-94

SEE
NORTH COUNTRY TRAIL -
MUNISING

CHATHAM
12 MI

1.1 MI

.25 .5 MI

Munising Ranger District, Hiawatha National Forest
RR 2, Box 400   906-387-2512
Munising, MI 49862

Forest Supervisor, Hiawatha National Forest
2727 N. Lincoln Rd.   906-786-4062
Escanaba, MI 49829

Michigan Atlas & Gazetteer Location: 102AB3

County Location: Alger

Directions To Trailhead:
6 miles SW of Munising on M94, to the parking lot on the south side of the road.

Trail Type: Hiking/Walking, Cross Country Skiing, Mountain Biking
Trail Distance: 30 km   Loops: Many   Shortest: 1.5 km Longest: 11 km
Trail Surface: Natural
Trail Use Fee: Yes, for skiing only
Method Of Ski Trail Grooming: Track set
Skiing Ability Suggested: Novice to advanced
Hiking Trail Difficulty: Moderate
Mountain Biking Ability Suggested: Novice to advanced
Terrain: Steep 15%, Hilly 35%, Moderate 30%, Flat 20%
Camping: AuTrain Campground, 7 miles west

Maintained by Munising Ranger District, Hiawatha National Forest
A well designed and groomed ski trail for all abilities.
A large trailhead cabin is open on weekends, with food service and ski rentals.
Outdoor toilet is available at the trailhead.
Forest cover includes hardwoods with conifer-ringed valleys.
Part of the North Country Trail - Munising.
Many other nearby trails.
Uses the same trailhead for the Valley Spur Mountain Bike Trail (see other listing)

VALLEY SPUR SKI TRAIL

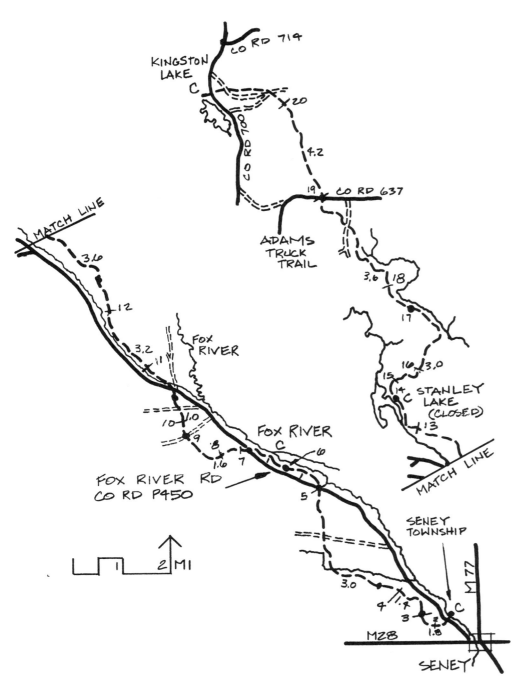

FOX RIVER PATHWAY

Shingleton Forest Area, Lake Superior State Forest
West M28, PO Box 67   906-452-6236
Shingleton, MI 49884

District Forest Manager, Lake Superior State Forest
South M123, PO Box 77   906-239-5131
Newberry, MI 49868

Michigan Atlas & Gazetteer Location: 103A78,104B1,115D78

County Location: Schoolcraft

Directions To Trailhead:
North trailhead - Kingston Lake Campground in Pictured Rocks NLonCo Rd 714 (H58) or Kingston Lake Rd.)
South trailhead - .5 mile north of Seney on Co Rd 450 (Fox River Rd.) at Seney Township Campground

Trail Type: Hiking/Walking, Mountain Biking, Interpretive
Trail Distance: 27.5 mi   Loops: NA   Shortest: NA   Longest: NA
Trail Surface: NA
Trail Use Fee: None
Method Of Ski Trail Grooming: NA
Skiing Ability Suggested: NA
Hiking Trail Difficulty: Moderate to difficult
Mountain Biking Ability Suggested: Novice to intermediate
Terrain: Steep 0%, Hilly 20%, Moderate 40%, Flat 40%
Camping: Four campgrounds available along the trail

Maintained by the DNR Forest Management Division
Not frequently used trail but does pass through some very beautiful and isolated land.
Since the trail is rather isolated, prepare well for the trip because emergency assistance will not be available.
Twenty-one marked locations along the trail provide interesting information about the history of the area.
Recent (1994) information about the condition of the trail is not favorable. The first few miles from the south trail are marked. However farther north the condition is very questionable. Contact the local DNR office listed above regarding current conditions before planning a trip.

Other contacts:
        DNR Forest Management Division Office, Lansing, 517-373-1275
        DNR Forest Management Region Office, Marquette, 906-228-6561

Shingleton Forest Area, Lake Superior State Forest
PO Box 67   906-452-6227
Shingleton, MI 49884

District Forest Manager, Lake Superior State Forest
PO Box 77   906-293-5151
Newberry, MI 49868

Michigan Atlas & Gazetteer Location: 103A6

County Location: Schoolcraft

Directions To Trailhead:
Northeast of Shingleton via north on H15, east on H58, then east on H52, then north on 454, then east on 450

Trail Type: Hiking/Walking

Trail Surface:
Trail Use Fee: None
Method Of Ski Trail Grooming:
Skiing Ability Suggested:
Hiking Trail Difficulty:
Mountain Biking Ability Suggested:
Terrain:
Camping: SFCG at the trailhead

Maintained by the DNR Forest Management Division
Currently under redevelopment (1994)
Contact DNR for current status.

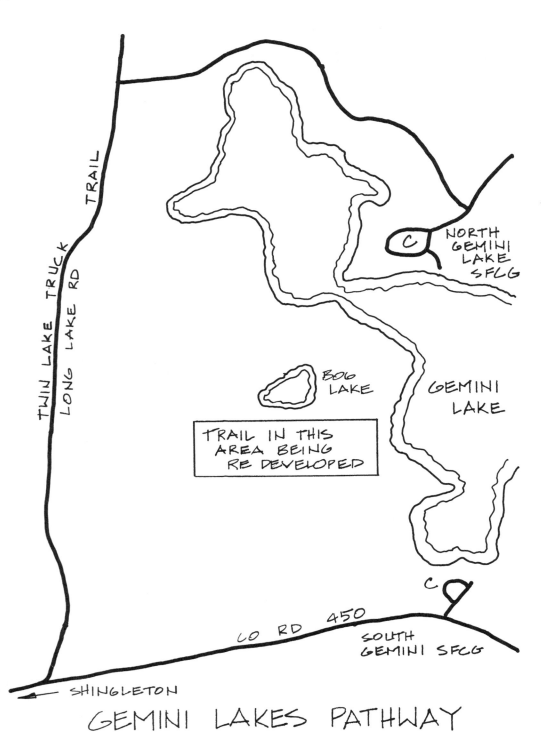

TWIN LAKE TRUCK TRAIL

LONG LAKE RD

NORTH GEMINI LAKE SFCG

BOG LAKE

GEMINI LAKE

TRAIL IN THIS AREA BEING RE DEVELOPED

CO RD 450

SOUTH GEMINI SFCG

← SHINGLETON

GEMINI LAKES PATHWAY

Seney National Wildlife Refuge
HCR2, Box 1   906-586-9851
Seney, MI 49883   906-586-9801

Michigan Atlas & Gazetteer Location: 103BC8,104BC1

County Location: Schoolcraft

Directions To Trailhead:
At Germfask on M77, just north of town.

Trail Type: Hiking/Walking, Cross Country Skiing, Mountain Biking, Interpretive
Trail Distance: 50+ mi   Loops: Many   Shortest: .8 mi   Longest: Long
Trail Surface: Gravel and natural
Trail Use Fee: Yes, vehicle entry fee at headquarters parking area only
Method Of Ski Trail Grooming: None
Skiing Ability Suggested: Novice
Hiking Trail Difficulty: Easy
Mountain Biking Ability Suggested: Novice
Terrain: Steep 0%, Hilly 0%, Moderate 30%, Flat 70%
Camping: None

Maintained by the Fish and Wildlife Service
Warming shelter available
Prohibited for use by ORV's and snowmobiles
Over 95,000 acres containing over 250 species of birds
Bike trails: 4.8 to 12.8 mile loops and greater on gravel dike roads
See also Northern Hardwoods Cross Country Ski Trails
Bike, canoe and ski rentals from Gronback-Northern Outfitters in Germfask
906-586-9801

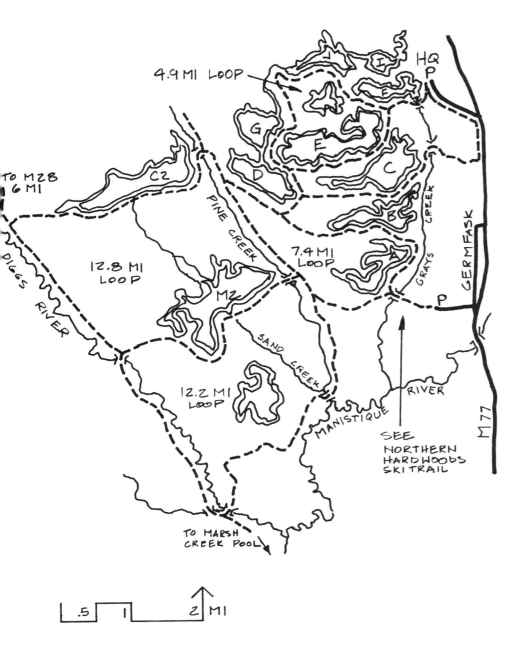

MOUNTAIN BIKE TRAIL
SENEY NATIONAL WILDLIFE REFUGE

SOUTH CURTIS RD.

CURTIS
1 MILE

SPRANG RD.

12
11
10
13
LOOP C
.5 MI
7
9 8
6
5
4 3
LOOP A
0.2 MI
LOOP D
.3 MI
14
1 2
BARRETT RD.
P
LOOP B
.3 MI

.125 MI

BARRETT ROAD SKI TRAILS.

Barrett Rd Cross Country Ski Trails

104

Curtis Area Chamber of Commerce
PO Box 477
Curtis, MI 49820

906-586-3700

Manilak Resort
RR3, Box 2620
Curtis, MI 49820

906-586-3285
or 6690

Michigan Atlas & Gazetteer Location: 104C2

County Location: Mackinac

Directions To Trailhead:
2 miles west and south of Curtis off Main St, then south on S. Curtis Rd and Sprang Rd, then west on Barrett Rd to the end of the road.

Trail Type: Cross Country Skiing
Trail Distance: 1.1 mi   Loops: 4   Shortest: .2 mi   Longest: .5 mi
Trail Surface: Natural
Trail Use Fee: Donations
Method Of Ski Trail Grooming: Skating
Skiing Ability Suggested: Novice
Hiking Trail Difficulty: NA
Mountain Biking Ability Suggested: NA
Terrain: Steep 0%, Hilly 15%, Moderate 25%, Flat 60%
Camping: None

Community maintained trail system.
Follow blue ribbons.
Another ski trail is in the area.

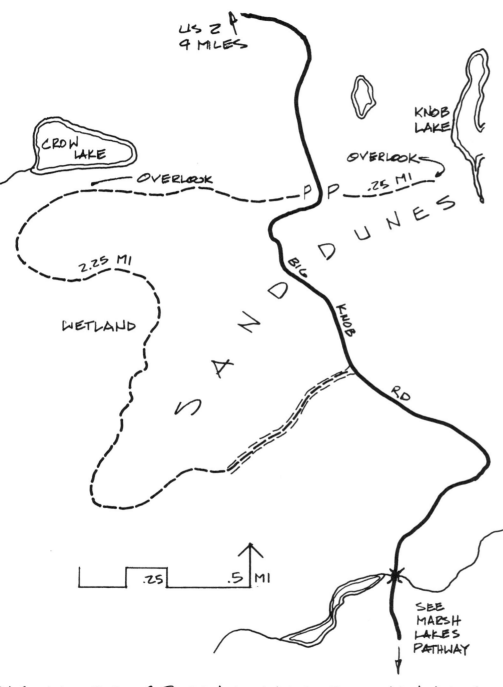

Naubinway Forest Area, Lake Superior State Forest
US2, PO Box 287   906-477-6048
Naubinway, MI 49762

District Forest Manager, Lake Superior State Forest
PO Box 77   906-293-5131
Newberry, MI 49868

Michigan Atlas & Gazetteer Location: 104D4

County Location: Mackinac

Directions To Trailhead:
About 55 miles west of the Mackinac Bridge, then 1.5 miles west of US2 & M123
intersection, then south 4 miles on Big Knob Rd. to the trailhead.

Trail Type: Hiking/Walking
Trail Distance: 2.75 mi   Loops: NA   Shortest: NA   Longest: NA
Trail Surface: Natural
Trail Use Fee: None
Method Of Ski Trail Grooming: NA
Skiing Ability Suggested: NA
Hiking Trail Difficulty: Easy to moderate
Mountain Biking Ability Suggested: NA
Terrain: Steep 20%, Hilly 20%, Moderate 30%, Flat 30%
Camping: On site at the Big Knob SFCG

Maintained by the DNR Forest Management Division
Scenic sand dune trail with 140' high overlook of Knob Lake
A loop route can be taken by using Big Knob Rd for the return trip to the
trailhead.
Marsh Lakes Pathway is nearby.
Other contacts:
    DNR Forest Management Division, Lansing 517-373-1270
    DNR Forest Management Division , Marquette 906-228-6561

BIG KNOB-CROW LAKE PATHWAY

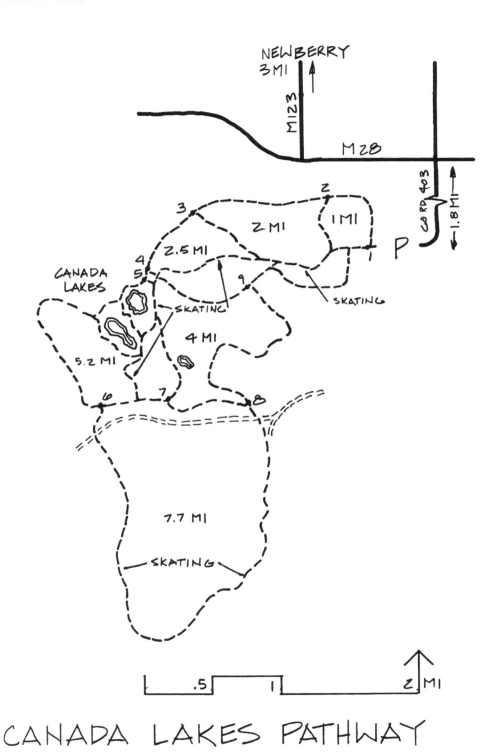

NEWBERRY
3 MI

M123

M28

CO RD 403

1.8 MI

P

2

1 MI

2 MI

3

2.5 MI

4

5

9

SKATING

SKATING

CANADA
LAKES

4 MI

5.2 MI

6

7

8

7.7 MI

SKATING

| .5 | 1 | 2 MI |

CANADA LAKES PATHWAY

Newberry Forest Area, Lake Superior State Forest
PO Box 428   906-293-3293
Newberry, MI 49868

District Forest Manager, Lake Superior State Forest
PO Box 77   906-293-5131
Newberry, MI 49868

Michigan Atlas & Gazetteer Location: 104B4,105B5

County Location: Luce

Directions To Trailhead:
5.5 miles SE of Newberry.
Trailhead - East 1 mile from the Jct of M123 and M28 to Co Rd 403, then south
1.5 miles to the parking lot trailhead.

Trail Type: Hiking/Walking, Cross Country Skiing, Mountain Biking
Trail Distance: 10+ mi   Loops: 6   Shortest: 1 mi   Longest: 7.7 mi
Trail Surface: Natural with sand
Trail Use Fee: Donation accepted at trailhead for grooming trails
Method Of Ski Trail Grooming: Track set
Skiing Ability Suggested: Novice and intermediate
Hiking Trail Difficulty: Easy
Mountain Biking Ability Suggested: Novice
Terrain: Steep 0%, Hilly 10%, Moderate 60%, Flat 30%
Camping: Public and private campgrounds in area

Maintained by the DNR Forest Management Division
Well groomed and very enjoyable skiing trail.
Some sections groomed for skating.
Site of an annual cross country ski race.
Campgrounds: North Country Campground, 4 miles north of Newberry on M123;
Natalie SFCG, 2 miles west of Newberry off Co Rd 405 and 434; KOA
Campground south of Newberry.
Logging museum in Newberry.
Other contacts:
        DNR Forest Manatement Division Office, Lansing, 517-373-1275
        DNR Forest Management Region Office, Marquette, 906-228-6561

Manilak Resort Ski Trails

Manilak Resort
RR3, Box 2620
McMillan, MI 49853

906-586-3285
906-586-6690

Michigan Atlas & Gazetteer Location: 104C3

County Location: Mackinac

Directions To Trailhead:
2 miles north of Curtis on H-33

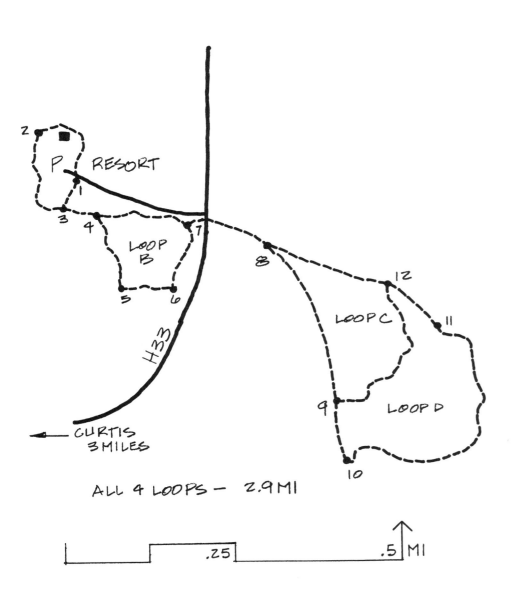

ALL 4 LOOPS — 2.9 MI

Trail Type: Hiking/Walking, Cross Country Skiing
Trail Distance: 2.9 mi   Loops: 4   Shortest: .3 mi   Longest: 1.1 mi
Trail Surface: Natural
Trail Use Fee: None, but donations accepted
Method Of Ski Trail Grooming: Packed
Skiing Ability Suggested: Novice
Hiking Trail Difficulty: NA
Mountain Biking Ability Suggested: NA
Terrain: Steep 0%, Hilly 0%, Moderate 15%, Flat 85%
Camping: None

Privately operated trail system open to the public

MANILAK RESORT
CROSS COUNTRY SKI TRAILS

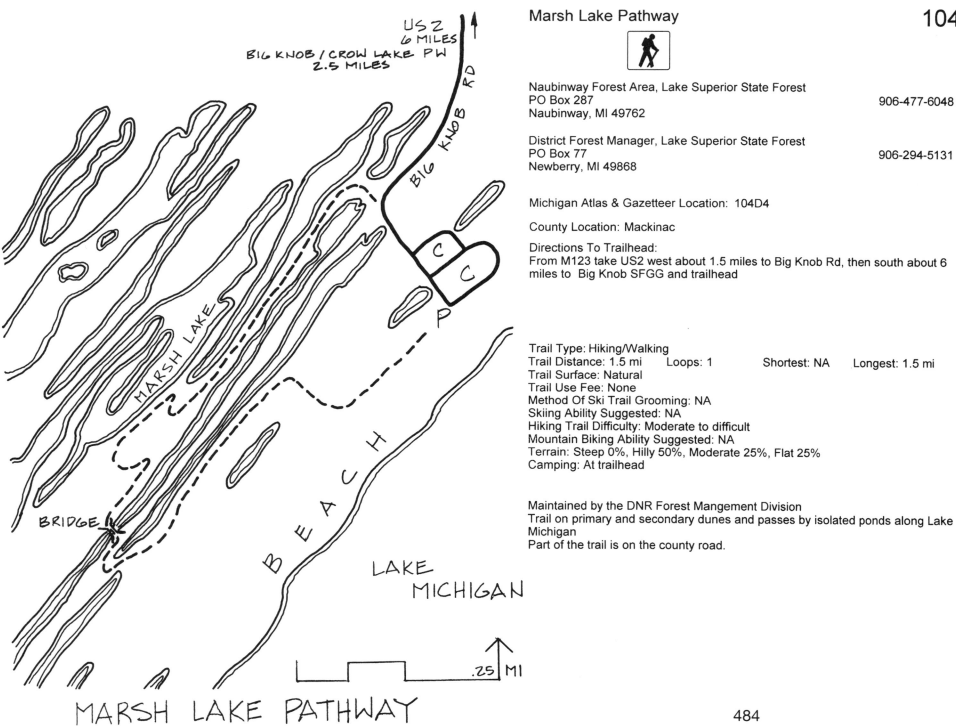

Naubinway Forest Area, Lake Superior State Forest
PO Box 287
Naubinway, MI 49762

906-477-6048

District Forest Manager, Lake Superior State Forest
PO Box 77
Newberry, MI 49868

906-294-5131

Michigan Atlas & Gazetteer Location: 104D4

County Location: Mackinac

Directions To Trailhead:
From M123 take US2 west about 1.5 miles to Big Knob Rd, then south about 6 miles to Big Knob SFGG and trailhead

Trail Type: Hiking/Walking
Trail Distance: 1.5 mi   Loops: 1   Shortest: NA   Longest: 1.5 mi
Trail Surface: Natural
Trail Use Fee: None
Method Of Ski Trail Grooming: NA
Skiing Ability Suggested: NA
Hiking Trail Difficulty: Moderate to difficult
Mountain Biking Ability Suggested: NA
Terrain: Steep 0%, Hilly 50%, Moderate 25%, Flat 25%
Camping: At trailhead

Maintained by the DNR Forest Mangement Division
Trail on primary and secondary dunes and passes by isolated ponds along Lake Michigan
Part of the trail is on the county road.

US2
6 MILES
BIG KNOB / CROW LAKE PW
2.5 MILES

BIG KNOB RD

MARSH LAKE

C
C
P

BEACH

BRIDGE

LAKE
MICHIGAN

.25 MI

MARSH LAKE PATHWAY

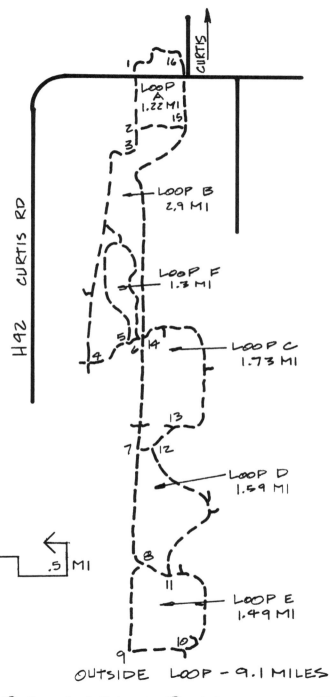

.5 MI

OUTSIDE LOOP - 9.1 MILES

NORTH CURTIS ROAD SKI TRAIL

Curtis Area Chamber of Commerce
Box 447
Curtis, MI 49820

Manilak Resort
RR3 Box 2620
Curtis, MI 49820

906-586-3285
906-586-6690

Michigan Atlas & Gazetteer Location: 104C2

County Location: Mackinac

Directions To Trailhead:
1 mile west of Curtis on Co Rd H-42 (North Curtis Rd) off Main St

Trail Type: Hiking/Walking, Cross Country Skiing, Mountain Biking
Trail Distance: 9.1 mi   Loops: 6   Shortest: 1.22 mi Longest: 2.92 mi
Trail Surface: Natural
Trail Use Fee: None
Method Of Ski Trail Grooming: Skating
Skiing Ability Suggested: Novice
Hiking Trail Difficulty: Easy
Mountain Biking Ability Suggested: Novice
Terrain: Steep 0%, Hilly 10%, Moderate 15%, Flat 75%
Camping: None

Maintained by the Manilak Resort on private property

Northern Hardwoods Cross Country Ski Trail

Seney National Wildlife Refuge
HCR2, Box 1
Seney, MI 49883

906-586-9851

Gronback-Northland Outfitters
PO Box 65
Germfask, MI 49836

l906-586-9801

Michigan Atlas & Gazetteer Location: 104BC1

County Location: Schoolcraft

Directions To Trailhead:
On M77 in Germfask, turn west on street just south of the Grace Lutheran
Church. Take road west to parking lot.
Trailhead is at the parking lot. In summer a gate limits vehicle access. However
actual use is not restricted.

Trail Type: Hiking/Walking, Cross Country Skiing
Trail Distance: 8.5 mi   Loops: 5   Shortest: .8 mi   Longest: 6 mi
Trail Surface: Natural
Trail Use Fee: None
Method Of Ski Trail Grooming: Track set
Skiing Ability Suggested: Novice to intermediate
Hiking Trail Difficulty: Easy
Mountain Biking Ability Suggested: NA
Terrain: Steep 0%, Hilly 0%, Moderate 30%, Flat 70%
Camping: None

Maintained by the Seney Wildlife Refuge and Gronback-Northland Outfitters

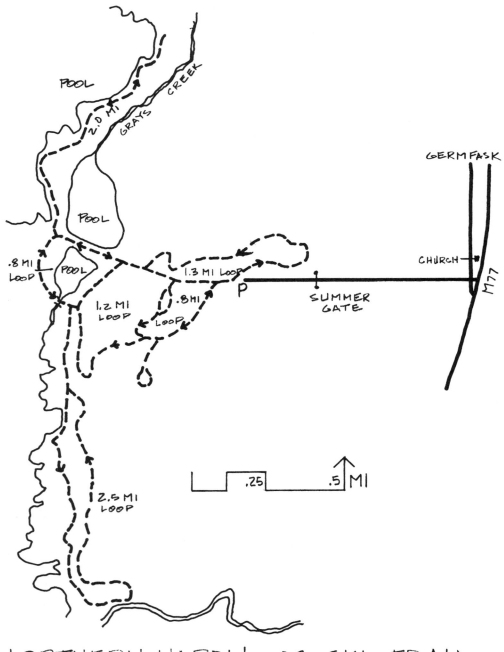

NORTHERN HARDWOODS SKI TRAIL
SENEY NATIONAL WILDLIFE REFUGE

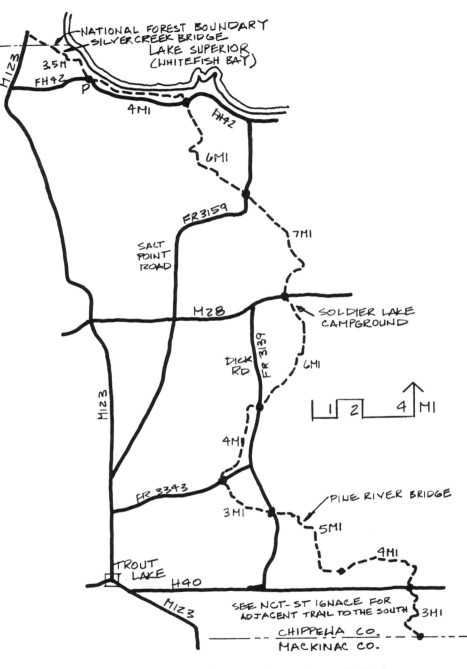

Sault Ste. Marie Ranger District, Hiawatha National Forest
4000 I-75 Business Loop   906-635-5311
Sault Ste Marie, MI 49783

Forest Supervisor, Hiawatha National Forest
2727 N. Lincoln Rd.   906-786-4062
Escanaba, MI 49829

Michigan Atlas & Gazetteer Location: 105A8,106ABC12,117D8

County Location: Chippewa

Directions To Trailhead:
Near East Lake at the Chippewa Co Line to Tahquamenon Falls State Park
South trailhead - Lookout on East Lake Dr. on Chippewa Co Line just south of H40
North trailhead - On FR 42(east of M123) .5 mile west of Lake Superior.

Trail Type: Hiking/Walking
Trail Distance: 42 mi   Loops: NA   Shortest: NA   Longest: NA
Trail Surface: Natural
Trail Use Fee: None
Method Of Ski Trail Grooming: NA
Skiing Ability Suggested: NA
Hiking Trail Difficulty: Moderate to difficult
Mountain Biking Ability Suggested: NA
Terrain: Flat to rolling
Camping: Campground at Soldier Lake and primitive campsites along the trail

Maintained by the Sault Ste. Marie Ranger District, Hiawatha National Forest
Connects to the North Country Trail - St. Ignace, on the south
Write the Sault Ste. Marie Ranger District for a detailed map. The trail continues north of the National Forest boundary for about 2 miles.
The trail can then be picked up at the River Unit campground of the Tahquamenon Falls State Park. See the state park for more detailed information on that section of the trail.
For more information contact the North Country Trail Association,   PO Box 311, White Cloud, MI 49349   616-689-1912
As with all of the North Country Trail in the national forest, wilderness camping is permitted 200' from the trail.

NORTH COUNTRY TRAIL- SAULT STE MARIE

Naubinway Forest Area, Lake Superior State Forest
PO Box 287   906-477-6048
Naubinway, MI 49762

District Forest Manager, Lake Superior State Forest
South M-123, PO Box 77   906-293-5131
Newberry, MI 49868

Michigan Atlas & Gazetteer Location: 105C5

County Location: Schoolcraft

Directions To Trailhead:
9 miles east of Engadine on Hiawatha Trail (H40) or 8 miles west of Rexton

Trail Type: Cross Country Skiing
Trail Distance: 1.6 mi   Loops: 1   Shortest: NA   Longest: 1.6 mi
Trail Surface: Natural
Trail Use Fee: None
Method Of Ski Trail Grooming: Yes
Skiing Ability Suggested: Novice
Hiking Trail Difficulty: NA
Mountain Biking Ability Suggested: NA
Terrain: 100% Flat
Camping: Black Creek State Forest Campground

Maintained by the DNR Forest Management Division
Trail designed for cross country skiing.
Used mostly by local skiers.

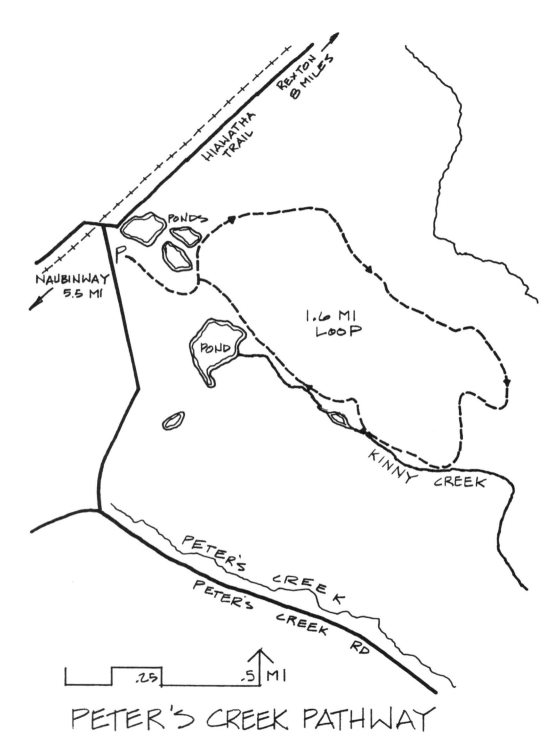

REXTON 8 MILES

HIAWATHA TRAIL

PONDS

P

NAUBINWAY 5.5 MI

POND

1.6 MI LOOP

POND

KINNY CREEK

PETER'S CREEK

PETER'S CREEK RD

.25   .5 MI

PETER'S CREEK PATHWAY

CO RD 520

P
C

LITTLE BREVORT LAKE

C

LAKE MICHIGAN

US 2

LITTLE HEAD RD

.5   1 MI

ST. IGNACE

Naubinway State Forest, Lake Superior State Forest
PO Box 287   906-477-6048
Naubinway, Mi 49762

District Forest Manager, Lake Superior State Forest
PO Box 77   906-477-6048
Newberry, MI 49762

Michigan Atlas & Gazetteer Location: 105D8

County Location: Mackinac

Directions To Trailhead:
East of Brevort on US2, 2 miles than north .5 mi to South Little Brevort Lake
SFCG and trailhead.

Trail Type: Hiking/Walking
Trail Distance: 2.5 mi   Loops: 1   Shortest: NA   Longest: 2.5 mi
Trail Surface: Natural
Trail Use Fee: None
Method Of Ski Trail Grooming: NA
Skiing Ability Suggested: NA
Hiking Trail Difficulty: Moderate
Mountain Biking Ability Suggested: NA
Terrain: Steep 0%, Hilly 60%, Moderate 40%, Flat 0%
Camping: At trailhead, along trail and neaby SFCG

Maintained by the DNR Forest Management Division
A pleasant short trail along LIttle Brevort Lake and River.

SWITCHBACK RIDGE PATHWAY

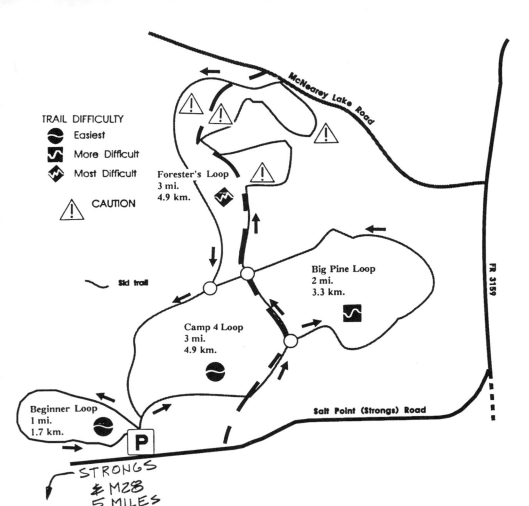

TRAIL DIFFICULTY
- Easiest
- More Difficult
- Most Difficult

⚠ CAUTION

Forester's Loop
3 mi.
4.9 km.

Sid trail

Big Pine Loop
2 mi.
3.3 km.

Camp 4 Loop
3 mi.
4.9 km.

Beginner Loop
1 mi.
1.7 km.

Salt Point (Strongs) Road

FR 3159

McNearey Lake Road

P

STRONGS
& M28
5 MILES

.25 .5 1 MI

McNEARNEY SKI TRAIL

McNearney Ski Trail

Sault Saint Marie Ranger District, Hiawatha National Forest
4000 I-75 Business Spur
Sault Ste. Marie, MI 49783   906-635-5311

Forest Supervisor, Hiawatha National Forest
2727 N. Lincoln Rd   906-786-4062
Escanaba, MI 49829

Michigan Atlas & Gazetteer Location: 106A1

County Location: Chippewa

Directions To Trailhead:
West of Sault Ste Marie. 4 miles north of M28 on FR 3159 (Salt Point Rd) north of Strongs.

Trail Type: Cross Country Skiing
Trail Distance: 8 mi   Loops: 4   Shortest: 1 mi   Longest: 3 mi
Trail Surface: Natural
Trail Use Fee: None
Method Of Ski Trail Grooming: None
Skiing Ability Suggested: Novice to intermediate
Hiking Trail Difficulty: NA
Mountain Biking Ability Suggested: NA
Terrain: Steep 0%, Hilly 33%, Moderate 23%, Flat 44%
Camping: Nearby at Solder Lake NFCG

Maintained by the Sault Ste Marie Ranger District, Hiawatha National Forest
Four loops with different skill levels requrried
North Country Trail - Sault Ste Marie passes this trail about 1.5 miles to the northeast

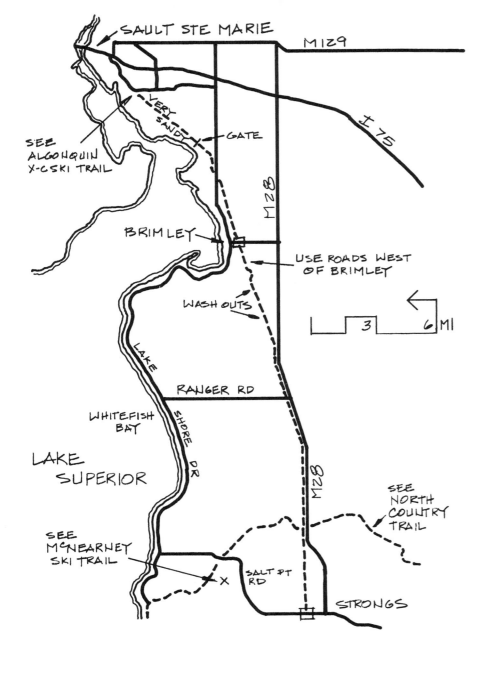

SOO-STRONGS RAIL-TRAIL

Sault Ste Marie Forest Area, Lake Superior State Forest
2001 Ashman, PO Box 798   906-635-5281
Sault Ste Marie, MI 49738

District Forest Manager, Lake Superior State Forest
PO Box 77   906-293-5131
Newberry, MI 49868

Michigan Atlas & Gazetteer Location: 106AB1234,107A5

County Location: Chippewa

Directions To Trailhead:
East trailhead - Exit I-75 at 3 mile Rd in Sault Ste Marie, then west on 3 Mile Rd
for about 1 mile, then right on 20th St for about 1.25 miles to trailhead.

Trail Type: Hiking/Walking, Mountain Biking
Trail Distance: 32 mi   Loops: NA   Shortest: NA   Longest: NA
Trail Surface: Natural and ballast
Trail Use Fee: None
Method Of Ski Trail Grooming: NA
Skiing Ability Suggested: NA
Hiking Trail Difficulty: Easy to moderate
Mountain Biking Ability Suggested: Intermediate
Terrain: 100% Flat
Camping: Campground at nearby Brimley State Park and NFCG

Maintained by the DNR Forest Management Division
The North Country Trail crosses at Soldier Lake NFCG access road.

Sault Ste. Marie Forest Area, Lake Superior State Forest
2001 Ashmun St., PO Box 798   906-635-5281
Sault Ste. Marie, MI 49783

District Forest Manager, Lake Superior State Forest
PO Box 77   906-293-5131
Newberry, MI 49868

Michigan Atlas & Gazetteer Location: 107A5

County Location: Chippewa

Directions To Trailhead:
2 miles west of I-75, SW of Sault Ste. Marie, Michigan.
Take 3 Mile Rd. exit off of I-75, then west on 3 Mile Rd about 1 mile to Baker Rd,
right on Baker Rd to 16th Ave. Left (west) on 16th Ave to trailhead which is
about 1 mile on the left.

Trail Type: Hiking/Walking, Cross Country Skiing
Trail Distance: 8.8 mi   Loops: 5   Shortest: 1 mi   Longest: 3 mi
Trail Surface: Natural
Trail Use Fee: None, but donations are accepted to groom the trail
Method Of Ski Trail Grooming: Track set
Skiing Ability Suggested: Novice to intermediate
Hiking Trail Difficulty: Easy
Mountain Biking Ability Suggested: NA
Terrain: Steep 0%, Hilly 0%, Moderate 10%, Flat 90%
Camping: Campgrounds avaialble locally

Maintained by the DNR Forest Management Division
Although near Sault Ste. Marie, the trail is very secluded in a mixed hardwood
and evergreen forest.
A very popular ski trail especially used by the local college students.
The Soo-Strongs Rail Trail passes through trail system, which is used for
snowmobiling in the winter months.

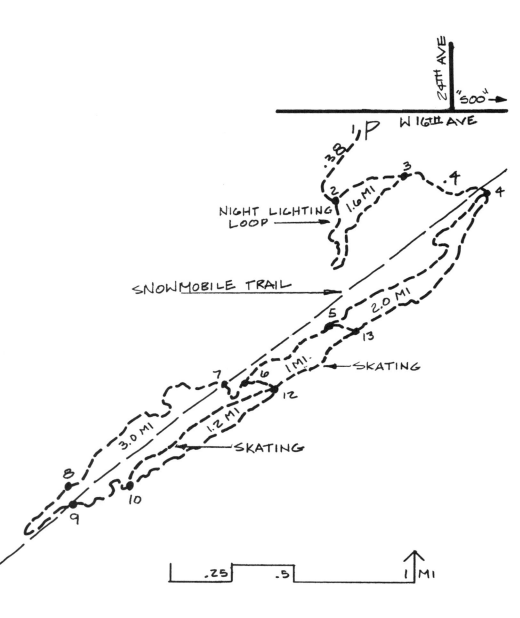

ALGONQUIN
CROSS COUNTRY SKI TRAIL

Sault Ste. Marie Forest Area, Lake Superior State Forest
2001 Ashmun St., PO Box 798   906-635-5281
Sault Ste Marie, MI 49783

District Forest Manager, Lake Superior State Forest
South M123, PO Box 77   906-293-5131
Newberry, MI 49868

Michigan Atlas & Gazetteer Location: 107C5

County Location: Chippewa

Directions To Trailhead:
16 miles south of Sault Ste. Marie on I-75 at the Kinross exit 378
Trailhead - Exit I-75 east on Tone Rd. 4 miles to Wilson Rd., then south .75 mile
to parking lot

Trail Type: Hiking/Walking, Cross Country Skiing, Mountain Biking
Trail Distance: 7.7 mi   Loops: 2   Shortest: 2 mi   Longest: 5.7 mi
Trail Surface: Track set
Trail Use Fee: Donations accepted at trailhead
Method Of Ski Trail Grooming: Track set weekly or more if needed
Skiing Ability Suggested: Novice
Hiking Trail Difficulty: Easy
Mountain Biking Ability Suggested: Novice to intermediate
Terrain: 100% Flat
Camping: None

Maintained by the DNR Forest Management Division
Wooded trails.
Food and lodging available in Kinross.
Popular trail with local skiers.
Other contacts:
        DNR Forest Management Division Office, Lansing, 517-373-1275
        DNR Forest Management Region Office, Marquette, 906-228-6561

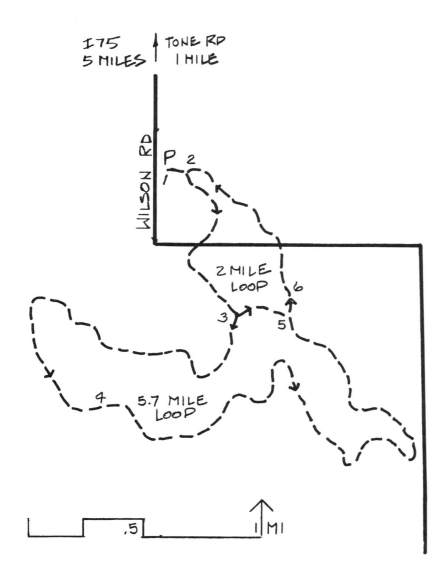

PINE BOWL PATHWAY

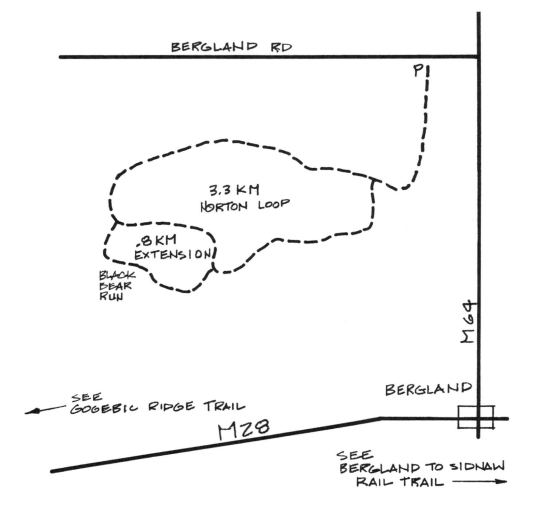

BERGLAND RD

P

3.3 KM
NORTON LOOP

.8 KM
EXTENSION

BLACK
BEAR
RUN

M 6

SEE
GOGEBIC RIDGE TRAIL

BERGLAND

M28

SEE
BERGLAND TO SIDNAW
RAIL TRAIL

.5 KM

BERGLAND SKI TRAIL

Bergland Ski Trail

Bergland Ranger District, Ottawa National Forest
M28, PO Box 126   906-575-3441
Bergland, MI 49910   906-575-3877TTY

Recreation Staff Officer, Ottawa National Forest
2100 E. Cloverland Drive   906-932-1330
Ironwood, MI 49938

Michigan Atlas & Gazetteer Location: 108D4

County Location: Ontonagon

Directions To Trailhead:
Trailhead - 1mile north of the Bergland on M6, then left (west) 100 yds to parking area and trailhead.

Trail Type: Cross Country Skiing
Trail Distance: 2.9 mi   Loops: 2   Shortest: 2.6 mi Longest: 2.9 mi
Trail Surface: Natural
Trail Use Fee: None
Method Of Ski Trail Grooming: Track set occasionally
Skiing Ability Suggested: Novice to intermediate
Hiking Trail Difficulty: NA
Mountain Biking Ability Suggested: NA
Terrain: Steep 0%, Hilly 15%, Moderate 35%, Flat 50%
Camping: Campground available at Lake Gogebic State Park

Maintained by the Bergland Ranger District, Ottawa National Forest
A well marked but not frequently used ski trail.
Food and lodging available in Bergland.
Other trails in the area are the Gogebic Ridge Hiking Trail and the North Country Trail - Bergland.

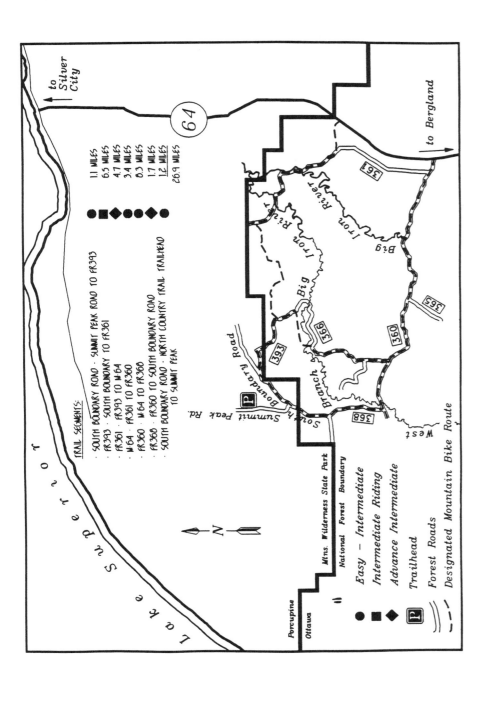

Bergland Ranger District, Ottawa National Forest
M28. PO Box 126   906-575-3441
Bergland, MI 49910

Recreation Staff Officer, Ottawa National Forest
2100 E. Cloverland Drive   906-932-1330
Ironwood, MI 49938

Michigan Atlas & Gazetteer Location: 108BC234

County Location: Ontonagon

Directions To Trailhead:
East Trailhead - West of M64, 5 miles north of Bergland on FR 360

Trail Type: Mountain Biking
Trail Distance: 26.9 mi   Loops: Shortest: Longest:
Trail Surface: Gravel, sand and natural
Trail Use Fee: None
Method Of Ski Trail Grooming: NA
Skiing Ability Suggested: NA
Hiking Trail Difficulty: NA
Mountain Biking Ability Suggested: Novice to advanced
Terrain: Steep 0%, Hilly 30%, Moderate 39%, Flat040%
Camping: Several Campgrounds in the area

Maintained by the Ottawa National Forest.
Trails designated in 1994.
From their literature,"Challenging trip through a northern hardwood forest, over
open gravel roads as well as closed, overgrown logging roads. There are many
beaver dams to navigate around   Hazards include beaver ponds, crossing the
West Branch of the Big Iron River (no bridge) and deep ruts in various locations.
Some parts of the trail are open roads used by commercial vehicles; some
closed roads also currently being used as parts of the North Country National
Scenic Hiking Trail. Check conditions of the Big Iron River crossing before
embarking on any trip. Check in at either the State Park or any National Forest
Offices to report any adverse trail conditons and to let the Forest Service know
how you liked the ride."

EHLCO MOUNTAIN BIKE COMLEX

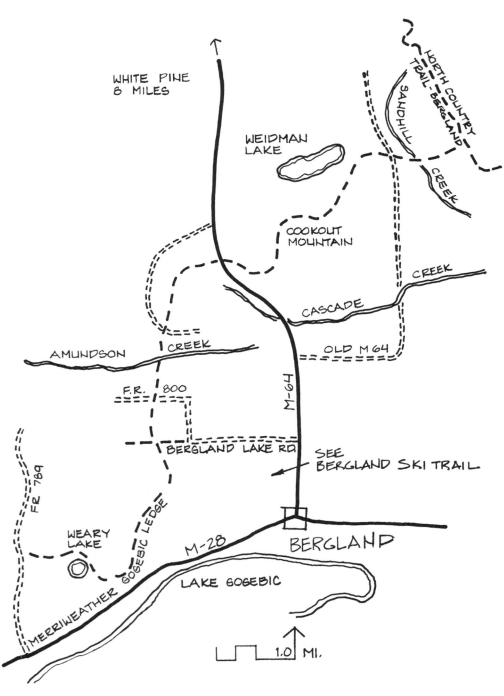

Bergland Ranger District, Ottawa National Forest
M28, PO Box 126
Bergland, MI 49910

906-575-3441

Recreation Staff Officer, Ottawa National Forest
2100 E. Cloverland Drive
Ironwood, MI 49938

906-932-1330

Michigan Atlas & Gazetteer Location: 108CD34

County Location: Ontonagon

Directions To Trailhead:
Bergland Trail trailhead - 3 miles north of Bergland on M64
West trailhead - 1.5 miles north of M28 on FR 789, 3 miles west of Bergland
East trailhead - North Country Trail - Bergland segment near the Sandhill Creek crossing

Trail Type: Hiking/Walking
Trail Distance: 9 mi   Loops: NA   Shortest: NA   Longest: NA
Trail Surface: Natural
Trail Use Fee: None
Method Of Ski Trail Grooming: NA
Skiing Ability Suggested: NA
Hiking Trail Difficulty: Moderate to difficult
Mountain Biking Ability Suggested: NA
Terrain: Rolling with some steep grades not suitable for skiing
Camping: Wilderness camping permitted 200' off trail

Maintained by the Bergland Ranger District, Ottawa National Forest
Connects to the North Country Trail - Bergland Segment

GOGEBIC RIDGE HIKING TRAIL

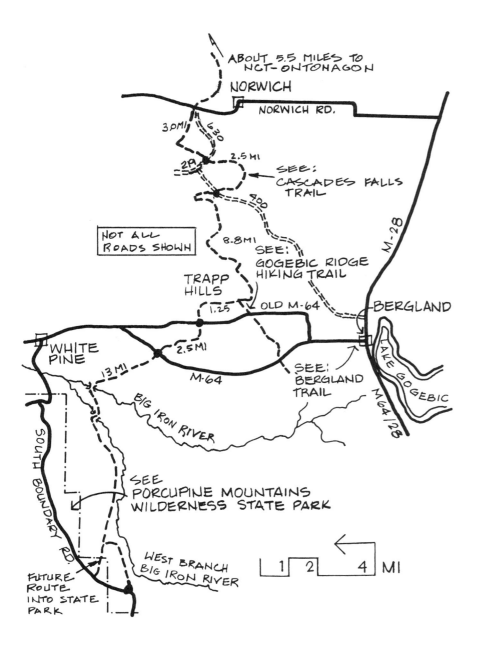

Bergland Ranger District, Ottawa National Forest
M28, PO Box 126   906-575-3441
Bergland, MI 49910

Recreation Staff Officer, Ottawa National Forest
2100 E. Cloverland Drive   906-932-1330
Ironwood, MI 49938   800-562-1201

Michigan Atlas & Gazetteer Location: 108C34,109C56

County Location: Ontonagon

Directions To Trailhead:
West trailhead-S. Boundary Rd adjacent to Procupine Mountains State Park
East trailhead-NE of Bergland, 10 miles north of M28 on Norwich Rd, at the
intersection of FH 219
Trailhead -7 miles north of Bergland on M64
Trailhead - Spur at Cascade Falls Trail
Trailhead - Norwich Rd at FR630

Trail Type: Hiking/Walking
Trail Distance: 37 mi   Loops: NA   Shortest: NA   Longest: NA
Trail Surface: Natural
Trail Use Fee: None
Method Of Ski Trail Grooming: NA
Skiing Ability Suggested: NA
Hiking Trail Difficulty: Difficult
Mountain Biking Ability Suggested: NA
Terrain: Steep 5%, Hilly 14%, Moderate 55%, Flat 26%
Camping: There are no developed campsites but wilderness camping is
permitted.

Maintained by the Bergland Ranger District, Ottawa National Forest
This is a point to point trail.
Connected to the east end of the Gogebic Ridge Trail.
Formally the Trap Falls section of the North Country Trail.
A more detailed trail map is available from the Bergland Ranger District.
Wilderness camping is permitted 200' from the trail.
For more information about the North Country Trail, contact the North Country
Trail Association, PO Box 311, White Cloud, MI 49349 616-689-1912

NORTH COUNTRY TRAIL-
BERGLAND

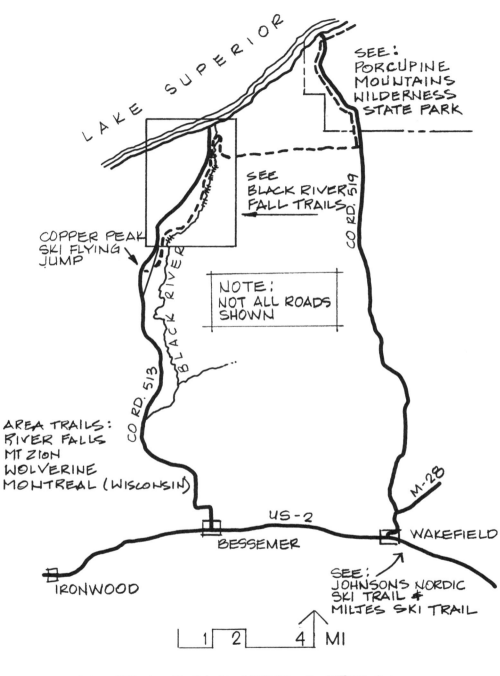

Bessemer Ranger District, Ottawa National Forest
500 N. Moore St.   906-667-0261
Bessemer , MI 49911

Recreation Staff Officer, Ottawa National Forest
2100 E. Cloverland Drive   906-932-1330
Ironwood, MI 49938   800-562-1201

Michigan Atlas & Gazetteer Location: 108C1, 113A8

County Location: Gogebic

Directions To Trailhead:
Trailhead-Co Rd 513, 11 miles north of Bessemer near Copper Peak
Trailhead-North of Wakefield on Co Rd 519, .5 mile south of the Porcupine
Mountains Wilderness State Park boundary

Trail Type: Hiking/Walking
Trail Distance: 12 mi   Loops: NA   Shortest: NA   Longest: NA
Trail Surface: Natural
Trail Use Fee: None
Method Of Ski Trail Grooming: NA
Skiing Ability Suggested: NA
Hiking Trail Difficulty: Difficult
Mountain Biking Ability Suggested: NA
Terrain: Steep 10%, Hilly 10%, Moderate 40%, Flat 4%
Camping: Campgound at Black River Harbor on Lake Superior

Maintained by the Bessemer Ranger District, Ottawa National Forest
This is a point to point trail.
Several falls are along the trail on the Black River.
Also as with all of the North Country Trail, wilderness camping is permitted 200'
from the trail . Drinking water is also available at the Potawatomi and Gorge
Falls Picnic Area.
Copper Peak is the largest ski jump in the United States.
For more information about the North Country Trail contact the North Country
Trail Association, PO Box 311, White Cloud, MI 49349 616-689-1912
A more detailed map is available from the Bessemer Ranger District office.

NORTH COUNTRY TRAIL- BESSEMER

TRAIL NOTES

Porcupine Mountains Wilderness State Park
599 M107
Ontonagon, MI 49953

906-885-5275

DNR Parks and Recreation Division

517-373-1270

Michigan Atlas & Gazetteer Location: 108B1234

County Location: Ontonagon & Gogebic

Directions To Trailhead:
17 miles west of Ontonagon on the shore of Lake Superior

SEE MAPS ON NEXT PAGE

Trail Type: Hiking/Walking, Cross Country Skiing
Trail Distance: 85+ mi   Loops: Many   Shortest: Longest:
Trail Surface: Natural
Trail Use Fee: None, but vehicle entry fee required
Method Of Ski Trail Grooming: Track set regularly
Skiing Ability Suggested: Novice to intermediate
Hiking Trail Difficulty: Easy to difficult
Mountain Biking Ability Suggested: NA
Terrain: Rolling to very hilly
Camping: Available in park, facilities may be limited during the winter

Maintained by the DNR Parks and Recreation Division
A unique state park at the shore of Lake Superior. Rentals, warming area, snack bar and alpine skiing available. Only about 25 mi of the trails were designed for skiing. Most of these ski trails are not used for hiking trails in the summer. Extensive wilderness hiking trail system has been developed throughout the park complete with shelters and cabins available for rent. One ski trail leads to the top of the alpine slope for a very spectacular panoramic view of Lake Superior. Back country cabins are available on a reservation basis for rent throughout the year. The North Country Trail uses Little Carp River, Lake Superior and LIly Pond Trails 17.5 mile segment. Lodging and restaurants are available in Ontonagon and Silver City. Note: there are two trail maps. One for skiing and another map at a larger scale for all hiking trails.

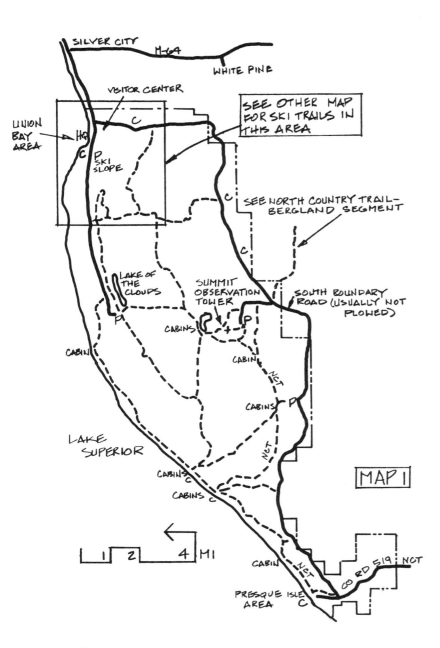

MAP 1

SILVER CITY M-64

WHITE PINE

VISITOR CENTER

SEE OTHER MAP FOR SKI TRAILS IN THIS AREA

UNION BAY AREA

HQ
C

C P SKI SLOPE

SEE NORTH COUNTRY TRAIL- BERGLAND SEGMENT

LAKE OF THE CLOUDS

SUMMIT OBSERVATION TOWER

SOUTH BOUNDARY ROAD (USUALLY NOT PLOWED)

CABINS

P

CABIN

CABIN

NCT

CABINS P

LAKE SUPERIOR

NCT

CABINS C

CABINS C

CABIN

NCT

CO RD 519 NCT

PRESQUE ISLE AREA C

1 2 4 MI

PORCUPINE MOUNTAINS WILDERNESS STATE PARK

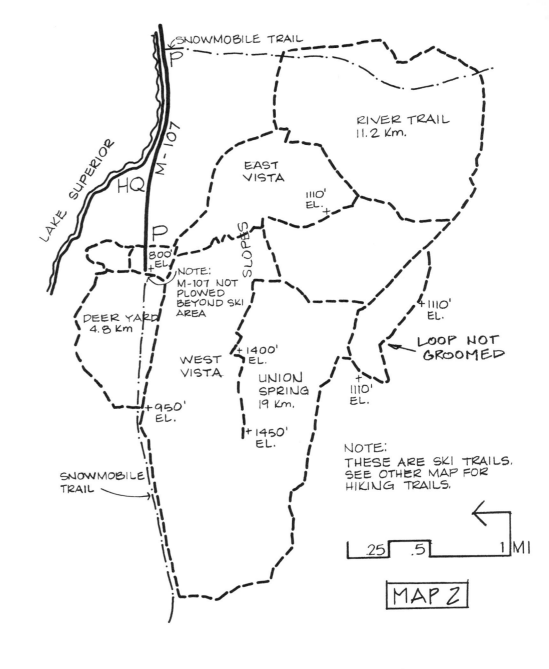

SNOWMOBILE TRAIL

P

RIVER TRAIL 11.2 Km.

LAKE SUPERIOR

HQ

M-107

P

EAST VISTA

1110' EL.

800 EL.

NOTE: M-107 NOT PLOWED BEYOND SKI AREA

DEER YARD 4.8 km

SLOPES

WEST VISTA

+1400' EL.

UNION SPRING 19 Km.

+1110' EL.

LOOP NOT GROOMED

+950' EL.

+1450' EL.

+1110' EL.

SNOWMOBILE TRAIL

NOTE: THESE ARE SKI TRAILS. SEE OTHER MAP FOR HIKING TRAILS.

.25 .5 1 MI

MAP 2

PORCUPINE MOUNTAINS WILDERNESS STATE PARK

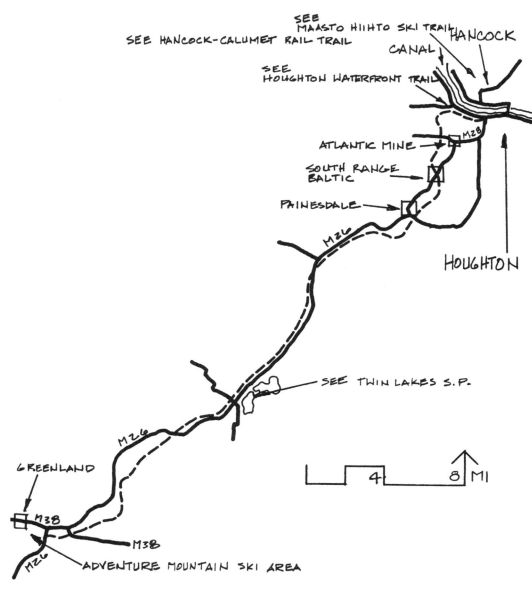

SEE
MAASTO HIIHTO SKI TRAIL
SEE HANCOCK-CALUMET RAIL TRAIL
HANCOCK
CANAL
SEE
HOUGHTON WATERFRONT TRAIL
ATLANTIC MINE
M28
SOUTH RANGE BALTIC
PAINESDALE
M26
HOUGHTON
SEE TWIN LAKES S.P.
M26
GREENLAND
M38
M38
M26
ADVENTURE MOUNTAIN SKI AREA
4   8 MI

BILL NICHOLLS RAIL TRAIL

Baraga Forest Area, Copper Country State Forest
PO Box 440
Baraga, MI 49908

906-353-6651

District Forest Manager, Copper Country State Forest
PO Box 440
Baraga, MI 49908

906-353-6651
517-373-1270

Michigan Atlas & Gazetteer Location: 109B8,118CD24

County Location: Houghton & Ontonagon

Directions To Trailhead:
North trailhead - Houghton, west of town on Canal Drive and the Houghton Waterfront Trail
South trailhead - Adventure Mountain Ski Area in Greenland
Other trailheads - South Range, trail crosses M26 and Toivola on south side of M26

Trail Type: Hiking/Walking, Mountain Biking
Trail Distance: 41   Loops: NA   Shortest: NA   Longest: NA
Trail Surface: Natrual and ballast
Trail Use Fee: None
Method Of Ski Trail Grooming: NA
Skiing Ability Suggested: NA
Hiking Trail Difficulty: Easy to moderate
Mountain Biking Ability Suggested: Novice
Terrain: 100%Flat
Camping: Twin Lakes SP, Emily Lake SFCG and City of Hancock campground

Managed by the DNR Forest Mangement Division.
This rail-trail is the former Copper Range Railroad that extended from Houghton to just south of Mass City.
Trail surface is original ballast, clay and sand.
Trail crosses three bridges with a total distance of 1,288 feet and 65,75 and 85 feet high
Trail connects with the two rail trails (Hancock to Calumet Rail-Trail and Keweenaw Rail-Trail in Hancock)
Used as a snowmobile trail from from December through April.

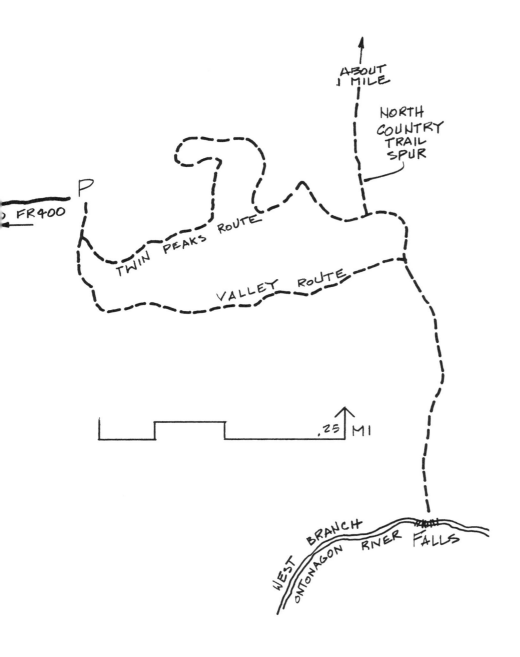

ABOUT 1 MILE

NORTH COUNTRY TRAIL SPUR

P

FR400

TWIN PEAKS ROUTE

VALLEY ROUTE

.25 MI

WEST BRANCH ONTONAGON RIVER FALLS

CASCADE FALLS HIKING TRAIL

Bergland Ranger District, Ottawa National Forest
M28, PO Box 126
Bergland, MI 49910
906-575-3441

Recreation Staff Officer, Ottawa National Forest
2100 E. Cloverland Drive
Ironwood, MI 49938
906-932-1330

Michigan Atlas & Gazetteer Location: 109C5

County Location: Ontonagon

Directions To Trailhead:
From Bergland, take M28 1 mile east to FR 400, then north 7 miles to sign leading to parking area and trailhead

Trail Type: Hiking/Walking
Trail Distance: 1.7 mi   Loops: 1   Shortest: NA   Longest: NA
Trail Surface: Natural
Trail Use Fee: None
Method Of Ski Trail Grooming: NA
Skiing Ability Suggested: NA
Hiking Trail Difficulty: Moderate
Mountain Biking Ability Suggested: NA
Terrain: Steep 15%, Hilly 30%, Moderate 25%, Flat 30%
Camping: None

Maintained by the Ottawa National Forest
Scenic trail to the Cascade Falls
Spur trail to the North Country Trail - Ontonagon

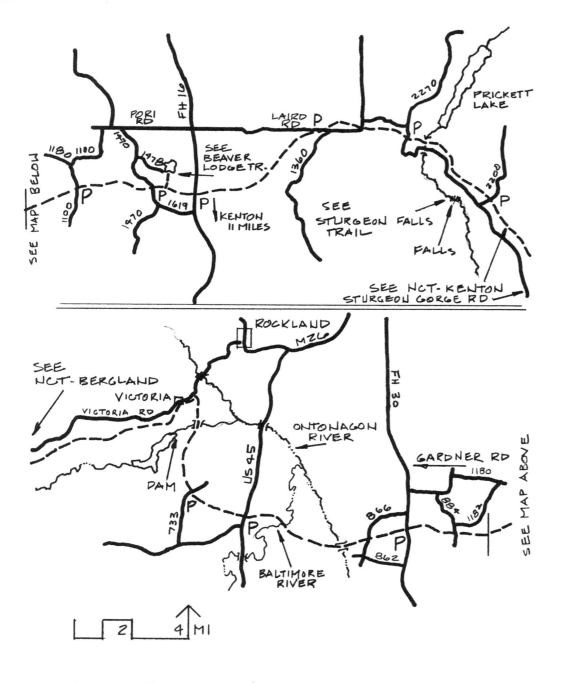

Ontonagon Ranger District - Ottawa National Forest
1209 Rockland Rd
Ontonagon, MI 49953

906-884-2085
906-884-2411

Recreation Staff Officer, Ottawa National Forest
2100 E. Cloverland Drive
Ironwood, MI 49938

906-932-1330
800-562-1201

Michigan Atlas & Gazetteer Location: 109C78,110C123

County Location: Ontonagon, Baraga, Houghton

Directions To Trailhead:
West trailhead - Victoria on Victoria Rd, Trailhead - on US45 about 5 miles south of M26 and US45 intersection located just east of Rockland.
Trailhead - Bob Lake NFCG.
Trailhead - Sturgeon River Falls.
Trail on east side of Sturgeon Gorge Rd and crosses FR 2200

Trail Type: Hiking/Walking
Trail Distance: 47 mi   Loops: NA   Shortest: NA   Longest: NA
Trail Surface: Natural
Trail Use Fee: None
Method Of Ski Trail Grooming: NA
Skiing Ability Suggested: NA
Hiking Trail Difficulty: Difficult
Mountain Biking Ability Suggested: NA
Terrain: Steep 30%, Hilly 40%, Moderate 20%, Flat 10%
Camping: Bob Lake CG and wilderness camping permitted 200' from trail

Maintained by the Ontonagon Ranger District - Ottawa National Forest
Very rugged, beautiful and isolated segment.
The Sturgeon Falls near the east end of the segment is worth the short side trip.
Detailed maps of the segment are available.
Plan to spend some time in the old historic mining town of Victoria.
The Bob Lake CG is very nice and the well water is available.
For further information about the North Country Trail contact the North Country Trail Association, PO Box 311, White Cloud, MI 49349 616-689-1912

NORTH COUNTRY TRAIL- ONTONAGON

Baraga State Park
Rte 1, Box 566
Baraga, MI 49908-9790

906-353-6558

McLain State Park
Rte 1, Box 82
Hancock, MI 49930

906-482-0278

Michigan Atlas & Gazetteer Location: 110B4, 111B4

County Location: Baraga

Directions To Trailhead:
One mile south of Baraga on US41along the Keweenaw Bay

Trail Type: Hiking/Walking, Interpretive
Trail Distance: .75 mi   Loops: 1   Shortest: NA   Longest: .75 mi
Trail Surface: Natural
Trail Use Fee: None, but vehicle entry permit required
Method Of Ski Trail Grooming: NA
Skiing Ability Suggested: NA
Hiking Trail Difficulty: Easy
Mountain Biking Ability Suggested: NA
Terrain: Steep 5%, Hilly 15%, Moderate 75%, Flat 5%
Camping: Campground on site

Maintained by the DNR Parks and Recreation Division
Compact park on the shore of the Keweenaw Bay, Lake Superior

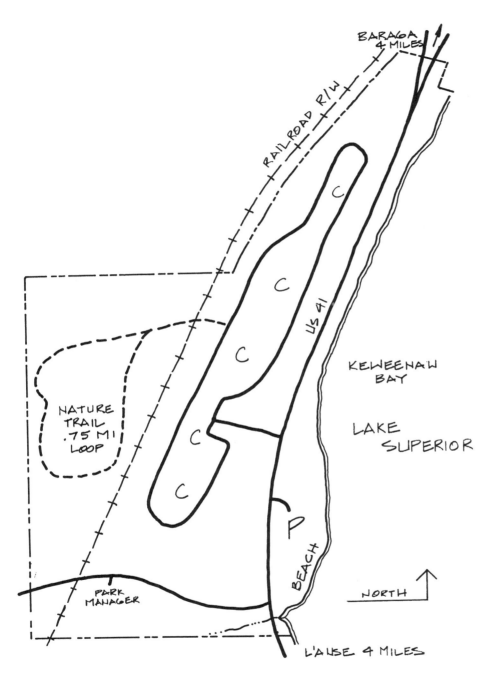

BARAGA STATE PARK

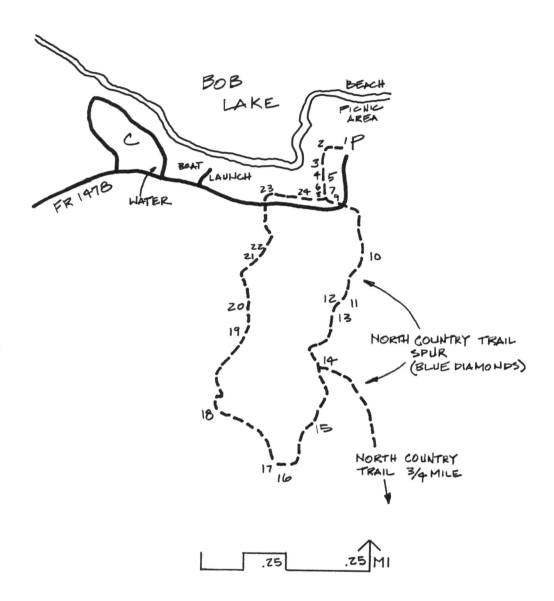

Ontonagon Ranger District, Ottawa National Forest
1209 Rockland Rd
Ontonagon, MI 49953
906-884-2411

Recreation Staff Officer, Ottawa National Forest
2100 E. Cloverland Drive
Ironwood, MI 49938
906-932-1330

Michigan Atlas & Gazetteer Location: 110C1

County Location: Houghton

Directions To Trailhead:
At the Bob Lake National Forest Campground. From Baraga, take M38 19 miles to FH 16, then south about 7.5 miles to Pori/South Laird Rd, then west 2.5 miles to FR 1470, then south 1.5 miles to campground. Trailhead at picnic area parking lot, beyond campground.

Trail Type: Hiking/Walking, Interpretive
Trail Distance: 1.25   Loops: 1   Shortest: NA   Longest: 1.25 mi
Trail Surface: Natural
Trail Use Fee: None
Method Of Ski Trail Grooming: None
Skiing Ability Suggested: NA
Hiking Trail Difficulty: Easy to moderate
Mountain Biking Ability Suggested: NA
Terrain: Steep 0%, Hilly 5%, Moderate 80%, Flat 10%
Camping: Campground at trailhead

Maintained by the Ottawa National Forest
Trail has 21 stations. A nature trail brochure is available.
Part of the trail was orginally a logging railroad.
At station 14, a spur trail begins to the North Country Trail - Ontonagon

BEAVER LODGE NATURE TRAIL

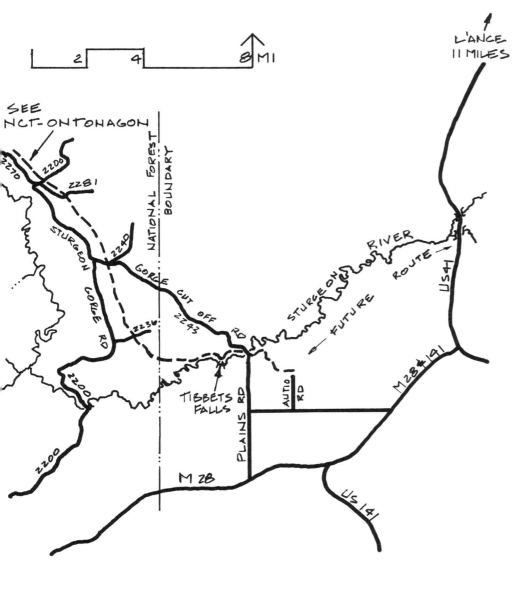

Kenton Ranger District, Ottawa National Forest
M28   906-852-3500
Kenton, MI 49943

Recreation Staff Officer, Ottawa National Forest
2100 E. Cloverland Drive   906-932-1330
Ironwood, MI 49938   800-562-1201

Michigan Atlas & Gazetteer Location: 110CD34

County Location: Ontonagon, Baraga

Directions To Trailhead:
 West trailhead - Take FR2200 north from M28 just east of Sidnaw for about 9 miles to the trail access point on east side of FR2200 near the Surgeon River Falls access trail.
East Tailhead - Two miles west of Covington on M-28, take Plains Rd north about two miles, then west 1 mile on Section 16 Rd to Autio Rd. North on Autio Rd to its end. Trail across Nestor Creek.

Trail Type: Hiking/Walking
Trail Distance: 7.6   Loops: No   Shortest: NA   Longest: NA
Trail Surface: Natural
Trail Use Fee: None
Method Of Ski Trail Grooming: None
Skiing Ability Suggested: NA
Hiking Trail Difficulty: Difficult
Mountain Biking Ability Suggested: NA
Terrain: Steep 0%, Hilly 5%, Moderate 55%, Flat 40%
Camping: There are no developed campsite but wilderness camping permitted

Maintained by the Kenton Ranger District, Ottawa National Forest.
Terrain and remoteness in the nearby Sturgeon River Gorge are exceptional, even for the upper peninsula.
A more detailed map is available from the Kenton Ranger District.
Like all of the North Country Trail, wilderness camping is permitted 200' from the trail
For more information about the North Country Trail, contact the North Country Trail Association, PO Box 311, White Cloud, MI 49349 616-689-1912

NORTH COUNTRY TRAIL
KENTON & TIBBETS FALLS

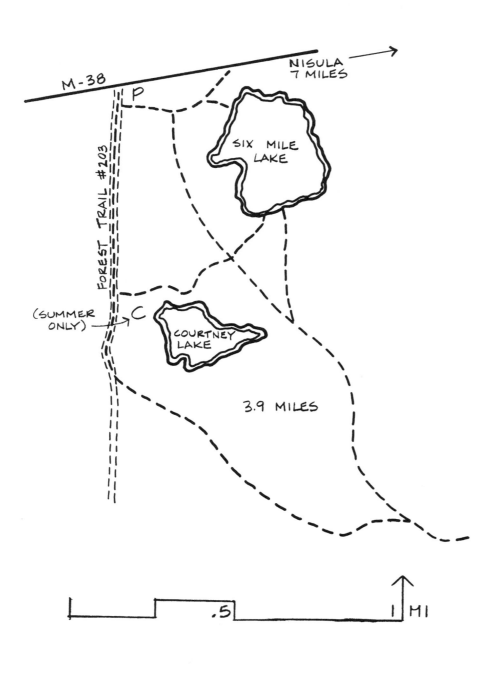

Ontonagon Ranger District, Ottawa National Forest
PO Box 217   906-884-2411
Ontonagon, MI 49953

Recreation Staff Officer, Ottawa National Forest
2100 Cloverland Drive   906-932-1330
Ironwood, MI 49938   800-562-1201

Michigan Atlas & Gazetteer Location: 110B1

County Location: Ontonagon

Directions To Trailhead:
West of Baraga on M38 7 miles west of Nisula at Courtney Lake Recreation
Area on FH203

Trail Type: Hiking/Walking, Cross Country Skiing
Trail Distance: 4.2 mi   Loops: 2   Shortest: 1.5 mi Longest: 4.2 mi
Trail Surface: Natural
Trail Use Fee: None
Method Of Ski Trail Grooming: None
Skiing Ability Suggested: Novice
Hiking Trail Difficulty: Easy
Mountain Biking Ability Suggested: NA
Terrain: Steep 0%, Hilly 10%, Moderate 40%, Flat 50%
Camping: Campgound at trailhead open in snowless months

Maintained by the Ontonagon Ranger District, Ottawa National Forest
Courtney Lake has a very nice swimming area.
Many other unmarked trails in the area for wilderness skiing.
Trail is not well marked.
FR 203 is plowed to some privately owned cabins near campground.

OLD GRADE SKI TRAIL

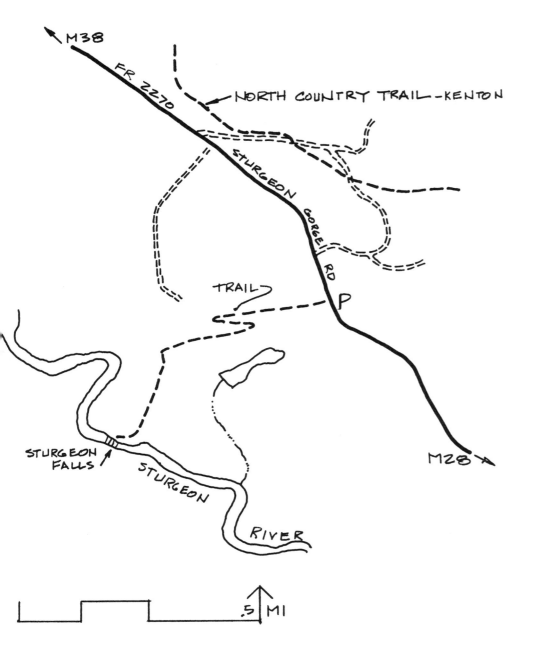

Kenton Ranger District, Ottawa National Forest
M28
Kenton, MI 49943

Recreation Staff Officer, Ottawa National Forest
2100 E. Cloverland Drive   906-932-1330
Ironwood, MI 49938

Michigan Atlas & Gazetteer Location: 110C3

County Location: Houghton

Directions To Trailhead:
14 miles north of Sidnaw via FR 2200 and 2270, or From M38 between Alstion and Baraga, follow Prickett Dam Rd and FR2270 south for 11 miles.

Trail Type: Hiking/Walking
Trail Distance: 1 mi   Loops: NA   Shortest: NA   Longest: NA
Trail Surface: Natural
Trail Use Fee: None
Method Of Ski Trail Grooming: NA
Skiing Ability Suggested: NA
Hiking Trail Difficulty: Moderate
Mountain Biking Ability Suggested: NA
Terrain: Steep 5%, Hilly 20%, Moderate 10%, Flat 65%
Camping: None

Maintained by the Kenton Ranger District, Ottawa National Forest
Spur trail to falls from parking lot and North Country Trail -Ontonagon that is across the road

STURGEON FALLS TRAIL

McLain State Park
RR!, Box 82 M203
Hancock, MI 49930

906-482-0278
906-288-3321

DNR Parks and Recreation Division

517-373-1270

Michigan Atlas & Gazetteer Location: 110A2

County Location: Houghton

Directions To Trailhead:
28 miles south of Houghton on M-26

Trail Type: Hiking/Walking, Cross Country Skiing, Interpretive
Trail Distance: 1.5 mi   Loops: 1   Shortest: NA   Longest: 1.5 mi
Trail Surface: Natural
Trail Use Fee: None, but vehicle entry fee required
Method Of Ski Trail Grooming: Track set once/week minimum
Skiing Ability Suggested: Novice
Hiking Trail Difficulty: Easy
Mountain Biking Ability Suggested: NA
Terrain: Steep 0%, Hilly 0%, Moderate 50%, Flat 50%
Camping: Seasonal camground on site

Maintained by the DNR Parks and Recreation Division
Two overlooks along the trail, which can permit a view of Lake Superior on a clear day .
A very popular state park opened only during the summer.
Located on one of the warmest lakes in the UP.

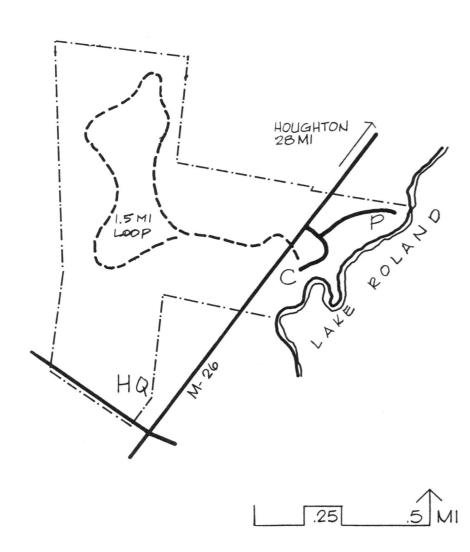

TWIN LAKES STATE PARK

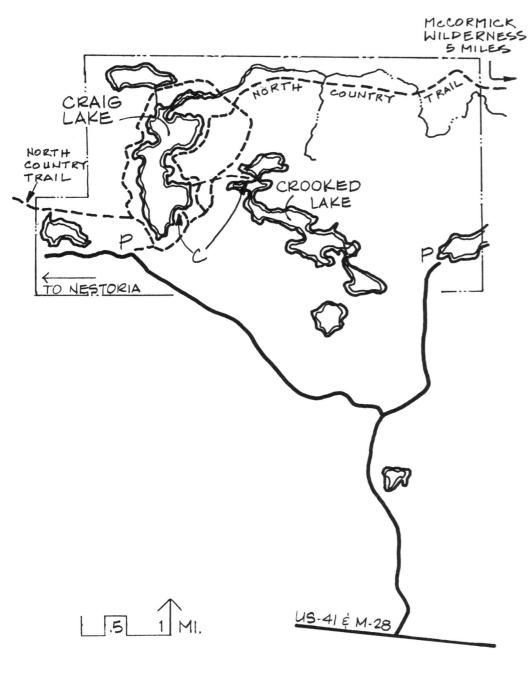

McCORMICK
WILDERNESS
5 MILES

CRAIG
LAKE

NORTH COUNTRY TRAIL

NORTH
COUNTRY
TRAIL

CROOKED
LAKE

P

P

C

TO NESTORIA

US-41 & M-28

.5   1 MI.

CRAIG LAKE STATE PARK

Van Riper State Park
PO Box 66
Champion , MI 49814

906-339-4461

DNR Parks and Recreation Division

517-373-1270

Michigan Atlas & Gazetteer Location: 111CD7

County Location: Marquette

Directions To Trailhead:
West of Marquette and 2 miles west of Michigamme on US41 at Craig Lake Rd.
Axquire detailed road map at Van Riper State Park before going to the park.

Trail Type: Hiking/Walking, Cross Country Skiing, Interpretive
Trail Distance: 6.8 mi   Loops: 1   Shortest: NA   Longest: 6.8 mi
Trail Surface: Natural
Trail Use Fee: None
Method Of Ski Trail Grooming: None - Wilderness area
Skiing Ability Suggested: Advanced
Hiking Trail Difficulty: Difficult
Mountain Biking Ability Suggested: NA
Terrain: Rolling to very hilly with rock outcrops
Camping: Cabin rentals and wilderness camping permitted

Maintained by the DNR Parks and Recreation Division
This is a state park with few facilities.
Suitable for skiing by those with winter survival skills only.
Two primitive campgrounds are located in the park. One is located 1mile from
the trailhead and another is located 1.8 miles from the trailhead.
Contact Van Riper State Park for more detailed information before leaving for
the park.. Wilderness camping permitted off existing trails.
Developed campground available at Van Riper State Park and private
campgrounds nearby.
Craig Lake State Park is managed by Van Riper State Park.

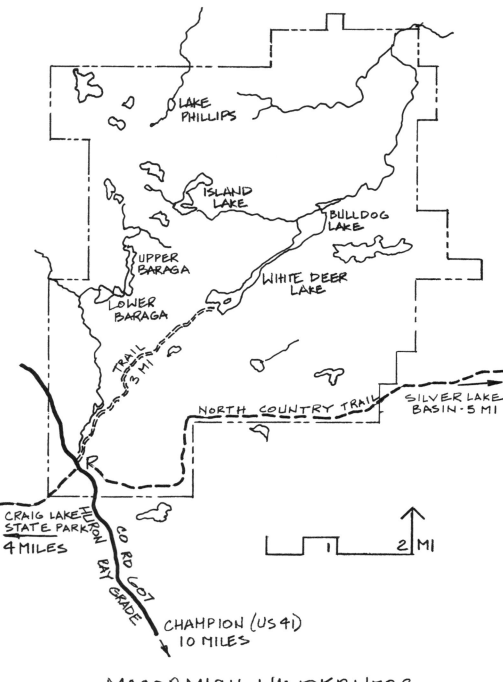

Kenton Ranger District, Ottawa National Forest
M28
Kenton, MI 49943   906-852-3500

Recreation Staff Officer, Ottawa National Forest
2100 Cloverdale Drive   906-932-1330
Ironwood , MI 49938   800-562-1201

Michigan Atlas & Gazetteer Location: 111C8,112C1

County Location: Marquette

Directions To Trailhead:
12 miles north of US41 from Champion on Co Rd 607 (Huron Bay Grade)

Trail Type: Hiking/Walking, Cross Country Skiing
Trail Distance: 8 mi   Loops: 2   Shortest: Longest:
Trail Surface: Natural
Trail Use Fee: None
Method Of Ski Trail Grooming: None
Skiing Ability Suggested: Advanced
Hiking Trail Difficulty: Moderate to difficult
Mountain Biking Ability Suggested: NA
Terrain: Steep 5%, Hilly 40%, Moderate 45%, Flat 10%
Camping: No developed campground, but wilderness camping is permitted

Maintained by the Kenton Ranger District, Ottawa National Forest
Formerly owned by Cyrus McCormick, son of the inventor of the reaper harvesting machine. Very rugged, isolated and scenic area.
Nearest developed campground is at Van Riper State Park on US41.
Recommended only for skiers with winter survival skills since the area is very isolated.
Total forest acreage is over 17,600 acres.

McCORMICK WILDERNESS

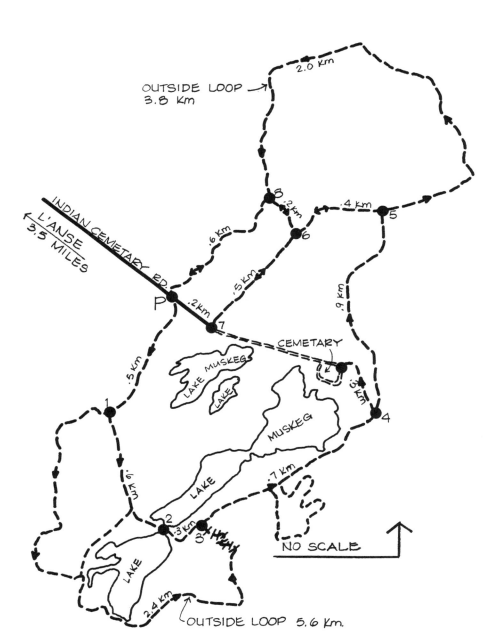

Baraga County Tourist Association
PO Box 556   906-524-7444
Baraga, MI 49908

Baragaland Cross Country Ski Club
c/o Indian Country Sales   906-524-6518
L'Anse, MI 49946

Michigan Atlas & Gazetteer Location: 111B5

County Location: Baraga

Directions To Trailhead:
From downtown L'Anse take Main St. north 1.6 miles to Indian Cemetery Rd.,
then right 2.5 miles to the trailhead. Park along the road.

Trail Type: Cross Country Skiing
Trail Distance: 8 mi   Loops: 4   Shortest: 1 mi   Longest: 3 mi
Trail Surface:
Trail Use Fee: Donations accepted at trailhead
Method Of Ski Trail Grooming: Track set with skating lane
Skiing Ability Suggested: Novice to advanced
Hiking Trail Difficulty: NA
Mountain Biking Ability Suggested: NA
Terrain: Steep 10%, Hilly 30%, Moderate 40%, Flat 20%
Camping: Available nearby

Maintained by the Baragaland Cross-Country Ski Club
Site of the Baragaland Cross-Country Ski Race held the 2nd Sunday in February

Indian Country Sales is the local ski shop in L'Anse.
Indian cemetary dating back to the 1840's is along the trail.
Well designed and maintained trail system.

PINERY LAKES TRAIL

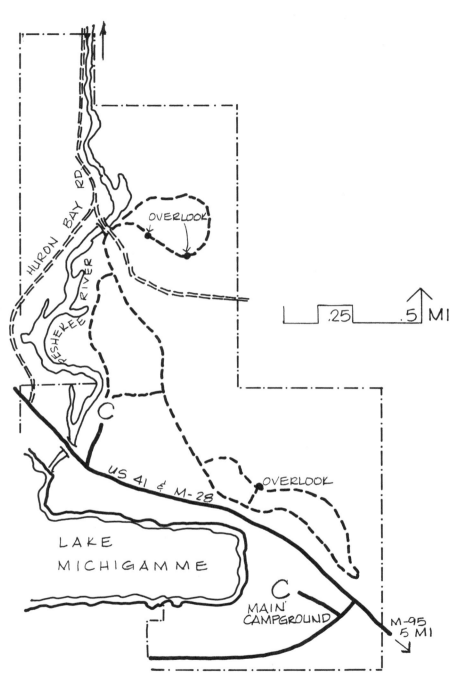

VAN RIPER STATE PARK

Van Riper State Park
Box 66
Champion, MI 49814

906-339-4461

DNR Parks and Recreation Division

517-373-1270
906-228-6561

Michigan Atlas & Gazetteer Location: 111D8,112D1

County Location: Marquette

Directions To Trailhead:
West of Marquette and 5 miles west of M95 on US41/M28
Trailhead is west of main park entrance on north side of US41/M28 at the rustic campground.

Trail Type: Hiking/Walking, Cross Country Skiing, Interpretive
Trail Distance: 4.5 mi   Loops: 4   Shortest: Longest:
Trail Surface: Natural
Trail Use Fee: None, but vehicle entry fee required
Method Of Ski Trail Grooming: None
Skiing Ability Suggested: Advanced
Hiking Trail Difficulty: Moderate to difficult
Mountain Biking Ability Suggested: NA
Terrain: Hilly
Camping: Campground available at trailhead and on Lake Michigamme

Maintained by the DNR Parks and Recreation Divison
Overlooks along the trail
Near the Peshekee to Clowry Rail Trail and the Republic to Champion Rail Trail.

City of Ishpeming
100 Division St.
Ishpeming, MI 49849

906-486-6181
906-486-8301

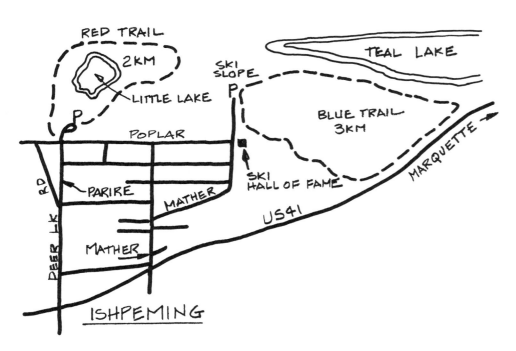

Michigan Atlas & Gazetteer Location: 112D3

County Location: Marquette

Directions To Trailhead:
Red Trailhead - From M41(stop light) in Ishpeming, turn north on Second St., continue straight onto Prairie St to the park entrance. Trailhead is just inside entrance on left side before "park" sign.
Blue Trailhead - Same as above, but right at park entrance on Poplar St. to the end of the street, then left (north) to the downhill ski area. Trailhead is at the right ski tow.

Trail Type: Cross Country Skiing
Trail Distance: 5 km   Loops: 2   Shortest: 2 km   Longest: 3 km
Trail Surface: Natural
Trail Use Fee: Yes, daily, season and family passes available
Method Of Ski Trail Grooming: Track set
Skiing Ability Suggested: Novice to intermediate
Hiking Trail Difficulty: NA
Mountain Biking Ability Suggested: NA
Terrain: Moderate to hilly
Camping: None

Maintained by the City of Ishpeming.
Trail not suitable for skating.
This trail is typical of the several community cross country ski trails in this area. They are relatively short but are designed well and well maintained.
Warming hut, restrooms and a small alpine slope are part of the area.
Sledding area and toboggan run that is 1500' long.
The trails were both very well designed and scenic along the shores of Little Lake and Teal Lake.

AL QUAAL RECREATION AREA

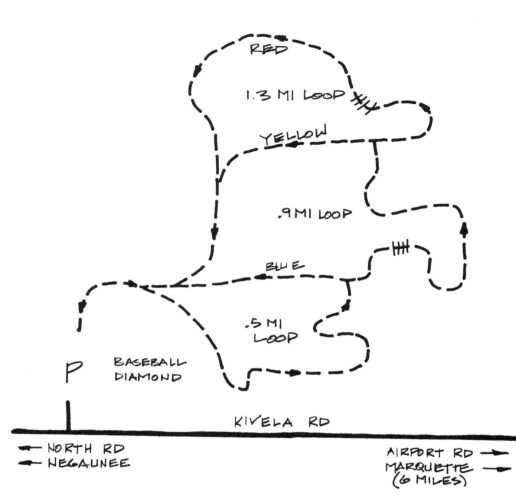

Kivela Road Trail

Negaunee Township
42 M35
Negaunee, MI 49866

906-475-7869

Michigan Atlas & Gazetteer Location: 112D4

County Location: Marquette

Directions To Trailhead:
North of US41via North Rd.and Kivela Rd. west of the county airport.

Trail Type: Hiking/Walking, Cross Country Skiing, Mountain Biking
Trail Distance: 3 mi   Loops: 3   Shortest: .5 mi   Longest: 1.3 mi
Trail Surface: Natural
Trail Use Fee: None
Method Of Ski Trail Grooming: Track set
Skiing Ability Suggested: Novice to advanced
Hiking Trail Difficulty: Easy to moderate
Mountain Biking Ability Suggested: Easy to moderate
Terrain: Steep 0%, Hilly 20%, Moderate 0%, Flat 80%
Camping: None at the trail

Owned by Negaunee Township
Designed for skiing but available for other uses.
Shortest loop - Novice - Blue trail marking
Middle loop - Intermediate - Yellow trail marking
Longest loop - Advanced - Red trail marking

KIVELA ROAD TRAIL

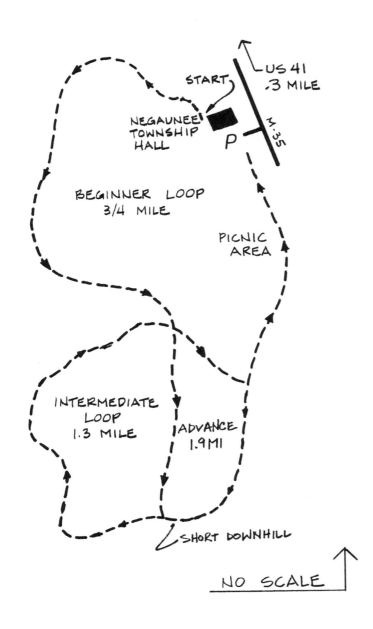

Negaunee Township Hall
RR, M35
Negaunee, MI 49866

906-475-7869

Michigan Atlas & Gazetteer Location: 112D4

County Location: Marquette

Directions To Trailhead:
Trailhead - NW corner of the Negaunee Township Offices located .4 mile south of US41 on M35 (intersection is just east of airport)

Trail Type: Hiking/Walking, Cross Country Skiing, Mountain Biking
Trail Distance: Loops: 3   Shortest: Longest: 3
Trail Surface: Natural
Trail Use Fee: None
Method Of Ski Trail Grooming: Track set on occasion
Skiing Ability Suggested: Novice to intermediate
Hiking Trail Difficulty: Easy
Mountain Biking Ability Suggested: Intermediate
Terrain: Steep 0%, Hilly 20%, Moderate 0%, Flat 80%
Camping: None

Maintained by Negaunee Township.
Small but well maintained trail with several long downhill sections

NEGAUNEE TOWNSHIP TOURING TRAIL

North Country Trail Association
PO Box 311   616-689-1912
White Cloud, MI 49349

North Country Trail Association
12 Middle Island   906-225-1704
Marquette, MI 49855

Michigan Atlas & Gazetteer Location: 112C4,113CD56

County Location: Marquette

Directions To Trailhead:
South trailhead - Lakeshore Drive at Hawley at the north end of town on Lake Superior.
Intermediate trailhead - Co Rd 550 between the Mead-Wetmore Pond Interpretive trailhead and the Harlow Lake Pathway trailhead. NCT crosses Co Rd 550. Trail crosses Co Rd 550 again about 2.5 miles north of previous intermediate trailhead. North trailhead - On Co Rd 550 at Garlic River bridge

Trail Type: Hiking/Walking, Cross Country Skiing
Trail Distance: 21 mi   Loops: NA   Shortest: NA   Longest: NA
Trail Surface: Natural
Trail Use Fee: None
Method Of Ski Trail Grooming: NA
Skiing Ability Suggested: Advanced
Hiking Trail Difficulty: Moderate to difficult
Mountain Biking Ability Suggested: NA
Terrain: Steep 10%, Hilly 10%, Moderate 20%, Flat 60%
Camping: Nearby SFCG and in Marquette (see below)

Recent addition to the North Country Trail being developed by local members. Future develop will extend to the west from Garlic Falls and south of Garlic Falls
Trail passes by several other trail systems including Harllow Lake Pathway, Sugar Loaf Mountain Natural Area, Little Presque Isle Tract and the Mead-Wetmore Pond Interpretive Trail.
Beautiful segment of the North Country Trail, some of which follows the shore of Lake Superior north of Marquette.
Total trail distance includes 3 miles south of Garlic Falls scheduled to be built in 1994.

SEE MAPS ON NEXT PAGE

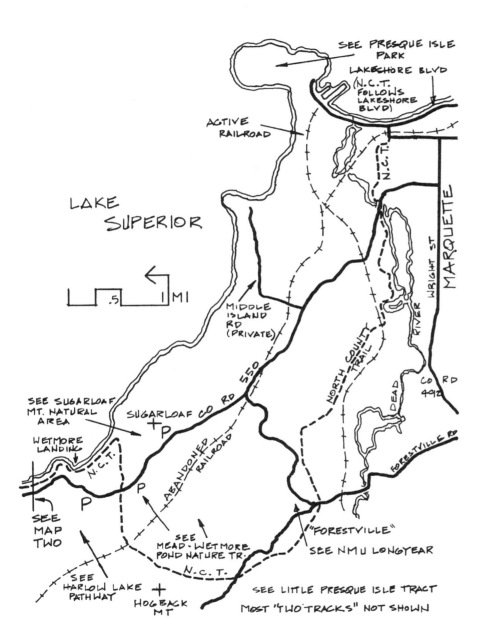

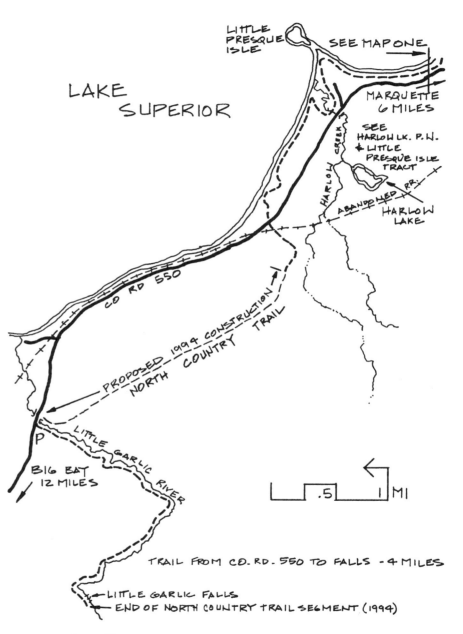

NORTH COUNTRY TRAIL - MARQUETTE (MAP 1)

Lake Superior

SEE PRESQUE ISLE PARK

LAKESHORE BLVD (N.C.T. FOLLOWS LAKESHORE BLVD)

ACTIVE RAILROAD

N.C.T.

LAKE SUPERIOR

MARQUETTE

WRIGHT ST

.5 1 MI

MIDDLE ISLAND RD (PRIVATE)

NORTH COUNTRY TRAIL

DEAD RIVER

CO RD 492

SUGARLOAF CO RD 550

SEE SUGARLOAF MT. NATURAL AREA

P

WETMORE LANDING

N.C.T.

ABANDONED RAILROAD

P

P

FORESTVILLE RD

SEE MAP TWO

SEE MEAD-WETMORE POND NATURE TR.

"FORESTVILLE"

SEE NMU LONGYEAR

N.C.T.

SEE HARLOW LAKE PATHWAY

HOGBACK MT

SEE LITTLE PRESQUE ISLE TRACT

MOST "TWO TRACKS" NOT SHOWN

NORTH COUNTRY TRAIL MARQUETTE (MAP 2)

LITTLE PRESQUE ISLE

SEE MAP ONE

LAKE SUPERIOR

MARQUETTE 6 MILES

SEE HARLOW LK. P.W. & LITTLE PRESQUE ISLE TRACT

HARLOW CREEK

ABANDONED RR

HARLOW LAKE

CO RD 550

PROPOSED 1994 CONSTRUCTION NORTH COUNTRY TRAIL

P

LITTLE GARLIC RIVER

BIG BAY 12 MILES

.5 1 MI

TRAIL FROM CO. RD. 550 TO FALLS - 4 MILES

LITTLE GARLIC FALLS

END OF NORTH COUNTRY TRAIL SEGMENT (1994)

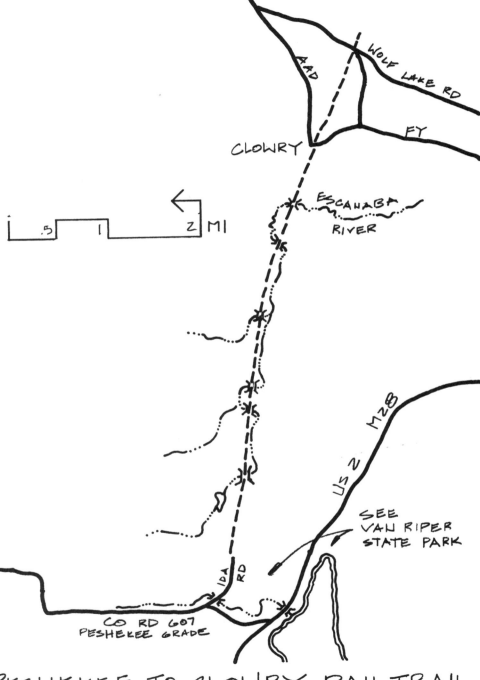

Ishpeming Forest Area, Escanaba River State Forest
1985 US 41 West   906-485-1031
Ishpeming, MI 48949

District Forest Manager, Escanaba River State Forest
6833 US2,41 and M35   906-786-2351
Gladstone, Mi 48937

Michigan Atlas & Gazetteer Location: 112D12

County Location: Marquette

Directions To Trailhead:
West trailhead - West of Champion 2 miles then north on Co Rd 607 1 mile,
theneast .25 mi on Ida Rd to trailhead
East trailhead - Wolf Lake Rd (Ax Rd). 1 mile past Clowry

Trail Type: Hiking/Walking, Mountain Biking
Trail Distance: 6 mi   Loops: NA   Shortest: NA   Longest: NA
Trail Surface: Original ballast and soil
Trail Use Fee: None
Method Of Ski Trail Grooming: NA
Skiing Ability Suggested: NA
Hiking Trail Difficulty: Easy
Mountain Biking Ability Suggested: Novice
Terrain: 100% Flat
Camping: Van Riper State Park at west end of trail.

Maintained by the DNR Forest Management Division
Used also for snowmobiles and ORV's
Outstanding bridges.
Best to park at Van Riper State Park

PESHEKEE TO CLOWRY RAILTRAIL

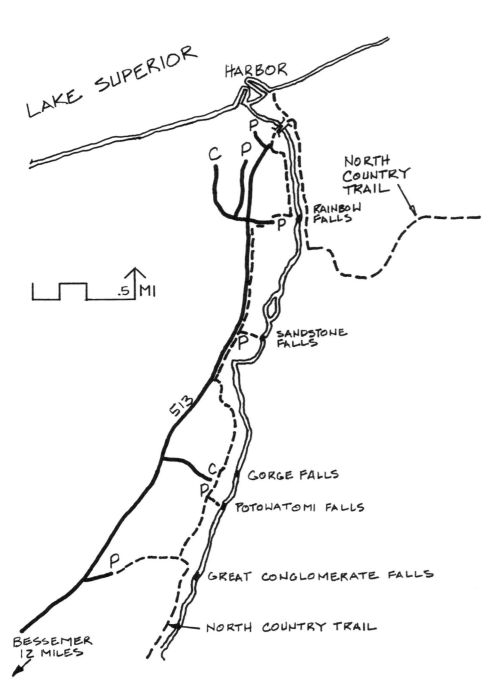

LAKE SUPERIOR

HARBOR

NORTH COUNTRY TRAIL

RAINBOW FALLS

.5 MI

513

SANDSTONE FALLS

GORGE FALLS

POTOWATOMI FALLS

GREAT CONGLOMERATE FALLS

NORTH COUNTRY TRAIL

BESSEMER 12 MILES

BLACK RIVER HARBOR TRAILS

Black River Harbor Trails

Bessemer Ranger District, Ottawa National Forest
500 N Moore St
Bessemer, MI 49911

906-667-0261

Recreation Staff Officer, Ottawa National Forest
2100 E. Cloverland Drive
Ironwood, MI 49938

906-932-1330

Michigan Atlas & Gazetteer Location: 113A8

County Location: Gogebic

Directions To Trailhead:
Along the Black River north of Bessemer to Lake Superior and Black River Harbor. First trail is 12 miles north of Bessemer and continuing north.

Trail Type: Hiking/Walking
Trail Distance: 5 mi   Loops: 5   Shortest: NA   Longest: NA
Trail Surface: Natural
Trail Use Fee: None
Method Of Ski Trail Grooming: NA
Skiing Ability Suggested: NA
Hiking Trail Difficulty: Moderate to difficult
Mountain Biking Ability Suggested: NA
Terrain: Varies with trail
Camping: Campground at Black River Harbor

Maintained by the Ottawa National Forest
Several individual trails from parking areas off Black River Rd to various falls. These are point to point trails, one way.
Great Conglomerate Falls Trail - .75 mile - 30% steep, 30% moderate, 40% flat
Gorge an Potawatomi Falls National Recreation Trail - .75 mile - 70% steep, 30% flat
Sandstone Falls Trail - .25 mile - 40% steep, 20% moderate, 40% flat
Rainbow Falls Trail, West - .5 mile - 80% steep, 20% moderate - stairs
Rainbow Falls Trail, East - .75 mile - 40% steep, 60% moderate - stairs

Trails are connected togeather by the North Country Trail. Rainbow Falls Trail -East is part of the North Country Trail.

Cedar Trail

Frontier Bar c/o John Innes
HCR Box 484
Saxon, WI 54559

715-893-2461

Michigan Atlas & Gazetteer Location: 113C7

County Location: Wisconsin

Directions To Trailhead:
IN Wisconsin, about 18 miles west of Ironwood on US2 at the intersection of US2 and Hwy 169.
South trailhead - Frontier Bar on US2 at Hwy 169.
North trailhead - Harbor Lights Bar on Co Rd A

Trail Type: Hiking/Walking, Cross Country Skiing, Interpretive
Trail Distance: 15 km   Loops: NA   Shortest: NA   Longest: NA
Trail Surface: Natural
Trail Use Fee: Donations accepted for trail maintenance only
Method Of Ski Trail Grooming: Track set
Skiing Ability Suggested: Intermediate
Hiking Trail Difficulty: Moderate
Mountain Biking Ability Suggested: NA
Terrain: Steep 0%, Hilly 10%, Moderate 20%, Flat 70%
Camping: Campground at south end of the trail

Maintained by volunteers.
The trail is located 18 miles west of the Wisconsin border.
Grooming done by the Frontier Bar. Donations accepted.
The trail has a 600 foot decent to Lake Superior.
Meals available at both trailhead taverns.
Picturesque ravines and mature forest along trail.
Camping: County park, campground and harbor at north trailhead. Private campground with showers and trailer hook-ups available at the south trailhead.

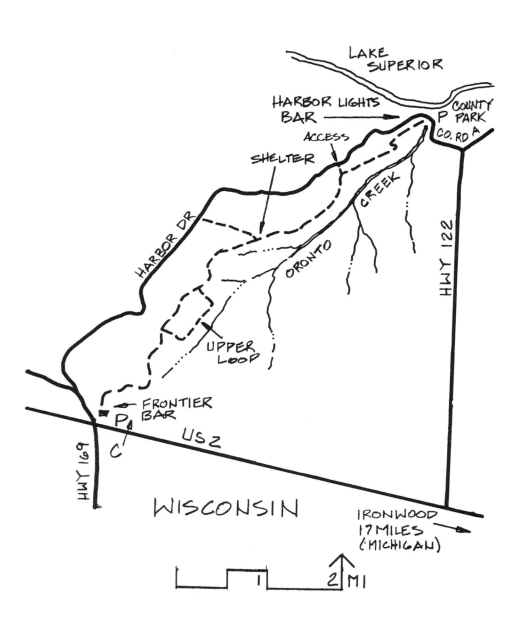

CEDAR TRAIL

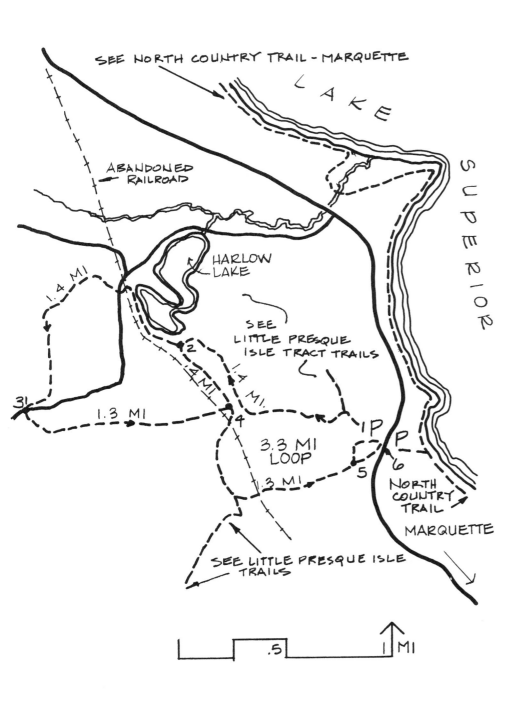

Ishpeming Forest Area, Escanaba River State Forest
1985 U.S. 41 West   906-485-1031
Ishpeming, MI 49849

Marquette Field Office, Eacanaba River State Forest
110 Ford Rd   906-249-1497
Marquette, MI 49855

Michigan Atlas & Gazetteer Location: 113D5

County Location: Marquette

Directions To Trailhead:
5 miles north of Marquette on Co Rd 550. Trail is on the west side of the road.
Parking in a former gravel pit.

Trail Type: Hiking/Walking, Cross Country Skiing, Mountain Biking
Trail Distance: 5.6 mi   Loops: 2   Shortest: 3.3 mi Longest: 5.6 mi
Trail Surface: Natrual
Trail Use Fee: None
Method Of Ski Trail Grooming: None
Skiing Ability Suggested: Intermediate
Hiking Trail Difficulty: Easy to moderate
Mountain Biking Ability Suggested: Novice to intermediate
Terrain: Steep 0%, Hilly 0%, Moderate 50%, Flat 50%
Camping: None

Maintained by the DNR Forest Management Divison.
Part of the Little Presque Isle Tract trails.
See map for additional trails that are nearby.
Other contacts:
        DNR Forest Management Division Office, Lansing, 517-373-1275
        DNR Forest Management District Office, Gladstone, 906-786-2351
        DNR Forest Management Region Office, Marquette, 906-228-6561

HARLOW LAKE PATHWAY

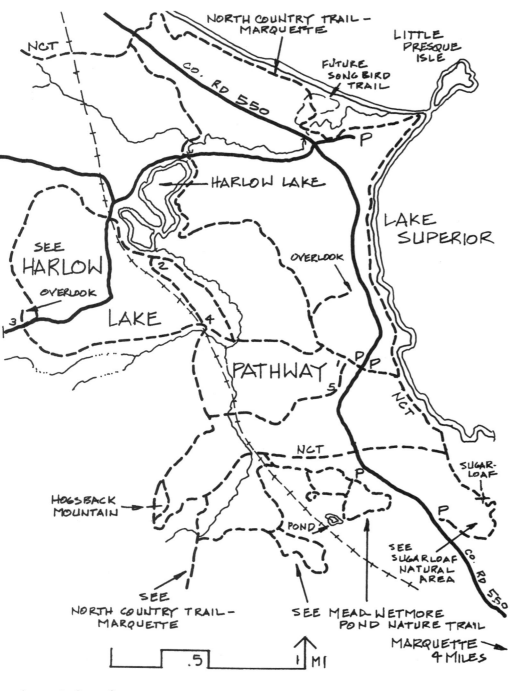

Ishpeming Forest Area, Escanaba River State Forest
1985 US 41 West   906-485-1031
Ishpeming, MI 49849

Marquette Field Office, Escanaba River State Forest
110 Ford Rd   906-249-1497
Marquette, MI 49855

Michigan Atlas & Gazetteer Location: 113CD5

County Location: Marquette

Directions To Trailhead:
6.5 miles north of Marquette on Co. Rd. 550 to parking lot just before the Harlow Creek bridge. Parking lot is located north of the Harlow Lake, Sugar Loaf and Mead-Wetmore Pond trailhead parking lots.

Trail Type: Hiking/Walking, Interpretive
Trail Distance: 18 mi   Loops: 4   Shortest: 3 mi   Longest: 7 mi
Trail Surface:
Trail Use Fee: None
Method Of Ski Trail Grooming: NA
Skiing Ability Suggested: NA
Hiking Trail Difficulty: Easy to moderate
Mountain Biking Ability Suggested:
Terrain: Steep 10%, Hilly 25%, Moderate 40%, Flat 25%
Camping: None

Maintained by the DNR Forest Management Division
Trail system connects the Mead - Wetmore Pond Interpretive Trail, Harlow Lake Pathway
and Sugar Loaf Mountain Natural Area trail.
Cross country skiing limited to the Harlow Lake Pathway portion of the Little Presque Isle
For more information contact:
        DNR Forest Management Region Office, Marquette 906-228-6561
        DNR Forest Management Division Office, Lansing 517-373-1275

LITTLE PRESQUE ISLE TRACT

Mercer MECCA Cross Country Ski Club
PO Box 76
Mercer, WI 54547

715-476-2938

(Map)

ABC -TRAILHEADS

CO RD FF

STATE 51

STATEHOUSE CIRCLE

MERCER

DNR STATION

STATEHOUSE DR.

SNOWS MARKET

[A]

TRAIL

MERCER LAKE

BEACHWAY DR.

POPKO'S CIRCLE

LITTLE PIKE LAKE RD.

LITTLE PIKE LAKE

LOON 5KM

BLUE

MERCER LK CIRCLE

LITTLE TURTLE FLOWAGE RD.

[B]

BOYER RD

TOWN RD

JOE'S SHACK RD.

LITTLE TURTLE 4KM TR.

MERCER SPRINGS 3KM

MERCER SPRINGS

6KM TR

VOSS LK TR

[C]

LOOP 3

LOOP 1

LOOP 2

CABIN

SPRUCE HILLS TRAIL 1KM

LITTLE TURTLE FLOWAGE

HOMESTEAD TRAIL 6KM

NORTH ↑

SNOWMOBILE TRAIL

Michigan Atlas & Gazetteer Location: 113 Wisconsin

County Location: Wisconsin

Directions To Trailhead:
23 miles south of Ironwood on US51 at Mercer Wisconsin.
Traihead A - About 1/8 mile north of Mercer on US51 to Statehouse Circle Rd,then follow signs.
Traihead B - .25 south of Mercer on US51 to Beachway Drive, then to Mercer Lake Circle Rd, then to Boyer Rd, then to Town Rd. (follow signs).   Trailhead C - From Mercer on US51 north 1 mile to CoRd FF and follow signs.

Trail Type: Cross Country Skiing
Trail Distance: 25 km   Loops: 4   Shortest: 3 km   Longest: 9 km
Trail Surface: Natural
Trail Use Fee: Donations accepted
Method Of Ski Trail Grooming: Track set weekly
Skiing Ability Suggested: Novice to intermediate
Hiking Trail Difficulty: NA
Mountain Biking Ability Suggested: NA
Terrain: Steep 5%, Hilly 20%, Moderate 60%, Flat 15%
Camping: None

Maintained by the MECCA Ski Club. A non-profit organization which maintains, grooms and promotes the trail.
Well designed and interesting ski trail.
This and other Iron County trails were developed through the close cooperation of various local citizen groups and the Iron County Wisconsin Forestry Department.
Strictly a ski trail. Not suitable for mountain biking or hiking because of the many swamps in the area along the trail.
Heated cabin along trail at a scenic wetland vista.
Donations by trail users are an essential part of the fund raising program to maintain these trails.
Several trailheads and a waterfall are along the trail.
Some of the trail is on private land. Please stay on the trail at all times.

MECCA X-C SKI TRAIL

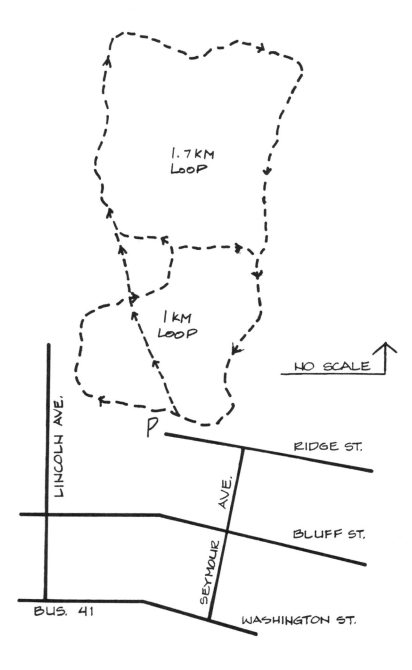

City of Marquette, Department of Parks and Recreation
300 Baraga Ave
Marquette, MI 49855

906-228-0460

Michigan Atlas & Gazetteer Location: 113D5

County Location: Marquette

Directions To Trailhead:
Take Washington St. .5 mile west of the downtown area to Seymour St, then proceed north to Ridge St., then west on Ridge St. to the parking lot. The trailhead is directly north of the parking lot.

Trail Type: Hiking/Walking, Cross Country Skiing, Interpretive
Trail Distance: 4.4 km   Loops: 3   Shortest: 1 km   Longest: 1.7 km
Trail Surface:
Trail Use Fee: Yes, donation for skiing only
Method Of Ski Trail Grooming: Track set with skating trail
Skiing Ability Suggested: Novice to intermediate
Hiking Trail Difficulty: Easy
Mountain Biking Ability Suggested: NA
Terrain: Steep 0%, Hilly 5%, Moderate 95%, Flat 5%
Camping: Available in the Marquette area

Maintained by the Parks Department, City of Marquette
1.7 km lighted loop to 11pm
Trails for traditional and skating styles

MARQUETTE FITNESS TRAIL

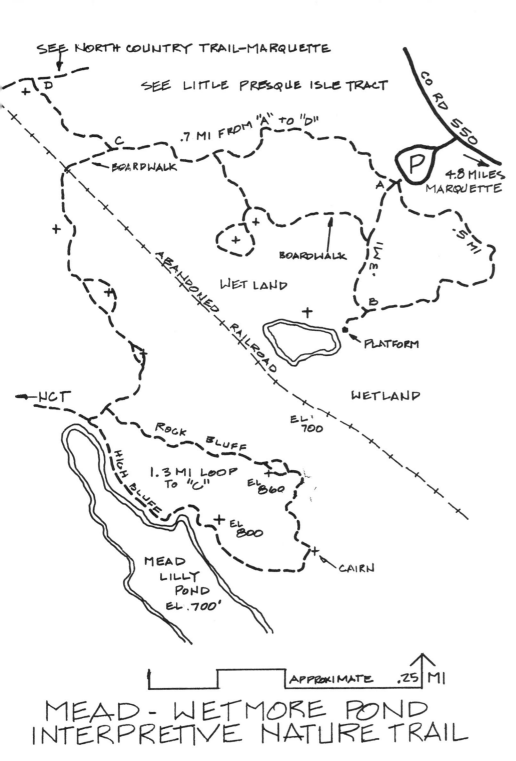

SEE NORTH COUNTRY TRAIL-MARQUETTE

SEE LITTLE PRESQUE ISLE TRACT

CO RD 550

+ D

.7 MI FROM "A" TO "D"

C

BOARDWALK

4.8 MILES MARQUETTE

P

A

+

+

+

BOARDWALK

WETLAND

.5 MI

B

+

PLATFORM

ABANDONED RAILROAD

WETLAND

NCT

EL' 700

ROCK BLUFF

1.3 MI LOOP TO "C"

EL 860

HIGH BLUFF

+ EL 800

+ EL 700

+ CAIRN

MEAD LILLY POND EL .700'

APPROXIMATE .25 MI

MEAD - WETMORE POND
INTERPRETIVE NATURE TRAIL

Mead-Wetmore Pond Nature Trail

Mead Paper, Woodlands Department
US41, West
Champion, MI 49814

906-339-2281

Mead Paper, Woodland Communications
PO Box 1008
Escanaba, MI 49829

906-786-1660
Ext. 2194

Michigan Atlas & Gazetteer Location: 113D5

County Location: Marquette

Directions To Trailhead:
4.5 miles north of Marquette on Co. Rd. 550. Between the Sugar Loaf and Harlow Lake trails.

Trail Type: Hiking/Walking, Cross Country Skiing, Interpretive
Trail Distance: 12 mi   Loops: 3   Shortest: Various Longest: Various
Trail Surface: Natural
Trail Use Fee: None
Method Of Ski Trail Grooming: None
Skiing Ability Suggested: Novice to intermediate
Hiking Trail Difficulty: Easy to moderate
Mountain Biking Ability Suggested: NA
Terrain: Steep 2%, Hilly 10%, Moderate 28%, Flat 60%
Camping: None

Owned and developed by Mead Paper.
Trails and facilities built by Mead and and volunteers including members of the North Country Trail Association, Michigan Department of Natural Resources, Northern Michigan University faculty and other volunteers.
Wetmore pond is a floating bog worth the time to view.
North County Trail - Marquette segment passes nearby the area.
Part of a trail system that connects together the North Country Trail, Harlow Lake Pathway and the Sugar Loaf Mountain Interpretive Trail. All are listed separately in the atlas.

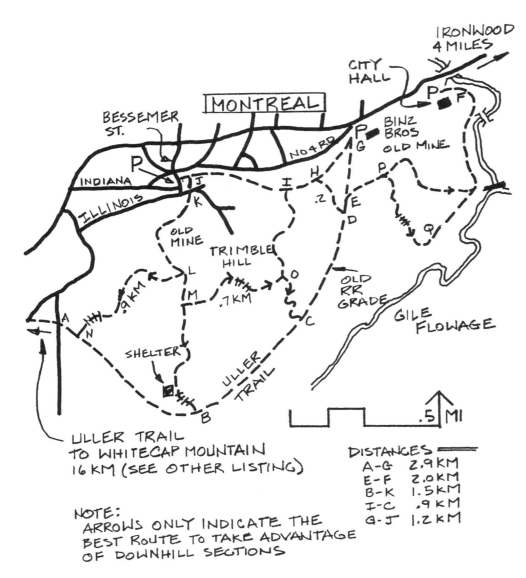

IRONWOOD
4 MILES

CITY
HALL

MONTREAL

BESSEMER
ST.

P

INDIANA

ILLINOIS

NO 4 RD

BINZ
BROS

OLD MINE

P

G

H

I

.2

E

D

Q

P

OLD
MINE

TRIMBLE
HILL

.9 KM

L

M

.7 KM

O

C

OLD
RR
GRADE

GILE
FLOWAGE

A

N

SHELTER

ULLER
TRAIL

B

.5 MI

ULLER TRAIL
TO WHITECAP MOUNTAIN
16 KM (SEE OTHER LISTING)

DISTANCES
A-G 2.9 KM
E-F 2.0 KM
B-K 1.5 KM
I-C .9 KM
G-J 1.2 KM

NOTE:
ARROWS ONLY INDICATE THE
BEST ROUTE TO TAKE ADVANTAGE
OF DOWNHILL SECTIONS

Iron County Extension Service
Court House
Hurley, WI 54534
715-561-2695

Penokee Rangers Inc.
301 Birch St.
Pence, WI 54553
715-561-5623

Michigan Atlas & Gazetteer Location: 113C6

County Location: Wisconsin

Directions To Trailhead:
4 miles west of Ironwood via US2 and Wisconsin Hwy 77
Trailhead - In Montreal take Bessemer south to trailheads(2) at the corners of 4
Rd & Bessemer & Illinois & Bessemer.
Trailhead - Montreal City Hall on Hwy 77
Trailhead - West end of Montreal on Spring Camp Rd

Trail Type: Hiking/Walking, Cross Country Skiing, Interpretive
Trail Distance: 15 km   Loops: 6   Shortest: .5 km   Longest: 11 km
Trail Surface: Natural
Trail Use Fee: Donation requested at trailhead
Method Of Ski Trail Grooming: Track set 3 to 4 times per week
Skiing Ability Suggested: Novice to intermediate
Hiking Trail Difficulty: Easy to moderate
Mountain Biking Ability Suggested: Intermediate to advanced
Terrain: Steep 10%, Hilly 40%, Moderate 20%, Flat 30%
Camping: None

Maintained by the Penokee Rangers (a local non-profit ski club)
A delightful trail system in the hills above Montreal.
Shelter cabin is along the trail Trail is well designed with several long downhill
runs and beautiful scenery.
The east end of the 16 km Uller Trail (see other listing) to Weber Lake.
Portion of the trail (Uller Trail) is double track on the old Montreal Iron Mine
railroad grade. Many historic remanents of the Montreal Mine (the deepest iron
mine in the world, almost 1 mile deep) are visible along the trail including tailing
piles, many old structures and the railroad grade cut through bedrock.

MONTREAL PUBLIC TRAIL

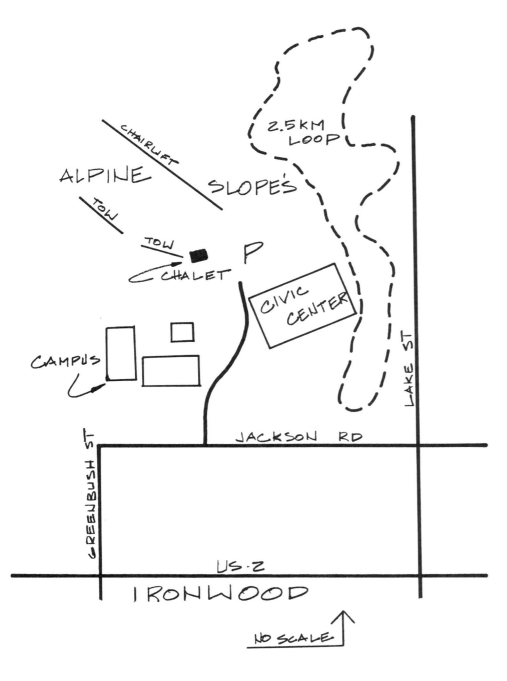

Gogebic Community College
E4946 Jackson Rd
Ironwood, MI 49938

906-932-3718

Michigan Atlas & Gazetteer Location: 113C7

County Location: Gogebic

Directions To Trailhead:
On the campus of Gogebic Community College, .5 mile north of US2

Trail Type: Hiking/Walking, Cross Country Skiing
Trail Distance: 2.5 km   Loops: 1   Shortest: Longest: 2.5 km
Trail Surface: Natural
Trail Use Fee: None
Method Of Ski Trail Grooming: Track set
Skiing Ability Suggested: Novice
Hiking Trail Difficulty: Easy
Mountain Biking Ability Suggested: NA
Terrain: Steep 0%, Hilly 0%, Moderate 10%, Flat 90%
Camping: None

Operated by Gogebic Community College

Athletic Department
Northern Michigan Univesity
Marquette, MI 49855

Michigan Atlas & Gazetteer Location: 113D5

County Location: Marquette

Directions To Trailhead:
From US41, take Wright St north to road to Forestville. After crossing Dead River at about 1.7 miles from US23 turn right over railroad tracks, then another right to trail

Trail Type: Cross Country Skiing
Trail Distance: 4.5 km   Loops: 2   Shortest: 2 km   Longest: 3 km
Trail Surface: Natrual
Trail Use Fee: None
Method Of Ski Trail Grooming: None
Skiing Ability Suggested: Intermediate
Hiking Trail Difficulty: NA
Mountain Biking Ability Suggested: NA
Terrain:
Camping: None

Maintained by Northern Michigan University

2KM LOOP

3KM LOOP

.3 MI

1.9 MI

CO RD HD

WRIGHT ST. 492

SIGN TO "FORESTVILLE"

NEGAUNEE   US 41   TO MARQUETTE

NORTH

NMU LONGYEAR

City of Marquette, Parks & Recreation Department
300 Baraga Ave
Marquette, MI 49855

906-228-8200
ext 213

800-544-4321

Michigan Atlas & Gazetteer Location: 113D6

County Location: Marquette

Directions To Trailhead:
2 miles north of Marquette along lakeshore at Presque Isle Park Take
Lakeshore Blvd north to Peter White Dr(2 miles) Trailhead-Adjacent to Peter
White Drive and plowed parking lots.

Trail Type: Hiking/Walking, Cross Country Skiing, Interpretive
Trail Distance: 5 km   Loops: 3   Shortest: 1.5 km Longest: 3.5 km
Trail Surface:
Trail Use Fee: Yes, donation for skiing only
Method Of Ski Trail Grooming: Track set as needed
Skiing Ability Suggested: Novice to intermediate
Hiking Trail Difficulty: Moderate
Mountain Biking Ability Suggested: NA
Terrain: Steep 0%, Hilly 25%, Moderate 35%, Flat 40%
Camping: Very nearby

Maintained by the City of Marquette, Parks and Recreation Department
Both wide (vehicle drive in summer) and narrow (foot paths) trails are available
to the skier A small city zoo is along the return trail Interior trails are through
dense forests.
Beautiful view of Lake Superior and winter ice formations. Also a snow shoe trail
avaialble which is not listed. Traditional and skating style trails. Skating is
goomed on about 70% of the trails.
Because of the warming effect of Lake Superior, this trail looses its snow cover
earlier than the inland trails in the Marquette and Ishpeming area.
Brochure is available for the 14 station interpretive trail.

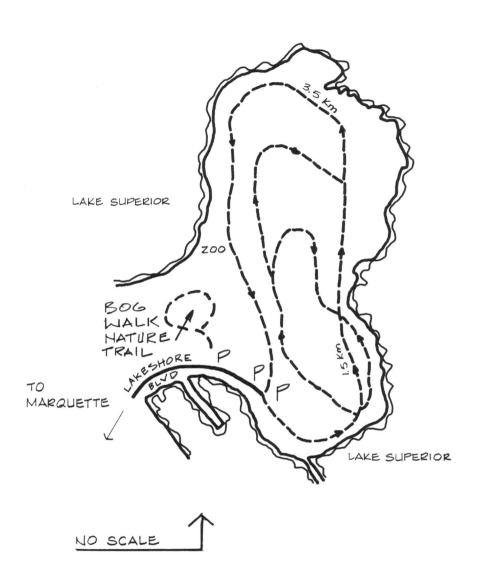

LAKE SUPERIOR

3.5 km

ZOO

1.5 km

BOG
WALK
NATURE
TRAIL

LAKESHORE
BLVD

P   P
  P   P

TO
MARQUETTE

LAKE SUPERIOR

NO SCALE

PRESQUE ISLE PARK

River Falls Outdoors
N10675 Junet Rd.
Ironwood , MI 49938

906-932-5638

Map labels

JUNET RD

OLSON RD

JUNET RD

SIS'S LOOP

PRIVATE RD

JUNET

HIGH POINT

RD

WET LAND

HIGH POINT

PRIVATE SMALL BLUFF SCENIC VIEW

HIGH BLUFF SCENIC VIEW

HIGH POINT

LODGE COMPOUND

PETERSON FALLS

HIGH RIDGE TRAIL

PRIVATE

WISCONSIN

US 2

HIGH POINT

UPPER FALLS

HIGH POINT

JUNET RD

SUPERIOR ST

CURRY TRAIL

MONTREAL RIVER

COUNTY FAIRGROUNDS

IRONWOOD MICHIGAN

HURLEY WISCONSIN

US 2

US 51

.25   .5 MI

McGUIRE'S RIVER FALLS TRAIL

Michigan Atlas & Gazetteer Location: 113C7

County Location: Gogebic

Directions To Trailhead:
Along the Montreal River 4 miles north of Ironwood.
Take Superior St. north to Junet Rd., west on Junet to the Lodge (follow signs)

Trail Type: Hiking/Walking, Cross Country Skiing, Mountain Biking, Interpretive
Trail Distance: 5.5 mi   Loops: 3   Shortest: 1 mi   Longest: 3 mi
Trail Surface: Natural
Trail Use Fee: Yes, for skiing
Method Of Ski Trail Grooming: Double track set
Skiing Ability Suggested: Novice to intermediate
Hiking Trail Difficulty: Easy to moderate
Mountain Biking Ability Suggested: Novice to intermediate
Terrain: Steep 10%, Hilly 30%, Moderate 30%, Flat 30%
Camping: Yes

Privately operated touring center and outfitter
Trails are free when staying at River Falls Outdoors.
Cottages and lodge with complete facilities including sauna and fireplace.
Overlooking the Montreal River and falls.
Outfitting services available for mountain bike trips, hiking trips in the Porcupine
Mountains and canoe trips in the Sylvania Area and area rivers.

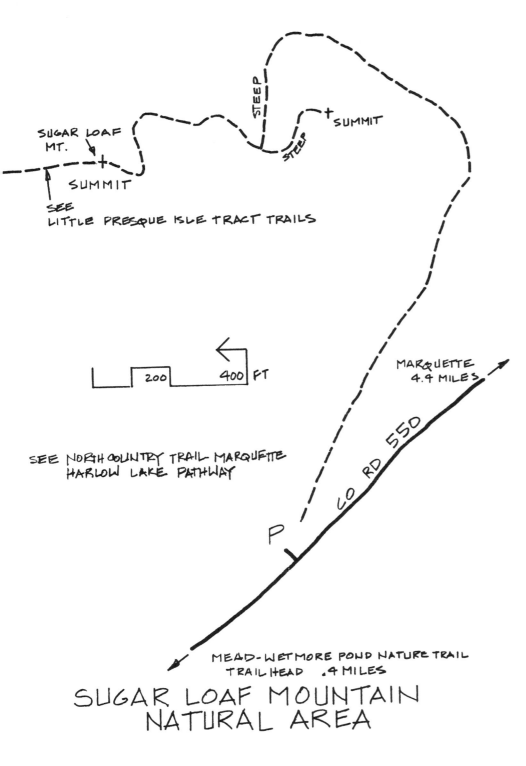

SUGAR LOAF
MT.

SUMMIT

SEE
LITTLE PRESQUE ISLE TRACT TRAILS

STEEP

STEEP

SUMMIT

200 400 FT

SEE NORTH COUNTRY TRAIL MARQUETTE
HARLOW LAKE PATHWAY

P

MARQUETTE
4.4 MILES

CO RD 550

MEAD-WETMORE POND NATURE TRAIL
TRAIL HEAD .4 MILES

SUGAR LOAF MOUNTAIN
NATURAL AREA

Marquette Co. Resource Management & Development Dept
234 Baraga   906-228-1535
Marquette, MI 49855

Michigan Atlas & Gazetteer Location: 113D5

County Location: Marquette

Directions To Trailhead:
North from Marquette about 4.4 miles along Lake Superior on Co Rd 550

Trail Type: Hiking/Walking, Interpretive
Trail Distance: .5 mi   Loops: NA   Shortest: NA   Longest: NA
Trail Surface: Natural
Trail Use Fee: None
Method Of Ski Trail Grooming: NA
Skiing Ability Suggested: NA
Hiking Trail Difficulty: Moderate
Mountain Biking Ability Suggested: NA
Terrain: Steep 35%, Hilly 45%, Moderate 15%, Flat 5%
Camping: None

Maintained by the Marquette County Road Commission.
Near Harlow Lake Pathway and the Mead-Wetmore Pond Interpretive Trail.
Very scenic changing panoramic views of the Lake Superior shoreline.

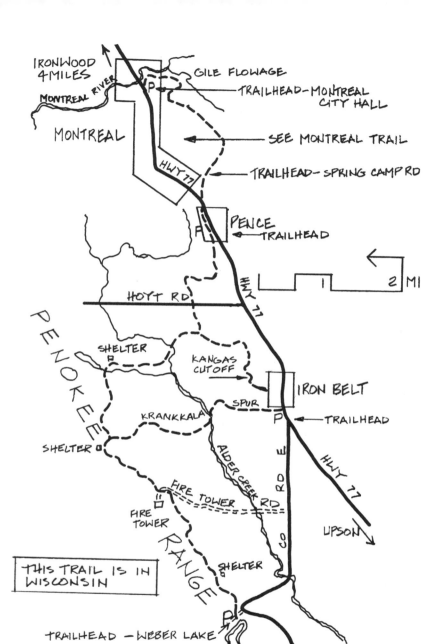

Penokee Rangers Inc.
301 Birch St
Pence, WI 54550

715-561-5623

Michigan Atlas & Gazetteer Location: 113C6

County Location: Wisconsin

Directions To Trailhead:
This trail is in Wisconsin. Gazetteer location is closest location in Michigan
East trailhead - Montreal Public Trail at the Montreal City Hall
Middle trailheads - On Hwy 77 at Pence and north side of Iron Belt (Krankkala
Spur and Kangas Cut-off)
West trailhead - Weber Lake next to Whitecap Mountainson Co Hwy E

Trail Type: Cross Country Skiing, Interpretive
Trail Distance: 25 km   Loops: NA   Shortest: NA   Longest: NA
Trail Surface: Natural
Trail Use Fee: Donation accepted
Method Of Ski Trail Grooming: Track set as needed
Skiing Ability Suggested: All levels
Hiking Trail Difficulty: All levels
Mountain Biking Ability Suggested: NA
Terrain: Steep 10%, Hilly 50%, Moderate 30%, Flat 10%
Camping: Along the trail at trailside shelters

Maintained by the Penokee Rangers Inc, a local non-profit cross-country ski club
The trail has 14 interpreted locations coveing geography, wildlife, forestry and
history.
A well established ski trail with little interferance from snowmobiles, even though
there are few signs to prohibit snowmobile use on the trail.
Since this trail is funded solely by the donations of its users, it is essential that
you make a donation to fund the grooming .
The Montreal Trail located at the east end of the Uller is also maintained by the
Penokee Rangers Inc.
This trail traverses the top of the scenic Penokee Mountains from Montreal to
Weber Lake. Two rustic shelters along the trail are available for overnight
accomodations.

ULLER TRAIL

Wolverine Nordic Ski Corporation
N12855 Lake Rd   906-932-3299
Ironwood, MI 49938

Outer Edge
E6298 US2   906-932-5566
Bessemer, MI 49911

Michigan Atlas & Gazetteer Location: 113BC78

County Location: Gogebic

Directions To Trailhead:
Wolverine Hill trailhead - East of Ironwood on US2 1 mile, then north on Section 12 Rd 1.25 miles, then east .5 mile on Sunset Rd to the ski jumps.
Trailhead also at Outer Edge store on US2

Trail Type: Cross Country Skiing
Trail Distance: 14 km   Loops: 5   Shortest: Longest:
Trail Surface:
Trail Use Fee: Donation of $2/day is requested to groom trails
Method Of Ski Trail Grooming: Track set usually Monday and Friday
Skiing Ability Suggested: Novice to intermediate
Hiking Trail Difficulty: NA
Mountain Biking Ability Suggested:
Terrain: Rolling to hilly with some flat sections
Camping: None

Maintained by the Wolverine Ski Club
The trail offers a variety of scenery, maple hardwood forests, old homesteads, scenic overlooks, streams, a beaver dam, "ice falls", and ski jumps.
Very popular trail, but large enough so you don't get the feeling of being crowded.
Well designed ski trail for the novice and intermediate skier.
Near many other trails including Johnson's in Wakefield, Snowcrest and several Wisconsin trails just across the state line.

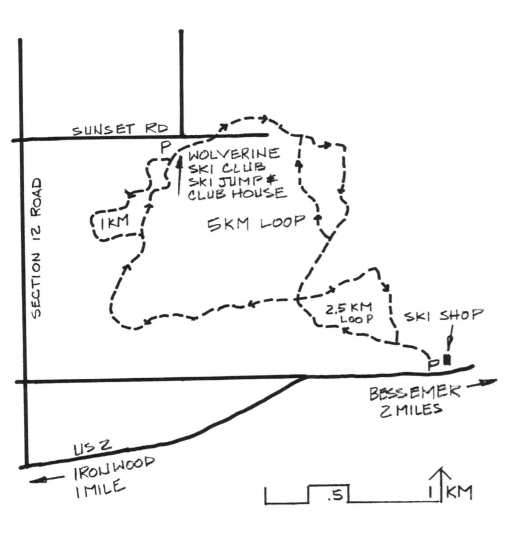

WOLVERINE SKI TRAIL

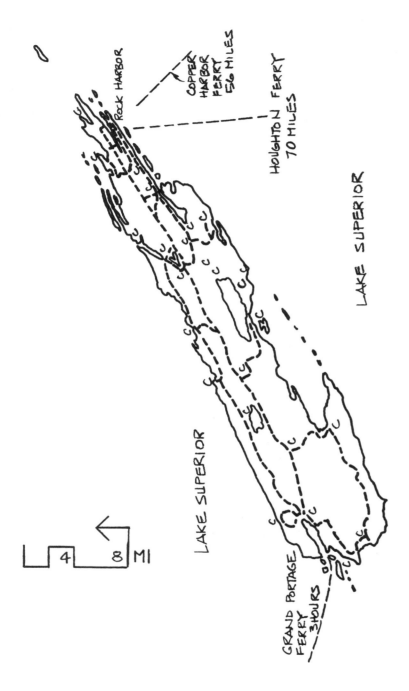

Isle Royale National Park
87 N. Ripley St
Houghton, MI 49931-1895

906-482-0984

Michigan Atlas & Gazetteer Location: 114all,115all

County Location: Keweenaw

Directions To Trailhead:
70 miles north of Houghton in Lake Superior Ferry services from Houghton,
Copper Harbor and Grand Portage Sea plane service from Houghton

Trail Type: Hiking/Walking, Interpretive
Trail Distance: 165 mi   Loops: Many   Shortest: Longest:
Trail Surface: Paved and mostly natural
Trail Use Fee: Yes
Method Of Ski Trail Grooming: NA
Skiing Ability Suggested: NA
Hiking Trail Difficulty: Easy to extremely difficult
Mountain Biking Ability Suggested: NA
Terrain: Steep 20%, Hilly 30%, Moderate 30%, Flat 20%
Camping: Available throughout the park

Maintained by the National Park Service
The most rugged and remote area in Michigan. The extreme beauty of this island
is a delight to the senses. Be completely prepared before attempting to do any
extensive hiking on the island. Write to the Park for information on
hiking/camping/boating recommendations before planning your trip. Complete
lodge facilities are available at Rock Harbor for those not interested in extensive
hiking but reservations must be made months in advance to assure
accomodation. Likewise, reservations on the two ferry boats should be made a
month in advance of departure to assure space on board. Write for information
brochures and catalog of publications available. Park season Apr 16th - Oct
31st. Full services are available June-August NOT OPEN IN THE WINTER.

ISLE ROYALE NATIONAL PARK

Pictured Rocks National Lakeshore
PO Box 40
Munising, MI 49862-0040

906-387-3700
906-387-2607

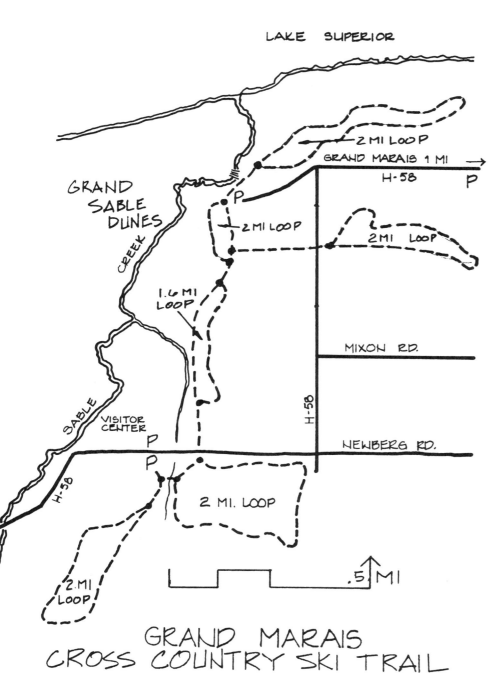

Michigan Atlas & Gazetteer Location: 115C8

County Location: Alger

Directions To Trailhead:
1 mile west of Grand Marais on H58 (just inside the park boundary) or 1 mile west of M77 on Newberg Rd.

Trail Type: Hiking/Walking, Cross Country Skiing
Trail Distance: 10 mi   Loops: 6   Shortest: Longest:
Trail Surface: Natural
Trail Use Fee: None
Method Of Ski Trail Grooming:
Skiing Ability Suggested: Novice to intermediate
Hiking Trail Difficulty: Easy
Mountain Biking Ability Suggested: NA
Terrain: Flat to rolling some steep hills
Camping: Campground available in summer only

Maintained by the Pictured Rocks National Lakeshore
Backcountry camping is permitted 200' off the trail.
View of Sable Falls and Lake Superior from the trail.
Ranger office is located near the trailhead.
A map is in place at each trail intersection.
Pets are not permitted on the ski trails.

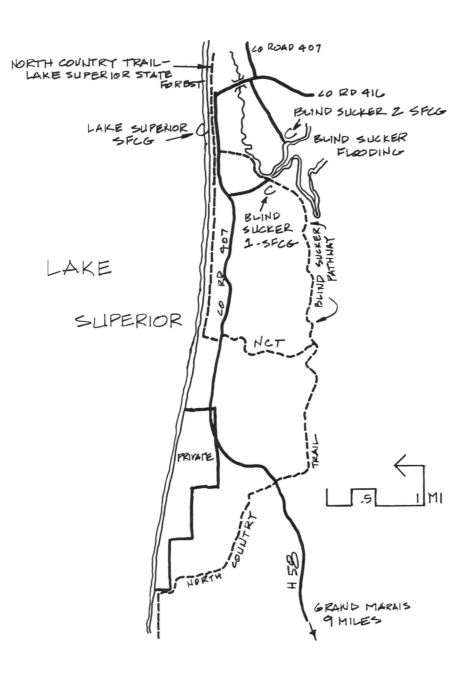

Newberry Forest Area, Lake Superior State Forest
PO Box 428   906-293-3293
Newberry, MI 49868

District Forest Manager, Lake Superior State Forest
PO Box 77   906-293-5132
Newberry, MI 49868

Michigan Atlas & Gazetteer Location: 116C2

County Location: Luce

Directions To Trailhead:
Along Lake Superior 10 miles east of Grand Marais on H 58 at Blind Sucker 1
State Forest Campground (SFCG)

Trail Type: Hiking/Walking
Trail Distance: 3+ mi   Loops: NA   Shortest: NA   Longest: NA
Trail Surface: Natural
Trail Use Fee: None
Method Of Ski Trail Grooming: NA
Skiing Ability Suggested: NA
Hiking Trail Difficulty: Moderate
Mountain Biking Ability Suggested: NA
Terrain: Steep 0%, Hilly 25%, Moderate 60%, Flat 15%
Camping: Campround along trail and also nearby

Maintained by the DNR Forest Management Division
The trail is a bypass section of the North Country Trail - Lake Superior State
Forest
Trail distance is approximate.
By also using the North Country Trail, a 7.6 mile loop can be made.
The trail is in a very scenic and isolated area.

BLIND SUCKER PATHWAY

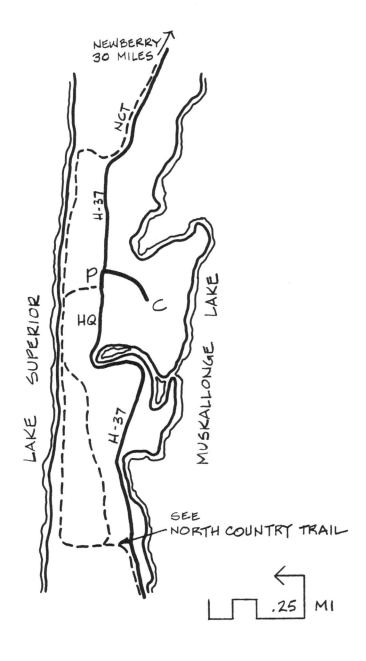

MUSKALLONGE LAKE
STATE PARK

Muskallonge Lake State Park
Rte 1, PO Box 245
Newberry, MI 49868

906-658-3338

DNR Parks and Recreation Division

517-373-1270
906-492-3415

Michigan Atlas & Gazetteer Location: 116C4

County Location: Luce

Directions To Trailhead:
30 miles north of Newberry on Co Rd 407 (H37) 18 miles east of Grand Marais on Co Rd 407

Trail Type: Hiking/Walking, Cross Country Skiing
Trail Distance: .75 mi   Loops: 1   Shortest: Longest: .75 mi
Trail Surface: Natural
Trail Use Fee: None, but vehicle entry fee required
Method Of Ski Trail Grooming: NA
Skiing Ability Suggested: NA
Hiking Trail Difficulty: Easy
Mountain Biking Ability Suggested: NA
Terrain: Steep 0%, Hilly 0%, Moderate 90%, Flat 10%
Camping: Campground in the park

Maintained by the DNR Parks and Recreation Division
Part of the North Country Pathway
Site of a logging town call Deer Park in the 1800's
Good agate hunting along Lake Superior near trail

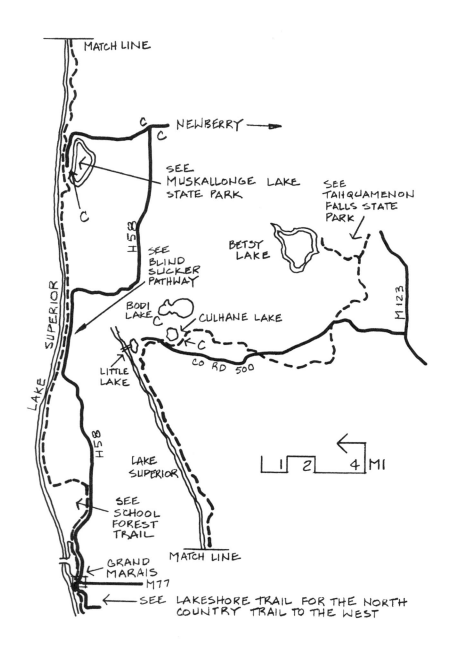

District Forest Manager, Lake Superior State Forest
PO Box 77   906-293-5131
Newberry, MI 49868

Tahquamenon Falls State Park
Rte 48, Box 225   906-492-3415
Paradise, MI 49768   517-373-1270

Michigan Atlas & Gazetteer Location: 116C1234,117CD567

County Location: Luce/Chippewa

Directions To Trailhead:
From Tahquamenon Falls State Park to Pictured Rocks National Lakeshore.
Trailheads - Grand Marais, Tahquamenon Falls SP, Muskallonge Lake SP,
Lake Superior SFCG and Two Hearted River SFCG.

Trail Type: Hiking/Walking
Trail Distance: 56 mi   Loops: NA   Shortest: NA   Longest: NA
Trail Surface: Natural
Trail Use Fee: None
Method Of Ski Trail Grooming: None
Skiing Ability Suggested: NA
Hiking Trail Difficulty: Moderate to difficult
Mountain Biking Ability Suggested: NA
Terrain: Steep 0%, Hilly 25%, Moderate 50%, Flat 25
Camping: Numerous campgrounds along the trail

Maintained by the DNR Forest Management Division.
Excellent wilderness hiking trail. Like the entire North Country Trail system, this
is a point to point trail.
Some sections have been reported to be not well maintained. Confirm
information before starting out on the trail.
For more information about the North Country Trail contact the North Country
Trail Association, PO Box 311, White Cloud, MI 49349 616-689-1912

NORTH COUNTRY TRAIL
LAKE SUPERIOR STATE FOREST

POSSIBLE ROUTE
NORTH COUNTRY TRAIL
SEE PAGE 105 OF
MICHIGAN SECTION—
HIKER GUIDE

5 MI
LOOP

SUCKER RIVER

2.4 MI
LOOP

1.2 MI
LOOP

GRAND
MARAIS
4 MI

P

H-58

NO SCALE

SCHOOL FOREST SKI TRAIL

Grand Marais Chamber of Commerce
PO Box 139
Grand Marais, MI 49839

906-494-2766

Kathleen R Baker
PO Box 118
Grand Marais, MI 49839

906-494-2766

Michigan Atlas & Gazetteer Location: 116C1

County Location: Alger

Directions To Trailhead:
4 miles east of Grand Marais on H58 just past the creek. Parking lot on right side of road. Short walk from parking lot to the trailhead (look for sign on left).

Trail Type: Hiking/Walking, Cross Country Skiing
Trail Distance: 6.8 mi   Loops: 5   Shortest: 1.2 mi Longest: 5 mi
Trail Surface: Natural
Trail Use Fee: None
Method Of Ski Trail Grooming: Track set weekly
Skiing Ability Suggested: Novice to intermediate
Hiking Trail Difficulty: Easy to moderate
Mountain Biking Ability Suggested: NA
Terrain: Steep 10%, Hilly 5%, Moderate 5%, Flat 80%
Camping: Camping not permitted

Maintained by the community of Grand Marais
Food and lodging in Grand Marais.
Connects with the North Country Trail - Lake Superior State Forest..
Site of the Polar Bear Cross Country Ski Race held the first week of February.
Well marked trail with beautiful north country scenery .
The North Country Trail may not be well marked in this area(1994).

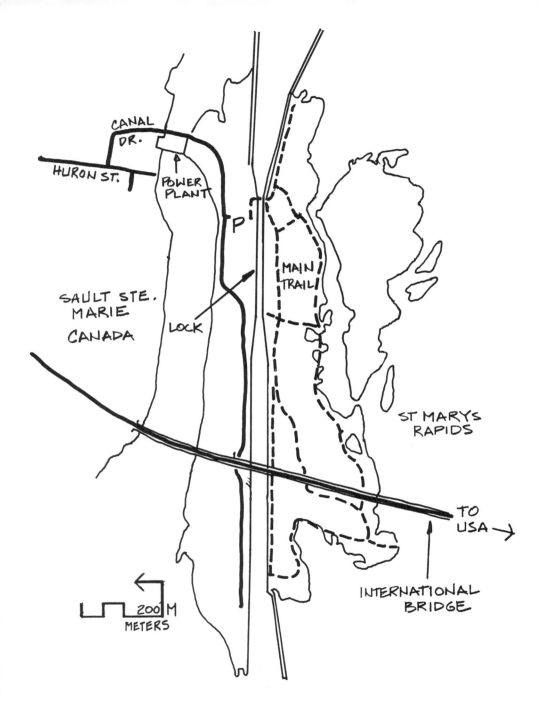

Attikamek Trail

Sault Canal National Historic Site
1 Canal Drive
Sault Ste Marie, Ontario, Canada P6A 6W4

705-942-6262

Michigan Atlas & Gazetteer Location: 117A6

County Location: Ontario, Canada

Directions To Trailhead:
Along the Canadian Soo Locks under the International Bridge. Turn right past customs and right again on Huron Street to Canal Drive, then left on Canal Drive past the power generating station to the Visitor Center.

Trail Type: Hiking/Walking, Cross Country Skiing, Interpretive
Trail Distance: 1.4 mi   Loops: 2   Shortest: Longest:
Trail Surface: Paved and natural
Trail Use Fee: None
Method Of Ski Trail Grooming: None
Skiing Ability Suggested: Novice
Hiking Trail Difficulty: Easy
Mountain Biking Ability Suggested: NA
Terrain: 100% Flat
Camping: None

Maintained by the Canadian Parks Service.
Interesting 13 station interpretive trail of the Canadian Soo locks.
Call or write for trail guide.

ATTIKAMEK TRAIL

Newberry Forest Area, Lake Superior State Forest
PO Box 428   906-293-3293
Newberry, Mi 49868

District Forest Manger, Lake Superior State Forest
PO Box 77   906-293-5131
Newberry, MI 49868

Michigan Atlas & Gazetteer Location: 117C6

County Location: Luce

Directions To Trailhead:
Near Lake Superior at Bodi Lake SFCG about 35 miles northeast of Newberry

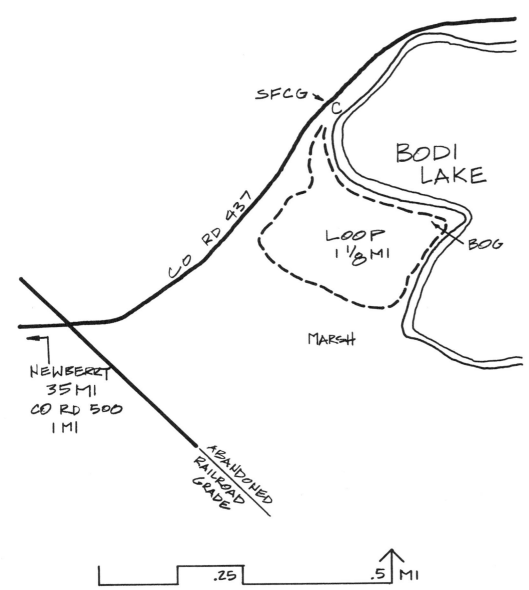

Trail Type: Hiking/Walking
Trail Distance: 1.8 mi   Loops: 1   Shortest: NA   Longest: 1.8 mi
Trail Surface: Natural
Trail Use Fee: None
Method Of Ski Trail Grooming: NA
Skiing Ability Suggested: NA
Hiking Trail Difficulty: Easy
Mountain Biking Ability Suggested: NA
Terrain: Steep 0%, Hilly 0%, Moderate 20%, Flat 80%
Camping: Campground on site

Maintained by the DNR Forest Management Division
Short pathway adjacent to the Bodi Lake SFCG.

BODI LAKE PATHWAY

Chadwick's Kwagama Lake Lodge
ACR 118.5
Hawk Junction, Ontario, Canada P0S 1G0

705-856-1104

Michigan Atlas & Gazetteer Location: 117 North

County Location: Canada

Directions To Trailhead:
Take the Algoma Central Railroad 118.5 miles north of Sault Ste Marie, Canada, then 9 miles by bike or skis
Departure location from the railroad is 4 miles north of the famous Agawa Canyon.

Trail Type: Hiking/Walking, Cross Country Skiing, Mountain Biking
Trail Distance: 50+ mi   Loops: 8+   Shortest: 1.5 mi Longest: 8 mi
Trail Surface: Natural
Trail Use Fee: Included in American Plan accomodations
Method Of Ski Trail Grooming: Packed
Skiing Ability Suggested: Intermediate to advanced
Hiking Trail Difficulty: Easy to difficult
Mountain Biking Ability Suggested: Intermediate to advanced
Terrain: Steep 10%, Hilly 50%, Moderate 30%, Flat 10%
Camping: None

Privately operated American Plan wilderness lodge on the Algoma Central Railway
Complete lodge facilities with private cabins.
Extensive trail system is maintained for the exclusive use of the guests.
Trail system is adjacent to the Lake Superior Provincial Park.
Guide service included in the package.
Call or write for more information.
Reservations are absolutely required.

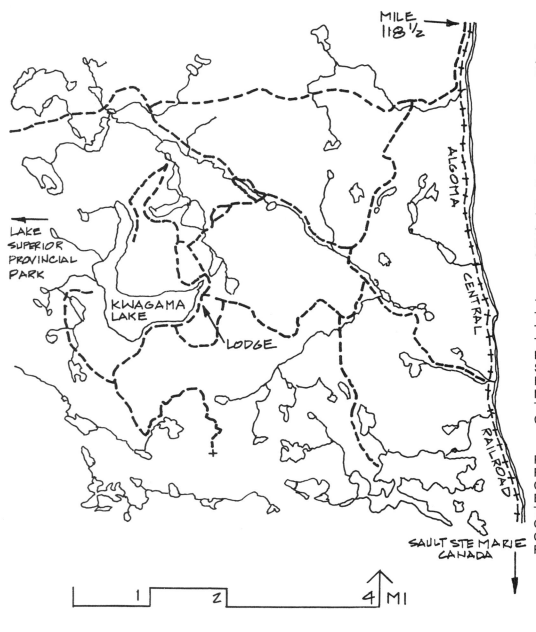

KWAGAMA LAKE LODGE

Sault Trails and Recreation Inc.
99 Foster Drive, PO Box 580   705-759-3898
Sault Ste Marie, Ontario, Canada P6A 5N1   705-942-0383

800-361-1522

Michigan Atlas & Gazetteer Location: 117A7

County Location: Ontario, Canada

Directions To Trailhead:
10 miles north of International Bridge, then take Hwy 17N to 5th Line, then right
2 miles to Hiawatha Lodge

Trail Type: Hiking/Walking, Cross Country Skiing
Trail Distance: 35 km   Loops: 12   Shortest: 1 km   Longest: 13+ km
Trail Surface: Natural
Trail Use Fee: Yes, daily, annual and family passes available
Method Of Ski Trail Grooming: Track set with a double track daily
Skiing Ability Suggested: Novice to advanced
Hiking Trail Difficulty: Easy to moderate
Mountain Biking Ability Suggested: NA
Terrain: Steep 5%, Hilly 25%, Moderate 50%, Flat 20%
Camping: None

Outstanding cross country ski area.
Lodge has a restaurant, snack bar, sauna, bar, ski rentals etc.
Expertly groomed trails.
The trail system has a biathlon range, a 150' vertical alpine slope.
Established over 40 years ago as a cross country ski area by Finnish residents
of the Soo. This area is one of the finest trail systems in the Great Lakes area.
2 km lighted trail with 2 tracks and a skating lane, 7 nights a week.
When you're in the Soo to ski Stokely Creek and Searchmont don't pass up this
one.

HIAWATHA HIGHLANDS
SKI TRAILS

Searchmont
Box 787
Sault Ste Marie, Ontario, Canada P6A 5N3

705-781-2340
800-663-2546

SEE MAPS ON NEXT PAGE

Michigan Atlas & Gazetteer Location: 117A6

County Location: Ontario, Canada

Directions To Trailhead:
8 miles north of Sault Ste. Marie, Canada on 17N, then east at Heyden on 556
for 17 miles to the town of Searchmont

Trail Type: Hiking/Walking, Cross Country Skiing, Mountain Biking
Trail Distance: See below Loops: Many   Shortest: Longest:
Trail Surface: Natural and gravel
Trail Use Fee: Yes for skiing
Method Of Ski Trail Grooming: Single track set 14' wide with a skating lane
Skiing Ability Suggested: Novice to advanced
Hiking Trail Difficulty: Easy to difficult
Mountain Biking Ability Suggested: Novice to advanced
Terrain: Below
Camping: None

Privately operated 4 season alpine, cross country ski and mountain bike resort.
Lodging, restaurant, rentals, lessons, ski shop and day nursery. Very fine well
designed trail system in the wooded area adjacent to the alpine slopes. Trails
are wide enough for skating with a single track on the right. Over 120 meter
elevation change in the intermediate/advanced trails.
Ski trails:50 km, 8 loops, terrain: 10% Steep, 40% Hilly, 30% Moderate, 10% Flat
Mountain bike trails: 150+ miles, terrain: 15% Steep, 20% Hilly, 35% Moderate,
30% Flat
Mountain bike trails are on public and private land with permission. Most
mountain bike trails are on vehicle roads and "2 tracks"(seldom used) and some
single track. Some tours use the train for part of the trip. Simply spectactular
scenery and challenging trails(if that's your desire)
Near Stokely Creek and Hiawatha Highlands ski trails.

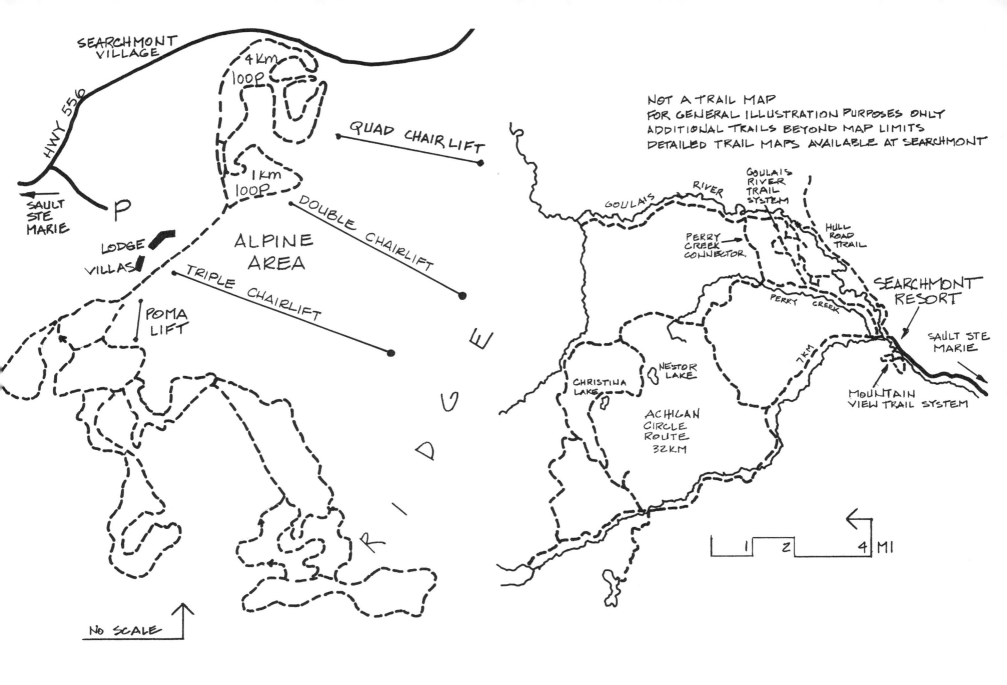

SEARCHMONT
VILLAGE

HWY 556

SAULT
STE
MARIE

P

4 Km
loop

1 Km
loop

QUAD CHAIR LIFT

DOUBLE CHAIRLIFT

LODGE
VILLAS

ALPINE
AREA

TRIPLE CHAIRLIFT

POMA
LIFT

R I D G E

NO SCALE

NOT A TRAIL MAP
FOR GENERAL ILLUSTRATION PURPOSES ONLY
ADDITIONAL TRAILS BEYOND MAP LIMITS
DETAILED TRAIL MAPS AVAILABLE AT SEARCHMONT

GOULAIS   RIVER

GOULAIS
RIVER
TRAIL
SYSTEM

HULL
ROAD
TRAIL

PERRY
CREEK
CONNECTOR

PERRY   CREEK

SEARCHMONT
RESORT

SAULT STE
MARIE

NESTOR
LAKE

CHRISTINA
LAKE

ACHIGAN
CIRCLE
ROUTE
32 KM

7 KM

MOUNTAIN
VIEW TRAIL SYSTEM

1   2   4 MI

SKI TRAILS
SEARCHMONT RESORT

MOUNTAIN BIKE TRAILS
SEARCHMONT RESORT   547

Stokely Creek Ski Touring Center
Karalash Corners   705-649-3421
Goulais River, Ontario, Canada P0S 1E0

HATS
99 Foster Drive, Level 3   800-461-6020
Sault Ste Marie, Ontario, Cananda P6A 5X6

Michigan Atlas & Gazetteer Location: 117 north of map

County Location: Ontario, Canada

Directions To Trailhead:
21 miles north of Sault Ste Marie Canada on 17N. Follow the signs east off Rte 17N just past the Buttermilk alpine ski area

Trail Type: Cross Country Skiing
Trail Distance: 150 km   Loops: Many   Shortest: Longest:
Trail Surface: Natural
Trail Use Fee: Yes
Method Of Ski Trail Grooming: Double track set with skating lane
Skiing Ability Suggested: Novice to advanced
Hiking Trail Difficulty: NA
Mountain Biking Ability Suggested: NA
Terrain: Steep 10%, Hilly 25%, Moderate 50%, Flat 15%
Camping: None

Privately operated ski touring center
One of the premier ski touring centers in the midwest. Named one of the best touring centers in North America by Cross Country Skier magazine.
Site of the annual Wabos Loppet, held in March each year. Good skiing is usually available through the end of March. The terrain and scenery is simply spectacular. One trail loop is 17 km with another trail going past the location of a former hang glider launching platform. Two trails have over 600 feet of vertical change. Day skiers lodge with bunkhouse and lodging is available. Winter lodging reservations should be made by Thanksgiving. You really have not skied the mid west until you have skied STOKELY CREEK. Don't pass up this one.

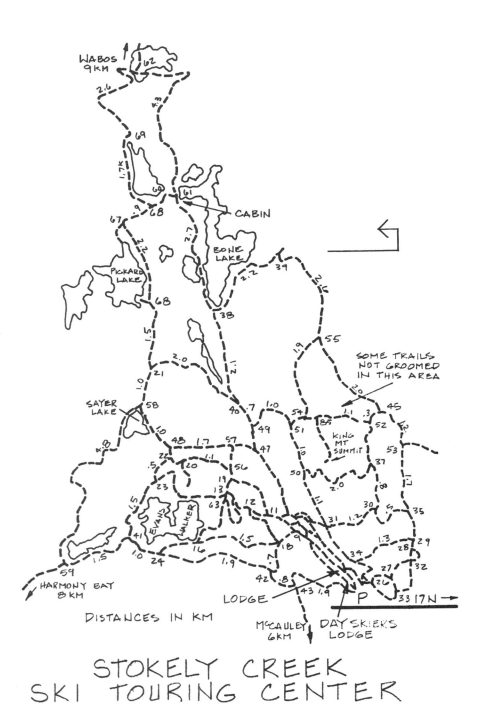

STOKELY CREEK
SKI TOURING CENTER

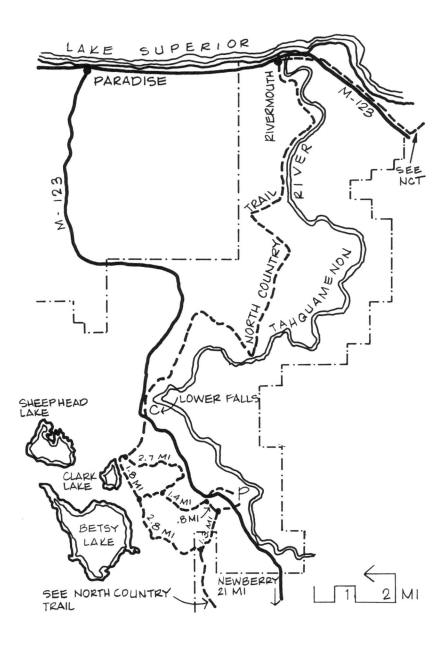

Tahquamenon Falls State Park
Rte 48, Box 225
Paradise, MI 49768

906-492-3415

DNR Parks and Recreation Division

517-373-1270

Michigan Atlas & Gazetteer Location: 117CD678

County Location: Chippewa

Directions To Trailhead:
12 miles west of Paradise on M123

Trail Type: Hiking/Walking, Cross Country Skiing, Interpretive
Trail Distance: 25 + mi   Loops: 4+   Shortest: 3.7 mi Longest: 13 mi
Trail Surface: Natural
Trail Use Fee: None, but vehicle entry fee required
Method Of Ski Trail Grooming: Track set
Skiing Ability Suggested: Novice to intermediate
Hiking Trail Difficulty: Easy to moderate
Mountain Biking Ability Suggested: NA
Terrain: Steep 0%, Hilly 0%, Moderate 20%, Flat 80%
Camping: Avaialble in the park in snowless months only

Maintained by the DNR Parks and Recreation Division.
Hiking and skiing trails are not all identical.
Ski trail length is less.
Food and lodging available in Paradise and Newberry .
Wilderness skiing is also possible but deep snow will make that quite difficult.
The North Country Trail passes through this park.

TAHQUAMENON FALLS STATE PARK

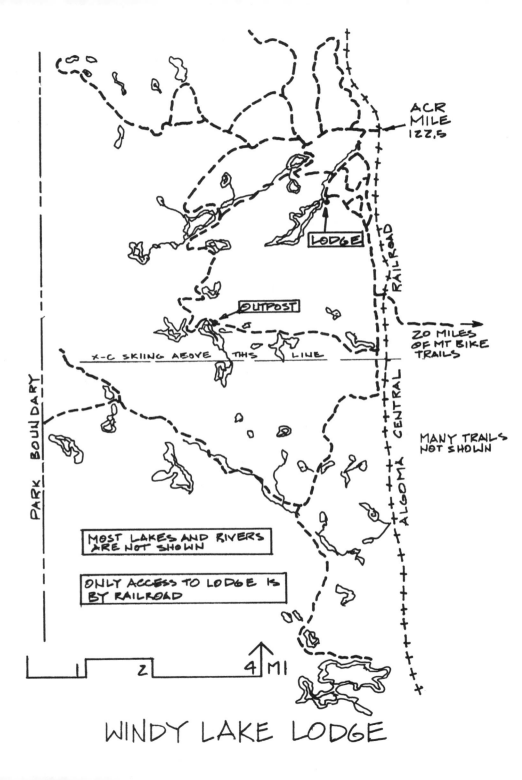

WIndy Lake Lodge
Mile 122.5 A.C.R.
Sault Ste Marie, Ontario, Canada P6A5N9

705-942-0525

Michigan Atlas & Gazetteer Location: 117A6

County Location: Ontario, Canada

Directions To Trailhead:
North of Sault Ste Marie, Canada. at mile post 122.5 Algoma Central Railway
Gazetteer location is not accurate

Trail Type: Hiking/Walking, Cross Country Skiing, Mountain Biking
Trail Distance: 50 + mi   Loops: Many   Shortest: Longest:
Trail Surface: Natural
Trail Use Fee: None, accomodation package includes trail fee
Method Of Ski Trail Grooming: Track set
Skiing Ability Suggested: Novice to advanced
Hiking Trail Difficulty: Easy to difficult
Mountain Biking Ability Suggested: intermediate to advanced
Terrain: Steep 5%, Hilly 15%, Moderate 40%, Flat 40%
Camping: None

A privately owned year around resort in the Canadian wilderness
Ski trail system has 50 km of groomed trails with 6 loops from 22.5 km to 5.2 km long
Accessable only by railroad from Sault Ste Marie, Canada via the Algoma Central Railroad
Extensive trail system of logging roads and 2 tracks.

Michigan Nature Association
PO Box 102
Avoca, MI 48006

810-324-2426

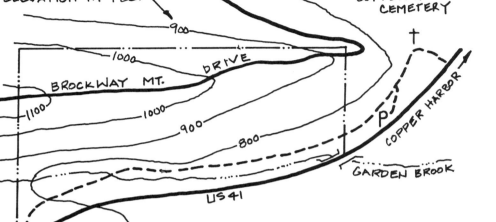

ELEVATION IN FEET

COPPER HARBOR CEMETERY

900

1000

BROCKWAY MT. DRIVE

1100

1000

900

COPPER HARBOR

P

800

GARDEN BROOK

US 41

.25 .5 MI

Michigan Atlas & Gazetteer Location: 118A1

County Location: Keweenaw

Directions To Trailhead:
Just south of Copper Harbor on US41 about .5 mile. Park near Garden Brook Bridge. Walk .5 mile on US 41 to a trail on the north(right) side of the road.

Trail Type: Hiking/Walking, Interpretive
Trail Distance: 1.6 mi   Loops: 1   Shortest: NA   Longest: 1.6 mi
Trail Surface: Natural
Trail Use Fee: None
Method Of Ski Trail Grooming: NA
Skiing Ability Suggested: NA
Hiking Trail Difficulty: Moderate
Mountain Biking Ability Suggested: NA
Terrain: Steep 0%, Hilly 50%, Moderate 50%, Flat 0%
Camping: Campground at Ft Wilkins State Park

Owned by the Michigan Nature Association
Sanctuary contains plants only found in the Keweenaw County.
Brockway Mountain is the highest point in the Copper Range.
Write or call for the sanctuary guidebook.

BROCKWAY MOUNTAIN NATURE SANCTUARY

Keweenaw Tourism Council
PO Box 336
Calumet, MI 49913

906-337-4579
800-338-7982

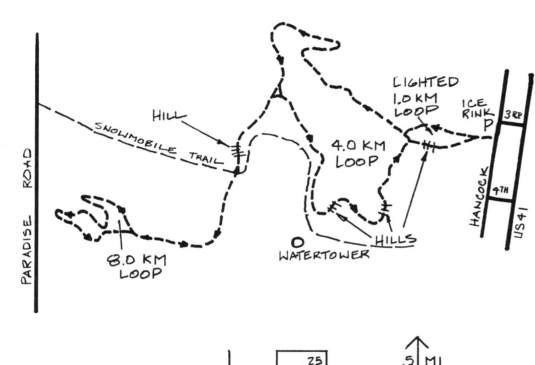

Michigan Atlas & Gazetteer Location: 118D4

County Location: Houghton

Directions To Trailhead:
In Chassell, 7 miles south of Houghton on US41.One block west of US41 on Hancock St. in Chassell next to the ice rink near the school at the north end of town. Trail starts on the left side of the warming building that is next to the ice rink .

Trail Type: Cross Country Skiing
Trail Distance: 8 km   Loops: 2   Shortest: 4 km   Longest: 8 km
Trail Surface: Natural
Trail Use Fee: None, donations accepted
Method Of Ski Trail Grooming: Track set
Skiing Ability Suggested: Novice to intermediate
Hiking Trail Difficulty: NA
Mountain Biking Ability Suggested: NA
Terrain: Steep 5%, Hilly 25%, Moderate 60%, Flat 10%
Camping: None

Maintained by the Villlage of Chassell with volunteers and the Chassell Recreation Club
Most of the trail is on private land so do not wander off the designated trail.
One km lighted trail.
Warming shelter available.
Trail not designed for skating.
A well designed trail that is a delight to ski.
The rolling terrain is used effectively to provide long rolling downhill runs with a minimum of climbing.
The mostly wooded with some open field skiing provides for a very pleasant experience.

CHASSEL CLASSIC SKI TRAIL

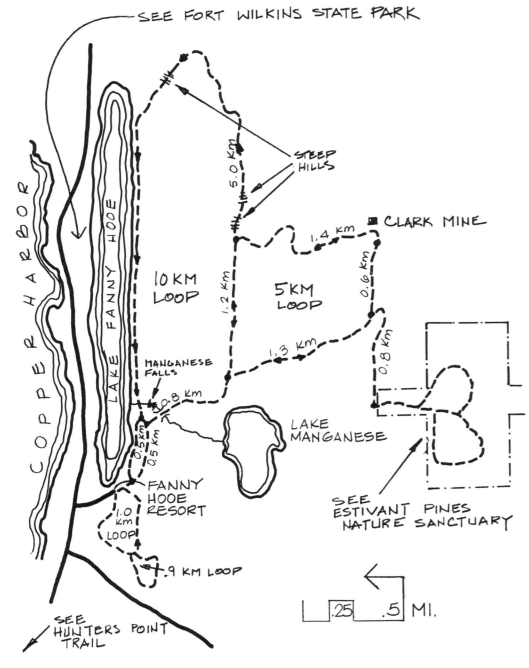

Baraga Forest Area, Copper Country State Forest
Box 440   906-353-6651
Baraga, MI 49908

Park Manager
Fort Wilkins State Park   906-289-4215
Copper Harbor, MI 49918

Michigan Atlas & Gazetteer Location: 118A12

County Location: Keweenaw

Directions To Trailhead:
Trailhead - West end of Lake Fanny Hooe near Lake Fanny Hooe Resort

Trail Type: Hiking/Walking, Cross Country Skiing, Mountain Biking, Interpretive
Trail Distance: 18.7 km   Loops: Several   Shortest: 1 km   Longest: 14 km
Trail Surface: Natural
Trail Use Fee: None
Method Of Ski Trail Grooming: Track set (some sections)
Skiing Ability Suggested: Intermediate to advanced
Hiking Trail Difficulty: Moderate
Mountain Biking Ability Suggested: Intermediate to advanced
Terrain: Rolling to hilly
Camping: Available at Fort Wilkins SP and Lake Fanny Hooe Resort

Maintained by the DNR Forest Management and, Parks and Recreation Divisions
Ski rentals and lodging available from Fanny Hooe Resort at the west end of Lake Fanny Hooe 906-289-4451.
Groomed by Fort Wilkins State Park.
Estivant Pines loop is owned by the Michigan Nature Association (see other listing).
Other contacts:
    DNR Forest Management Region Office, Marquette, 906-228-6561
    DNR Forest Management Division Office, Lansing, 517-373-1275
    Keweenaw Tourism Council 906-482-2388 or 800-338-7982

COPPER HARBOR PATHWAY

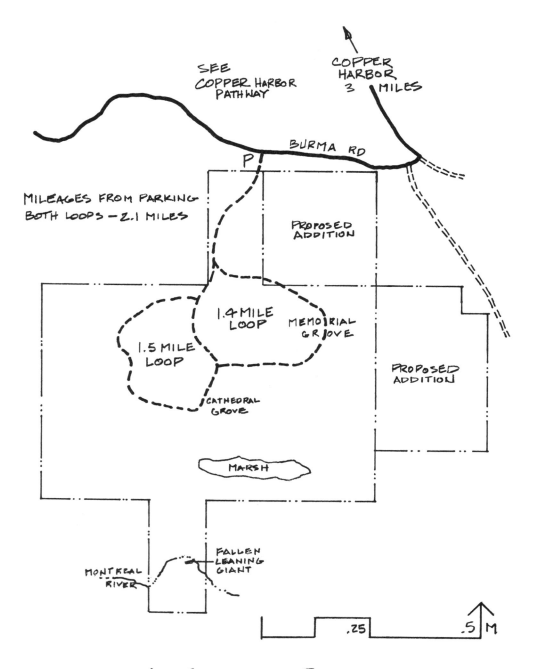

SEE
COPPER HARBOR
PATHWAY

COPPER
HARBOR
3 MILES

BURMA RD

P

MILEAGES FROM PARKING
BOTH LOOPS — 2.1 MILES

PROPOSED
ADDITION

1.4 MILE
LOOP

MEMORIAL
GROVE

1.5 MILE
LOOP

CATHEDRAL
GROVE

PROPOSED
ADDITION

MARSH

FALLEN
LEANING
GIANT

MONTREAL
RIVER

.25   .5 M

ESTIVANT PINES
NATURE SANCTUARY

Estivant Pines Nature Sanctuary

Michigan Nature Association
PO Box 102
Avoca, MI 48006

810-324-2626

Michigan Atlas & Gazetteer Location: 118A12

County Location: Keweenaw

Directions To Trailhead:
From the blinker light at US41 in Copper Harbor, turn right (east) .2 mile, then turn south (right) toward Lake Managanese. Then proceed 1.3 miles past Lake Manganese, then turn left (west) on Burma Rd, then bo .65 mile to the sanctuary.

Trail Type: Hiking/Walking, Cross Country Skiing, Interpretive
Trail Distance: 2.5   Loops: 2   Shortest: 1.4 mi Longest: 2.1 mii
Trail Surface: Natural
Trail Use Fee: None
Method Of Ski Trail Grooming: None
Skiing Ability Suggested: Intermediate
Hiking Trail Difficulty: Easy to moderate
Mountain Biking Ability Suggested: NA
Terrain: Steep 20%, Hilly 20%, Moderate 20%, Flat 40%
Camping: At Copper Harbor State Park

Owned by the Michigan Nature Association
One of the few remaining stands of virgin white pine in the state.
Worth the effort to get to this sanctuary.

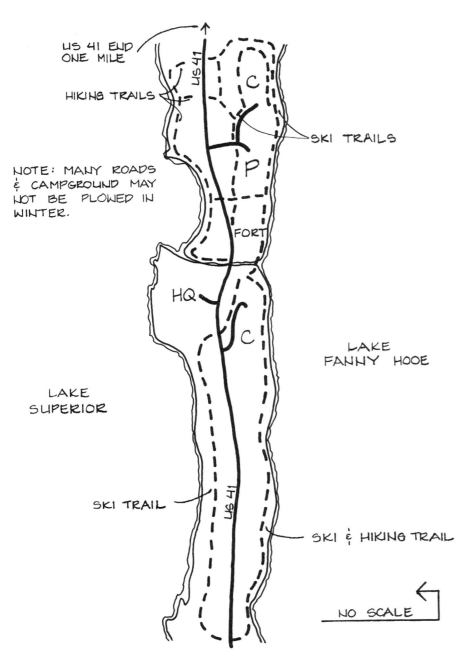

US 41 END
ONE MILE

HIKING TRAILS

US 41

C

SKI TRAILS

NOTE: MANY ROADS
& CAMPGROUND MAY
NOT BE PLOWED IN
WINTER.

P

FORT

HQ

C

LAKE
FANNY HOOE

LAKE
SUPERIOR

SKI TRAIL

US 41

SKI & HIKING TRAIL

NO SCALE

FORT WILKINS STATE PARK

Fort Wilkins State Park
US41 East
Copper Harbor, MI 49918   906-289-4215

DNR Parks and Recreation Division

517-373-1270
906-228-6561

Michigan Atlas & Gazetteer Location: 118A2

County Location: Keweenaw

Directions To Trailhead:
Just east of Copper Harbor on US41

Trail Type: Hiking/Walking, Cross Country Skiing, Interpretive
Trail Distance: 5 km   Loops: Several   Shortest: 1 km   Longest: 3.4 km
Trail Surface: Gravel and natural
Trail Use Fee: None, but vehicle entry fee required
Method Of Ski Trail Grooming: Track set
Skiing Ability Suggested: Novice
Hiking Trail Difficulty: Easy
Mountain Biking Ability Suggested: NA
Terrain: Steep 0%, Hilly 10%, Moderate 50%, Flat 40%
Camping: Campground in the park

Maintained by the DNR Parks and Recreation Division
Restored historic Fort built to protect the copper miners in the 1800's
Ski rentals available at the Lake Fanny Hooe Resort at the west end of Lake
Fanny Hooe 906-289-4451
Hiking and ski trailsare not all identical
Copper Harbor Pathway and several other trails are nearby. See other listings.

LAKE SUPERIOR

LAKESHORE ROAD

CALUMET WATER-WORKS ROAD

P

CALUMET 7 MI

P LOGGING EXHIBIT

P

PICNIC-REST AREA

WILDFLOWERS

GARDENERS CREEK

.25 MI.

GARDENERS CREEK NATURE TRAIL

Calumet Township
106 Red Jacket Rd
Calumet, MI 49913

906-337-2410

Michigan Atlas & Gazetteer Location: 118B4

County Location: Houghton

Directions To Trailhead:
2 miles northwest of M203 on Waterworks Rd, west of Calumet

Trail Type: Interpretive
Trail Distance: 1 mi   Loops: 1   Shortest: NA   Longest: 1 mi
Trail Surface: Natural with hardwood chips
Trail Use Fee: None
Method Of Ski Trail Grooming: NA
Skiing Ability Suggested: NA
Hiking Trail Difficulty: Easy
Mountain Biking Ability Suggested: NA
Terrain: Steep 0%, Hilly 0%, Moderate 95%, Flat 5%
Camping: Primitive camping for up to 50 people and shelter for 6 people

Owned by the Township of Calumet
Logging exhibit, picnic area along the shore of Lake Superior
Trail includes:
        40 tree and shrubs identified
        mounted maps at intersections
        displays of native pine, cedar and hemlock logs
        3 bridges across Gardeners Creek
Adjacent to Calumet Township Lakeshore park with beach, playgrounds and picnic pavilion

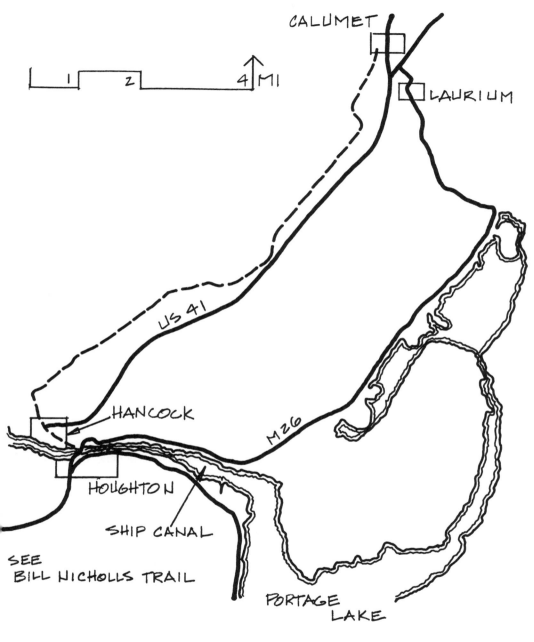

Baraga Forest Area, Copper Country State Forest
Box 440   906-353-6651
Baraga, MI 49908

District Forest Manager, Copper Country State Forest
Box 440   906-353-6651
Baraga, MI 49908

Michigan Atlas & Gazetteer Location: 118BC345

County Location: Houghton

Directions To Trailhead:
Between Hancock to Calumet along US41
South trailhead - Poorvoo Park on the Portage Lake Ship Canal on Tezcuco St in Hancock
North trailhead - Calumet depot at 9th St. and Oak St on the west edge of town

Trail Type: Hiking/Walking, Mountain Biking
Trail Distance: 13 mi   Loops: NA   Shortest: NA   Longest: NA
Trail Surface: Natural and ballast
Trail Use Fee: None
Method Of Ski Trail Grooming: NA
Skiing Ability Suggested: NA
Hiking Trail Difficulty: Easy
Mountain Biking Ability Suggested: Novice
Terrain: 100% Flat
Camping: None

Managed by the DNR Forest Management Division
A rail trail of the former Mineral Range Railroad built in 1908 to haul copper from the Red Jacket and other mines in the area and abandon in 1979 by the Soo Line.

HANCOCK/CALUMENT TRAIL

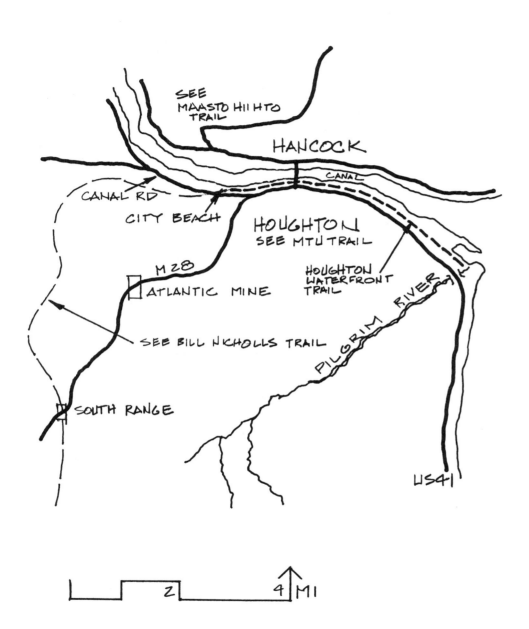

City of Houghton
PO Box 406
Houghton, MI 49931

906-482-1700

Michigan Atlas & Gazetteer Location: 118C4

County Location: Houghton

Directions To Trailhead:
Along the waterfront from the city beach on the west end to Pilgrim River on the east end.

Trail Type: Hiking/Walking
Trail Distance: 4.5 mi   Loops: NA   Shortest: NA   Longest: NA
Trail Surface: Paved
Trail Use Fee: None
Method Of Ski Trail Grooming: NA
Skiing Ability Suggested: NA
Hiking Trail Difficulty: Easy
Mountain Biking Ability Suggested: Novice
Terrain: 100% Flat
Camping: None nearby but state parks and state forest campgrounds in the area

Owned by the City of Houghton.
A paved waterfront trail along the canal that separates Houghton from Hancock.
The west end of the trail connects closely to the Bill Nicholls Rail Trail.
See many other trails in the area.

HOUGHTON WATERFRONT TRAIL

Copper Harbor Downtown Development Association
Fanny Hooe Resort   906-289-4451
Copper Harbor, MI 49918

Keweenaw Tourism Council

800-338-7982
906-482-2388

Michigan Atlas & Gazetteer Location: 118A1

County Location: Keweenaw

Directions To Trailhead:
Trailhead - West side of the Copper Harbor Marina which is just west of the downtown area.

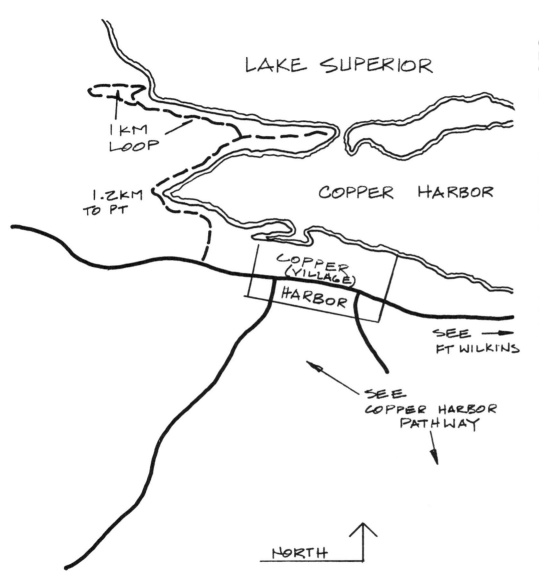

Trail Type: Hiking/Walking, Cross Country Skiing, Interpretive
Trail Distance: 4 km   Loops: NA   Shortest: NA   Longest: NA
Trail Surface: Natural
Trail Use Fee: None
Method Of Ski Trail Grooming: None
Skiing Ability Suggested: Novice
Hiking Trail Difficulty: Easy
Mountain Biking Ability Suggested: NA
Terrain: Steep 0%, Hilly 0%, Moderate 10%, Flat 90%
Camping: At Fort Wilkins State Park and Fanny Hooe Resort in Copper Harbor

Local trail maintained by the community of Copper Harbor
Easy trail for the entire family along the Lake Superior shoreline

HUNTERS POINT TRAIL

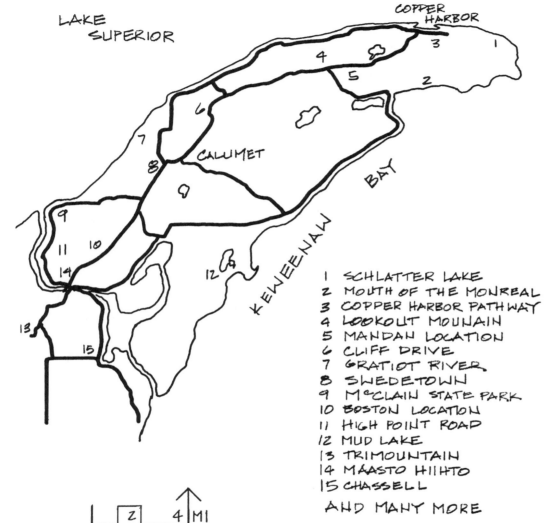

LAKE SUPERIOR

COPPER HARBOR

CALUMET

KEWEENAW BAY

1 SCHLATTER LAKE
2 MOUTH OF THE MONREAL
3 COPPER HARBOR PATHWAY
4 LOOKOUT MOUNAIN
5 MANDAN LOCATION
6 CLIFF DRIVE
7 GRATIOT RIVER
8 SWEDETOWN
9 M°CLAIN STATE PARK
10 BOSTON LOCATION
11 HIGH POINT ROAD
12 MUD LAKE
13 TRIMOUNTAIN
14 MAASTO HIIHTO
15 CHASSELL

AND MANY MORE

2 4 MI

Keweenaw Tourism Council
1197 Calumet Ave., PO Box 336
Calumet, MI 49913

800-338-7982
906-337-4579

Cross Country Sports
507 Oak St
Calumet, MI 49913

906-337-4520

Michigan Atlas & Gazetteer Location: 118all,119all

County Location: Keweenaw

Directions To Trailhead:
North of Houghton across the Portage Lake ship canal

Trail Type: Hiking/Walking, Cross Country Skiing, Mountain Biking
Trail Distance: 100+ mi   Loops: Shortest: Longest:
Trail Surface: Natural, gravel and rock
Trail Use Fee: None
Method Of Ski Trail Grooming: Varies
Skiing Ability Suggested: Novice to advanced
Hiking Trail Difficulty: Easy to difficult
Mountain Biking Ability Suggested: Novice to advance
Terrain: All types
Camping: Throughout the Keweenaw Peninsula

In addition to those locations shown on the map (some of which are described elsewhere in this atlas) there are many miles of old mining roads and forest trails to explore the beautiful Copper Island.
Because of the isolated location, good compass and map reading skills are essential to explore this area.
For ideas on where to go, see Rick at Cross Country Sports in Calumet (listed above). His complete bike and cross country ski shop will also come in handy if you need repairs or supplies.

KEWEENAW PENINSULA

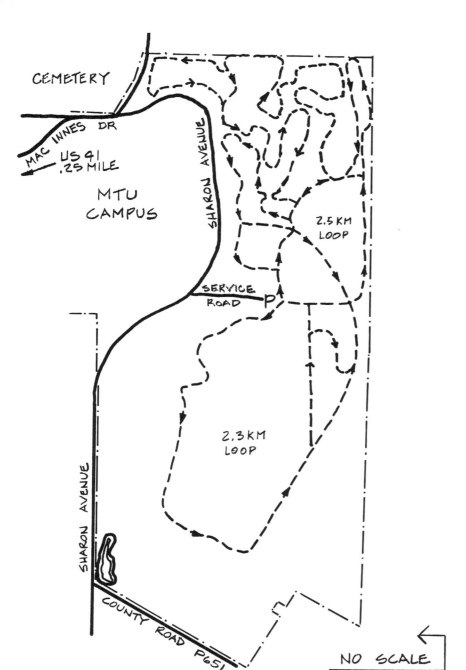

MTU TRAIL

Michigan Technological University-Athletic Department
1400 Townsend Drive   906-487-3070
Houghton, MI 49931-1295

Keweenaw Tourism Council
1197 Calumet   906-337-4579
Calumet, MI 49931   800-338-7982

Michigan Atlas & Gazetteer Location: 118D4

County Location: Houghton

Directions To Trailhead:
On the MTU campus between Sharon Ave and Manninen Rd. Entrance to trail on Sharon Ave.

Trail Type: Hiking/Walking, Cross Country Skiing, Mountain Biking
Trail Distance: 9.2 km   Loops: 7   Shortest: .6 km   Longest: 8.5 km
Trail Surface: Natural
Trail Use Fee: None
Method Of Ski Trail Grooming: Track Set with skating lane
Skiing Ability Suggested: Novice to advanced
Hiking Trail Difficulty: Easy to moderate
Mountain Biking Ability Suggested: Novice to advanced
Terrain: Steep 15%, Hilly 25%, Moderate 25%, Flat 35%
Camping: Camping available in area

Trails maintained on a regular basis by Michigan Technological University.
Cut offs from the main loop will bypass the most difficult trail sections which would reduce the required ability from advanced to an intermediate-novice.
A beautiful wooded trail system on the edge of the MTU campus.
Maintenance of the trail in the summer for mountain biking has not been consistant.

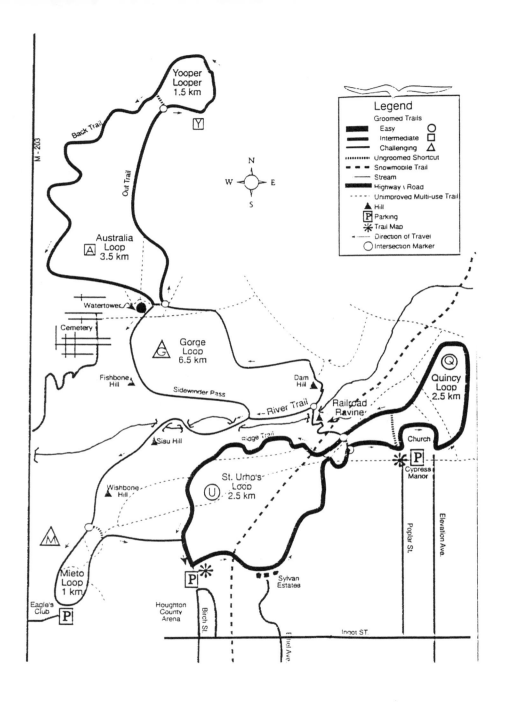

Houghton-Hancock Ski Club c/o City of Hancock
City Hall   906-483-1770
Hancock, MI 49930

Kewennaw Tourism Council
PO Box 336, 1197 Calumet Ave   800-338-7982
Calumet, MI 49913   906-337-4579

Michigan Atlas & Gazetteer Location: 118C4

County Location: Houghton

Directions To Trailhead:
Northwest edge of Hancock
Trailhead - Behind the Houghton County Arena at Birch and Ingot Streets
Trailhead - North end of Popular St Trailhead - Off M203 behind the Eagles
Club, NW of town

Trail Type: Hiking/Walking, Cross Country Skiing, Mountain Biking
Trail Distance: 17.5+ km Loops: 9+   Shortest: 1 km   Longest: 6.5 km
Trail Surface: Natural
Trail Use Fee: Donations accepted
Method Of Ski Trail Grooming: Track set occasionally
Skiing Ability Suggested: Intermediate to Advanced
Hiking Trail Difficulty: Moderate
Mountain Biking Ability Suggested: Novice to advanced
Terrain: Hilly
Camping: Campground not available nearby

Maintained by the Houghton-Hancock Ski Club and the City of Hancock
Maintained when funds are available - call ahead
Well designed ski trail.

MAASTO HIIHTO SKI TRAIL

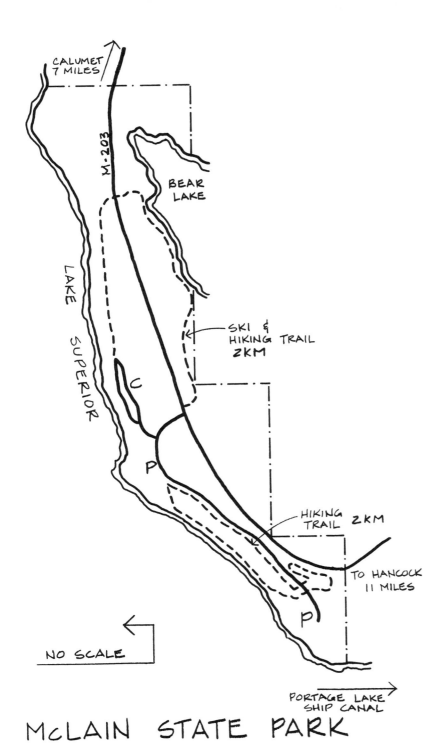

NO SCALE

MCLAIN STATE PARK

McLain State Park
M 203
Hancock, MI 49930

906-482-0278

DNR Parks and Recreation Division

517-373-1270

Michigan Atlas & Gazetteer Location: 118BC34

County Location: Houghton

Directions To Trailhead:
7 miles west of Calument on M-203 and 11 miles west of Hancock on M-203

Trail Type: Hiking/Walking, Cross Country Skiing, Interpretive
Trail Distance: 6 km   Loops: 2   Shortest: 2 km   Longest: 4 km
Trail Surface: Natural
Trail Use Fee: None, but vehicle entry fee required
Method Of Ski Trail Grooming: Packed as needed
Skiing Ability Suggested: Novice
Hiking Trail Difficulty: Easy
Mountain Biking Ability Suggested: NA
Terrain: Steep 0%, Hilly 0%, Moderate 4%, Flat 96%
Camping: Campground on site

Maintained by the DNR Parks and Recreation Divsion
Snowmobiles permited in park. Ski carefully

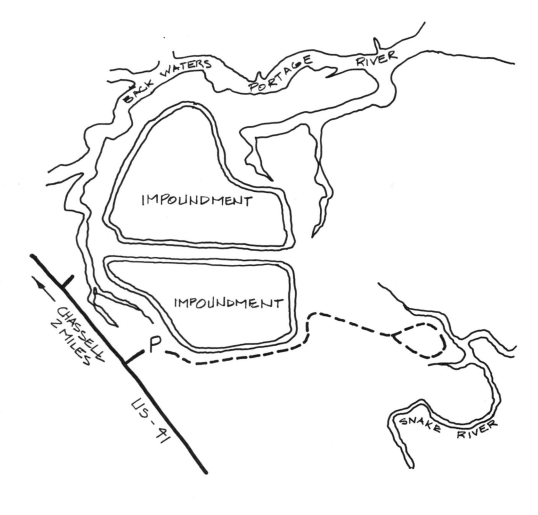

Baraga District Office, DNR Wildlife Division
PO Box 440
Baraga, MI 49908

906-353-6651

DNR Wildlife Division, Region 1 HQ
1990 US41 South
Marquette, MI 49855

517-373-1263

Michigan Atlas & Gazetteer Location: 199D5

County Location:

Directions To Trailhead:
2 miles southwest of Chassell on US41

Trail Type: Hiking/Walking, Interpretive
Trail Distance: .9 mi   Loops: 1   Shortest: Longest: .9 mi
Trail Surface: Natural
Trail Use Fee: None
Method Of Ski Trail Grooming: NA
Skiing Ability Suggested: NA
Hiking Trail Difficulty: Easy
Mountain Biking Ability Suggested: NA
Terrain: 100%Flat
Camping: None but campground at state park in Baraga

Maintained by the DNR Wildlife Divison
Observation platform along trail
Picnic pavilion at the trailhead

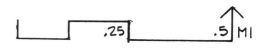

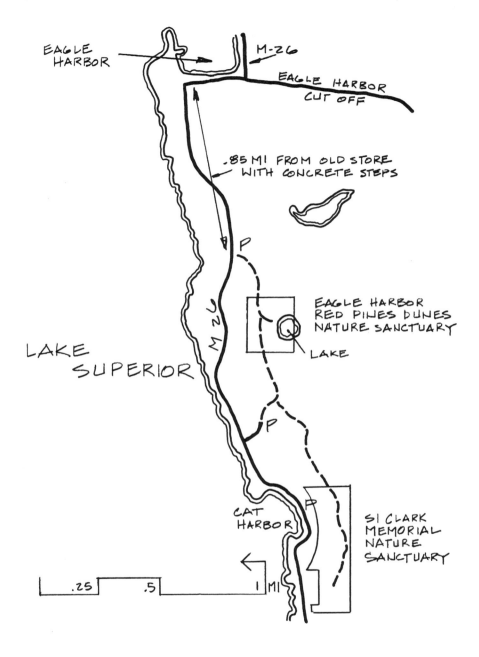

EAGLE HARBOR

M-26

EAGLE HARBOR CUT OFF

.85 MI FROM OLD STORE WITH CONCRETE STEPS

P

M 26

LAKE SUPERIOR

EAGLE HARBOR RED PINES DUNES NATURE SANCTUARY

LAKE

P

P

CAT HARBOR

SI CLARK MEMORIAL NATURE SANCTUARY

.25   .5   1 MI

Michigan Nature Association
PO Box 102
Avoca, MI 48006

810-324-2626

Michigan Atlas & Gazetteer Location: 119A7

County Location: Keweenaw

Directions To Trailhead:
From the old store in Eagle Harbor, go .85 mile west on M26 to a 2 track road.
From there, walk on the road as indicated on the map to the two sanctuaries

Trail Type: Hiking/Walking, Cross Country Skiing, Interpretive
Trail Distance: 4.3 mi   Loops: 2   Shortest: 1.8 mi Longest: 4.3 mi
Trail Surface: Natural
Trail Use Fee: None
Method Of Ski Trail Grooming: None
Skiing Ability Suggested: Intermediate to advanced
Hiking Trail Difficulty: Moderate
Mountain Biking Ability Suggested: NA
Terrain: Steep 10%, Hilly 20%, Moderate 20%, Flat 50%
Camping: None

Maintained by the Michigan Nature Association
Complete name is "Eagle Harbor Red Pines Dunes and Si Clark Memorial
Nature Sanctuaries
Red Pines Dunes is 25 acres
Si Clark is 37 acres

EAGLE HARBOR RED PINES DUNES
SI CLARK MEMORIAL NATURE SANCTURIES

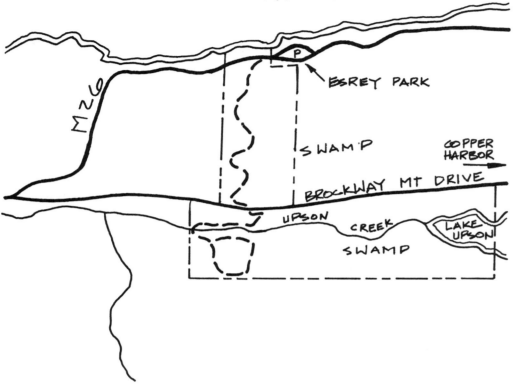

LAKE SUPERIOR

ESREY PARK

SWAMP

COPPER HARBOR

BROCKWAY Mt DRIVE

UPSON CREEK

LAKE UPSON

SWAMP

M26

.25 .5 MI

KEWEENAW SHORE NO. 1 NATURE SANCTUARY

Michigan Nature Association
PO Box 102
Avoca, MI 48006

810-324-2626

Michigan Atlas & Gazetteer Location: 119A8

County Location: Keweenaw

Directions To Trailhead:
East from Eagle Harbor on M26 about 5 miles to the west entrance of Esrey Park. Entrance to the sanctuary is 200 feet west on the south side of M26.

Trail Type: Hiking/Walking, Interpretive
Trail Distance: 2 mi   Loops: 1   Shortest: Longest: 2 mi
Trail Surface: Natural
Trail Use Fee: None
Method Of Ski Trail Grooming: NA
Skiing Ability Suggested: NA
Hiking Trail Difficulty: Difficult
Mountain Biking Ability Suggested: NA
Terrain: Steep 80%, Hilly 0%, Moderate 20%, Flat 0%
Camping: Campground in Copper Harbor

Owned by the Michigan Nature Association
Simply one of the most representative tracts in the Keweenaw.
Boreal forest of spruce, balsam fir, aspen and birch, conglomerate outcrop, sharp ridges, forests of pine, aspen, birch and red maple, swamp grass, alder, sphagnum bog, black spruce, pitcher plants and much more are all along the trail.
"If a person wanted to show some one unfamiliar to the Keweenaw an example of the Peninsula's varied plant communities andrugged ridge valley topography, this trail would be the best place to go." from MNA publication.

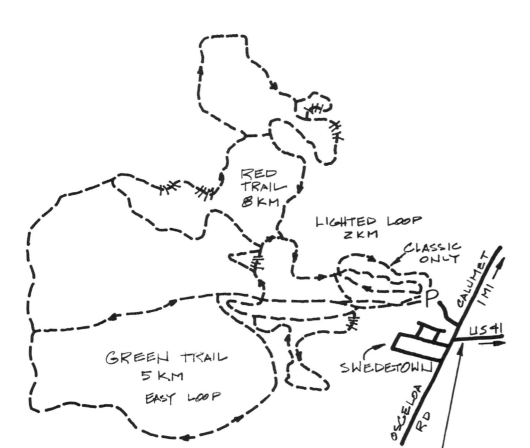

RED TRAIL 8 KM

LIGHTED LOOP 2 KM

CLASSIC ONLY

P

CALUMET 1 MI

US 41

GREEN TRAIL 5 KM

EASY LOOP

SWEDETOWN

OSCELOA RD

SWEDETOWN RD

SCALE NOT KNOWN

Copper Island Cross Country Ski Club
PO Box 214
Calumet, MI 49913

906-337-1170

Keweenaw Tourism Council
1197 Calumet Ave., PO Box 336
Calumet, MI 49913

800-338-7982
906-337-4579

Michigan Atlas & Gazetteer Location: 119C5

County Location: Houghton

Directions To Trailhead:
1 mile SW of Calumet on Osceloa Rd
Trailhead - Take Swedetown Rd west from US41 (just before tourist office, sign at intersection), then left on Osceloa Rd to trailhead. Follow signs from US 41 in Calumet.

Trail Type: Cross Country Skiing
Trail Distance: 20 km   Loops: Several   Shortest: 13 km Longest: 2 km
Trail Surface: Natural
Trail Use Fee: Donations accepted
Method Of Ski Trail Grooming: Track set with skating lane, 4 times/week
Skiing Ability Suggested: Novice to intermediate
Hiking Trail Difficulty: NA
Mountain Biking Ability Suggested: NA
Terrain: Steep 2%, Hilly 20%, Moderate 60%, Flat 18%
Camping: None

Maintained by Copper Island Cross-Country Ski Club
Beautifully designed and maintained trail system by local skiers. Site of several events yearly. Normal ski season begins in November and goes through March. Skiing available on the Keweenaw Peninsula through April.   Accomodations and food available in Calumet and Houghton/Hancock.
Rentals and ski shop at the Cross-Country Sports, 507 Oak St., Calumet, 337-4520.
Other contact: Keweenaw Peninsula Chamber of Commerce, 326 Shelden Ave., Houghton, MI 49931 906-482-5240

SWEDETOWN SKI TRAIL

Additional Reading Sources

Allen, Pat and DeRuiter, Gerald, *Backpacking In Michigan - 3rd Ed.*. Ann Arbor, MI: The University of Michigan Press (1994)

DuFresne, Jim, *Fifty Hikes in Lower Michigan*.Woodstock, VT: The Countryman Press, Inc.(1991)

DuFresne, Jim, *Michigan's Porcupine Mountains Wilderness State Park*, Clarkston, MI: Glovebox Guidebooks (1993), P.O. Box 852, Clarkston, MI 48347

DuFresne, Jim, *Lower Michigan's 75 Best Campgrounds*, Clarkston, MI: Glovebox Guidebooks (1993), P.O. Box 852, Clarkston, MI 48347

DuFresne, Jim, *OutdoorAdventures With Children*. Seattle: The Mountaineers (1990)

Gentry, Karen, *Cycling Michigan*. Clarkston, Ml: Glovebox Guidebooks (1993), PO Box 852, Clarkston, Ml. 48347

Johnson, Arden, *North Country National Scenic Trail - Michigan Section Hiker Guide*, North Country Trail Association Bookstore, PO Box 311, White Cloud, Ml 49349 (under constant revision). The entire guide of 117 maps can be purchased in its entirety, or prepackaged mapsets of various sections of the trail can be purchased separately. Write for an order form. Allow considerable time for a response and/or purchase since the NCTA operates with all volunteers including the bookstore.

Kraut, Ruth, *Footloose in Washtenaw, 2nd Ed.*, Ann Arbor, Ml: Ecology Center of Ann Arbor (1990)

Michigan Nature Association Sanctuary Guidebook (most current edition), Michigan Nature Association, PO Box 102, Avoca, Ml 48006 (810) 324-2626 Other pubications of selected sanctuaries and groups of sanctuaries are available.

Penrose, Laurie, Bill T., Ruth, Bill J., *Michigan Waterfalls*. Davison, MI: Friede Publications, 2339 Venezia, 48423 (1988)

Powers, Tom, *Natural Michigan*. Davison, MI: Friede Publications, 2339 Venezia, 48423 (1987)

Powers, Tom, *More Natural Michigan*. Davison, MI: Friede Publications, 2339 Venezia, 48423 (1992)

Powers, Tom, *Michigan State Parks*, Davison, MI: Friede Publications, 2339 Venezia, 48423 (1994)

Ruchhoft, Robert H., *Exploring North Manitou, South Manitou, High and Garden Islands, Of the Lake Michigan Archipelago*. Cincinnati, OH: The Pucelle Press, P.O. Box 19161, Cincinnati, 45219 (1991)

Storm, Roger; Wedzel, Susan; Ryan, Karen-Lee and Ulm, Mike, 40 *Great Rail-Trails*. Washington, D.C.:Rails to Trails Conservancy (1994)

Phone Numbers for Chamber of Commerce/Tourist Bureau/Visitors Bureau

ADA BUSINESS ASSOCIATION	(616)676-6482
ANCHOR BAY CHAMBER OF COMMERCE	(810)949-4120
ALBION CHAMBER OF COMMERCE	(517)629-5533
ALGER COUNTY CHAMBER OF COMMERCE	(906)387-2138
ALGONAC CHAMBER OF COMMERCE	(810)794-5511
ALLEGAN COUNTY TOURISM AND RECREATION COUNCIL	(616)673-2479
ALLEGAN AREA CHAMBER OF COMMERCE	(616)673-2479
ALLEGAN COUNTY	(616)673-8471
ALLEN CHAMBER OF COMMERCE	(517)439-4341
ALLEN PARK CHAMBER OF COMMERCE	(313)382-7303
	(313)388-5207
ALMA CHAMBER OF COMMERCE	(517)463-5525
	(517)463-8979
ALPENA AREA CHAMBER OF COMMERCE	(800)582-1906
	(517)354-4181
AMERICAN-ISREAL CHAMBER OF COMMERCE OF MICHIGAN	(810)661-1948
ANN ARBOR AREA CHAMBER OF COMMERCE	(313)665-4433
ANN ARBOR CVB	(313)995-7281
ARCADIA CHAMBER OF COMMERCE	(616)723-2575
ASSOCIATION OF COMMERCE & INDUSTRY OF OTTAWA CO	(616)842-4910
ATLANTA CHAMBER OF COMMERCE	(517)785-3400
AU GRES CHAMBER OF COMMERCE	(517)876-6688
AUBURN AREA CHAMBER OF COMMERCE	(517)662-4001
AUBURN HILLS CHAMBER OF COMMERCE	(810)853-7862
BAD AXE CHAMBER OF COMMERCE	(517)269-7411
BALDWIN CHAMBER OF COMMERCE	(616)745-4331
BARAGA COUNTY TOURIST & RECREATION ASSOCIATION	(906)524-7444
BATTLE CREEK AREA CHAMBER OF COMMERCE	(616)962-4076
BATTLE CREEK/CALHOUN CO VIS & CONVENTION BUREAU	(616)962-2240
BAY AREA CHAMBER OF COMMERCE	(517)893-4567
BAY AREA CVB	(800)424-5114
	(517)893-1222
BEAR LAKE CHAMBER OF COMMERCE	(616)723-2575
BEAVER ISLAND CHAMBER OF COMMERCE	(616)448-2505
BELDING CHAMBER OF COMMERCE	(616)794-2210
BELLAIRE CHAMBER OF COMMERCE	(616)533-6023
	(616)533-6473
BELLEVILLE CHAMBER OF COMMERCE	(313)697-7151
BELLEVUE CHAMBER OF COMMERCE	(616)763-9571
BENZIE COUNTY CHAMBER OF COMMERCE	(616)882-5802
BERRIEN SPRINGS/EAU CLAIRE CHAMBER OF COMMERCE	(616)471-9680

BESSEMER CHAMBER OF COMMERCE	(906)663-4542
BEULAH CHAMBER OF COMMERCE	(616)882-5802
BIG RAPIDS CHAMBER OF COMMERCE	(616)796-7649
BIRCH RUN CHAMBER OF COMMERCE-TOURISM DEPT	(517)624-9193
BIRMINGHAM/BLOOMFIELD CHAMBER OF COMMERCE	(810)644-1700
BLISSFIELD CHAMBER OF COMMERCE	(517)486-3642
	(517)486-2236
BLUE WATER AREA TOURIST BUREAU	(810)987-8687
	(800)852-4242
BOYNE COUNTRY CONVENTION AND VISITORS BUREAU	(616)348-2755
	(800)845-2828
BOYNE CITY CHAMBER OF COMMERCE	(616)582-6222
BOYNE COUNTRY CONVENTION AND VISITORS BUREAU	(800)456-0197
BERRIEN CHAMBER OF COMMERCE	(616)723-2575
BRIDGEPORT AREA CHAMBER OF COMMERCE	(517)777-9180
BRONSON CHAMBER OF COMMERCE	(517)369-5085
BROOKLYN CHAMBER OF COMMERCE	(517)592-8907
BUCHANAN AREA CHAMBER OF COMMERCE	(616)695-3291
BURR OAK CHAMBER OF COMMERCE	(616)489-5075
CADILLAC AREA CHAMBER OF COMMERCE	(616)775-9776
CADILLAC AREA VISITORS BUREAU	(800)22-LAKES
CANTON CHAMBER OF COMMERCE	(313)453-4040
CAPAC AREA CHAMBER OF COMMERCE	(810)395-2243
	(810)395-4321
CARO CHAMBER OF COMMERCE	(517)673-5211
CARSON CITY AREA CHAMBER OF COMMERCE	(517)584-6543
CASEVILLE CHAMBER OF COMMERCE	(517)856-3818
CASPIAN CHAMBER OF COMMERCE	(906)265-3822
CASS CITY CHAMBER OF COMMERCE	(517)872-3434
CASSOPOLIS AREA CHAMBER OF COMMERCE	(616)445-2703
CEDAR SPRINGS CHAMBER OF COMMERCE	(616)696-3260
CEDAR/MAPLE CITY CHAMBER OF COMMERCE	(616)228-6077
CEDARVILLE CHAMBER OF COMMERCE	(906)484-3935
CENTRAL LAKE AREA CHAMBER OF COMMERCE	(616)544-3322
	(616)544-5015
	(616)533-6114
CENTRAL MACOMB COUNTY CHAMBER OF COMMERCE	(810)463-1528
CHARLEVOIX AREA CONVENTION AND VISITORS BUREAU	(800)367-8557
CHARLEVOIX CHAMBER OF COMMERCE	(616)547-2101
CHARLOTTE CHAMBER OF COMMERCE	(517)543-0400
CHEBOYGAN AREA CHAMBER OF COMMERCE	(800)968-3302

CHEBOYGAN AREA TOURIST BUREAU	(616)627-7183	FERNDALE CHAMBER OF COMMERCE	(810)542-2160
CHELSEA CHAMBER OF COMMERCE	(313)475-1145	FIFE LAKE CHAMBER OF COMMERCE	(616)879-4471
CHESANING CHAMBER OF COMMERCE	(517)845-3055	FIFE LAKE AREA CHAMBER OF COMMERCE	(616)879-4287
CIRCLE MICHIGAN, INC	(800)513-MICH	FLINT AREA CHAMBER OF COMMERCE	(810)232-7101
	(616)941-4994	FLINT AREA CHAMBER OF COMMERCE	(810)233-7437
CLARE CHAMBER OF COMMERCE	(517)386-2442	FLINT AREA CVB	(800)288-8040
CLARKSTON CHAMBER OF COMMERCE	(810)625-8055		(810)232-8900
CLAWSON CHAMBER OF COMMERCE	(810)435-2450	FLUSHING AREA CHAMBER OF COMMERCE	(810)659-4141
COLDWATER CHAMBER OF COMMERCE	(517)278-5985	FOUR FLAGS AREA COUNCIL ON TOURISM	(616)683-3720
COLOMA CHAMBER OF COMMERCE	(616)468-3377	FRANKENMUTH CHAMBER OF COMMERCE	(517)652-6106
COLON CHAMBER OF COMMERCE	(517)278-5985	FRANKENMUTH CVB	(800)FUN TOWN
	(616)432-2403		(517)652-6106
	(616)432-2532	FRANKFORT/ELBERTA CHAMBER OF COMMERCE	(616)352-7251
COOPERSVILLE AREA CHAMBER OF COMMERCE	(616)837-9731	FRANKFORT VISITORS BUREAU	(616)352-7251
COPPER HARBOR IMPROVEMENT ASSOCIATION	(906)289-4287	FREELAND AREA CHAMBER OF COMMERCE	(517)695-6620
CORNERSTONE ALLIANCE	(616)925-6100	FREMONT CHAMBER OF COMMERCE	(616)924-0770
CRYSTAL FALLS CHAMBER OF COMMERCE	(906)265-3822	GARDEN CHAMBER OF COMMERCE	(906)786-2192
CRYSTAL FALLS INFORMATION CENTER	(906)875-4454	GARDEN CITY CHAMBER OF COMMERCE	(313)422-4448
CURTIS AREA CHAMBER OF COMMERCE	(906)586-3700	GAYLORD GOLF MECCA	(517)732-6333
DAVISON AREA CHAMBER OF COMMERCE	(810)658-5355		(800)345-8621
DAVISON CHAMBER OF COMMERCE	(810)653-6266	GAYLORD/OTSEGO CHAMBER OF COMMERCE	(517)732-4000
DE TOUR VILLAGE CHAMBER OF COMMERCE	(906)297-5987	GAYLORD AREA CONVENTION & TOURISM BUREAU	(517)732-6333
DEARBORN CHAMBER OF COMMERCE	(313)584-6100		(800)345-8621
DEARBORN HEIGHTS CHAMBER OF COMMERCE	(313)274-7480	GLADSTONE CHAMBER OF COMMERCE	(906)786-2192
DELTA COUNTY TOURIST & CONVENTION BUREAU	(800)437-7496	GLADWIN CHAMBER OF COMMERCE	(517)426-5451
DELTA COUNTY CHAMBER OF COMMERCE	(906)786-2192	GLEN LAKE/SLEEPING BEAR CHAMBER OF COMMERCE	(616)334-3238
DICKINSON COUNTY TOURISM ASSOCIATION	(906)774-2002	GOGEBIC AREA CVB	(800)272-7000
DICKINSON COUNTY CHAMBER OF COMMERCE	(800)236-2447		(906)932-4850
DISCOVER GOLF ON MICHIGAN'S SUNRISE SIDE	(517)742-4350	GRAND RAPIDS AREA CVB	(800)678-9859
	(800)729-9373		(616)459-8187
DOUGLAS	(616)857-1701	GRAND LEDGE AREA CHAMBER OF COMMERCE	(517)627-2383
DOWAGIAC CHAMBER OF COMMERCE	(616)782-8212	GRAND BEACH CHAMBER OF COMMERCE	(616)469-5409
DRUMMOND ISLAND CHAMBER OF COMMERCE	(906)493-5245	GRAND BLANC CHAMBER OF COMMERCE	(810)695-4222
DURAND CHAMBER OF COMMERCE	(517)288-3715	GRAND RAPIDS AREA CHAMBER OF COMMERCE	(616)771-0300
EAST JORDAN CHAMBER OF COMMERCE	(616)536-7351	GRAND RAPIDS AREA CVB	(800)678-9859
EASTPOINTE (DETROIT) CHAMBER OF COMMERCE	(810)776-5520		(616)459-8287
EDMORE AREA CHAMBER OF COMMERCE	(517)427-5821	GRAND HAVEN/SPRING LAKE VISITORS BUREAU	(616)842-4499
EDWARDSBURG CHAMBER OF COMMERCE	(616)663-2023	GRAND MARAIS CHAMBER OF COMMERCE	(906)494-2766
ELBERTA CHAMBER OF COMMERCE	(616)352-7251	GRANDVILLE CHAMBER OF COMMERCE	(616)531-8890
ELK COUNTRY VISITORS BUREAU	(517)742-4350	GRAYLING AREA VISITORS COUNCIL	(517)348-2921
ELK RAPIDS CHAMBER OF COMMERCE	(616)264-8202		(800)937-8837
EMPIRE BUSINESS ASSOCIATION	(616)326-5287	GRAYLING REGIONAL CHAMBER OF COMMERCE	(517)348-2921
	(616)326-5157	GREATER BATTLE CREEK/CALHOUN CO VISITORS &	
ESCANABA CHAMBER OF COMMERCE	(906)786-2192	CONVENTION BUREAU	(800)397-2240
EVART CHAMBER OF COMMERCE	(616)734-5554	GREATER BERKLEY CHAMBER OF COMMERCE	(810)544-9464
FARMINGTON CHAMBER OF COMMERCE	(810)474-3440	GREATER BRIGHTON AREA CHAMBER OF COMMERCE	(810)227-5086
FENNVILLE CHAMBER OF COMMERCE	(616)561-5013	GREATER CROSWELL/LEXINGTON CHAMBER OF COMMERCE	(810)359-2262
	(616)561-6311	GREATER DETROIT CHAMBER OF COMMERCE	(313)964-4000
FENTON CHAMBER OF COMMERCE	(810)629-5447	GREATER JACKSON CHAMBER OF COMMERCE	(517)782-8221

GREATER KALKASKA AREA CHAMBER OF COMMERCE	(616)258-4906
GREATER LANSING CVB	(517)487-6800
	(800)648-6630
GREATER ORTONVILLE CHAMBER OF COMMERCE	(810)627-2811
GREATER ROMULUS CHAMBER OF COMMERCE	(313)326-4290
GREENBUSH CHAMBER OF COMMERCE	(517)739-7635
GREENBUSH-OSCODA-AU SABLE LODGING ASSOCIATION	(517)739-5156
	(800)235-GOAL
GREENVILLE CHAMBER OF COMMERCE	(616)754-4697
GROSSE POINTE SHORES CHAMBER OF COMMERCE	(810)777-2741
GUN LAKE AREA CHAMBER OF COMMERCE	(616)672-7822
HALE AREA CHAMBER OF COMMERCE	(517)728-2051
	(800)722-8229
HAMTRAMCK CHAMBER OF COMMERCE	(313)875-7877
HARBERT CHAMBER OF COMMERCE	(616)469-5409
HARBOR BEACH CHAMBER OF COMMERCE	(517)479-6450
HARBOR COUNTRY CHAMBER OF COMMERCE	(616)469-5409
HARBOR COUNTRY LODGING ASSOCIATION	(800)362-7251
HARBOR SPRINGS CHAMBER OF COMMERCE	(616)347-4150
HARRISON CHAMBER OF COMMERCE	(517)539-6011
HARRISVILLE CHAMBER OF COMMERCE	(517)724-5107
HART/SILVER LAKE CHAMBER OF COMMERCE	(616)873-2247
HARTLAND TOURIST ASSN	(616)754-5697
HASTINGS CHAMBER OF COMMERCE	(616)945-2454
HAZEL PARK CHAMBER OF COMMERCE	(810)543-8556
HESPERIA AREA CHAMBER OF COMMERCE	(616)854-3695
HIGHLAND PARK CHAMBER OF COMMERCE	(313)868-6420
HILLMAN AREA CHAMBER OF COMMERCE	(517)742-3739
HILLSDALE CHAMBER OF COMMERCE	(517)439-4341
HOLLAND AREA CVB	(616)396-4221
	(800)822-2770
HOLLAND CHAMBER OF COMMERCE	(616)392-2389
HOLLY AREA CHAMBER OF COMMERCE	(810)634-1900
HONOR CHAMBER OF COMMERCE	(616)882-5802
HOUGHTON LAKE CHAMBER OF COMMERCE	(517)366-5644
HOUGHTON LAKE CHAMBER OF COMMERCE	(800)248-LAKE
	(800)292-9071
HOWELL CHAMBER OF COMMERCE	(517)546-3920
HUBBARD LAKE CHAMBER OF COMMERCE	(517)736-8111
	(517)727-9919
HUDSON AREA CHAMBER OF COMMERCE	(517)448-8983
HUDSONVILLE CHAMBER OF COMMERCE	(616)896-9020
HURON COUNTY VISITORS BUREAU	(800)35-THUMB
HURON COUNTY VISITORS BUREAU	(517)269-6413
HURON SHORES CHAMBER OF COMMERCE	(800)423-2823
	(517)724-5107
HURON TOWNSHIP CHAMBER OF COMMERCE	(313)753-4220
HURON VALLEY AREA CHAMBER OF COMMERCE	(313)685-7129

IDLEWILD CHAMBER OF COMMERCE	(616)745-4331
IMLAY CITY AREA CHAMBER OF COMMERCE	(313)724-1361
INDIAN RIVER TOURIST BUREAU	(616)238-9325
INTERLOCHEN CHAMBER OF COMMERCE	(616)276-7141
IONIA CHAMBER OF COMMERCE	(616)527-2560
IRON COUNTY TOURISM COUNCIL	(906)265-3822
	(800)255-3620
IRON RIVER CHAMBER OF COMMERCE	(906)265-3822
IRONS AREA TOURIST ASSN	(616)266-8101
IRONS AREA TOURIST ASSN	(616)266-5317
IRONWOOD TOURISM COUNCIL	(906)932-1000
IRONWOOD AREA CHAMBER OF COMMERCE	(906)932-1122
ISABELLA COUNTY CVB	(800)77-CHIEF
	(517)772-4433
ISHPEMING-NEGAUNEE AREA CHAMBER OF COMMERCE	(906)486-4841
ITHACA CHAMBER OF COMMERCE	(517)875-3640
	(517)875-3456
JACKSON CONVENTION & TOURIST BUREAU	(800)245-5282
	(517)764-4440
JENISON CHAMBER OF COMMERCE	(616)457-5610
JONESVILLE CHAMBER OF COMMERCE	(517)439-4341
KALAMAZOO COUNTY CVB	(616)381-4003
	(800)945-KALA
KALEVA CHAMBER OF COMMERCE	(616)723-2575
KALKASKA COUNTY CHAMBER OF COMMERCE	(616)258-9103
KEWEENAW TOURISM COUNCIL	(906)337-4579
	(800)338-7982
	(906)482-2388
KEWEENAW PENINSULA CHAMBER OF COMMERCE	(906)482-5240
LAKE CITY AREA CHAMBER OF COMMERCE	(616)839-4969
LAKE COUNTY CHAMBER OF COMMERCE	(616)745-4331
LAKE GOGEBIC AREA CHAMBER OF COMMERCE	(906)575-3265
LAKE MICHIGAN CVB	(616)925-0044
	(616)925-6100
LAKE ODESSA AREA CHAMBER OF COMMERCE	(616)374-0766
LAKES AREA CHAMBER OF COMMERCE	(810)624-2826
LAKESHORE CHAMBER OF COMMERCE	(616)429-1170
LAKESHORE CVB	(616)637-5252
LAKESIDE CHAMBER OF COMMERCE	(616)469-5409
LANSING REGIONAL CHAMBER OF COMMERCE	(517)487-6340
LAPEER AREA CHAMBER OF COMMERCE	(810)664-6641
LEELANAU PENINSULA CHAMBER OF COMMERCE	(616)256-9895
LELAND BUSINESS ASSOCIATION	(616)256-9382
LENAWEE COUNTY CHAMBER OF COMMERCE	(517)265-5141
	(800)682-6580
LENAWEE COUNTY CONFERENCE & VISITORS BUREAU	(517)263-7000
	(800)536-2933
LEROY CHAMBER OF COMMERCE	(616)768-4443

LES CHENEAUX CHAMBER OF COMMERCE	(906)484-3935	METRO EAST CHAMBER OF COMMERCE	(810)777-2741
LEWISTON CHAMBER OF COMMERCE	(517)786-2293	METROPOLITAN DETROIT CVB	(800)DE-TROIT
	(800)428-2293		(313)259-4333
	(517)786-2112	MICHIANA CHAMBER OF COMMERCE	(616)469-5409
LEXINGTON CHAMBER OF COMMERCE	(810)359-2262	MICHIGAN DEPARTMENT OF NATURAL RESOURCES	(517)373-1204
LINCOLN PARK CHAMBER OF COMMERCE	(313)386-0140	MICHIGAN STATE CHAMBER OF COMMERCE	(517)371-2100
LINDEN/ARGENTINE CHAMBER OF COMMERCE	(810)750-8794	MICHIGAN TRAVEL & TOURISM ASSOCIATION	(517)485-8000
LITCHFIELD CHAMBER OF COMMERCE	(313)542-2351	MICHIGAN CHARTER BOAT ASSOCIATION	(517)886-3999
LIVINGSTON COUNTY VISITORS BUREAU	(800)686-8474	MICHIGAN BICYCLE TOURING GUIDE	(616)263-5885
	(517)548-1795	MICHIGAN RIVER GUIDES ASSOCIATION	(616)848-4597
LIVONIA CHAMBER OF COMMERCE	(313)427-2122	MICHIGAN TRAVEL BUREAU	(800)5432-YES
LOWELL AREA CHAMBER OF COMMERCE	(616)897-9161	MICHIGAN BED & BREAKFAST DIRECTORY	(800)832-6657
LUCE COUNTY ECONOMIC DEVELOPMENT CORP	(906)293-3307	MICHIGAN UNDERWATER PRESERVES COUNCIL	(906)643-8717
	(906)293-5982	MICHIGAN'S SUNRISE SIDE, INC	(800)424-3022
LUDINGTON AREA CHAMBER OF COMMERCE	(800)542-4600		(517)469-4544
LUDINGTON AREA CVB	(616)845-0324	MIDLAND COUNTY CVB	(517)839-9901
MACKINAC ISLAND CHAMBER OF COMMERCE	(906)847-3783	MILAN CHAMBER OF COMMERCE	(313)439-7932
	(906)847-6418	MILFORD CHAMBER OF COMMERCE	(810)685-7129
MACKINAW CITY CHAMBER OF COMMERCE	(616)436-5574	MIO CHAMBER OF COMMERCE	(517)826-3331
MACKINAW AREA TOURIST BUREAU	(616)436-5664	MONROE COUNTY CHAMBER OF COMMERCE	(313)242-3366
	(800)666-0160	MONROE COUNTY CONVENTION & TOURISM BUREAU	(800)252-3011
MADISON HEIGHTS CHAMBER OF COMMERCE	(810)542-5010		(313)457-1030
MANCHESTER CHAMBER OF COMMERCE	(313)428-7722	MONTAGUE CHAMBER OF COMMERCE	(616)893-4585
	(313)747-1294	MONTMORENCY COUNTY TOURISM BUREAU	(517)742-4347
MANISTEE AREA CHAMBER OF COMMERCE	(616)723-2575	MONTMORENCY COUNTY TOURISM BUREAU	(517)742-3739
MANISTEE FILER AREA TOURIST ASSOCIATION	(616)723-8385		(517)742-4350
MANISTIQUE AREA TOURIST COUNCIL	(906)341-5838	MONTROSE AREA CHAMBER OF COMMERCE	(810)639-3475
	(800)342-4282	MOUNT CLEMENS CHAMBER OF COMMERCE	(810)463-1528
MANISTIQUE CHAMBER OF COMMERCE	(906)341-5010	MOUNT PLEASANT AREA CHAMBER OF COMMERCE	(517)772-2396
MANISTIQUE LAKES AREA TOURISM BUREAU	(906)586-9732	MUNISING VISITORS BUREAU	(906)387-2138
MANTON AREA CHAMBER OF COMMERCE	(616)824-4158	MUSKEGON COUNTY CVB	(800)235-FUNN
MARINE CITY CHAMBER OF COMMERCE	(810)765-4501		(616)722-3751
MARION CHAMBER OF COMMERCE	(616)743-2461		(616)893-4585
MARLETTE AREA CHAMBER OF COMMERCE	(517)635-2429	MUSKEGON ECONOMIC GROWTH ALLIANCE	(616)722-3751
MARQUETTE AREA CHAMBER OF COMMERCE	(906)226-6591		(616)728-7251
MARQUETTE COUNTRY CVB	(800)544-4321	NASHVILLE CHAMBER OF COMMERCE	(517)852-0845
	(906)228-7749	NAUBINWAY/ENGADINE MERCHANTS ASSOCIATION	(906)477-6271
MARSHALL CHAMBER OF COMMERCE	(616)781-5163	NEGAUNEE CHAMBER OF COMMERCE	(906)226-6591
MARYSVILLE CHAMBER OF COMMERCE	(810)364-6180	NEGAUNEE/ISHPEMING AREA CHAMBER OF COMMERCE	(906)486-4841
MASON AREA CHAMBER OF COMMERCE	(517)676-1016	NEW BUFFALO CHAMBER OF COMMERCE	(616)469-5409
MASON COUNTY CVB	(616)845-0324	NEW ERA CHAMBER OF COMMERCE	(616)861-4303
MASON COUNTY CVB	(800)542-4600	NEWAGO CHAMBER OF COMMERCE	(616)652-3068
MCBAIN AREA CHAMBER OF COMMERCE	(616)825-2387	NEWAGO COUNTY TOURIST COUNCIL	(616)652-9298
MCBAIN CHAMBER OF COMMERCE	(616)825-2416	NEWBERRY AREA TOURISM ASSOCIATION	(800)831-7292
MECOSTA COUNTY CHAMBER OF COMMERCE	(616)796-7649	NEWBERRY MERCHANTS ASSOCIATION	(906)293-3931
MECOSTA COUNTY CVB	(800)833-6697	NEWBERRY AREA CHAMBER OF COMMERCE & TOURIST ASSN	(906)293-5562
MECOSTA COUNTY CVB	(616)796-7640	NILES FOUR FLAGS AREA	(616)683-3720
MENOMINEE AREA CHAMBER OF COMMERCE	(906)863-2679	HORTHPORT CHAMBER OF COMMERCE	(616)386-5806
MESICK CHAMBER OF COMMERCE	(616)885-1280	HORTHVILLE CHAMBER OF COMMERCE	(810)349-7640

NORTHWEST MICHIGAN GOLF COUNCIL	(800)937-7272	ROCHESTER CHAMBER OF COMMERCE	(810)651-6700
NOVI CHAMBER OF COMMERCE	(810)349-3743	ROCKFORD CHAMBER OF COMMERCE	(616)866-2000
OAKLAND COUNTY CHAMBER OF COMMERCE	(810)456-8600	ROGERS CITY CHAMBER OF COMMERCE	(517)734-2535
OCEANA COUNTY TRAVEL BUREAU	(616)873-7141		(800)622-4148
ONAWAY CHAMBER OF COMMERCE	(517)733-2874	ROMEO CHAMBER OF COMMERCE	(810)752-4436
ONEKAMA CHAMBER OF COMMERCE	(616)723-2575	ROTHBURY CHAMBER OF COMMERCE	(616)894-2385
ONTONAGON TOURISM COUNCIL	(906)884-4735	ROYAL OAK CHAMBER OF COMMERCE	(810)547-4000
ORION AREA CHAMBER OF COMMERCE	(810)693-6300	RV & CAMPSITE DIRECTORY	(800)422-6478
OSCODA CHAMBER OF COMMERCE	(616)694-6880		(517)349-8881
	(517)739-7322	SAGINAW COUNTY CHAMBER OF COMMERCE	(517)752-7161
OSCODA COUNTY (MIO) CHAMBER OF COMMERCE	(517)826-3606	SAGINAW COUNTY CVB	(800)444-9979
	(517)826-3331		(517)752-7164
	(800)800-6133	SAINT CHARLES AREA CHAMBER OF COMMERCE	(517)865-8287
OSCODA/AUSABLE CHAMBER OF COMMERCE	(800)235-GOAL	SAINT LOUIS AREA CHAMBER OF COMMERCE	(517)681-3825
OSSINEKE CHAMBER OF COMMERCE	(517)471-2493	SALINE CHAMBER OF COMMERCE	(313)429-4494
OTSEGO CHAMBER OF COMMERCE	(616)694-6880	SANDUSKY CHAMBER OF COMMERCE	(810)648-4445
OWOSSO CHAMBER OF COMMERCE	(517)723-5149	SANFORD AREA CHAMBER OF COMMERCE	(517)687-2800
OXFORD CHAMBER OF COMMERCE	(810)628-0410	SANILAC TOURISM COUNCIL	(313)679-2300
PARADISE AREA TOURISM COUNCIL	(906)492-3310	SAUGATUCK/DOUGLAS CVB	(616)857-1701
PAW PAW CHAMBER OF COMMERCE	(616)657-5395	SAULT AREA CHAMBER OF COMMERCE	(906)632-3301
PENTWATER CHAMBER OF COMMERCE	(616)869-4150	SAULT STE MARIE TOURIST BUREAU	(800)MI-SAULT
PETOSKEY REGIONAL CHAMBER OF COMMERCE	(616)347-4150		(906)632-3301
PETOSKEY BOYNE COUNTRY CVB	(800)845-2828	SAWYER CHAMBER OF COMMERCE	(616)469-5409
	(800)456-0197	SCHOOLCRAFT COUNTY CHAMBER OF COMMERCE	(906)341-5010
PIGEON CHAMBER OF COMMERCE	(517)453-3441	SCHOOLCRAFT COUNTY ECONOMIC DEVELOPMENT CORP	(906)341-5126
	(517)453-2733	SCOTTVILLE CHAMBER OF COMMERCE	(616)757-4729
PINCONNING CHAMBER OF COMMERCE	(800)44-PINNY		(616)757-4304
	(517)879-2816		(616)757-3673
PLAINWELL CHAMBER OF COMMERCE	(616)685-8877	SEBEWAING CHAMBER OF COMMERCE	(517)883-2150
PLYMOUTH CHAMBER OF COMMERCE	(313)453-1540	SHELBY CHAMBER OF COMMERCE	(616)861-4054
PONTIAC CHAMBER OF COMMERCE	(810)335-9600	SHEPHERD AREA CHAMBER OF COMMERCE	(517)828-6683
	(810)683-4747	SILVER LAKE AREA CHAMBER OF COMMERCE	(616)873-2247
	(313)335-9190	SKIDWAY LAKE AREA CHAMBER OF COMMERCE	(517)873-4150
PORCUPINE MT PROMOTIONAL CHAMBER	(906)885-5885	SOUTH HAVEN CHAMBER OF COMMERCE	(616)637-5171
PORT HURON CHAMBER OF COMMERCE	(810)985-7101	SOUTH LYON CHAMBER OF COMMERCE	(810)437-3257
PORTLAND AREA CHAMBER OF COMMERCE	(517)647-2100	SOUTHERN WAYNE COUNTY CHAMBER OF COMMERCE	(313)284-6000
POSEN CHAMBER OF COMMERCE	(517)766-8128	SOUTHFIELD CHAMBER OF COMMERCE	(810)557-6400
PRESQUE ISLE AREA COMMERCE COMMITTEE	(517)595-5095	SOUTHWEST MICHIGAN TOURIST COUNCIL	(616)925-6301
	(517)595-6970	SPARTA CHAMBER OF COMMERCE	(616)887-2454
QUINCY CHAMBER OF COMMERCE	(517)639-3745	SPRING LAKE VISITORS BUREAU	(616)842-4499
RAPID RIVER CHAMBER OF COMMERCE	(906)786-2192	ST. CLAIR SHORES CHAMBER OF COMMERCE	(810)777-2741
RAVENNA CHAMBER OF COMMERCE	(616)853-2241	ST. HELEN CHAMBER OF COMMERCE	(517)389-3725
RECREATIONAL CANOEING ASSOCIATION	(906)238-7868	ST. IGNACE AREA TOURIST ASSOCIATION	(800)338-6660
REDFORD TOWNSHIP CHAMBER OF COMMERCE	(313)535-0960	ST. IGNACE CHAMBER OF COMMERCE	(906)463-8717
REED CITY CHAMBER OF COMMERCE	(616)832-5431	ST. JAMES CHAMBER OF COMMERCE	(616)448-2505
REESE CHAMBER OF COMMERCE	(517)776-7525	ST. JOHNS CHAMBER OF COMMERCE	(517)224-7248
RICHMOND AREA CHAMBER OF COMMERCE	(810)727-3975	ST. JOSEPH LAKE MICHIGAN CVB	(616)925-0044
	(810)727-7513	ST. JOSEPH TODAY	(616)982-6739
RIVER COUNTRY TOURISM COUNCIL	(616)467-4505	STANDISH CHAMBER OF COMMERCE	(517)846-7867

STERLING HEIGHTS AREA CHAMBER OF COMMERCE	(810)731-5400
STEVENSVILLE CHAMBER OF COMMERCE	(616)429-1170
STURGIS CHAMBER OF COMMERCE	(616)651-5758
SUTTONS BAY CHAMBER OF COMMERCE	(616)271-4444
SWARTZ CREEK CHAMBER OF COMMERCE	(810)635-9643
TAWAS BAY TOURIST & CONVENTION BUREAU	(517)362-8643
TAWAS CITY (INC. TAWAS BAY) CHAMBER OF COMMERCE	(800)55-TAWAS
	(517)362-8643
TECUMSEH CHAMBER OF COMMERCE	(517)423-3740
THOMPSONVILLE CHAMBER OF COMMERCE	(616)882-5802
THREE RIVERS CHAMBER OF COMMERCE	(616)278-8193
THREE OAKS CHAMBER OF COMMERCE	(616)469-5409
THUNDER BAY REGION	(800)582-1906
	(517)354-4181
TIPTON CHAMBER OF COMMERCE	(517)592-8907
TRAVERSE CITY CVB	(800)TRAVERS
	(616)947-1120
TRAVERSE CITY AREA CHAMBER OF COMMERCE	(616)947-5075
TROY CHAMBER OF COMMERCE	(810)641-8151
TRUFANT CHAMBER OF COMMERCE	(616)984-2555
TWIN CITIES AREA CHAMBER OF COMMERCE	(616)925-0044
UNION CITY CHAMBER OF COMMERCE	(517)278-5985
UNION CITY BETTERMENT ASSOCIATION	(517)741-5861
UNION PIER CHAMBER OF COMMERCE	(616)469-5409
UPPER PENINSULA TRAVEL & RECREATION ASSOCIATION	(800)562-7134
	(906)774-5480
UTICA CHAMBER OF COMMERCE	(810)731-5400

VASSAR CHAMBER OF COMMERCE	(517)823-2601
WAKEFIELD CHAMBER OF COMMERCE	(906)224-2222
	(906)229-5122
WARREN, CENTER LINE, STERLING HTS CHAMBER OF COMMERCE	(313)751-3939
WATERSMEET CHAMBER OF COMMERCE	(906)358-4569
	(906)358-4766
WAYLAND CHAMBER OF COMMERCE	(616)792-2265
WAYNE CHAMBER OF COMMERCE	(313)721-0100
WELLSTON AREA TOURIST ASSOCIATION	(616)848-4896
WELLSTON CHAMBER OF COMMERCE	(616)723-2575
WEST BRANCH - OGEMAW TRAVEL & VISITORS BUREAU	(517)345-2821
WEST MICHIGAN TOURIST ASSOCIATION	(616)456-8557
WEST BRANCH-OGEMAW TRAVEL & VISITORS BUREAU	(800)755-9091
WEST BLOOMFIELD CHAMBER OF COMMERCE	(810)626-3636
WESTLAND CHAMBER OF COMMERCE	(313)326-7222
WHITE LAKE AREA CHAMBER OF COMMERCE	(616)893-4585
WHITE CLOUD CHAMBER OF COMMERCE	(616)689-6607
WHITE LAKE AREA CHAMBER OF COMMERCE	(800)497-4580
WHITEHALL CHAMBER OF COMMERCE	(616)893-4585
WHITMORE LAKE CHAMBER OF COMMERCE	(313)449-8540
WILLIAMSTON CHAMBER OF COMMERCE	(517)655-1549
WYOMING CHAMBER OF COMMERCE	(616)531-5990
YPSILANTI CHAMBER OF COMMERCE	(313)482-5920
YPSILANTI CVB	(313)483-4444
ZEELAND CHAMBER OF COMMERCE	(616)772-2494

Land Preservation Organizations

Grand Traverse Regional Land Conservancy The Grand Traverse Regional Land Conservancy was incorporated in 1991 with the mission to protect significant natural, agricultural, scenic areas and advance land stewardship in Antrim, Benzie, Grand Traverse and Kalkaska Counties now and for future generations. For more information call or write them at 624 Third St., Traverse City, Ml 49684 (616) 9297911

The Nature Conservancy The Nature Conservancy is an international nonprofit organization with one mission: *To Protect Rare Plants, Animals, and Natural Communities by Preserving the Critical Lands and Waters They Need to Survive.* In Michigan, the Nature Conservancy has helped protect over 43,000 acres of our states finest wetlands, forests, shorelines and prairies. Please treat all nature preserves with the respect they deserve for being the original nature of Michigan. For more information call or write, the Michigan Chapter, 2840 E. Grand River, Suite 5, East Lansing, Ml 48823 (517) 332-1741.

Michigan Nature Association The Michigan Nature Association (MNA) is a private, non-profit citizens' organization which is not affiliated with any other conservation group. Beginning in 1960, it pioneered a program of *acquiring natural areas in Michigan without the use of government funds.* Most of the work is done by volunteers. The MNA now has 140 preservation projects in fifty counties. Many are easy to visit while others require a guide. To obtain a MNA sanctuary guidebook or for more information, write or call, the MNA, PO Box 102, Avoca, Ml 48006 (810) 324-2626.

Little Traverse Conservancy The Little Traverse Conservancy is a non-profit conservation organization working to protect the natural diversity and beauty of northern Michigan by preserving significant land and scenic areas and fostering appreciation and understanding of the environment. Since 1972, over 3,000 acres of land have been acquired which are open to the public. Also the Conservancy uses conservation easements to protect significant natural and scenic features of northern Michigan. Hiking, bird watching, nature study, photography are encouraged. Hunting and overnight use is allowed only with permission. For more information, call or write the Little Traverse Conservancy, 3264 Powell Rd., Harbor Springs, Ml 49740 (616) 347-0991.

Trail Advocacy Organizations

Rails to Trails Conservancy The mission of the Rails-to-Trails Conservancy is to *enhance America's communities and countrysides by converting thousands of miles of abandoned rail corridors, and connecting open space, into a nationwide network of public trails.* The goal of the Michigan Chapter is the creation of the Discover Michigan Trail, an interconnecting statewide trail system largely on abandoned railroad rights-of-way. Toward that end, the Michigan Chapter works to: educate the public and officials about rail-trails; help organize local groups to promote specific trail segments; provide technical assistance to local groups and governmental agencies; support appropriate state and local legislation, policy, and planning regarding rail-trails. For more information call or write the Rails-to-Trails Conservancy, Michigan Chapter, 913 W. Holmes, Suite 145, Lansing, Ml 48910-0411 (517) 393-6022, fax 393-1960.

North Country Trail Association The North Country Trail Association is a non-profit organization, with local chapters, whose purpose is to promote and develop the North Country National Scenic Trail. For more information and addresses of local chapters, write the NCTA, PO Box 311, White Cloud, Ml 49349. (616) 689-1912

Michigan Mountain Biking Association The Michigan Mountain Biking Association (MMBA) is a non-profit organization, with regional chapters. It was established in 1990 for the purpose of providing riding opportunities by promoting responsible riding and sharing the responsibility for developing and maintaining trails. With over 1,000 members statewide, the MMBA is active in keeping the existing trails open to mountain bikes and developing new trails throughout the state. For more information call or write the MMBA, PO Box 29 Belmont, Ml (616) 784-9327 fax 785-0120.

Pigeon River Country Association The Pigeon River Country Association was established in 1971 to be a citizen advocacy group for the Pigeon River Country State Forest. Part of that charge includes the development and promotion of the High Country Pathway. The association sells a detailed trail guidebook, forest map and book titled *Pigeon River Country, A Michigan Forest.* For more information or to purchase the publications write the Pigeon River Country Association, P.O. Box 122, Gaylord, Ml 49735. The publications can also be purchased through the DNR Gaylord office.

League of Michigan Cyclists The League of Michigan Bicyclists, a statewide organization of bicyclists, was formed in 1982. With a membership of over 1500 (1994) individuals and 18 affiliated clubs, LMB is responsive to the interests of those members and the bicycling conditions of Michigan. LMB sponsors various weekend conferences about transportation issues, bicycle safety education and in club leadership. They have compiled the Bicycle Michigan Poster-Calendar of events for several years, which is distributed at MDOT Welcome Centers. Since 1993, the League has produced PSAs on bicycling for TV, a video for law enforcement officers "The Law's for All", and a bicycle safety literature program. The League promotes the Shoreline Bicycle Tours - West, East and North routes. These tours effectively promote "proper" bicycling on the roads both for the riders and the public, as well as provide the funding for their programs. For more information write or call PO Box 16201, Lansing, Ml 48901, (313) 379-2453

Sierra Club The Sierra Club is an international environmental organization involved in both advocacy and outdoor activities. In Michigan, the Mackinac Chapter and its 15 regional groups are active in hiking, canoeing and cross country skiing, as well as lobbying for protection of public lands and clean and healthy environment. For more information contact the Mackinaw Chapter, 300 North Washington Square, Suite 411, Lansing, Ml 48933. (517) 484-2372

Outdoors Forever Outdoors Forever is a non-profit organization established in 1968 dedicated to promoting life-long "inclusive" outdoor recreation. The organization philosophy is that everyone should be able to hunt, fish, camp, hike, picnic, bird watch or enjoy any other outdoor recreational activity for as long as they WANT to, regardless of age or physical abilities. For more information, contact them at PO Box 4832, East Lansing, Ml 48823 (517) 337-0018.

Cross Country Ski Trails

Addison Oaks County Park
Agonikak Trail
Al Quaal Recreation Area
Albert C. Keppel Forest Preserve
Algonac State Park
Algonquin Cross Country Ski Trail
Allegan State Game Area
Alligator Hill Trail
Aman Park
Anderson Lake Pathway
Attikamek Trail
Avalanche Preserve
Bald Mountain Recreation Area
Barrett Rd Cross Country Ski Trails
Battle Creek Linear Park
Baw Beese Trail
Bay City State Park/Tobico Marsh Wildlife
    Refuge
Bay View Ski Trail
Bear River Park
Beaver Island
Bergland Ski Trail
Bertha Brock Park
Betsie River Pathway
Bewabic State Park
Big M Cross Country Ski Area
Binder Park Inc.
Bintz Apple Mountain Ski Area
Birchwood Farms Golf and Country Club
Black Mountain Recreation Area
Blandford Nature Center
Blood Creek Cross Country Ski Trail
Bloomer Park
Blueberry Ridge Pathway
Bowman Lake Foot Travel Area
Boyne Highlands
Boyne Nordican
Brighton Recreation Area

Briley Township Trail
Bruno's Run Trail
Buckhorn Cross Country Ski Trail
Burt Lake State Park
Buttles Road Pathway
Cadillac Pathway
Canada Lakes Pathway
Cannonsburg State Game Area
Cedar River Pathway
Cedar Trail
Central Park
Chadwick's Kwagama Lake Lodge
Chalet Cross Country
Chandler Lake Pathway
Charles Ranson Nature Preserve
Charlton Park Village and Museum
Chassell Classic Ski Trail
Cheboygan State Park
Chlppewa Hills Pathway
Chippewa Nature Center
Christmas Cross Country Ski Trail
Clear Lake State Park
Cleveland Cross Country Ski Trail
Coldbrook County Park
Colonial Point Memorial Forest
Cool Cross Country Ski Area
Copper Harbor Pathway
Corsair Trails
County Farm Park
Craig Lake State Park
Cross Country Ski Headquarters
Cross Country Ski Shop
Crossroads Rail Trail & Reed City Linear Park
Crystal Mountain Resort
Dahlem Environmental Education Center
Days River Pathway
De Graaf Nature Center
DeTour Cross Country Ski Trail

Deerfield Nature Park
Dr. T.K. Lawless County Park
Drayton Plains Nature Center
Eagle Harbor Dunes & Clark Nature
    Sanctuaries
Eagle Run
Eastgate Park
Egypt Valley Trail
Elizabeth Park
Empire Bluff Trail
Escanaba Cross Country Ski Pathway
Estivant Pines Nature Sanctuary
Fayette State Park
Fishermanls Island State Park
Fitzgerald Park
For-Mar Nature Preserve
Forbush Corner
Fort Custer Recreation Area
Fort Wilkins State Park
Fox Park
Fred Russ Forest Park
Freedom Hill County Park
Fumee Lake Trail
Furstenberg Park
Gallup Park
Garland
George Young Recreation Complex
Gladstone Cross Country Ski Trail
Glen Oaks Golf Course
Good Harbor Bay Ski Trail
Grand Island National Recreation Area
Grand Marais Cross Country Ski Trail
Grand Mere State Park
Grand River Park
Grand Traverse County Civic Center Trail
Grand Traverse Natural Education Preserve
Grand Traverse Resort Village
Grass River Natural Area

Green Pine Lake Pathway
Green Point Nature Center
Hager Park
Hanson Hills Recreation Area
Harlow Lake Pathway
Harris Center
Hart-Montague Bicycle Trail State Park
Hartwick Pines State Park
Hayo-Went-Ha Nordic Ski Center
Heartland Trail
Heritage Park
Herman Vogler Conservation Area
Hiawatha Highlands
Hiawatha Ski Trail
Hickory Hills
Highbanks Trail
Highland Recreation Area
Hinchman Acres Resort
Hoeft State Park
Hoffmaster State Park
Hofma Park
Hoist Lakes Foot Travel Area
Holly Recreation Area
Howard Christensen Nature Center
Howell Conference and Nature Center
Hudson-Mills Metropark
Hungerford Trail
Hunter's Point Trail
Huron Hills Cross Country Ski Center
Huron Meadows Metropark
Imerman Memorial Park
Independence Lake County Park
Independence Oaks County Park
Indian Lake Pathway
Indian Springs Metropark
Indian Trails
Interlochen State Park
Ionia State Recreation Area
Iron Mountain City Park
Island Lake Recreation Area
Ithaca Jailhouse Trail
Jewel Lake Trail
Johnsonls Nordic Trails
Kal-Haven Trail Sesquicentennial State Park
Kalamazoo Nature Center
Keehne Environmental Area

Kensington Metropark
Kent County Airport Cross Country Ski Trail
Kent Trails
Keweenaw Peninsula
Kirk Park
Kivela Road Trail
Kiwanis Trail
Lake Ann Pathway
Lake Erie Metropark
Lake Lansing Park - North
Lake Mary Plains Pathway
Lake Ottawa Recreation Area
LakeView Hills Country Inn and Nordic Ski
    Center
Lakelands Trail State Park
Lakes of the North
Lakeslide Trail around Spring Lake
Lamoreaux Park
Laughing Whitefish Falls Scenic Site
Leelanau State Park
Legg Park
Ligon Outdoor Center
Lincoln Brick Park
Little Traverse Wheelway
Lost Lake Pathway
Lost Tamarack Pathway
Lost Twin Lakes Pathway
Loud Creek Cross Country Ski Trail
Love Creek County Park & Nature Center
Lower Huron Metropark
Ludington State Park
MECCA Ski Trail
MTU Trail
Maasto Hiihto Ski Trail
MacKenzie National Recreation Trail
Mackinac Island
Madeline Bertrand County Park
Magoon Creek Natural Area
Manilak Resort Ski Trails
Maple Lane Touring Center
Marquette Fitness Trail
Marsh Ridge
Mason Tract Pathway
Maybury State Park
McClure Riverfront Park
McCormick Wilderness

McCune Nature Preserve
McGuires Resort
McKeever Hills
McLain State Park
McNearney Ski Trail
Mead-Wetmore Pond Nature Trail
Merriman East Pathway
Metamora-Hadley Recreation Area
Metro Beach Metropark
Michaywe Slopes
Middle Rouge Parkway Trail
Midland - Mackinac Trail
Milje's Cross Country Ski Trails
Mill Creek State Park
Mitchell State Park
Montreal Public Trail
Mt. McSauba Recreation Area
Mt. Zion
Muncie Lakes Pathway
Munising Cross Country Ski Trail
Muskallonge Lake State Park
Muskegon State Park
NMU Longear Ski T rail
National Mine Ski Area
Negaunee Township Touring Trail
Neithercut Woodland
Nichols Arboretum
Nordhouse Dunes Wilderness
North Central Michigan College
North Country Trail - Marquette
North Country Trail - Rouge River State Game
    Area
North Curtis Road Cross Country Ski Trails
North Higgins Lake State Park
North Point Nature Preserve
Northern Hardwoods Cross Country Ski Trail
Norway Ridge Pathway
Nub's Nob
Oakwoods Metropark
Ocqueoc Falls Bicentennial Pathway
Ogemaw Hills Pathway
Old Grade Ski Trail
Old Indian Trail
Old Mission State Park
Orchard Beach State Park
Orion Oaks County Park

Ortonville Recreation Area
Ossineke Pathway
Ottawa - Muskegon Rail Trail
Paint Creek Trail
Palmer Park
Pando Ski Area
Pentwater Pathway
Pere Marquette Trail (Clare to Baldwin)
Pere Marquette Trail of Mid-Michigan
Peters Creek Ski Trail
Petoskey State Park
Pickerel Lake Pathway
Pigeon Creek Ski Trail
Pinckney Recreation Area
Pinconning Park
Pine Baron Pathway
Pine Bowl Pathway
Pine Forest Pathway
Pine Haven Recreation Area
Pine Mountain Ski and Recreation
Pine Valleys Pathway
Pinery Lakes Trail
Platte Plains Trail
Pontiac Lake Recreation Area
Porcupine Mountains Wilderness State Park
Port Crescent State Park
Portage Creek Bicentennial Park
Portland Rivertrail Park
Prairie View Park
Presque Isle Park
Price Nature Center
Proud Lake Recreation Area
Provin Trails Park
Pyatt Lake Natural Area
Rapid River National Cross Country Ski Trail
Reffitt Nature Preserve
Reid Lake Foot Travel Area
Rifle River Recreation Area
Riley Trails
Ringwood Forest
River Bluff Nature Trail
River Falls Trail
River Oaks County Park

River Road Sports Complex
Rolling Hills County Park
Rose Lake Wildlife Research Area
Round Lake Nature Preserve
Sand Dunes Cross Country Ski Trail
Sand Lakes Quiet Area
Sanford Natural Area
Sarett Nature Center
Saugatuck Dunes State Park
Scenic Drive Cross Country Ski Trail
School Forest Ski Trail
Schoolcraft County Environmental Lab
Schrier Park
Scotts Woods Park
Seagull Point Park
Searchmont
Searles Audubon Nature Preserve
Seidman Park
Seney National Wildlife Refuge
Seven Lakes State Park
Seven Ponds Nature Center
Shanty Creek/Schuss Mountain Resorts
Sheep Ranch Pathway
Shiawassee National Wildlife Refuge
Shingle Mill Pathway
Silver Creek County Park
Silver Creek Pathway
Sinkhole Pathway
Skegemog Pathway
Ski Brule/Ski Homestead
Sleeper State Park
Sleepy Hollow Nature Preserve
Sleepy Hollow State Park
South Higgins Lake State Park
South Lyons Rail Trail
Spring Brook Pathway
Springfield Oaks Golf Course
St Martin Cross Country Ski Trail
Stokely Creek Ski Touring Center
Stony Creek Metropark
Sugar Loaf Resort
Suicide Bowl
Swedetown Ski Trail

Sylvania Wilderness
Tabor Hill Winery and Restaurant
Tahquamenon Falls State Park
Thompson Harbor State Park
Thornapple Rail Trail
Thunder Bay Resort
Tisdale Triangle Pathway
Treetops Sylvan Resort
Trout Lake Pathway
Twin Lakes State Park
Uller Trail
Valley Spur Ski Trail
Van Buren Trail State Park
Van Riper State Park
Vasa Trail
Wagener County Park
Wah-Wah-Tas-See Pathway
Wahlfield Park
Wakeley Lake Non-Motorized Area
Warner Creek Pathway
Warren Dunes State Park
Warren Valley Golf Course
Warren Woods State Park
Waterloo Recreation Area
Waterloo-Pinckney Hiking Trail
Watersmeet Ski Trail
Wells State Park
West Bloomfield Nature Preserve
West Bloomfield Trail Network
West Higgins Lake Cross Country Ski Trail
West Lake Nature Preserve
White Lake Oaks Golf Course
White Pine Trail State Park
Whitewater Park
Wilderness State Park
Wilderness Valley Cross Country Ski Center
Wildwood Hills Pathway
Willow Metropark
Windy Lake Lodge
Woldumar Nature Center
Wolverine Ski Trail
Yankee Springs Recreation Area
Young State Park

Hiking Trails

Addison Oaks County Park
Agate Falls Scenic Site
Agonikak Trail
Albert C. Keppel Forest Preserve
Algonac State Park
Algonquin Cross Country Ski Trail
Alice W. Moore Woods Nature Sanctuary
Allegan State Game Area
Alligator Hill Trail
Aman Park
Anderson Lake Pathway
Arboretum Trail
Attikamek Trail
Au Train Songbird Trail
Avalanche Preserve
Baker Sanctuary
Baker Woodlot
Bald Mountain Recreation Area
Baraga State Park
Battle Creek Linear Park
Baw Beese Trail
Bay City State Park/Tobico Marsh Wildlife
    Refuge
Bay De Noc-Grand Island National Recreation
    Trail
Bay Hampton Rail Trail and Bay City
    Riverwalk
Bay View Ski Trail
Bear River Park
Beaver Island
Beaver Lodge Nature Trail
Bergland to Sidnaw Rail Trail
Bert DeVriendt Nature Trail
Bertha Brock Park
Besser Bell Pathway
Betsie River Pathway
Bewabic State Park
Big Bear Lake Nature Pathway

Big Knob-Crow Lake Pathway
Bill Nicholls Trail
Binder Park Inc.
Black Mountain Recreation Area
Black River Harbor Trails
Blandford Nature Center
Blind Sucker Pathway
Bloomer Park
Blueberry Ridge Pathway
Bodi Lake Pathway
Bond Falls Trail
Bowman Lake Foot Travel Area
Brennan Memorial Nature Sanctuary
Brighton Recreation Area
Brockway Mountain Nature Sanctuary
Bruno's Run Trail
Burt Lake State Park
Buttles Road Pathway
Cadillac Pathway
Canada Lakes Pathway
Cannonsburg State Game Area
Cascades Falls Hiking Trail
Cass City Trail
Cedar River Pathway
Cedar Trail
Central Park
Chadwick's Kwagama Lake Lodge
Chandler Lake Pathway
Charles Ranson Nature Preserve
Charlton Park Village and Museum
Cheboygan State Park
Chippewa Hills Pathway
Chippewa Nature Center
Christmas Cross Country Ski Trail
Clear Lake - Jackson Lake Pathway
Clear Lake State Park
Coldbrook County Park
Colonial Point Memorial Forest

Cool Cross Country Ski Area
Copper Harbor Pathway
Corsair Trails
Cottonwood Trail
County Farm Park
Craig Lake State Park
Cross Country Ski Headquarters
Crossroads Rail Trail & Reed City Linear Park
Crystal Mountain Resort
Dahlem Environmental Education Center
Days River Pathway
De Graaf Nature Center
Dearborn Environmental Study Area
Deerfield Nature Park
Dinosaur Hill Nature Preserve
Dowagiac Woods Nature Sanctuary
Dr. T. K. Lawless County Park
Drayton Plains Nature Center
Dunes Trail
E.J. Johnson Nature Center
Eagle Harbor Dunes & Clark Nature
    Sanctuaries
Eagle Run
Eastgate Park
Egypt Valley Trail
Elizabeth Park
Empire Bluff Trail
Estivant Pines Nature Sanctuary
Fayette State Park
Felch Grade Rail Trail
Fenner Arboretum
Fernwood Botanic Garden
Fish Point Wlldlife Area
Fisherman's Island State Park
Fitzgerald Park
For-Mar Nature Preserve
Fort Custer Recreation Area
Fort Wilkins State Park

Fox Park
Fox River Pathway
Fred Russ Forest Park
Fumee Lake Trail
Furstenberg Park
Gallup Park
Gemini Lakes Pathway
Genes Pond Pathway
Genesee Recreation Area
George Young Recreation Complex
Gladstone Cross Country Ski Trail
Gogebic Ridge Hiking Trail
Good Harbor Bay Ski Trail
Grand Island National Recreation Area
Grand Marais Cross Country Ski Trail
Grand Mere State Park
Grand River Park
Grand Traverse County Civic Center Trail
Grand Traverse Natural Education Preserve
Grand Traverse Resort Village
Grass River Natural Area
Green Pine Lake Pathway
Green Point Nature Center
Hager Park
Hancock/Calument Trail
Hanson Hills Recreation Area
Harlow Lake Pathway
Harris Center
Hart-Montague Bicycle Trail State Park
Hartwick Pines State Park
Haymeadow Falls Trail
Haywire Rail Trail
Heartland Trail
Henning Park
Heritage Park
Herman Vogler Conservation Area
Hiawatha Highlands
Hiawatha Ski Trail
Hickory Hills
Hidden Lake Gardens
High Country Pathway
Highbanks Trail
Highland Recreation Area
Hinchman Acres Resort
Hoeft State Park
Hoffmaster State Park

Hofma Park
Hoist Lakes Foot Travel Area
Holliday Nature Preserve
Holly Recreation Area
Horseshoe Bay Hiking Trail
Horseshoe Lake Nature Trail
Houghton Waterfront Trail
Howard Christensen Nature Center
Howell Conference and Nature Center
Hudson-Mills Metropark
Hungerford Trail
Hunter's Point Trail
I-275 Bike Path
Imerman Memorial Park
Independence Lake County Park
Independence Oaks County Park
Indian Lake Pathway
Indian Lake State Park
Indian Springs Metropark
Interlochen State Park
Ionia State Recreation Area
Iron Mountain City Park
Iron Range Rail Trail
Island Lake Nature Trail
Island Lake Recreation Area
Island Park
Isle Royale National Park
Ithaca Jailhouse Trail
Jewel Lake Trail
Jordan Valley Pathway
Kal-Haven Trail Sesquicentennial State Park
Kalamazoo Nature Center
Keehne Environmental Area
Keith McKellop Walkway
Kellogg Forest
Kensington Metropark
Kent Trails
Keweenaw Peninsula
Keweenaw Shore No. 1 Nature Sanctuary
Kirk Park
Kitchel-Lindquist Dune Preserve
Kivela Road Trail
Kiwanis Trail
Lake Ann Pathway
Lake Bluff Audubon Center
Lake Gogebic State Park

Lake Lansing Park-North
Lake Mary Plains Pathway
Lake Michigan Recreation Area Bike Trail
Lake Ottawa Recreation Area
LakeView Hills Country Inn and Nordic Ski
    Center
Lakelands Trail State Park
Lakeshore Trail
Lakeside Trail around Spring Lake
Lamoreaux Park
Lansing River Trail
Laughing Whitefish Falls Scenic Site
Leelanau State Park
Legg Park
Ligon Outdoor Center
Lincoln Brick Park
Little Bay De Noc Recreation Area
Little Falls Trail
Little Presque Isle Tract
Little Traverse Wheelway
Littlejohn Lake County Park
Lloyd A Stage Outdoor Education Center
Lost Lake Pathway
Lost Tamarack Pathway
Lost Twin Lakes Pathway
Loud Creek Cross Country Ski Trail
Love Creek County Park & Nature Center
Lower Huron Metropark
Ludington State Park
MTU Trail
Maasto Hiihto Ski Trail
MacKenzie National Recreation Trail
Mackinac Island
Mackinaw / Alanson Rail Trail
Madeline Bertrand County Park
Magoon Creek Natural Area
Manilak Resort Ski Trails
Manistee River Trail
Marquette Fitness Trail
Marsh Lake Pathway
Mason Tract Pathway
Matthaei Botanical Gardens
Maybury State Park
McClure Riverfront Park
McCormick Wilderness
McCune Nature Preserve

McKeever Hills
McLain State Park
Mead-Wetmore Pond Nature Trail
Merriman East Pathway
Metamora-Hadley Recreation Area
Metro Beach Metropark
Michaywe Slopes
Middle Rouge Parkway Trail
Midland-Mackinac Trail
Mill Creek State Park
Mitchell State Park
Montreal Public Trail
Mt. McSauba Recreation Area
Mt. Zion
Muncie Lakes Pathway
Munising Cross Country Ski Trail
Muskallonge Lake State Park
Muskegon State Park
Myron & Isabel Zucker Nature Sanctuary
Nahma Marsh Hiking Trail
National Mine Ski Area
Negaunee Township Touring Trail
Negwegon State Park
Neithercut Woodland
Nichols Arboretum
Ninga Aki Pathway
Nipissing Dune Trails
Nordhouse Dunes Wilderness
North Central Michigan College
North Country Trail-Baldwin
North Country Trail-Bergland
North Country Trail-Bessemer
North Country Trail-Connector
North Country Trail-Kenton & Tibbits Falls
North Country Trail-Lake Superior State
    Forest
North Country Trail-Mackinaw State Forest 2
North Country Trail-Mackinaw State Forest 3
North Country Trail-Manistee
North Country Trail-Marquette
North Country Trail-Munising
North Country Trail-Ontonagon
North Country Trail-Pere Marquette State
    Forest 1
North Country Trail-Rouge River State Game
    Area

North Country Trail-Sault Ste. Marie
North Country Trail - St. Ignace
North Country Trail - White Cloud
North Country Trail-Pere Marquette 2/
    Mackinaw 1
North Curtis Road Cross Country Ski Trails
North Higgins Lake State Park
North Manitou Island
North Point Nature Preserve
Northern Hardwoods Cross Country Ski Trail
Norway Ridge Pathway
Oakwoods Metropark
Ocqueoc Falls Bicentennial Pathway
Old Grade Ski Trail
Old Indian Trail
Old Mission State Park
Onaway State Park
Orchard Beach State Park
Orion Oaks County Park
Ortonville Recreation Area
Osborne Mill Preserve Nature Trail
Osceola Pathway
Ossineke Pathway
Ottawa-Muskegon Rail Trail
Paint Creek Trail
Palmer Park
Park Lyndon
Peninsula Point Hiking Trail
Pentwater Pathway
Pere Marquette Trail (Clare to Baldwin)
Pere Marquette Trail of Mid-Michigan
Peshekee to Clowry Rail Trail
Petoskey State Park
Pickerel Lake Pathway
Pictured Rocks National Lakeshore-Day Hikes
Pigeon Creek Ski Trail
Pinckney Recreation Area
Pinconning Park
Pine Baron Pathway
Pine Bowl Pathway
Pine Forest Pathway
Pine Haven Recreation Area
Pine Mountain Ski and Recreation
Pine Valleys Pathway
Pines Point Trail
Platte Plains Trail

Platte Springs Pathway
Pontiac Lake Recreation Area
Porcupine Mountains Wilderness State Park
Port Crescent State Park
Portage Creek Bicentennial Park
Portland Rivertrail Park
Power Island and Bassett Island
Prairie View Park
Presque Isle Lighthouse Park
Presque Isle Park
Price Nature Center
Proud Lake Recreation Area
Provin Trails Park
Pyatt Lake Natural Area
Pyramid Point Trail
Rapid River National Cross Country Ski Trail
Red Buck Trail
Red Pine Natural Area
Reffitt Nature Preserve
Reid Lake Foot Travel Area
Rifle River Recreation Area
Riley Trails
Ringwood Forest
River Bluff Nature Trail
River Falls TrailRiver Oaks County Park
River Road Sports Complex
Rolling Hills County Park
Rose Lake Wildlife Research Area
Round Lake Nature Preserve
Sand Dunes Cross Country Ski Trail
Sand Lakes Quiet Area
Sanford Natural Area
Sarett Nature Center
Saugatuck Dunes State Park
School Forest Ski Trail
Schoolcraft County Environmental Lab
Schrier Park
Scotts Woods Park
Seagull Point Park
Searchmont
Searles Audubon Nature Preserve
Seidman Park
Seney National Wildlife Refuge
Seven Lakes State Park
Seven Ponds Nature Center
Shannon Nature Sanctuary

Shanty Creek/Schuss Mountain Resorts
Shauger Hill Hiking Trail
Sheep Ranch Pathway
Shiawassee National Wildlife Refuge
Shingle Mill Pathway
Shore To Shore Trail-Segment A
Shore To Shore Trail-Segment B
Shore To Shore Trail-Segment C
Shore to Shore Trail
Silver Creek County Park
Silver Creek Pathway
Silver Lake Trail
Sinkhole Pathway
Skegemog Pathway
Ski Brule/Ski Homestead
Sleeper State Park
Sleepy Hollow Nature Preserve
Sleepy Hollow State Park
Soo Strongs Rail Trail
South Higgins Lake State Park
South Lyons Rail Trail
South Manitou Island
Spring Brook Pathway
St. Ignace-Trout Lake Rail Trail
St. Martin Cross Country Ski Trail
State Line Rail Trail
Sterling State Park
Stony Creek Metropark

Sturgeon Falls Trail
Sugar Loaf Mountain Natural Area
Sugar Loaf Resort
Switchback Ridge Pathway
Sylvania Visitor Center Interpretive Trail
Sylvania Wilderness
Tahquamenon Falls State Park
Thompson Harbor State Park
Thornapple Rail Trail
Thunder Bay Resort
Timberland Swamp Nature Sanctuary
Tisdale Triangle Pathway
Traverse City Recreational Trail
Treaty Tree Trail
Trillium Trail Nature Sanctuary
Trout Lake Pathway
Twin Lakes State Park
Tyoga Historical Pathway
Valley Spur Mountain Bike Trail
Valley Spur Ski Trail
Van Buren Trail State Park
Van Raalte Historical Farm and Recreation
    Area
Van Riper State Park
Vasa Trail
Veterans Memorial Park
Votey Trail
Wagener County Park

Wah-Wah-Tas-See Pathway
Wahlfield Park
Wakeley Lake Non-Motorized Area
Warner Creek Pathway
Warren Dunes State Park
Warren Woods State Park
Waterloo Recreation Area
Waterloo-Pinckney Hiking Trail
Watersmeet Ski Trail
Watersmeet/Land O' Lakes Trail
Wells State Park
West Bloomfield Nature Preserve
West Bloomfield Trail Network
West Branch Pathway
West Lake Nature Preserve
White Pine Trail State Park
Whitehouse Nature Center
Whitewater Park
Wilcox-Warnes Memorial Nature Sanctuary
Wilderness State Park
Wildwood Hills Pathway
Windy Lake Lodge
Windy Moraine Trail
Woldumar Nature Center
Yankee Springs Recreation Area
Young State Park

Mountain Bike Trails

Addison Oaks County Park
Agonikak Trail
Albert C. Keppel Forest Preserve
Allegan State Game Area
Aman Park
Anderson Lake Pathway
Avalanche Preserve
Bald Mountain Recreation Area
Bay City State Park/Tobico Marsh Wildlife
    Refuge
Bay De Noc-Grand Island National Recreation
    Trail
Bear River Park
Beaver Island
Bergland to Sidnaw Rail Trail
Betsie River Pathway
Bill Nicholls Trail
Black Mountain Recreation Area
Bloomer Park
Blueberry Ridge Pathway
Bois Blanc Island
Boyne Nordican
Brighton Recreation Area
Bruno's Run Trail
Buttles Road Pathway
Cadillac Pathway
Canada Lakes Pathway
Cannonsburg State Game Area
Cedar River Pathway
Chadwick's Kwagama Lake Lodge
Chandler Lake Pathway
Charlton Park Village and Museum
Chippewa Hills Pathway
Clear Lake-Jackson Lake Pathway
Cool Cross Country Ski Area
Copper Harbor Pathway
Crystal Mountain Resort
Days River Pathway

Deerfield Nature Park
Eagle Run
Ehlco Mountain Bike Complex
Felch Grade Rail Trail
Fisherman's Island State Park
Fort Custer Recreation Area
Fox River Pathway
Fumee Lake Trail
George Young Recreation Complex
Gladstone Cross Country Ski Trail
Grand Island National Recreation Area
Grand River Park
Green Pine Lake Pathway
Hancock/Calument Trail
Hanson Hills Recreation Area
Harlow Lake Pathway
Hartwick Pines State Park
Haywire Rail Trail
Heartland Trail
Herman Vogler Conservation Area
Hidden Valley Resort
High Country Pathway
Highland Recreation Area
Hinchman Acres Resort
Hofma Park
Holly Recreation Area
Hungerford Trail
Imerman Memorial Park
Indian Lake Pathway
Ionia State Recreation Area
Iron Mountain City Park
Iron Range Rail Trail
Island Lake Recreation Area
Ithaca Jailhouse Trail
Kal-Haven Trail Sesquicentennial State Park
Keweenaw Peninsula
Kivela Road Trail
Lake Ann Pathway

Lake Mary Plains Pathway
Lake Michigan Recreation Area Bike Trail
LakeView Hills Country Inn and Nordic Ski
    Center
Lakelands Trail State Park
Little Bay De Noc Recreation Area
Little Falls Trail
Lost Lake Pathway
Lost Tamarack Pathway
Lost Twin Lakes Pathway
MTU Trail
Maasto Hiihto Ski Trail
MacKenzie National Recreation Trail
Mackinac Island
Mackinaw/Alanson Rail Trail
Maybury State Park
McClure Riverfront Park
Merriman East Pathway
Midland - Mackinac Trail
Muncie Lakes Pathway
National Mine Ski Area
Negaunee Township Touring Trail
Negwegon State Park
North Country Trail-Baldwin
North Country Trail-Mackinaw State Forest 2
North Country Trail-Mackinaw State Forest 3
North Country Trail-Manistee
North Country Trail-Pere Marquette State
    Forest 1
North Country Trail-Rouge River State Game
    Area
North Country Trail-White Cloud
North Country Trail-Pere Marquette
    2/Mackinaw 1
North Curtis Road Cross Country Ski Trails
North Higgins Lake State Park
Norway Ridge Pathway
Ocqueoc Falls Bicentennial Pathway

584

Ortonville Recreation Area
Ottawa-Muskegon Rail Trail
Paint Creek Trail
Pando Ski Area
Pentwater Pathway
Pere Marquette Trail of Mid-Michigan
Peshekee to Clowry Rail Trail
Pinckney Recreation Area
Pine Bowl Pathway
Pine Haven Recreation Area
Pine Mountain Ski and Recreation
Pine Valleys Pathway
Pomeroy/Henry Lake Mountain Bike
    Complex
Pontiac Lake Recreation Area
Proud Lake Recreation Area
Republic/Champion Grade Trail
Rifle River Recreation Area
Riley Trails
Ringwood Forest
River Falls Trail
Rose Lake Wildlife Research Area

Sand Lakes Quiet Area
Searchmont
Seney National Wildlife Refuge
Seven Lakes State Park
Shanty Creek/Schuss Mountain Resorts
Sheep Ranch Pathway
Shiawassee National Wildlife Refuge
Shingle Mill Pathway
Shore To Shore Trail-Segment A
Shore To Shore Trail-Segment B
Shore To Shore Trail-Segment C
Shore to Shore Trail
Silver Creek County Park
Silver Creek Pathway
Silver Lake Trail
Sinkhole Pathway
Skegemog Pathway
Sleeper State Park
Sleepy Hollow State Park
Soo-Strongs Rail Trail
South Higgins Lake State Park
Spring Brook Pathway

St Ignace-Trout Lake Rail Trail
State Line Rail Trail
Sugar Loaf Resort
Thompson Harbor State Park
Thornapple Rail Trail
Tisdale Triangle Pathway
Trout Lake Pathway
Valley Spur Mountain Bike Trail
Valley Spur Ski Trail
Van Buren Trail State Park
Vasa Trail
Wakeley Lake Non-Motorized Area
Warner Creek Pathway
Watersmeet Ski Trail
Watersmeet/Land O'Lakes Trail
West Bloomfield Trail Network
White Pine Trail State Park
Wilderness State Park
Wildwood Hills Pathway
Windy Lake Lodge
Yankee Springs Recreation Area

Interpretive Trails

Albert C. Keppel Forest Preserve
Alice W. Moore Woods Nature Sanctuary
Allegan State Game Area
Anderson Lake Pathway
Arboretum Trail
Attikamek Trail
Avalanche Preserve
Baker Sanctuary
Baker Woodlot
Baraga State Park
Battle Creek Linear Park
Bay City State Park/Tobico Marsh Wildlife
    Refuge
Beaver Lodge Nature Trail
Bert DeVriendt Nature Trail
Bertha Brock Park
Besser Bell Pathway
Bewabic State Park
Big Bear Lake Nature Pathway
Black Mountain Recreation Area
Blandford Nature Center
Bloomer Park
Brennan Memorial Nature Sanctuary
Brockway Mountain Nature Sanctuary
Burt Lake State Park
Cass City Trail
Cedar Trail
Central Park
Charles Ranson Nature Preserve
Charlton Park Village and Museum
Cheboygan State Park
Chippewa Nature Center
Clear Lake-Jackson Lake Pathway
Clear Lake State Park
Colonial Point Memorial Forest
Cool Cross Country Ski Area
Copper Harbor Pathway
Corsair Trails

County Farm Park
Craig Lake State Park
Cross Country Ski Headquarters
Dahlem Environmental Education Center
De Graaf Nature Center
Dearborn Environmental Study Area
Dinosaur Hill Nature Preserve
Dowagiac Woods Nature Sanctuary
Dr. T. K. Lawless County Park
Drayton Plains Nature Center
E.J. Johnson Nature Center
Eagle Harbor Dunes & Clark Nature
    Sanctuaries
Eastgate Park
Empire Bluff Trail
Erie Marsh Preserve
Estivant Pines Nature Sanctuary
Fayette State Park
Fernwood Botanic Garden
Fish Point WIldlife Area
Fisherman's Island State Park
Fitzgerald Park
For-Mar Nature Preserve
Fort Custer Recreation Area
Fort Wilkins State Park
Fox Park
Fox River Pathway
Fred Russ Forest Park
Fumee Lake Trail
Furstenberg Park
Gallup Park
Gardner's Creek Nature Trail
Genes Pond Pathway
George Young Recreation Complex
Grand Island National Recreation Area
Grand Mere State Park
Grand Traverse Natural Education Preserve
Grass River Natural Area

Green Point Nature Center
Hager Park
Harris Center
Harrisville State Park
Hart-Montague Bicycle Trail State Park
Hartwick Pines State Park
Henning Park
Heritage Park
Herman Vogler Conservation Area
Hidden Lake Gardens
Highbanks Trail
Hoeft State Park
Hoffmaster State Park
Holliday Nature Preserve
Holly Recreation Area
Howard Christensen Nature Center
Howell Conference and Nature Center
Hudson-Mills Metropark
Hunter's Point Trail
Imerman Memorial Park
Independence Lake County Park
Independence Oaks County Park
Indian Lake State Park
Indian Springs Metropark
Interlochen State Park
Island Lake Nature Trail
Island Park
Isle Royale National Park
Joan Rodman Memorial Plant Preserve
Jordan Valley Pathway
Kalamazoo Nature Center
Keehne Environmental Area
Kellogg Forest
Kensington Metropark
Kernan Sanctuary & Sonnenberg Plant
    Preserve
Keweenaw Shore No. 1 Nature Sanctuary
Kitchel-Lindquist Dune Preserve

Lake Bluff Audubon Center
Lake Erie Metropark
Lake Gogebic State Park
LakeView Hills Country Inn and Nordic Ski
    Center
Leelanau State Park
Legg Park
Ligon Outdoor Center
Little Presque Isle Tract
Lloyd A Stage Outdoor Education Center
Lost Lake Pathway
Love Creek County Park & Nature Center
Lower Huron Metropark
Ludington State Park
Mackinac Island
Madeline Bertrand County Park
Magoon Creek Natural Area
Marquette Fitness Trail
Matthaei Botanical Gardens
Maybury State Park
McCune Nature Preserve
McLain State Park
Mead-Wetmore Pond Nature Trail
Metamora-Hadley Recreation Area
Metro Beach Metropark
Mill Creek State Park
Mitchell State Park
Montreal Public Trail
Myron & Isabel Zucker Nature Sanctuary
Nahma Marsh Hiking Trail
Nichols Arboretum
Ninga Aki Pathway
Nipissing Dune Trails
North Central Michigan College
North Higgins Lake State Park
North Manitou Island
North Point Nature Preserve
Oakwoods Metropark
Ocqueoc Falls Bicentennial Pathway
Orchard Beach State Park
Osborne Mill Preserve Nature Trail

Ossineke Pathway
Paint Creek Trail
Park Lyndon
Peninsula Point Hiking Trail
Petoskey State Park
Petroglyph Park Nature Trail
Pictured Rocks National Lakeshore-Day Hikes
Pinckney Recreation Area
Pinconning Park
Pine Haven Recreation Area
Platte Springs Pathway
Pontiac Lake Recreation Area
Port Crescent State Park
Portage Creek Bicentennial Park
Portland Rivertrail Park
Presque Isle Lighthouse Park
Presque Isle Park
Price Nature Center
Proud Lake Recreation Area
Pyatt Lake Natural Area
Red Pine Natural Area
Reffitt Nature Preserve
Rifle River Recreation Area
Ringwood Forest
River Bluff Nature Trail
River Falls Trail
Rolling Hills County Park
Round Lake Nature Preserve
Sanford Natural Area
Sarett Nature Center
Schoolcraft County Environmental Lab
Schrier Park
Scotts Mill Park
Seagull Point Park
Searles Audubon Nature Preserve
Seney National Wildlife Refuge
Seven Lakes State Park
Seven Ponds Nature Center
Shannon Nature Sanctuary
Shiawassee National Wildlife Refuge
Silver Creek County Park

Silver Lake Trail
Skegemog Pathway
Sleeper State Park
Sleepy Hollow Nature Preserve
South Manitou Island
Stephen M. Polovich Memorial Nature
    Sanctuary
Stony Creek Metropark
Sugar Loaf Mountain Natural Area
Sylvania Visitor Center Interpretive Trail
Tahquamenon Falls State Park
Tawas Point State Park
Thorne Swift Nature Preserve
Timberland Swamp Nature Sanctuary
Trillium Trail Nature Sanctuary
Twin Lakes State Park
Tyoga Historical Pathway
Uller Trail
Van Raalte Historical Farm and Recreation
    Area
Van Riper State Park
Veterans Memorial Park
Votey Trail
Wagener County Park
Wah-Wah-Tas-See Pathway
Warren Dunes State Park
Warren Woods State Park
Waterloo Recreation Area
West Bloomfield Nature Preserve
West Bloomfield Trail Network
West Branch Pathway
West Lake Nature Preserve
Whitehouse Nature Center
Whitewater Park
Wilcox-Warnes Memorial Nature Sanctuary
Wilderness State Park
Windy Moraine Trail
Woldumar Nature Center
Woodland Management Trail
Yankee Springs Recreation Area
Young State Park

Paved Trails

Addison Oaks County Park
Attikamek Trail
Baker Sanctuary
Battle Creek Linear Park
Baw Beese Trail
Bay City State Park/Tobico Marsh Wildlife Refuge
Bay Hampton Rail Trail and Bay City Riverwalk
Beaver Island
Blandford Nature Center
Chippewa Nature Center
Crossroads Rail Trail & Reed City Linear Park
Dahlem Environmental Education Center
De Graaf Nature Center
Dearborn Environmental Study Area
Fenner Arboretum
Fernwood Botanic Garden
For-Mar Nature Preserve
Fort Custer Recreation Area

Furstenberg Park
Gallup Park
Genesee Recreation Area
Grand Mere State Park
Grand Traverse County Civic Center Trail
Grand Traverse Resort Village
Hart-Montague Bicycle Trail State Park
Heritage Park
Hidden Lake Gardens
Hoffmaster State Park
Houghton Waterfront Trail
Howard Christensen Nature Center
Hudson-Mills Metropark
I-275 Bike Path
Independence Oaks County Park
Indian Springs Metropark
Isle Royale National Park
Keith McKellop Walkway
Kensington Metropark
Kent Trails
Kiwanis Trail
Lakeside Trail around Spring Lake

Little Bay De Noc Recreation Area
Little Traverse Wheelway
Lower Huron Metropark
Ludington State Park
Mackinac Island
Maybury State Park
Mill Creek State Park
Mitchell State Park
North Country Trail-White Cloud
Paint Creek Trail
Pere Marquette Trail of Mid-Michigan
Pictured Rocks National Lakeshore-Day Hikes
Portage Creek Bicentennial Park
Portland Rivertrail Park
Schrier Park
Shanty Creek/Schuss Mountain Resorts
South Lyons Rail Trail
Stony Creek Metropark
Traverse City Recreational Trail
West Bloomfield Nature Preserve
West Lake Nature Preserve

Handicapper Trails

Addison Oaks County Park
Battle Creek Linear Park
Baw Beese Trail
Bay City State Park/Tobico Marsh Wildlife Refuge
Bay Hampton Rail Trail and Bay City Riverwalk
Black River Harbor Trails
Blandford Nature Center
Chippewa Nature Center
Crossroads Rail Trail & Reed City Linear Park
Dahlem Environmental Education Center
De Graaf Nature Center
Fenner Arboretum
Fernwood Botanic Garden
For-Mar Nature Preserve
Furstenberg Park
Gallup Park
Genesee Recreation Area
Grand Mere State Park
Grand Traverse County Civic Center Trail
Hart-Montague Bicycle Trail State Park
Heritage Park
Hickory Hills

Hidden Lake Gardens
Highbanks Trail
Hoffmaster State Park
Houghton Waterfront Trail
Howard Christensen Nature Center
Hudson-Mills Metropark
I-275 Bike Path
Independence Oaks County Park
Indian Springs Metropark
Island Park
Kal-Haven Trail Sesquicentennial State Park
Kensington Metropark
Kent Trails
Kiwanis Trail
Lakeside Trail around Spring Lake
Lansing River Trail
Ligon Outdoor Center
Little Bay De Noc Recreation Area
Little Traverse Wheelway
Lower Huron Metropark
Ludington State Park
Mackinac Island

Marquette Fitness Trail
Matthaei Botanical Gardens
Maybury State Park
Middle Rouge Parkway Trail
Mill Creek State Park
Mitchell State Park
Nahma Marsh Hiking Trail
Oakwoods Metropark
Paint Creek Trail
Pere Marquette Trail of Mid-Michigan
Pictured Rocks National Lakeshore - Day Hikes
Portage Creek Bicentennial Park
Portland Rivertrail Park
Reffitt Nature Preserve
Schrier Park
South Lyons Rail Trail
Stony Creek Metropark
Traverse City Recreational Trail
Treaty Tree Trail
West Bloomfield Nature Preserve
West Lake Nature Preserve
Whitehouse Nature Center

Multiple Grid Trails

27	Kal-Haven Trail SP
28	Kal-Haven Trail SP
31	Lakelands Trail SP, Waterloo RA, Waterloo-Pinckney Hiking Trail
32	Island Lake RA, Lakelands Trail SP, Waterloo RA, Waterloo-Pinckney Hiking Trail
36	Thornapple RT
37	Thornapple RT
40	Island Lake RA
41	Bald Mountain RA
42	Bald Mountain RA
44	Hart-Montague Bicycle Trail SP, Ottawa-Muskegon RT
45	Hart-Montague Bicycle Trail SP
46	NCT-White Cloud, White Pine Trail SP
47	Heartland Trail
48	Heartland Trail
54	Ludington SP
55	NCT-Baldwin, NCT- White Cloud
56	NCT-White Cloud, Pere Marquette Trail (Clare to Baldwin), White Pine Trail SP
57	Pere Marquette Trail (Clare to Baldwin)
58	Pere Marquette Trail (Clare to Baldwin), Pere Marquette Trail of Mid-Michigan
59	Midland-Mackinac Trail, Pere Marquette Trail of Mid-Michigan
64	Ludington SP
65	NCT-Baldwin, NCT-Manistee
66	NCT-Manistee, NCT-Pere Marquette SF 1, White Pine Trail SP
67	NCT-Pere Marquette SF 1, Shore to Shore Trail, White Pine Trail SP
68	Trout Lake PW
69	Midland-Mackinac Trail, Trout Lake PW
70	Shore to Shore Trail - Segment A
71	Shore to Shore Trail - Segment A
73	Shore to Shore Trail
74	Muncie Lakes PW, NCT- Pere Marquette SF 1, Shore to Shore Trail, Vasa Trail
75	Muncie Lakes PW, NCT- Pere Marquette SF 1, Shore to Shore Trail, Vasa Trail
76	Shore to Shore Trail, Tisdale Triangle PW
77	Midland-Mackinac Trail, Shore to Shore Trail, Tisdale Triangle PW
78	Shore to Shore Trail - Segment A
79	Shore to Shore Trail
81	Jordan River PW
82	Jordan River PW, Mackinaw-Alanson RT
83	Black Mountain RA, Midland-Mackinac Trail
87	Iron Range RT, State Line RT
88	Felch Grade RT
89	Felch Grade RT
90	Bay De Noc-Grand Island National Receation Trail, Days River PW, Rapid River National Cross Country Ski Trail
91	Haywire RT, Indian Lake PW
92	Beaver Island
93	Beaver Island
94	Bois Blanc Island, Mackinaw-Alanson RT, Midland-Mackinac Trail, NCT-St. Ignace, St. Ignace - Trout Lake RT, St. Martin Cross Country Ski Trail
95	Black Mountain RA, Bois Blanc Island, DeTour Cross Country Ski Trail
96	Pomeroy/Henry Lake Mountain Bike Complex, State Line RT
97	Bergland to Sidnaw RT, Pomeroy/Henry Lake Mountain Bike Complex
98	Bergland to Sidnaw RT, Iron Range RT, State Line RT
99	Iron Range RT, State Line RT
100	Republic/Champion Grade Trail
102	Bay De Noc-Grand Island National Recreation Trail, Days River PW, Grand Island National Recreation Area, Lakeshore Trail, PRNL - Day Hikes, Rapid River National Cross Country Ski Trail
103	Fox River PW, Haywire RT, Indian Lake PW, Seney National Wildlife Refuge
104	Canada Lakes PW, Fox River PW, Seney National Wildlife Refuge
105	Canada Lakes PW, NCT-Sault Saint Marie, St. Ignace-Trout Lake RT
106	NCT-Sault Saint Marie, NCT-St. Ignace, Soo-Strongs RT, St. Ignace-Trout Lake RT, St. Martin Cross Country Ski Trail
107	Soo Strongs RT
108	Bergland to Sidnaw RT, NCT-Bergland, NCT-Bessemer
109	Bergland to Sidnaw RT, Bill Nicholls Trail, NCT-Bergland, NCT-Ontonagon
110	Baraga SP, Bergland to Sidnaw RT, NCT-Ontonagon
111	Barage SP, McCormick Wilderness, Van Riper SP
112	McCormick Wilderness, NCT-Marquette, Republic/Champion Grade Trail, Van Riper SP
113	NCT-Bessemer, NCT-Marquette
114	Grand Island National Recreation Area, Isle Royale National Park, Lakeshore Trail
115	Fox River PW, Isle Royale National Park, Lakeshore Trail, PRNL-Day Hikes
116	DeTour Cross Country Ski Trail, NCT-Lake Superior SF
117	Chadwick's Kawagama Lake Lodge, NCT-Lake Superior SF, NCT-Sault Saint Marie, Stokely Creek Ski Touring Center
118	Bill Nicholls Trail, Keweenaw Peninsula
119	Keweenaw Peninsula

SP- State Park
RA - Recreation Area
PW - Pathway
RT- Rail Trail
NCT-North Country Trail
SF-State Forest
PRNL - Pictured Rocks National Lakeshore

INDEX

TRAIL NOTES

TRAIL NOTES